Portraits of Zhong Kui by Timeless Masters

Compiled by Xu Xiwen and Dai Xinwei

LIGHTH USE

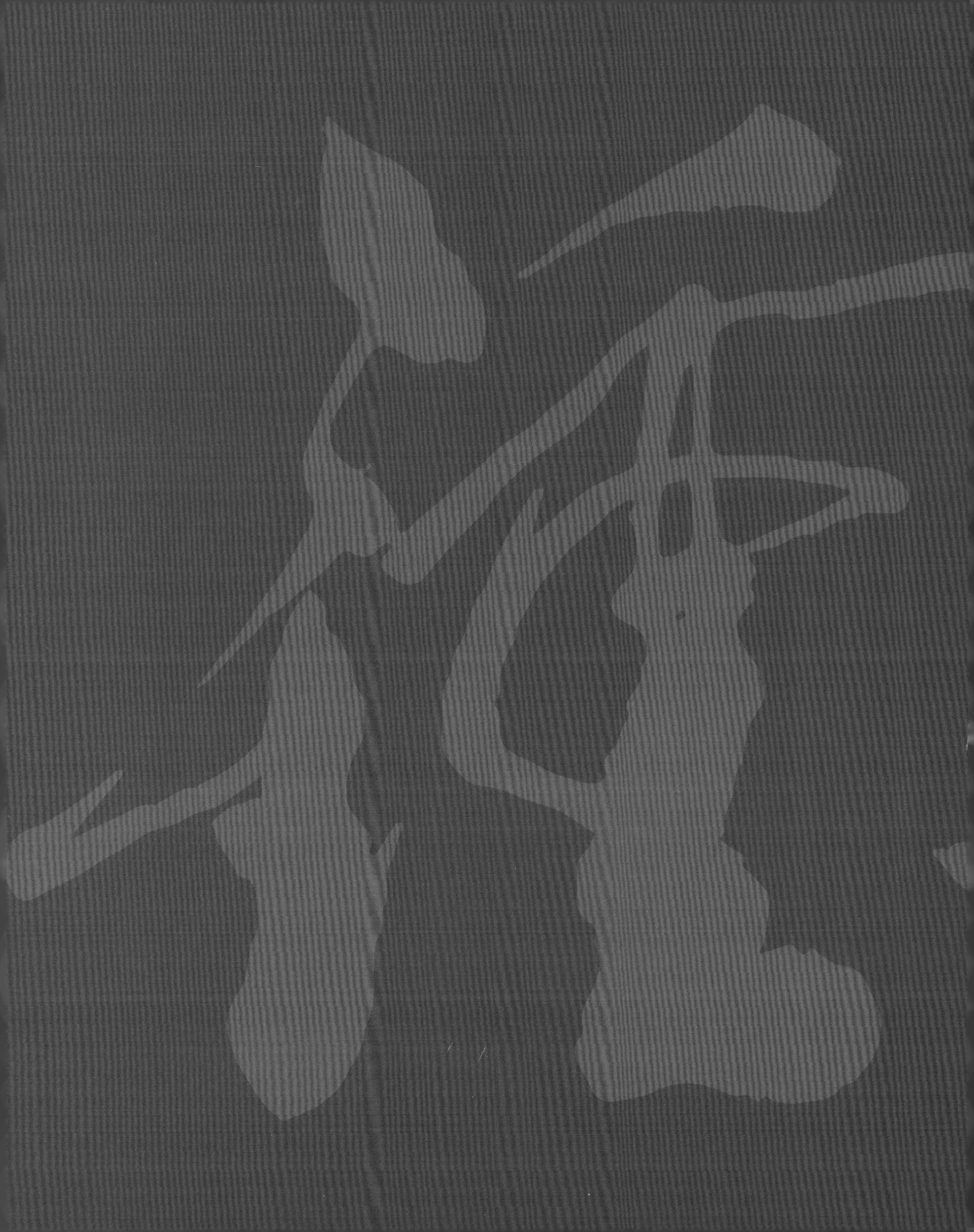

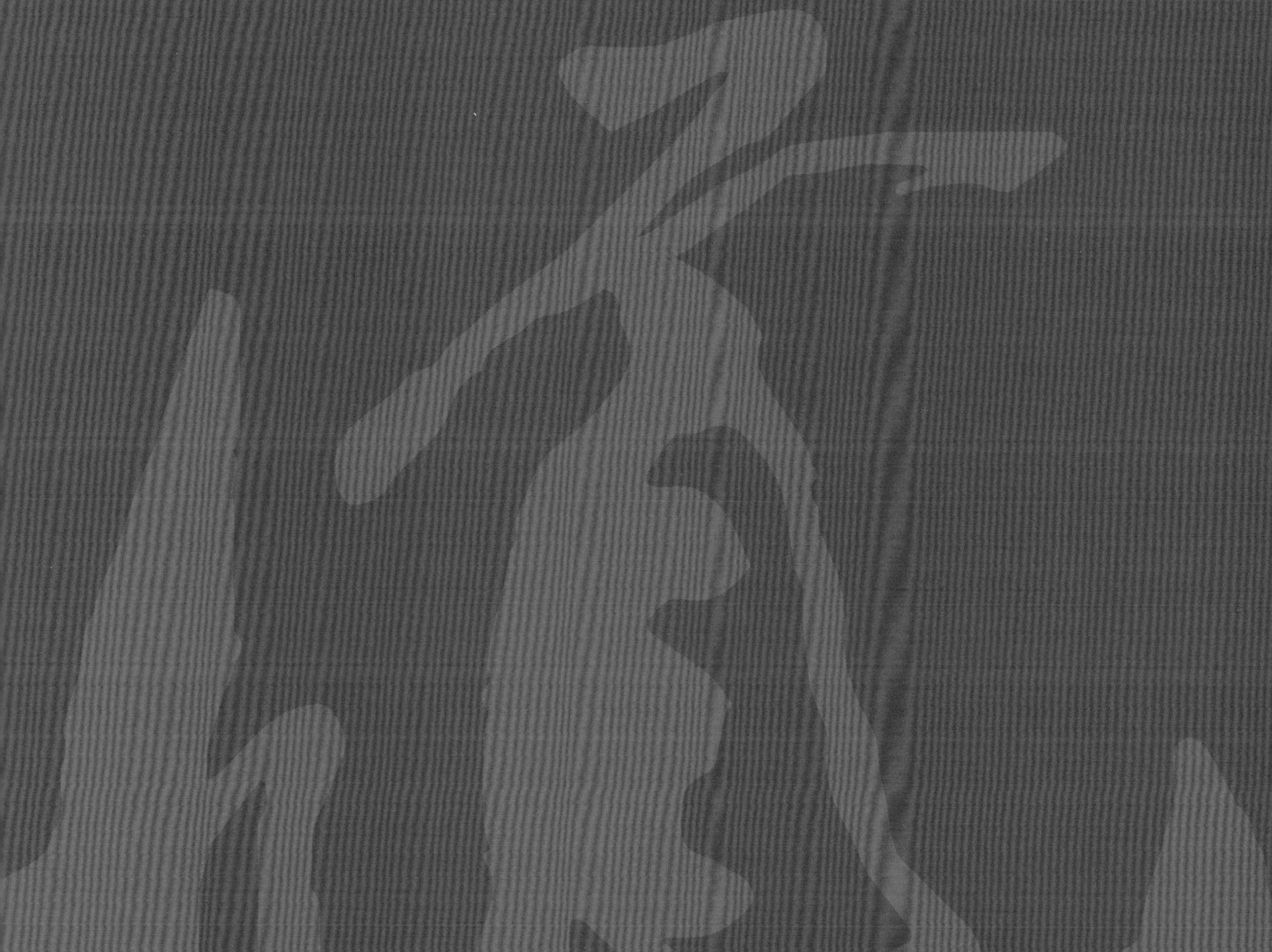

Within the tapestry of China's age-old myths, Zhong Kui emerges as a distinctive figure of significance.

To some, he is the formidable "Ghost King," to others, a valiant "Ghost Hero," and a few revere him as the divine "Kui God."

However, in the realm of mortals, there exists no private estate, no descendants, no stone inscriptions, and no temples in his name. He is not a constantly revered god of great renown; rather, it is during occasions like the Dragon Boat Festival or the Lunar New Year festivities that people recall his prowess in exorcising and dispelling malevolent spirits.

While interpretations of him might diverge, the shared hope he symbolizes in protecting against evil and ushering in prosperity remains constant in people's hearts.

Lord Zhong

Jinshi Zhong

Possessing the power to soar through the heavens and delve into the depths of the earth, he was not content to simply enjoy peace and prosperity in the celestial palace. Neither did he wish to hold office for personal enrichment in the underworld. Instead, he chose to dedicate himself to protecting the human realm, taking pride in banishing evil spirits and capturing malevolent ghosts for the well-being of the people.

Bearded Lord

Elder Beard

Ever since the myths and legends of Zhong Kui emerged, he has been revered as a magnanimous and just guardian in the annals of folklore. Throughout history, the public has held him in affectionate regard, bestowing upon him cherished names such as "Lord Zhong," "Jinshi[1] Zhong," "Bearded Lord," "Elder Beard," "Kui," and "Elder Kui," among others.

Kui

Elder Kui

[1] An esteemed academic title conferred upon those who successfully passed the highest level of the imperial examination in ancient China.

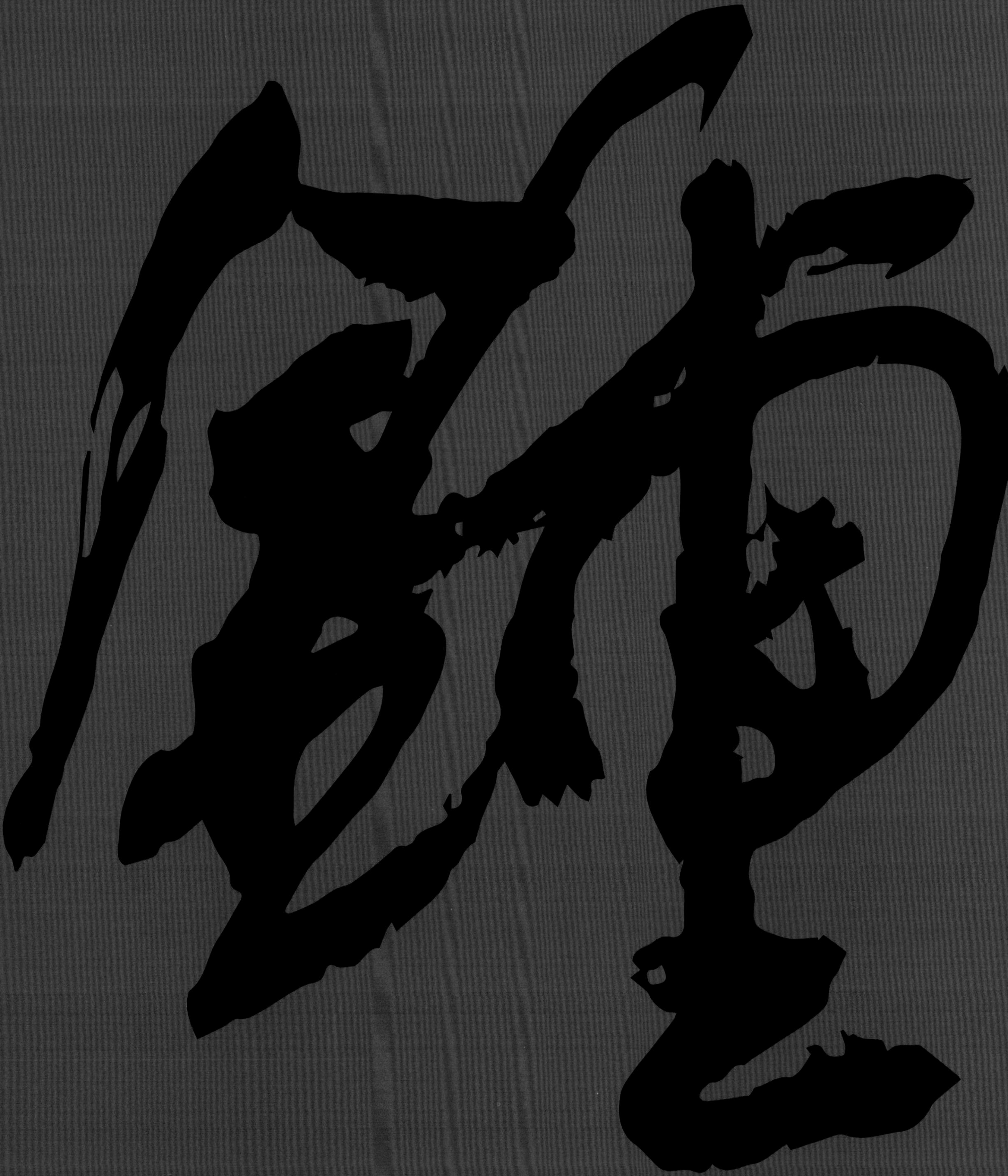

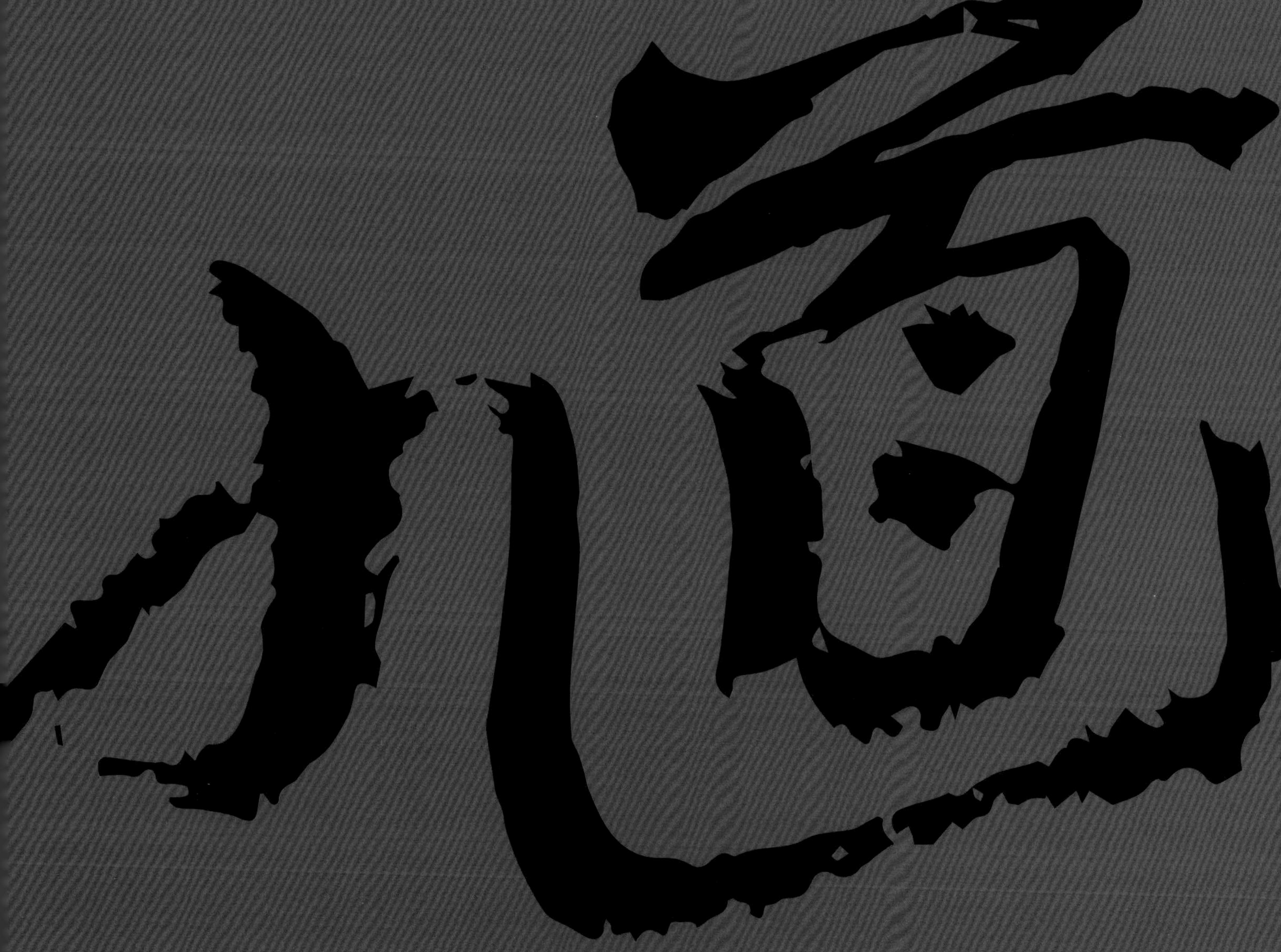

CChinese name: Zhong Kui
English name: Zhong Kui
Other names: Zhong Zhengnan, Zhong Jinshi, Zhong Tianshi
Mythological systems: Taoism, China (Tang Dynasty)
Owned by: Han Nationality
Residence: Zhongnan County, Zhongnan Mountain
Master: The underworld, life and death, judge, door God, ghost hunting, God of wealth
Symbol: exorcism, justice, blessing of the house, good fortune
Siblings: Zhong Mei'er
Gender: Malehinese name: Zhong Kui
English name: Zhong Kui
Other names: Zhong Zhengnan, Zhong Jinshi, Zhong Tianshi
Mythological systems: Taoism, China (Tang Dynasty)
Owned by: Han Nationality
Residence: Zhongnan County, Zhongnan Mountain
Master: The underworld, life and death, judge, door God, ghost hunting, God of wealth
Symbol: exorcism, justice, blessing of the house, good fortune
Siblings: Zhong Mei'er
Gender: Male

Preface

Wielding a treasured blade, clad in tattered boots and a blue robe, with fierce eyes and a coiled beard, travelling by palanquin or by boat, accompanied by a few mischievous spirits, with bats circling overhead... This captures the iconic image of Zhong Kui, known to the Chinese as Jinshi Zhong. Such a rugged and fierce visage, yet the Chinese do not see him as a malevolent deity. Instead, they hold him in great affection, welcoming him into their homes and cherishing his presence day and night. For countless generations, images of Zhong Kui have been hung in homes during the eve of the Lunar New Year and on the Tianzhong Festival (also known as the Dragon Boat Festival, marked on the fifth day of the fifth lunar month). In years of hardship and scant harvests, people turn to him seeking blessings; during times of peace and prosperity, he is deeply appreciated for warding off evil spirits. Consequently, Zhong Kui has seamlessly woven himself into the tapestry of Chinese traditional culture, simultaneously emerging as a dominant theme in the arts of painting and calligraphy. Embedded in his persona is the common folk's aversion to and abhorrence of dark forces, a reflection of their desire to eradicate evil and pursue justice. This emblematic figure not only encapsulates the aesthetic ideal of "ferocious beauty," as phrased by Mr. Li Zehou, but also exemplifies the Chinese people's deep-rooted moral values of upholding righteousness.

The tale of Zhong Kui traces its roots deep into antiquity. One of the most recounted tales is linked to Emperor Xuanzong of Tang. In a dream, the emperor beheld Zhong Kui, a Jinshi who was once dismissed, reclaiming treasures on the emperor's behalf and consuming thieving spirits. Inspired by the emperor's recounting, the illustrious artist Wu Daozi rendered a portrait capturing Zhong Kui's distinctive visage. Yet, this record, validated by scholars and experts, is not the sole testament to Zhong Kui's origins; some believe his legend might reach back into the mists of prehistory. In truth, the image of Zhong Kui has evolved and matured over centuries of tales and recordings. As these narratives accumulated, Zhong Kui's portrayal grew richer, gaining a consistent appearance, attire, backdrop, and narrative arc. His unwavering mission remains consistent — to vanquish evil spirits, usher in good fortune, and bestow happiness. As early as the Tang and Five Dynasties periods, esteemed court painters like Wu Daozi and Huang Quan chronicled the creation of Zhong Kui portraits, hung as talismans against malevolence. This custom, initially embraced by the imperial elite, gradually permeated the common households, establishing itself as a favoured genre among the masses. Especially notable is the transformation when the Chinese literati began contributing to this narrative. Whether it was in character depiction, themes, stories, artistic techniques, or presentation forms, significant shifts were observed. It was the evolving aesthetics and tastes of China's literati, coupled with their distinctive brushwork, that infused the image of Zhong Kui with profound cultural significance.

In the early Qing Dynasty, the renowned painter Gao Qipei was particularly skilled in painting with his fingers. Among the artworks he created during the Kangxi period is the "Songzhou Ten Poems Scroll," which features a portrayal of Zhong Kui. Gao wrote in the inscription, "Commissioned to oversee the grain reserves in Songzhou, I have spent nine months here. What I have heard and witnessed is unspeakable. These drawings accompany ten poems, aiming to preserve them for posterity." A mythical figure, embedded amidst the "natural sketches" of a rugged and untamed land, this depiction not only illuminates the harsh conditions of the time but also highlights the diverse renditions of Zhong Kui by the scholarly artists. In matters of spectral beings, one cannot overlook Luo Pin (Liangfeng), from the Qing Dynasty. In his painting "Zhong Kui with Sword and Guqin[2]," Zhong Kui is depicted holding a sword, while the accompanying spirit, once rendered fearsome, now resembles a celestial child. Most intriguingly, their belongings are no longer mundane items but a guqin. "With a guqin and a sword as travel mates, my chest brims with poetry, elevating my spirit," the inscription exudes a scholarly aura, bestowing upon Zhong Kui a fresh narrative. "In ancient times, artists crafted delicate portraits of Jinshi Zhong, presenting them to the imperial court every New Year's Eve to ward off misfortune. Yet, in this present age, such practices are reserved especially for the fifth day of the fifth month," such an inscription undeniably stands as a significant testament in the artistic history of Zhong Kui.

From the early to the mid-late Qing Dynasty, eminent artists like Wang Gang, Qian Du, Zeng Yandong, Lu Hui, and Ju Lian crafted portrayals of Zhong Kui imbued with ancient charm. Transitioning into the Republic era, works by Qi Baishi, Zhang Daqian, Pu Ru, Pu Quan, Xia Jingguan, Pan He, Huang Shaoqiang, Deng Fen, and Chen Yuandu not only carried the legacy of the preceding dynasty but also exuded the zeitgeist of their time, reflecting an exceptionally strong literati flavour characteristic of the Republic period. From the artworks centred on Zhong Kui, it is evident that between the Qing Dynasty and the Republic era, there was a deep-seated tradition of portraying Zhong Kui. This was not just a reflection of popular customs but also signalled a vibrant exchange among the literati in the realms of painting and calligraphy. Take, for instance, the Zhong Kui painting jointly created by Feng Runzhi and Rong Zuchun, with inscriptions added by Cheng Jingxuan and Yi Dachang, gifted to Zhao Haogong. While this was indeed a festive offering for the Tianzhong Festival, it also subtly hints at the "cultural debts" often shared among Chinese literati. In modern times, Huang Zhou's painting of Zhong Kui, titled "Expelling Evil and Attracting Blessings," was inscribed by Liu Haisu and retouched by Xie Zhiliu, Cheng Shifa, and others, indicating the continuation of this artistic tradition. As we admire the diverse depictions of Zhong Kui by artists from the Qing Dynasty to the Republic era, we must not forget the aspirations expressed in the painters' brushstrokes during an age transitioning from prosperity to decline and fraught with frequent wars, as well as the central wishes of the art collectors.

---

[2] Guqin (古琴) is a traditional Chinese seven-stringed zither, revered for its refined and profound sound, often associated with scholars and sages.

As a mythical figure beloved by the masses, Zhong Kui possesses a recognizable visage with certain "standard features," such as his facial appearance and attire. Throughout the annals of artistic creation, there emerges a noteworthy trend: this iconic image has inspired countless reproductions. Rather than merely portraying the same figure, many artists have directly emulated or meticulously replicated Zhong Kui paintings of their predecessors. In the Ming Dynasty, Emperor Xianzong, Zhu Jianshen, crafted a painting titled "Welcoming Blessings of Good Fortune," in which Zhong Kui is depicted holding a Ruyi sceptre, accompanied by a young spirit presenting persimmons. During the Republican era, artist Wu Yongxiang's "All Matters Go Smoothly" faithfully replicated this portrayal. Gao Zhenbai's "Zhong Kui in the Chilly Woods" was directly copied from Li Lin's Ming Dynasty work, "Zhong Kui in the Chilly Woods." Furthermore, "Zhong Kui Attending the Morning Court" closely replicated Pu Ru's composition on the same theme. These artistic works highlight the unique creative attributes associated with the theme of Zhong Kui. During the new era, the trend of such creative expression continued. For instance, during the early days of the reform and opening-up period, Tang Yun crafted "Exorcising Ominous Signs" in Guangzhou. Huang Zhou followed by creating an imitation of this piece, titled "Imitating Tang Dashi's 'Exorcising Ominous Signs'." These two Zhong Kui depictions were produced during the same era and share visual similarities. However, they allow us to appreciate the unique stylistic features and the charm of the brushwork of each artist, offering a glimpse into a fascinating art world anecdote.

In addition to preserving the iconic image of Zhong Kui, artists over the ages have greatly expanded upon the theme, adding a wealth of new content. Beyond the primary role of exorcising evil and bestowing blessings, depictions have evolved to show Zhong Kui in various other aspects of life: attending the imperial morning court, arranging his sister's marriage, travelling, playing chess, drinking, reading, and more, thus greatly enriching the narrative surrounding him. In recent times, the engagement of renowned artists has lent this character a fresh dynamism: Pu Ru's portrayals brim with a whimsical charm; Zhang Daqian reimagined Zhong Kui, styling him as a scholar-official rather than a brusque figure; the cartoonist Fang Cheng presented Zhong Kui with endearing comic attributes, even depicting tussles between the genuine and counterfeit Zhong Kuis. Each of these creative ventures has set a new precedent in the artistic rendition of Zhong Kui.

As Zhong Kui has remained a pervasive subject within the realm of painting, he has inspired the artistic endeavours of myriad artists throughout successive eras. With the ebb and flow of the history of painting, certain artists who once depicted him have now receded into obscurity, their stories demanding rediscovery and scholarly attention. Among them was Liang Junqing, who painted a depiction of Zhong Kui complemented by the inscriptions of Bai Jiao. While Bai Jiao's reputation endures, widely recognized for his contributions, Liang Junqing is a distinguished doctor from Shanghai. In the 1940s, he was the trusted physician for Zheng Zhenduo, a luminary in the cultural sphere, and his family. The act of a doctor, one who dedicated his life to healing others, in painting Zhong Kui—a symbol traditionally associated with health and the expulsion of evil—is seen as an exemplary convergence of his professional life with artistic expression.

Throughout the extensive history of Zhong Kui's image, in every era and at every level of society, creators have endowed this figure with the power to uphold justice. An innate repulsion to evil and a sincere longing for goodness are common sentiments shared by humanity across ages. In the past, people would hang images of Zhong Kui during significant times such as Sui Chu (Lunar New Year's Eve) and Tian Zhong (Dragon Boat Festival), aiming to purge misfortune and pray for peace and happiness. As we approach the end of the year of Wuxu, compiling this volume *Portraits of Zhong Kui by Timeless Masters* follows this ancient practice, echoes this enduring sentiment, and invites connoisseurs from all walks to provide their valued corrections and insights.

Dai Xinwei
October 2018

Catalogue

002 Origin of the Image of Zhong Kui

006 The Ideological Significance and Aesthetic Characteristics of Zhong Kui Paintings

012 Historical Evolution of Zhong Kui Paintings

039 **Zhong Kui with Plum Blossoms and Sparrows**
Artist: Yang Jin, Xu Wen, Gu Fang, Xu Yunlu

047 **Zhong Kui**
Artist: Gao Qipei

051 **Jinshi Zhong**
Artist: Wang Gang

055 **Celestial Feast at the Zenith**
Artist: Wang Yuanxun

057 **Zhong Kui with Sword and Guqin**
Artist: Luo Pin

059 **Welcoming Fortune**
Artist: Zeng Yandong

063 **Zhong Kui**
Artist: Qian Du

067 **Zhong Kui**
Artist: Wang Gong

071 **Zhong Kui Drunk**
Artist: Ma Genxian

075 **Zhong Kui**
Artist: Lai Liansu

079 **Chess at Zhongnan Mountain**
Artist: Xiang Kun

083 **The Portrait of Zhong Kui**
Artist: Ou Shaoyan

085 **Jinshi Zhong**
Artist: Pan Jin

089 **Zhong Kui**
Artist: Zhang Zhirong

093 **Good Fortune Arrives**
Artist: Jiang Danxu

097 **Good News Heard**
(Qing Dynasty kesi silk tapestry)

105 **Zhong Kui Playing Chess**
Artist: Pan Panseng

109 **Standing to Hear Good Tidings**
Artist: Zhao Bi

113 **Zhong Kui**
Artist: Zhu Hang

115 **The Venerable Zhong Entering the Court to Offer Earnest Admonitions**
Artist: Wu Yun

119 **Blessings Descend from Heaven**
Artist: Ju Lian

123 **Weighing Ghosts**
Artist: Chen Zhao

127 **Splashed Ink Zhong Kui**
Artist: Ren Bonian

131 **Zhong Kui's Little Sister**
Artist: Ren Bonian

135 **Zhong Kui Capturing Ghosts**
Artist: Ren Bonian

139 **Companions Inebriated Beneath the Paulownia Shade**
Artist: Li Yu

143 **Zhong Kui Dancing with a Sword**
Artist: Wu Youru, Zhong Junsheng

145 **Zhong Kui**
Artist: Lu Hui

149 **Zhong Kui**
Artist: Lu Hui |
Inscription by Wu Changshuo

153 **Blessings from Heaven**
Artist: Jiang Qia, Su Shijie

157 **Zhong Kui Adds Fortune**
Artist: Feng Runzhi, Rong Zuchun

161 **Blessings from Heaven**
Artist: Rong Zuchun

165 **Three Indifferents**
Artist: Pan He

169 **Zhong Kui Marrying Off His Sister**
Artist: Shen Xinhan

173 **Jinshi Zhong Marrying Off His Sister**
Artist: Shen Xinhan

177 **Zhong Kui Returning from the Night Banquet**
Artist: Shen Xinhan

181 **Expelling Evil and Cleansing Aura**
Artist: Shen Xinhan

185 **Return from the Night Banquet**
Artist: Shen Xinhan

189 **Building Happiness and Receiving Joy**
Artist: Shen Xinhan

193 **Zhong Kui with a Flower in His Hair**
Artist: Shen Xinhan

197 **Only Seeing Fortune Arrive**
Artist: Shen Xinhai

201 **Evening Ferry across the Spring River**
Artist: Shen Xinhan

205 **Exhaustively Eliminating Toxins**
Artist: Shen Xinhan

209 **Only Seeing Fortune Arrive**
Artist: Shen Xinhan

213 **Jinshi of Zhongnan**
Artist: Qi Baishi

217 **Zhong Kui Marrying Off His Sister**
Artist: Chen Kanghou, Bian Fuchang

221 **Flower Hairpin**
Artist: Wang Yun

225 **Zhong Kui**
Artist: Xia Jingguan, Wu Yongwei

227 **Zhong Kui's Nightly Patrol**
Artist: Chen Banding

231 **Zhong Kui Suppressing Evil**
Artist: Zhu Jun

235 **Zhong Kui Marrying Off His Sister**
Artist: Li Fangyuan

239 **Blessings from Heaven**
Artist: Liu Kuiling

243 **Zhong Kui Fearing Dog**
Artists: Wang Mengbai, Wu Kaisheng

247 **Mountain Forest Noble Guest**
Artist: Mei Yutian

251 **Zhong Kui Marrying Off His Sister**
Artist: Chen Da

255 **Zhong Kui Marrying Off His Sister**
Artist: Gu Xiaoyan

257 **Cinnabar Zhong Kui**
Artist: Deng Fen

259 **Blessings from Heaven**
Artist: Fang Zaiyong

263 **Shortcut to Zhongnan**
Artists: Zhang Lusheng, Yuan Xilian

267 **The New Year's Eve Excursion of Zhong Kui**
Artist: Qian Yunhe

271 **Zhong Kui**
Artist: Li Xian

275 **Zhong Kui's Outing**
Artists: Song Luo, Li You

277 **Zhong Kui**
Artist: Xu Beihong

279 **Zhong Kui and the Little Ghosts**
Artist: Xu Beihong

283 **Zhong Kui Expelling Malevolence**
Artist: Pu Ru

285 **Jinshi Zhong**
Artist: Pu Ru

287 **Blessings Abundant**
Artist: Pu Ru

291 **Zhong Kui Repelling Ghosts**
Artists: Xu Cao, Zhang Wenlian

295 **Zhong Kui**
Artist: Qian Songyan

299 **Zhong Kui Reading**
Artist: Zhang Daqian

303 **Descending Blessings and Banishing Evil**
Artist: Zhang Daqian

305 **Zhong Kui**
Artist: Guan Liang

307 **Zhong Kui**
Artist: Huang Shaoqiang

309 **Zhong Kui**
Artist: Chen Yuandu

313 **Jinshi Zhong Playing with Children**
Artist: Chen Yuandu

317 **Zhong Kui Drunk**
Artist: Shen Zicheng

321 **Jinshi Zhong**
Artist: Fu Baoshi

325 **Zhong Kui Attending the Morning Court**
Artist: Gao Zhenbai

327 **Zhong Kui's Outing**
Artist: Gao Zhenbai

329 **Zhongnan's Jinshi Welcoming Spring**
Artist: Gao Zhenbai

333 **Zhong Kui in the Chilly Woods**
Artist: Gao Zhenbai

335 **Jinshi Zhong**
Artist: Li Keran

337 **Zhong Kui Wielding a Sword**
Artist: Li Keran

341 **Zhong Kui Giving His Sister Away in Marriage**
Artist: Li Keran

349 **Jinshi Zhong's Outing**
Artist: Wu Guangyu

353 **Zhong Kui**
Artist: Cai Heting

355 **Red-Robed Zhong Kui**
Artist: Lu Yanshao

359 **Zhong Kui Drunk**
Artist: Liang Junqing

363 **Zhong Kui Under the Moon**
Artist: Tang Yun

367 **Exorcising Misfortune**
Artist: Tang Yun

369 **Dispelling Evil and Condensing Auspiciousness**
Artist: Wang Lanruo

371 **Righteousness Prevails in the Human World**
Artist: Guan Shanyue

375 **Everything Goes Well**
Artist: Wu Yongxiang

379 **Red-Robed Zhong Kui**
Artist: Pu Quan

381 **Green-Robed Zhong Kui**
Artist: Lai Shaoqi

383 **Celebrating Longevity**
Artist: Lin Qin

387 **Red-Robed Zhong Kui**
Artist: Fang Cheng

389 **True and False Zhong Kui**
Artist: Fang Cheng

391 **Zhong Kui Wielding Sword**
Artist: Lü Lin

393 **Zhong Kui Holding Fan**
Artist: Lü Lin

395 **Zhong Kui with Sword**
Artist: Kang Shiyao

397 **Bingyin Zhong Kui**
Artist: Cheng Shifa

401 **Zhong Kui Marrying Off His Sister**
Artist: Huang Zhou

403 **Expelling Evil and Attracting Blessings**
Artist: Huang Zhou

405 **Imitating Tang Yun's "Exorcising Misfortune"**
Artist: Huang Zhou

407 Seeking Out Flattery and Deceit in the Human Realm
Artist: Huang Zhou

409 Zhong Kui
Artist: Yang Guoxun

411 Zhong Kui Fearing Ghosts
Artist: Chen Dexi

413 Zhong Kui with Elegant Interests
Artist: Fan Zeng

415 Evil Cannot Suppress the Righteous
Artist: Fan Zeng

417 Zhong Kui Welcoming Fortune
Artist: Liu Yuesheng

421 Holding the Sword
Artist: Lin Yong

423 Zhong Kui Settling Accounts
Artist: Lin Yong

427 Zhong Kui Watching Ducks
Artist: Lin Yong

431 Zhong Kui with Flowers in His Hair
Artist: Liu Sifen

435 Zhong Kui Welcoming Fortune
Artist: Wang Xijing

437 Zhong Kui
Artist: Jia Haoyi

439 Elegant Interests
Artist: Zhou Siyin

440 Compilation of Zhong Kui Resources

448 A Collection of Poetic Inscriptions on Portraits of Zhong Kui by Renowned Masters

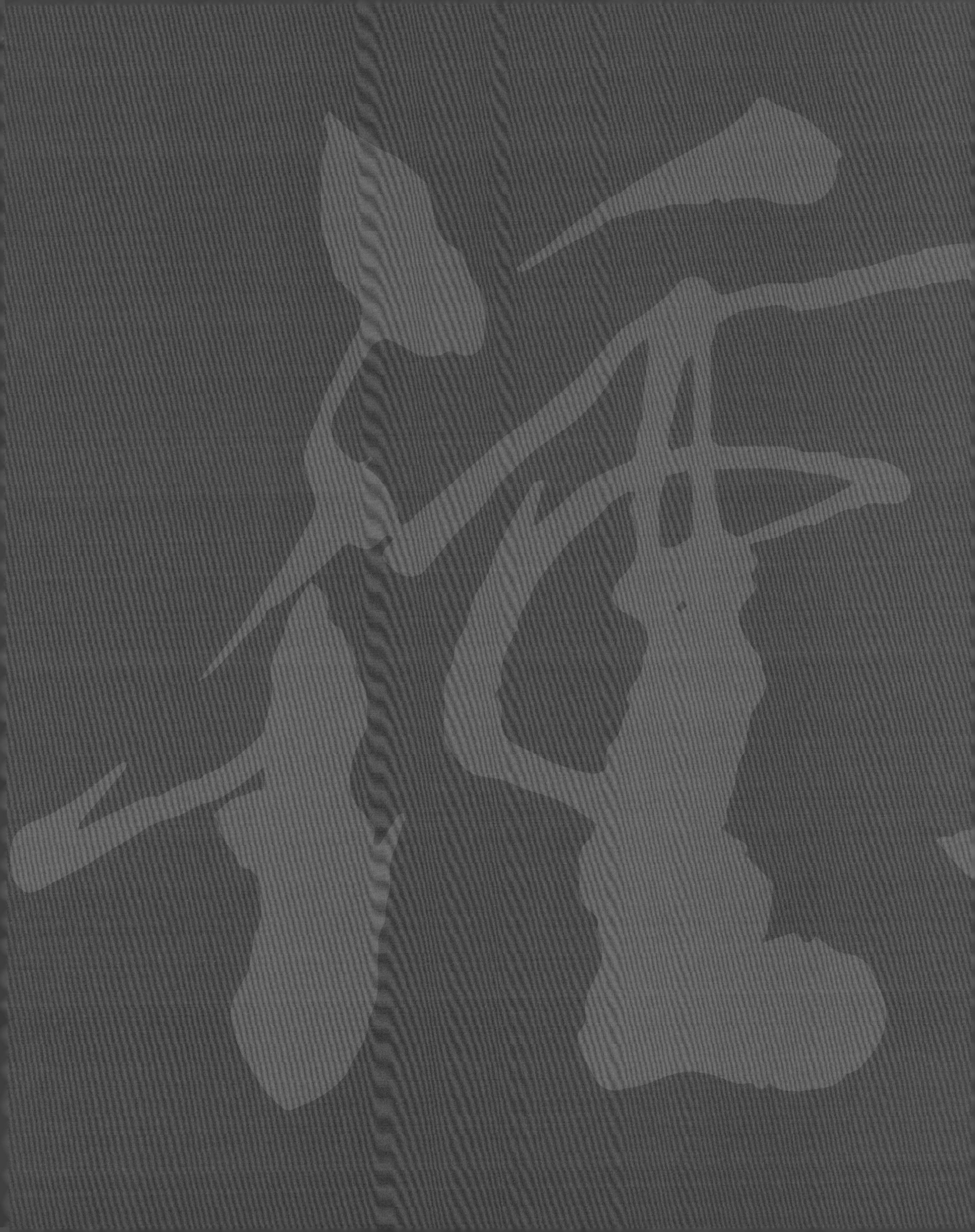

Origin of the Image of Zhong Kui

As recounted in Wang Yuncheng's Wang Yuncheng's *Tales of the Unrecorded and Extraordinary* from the Ming Dynasty era, Zhong Kui was a luminary of the Tang Dynasty—a paragon of both the pen and the sword, blessed with striking looks. In the pivotal year of the imperial examination, alongside his fellow scholar, Du Ping, he set out for the capital to take the prestigious test. Tragically, on their way, they unwittingly stumbled upon a haunt of spectral beings. After enduring a night of ridicule and torment at the hands of these spirits, Zhong Kui emerged marred and grotesque. This unfortunate transformation resulted in the Tang Emperor barring him from the examination, plunging Zhong Kui into such depths of despair that he took his own life. Moved by the injustice, Du Ping penned a heartfelt appeal to the emperor on Zhong Kui's behalf. The Tang Emperor, wracked with guilt, posthumously honoured Zhong Kui with the distinguished title of a Jinshi from Zhongnan Mountain. He was also given the sacred responsibility of guarding the imperial palace's back gate and was revered as a guardian deity against evil and malevolence. Deeply indebted to Du Ping, Zhong Kui, in a bid to honour a past vow, courageously bridged the chasm between the realms of the dead and the living, ensuring that his sister became Du Ping's bride. However, the *Catalogue with Critical Abstracts of the Complete Opera Collection* narrates a slightly different tale. It mentions that Zhong Kui, who was recognized as a Jinshi from Zhongnan Mountain during the Tang era, inadvertently entered a temple one day while inebriated. Upon witnessing numerous monks conducting a spiritual ceremony for his close friend Du Ping, he was consumed by sudden fury. Lashing out, he attacked the monks, declaring, "Our destinies are in the hands of the heavens! Why turn to spirits for safeguarding? If these entities ever intend to harm, they are true malefactors, deserving to be vanquished and devoured!" Horrified by what transpired, a horde of spirits sought refuge with the Bodhisattva Guanyin, recounting their grievances. Guanyin, swayed by their deceitful words, chose to shorten Zhong Kui's lifespan. Indeed, on his way to the imperial examination, these malevolent spirits marred Zhong Kui's visage. Despite earning honours in the exam, his grotesque appearance led to his eventual dismissal. Overwhelmed by fury, he met his end by hurling himself against a set of stairs. When the Jade Emperor heard of this tragic tale, he honoured Zhong Kui with the esteemed title of "General Who Vanquishes Malice." Such evocative myths about Zhong Kui imbue his character with a deep, mesmerizing mystique, giving rise to a captivating and enigmatic artistic allure.

The origin of Zhong Kui's image has always been the subject of varied tales. Collating these, we arrive at six predominant theories:

Firstly, it is believed that Zhong Kui truly existed in history. Born during the Tang Dynasty, Zhong Kui was characterized as a man of unwavering integrity and bravery. Upholding justice and righteousness, he was exceptionally talented. Through the imperial examination, he ranked at the very top. However, ensnared by malicious accusations, his life was tragically cut short amidst grievous injustice. Inspired by his impeccable virtue, subsequent narratives emerged, upholding justice and admonishing the deceitful. Such an interpretation is echoed in Wang Yuncheng's Tales of the Unrecorded and Extraordinary from the Ming Dynasty and Zhang Dafu's *Joy Across the World* from the Qing Dynasty.

Secondly, it is believed that the image of Zhong Kui (钟馗) traces back to the Zhong Kui (终葵) Clan of the Yin people. As documented in Zuo Zhuan, Annals of Duke Ding, King Cheng of Zhou allocated the people of Yin (previously of the Shang Dynasty) to his uncle, Kang Shu, and organized them into seven clans. Among these, the Zhong Kui (终葵) Clan stood out, especially renowned for their expertise in crafting "zhui" (ritual spikes) (Refer to Rites of Zhou, Office of Winter). These spikes were not merely essential tools in ancient times but were also utilized to expel malevolent spirits. Since these spikes were crafted by the Zhong Kui (终葵) Clan, they were sometimes referred to as "Zhong Kui" (钟葵), synonymous with "zhui". Due to the phonetic resemblance between Zhong Kui (钟葵) and Zhong Kui (钟馗), the former, celebrated for crafting evil-warding "zhui", gradually became associated with the latter, revered as the deity of exorcism. Notably, both Yang Shen in his Chronicles of Unusual Histories during the Ming Dynasty and Gu Yanwu in Records of Daily Enlightenment during the Qing Dynasty explored the origins of Zhong Kui (钟馗), drawing on the phonetic links that connect Zhong Kui (钟馗) with both Zhong Kui (钟葵) and Zhong Kui (终葵). [3]

Thirdly, it is believed that Zhong Kui's iconic image finds its roots in the Fang Xiang Clan, custodians of traditional ceremonies. As per the *Rites of Zhou, Offices of Summer, Sima Xia*, in days of yore, a profound ritual named the "Grand Ceremony of the Nuo Folk Religion[4]" was held to banish spirits and malevolent entities. In the grand ceremony, the Fang Xiang clan assumed a mystic form: hands cloaked in bear hide, a face with four golden eyes, draped in somber garb and crimson skirts, with halberd in hand and shield held high. He danced and roared, leading legions from palace halls to forgotten graves, banishing spectres and spirits with a force that echoed through the ages. Mr. Chang Renxia elucidated that the origins of the "Grand Ceremony of the Nuo Folk Religion" can be traced back to the ancient rites of man battling beasts, symbolizing a sacred dance to ward off malevolent spirits. The commanding garb of the Fang Xiang clan, their ghastly visages, coupled with the wild cries of their entourage, all echo the primal gestures reminiscent of man's ancient struggles with wild beasts. Esteemed annals like the *Analects, Book of Rites, Lüshi Chunqiu, Huainanzi,* and others chronicle this "Nuo Folk Religion". Historical accounts, such as those in Fan Ye's *Book of the Later Han* and Zhang Heng's *Fu on Eastern Metropolises*, reveal that by the Han Dynasty, the "Grand Ceremony of the Nuo Folk Religion" emerged as a paramount end-of-year ritual within the confines of the royal palace. This venerable tradition persisted into the early phases of the Tang Dynasty, only to be incrementally overshadowed by the evolving practices of Zhong Kui dance performances and the adorning of Zhong Kui divine effigies. The Ming scholar Xie Zhaozhe in his work *Miscellany of Five Assorted Offerings* and the Qing scholar Gu Lu in *The Records of Qing's Auspiciousness* both posited this perspective.

---

[3] In this paragraph, the three names Zhong Kui (钟馗), Zhong Kui (钟葵), and Zhong Kui (终葵) share phonetic similarities in Chinese, all pronounced as "Zhong Kui". With their different character forms come distinct significances for each term:
Zhong Kui (钟馗): Refers to the renowned figure in Chinese mythology. He is the primary subject of our discussion and is the most commonly used of the three.
Zhong Kui (终葵): Referring to a distinct character, this term is associated with the lineage of the Yin people, specifically the Zhong Kui Clan.
Zhong Kui (钟葵): While sharing the same pronunciation as the former, this represents an alternative written form of "终葵" in historical texts.

[4] The "Nuo Folk Religion" is a traditional Chinese sacrificial activity. Its primary objectives are exorcising demons, banishing epidemics, expressing gratitude to deities, and ushering in good fortune. Centred around shamanic rituals, it manifests the beliefs in the worship of nature, ancestors, spirits, and the animistic idea that every entity possesses a soul.

Fourthly, contemporary scholars, Mrs. Su Xuelin and Mr. Mao Yibo, contend that "Zhong Kui is also considered as the star deity Kui Xing (魁星), evolving from the mythic figure Kui (夔)." They elaborate by stating, "The Kui Xing (魁星) actually corresponds to the Kui constellation (奎宿). What is referred to as Kui (夔), in essence, stems from Zhong Kui (终葵), also known as Zhong Kui (钟葵), and ultimately Zhong Kui (钟馗); these are but transformations of character forms driven by phonetic resemblances." The Kui Xing (魁星), also known as the "Kui constellation (奎宿)," is one of the twenty-eight lunar mansions in ancient astronomy. Han dynasty texts such as The Divine Covenant of Filial Piety mention the concept that "Kui (奎) presides over literature", and the Han people erected the Kui Star (奎星) Pavilion in reverence. Subsequently, feudal scholars venerated it as the deity governing the rise and fall of literary fortune. The deity Kui (魁), though homely and ghost-like in appearance, indeed bears a striking resemblance to Zhong Kui (钟馗), as if their images are matching halves of a tally. As for "Kui" (夔), according to the records in the Book of Documents, Canon of Yao, Kui (夔) was a music official during the era of the sage kings Yao and Shun, entrusted with the duties of ritual music and offerings. With the deification of Yao and Shun, Kui (夔) too was deified, thereby transcending into a spiritual being, becoming a constellation, which is a logical progression of events.[5]

Fifthly, it is posited that Zhong Kui (钟馗) originates from "Zhong Kui (钟夔)." The phonetic series in the *Jiyun* dictionary clarifies that the characters Kui (馗), Kui (夔), and Kui (逵) are interchangeable. "Zhong Kui (钟夔)," in the lexicon of the Chinese character classification, "Zhong" embodies the meaning of exhaustion and finality. The *Annals of Confucius and His Descendants* refers to "earthly and stony spectres" as such Kui (夔), the so-called Mōryō[6]. To exhaustively control evil spirits, thus, they are named Zhong Kui (终夔). In the Han Dynasty, Zhang Heng's *Fu on Eastern Metropolises* contains the phrase "the ravages of Kui (夔), Xuan[7], and Wang Xiang[8]." Xue Zong comments: "Ravages, akin to slaying. Kui (夔), the spectre of wood and stone, is like a dragon with horns, its scales and armor gleaming like the sun and moon, foretelling a severe drought upon its sighting." The *Classic of Mountains and Seas* also speaks of Kui (夔) as a spiritual beast in the mountains with a single foot. Such interpretations were once prevalent during the Ming dynasty.

Sixthly, the Ming scholar Hu Yinglin, in his work *Notes from the Shaoshi Mountain Studio*, regards Zhong Kui as merely a name amongst gods and spirits. "Before the Six Dynasties, such entities were believed to exist, and the tales of their ghost-binding endeavours have been handed down for more than a day." Consequently, one need not delve too deeply into the mythology of Zhong Kui, nor should interpretations be forcefully contrived or far-fetched.

If one were to compare horizontally these six perspectives, it is not difficult to deduce the following conclusion: The image of Zhong Kui evolved gradually from ancient myths and various customary rites, rather than being based on a historical figure. If we accept the claims of scholars like Zhang Dafu, who posit that Zhong Kui was a creation of the Tang Dynasty, based on the life of an actual person who became the foundation of the Zhong Kui myth, then we cannot explain the historical fact noted by Yang Shen, Hu Yinglin, and Gu Yanwu that during the Northern and Southern Dynasties, there was a popular trend of naming people after Zhong Kui. In the historical records, the Northern Wei had figures such as Yao Xuan (originally named Zhong Kui (钟葵), with the courtesy name Bi Xie[9]), Zong Zhongkui (仲葵), Yang Zhongkui (仲葵) (military governor of Fuhan), Zhang Zhongkui (仲葵) (grandson of Dorgon), Yu Zhongkui (仲葵) (known as Jing), and Li Zhongkui (仲葵) (King of Dunqiu); the Northern Qi had Gong Zhongkui (钟馗) (eunuch) and Murong Zhongkui (钟馗); the Sui dynasty included Yang Zhongkui (钟馗) (of the imperial clan), Qiao Zhongkui (钟馗) (a general under Prince Liang), Duan Zhongkui (钟葵), among others. In *The History of the Northern Dynasties, Biography of En'xing,* Gong Zhongkui (钟葵) is also written as Gong Zhongkui (钟馗); similarly, in the *Biography of the Sui Commoner Liang* from the same book, Qiao Zhongkui (钟葵) is also referred to as Qiao Zhongkui (钟馗). This serves as evidence that "Zhong Kui (钟葵)" was indeed synonymous with "Zhong Kui (钟馗)." Furthermore, the *Xuanhe Painting Catalog* contains an entry on ancient steles from the Six Dynasties period found among ruins and tombs, on which the name Zhong Kui (钟馗) is inscribed, presumably the name of the tomb's occupant. Shen Kuo mentioned in his *Dream Pool Essays* that during the reign of Emperor Renzong of the Song dynasty, a tomb was excavated in Shangyuan County, Jinling (present-day Nanjing), revealing it to be the final resting place of Lady Zheng, mother of the General of Western Conquest, Zong Que, from the Song of Southern dynasties. The epitaph on the tomb stele also recorded that Zong Que had a sister named Zhong Kui (钟馗), indicating that the name of Zhong Kui (钟馗) has ancient origins. Furthermore, in *Zizhi Tongjian, Tang Annals,* a military officer under Wang Wujun named Zhang Zhongkui (仲葵), is also referred to as Zhang Zhongkui (终葵), validating that "Zhong Kui (钟葵)" and "Zhong Kui (终葵)" are indeed one and the same. Looking into *The Complete Works of the Tang Dynasty* and ancient texts like Wang Renxiu's *Qieyun* from the Tang era, it is evident that the tradition of painting Zhong Kui (钟馗) at the year's end, intended as a screen to dispel malign forces and to avert disasters while bringing blessings, was already widespread during the flourishing period of the Tang Dynasty.

Excerpted from Li Tianxiu and Wang Zhende's *Reflections on Zhong Kui and Zhong Kui Paintings*

—— Republished in *Masters of Calligraphy and Painting: Zhong Kui Special Edition*

---

[5] In this paragraph, various forms of the name "Kui" are used to reference different historical and mythological concepts, all of which are homophones in Chinese, pronounced "Kui".

[6] Mōryō (罔两, also written as "魍魉"), a spirit from Chinese mythology, was originally one of the youngest sons of the ancient Emperor Zhuanxu. Following his death, he became associated with pestilence and is often depicted as an eerie being responsible for epidemics, as described in texts such as Huainanzi and In Search of the Supernatural. In folklore, he's known to haunt rivers, palaces, and scare children, contributing to various diseases.

[7] The Xuan (魖) is described in ancient Chinese mythology as a fierce and formidable beast.

[8] The Wang Xiang, (罔象, also written as "魍象") is a legendary aquatic creature or a terrestrial spectre of wood and stone from ancient Chinese mythology.

[9] In Chinese culture, "Bi Xie" (辟邪) refers to the practice or belief in warding off evil spirits or influences. It is often associated with talismans, figures, or rituals believed to have protective properties against misfortune or malevolent forces.

The Ideological Significance and Aesthetic Characteristics of Zhong Kui Paintings

One might wonder: given that Zhong Kui originated from dreams and fabrications, how has his tale spread so widely and endured for a millennium, still vivid in the minds of people today? What is the fundamental reason for this enduring presence? Is it the absurdity of his story that captures the intense fascination of people? Or is it the rich intellectual content and profound philosophy embodied in the image of Zhong Kui that invite lingering contemplation? Or perhaps it is the aesthetic value of Zhong Kui's image in the history of art that exerts an endless charm? It must be said that all three aspects contribute. There are political, social, and psychological reasons, as well as artistic ones. Otherwise, a hollow and insubstantial figure, no matter how bizarrely adorned, could not remain significant over time. Below is an analysis of the aesthetic value of Zhong Kui paintings:

1. The synergy of ideal beauty

Why does Zhong Kui, a fantastical character from Emperor Xuanzong of Tang's dreams, and a figure from myth with no counterpart in reality, possess an appearance that blurs the line between semblance and essence, between illusion and truth? We believe that while Zhong Kui may be a creation of fantasy, he resonates with the wishes and ideals of many across various eras to a significant degree. It is these collective desires and ideals that form the synergy necessary for the enduring legacy of Zhong Kui's image. For the Tang dynasty and the feudal rulers that followed, such a figure was much needed. During the transition from prosperity to decline, Emperor Xuanzong of the Tang Dynasty seemed to have a premonition of the impending An Lushan[10] Rebellion; hence, even during his indulgent escapades to the Li Mountain Palace, he still engaged in martial exercises. Amidst his life of unrestrained debauchery, a nameless sense of insecurity frequently assailed his fragile heart. Indeed, wasn't it a brazen demon that boldly stole his jade flute and the noble consort's purple sachet, even daring to "secretly pluck red lotuses from beneath the autumn waters" (as depicted in the Yuan poet Sa Duci's "Ode of the Zhongnan Scholar")? This left him not only concerned for the defence at the front gates but also wary of the peace at the back. At the same time, the masses of impoverished scholars, bewildered by the civil examination system and living in destitution, gradually became a profound social issue stirring the emperor's compassion. This likely contributed to the genetic makeup of Xuanzong's compelling narrative about Zhong Kui in his dream — the "scholar unsuccessful in martial examinations" — and was the impetus for his command to Wu Daozi to paint Zhong Kui, which he then affixed to the gates of the inner palace. Emperor Xuanzong's dream of Zhong Kui, in essence, was an ephemeral model erected for the disillusioned and despondent scholars of lower social standing, offering them an idol for solace when all paths seemed barred—a reflection of an ideal or wish among the rulers of the declining Tang Dynasty and those of subsequent feudal eras. Hence, the legend of Zhong Kui was not the reason for any rational delusion on the part of rulers like Xuanzong but rather the outcome of it. From this, can we not discern a truth: though legends are fabrications, often embodying elements of falsehood, they always sensitively echo real life. Zhong Kui's ability to vanquish demons and expel evil was not only welcomed by the emperor but also yearned for by the entire ruling class. Regarding the vast number of lower-class literati who held grievances against the Yang siblings[11], their admiration for Zhong Kui was predicated on a different set of thoughts. As the Ming literatus Wu Kuan lamented in his poem inscribed on "The New Year's Eve Excursion of Zhong Kui": "Alas! Old Zhong Kui is indeed a hero among spectres. Hence, the Tang Emperor, envisioning his likeness, decreed Wu Daozi to paint it with a brush of five colours. Recalling the days of the Tang Dynastycs Tianbao era, when ghosts were in abundance; Yang Guifei seduced with her fox-like charm in the Palace of Eternal Purity[12], and An Lushan roared in the imperial halls. Had Zhong Kui been present, these two spectres would not have escaped." Similarly, Wang Shizhen commented in "A Playful Inscription on Qian Shubao's Rendering of Zhong Kui's Relocation": "Within the palace of Kaiyuan, ghosts hailed a mother's name; The chancellors and viceroys indulged in hexes, to their shame. The Emperor bestowed upon Lord Zhong, the Yellow Thearch's[13] fame; Yet unrewarded ghostly chases, doomed him to the brine." As for what the Yuan dynasty poets articulated even more clearly: " The Emperor of Kaiyuan's realm in human cares has ceased; The haunted palace seeks the strength of this ghost-subduing beast." (as noted by Wang Xiaoweng in "Zhongshan Going on Excursion"). "In twilight years, the sun dims as thunder slays the light; Within jade halls, the spectres wail, recoiling from the sight." (as seen in Sa Duci's "Ode of the Zhongnan Scholar"). It is evident that later generations' views diverged from the legendary narrative of Zhong Kui protecting Emperor Xuanzong and Yang Guifei. Instead, they directed unstoppable righteous indignation towards the bewitching demons at Xuanzong's side, such as the pernicious Yang Guifei and An Lushan. In their indignation, they harboured hopes: not only did they wish for a Zhong Kui in their time to eradicate the evil spirits, but they also aspired for "heaven to always bring forth such individuals." Certainly, among those literati deeply intoxicated by the feudal elite's vision of posthumous honour, there were not a few who fantasized

---

[10] A general who launched a devastating rebellion against the Tang Dynasty, known as the An Lushan Rebellion.

[11] The "Yang siblings" refers to Yang Guifei, one of the Four Beauties of ancient China, and her brother Yang Guozhong. Their influence over Emperor Xuanzong and the Tang court is often blamed for contributing to the decline of the Tang Dynasty, particularly in the context of the An Lushan Rebellion.

[12] A palace in the Tang Dynasty's imperial complex, associated with Yang Guifei.

[13] An alternative title for the Yellow Emperor, a legendary Chinese sovereign and cultural hero.

about receiving imperial ennoblement after death, as Zhong Kui did. The Yuan poet Tang Su's poem "Zhong Kui" expresses such longing: "A soul of loyalty beyond the mortal call; In dreams, imperial robes from heaven fall. Alive, he shunned a thousand measures of grain; In death, his valour for nations does remain." While the common people's thoughts diverged greatly from those of the feudal rulers, their inevitable influence by the ruling class's ideology was undeniable. Moreover, Zhong Kui's purpose to rid the world of malevolent spirits, including those causing malarial fevers, undoubtedly aligned with the people's ideals and wishes. For compared to the ruling class, the common folk suffered more extensively and variedly from diseases, and they yearned even more for a righteous figure like Zhong Kui to shelter them. In this aspect, their thoughts found common ground with those of the rulers. Thus, it appears that Zhong Kui truly is an artistic figure who could be widely accepted and who has touched the hearts of many across generations (although this image was for a significant length of history, and in a considerable scope, associated with superstitious customs). Admittedly, people from different classes and social strata may have divergent aesthetic appraisals of Zhong Kui, yet they all invest their ideals of exorcising evil and summoning auspiciousness in him, thereby creating a collective force of ideal beauty within the image of Zhong Kui.

2. The unity of beauty and ugliness

As a formidable "great ghost," Zhong Kui's image is naturally ferocious and ugly. A vivid depiction by the Ming writer Ling Yunhan while eulogizing a painting of Zhong Kui goes, "A scholar from Zhongnan stands with sudden, stubborn mien; Deep in thought, his grin like a hedgehog, teeth unseen. Clad in blue with horned belt, his figure looms immense; His black hat shadows his face, boots baring digits hence." Zhong Kui's image has never strayed from the character "ugly." Yet within this ugliness, there lies the grievance of his forced ugliness, the bright glow of his righteous and altruistic soul. Thus, people do not find Zhong Kui frighteningly hideous, but rather, his ugliness is endearing, embodying a form of "beautiful ugliness." The Yuan poet Song Wu wrote in "Inscription on Gong Cuiyan's 'Zhongshan Going on Excursion'": "Turning back, old Kui observes, their eyes in silent battle; Seeming not to scorn Kui's looks, nor by his visage rattled." The Qing poet Gao Qipei in his "Self-Inscription on 'Zhong Kui Watching a Sword'" muses, "Rising to the heavens, poised as if a dragon in flight; Who would say this noble sir lacks a visage bright?" To this, the scholar Wang Chaowen has offered a brilliant analysis, noting that "in art, sometimes to reveal beauty and to enhance its perception, an emphasis on the opposing element is precisely needed..." The veteran actor Hou Yushan, in the play "Marrying Off Sister," portrays a Zhong Kui who, though sometimes childlike, never conceals the sorrow borne of misfortune or the joy of fulfilling his sister's wish to marry, overcoming the barriers of the dead and the living. His acting, singing, and dancing impart a clear sense that Zhong Kui is not a terrifying, malevolent ghost, but a being of goodness, innocence, forthrightness, and tender sentiment. "Marrying Off Sister" shows him to be a responsible and endearing person; his joyous Yangge[14] steps intertwine to amuse and evoke sympathy for his fate—a genius destroyed. "Beauty does not equate to being visually pleasing; regardless of Zhong Kui's looks, the audience distinctly feels that it is the inner character's beauty that is decisive," (from *Zhong Kui Is Not Ugly*). Regarding the beauty of character expressed through a grotesque and deformed exterior, the renowned 19th-century French sculptor Auguste Rodin also had insights, asserting, "What is deemed ugly in nature often reveals its 'character' more than that which is considered beautiful, for inner truth is more evidently manifested in the sorrowful countenance of illness, in the wrinkled and vile thin face, and in all forms of deformity and incompleteness, than in a countenance that is normal and whole." He believed that it is the power of "character" (in a broad sense) that creates artistic beauty (from *Art by Auguste Rodin*). Whether Rodin's assertions are comprehensive is a discussion for another time, but his emphasis on the necessity of an artistic image possessing the inner character's beauty is indeed insightful. We must not assume that a deformed and incomplete appearance is the best form to showcase the beauty of the soul, nor should we believe that a beautiful soul can only be revealed through an ugly exterior; however, it is a fact that due to the stark contrast, the expression of beauty is more pronounced. Our ancestors have always valued a fine tradition of emphasizing "inner beauty." Unlike the ancient Western custom of exploring beauty from an objective standpoint, they consistently intertwined beauty with ethical and moral virtues (equated with "goodness"), believing that virtue could manifest through a handsome appearance as well as an ugly or deformed one. They never endorsed the superficial judgment of "judging a book by its cover" and particularly despised characters who appeared dignified on the surface but were sordid at heart. Confucius expressed such views, stating, "It is virtuous manners which constitute the excellence of a neighbourhood," "If they will be set on virtue, there will be no practice of wickedness," "Fine words and an insinuating appearance are seldom associated with true virtue" (from *The Analects*). Clearly, Confucius regarded the inner quality of "benevolence" as the foundation of aesthetic judgment. He even considered pleasing words and feigned amiability as indications of a lack of virtue. Zhuangzi, who held views quite distinct from those of the Confucian school, nonetheless shares common ground with Confucius and Mencius in his veneration of inner beauty. The "perfected individuals" and "ultimate humans" celebrated in Zhuangzi, De Chong Fu are often cripples, blind, or ugly. He emphasized that "when one's virtue is extraordinary, (any deficiency in) his bodily form may be forgotten"; "What they had loved in their mother was not her bodily figure, but what had given animation to her figure"; and one should "wander within the realm of the corporeal form," and not "seek outside of it." It is evident that Zhuangzi did not focus on physical appearance but instead underscored inner virtue. The celebrated lyric epic *Li Sao* by Qu Yuan is a masterful ode that repeatedly affirms and extols "inner beauty." He professes time and again: "Abundant within me lies this inner beauty, further adorned by cultivated abilities." Qu Yuan's unwavering commitment to inner beauty also speaks to intrinsic virtues. The *Record of Music* states: "Music is the flourish of virtue, the vigourous spirit that transforms into divine." Mengzi proclaims: "A man who commands our liking is what is called a good man. He whose goodness is part of himself is what is called a real man. He whose goodness has been filled up is what is called a beautiful man." All these texts attribute beauty as the offspring of "virtue," "goodness," or "sincerity." And such internal beauty, when manifested through an ugly exterior, often appears even more striking and profound. History has seen its share of remarkable individuals whose less favourable appearance belied their unparalleled talents. Take, for example, Wei Zheng, the famous remonstrative official of early Tang, who, "though not exceeding an ordinary appearance," possessed "innate courage and wisdom" and dared to "offer candid admonitions," fully displaying the virtues of concern for the state and the people, fearlessly devoted to his cause. Emperor Taizong did not disdain his looks; on the contrary, he found them "charming" (as recorded in *The Old Book of Tang: Biographies, Section Twenty-One*). In the numerous depictions of Zhong Kui, a sharp contrast and yet a harmonious unity is achieved between "external ugliness" and "internal beauty." Take, for example, Gao Qipei's "Furious Zhong Kui," painted during the Dragon Boat Festival in the sixth year of the Yongzheng era (1728). On the terrifying visage, nearly every muscle appears to twitch; the full cheeks of his beard are like tufts of grass tossed in a tempest, each strand standing on end. The entire face is tightly drawn into a tense, flattened oval. The two wide eyes, brimming with uncontainable rage, emit a glare sharp as swords, while the tattered headdress quivers above his lowered brow. Zhong Kui's hands point directly ahead, and although no ghosts are depicted, one imagines the spirits causing chaos exactly where he points, unable to escape his righteous punishment. This portrayal, in terms of Zhong Kui's likeness, is undoubtedly hideous, even ferociously menacing. Yet, it is through such a figure, seething with rage, that the painter brilliantly captures the admirable virtues of hating evil as one would an enemy, of unyielding integrity, and valour that is hard to suppress. The "ugliness" here is precisely the revelation and manifestation of "beauty." That is to say, the more fiercely ugly, the more intensely beautiful. This stark contrast and successful union of beauty and ugliness poignantly convey the tragic grandeur of Zhong Kui's image. Of course, this unity is grounded in its profound historical substance and aesthetic ideal. For it allows a hero, indignant and unavenged in life, to display his divine might after death; it enables a hero, once uncelebrated, to vanquish demons for the world; it allows a hero, obscure in life, to achieve resounding fame, echoing through the ages. This suffices to stir a complex blend of poignancy and gratifying sorrow, inducing a rapture tinged with regret. Therefore, compared to a beauty that is superficially alluring, fleeting, and cheap, it opens the heart, invites deeper reflection, and engenders an artistic allure that endures through time.

3. The fusion of the "refined" and the "rustic"

Art has always had a distinction between the refined and the rustic. In bygone days, literati often esteemed the "refined" as elegant and dismissed the "rustic" as crude, not realizing that the "refined" often originated from the "rustic." Lu Xun once said: "The gentry often seize things from the folk, turning bamboo branch songs into classical Chinese, and the 'girl-next-door' into a concubine, but once these things touch their hands, they perish along with them" (from Lu Xun's *Reflections on Mei Lanfang and Others*). However, Zhong Kui paintings might be considered an exception, for although they too have been touched by the literati, they have managed to maintain a long-standing connection with the common folk due to historical inertia. On one hand, folk artists during festive seasons often consciously or unconsciously processed and created "Zhong Kui figures"; on the other hand, court painters and scholarly artists, in creating Zhong Kui paintings, continually drew nourishment from folk art (a trend that became particularly evident among rustic artists post the Yuan dynasty). Through such a cyclical process of variation and development, the historical Zhong Kui paintings ultimately condensed the aesthetic tastes of everyone, from emperors and high officials to the common people, forging a mutual intermingling of the refined and the rustic within a specific domain. Here, we might venture to compare the folk Zhong Kui paintings with those attributed to the Emperor Xianzong of Ming. Dutch Sinologist Jan. J. M. de Groot, in his book *The Religious System of China*, includes a folk painting of Zhong Kui. The painting depicts the fierce and menacing Zhong Kui voraciously devouring the head of a small demon, while another kneels at his feet begging for mercy; a bat serenely flits through the air, creating a cheerful swirl of exorcism and blessing. The Zhong Kui painted by Emperor Xianzong also shows a ferociously grim visage, with a demon attendant bearing fresh fruit beside him and a bat leading the way in front. Both are painted for the New Year to invite blessings, and while their styles may differ, the aspiration for happiness and the desire to expel evil spirits are consistent. It is evident that the brushstrokes of court painters often incorporate the wild spirit of folk art, while folk artisans continually imbibe the refined essence of courtly creations. The interplay between the refined and the rustic is manifestly apparent, both in the conceptual intentions and the artistic techniques employed. However, the fusion of the refined and the rustic does not equate to their mutual substitution, nor does it mean their homogenization. Rather, in their melding, they consistently maintain their distinct styles and characteristics. It goes without saying that without a clear distinction between the refined and the rustic, there can be no fusion. It is precisely because of the continuous blending of the refined with the rustic, and vice versa, over thousands of years, that Zhong Kui paintings have flourished in both spheres: rustic with refined undertones and refined with rustic nuances, ever-painting, ever-renewing. In summary, the myth of Zhong Kui and the various tales associated with him is a continuum from ancient to modern times, like streams flowing from distant eras and old folk customs. Emerging from an atmosphere of mysterious haze, they shimmer with a deep, ethereal brilliance, encompassing a complex aesthetic richness and possessing a vivid, potent symbolism. They seem to have avoided falling into the quagmire of feudal superstition, uniquely favoured in the realm of art to be ever-renewed and immortalized.

Excerpted from Li Tianxiu and Wang Zhende's *Reflections on Zhong Kui and Zhong Kui Paintings*

—— Republished in Masters of *Calligraphy and Painting: Zhong Kui Special Edition*

Historical Evolution of Zhong Kui Paintings

From the legends recounted in books, it is known that Zhong Kui paintings originated during the Tang Dynasty. It is said that the great painter Wu Daozi of Emperor Xuanzong's era was the pioneer of Zhong Kui paintings. Wu Daozi's depiction of Zhong Kui, known as the "Zhong Kui style," became a model of the time. It spread far and wide through the replication by countless artists. On this subject, Shen Kuo of the Northern Song Dynasty provided a vivid account in his *Supplementary Discourses to the Dream Pool Essays*:

The imperial palace has long possessed a painting of Zhong Kui by Wu Daozi, prefaced with an inscription by a Tang dynasty individual that reads: "Emperor Xuanzong of Tang, during his martial exercises at Li Mountain in the open year, returned to the palace by the end of the year feeling discontent and subsequently fell ill. As the illness persisted for nearly a month, no physician or sorcerer could bring about a recovery. One night, he dreamt of two ghosts, one large and one small. The smaller one, with a red calf's nose, wore one shoe and was barefoot with the other, carrying the spare shoe, and stealing Yang Guifei's purple sachet and the Emperor's jade flute while running around the palace. The larger ghost, in a hat and blue robe with one arm bare and both feet shod, caught the smaller one, gouged out its eyes, then tore it apart to devour. The Emperor inquired who the larger ghost was, to which it replied: 'I am Zhong Kui, a man who failed the military examinations but swore to rid the world of demons for Your Majesty.' Upon awakening, the Emperor found his illness had miraculously improved, and his vigour renewed. He then commanded the painter Wu Daozi to depict the scene from his dream, saying: 'Try to paint for me as seen in the dream.' Wu Daozi followed the decree, and as if having witnessed it himself, quickly completed the painting and presented it. The Emperor, gazing at it intently, said: 'It's as if you shared the dream with me. How strikingly similar it is!' Wu Daozi approached and said: 'Your Majesty, your constant labours day and night, often at the expense of meals, brought on the illness. If evil spirits were indeed dispelled, it was to protect Your Sacred Virtue.' Then, dancing, he wished the Emperor tens of thousands of years of life. The Emperor, overjoyed, rewarded him with a hundred gold pieces and decreed: 'The divine spirit responded in a dream, and the affliction was completely cured. A valiant man who expels demons truly deserves commendation. Since the painting is extraordinary, let it be shown to the officials. Used at the year's end to drive away evil, it should be easily recognized. To remove demonic influences and calm the malevolent atmosphere. Let it be known throughout the land, and let all be informed.'"

Similar records are also found in Gao Cheng's *Records of the Origins of Matters and Things* from the Northern Song and the Ming scholar Chen Yaowen's *Tianzhong Records*. The Zhong Kui story in the *Tianzhong Records* is cited from *The Unofficial History of Tang*, regrettably, the original text of which is no longer extant. From these records, it can be discerned that Wu Daozi's depiction of Zhong Kui was based on Emperor Xuanzong's peculiar dream, further enhanced by artistic imagination. Although the original work has not survived to the present day, the vivid image can still be envisioned from the inscriptions by the Tang people. Undoubtedly, it must have been an ethereal and soul-stirring masterpiece. Thereafter, Zhong Kui, with his ugly appearance and demon-devouring aura, began to shine with noticeable brilliance in the realm of art. The reasons for his enduring luminance through history's layered peaks are manifold; however, the origins of his inception can be summarized into three main points. Firstly, the advocacy by Emperor Xuanzong. Since it was a bizarre dream of the romantic sovereign of the Kaiyuan zenith, since the emperor commanded the painter to "depict the dream," and then "bestowed it upon officials," rewarding his favoured courtiers, and even "proclaimed it throughout the realm, ordering all to be informed," it naturally created a response as if mountains and seas were calling out in unison. Secondly, it emerged from the brush of "The Sage of Painting," Wu Daozi. Wu Daozi's painting of Zhong Kui did not only receive Shen Kuo's repeated praises but was also highly esteemed in Guo Ruoxu's *Records of Picture Seeing and Hearing*, which states: "Wu Daozi depicted Zhong Kui in a blue robe, standing on one foot, with one squinting eye, a Hu[15] at his waist, and dishevelled hair, seizing a demon with his left hand and gouging out its eyes with his right. The brushwork was forceful and vigourous, truly an exceptional piece of painted work." The commissioning of Wu Daozi to paint Zhong Kui was undoubtedly seen as a sensational event within the art circles of the time. It was not only Wu Daozi's reputation as an artist that stirred the era but also because this masterpiece pioneered a new domain within religious themes, enriching the genre with fresh content. Hence, it won Emperor Xuanzong's earnest admiration and the veneration and emulation of Daozi's disciples, such as Qu Yan, Zhang Cang, and Lu Lenga, and also drew the attention of countless other artists, both within the court and beyond. Thirdly, the figure of Zhong Kui garnered widespread resonance among the populace. Wu Daozi's Zhong Kui, who expelled the diminutive demons spreading malaria, did not act merely for the emperor but as a "banisher of malevolence from all under heaven." The desire to eliminate such malevolence easily stirred the common people, who lived under the threat of pestilence and evil spirits. It also aligned with the ancient folk custom of expelling the old and ushering in the new on New Year's Eve. Thus, when Emperor Xuanzong decreed Zhong Kui's image to be used as a talisman for driving away evil spirits at the year's end, it swiftly spread among the populace and gradually became part of the national traditional customs. Mr. Bo Songnian, in his *A Brief History of Door Paintings*, discusses Zhong Kui, known as the "God of the Rear Gate," and writes: "The tradition of depicting Zhong Kui as the deity who wards off evil and slays demons during festive seasons began in the late Tang Dynasty and continued robustly through the Ming and Qing dynasties. Initially, the images were mostly hung in halls, as described in the novel *Biographies of Ghost Pacification*, which states: 'To this day, on the New Year's Day festival, every household depicts the image of the god Zhong Kui: eyes on bats, sword in hand, suspended in the central hall.' Liu Ruoyu's *The Chronicles from the Wine Medium* from the Ming also records the custom of hanging paintings of the God of Fortune and Zhong Kui inside homes on New Year's Eve." Mr. Bo Songnian has demonstrated the widespread popularity of Zhong Kui paintings in folk culture.

However, his assertion that Zhong Kui paintings began as festive decorations at the end of the Tang Dynasty is still a matter open to further discussion. From the The Complete Works of the Tang Dynasty, we not only encounter *Acknowledgment for the Imperial Bestowal of Zhong Kui Painting and the Calendar* written by the minister Zhang Yue during Emperor Xuanzong's reign, but also *Acknowledgment to Duke Du of Huainan for the Imperial Bestowal of the Zhong Kui Calendar* by Liu Yuxi from Emperor Dezong's time, which says: 'Prostrate before the painted mighty deity, dispelling the gathering threats, promulgating the laws of time, reverently bestowing the seasons, the stern display adds prestige to the gates. The constant use of this auspicious talisman is indeed treasured.' It is evident that Zhong Kui paintings as New Year's decorations possibly started at the turn of the High and Mid Tang periods, likely spreading by the end of the Tianbao era. It is worth noting that although the earliest recorded Zhong Kui painting was by Wu Daozi of the Tang Dynasty, the myth of Zhong Kui did not originate in the Tang but is a continuation of ancient folk customs of exorcism, even tracing back to the grand Nuo rites of antiquity."

It is generally said that, due to the advocacy of the contemporary emperor during the Tang Dynasty, the artists merely fixated on replicating Wu Daozi's "Zhong Kui style," fervently imitating his works. However, with the fall of the Tang Dynasty and the continuous development of painting, the blind faith and adoration for Wu Daozi's "Zhong Kui style" were eventually shattered, giving rise to bold variations and renewals of the "Zhong Kui style." *Records of Picture Seeing and Hearing and Xuanhe Painting Catalog* both recount a widely beloved tale: after the fall of the Tang Dynasty, a painting of Zhong Kui by Wu Daozi held in the palace was scattered among the people. In the early 10th century, this treasured piece was presented to the Later Shu ruler, Wang Yan, who treasured it, hanging it in his bedroom for continuous admiration. At that time, the great artist Huang Quan was serving as an imperial calligrapher in Former Shu. One day, Wang Yan summoned Huang Quan to the inner palace to view Wu Daozi's painting of Zhong Kui. Huang Quan was awestruck at the sight. Wang Yan then said to Huang Quan: "In this painting by Wu Daozi, Zhong Kui uses the second finger of his right hand to gouge out the demon's eye. It would appear more forceful if he used his thumb instead. Could you make this change for me?" Following the order, Huang Quan took the painting home, pondered over it for several days, and finally decided to paint a new Zhong Kui on fresh silk, this time gouging the demon's eye with the thumb. The next day, Huang Quan presented both Wu Daozi's original and his new work to Wang Yan. The ruler questioned why he had not simply made the requested change, "I only commanded you to alter one finger, why have you painted an entirely new picture on another piece of paper?" Huang Quan explained: "In Wu Daozi's Zhong Kui, the strength and profound expression are all concentrated on the index finger of the right hand, not on the thumb. Thus, a casual alteration of the finger would have ruined the original work. In my new painting, I have shifted all the vigour and expression to the thumb." These words led Wang Yan to an epiphany, and he sighed deeply, praising Huang Quan for his meticulous approach to painting and his refusal to rashly apply his brush. Wu Daozi's original work depicted Zhong Kui using his index finger to gouge out the demon's eye, a clear intention to combat the red-clad little demon causing malaria. It was unnecessary to use the thumb; the index finger alone sufficed, embodying the adage, "Why use a cleaver to carve a chicken?" In the Tang Dynasty, this was perhaps a point of delighted conversation among the people. But by the Five Dynasties, people were no longer content with simply preserving the artistic creations of their predecessors. The new work commissioned by the Later Shu ruler from Huang Quan certainly demonstrates the painter's meticulous approach to the organic unity of motion and spirit in his subjects, as well as Huang Quan's reverence for the works of earlier masters. The historical fact is quite clear: a strong desire to break free from the "Zhong Kui style" and to create a Zhong Kui image for their own era was driving painters in their quest for new explorations. During the Five Dynasties, the painter Wang Daoqiu, despite his admiration for the styles of Wu Daozi and Lu Lengjia, made changes to Wu Daozi's "Zhong Kui style" in his mural "Zhong Kui Carrying a Ghost" for the Xiangguo Temple. In the same era, Zhou Wenju of Southern Tang was also renowned for his depictions of Zhong Kui. The imperial collection of the Song Dynasty once held seven of his Zhong Kui works, including five titled "Zhong Kui's Little Sister," indicating a shift from merely portraying Zhong Kui capturing ghosts to exploring his family background and personal life. Song Dynasty artists such as Yang Fei, Shi Ke, Pu Sheng, Sun Zhiwei, Li Gonglin, Ma Hezhi, Ma Lin, Liang Kai, and Gong Kai all painted the figure of Zhong Kui. Yang Fei essentially employed Wu Daozi's "sparse style" with slight variations. Shi Ke, known for his witty and eloquent nature, rendered Zhong Kui in a free, wild, and eccentric manner, refusing to be confined by the established methods of his predecessors. Pu Sheng's Zhong Kui, astride a massive ox and surrounded by servants, made the demons tremble and unsure of where to turn, earning praise from Wen Tong. Li Gonglin, lauded as "the foremost painter of the Song," also created "Zhong Kui Marrying Off His Sister." During the Southern Song period, Liang Kai took a fresh approach to depicting Zhong Kui, eschewing the grandiose acts of binding demons and the popular theme of his sister's marriage. Instead, he concocted leisurely scenarios like "stealing flowers and flutes," further enriching the character and image of Zhong Kui. The poem "Inscription on Liang Kai's Painting of Zhong Kui" by the Ming scholar Jiang Zhuxiao captures this sentiment exquisitely: "With a tiger's maw and bristled whiskers fierce; How can he not untie the fiends that humans pierce? To pilfer blooms and flutes, mere trifles they beseech; Can he endure a ghoul's mischief on the bridge that spans so reach?" As a bold and studious painter who dared to innovate, Liang Kai's Zhong Kui paintings achieved remarkable feats in both subject matter and technique. Ma Lin, following Ma Yuan's brushwork, created "Zhong Kui's Night Hunt," a scene of splendid vibrancy frequently mentioned in ancient texts, though the whereabouts of the original work are unknown. Yan Hui, a renowned painter at the turn of the Song and Yuan dynasties, once made "Zhong Kui's Hunting Procession," in which Zhong Kui has stiff horns on his head, a fierce expression like a wicked ghost, bare-bodied with a steel fork in hand, one foot kicking back. Some believe this to be a representation of the original form of Zhong Kui as Kui

Xing (from Mao Yibo's *Supplemental Records of Erlang Shen, the Three Great Emperor-Officials, and Zhong Kui*). Another of Yan Hui's works, "Zhong Kui's Moonlit Journey" (currently held at the Nelson-Atkins Museum of Art in the United States), presents a serene and chilly scene with a profound and subtle image, considered one of the finest depictions of Zhong Kui. Surveying the Song Dynasty's Zhong Kui paintings, as commented in the *Xuanhe Painting Catalog* regarding Yang Fei: "Although recent depictions of Zhong Kui are numerous, tracing back to the origin, some say: 'Emperor Xuanzong, suffering from malaria, dreamt of Zhong Kui dancing before him, banishing the disease. Subsequently, his likeness was transcribed and came to be known in the world, marking the origin of Zhong Kui's image. Over time, though the portrayals underwent minor transformations, the general depiction remained consistent, with variations only in how the Danqing[16] artists chose to adorn it" This broadly delineates two periods: one is the era of replicating Wu Daozi's "Zhong Kui style," the"era of replicating the likeness"; the second is the "time of change" and "only the Danqing artists chose to adorn it," which we refer to as "the stage of evolution in Zhong Kui paintings."

After the Yuan Dynasty, "Zhong Kui Paintings" entered their third phase of development, which continued until before the liberation. This phase could be termed the era of allegorical expression. Over these six hundred years, China's protracted feudal society declined precipitously towards eventual extinction. Society was often in turmoil, and upright literati and scholars frequently suffered persecution in literary inquisitions. At times, they were compelled to adopt more indirect methods. Consequently, their depictions of Zhong Kui often transcended the mere banishment of evil; they involuntarily used Zhong Kui as a vehicle to express their melancholy, indignation, hopes, and aspirations. Thus, many representations of Zhong Kui essentially became avatars and shadows of the artists themselves. Zheng Ji of the Qing Dynasty eloquently stated in his *A Concise Study of Painting at the Dream Fantasy Abode*: "Many renowned predecessors painted ghosts and deities, which the vulgar eye finds bizarre and hence discards. They do not realize that the ancients did not paint to simply please the world with their depictions, but rather used brush and ink to express the emotions harbored within their hearts. Such ordinary paintings are common and nothing novel. Without the guise of ghosts and deities, how could one release the boundless spirit?" However, to use this statement to describe the works of Wu Daozi, in my opinion, is not quite fitting. Wu Daozi's works are generally thematic, purposefully serving the court and temples. The characteristic of "using brush and ink to express what is held in the heart" is not particularly prominent. If this passage were used to describe the Zhong Kui paintings by some artists after the Yuan Dynasty, it would be exceedingly apt. Take, for example, Gong Kai's "Zhongshan Going on Excursion," which is housed in the Freer Gallery of Art in Washington, D.C. The painting depicts Zhong Kui and his sister on an excursion in a palanquin. They are accompanied by a host of strangely shaped little spirits, varying in size and form. Some carry the palanquin, others shoulder jars, some haul luggage, and others carry bundles, all bustling about in a flurry. Although Zhong Kui is also depicted with a bizarre ugliness, he is not as imbued with the sword-sharp, murderous aura of previous portrayals, but rather appears as a martial officer with a certain scholarly air. His sister and the maids behind her, using ink as a rouge to dab on their cheeks, are so whimsically portrayed they provoke silent laughter. Gong Kai's innovative imagination thus elicited strong interest in this painting. Many literati of the time, such as Wang Xiaoweng, Han Xing, Li Mingfeng, Shi Zongyan, and Song Wu, wrote poems and commentaries on this painting. Song Wu praised it, saying, "The Cuiyan hermit (Gong Kai), his mind serene and plain; Why knows he so the hearts of ghosts, their sentiments and pain? Behold, his brush strokes frighten those from the nether ring; Once the poem is complete, we'll hear the spectres sing. To this day, upon this scroll, a chill wind still does blow" (from "Inscription on Gong Cuiyan's 'Zhongshan Going on Excursion'"). Li Mingfeng's critique is even more whimsically expressive: "One must chuckle at Lord Gong's jest with spirits and ghosts; His bold strokes craft visions that rival celestial hosts. In poverty, I dare not unveil such art to gaze; Lest in jest, they find in me, a subject to amuse and amaze" (from "Zhongshan Going on Excursion"). However, why did Gong Kai choose to "jest with spirits and ghosts"? Clearly, there was an allegory intended. Mr. Wen Tingkuan makes a sensible point: "Gong Kai lived during the transition from the Song to the Yuan Dynasty and is said to have adamantly refused official positions after the fall of the Song, despite being so poor he had 'hardly a mat to sit on.' He used his brush to resist the Yuan, instructing his son to lie on a couch 'pressing down paper' for him to paint. This painting harbours the sentiment of loyalty to the fallen country, wishing to expel the rule of the Yuan Dynasty. Yuan scholars Chen Fang and Zhou Geng both recognized in their poetic postscripts that they likened Zhong Kui to his own aspirations, painting him 'with a spirit that could swallow thousands,' while depicting the servants of the Yuan rulers as little demons, dishevelled and grotesque, to inspire himself and others to resist the Yuan" (from *Ruminations on Freehand Paintings of Antiquity*). Considering Gong Kai's bold and refined brushwork, it represents a development from the "reduced brush figures" of Shi Ke and Liang Kai, indeed meriting the role of a bridge from the Song to the beginning of the Yuan. Additionally, renowned Yuan Dynasty painters Chen Lin and Wang Meng both have surviving works titled "Zhong Kui in the Chilly Woods." Wang Meng is known for his meticulous and detailed style, while Chen Lin is celebrated for his vigorous and profound expressiveness. Yet, their depictions of Zhong Kui share a common thread: both artists imbued their paintings with a sense of lofty solitude, tranquility, and a poignant spirit. "Using painting to express one's aspirations" is a significant characteristic

---

[16] "Danqing" (丹青) refers to the traditional Chinese fine brush painting, often using cinnabar (丹) and azurite (青) pigments.

of many works by Yuan artists and is also a distinctive feature of some Yuan Dynasty Zhong Kui paintings.

In the Ming Dynasty, there was no shortage of painters who used their art to express personal feelings and convictions. Let's take Dai Jin, the founder of the Zhejiang School of Painting, as an example. Dai Jin's figures were often depicted using techniques like orchid leaf strokes[17] combined with the silkworm head and rat tail strokes[18], creating a sense of rhythm and pause that earned him the reputation as the leading figure in the painting circles of the Ming era. Yet he suffered the misfortune of being slandered for painting a hermit in a red robe fishing by the river, which was maliciously construed as a desecration of the "red official robes" of the court. This accusation led to his dismissal from official position and exile back to his hometown, where he lived out his days in bitterness and poverty, nursing a sense of grievance. The surviving "Zhong Kui's Nightly Wanderings" by Dai Jin portrays a desolate scene of cold mountains and withered grass, shrouded in a bleak and confused atmosphere. Underneath a tattered umbrella stands Zhong Kui in an ill-fitting, broad dark robe with crossed feet, his face bearing a bitter look of illness, with a furrowed brow and downturned mouth betraying feelings of sorrow and suppressed anger. This clearly embodies the artist's own sense of drift and displacement, faintly conveying the depressive mood and resilient determination of Dai Jin after his disillusionment with officialdom. Isn't it so, that the legendary Zhong Kui, though a hero of unmatched talent, was not utilized by the world? This mirrors the life of Dai Jin, an unparalleled painter who could not find his footing in the world of politics. The difference lies in that Zhong Kui was even more unfortunate in life, and Dai Jin could not expect any posthumous honour. It is evident that rather than simply painting Zhong Kui, Dai Jin was subtly expressing his own heart and mind through the character of Zhong Kui. During the Ming Dynasty, Qian Geng's "Zhong Kui in the New Year" depicts Zhong Kui holding a Hu, with several blossoms of spring flowers tucked into his hat, his joy bubbling forth, eager to dance, presenting an entirely different elegance. This likely correlates with the vibrant urban economy of the mid-Ming to early Qing periods and the increasingly prominent trend in fine arts to symbolize good fortune. It also reflects the painter's own joyous sentiment while freely expressing himself through his art. The creation of Zhong Kui paintings reached its zenith during the Qing Dynasty, with many renowned painters, such as Gu Jianlong, Gao Qipei, Hua Xinluo, Jin Nong, Huang Shen, Luo Pin, Min Zhen, Zhao Zhiqian, Ren Xiong, Ren Bonian, and others excelling in this genre. Their works were numerous and artistically distinctive. Zhong Kui's portrayal varied from artist to artist, covering an incredibly broad range of content. For instance, Gao Qipei would paint several Zhong Kui paintings each year, and his works are now housed in the Palace Museum in Beijing, Liaoning Provincial Museum, National Museum of China, Shanghai Museum, and even in the collections of Kyosai Kawanabe in Japan. The Palace Museum alone possesses a *Metamorphic Forms of Zhong Kui Album* which comprises twelve pages of various Zhong Kuis, including scenes of him watching a sword, leaving a banquet, riding on ghosts, in the mirror, ascending the altar, wind and thunder, subduing demons, embracing his knees, sealing scroll, muffled laugh, reading, and dozing off – virtually encompassing all conceivable aspects of Zhong Kui's life. These depictions go beyond mere adherence to folk customs, warding off evil, or exorcising ghosts; they are infused with the artists' loathing for a corrupted reality, their ridicule of those incessantly pursuing wealth and status, and their mockery of the pedantic and small-minded, among other sentiments. It goes without saying that the Zhong Kui envisioned by the painter carries with it a certain symbolic meaning. The use of finger-painting in this artwork marks Gao Qipei's advantage over his predecessors. He also frequently employed cinnabar for painting Zhong Kui, catering to the folk customs of the time, which could be seen as an innovation in colour application by Qing Dynasty artists in their Zhong Kui creations (the exclusive use of cinnabar was not unique to the Qing Dynasty; Song Dynasty artists like Su Shi had painted bamboo in cinnabar). Later, during the Qianlong era, the prominent "Yangzhou School" came into vogue. These painters, either fallen from grace in officialdom or hopeless in their bureaucratic aspirations, lived by selling their paintings. They were different from the orthodox painters in the Qing court's Imperial Atelier, often regarded as eccentric and heterodox. Among them, artists like Huang Shen, Jin Nong, Hua Xinluo, and Luo Pin all have surviving works of Zhong Kui. In Huang Shen's "Portrait of Zhong Kui," the figure leans against a crooked old tree, his hat brim flared outward, eyes wide and white, gazing into the distance, seemingly filled with doubts, anxiety, and frustration. This recalls his use of the defiant Wei-Jin period figure Ji Kang in his *Jiaohu Poetry Collection*, to express his unwavering stance against all evil spirits and demons. His poem reads: "Ji Kang lights a lamp, illuminating the demons; disdainful to compete for brilliance, he plays the guqin and extinguishes the torch." On one hand, Huang Shen refuses to compete with malevolence, unwilling to associate with the corrupt; on the other hand, he deeply sympathizes with the downtrodden literati. In his poem "The Hardships of Travel," he expresses: "I wish to topple the southern peaks, turn them to feast; Exhaust the Eastern Sea to fill the cups of every least. To heartily feed all beneath the heavens, comfort the shivering scholars; That my name might race across the ages, unfading in its valour." Despite his own uncertain livelihood, he aspires to "feed all beneath the heavens," reflecting a remarkably noble and magnanimous spirit. Yet, his lofty ambitions remained unfulfilled. Despite his poverty, he did not belittle himself, and although his aspirations were high, he never sought to curry

[17]A painting technique that characterized by uneven pressure, the brush movement varies between lifting and pressing down, creating lines that are alternately thick and thin, resembling the shape of orchid leaves.

[18]A Chinese painting technique characterized by the way the brush is handled to create strokes that are thick at the beginning and taper off to a fine point, much like the head of a silkworm is broader and it narrows down to a tail, similar to that of a rat's thin tail.

favour with the powerful. Therefore, the Zhong Kui he painted, while dishevelled in appearance, is depicted with a grand and noble spirit, rarely tainted by the air of wealth and vulgarity. Hua Xinluo's thoughts wavered between Taoist and Buddhist philosophies, his yearning for a transcendental paradise often overshadowed by melancholy for the harsh realities of life. Hence, his works exude a breezy, ethereal, and elegant quality. His "Zhong Kui Marrying Off His Sister" depicts a cavalcade of celestial horses and chariots, resplendent with lights, amid a bustling procession, all to the accompaniment of rolling drums and music, conveying a vision of boundless and unrestrained imagination that transcends the earthly realm. Another piece, "Zhong Kui Devouring a Demon," captures Zhong Kui's hearty delight in gobbling up a demon under a willow tree, a scene rendered with distinctive flair. Furthermore, Qing Dynasty depictions of Zhong Kui seem to proliferate around the Dragon Boat Festival in May, a tradition that began at the Ming-Qing transition and flourished during the Qing era. Qing literati, cautious of the oppressive literary inquisitions, rarely engaged in risky political discourse, preferring to delve into ancient nostalgia, hence their extensive reading of classical texts and striving to accumulate the wisdom of the ancients. Their research and exploration of Zhong Kui paintings from past dynasties took a significant leap forward. In this regard, Jin Nong achieved notable success. At the age of seventy-five, he purposely used rice solution and ink from a Buddhist temple to paint "Drunken Zhong Kui" at the Dragon Boat Festival. His inscription reads: "During the Tang Dynasty, Wu Daozi created the 'Zhong Kui Entering the Palace' painting, while Zhang Wo depicted 'Zhong Kui Holding Hu.' From the Five Dynasties, Mou Yuande is known for the 'Zhong Kui Striking Ghosts' painting. In the Song Dynasty, Shi Ke produced 'Zhong Kui and His Little Sister,' Sun Zhiwei offered 'Zhong Kui in the Snow,' Li Gonglin composed 'Zhong Kui Marrying Off His Sister,' Liang Kai created 'Zhong Kui Seeking Plums on a Lame Horse,' and Ma Hezhi gave us 'Zhong Kui Reading Under the Pine.' From the Yuan Dynasty, Wang Meng painted 'Zhong Kui in the Chilly Woods,' Qian Gu portrayed 'Old Zhong Kui Relocating,' Guo Xu presented 'Zhong Kui Kicking a Ball,' and Chen Hongshou illustrated 'The New Year's Eve Excursion of Zhong Kui.' No one had ever painted a drunken Zhong Kui before, so I, using the Zen practice of mixing rice juice with ink, sucked the brush and depicted Zhong Kui inebriated. This painting not only serves to exorcise evil and ward off malevolence, but its portrayal of drunkenness is charmingly endearing, evoking the image of a jubilant scholar from Mount Zhongnan revelling in the festive celebrations of a golden age, basking in the peace of prosperous times. In the past, people would paint small images of Zhong Kui to offer to officials at year's end to dispel inauspiciousness, but now it is customarily done on the fifth day of the fifth month. On a summer day of the Xinwei year..."

In this inscription, Jin Nong enumerates twelve masters who have painted Zhong Kui from the Tang to the Qing dynasties, declaring his depiction of "Drunken Zhong Kui" to be an original creation, penned with the unique method of "using Zen rice juice mixed with ink." This breaks from the tradition of painting Zhong Kui for officials at year's end. Now, his eyes blaze with lightning-like ferocity, embodying the perceptive power to discern the finest details. The portrayal is meticulous, the posture vigorous, and the brushwork refined, revealing a distinct personal style. Moreover, the Zhong Kui paintings of Chen Shizeng, Zhang Daqian, Xu Beihong, Pu Xinshe, Chen Shaomei, Xu Yanxun, Li Keran, and Du Ziling have all been acclaimed by domestic and international audiences. In folk culture, the number of New Year paintings, door paintings, clay sculptures, toy figurines, shadow puppets, and paper cuttings featuring Zhong Kui themes is countless. Given the vast number of artists across dynasties, each with their unique style, connotations, and prolific creations, the study of Zhong Kui paintings has evolved into a specialized field of inquiry.

Excerpted from Li Tianxiu and Wang Zhende's *Reflections on Zhong Kui and Zhong Kui Paintings*

—— Republished in *Masters of Calligraphy and Painting: Zhong Kui Special Edition*

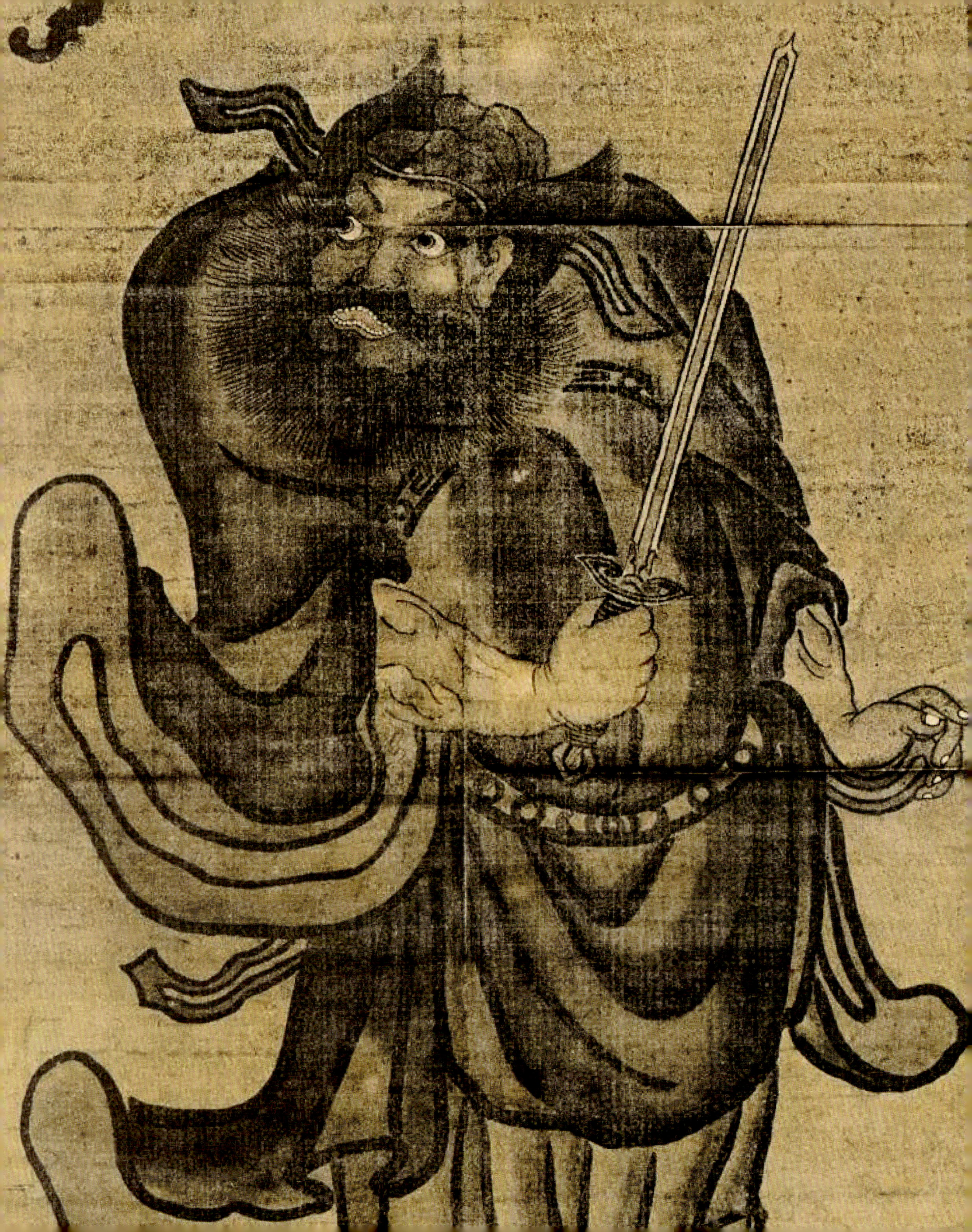

Originating in the Tang Dynasty

Throughout the long span of the Tang Dynasty, both court painters and folk artists used the "Zhong Kui style" of the Wu school as their model for replication. Thus, Zhong Kui, Zhong Kui paintings, and the belief in him, bolstered by historical associations, folk deification, imperial dreams, and the divine strokes of the master painter, have been perpetuated through the ages, enduring the test of time.

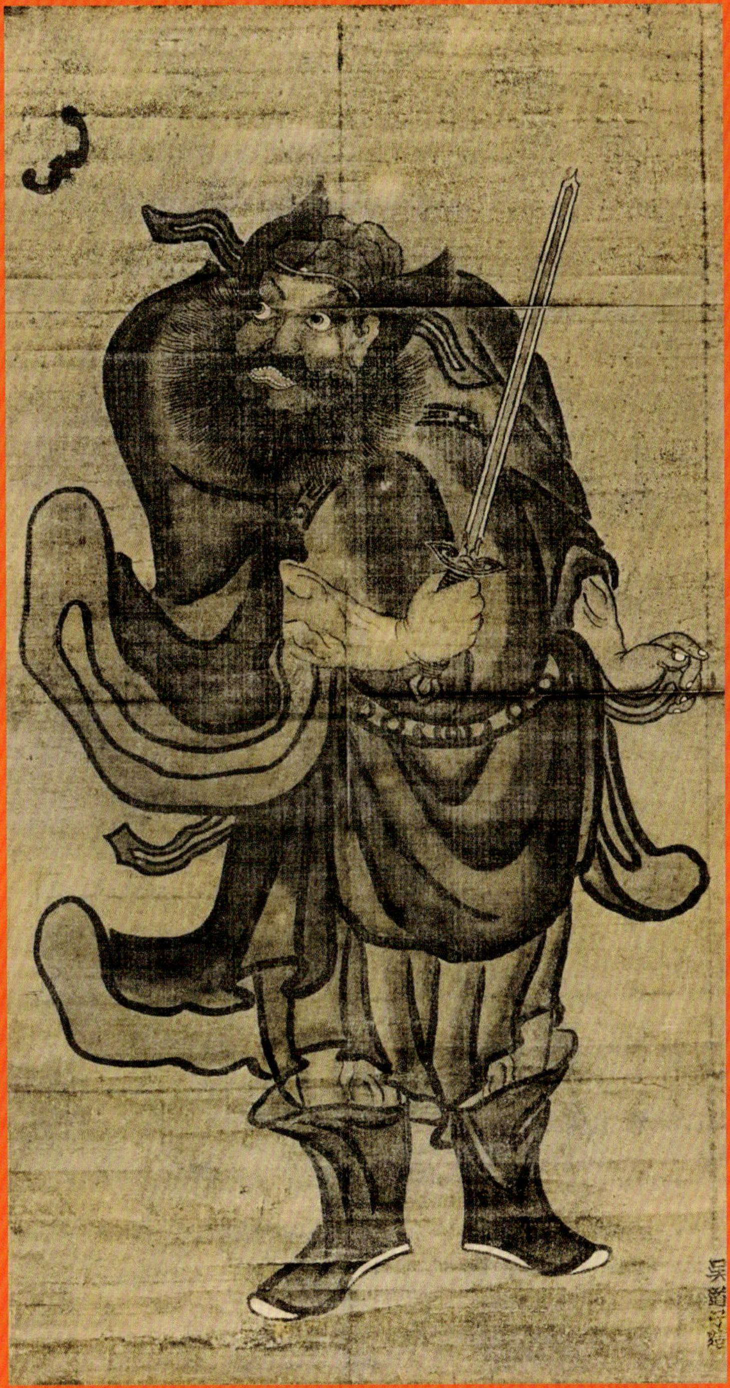

Zhong Kui

Wu Daozi

[Tang Dynasty]

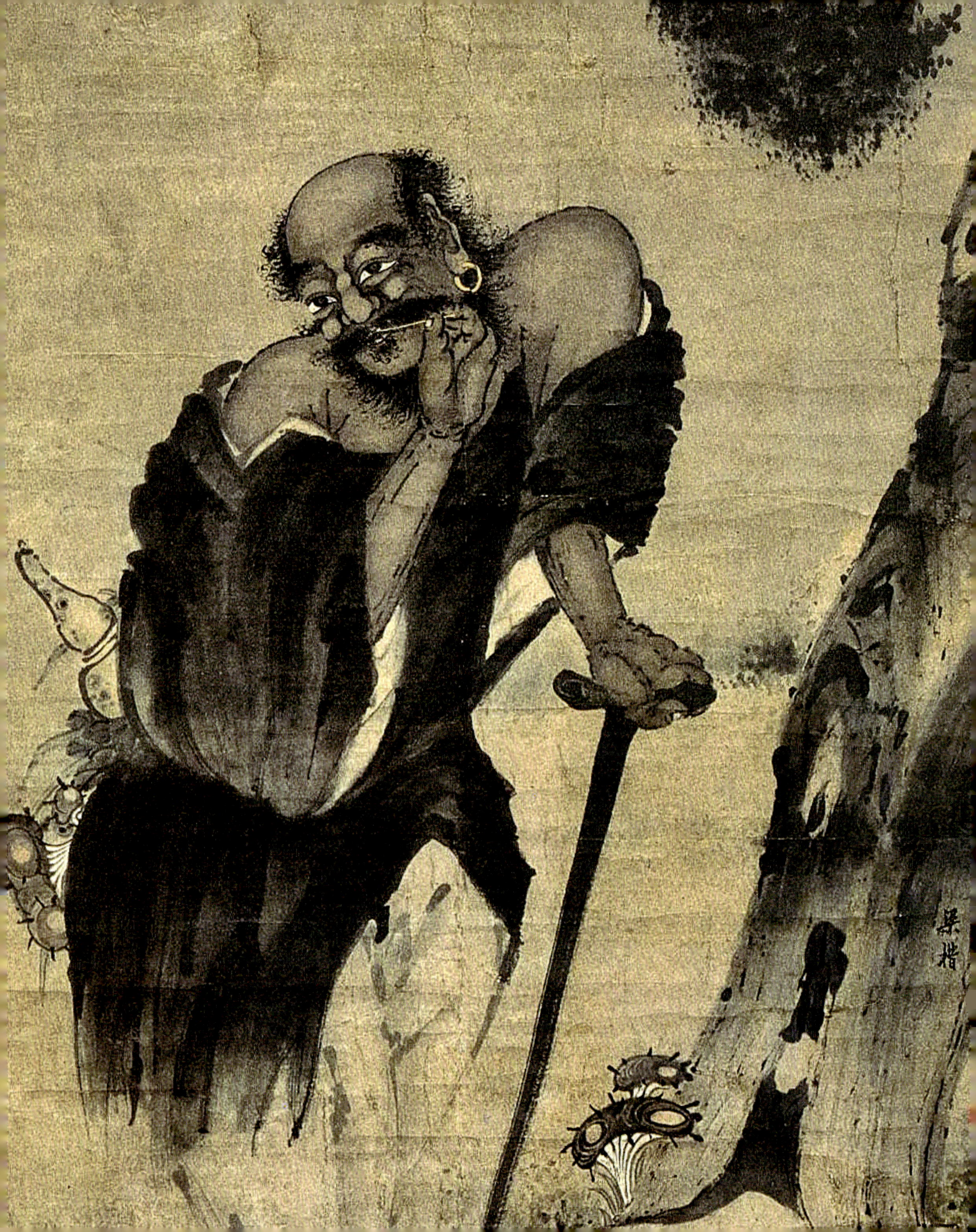
梁楷

The Second Peak from the Five Dynasties to the Northern and Southern Dynasties

With the fall of the Tang Dynasty and the continuous evolution of painting, Wu Daozi's "Zhong Kui style" began to be deconstructed. Huang Quan of the Five Dynasties paid meticulous attention to the spirit and movement of figures, showing reverence for the work of his predecessors while also breaking free from the constraints of Wu Daozi's "Zhong Kui style," establishing his own unique approach.

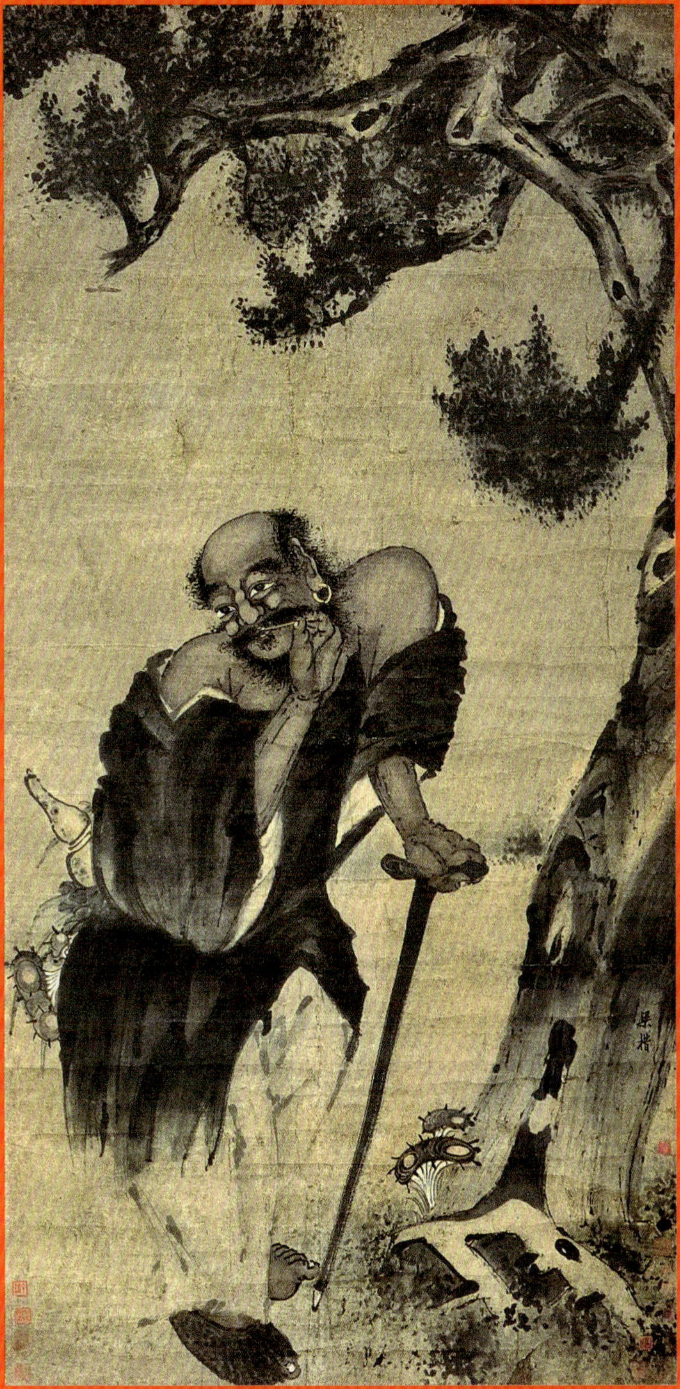

Zhong Kui

Liang Kai

[Five Dynasties]

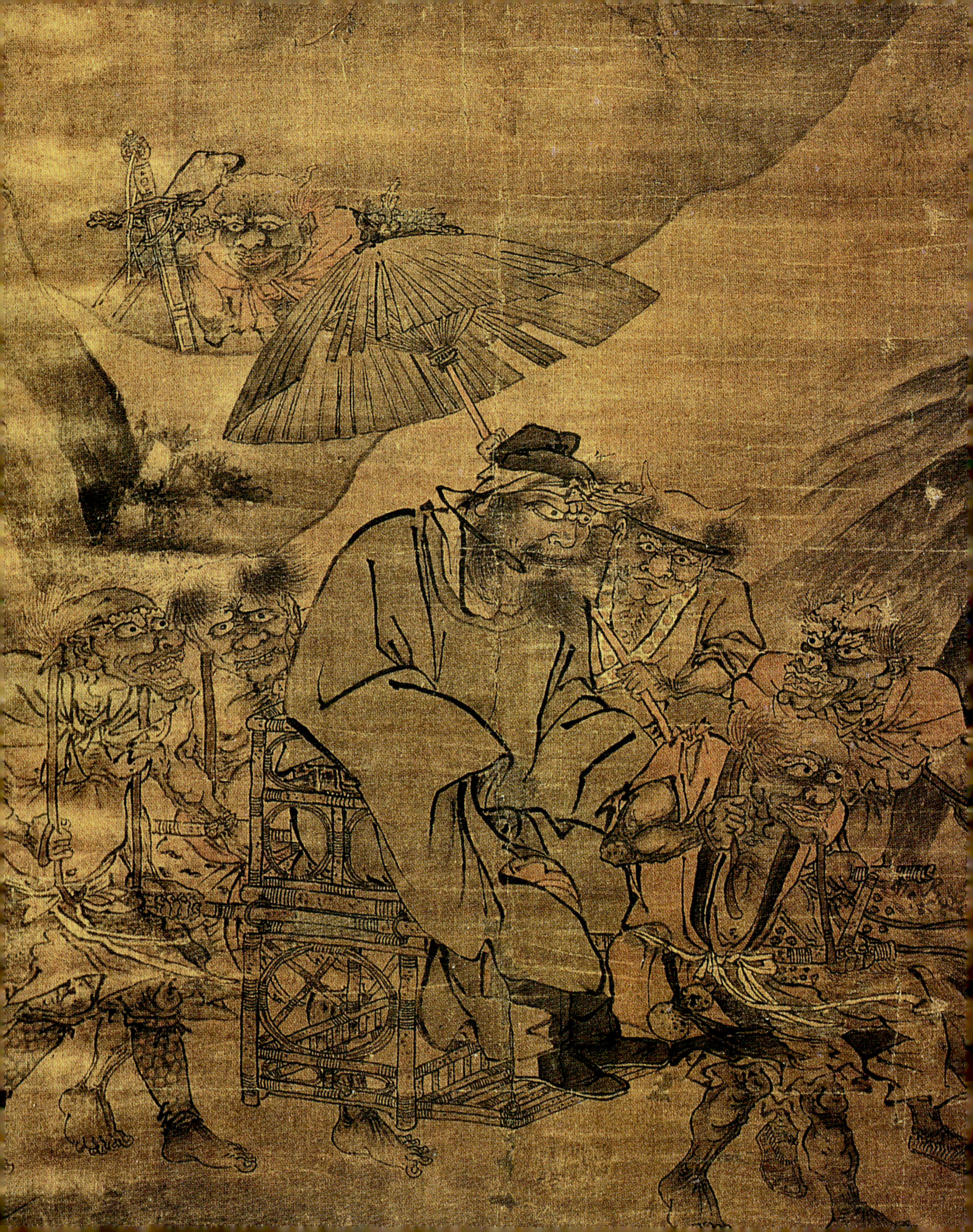

From the Yuan to the Late Qing and Early Republican Era

This period can be summarized as the "stage of emotional expression and implied meanings." The Qing scholar Zheng Ji stated in *A Concise Study of Painting at the Dream Fantasy Abode*: "Many esteemed predecessors painted ghosts and deities. Common viewers regard them as peculiar, not considering that the ancients did not paint merely for the pleasure of depiction, but rather used brush and ink to express the emotions within their hearts."

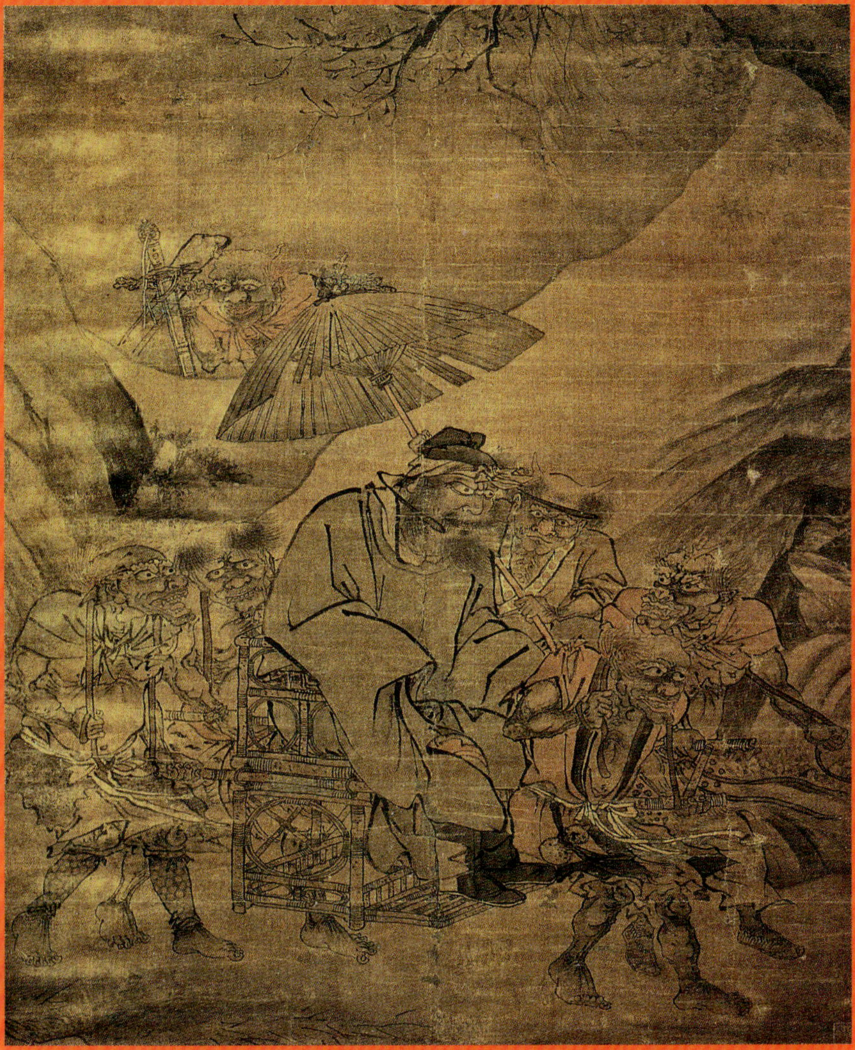

Zhong Kui's Hunting Procession

Yan Hui

[Yuan Dynasty]

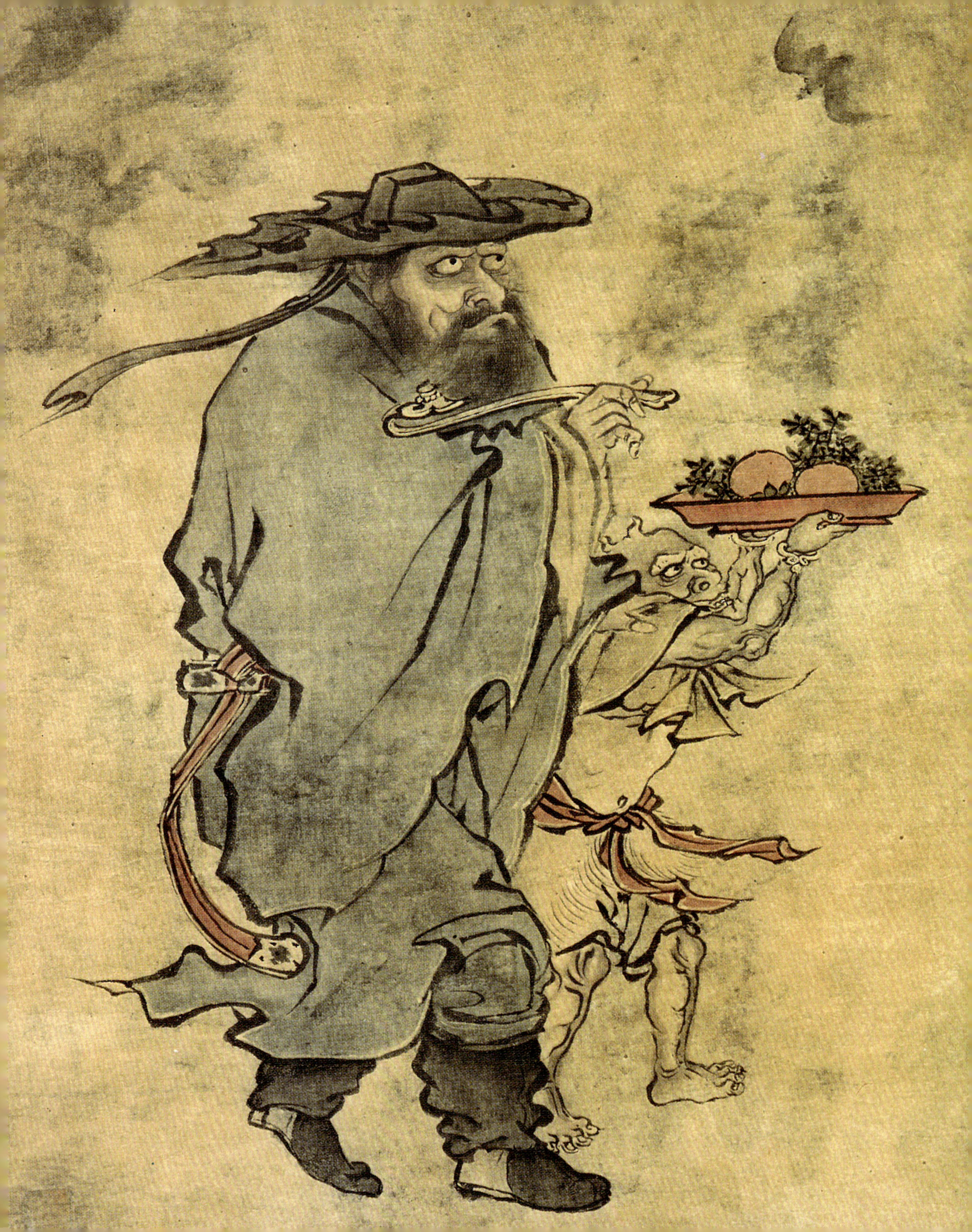

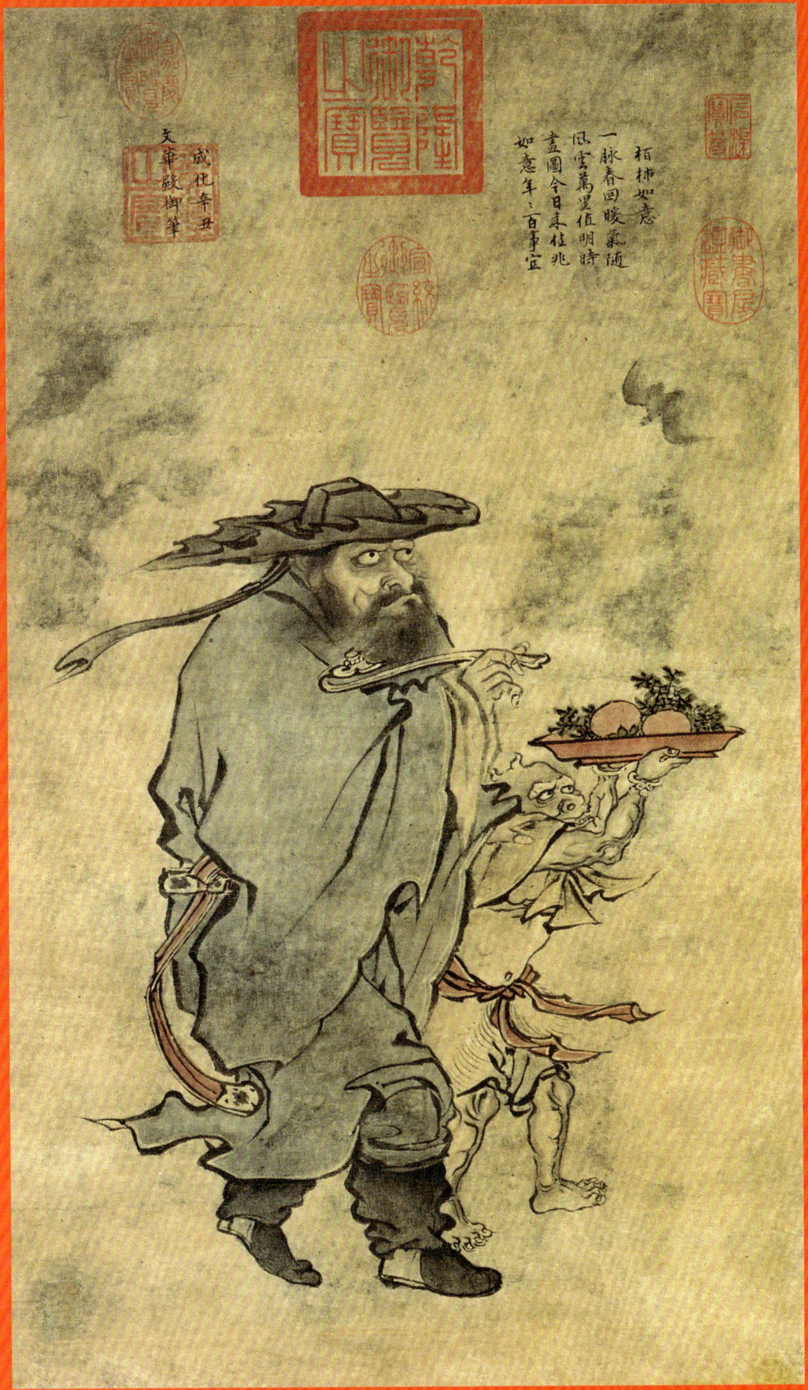

Imperial brushwork Welcoming Blessings of Good Fortune

Emperor Xianzong, Zhu Jianshen

[Ming Dynasty]

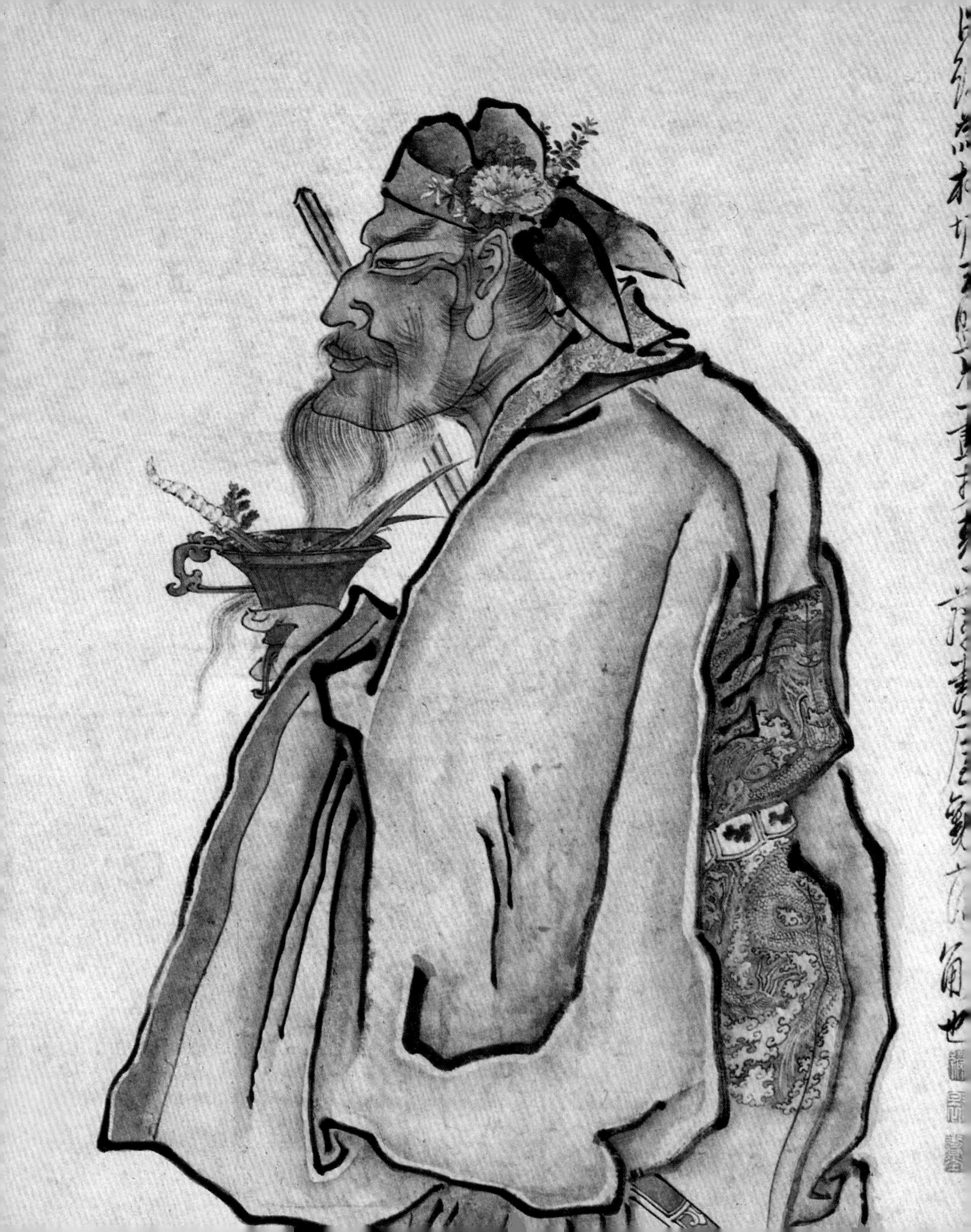

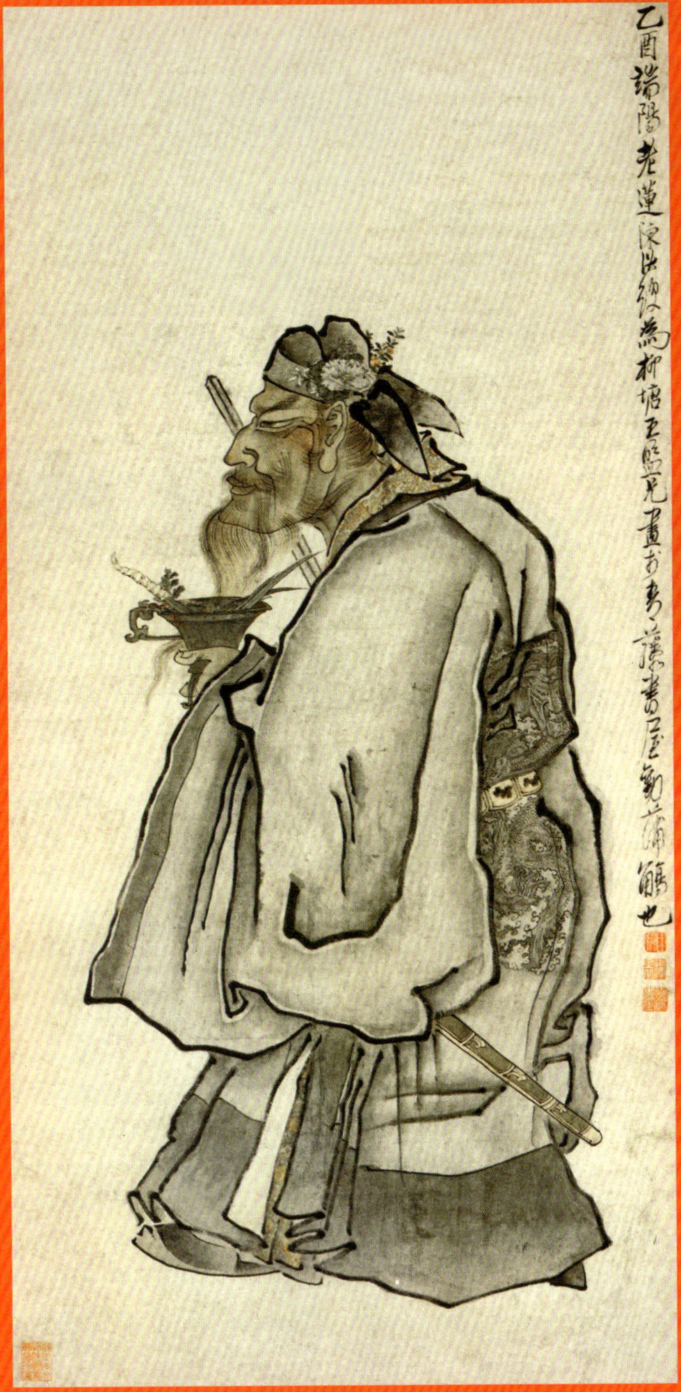

Portrait Scroll of Zhong Kui

Chen Hongshou

[Ming Dynasty]

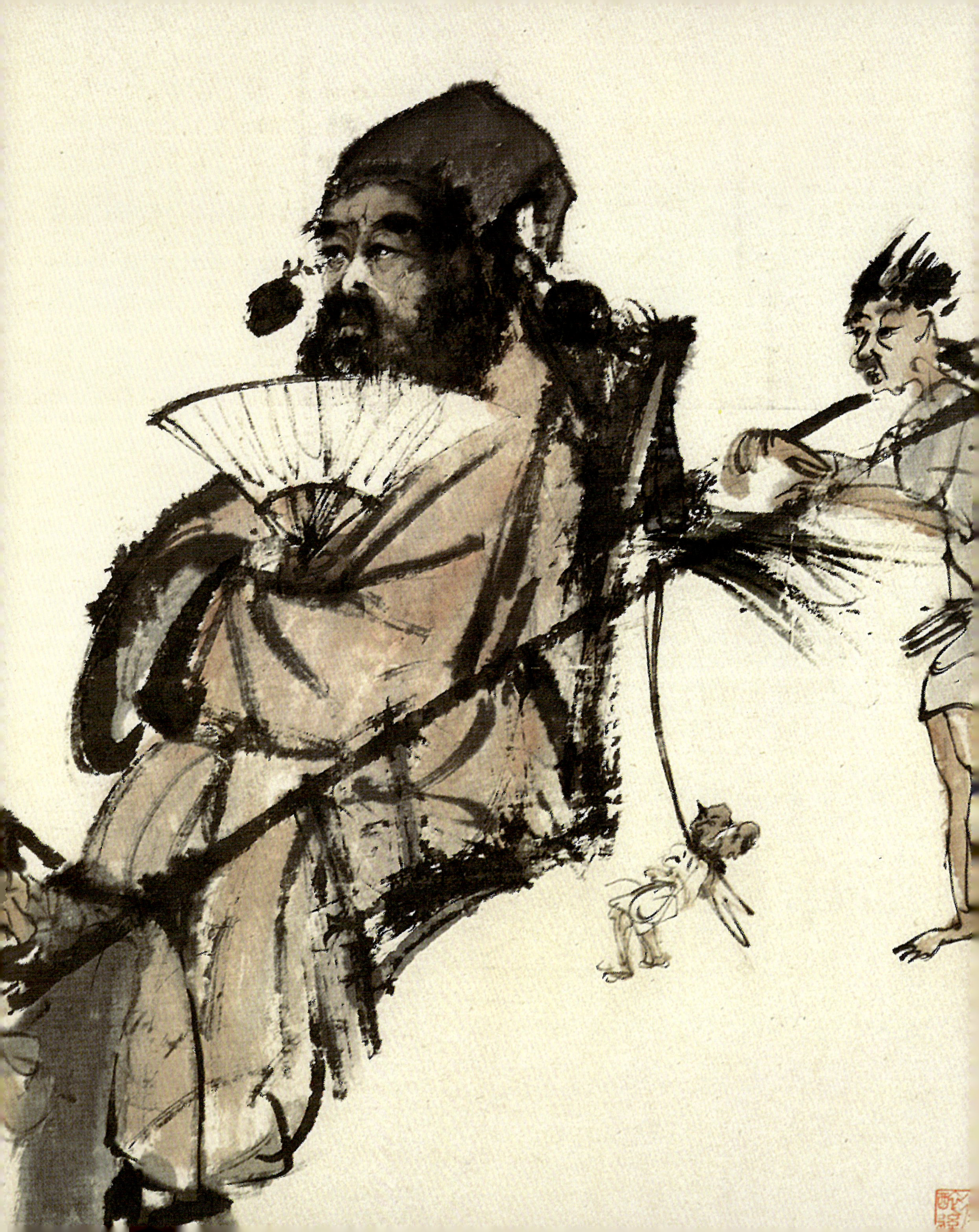

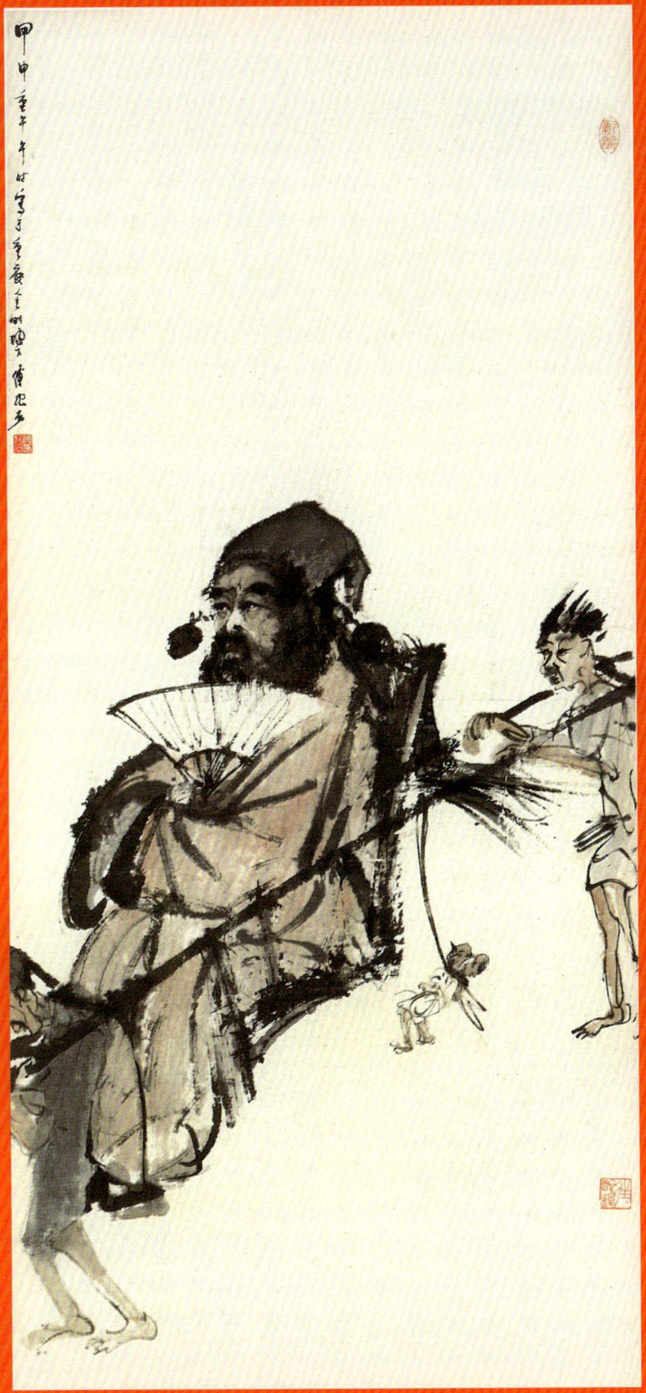

Zhong Kui

Fu Baoshi

[Contemporary]

He bridges the realms of heaven, earth, and humanity

Roaming among the worlds of mortals, ghosts, and gods

A deity of unique and extraordinary nature

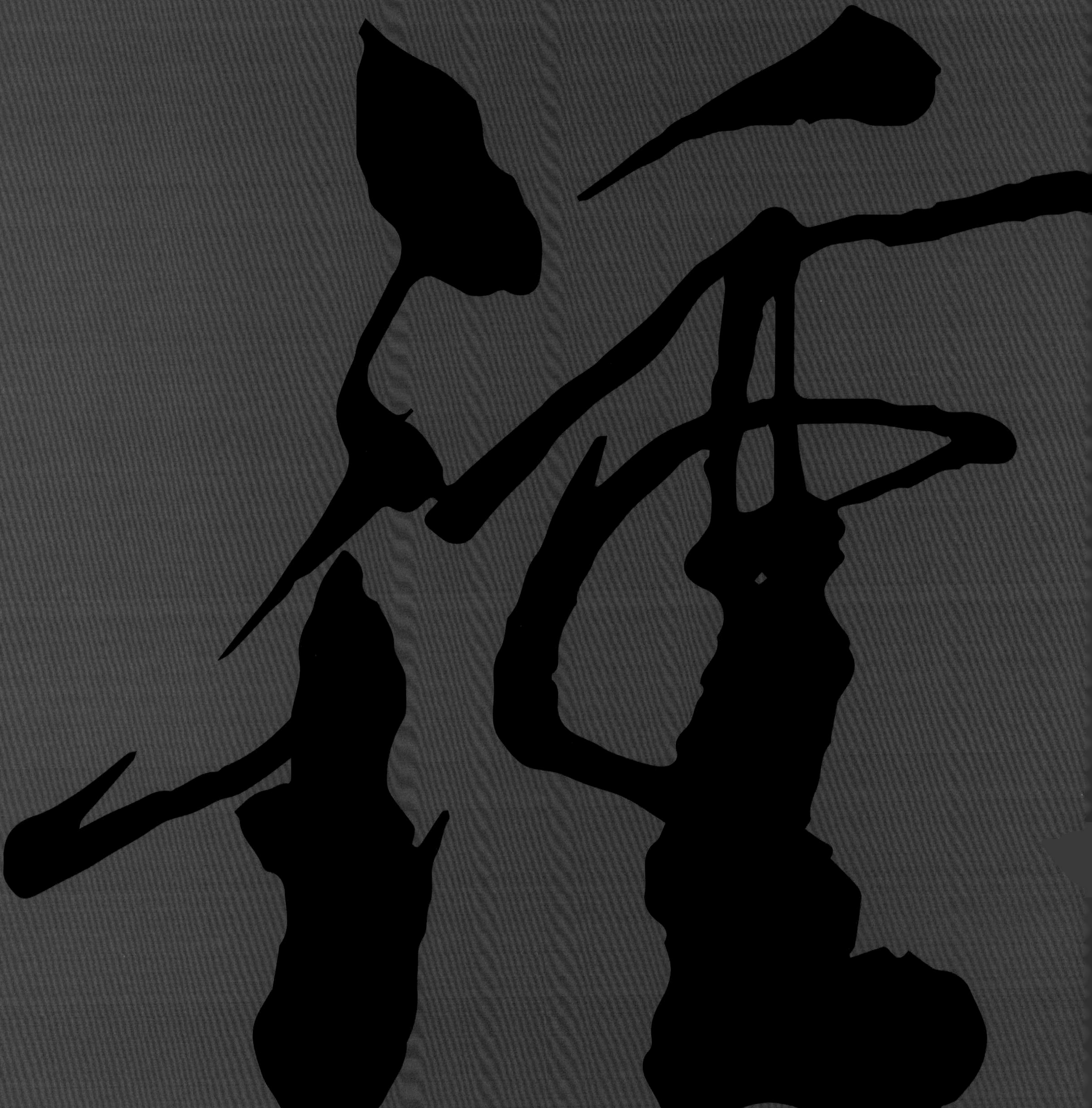

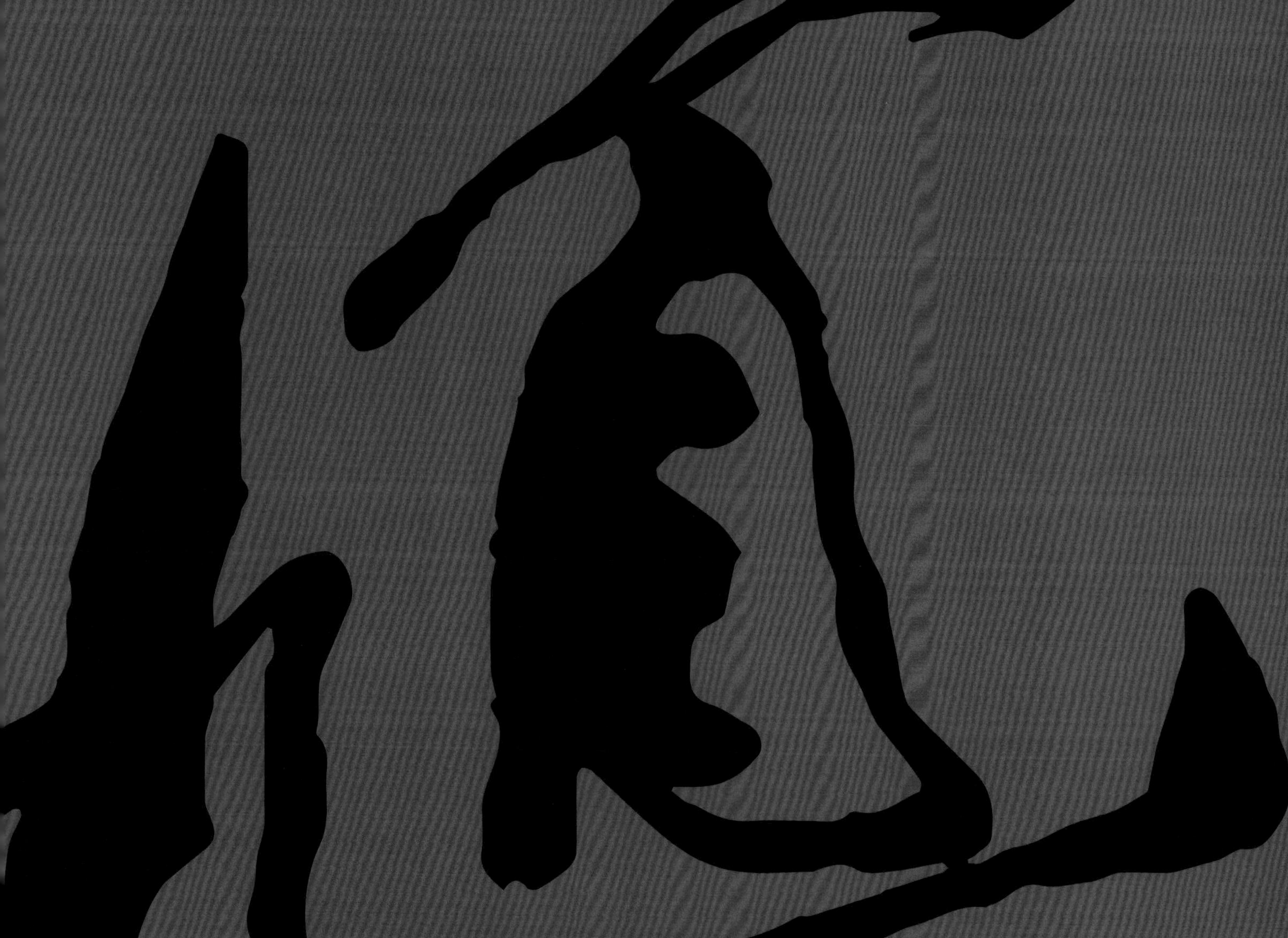

壬申春仲楊晉補梅竹

吳門徐玟添喜鵲

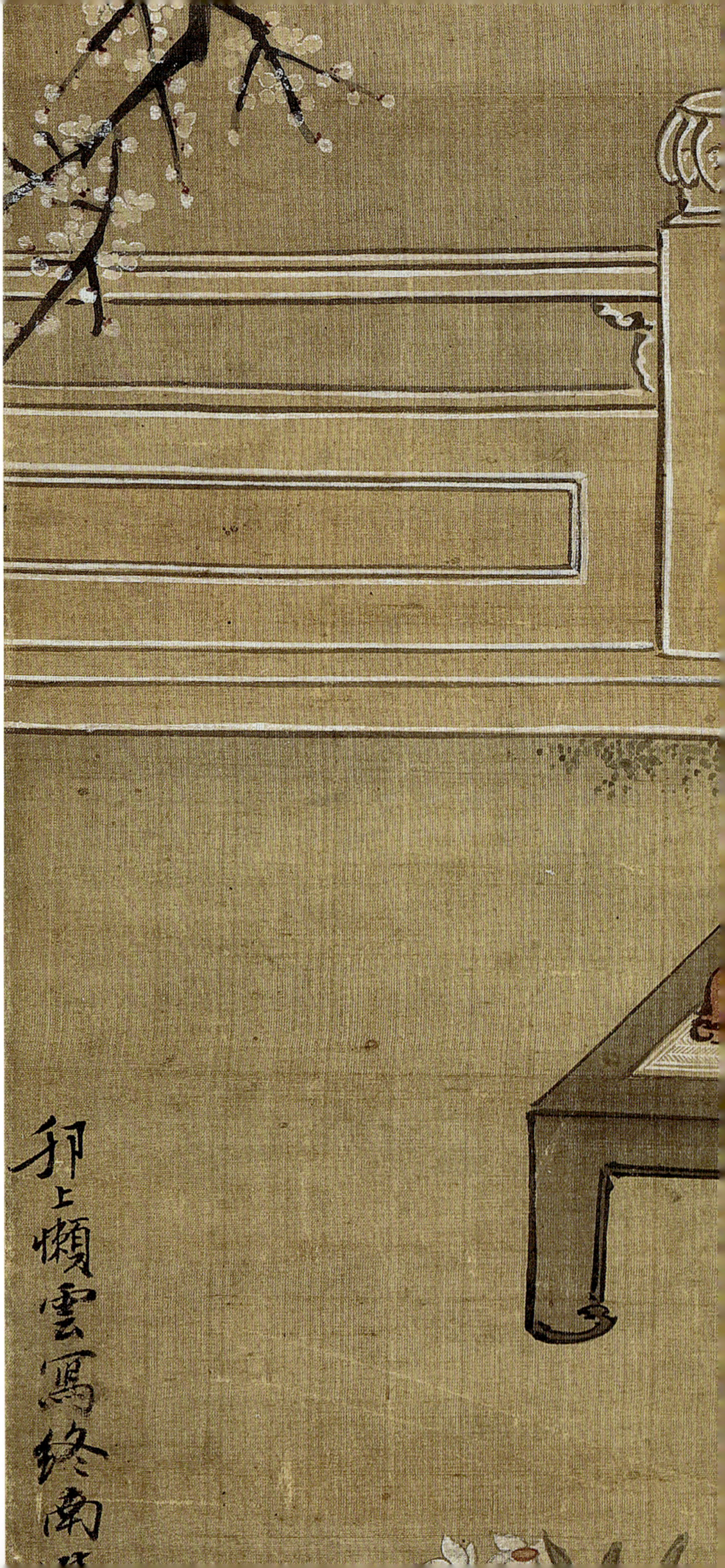

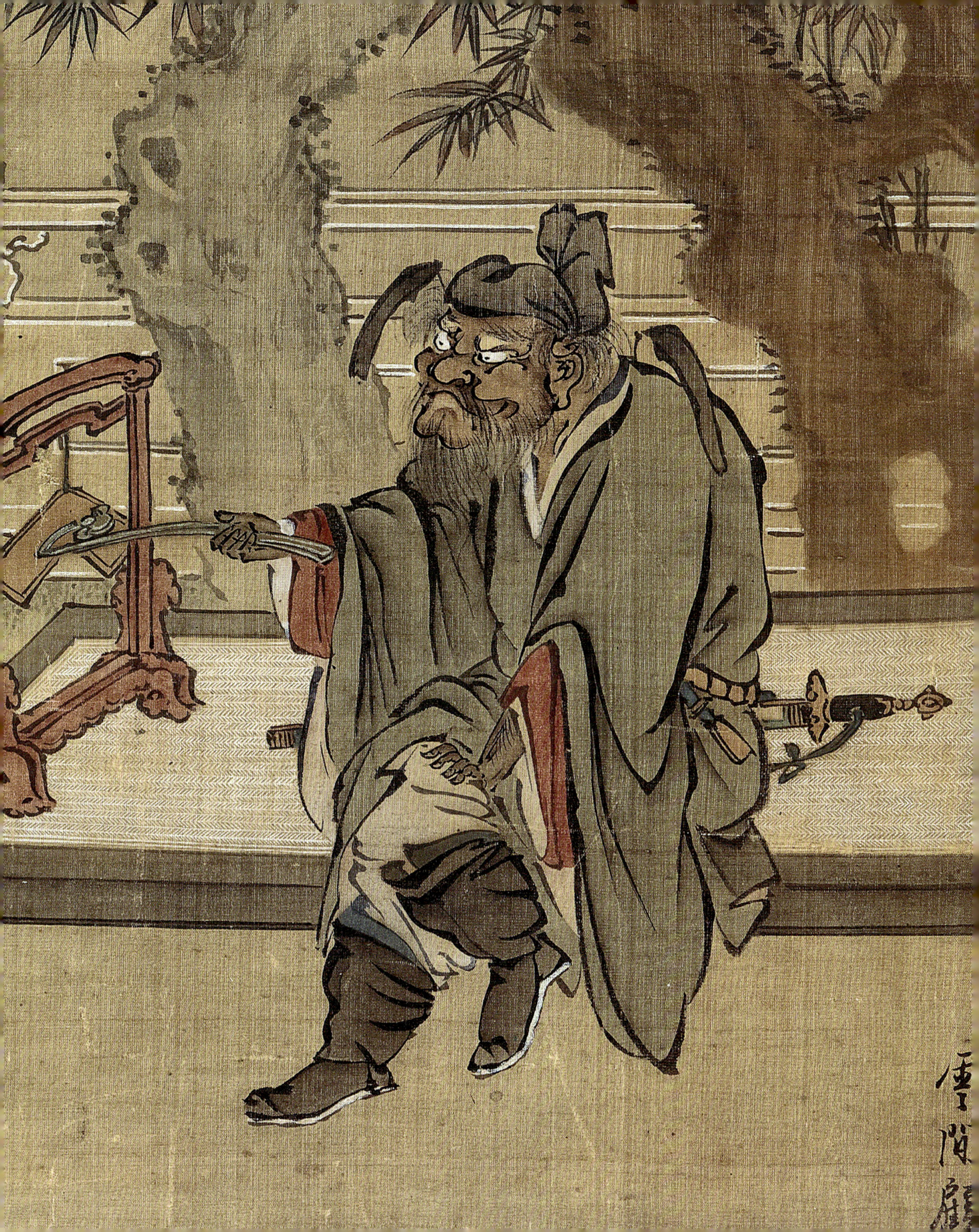

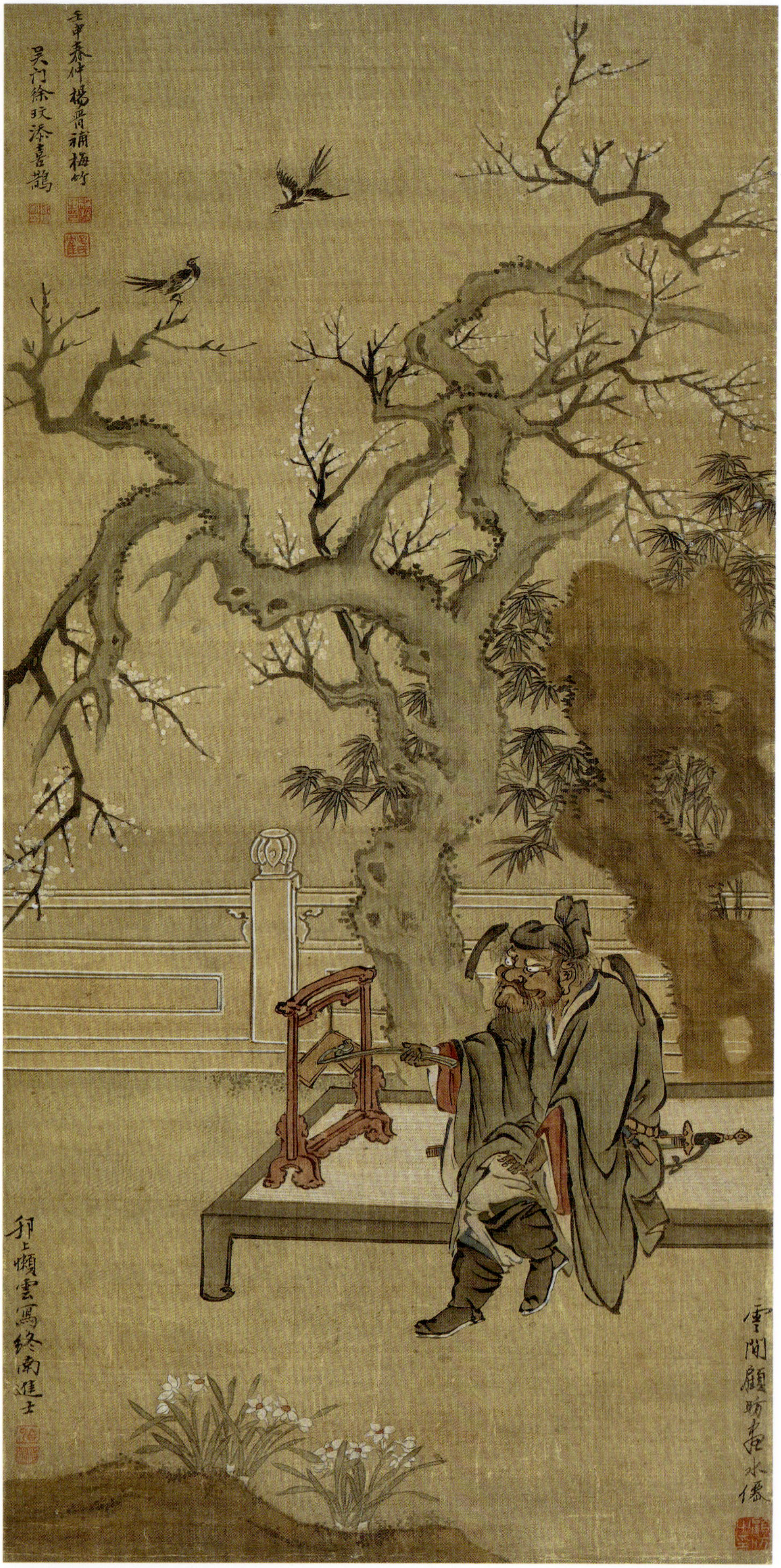
壬申春仲楊晉補梅竹
吳门徐玫添喜鵲
邗上懶雲寫終南進士
雲間顧昉畫水僊

Artists:
Yang Jin, Xu Wen, Gu Fang, Xu Yunlu

Medium:
Color on silk, Hanging scroll

Dimensions:
73.5 cm × 36 cm

Zhong Kui with Plum Blossoms and Sparrows

Inscription:
In the spring of the Renshen year,
Yang Jin added the bamboo and plum blossom

Seal:
The seal of Yang Jin, Zi He

Inscription:
Xu Wen of Wu School adds the joyous magpie

Seal:
Personal seal of Xu Wen

Inscription:
Painted by Gu Fang from "Among the Clouds", depicting the daffodils

Seal:
The seal of Gu Fang

Inscription:
Penned by Han Lan from Han, a Jinshi from Zhongnan

Seal:
He Yun, Han Lan

Yang Jin (1644-1728)
Courtesy name Zi He, styled as Xiting. He also identified himself as the Woodcutter of the Valley and the Crane Taoist, and occasionally signed his works as the Wild Crane. A native of Changshu, Jiangsu, he was a direct disciple of Wang Hui.

Xu Wen
Courtesy name Cai Ruo. A native of Wu County, Jiangsu. A poet and painter of the Qing dynasty. Skilled in poetry and prose, he excelled in landscape painting. Drawing inspiration from Song dynasty artists, his works exuded a distant, graceful charm. Later in life, he studied the Tang dynasty's Six Masters, always managing to convey a unique essence.

Gu Fang
Courtesy name Ri Fang and also known as Fu Shi. Styled as Ruo Zhou and also styled as Wan Gao. Originating from Huating (present-day Shanghai), he was a Qing dynasty painter. He specialized in landscapes following the styles of Dong Yuan, Juran, and the Four Masters of the Yuan dynasty. He traveled to the capital, where Wang Hui praised his brushwork as being free of any trivialities, and his ink as vibrant as a spectrum of colors. He once collaborated with Wang Hui on a painting of the Southern Inspection Tour. Later, he traveled through the two Guang provinces and southern Jiangxi, where his reputation and demand grew. He was particularly skilled in imitation.

Xu Yunlu
Courtesy name Qi Wan. Styled as Lan Yun. He was a scholar from Kunshan, Jiangsu. Skilled in poetry and prose, he particularly excelled in lyrics. When painting plum blossoms, he followed the style of Wang Mian.

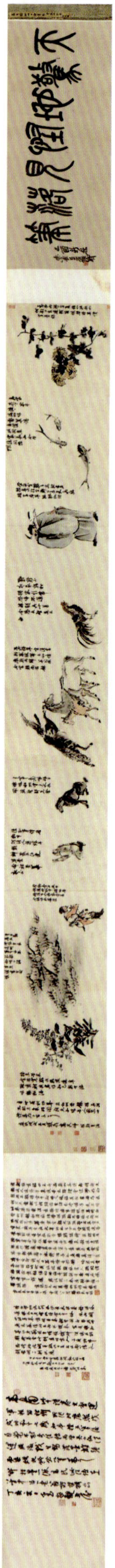

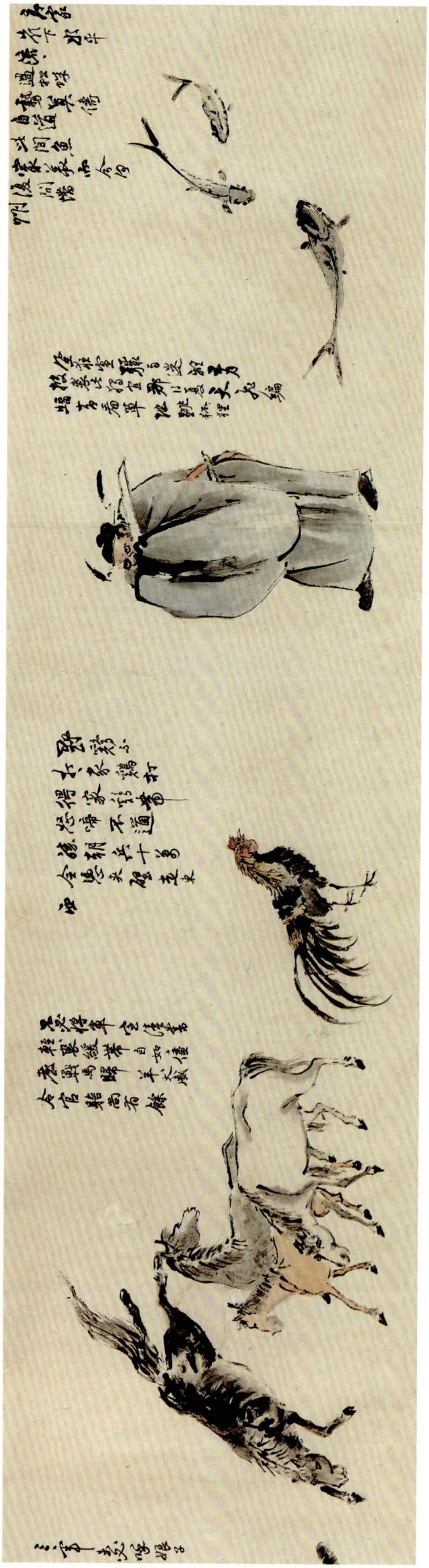

Artists:
Gao Qipei

Medium:
Color on paper, Long scroll (partial)

Dimensions:
44 cm × 368 cm

Zhong Kui

Inscription:
The wild wind and sudden snow bring disarray; in May, only cloaked in furs does one rightly stay.
How could bats fly in the summer's sphere? Yet on the grass, foxes leap, and here they appear.

Gao Qipei (1660-1734)
Courtesy name Wei Zhi, styled as Qe Yuan, Nan Cun, and Qe Dao Ren, among other pseudonyms such as "Man from Beyond the Shanhai Pass" and "Creative Craftsman". A native of Liaoyang, Fengtian, he was registered under the Han Army. An official and painter during the Qing dynasty, Gao is known as the pioneer of finger painting. During the Kangxi Emperor's reign, benefiting from hereditary privilege, he was first appointed as the Subprefectural Magistrate of Suzhou, then transferred to serve as the Surveillance Commissioner of Sichuan. Under the Yongzheng Emperor, he was promoted to Military Commander, but was later dismissed from his post. He was skilled in poetry and adept at painting, especially known for his landscapes and figures which exuded a bold and profound vigor. In his later years, he forsook the use of the brush in favor of finger painting.

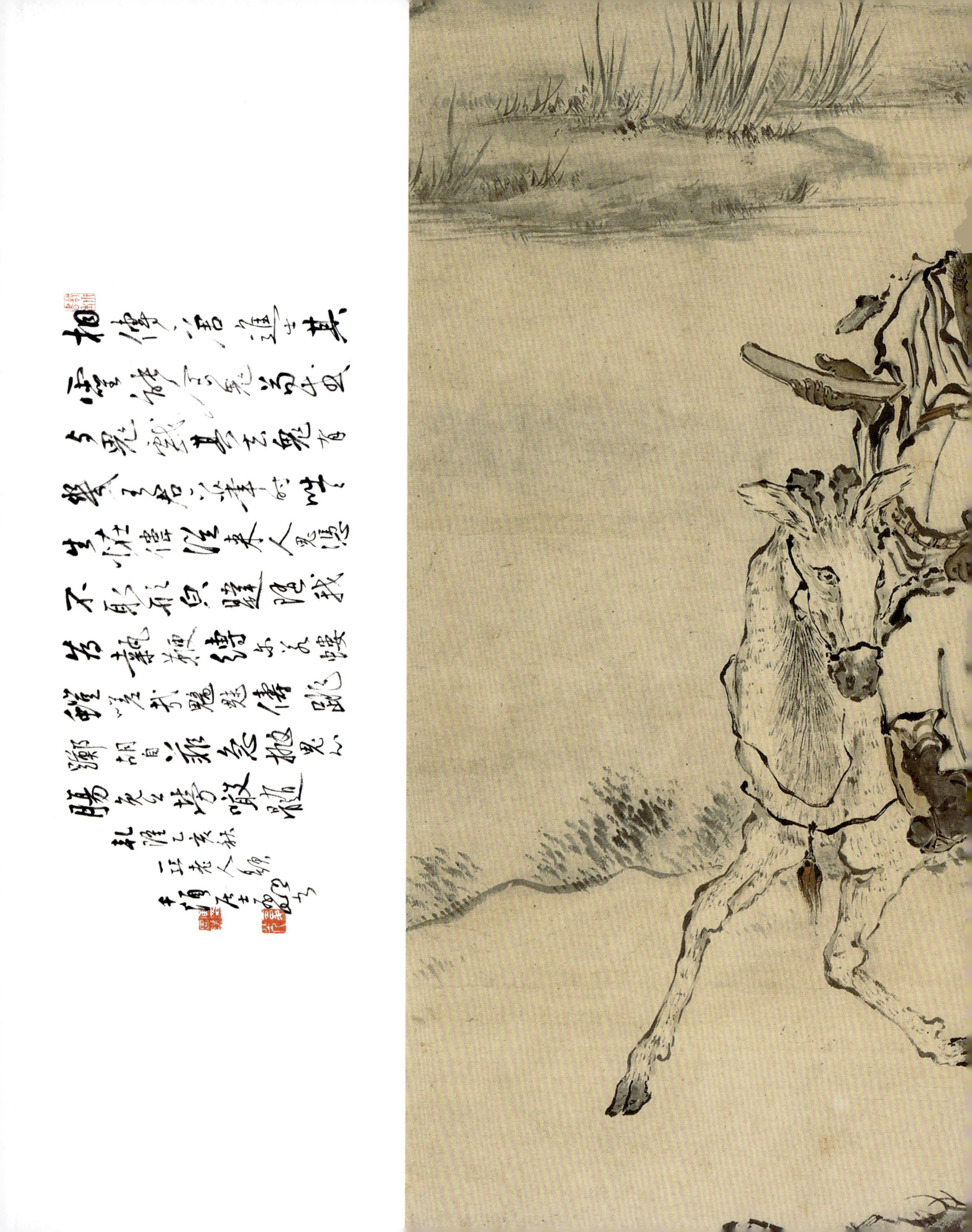

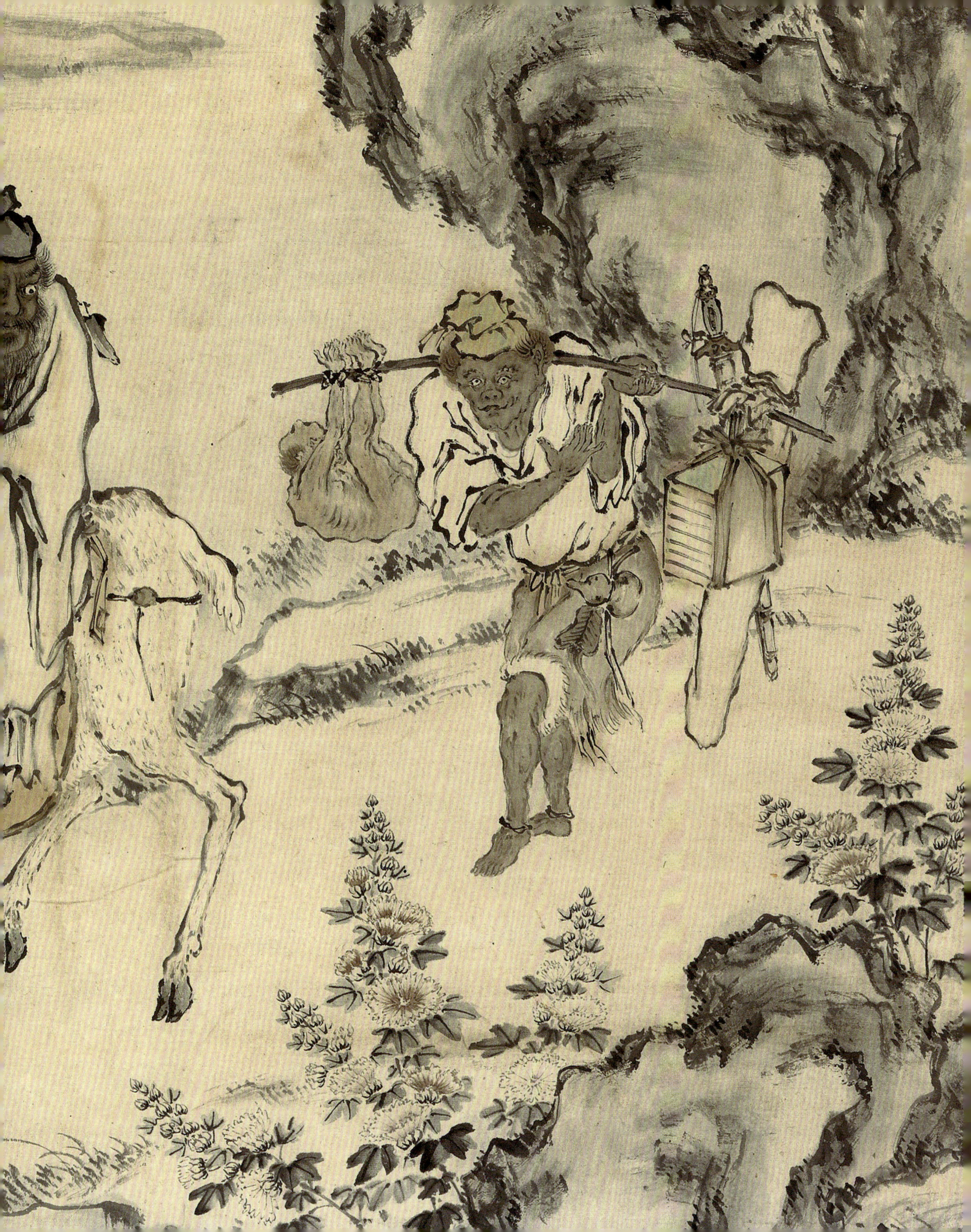

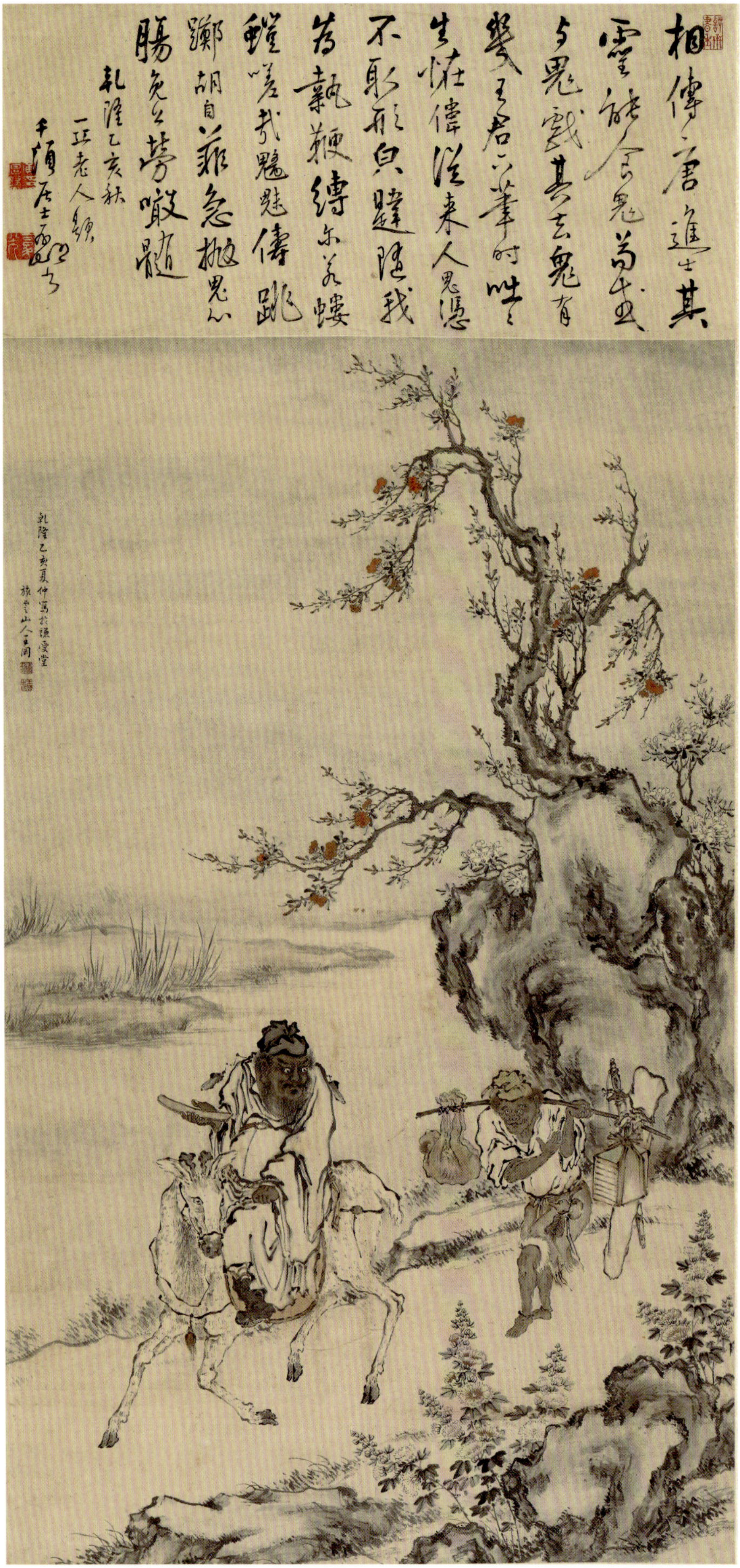

Artist:
Wang Gang

Medium:
Color on paper, Hanging scroll

Dimensions:
105.5 cm × 63 cm

Jinshi Zhong

Inscription:
In the summer of the Yihai year under Qianlong's reign, I inscribed this painting at the Qianshou Hall. Man of the Wandering Clouds, artist Wang Gang.

Seal:
Poetry Column

Inscription:
Legends tell of a Tang scholar who could devour ghosts at will. Should he frolic with these specters, few would manage to escape. When Master Wang wields his brush, formidable and eerie figures spring to life. Since time immemorial, portrayals of men and ghosts rely not on appearance but on spirit. Join me in brandishing the whip, binding them as trivial as ants. Oh, the folly of these demonic mates, prancing about in vain self-importance. Cast aside your ghastly desires, and spare yourself the toil of being consumed marrow and all. In the autumn of the Yihai year, the Elder of Yiqiu inscribed this in the study of the Qianqing Lay Scholar, Housui.

Seal:
The seal of Huang Housui, Fu Guang, Jiexuan Scholar

Wang Gang (1677–1770, though some sources indicate 1697–1770)
Courtesy name Nanshi, styled as "Man of the Wandering Clouds", was a native of Shanghai. A painter of the Qing dynasty, he was skilled in florals and portraits, seamlessly blending realism with his own unique style. His depictions of aquatic plants and insects were noted for their vividness. He also excelled in landscapes and was once a distinguished guest of Dong Bangda in the capital, with many of the imperial art commissions credited to his hand. His proudest works were stylistically akin to those of the master Ni Zan. He lived to the age of ninety-four, or as some records suggest, seventy-four.

天中瑞譣圖

丁巳春仲 作於武林寓館

山陰王元畫

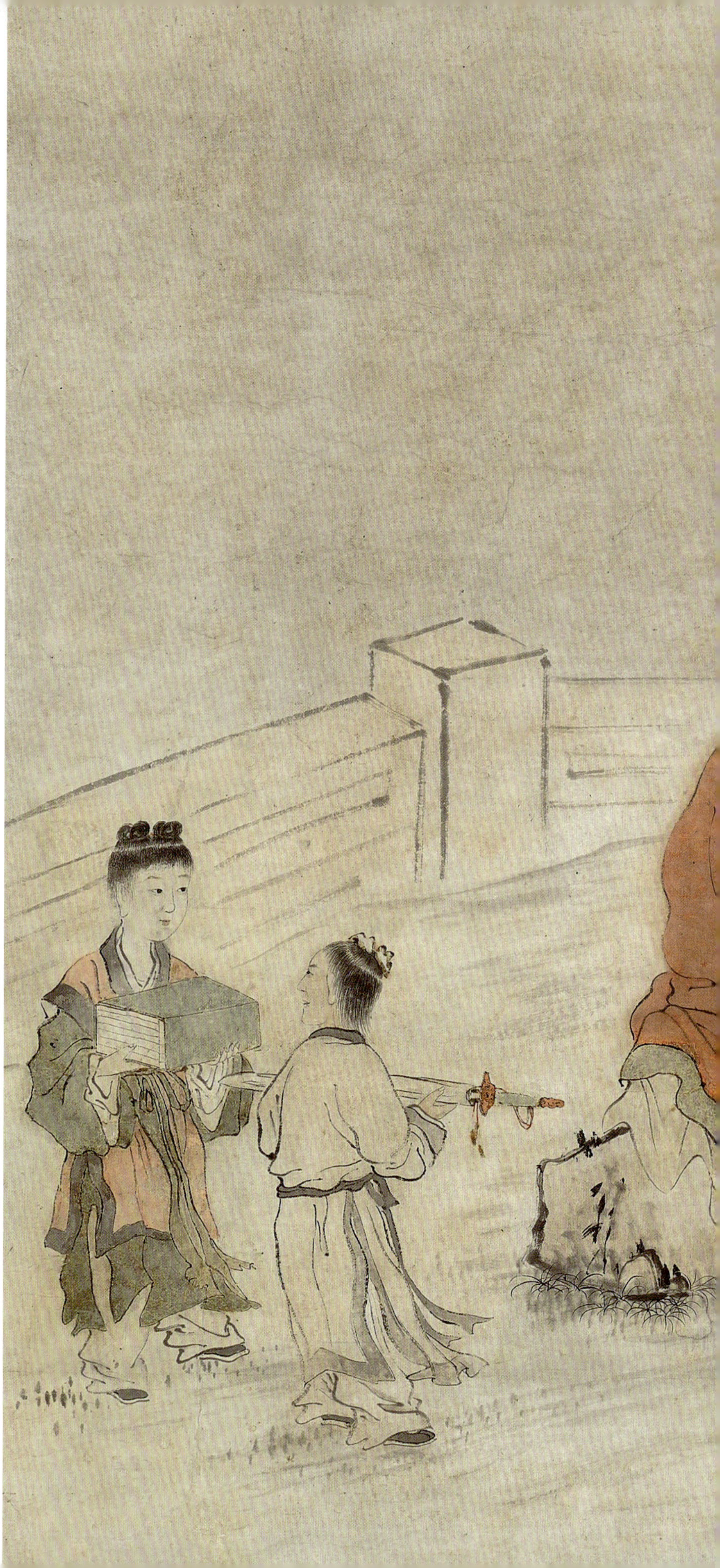

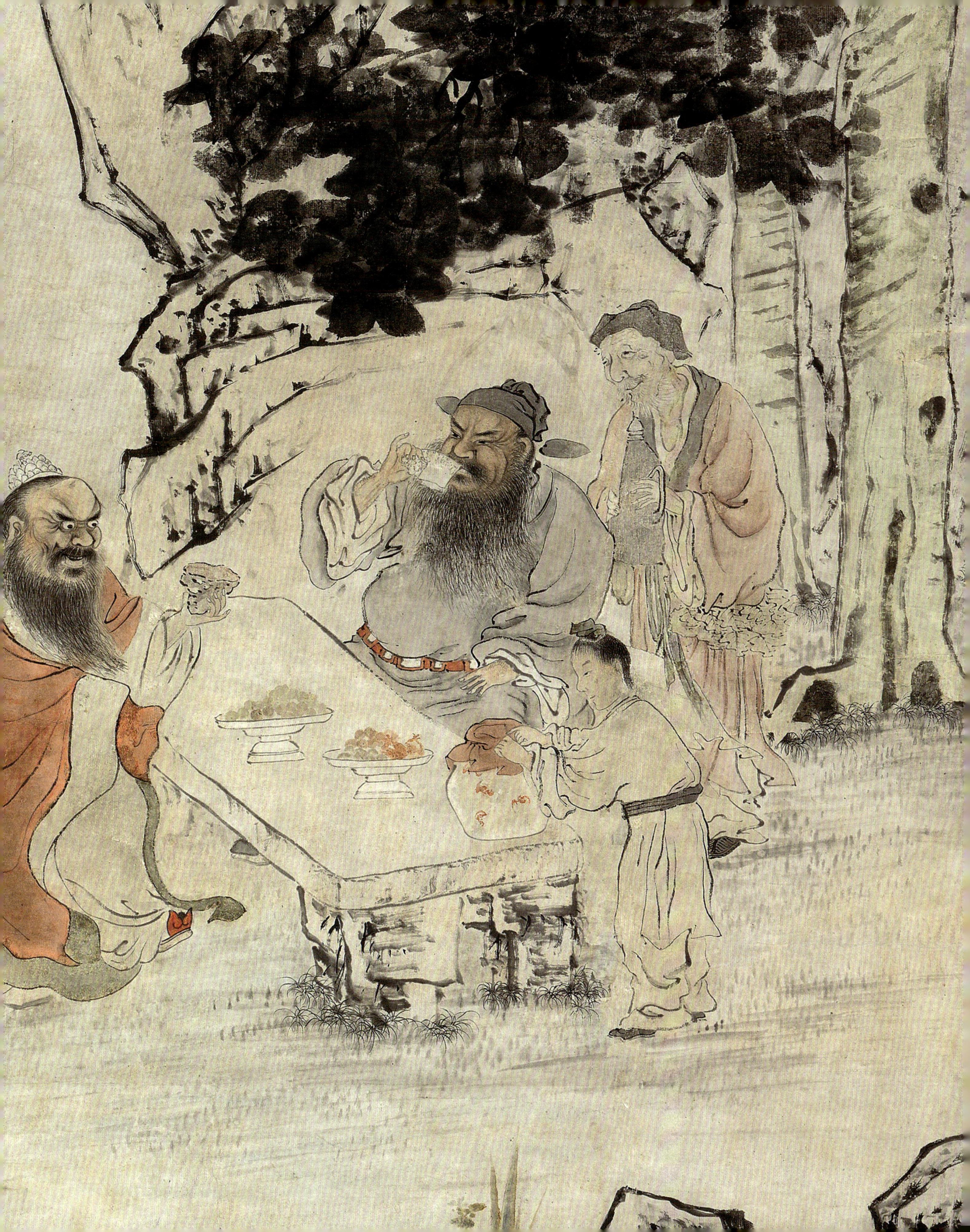

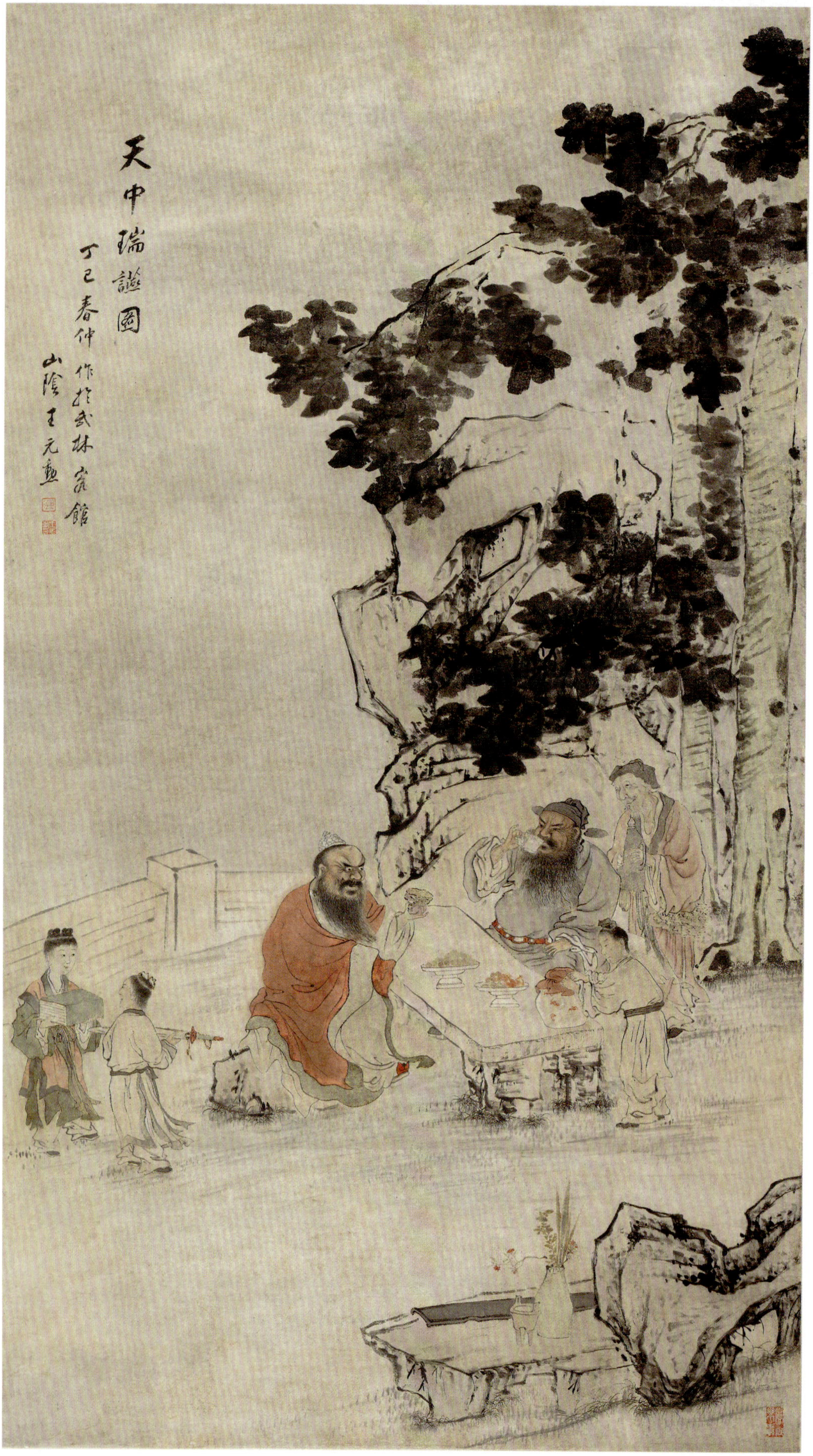
天中瑞讌圖
丁巳春仲作於武林寓館
山陰王元畫

Artist:
Wang Yuanxun

Medium:
Color on paper, Hanging scroll

Dimensions:
165 cm × 91 cm

Celestial Feast at the Zenith

Inscription:
Celestial Feast at the Zenith, crafted in the midst of spring in the year of Dingsi at the Wulin Guest House by Wang Yuanxun from Shanyin.

Seal:
Xiangzhou, The seal of Wang Yuanxun, Delightful Pleasures

Wang Yuanxun (1728–1807)
iled from Shanyin (present-day Shaoxing, Zhejiang). He was a Qing dynasty painter proficient in depicting figures, landscapes, birds, flowers, and insects, with a particular talent for vivid portraiture, rendering court ladies with enchanting allure. His son Wang Jingxian followed in his footsteps, sustaining the family's artistic legacy.

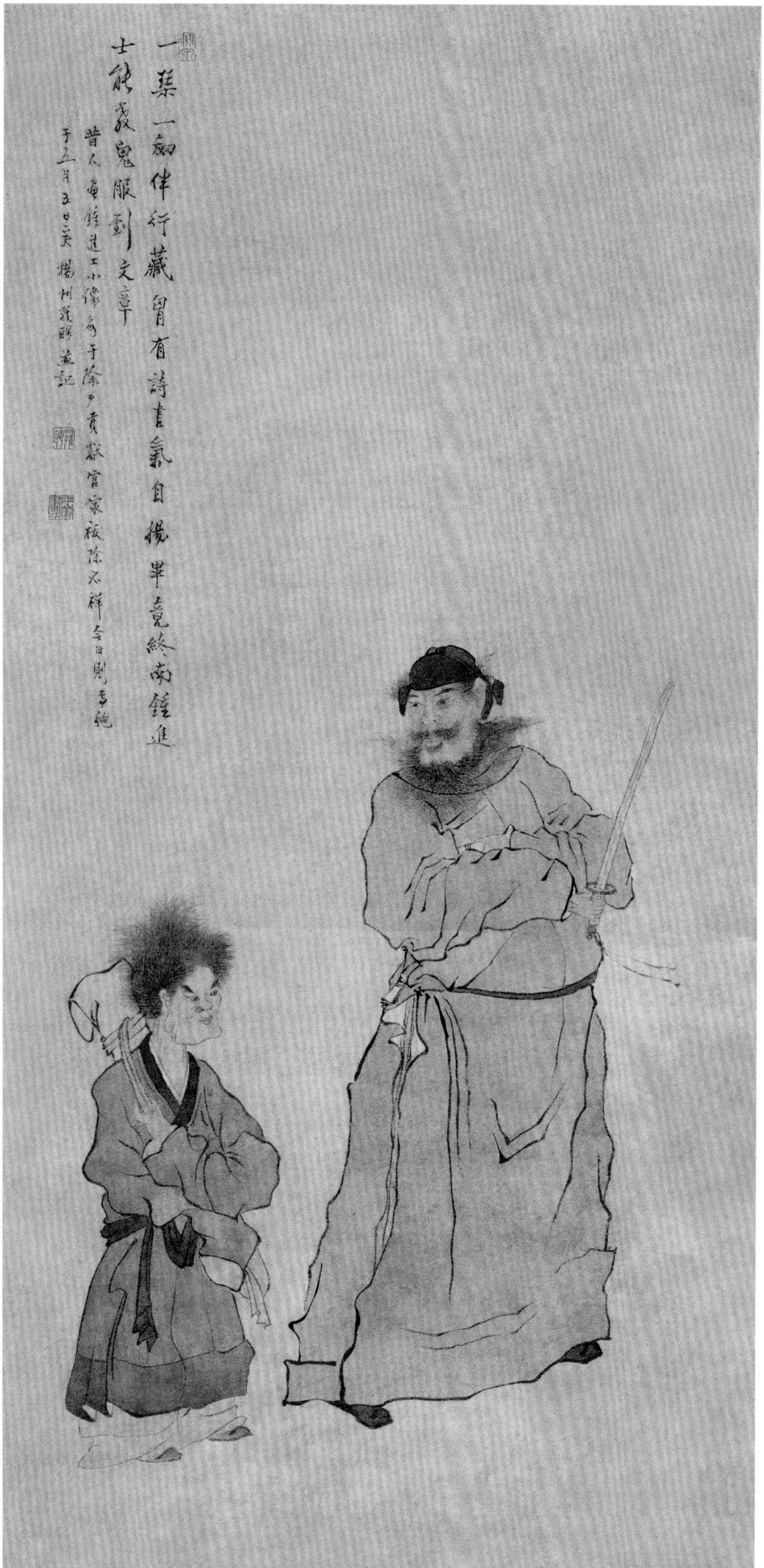
一琹一劍伴行藏 胷有詩書氣自揚 畢竟終南鍾進士 能教鬼服到文章
揚州羅聘並記

Artist:
Luo Pin

Medium:
Color on paper, Hanging scroll

Dimensions:
113 cm × 54 cm

Zhong Kui with Sword and Guqin

Inscription:
With a guqin and a sword as travel mates, my chest brims with poetry, elevating my spirit. After all, as a scholar from Zhongnan, my words can command ghosts to yield. In ancient times, artists crafted delicate portraits of Jinshi Zhong, presenting them to the imperial court every New Year's Eve to ward off misfortune. Yet, in this present age, such practices are reserved especially for the fifth day of the fifth month. Recorded by Luo Pin of Yangzhou.

Seal:
Luo Pin, Liangfeng's Artistic Record, Zhu Quan

Luo Pin (1733–1799)
Courtesy name Dunfu, styled as Liangfeng, also known by various sobriquets such as Yiyun, Monk of the Flower Temple, Jinniu Mountain Man, and Old Master Shi Lian. His ancestral home was in She County, Anhui, but his forebears had settled in Yangzhou. He was also skilled in seal carving and was one of the celebrated "Eight Eccentrics of Yangzhou". A direct disciple of Jin Nong, he led a simple life and enjoyed traveling.

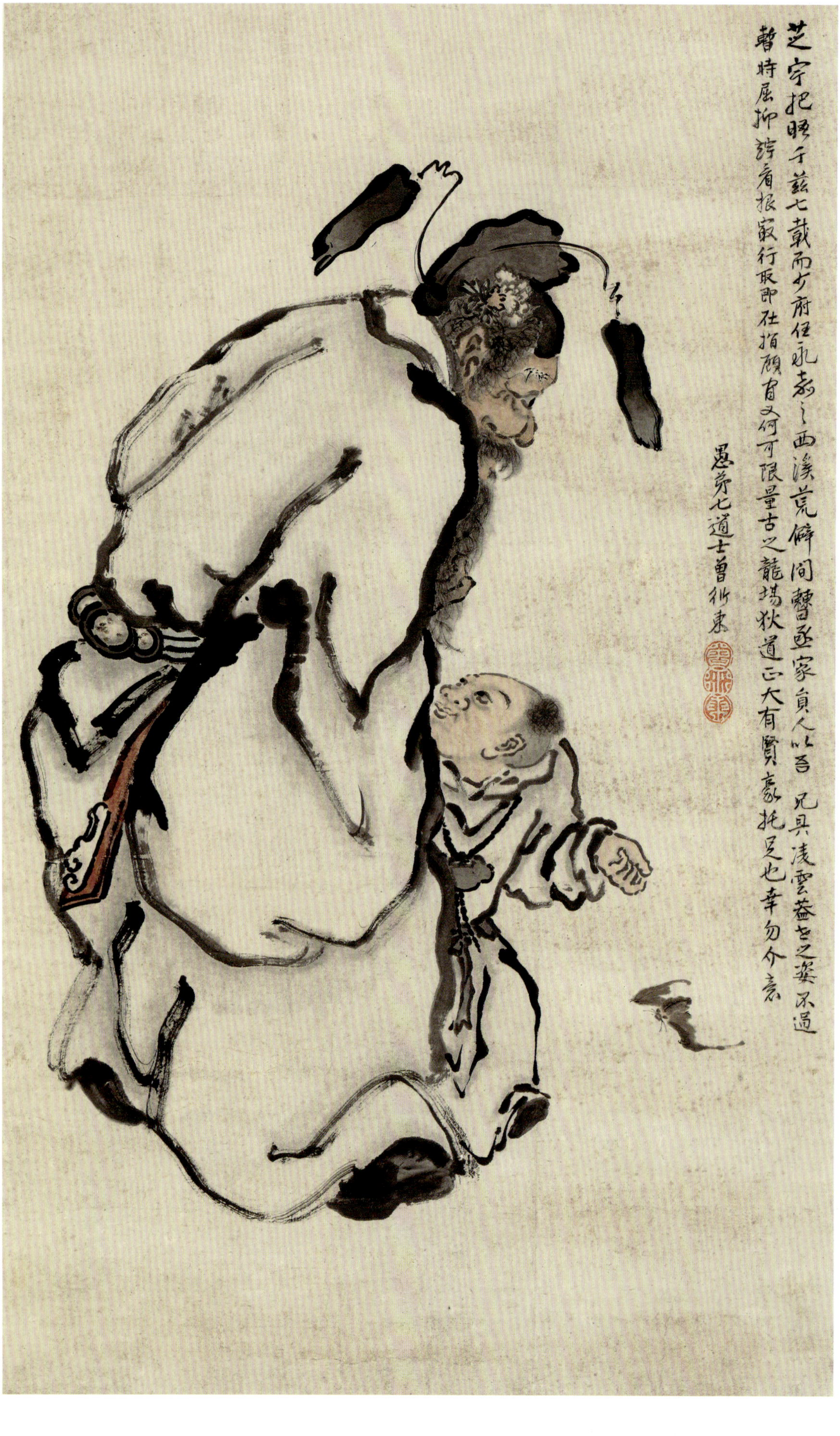

Artist:
Zeng Yandong

Medium:
Color on paper, Hanging scroll

Dimensions:
110 cm × 66 cm

Welcoming Fortune

Inscription:
Seven years have passed since our last encounter, dear brother, in your secluded post at West Creek. I often tell others of your exceptional character, merely temporarily subdued. Await the moment to soar high, success is but a fingertip away. Places like Longchang and Didao have been the cradle of the eminent. Pray, take no offense. Your foolish brother, Qi Taoist, Zeng Yandong.

Seal:
Zeng Yandong

Zeng Yandong (1750–unknown)
Courtesy name Qingzhan, also known as Qiru, styled as Qiru Lay Scholar and Qi Taoist, was originally from Jiaxiang, Shandong. He was the sixty-seventh-generation descendant of the Confucian scholar Zengzi. He achieved the status of a Juren in the Renzi year of the Qianlong reign. Zeng was a man of many talents, excelling as a painter, novelist, and Zaju[1] playwright.

[1] A form of traditional Chinese drama or opera.

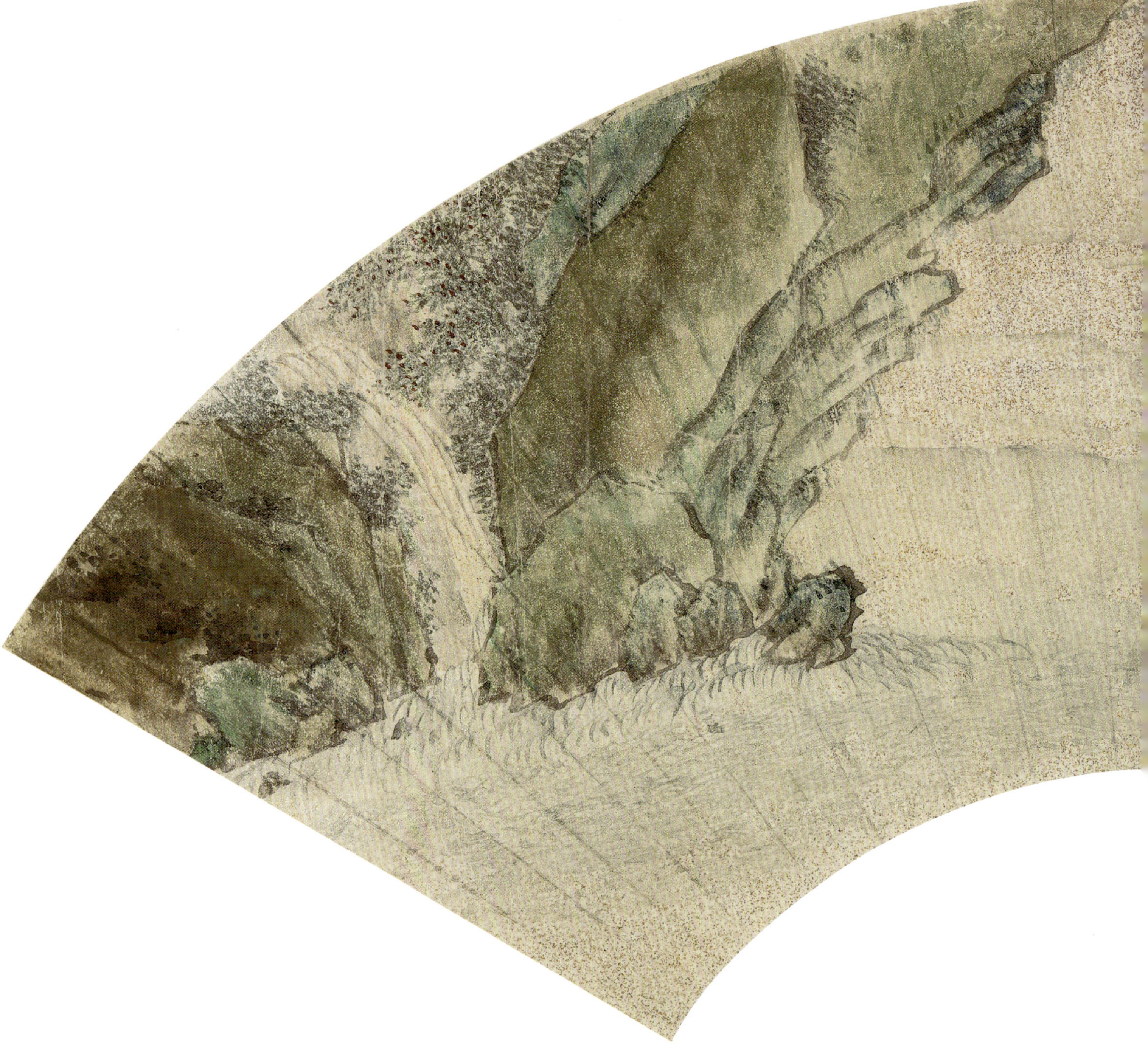

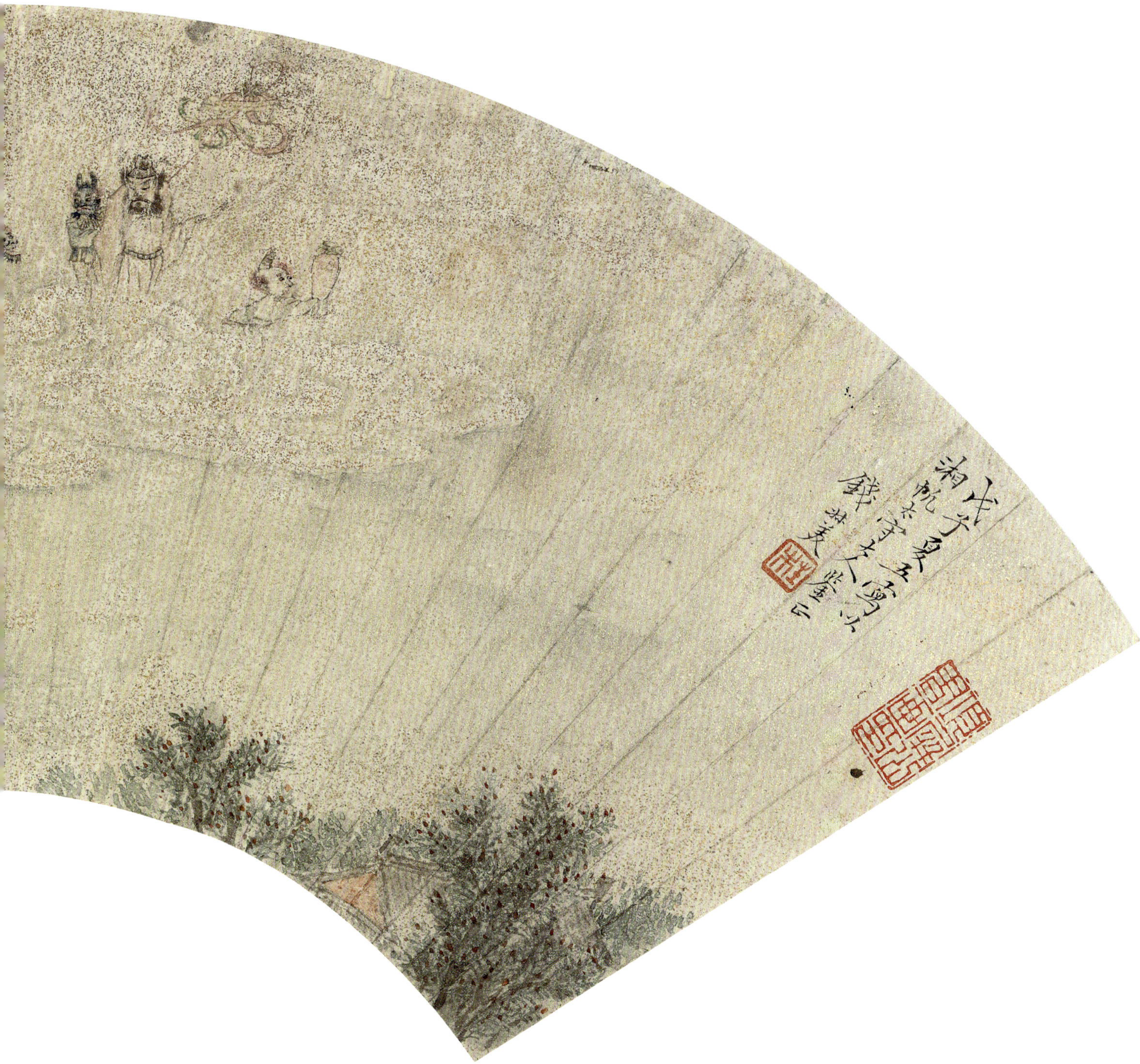
戊子夏五寫以
湘帆先生大人鑒正
錢杜叔美

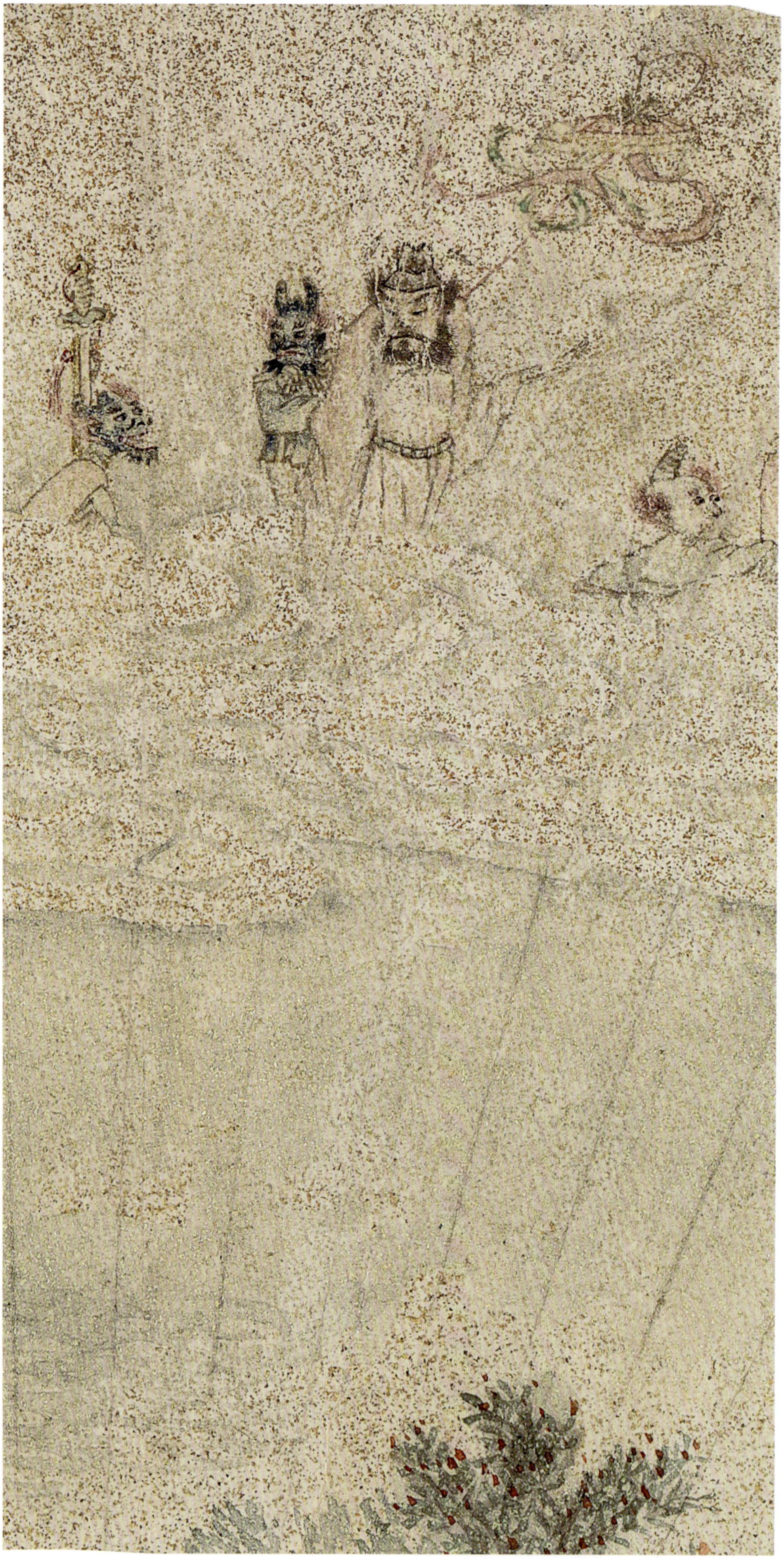

Artist:
Qian Du

Medium:
Color on letter paper; Fan-shaped

Dimensions:
18 cm × 54 cm

Zhong Kui

Inscription:
On the fifth day of summer in the Wuzi year, [the painting] was created in imitation of the style of the esteemed Prefect Xiangfan and was authenticated. By Qian Shumei.

Seal:
Du

Qian Du (1764–1845)
Initially named Yu, with the courtesy name Shumei, later changed to Du. Styled as Songhu Xiaoyin, also known as Songhu, and sometimes referred to as Hugong, he was a Lay Scholar from Qiantang. The younger brother of Qian Shu, he came from a family of officials. He became a Jinshi during the fifth year of the Jiaqing Emperor's reign and served as a Secretary. He is the author of works such as "Secrets of Songhu Painting" and "Memories of Songhu Painting".

欽青鋒耀白日飈未同兩大奔逸科頭
箕踞泛濩庖那憶金門對策時
嘉慶甲子五月道堅子汪泰謹寫

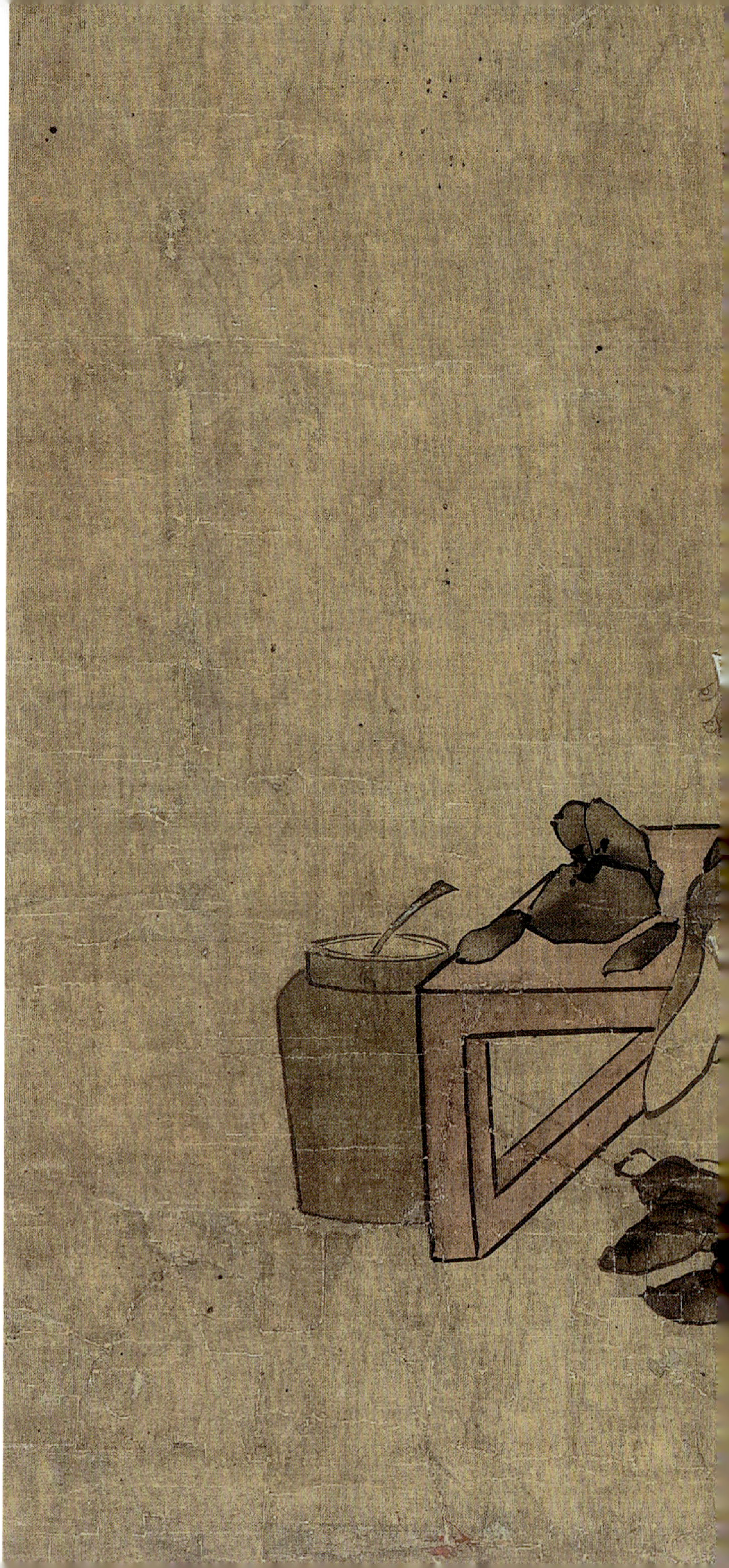

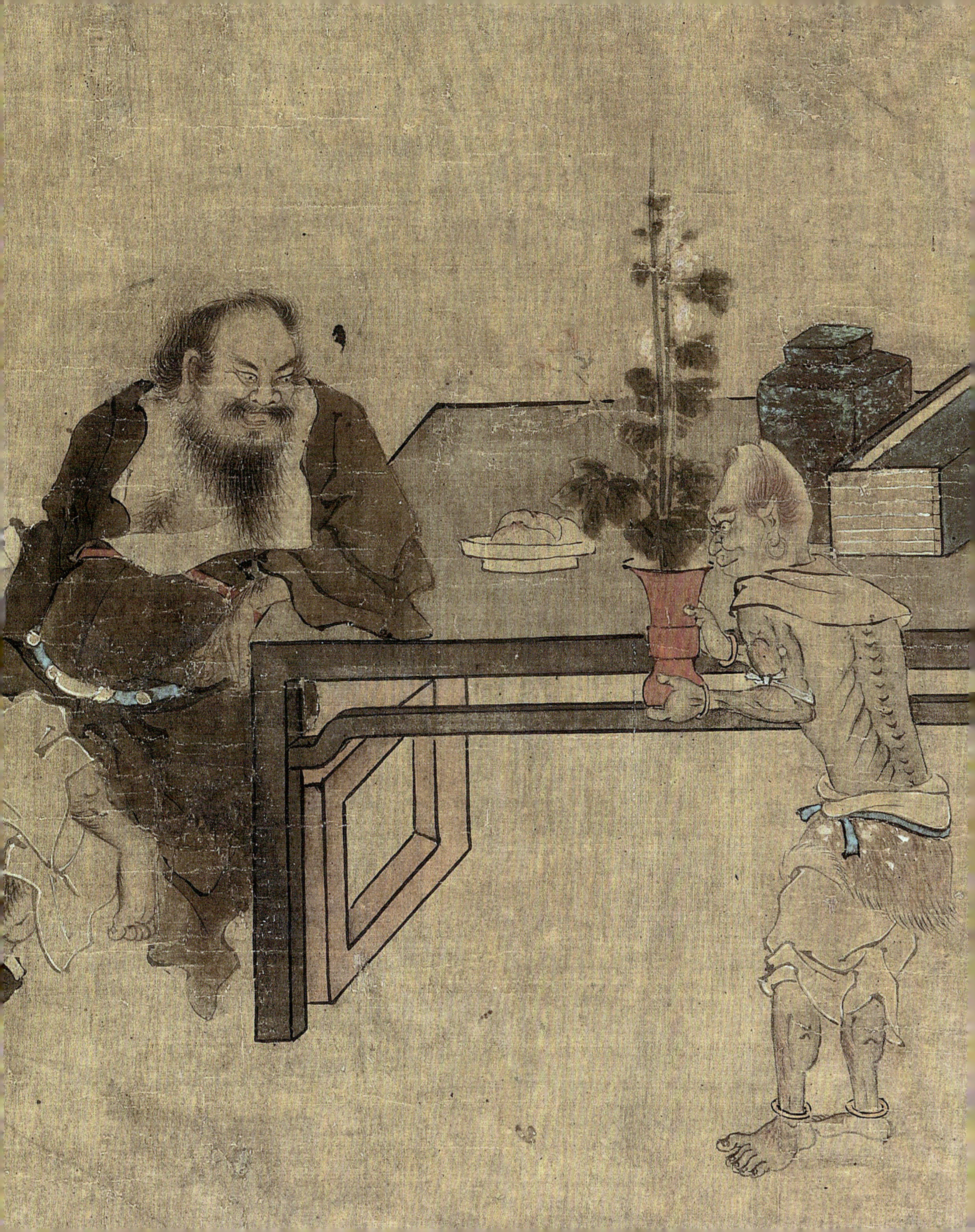

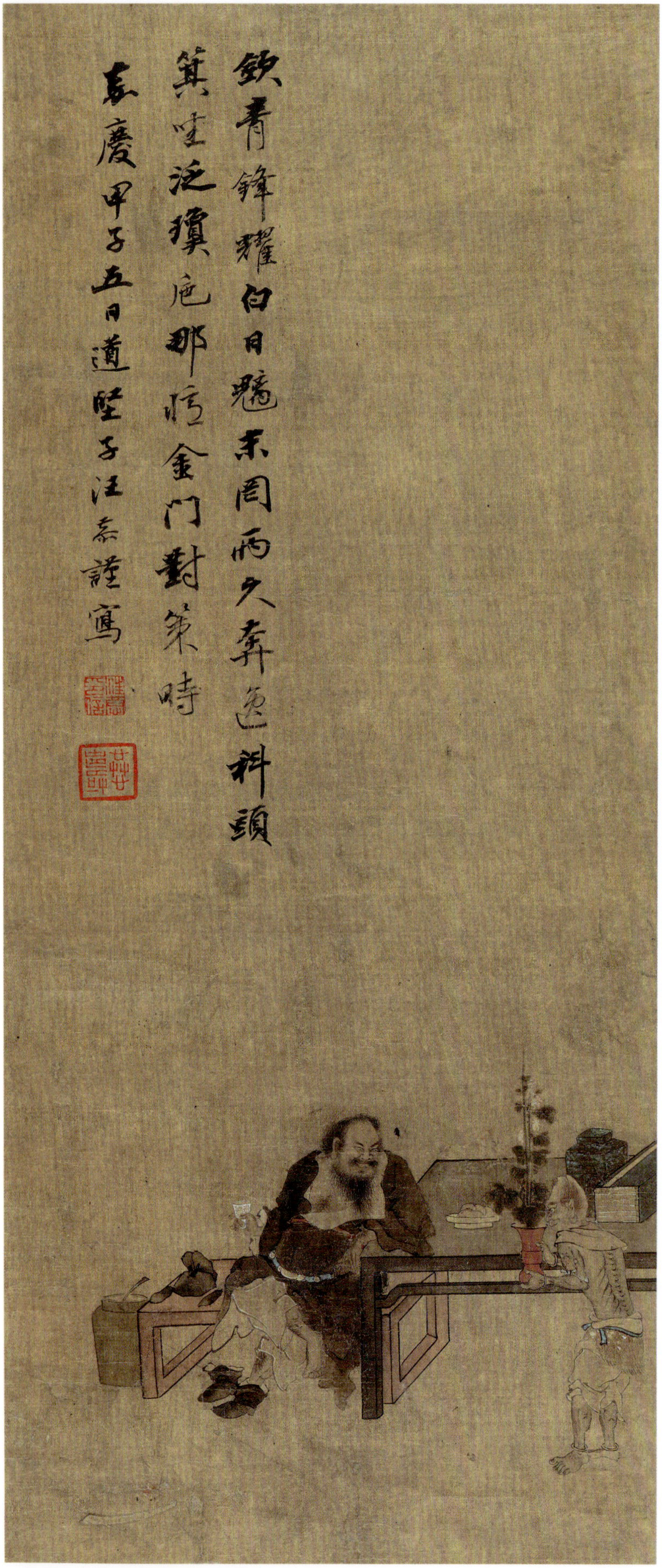
欽青鋒耀白日魑末罔兩久奔逸料頭
箕踞泛瓊卮那憶金門對策時
嘉慶甲子五日道墅子汪恭謹寫

Artist:
Wang Gong

Medium:
Color on silk, Hanging scroll

Dimensions:
88 cm × 37 cm

Zhong Kui

Inscription:
I've sheathed my sharpness, which shines as the bright sun. Malevolent spirits cannot linger, they flee swiftly. Seated with my examination hat during the tests, sipping fine wine, how could one forget the moments of strategizing at Jinmen. In the fifth month of the Jiawu year of Jiaqing reign, a cautious script by Qiujianzi Wang Gong.

Seal:
Wang Gong's Seal of Approval, Gong Shou

Wang Gong
Courtesy name Gongshou. Styled as Zhuping Lay Scholar, Shouyuan Hermit, Man of the Zishi Mountain, and Jinsha Historian. A native of Xiuning, Anhui, he once resided in Suzhou. A painter of the Qing dynasty, he was a connoisseur of musical rhythm and especially skilled in running and regular script, inheriting the methods of artists Liang Tongshu and Wang Wenzhi, with a close friendship with Cheng Tang.

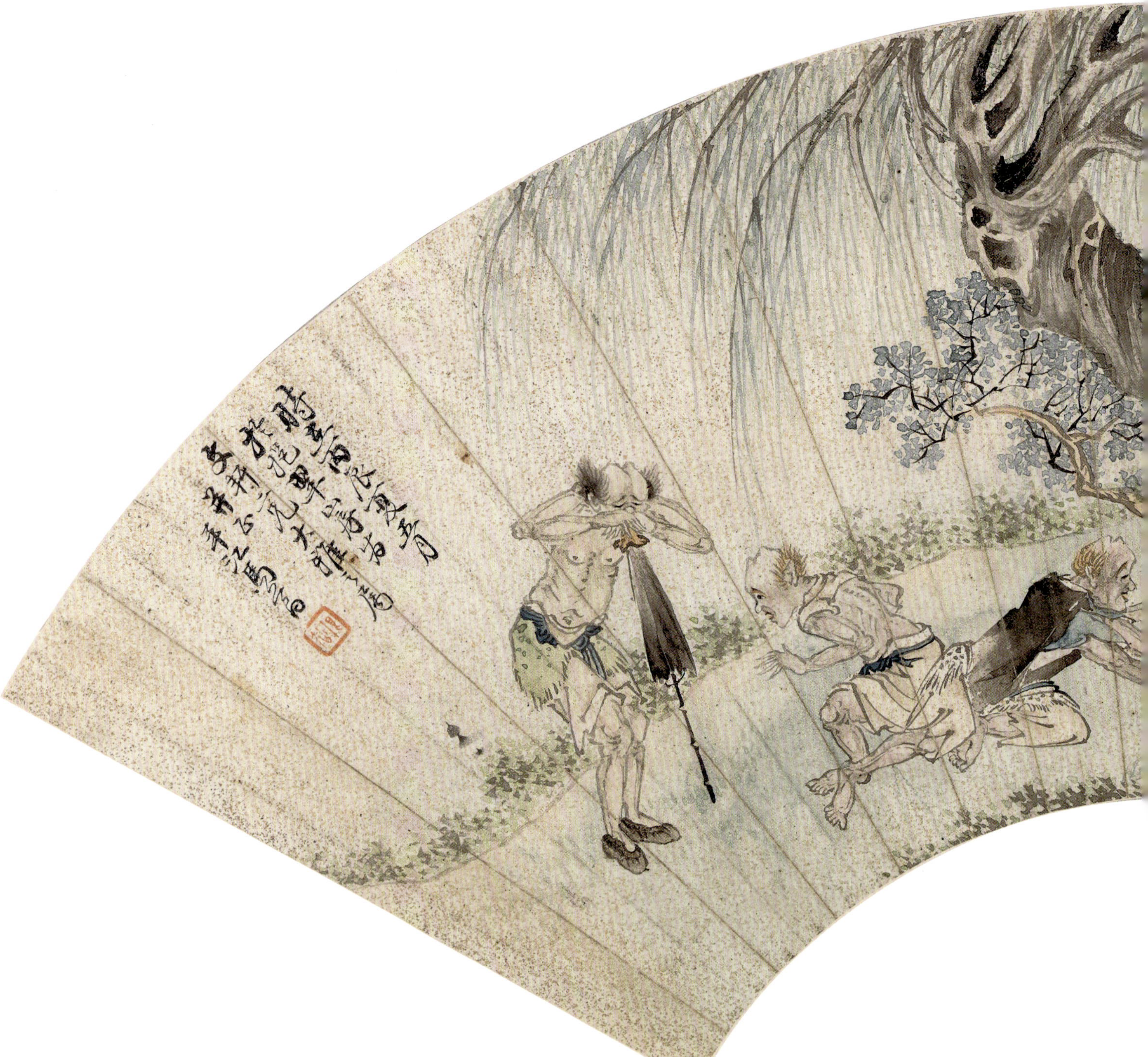

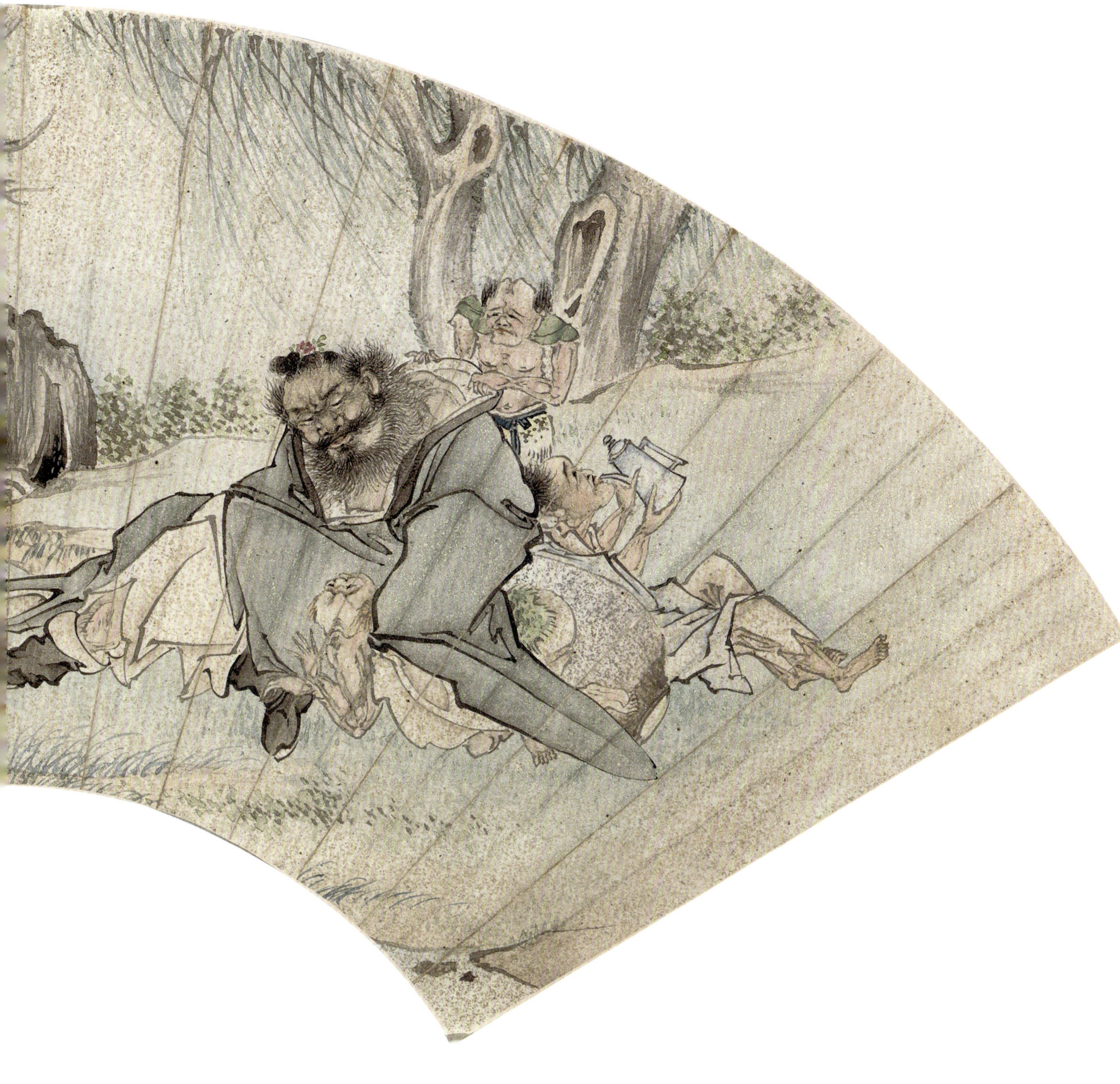

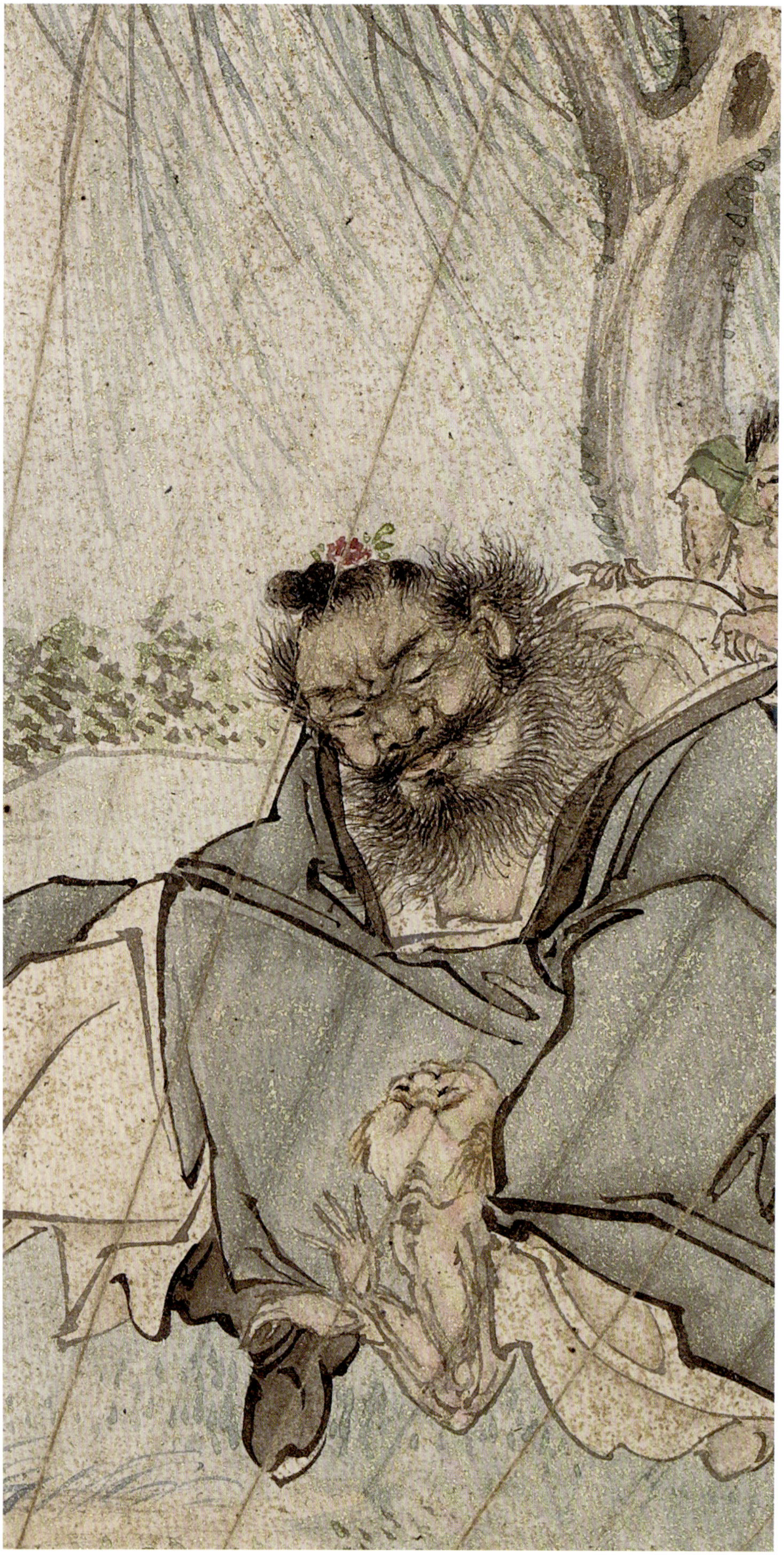

Artist:
Ma Genxian

Medium:
Color on letter paper, Fan-shaped

Dimensions:
18 cm × 53 cm

Zhong Kui Drunk

Inscription:
In the fifth month of the summer in the Bingchen year, at the Yicui Mountain House, I have made corrections for the grand elegance attributed to my second elder brother Wenxuan, by Ma Chang from Pingjiang.

Ma Genxian
A native of Suzhou, Jiangsu. A Qing dynasty painter who carried on his family's painting tradition and was skilled in playing the guqin. He specialized in carving fan ribs, creating exquisite designs of flowers and court ladies with such masterful intricacy that none could rival his craftsmanship.

破傘孤燈兩脚泥
莫符南北與東西
祇因今夜歸來晚
反怕無端着鬼迷

戊子冬月畫爲

聖廣表棣粲正

南柳賴廛肅

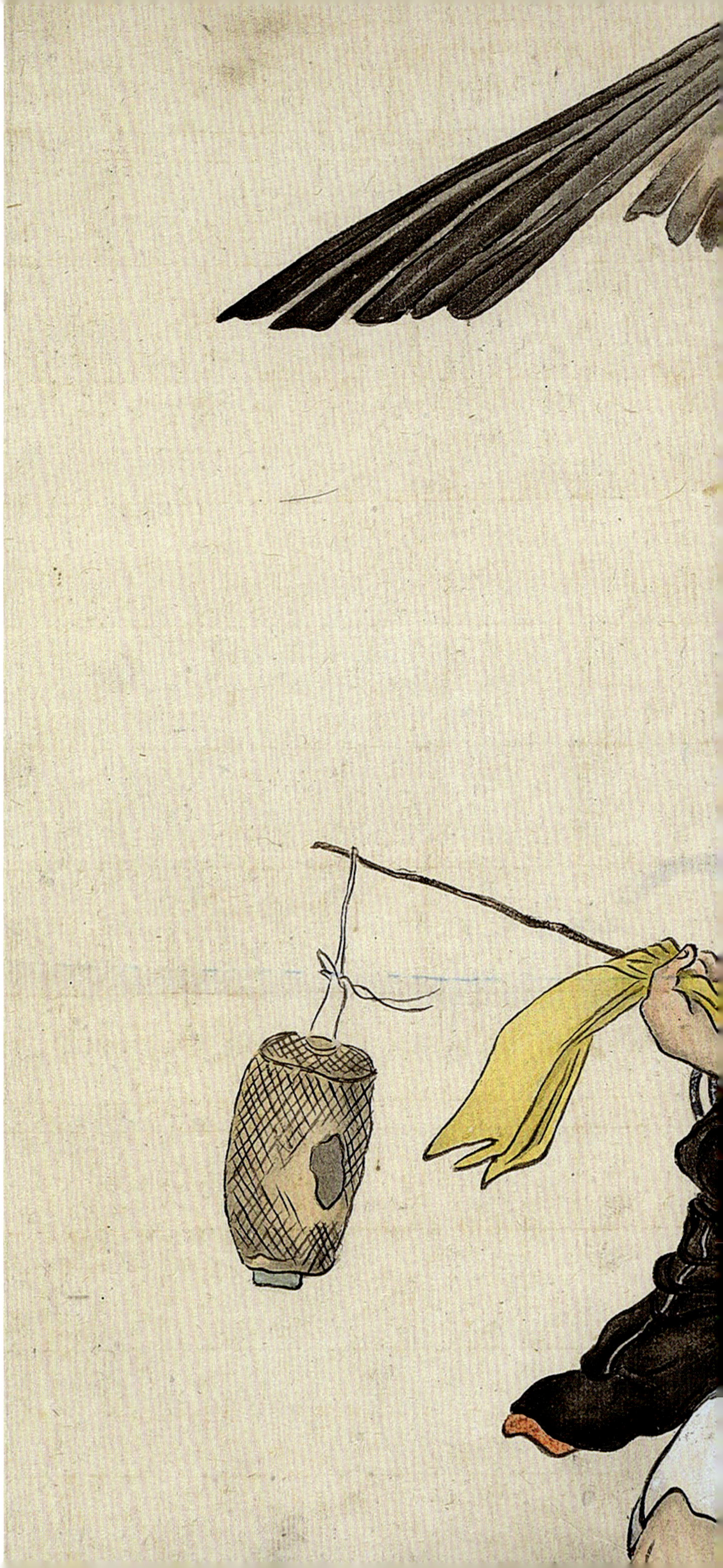

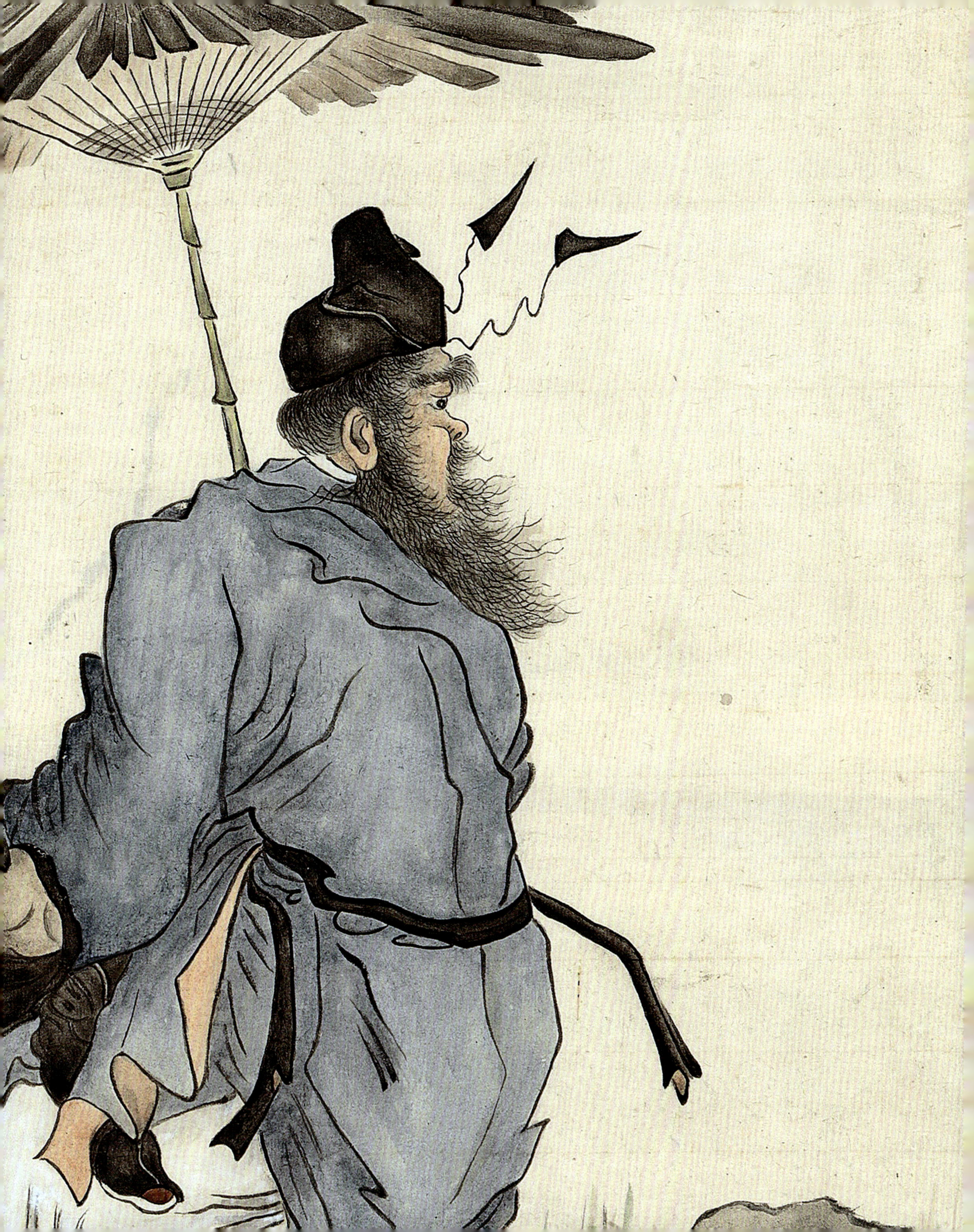

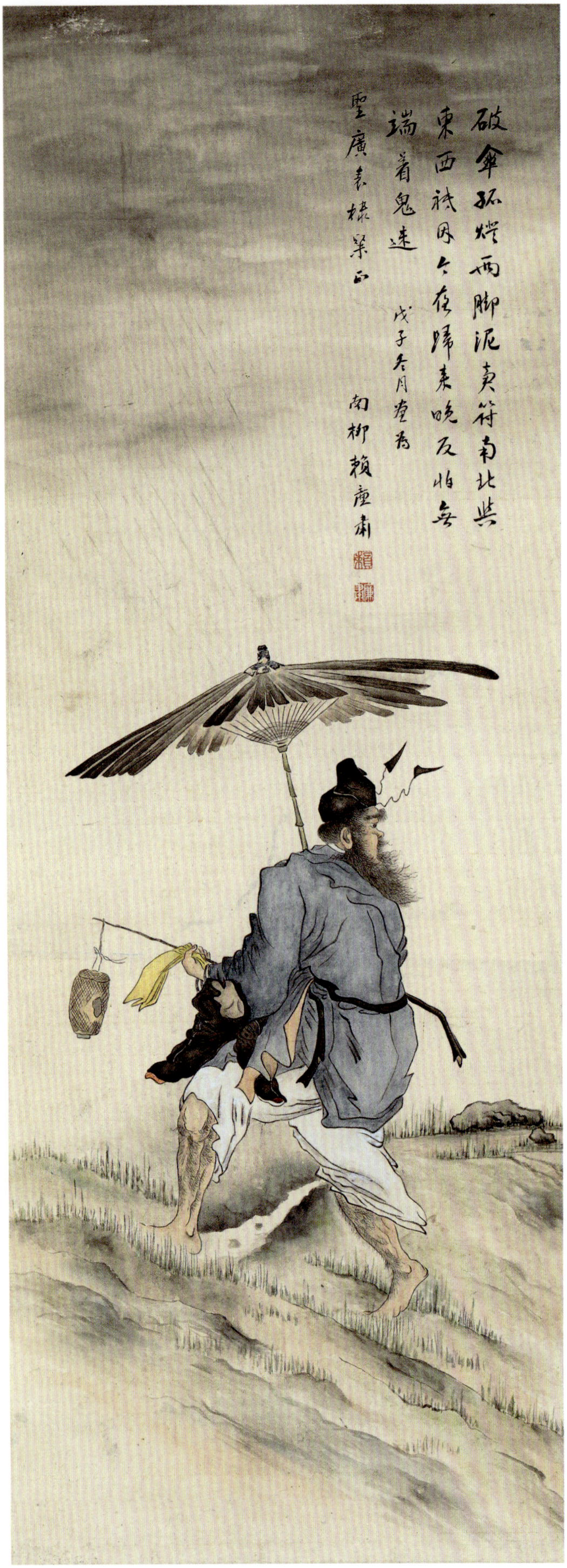
破傘孤燈雨腳泥夷符南北與
東西祇因今夜歸來晚反怕無
端着鬼迷
戊子冬月畫爲
聖廣表棣粲正

Artist:
Lai Liansu

Medium:
Color on paper, Hanging scroll

Dimensions:
95 cm × 34 cm

Zhong Kui

Inscription:
With broken umbrella and lone light, feet caked in mud, from left to right,
I peddle charms from north to south, east to west, under night's shroud.
It's just because I return late this eve, I fear that ghosts may deceive.
This painting was created in the winter month of the Wuzi year for my esteemed cousin Shengguang, styled Canzheng. By Lai Liansu, Nanliu.

Seal:
Lai, Liansu

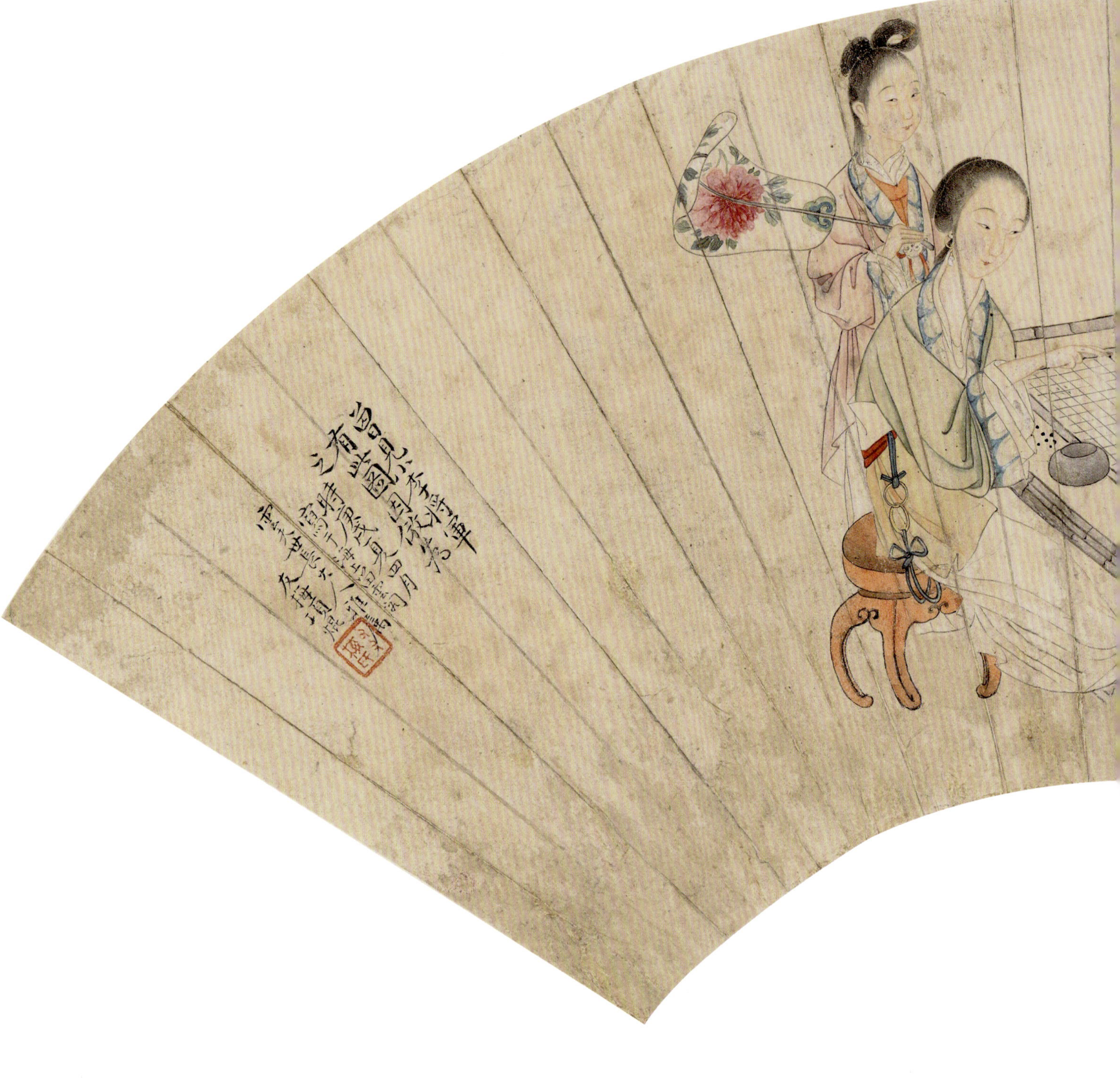

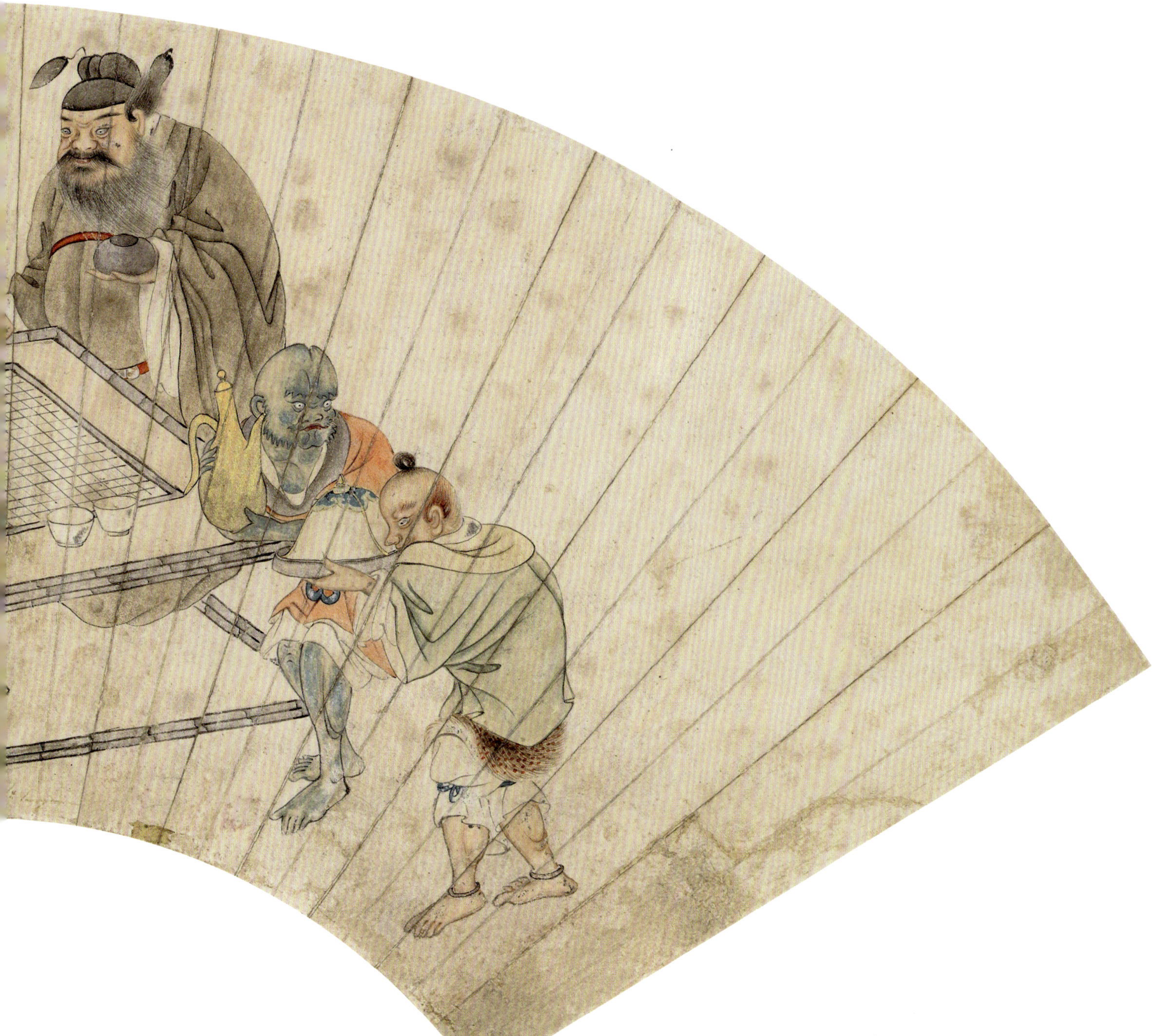

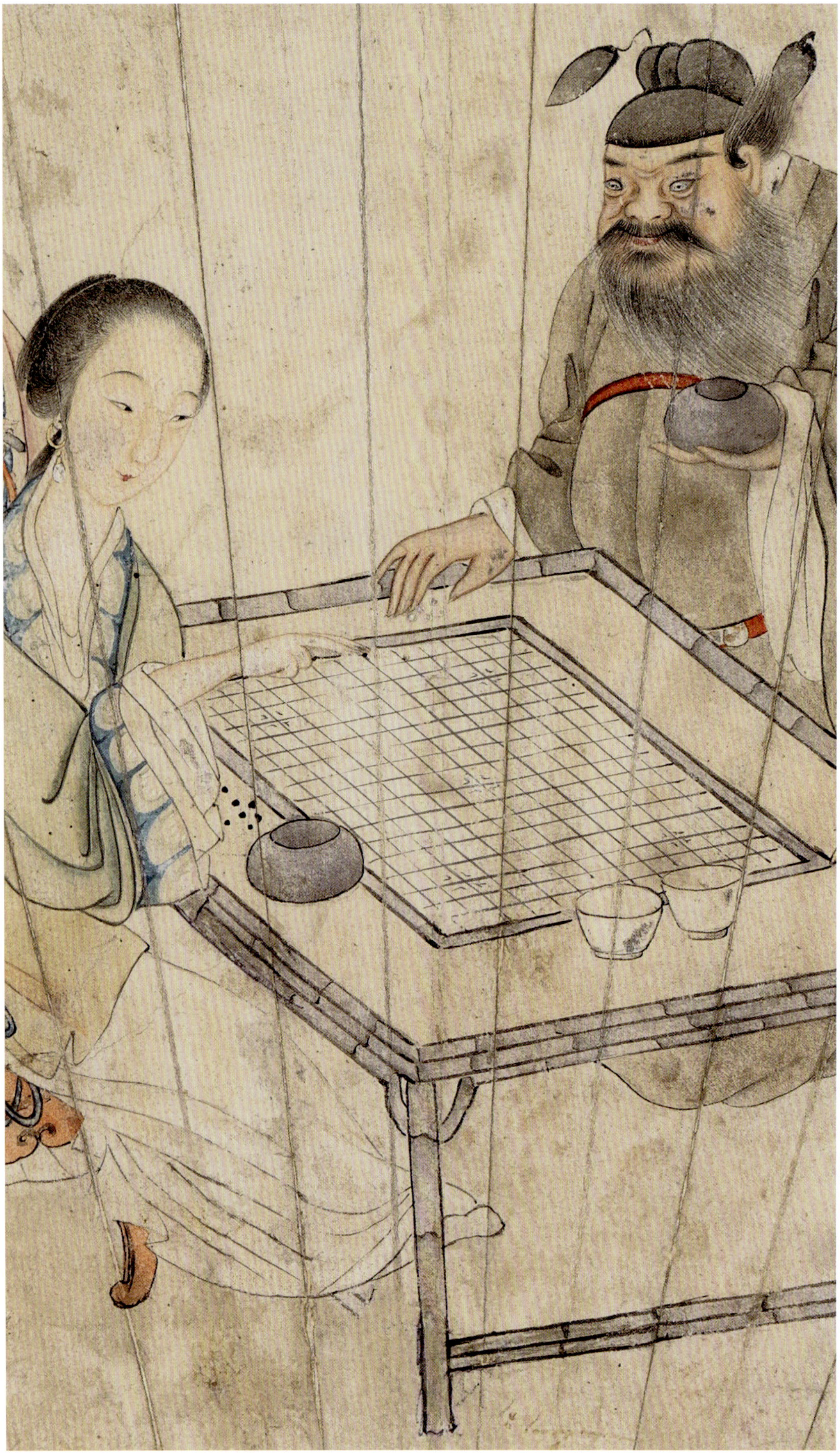

Artist:
Xiang Kun

Medium:
Color on paper, Fan-shaped

Dimensions:
17 cm × 51 cm

Chess at Zhongnan Mountain

Inscription:
Upon beholding a painting in General Xiao Li's possession, I was thus moved to craft a replica. Penned in the fourth month of the Gengxu summer at the Liuyun Pavilion by the sea, this work is born of the distinguished elder Yunfu's cultivated tastes. By Xiang Kun, Youmei.

Seal:
Youmei

Xiang Kun
Courtesy name Youmei, a native of Taicang, Jiangsu. He excelled in painting flowers and figures, distinguished by their exquisite beauty and delicate finesse.

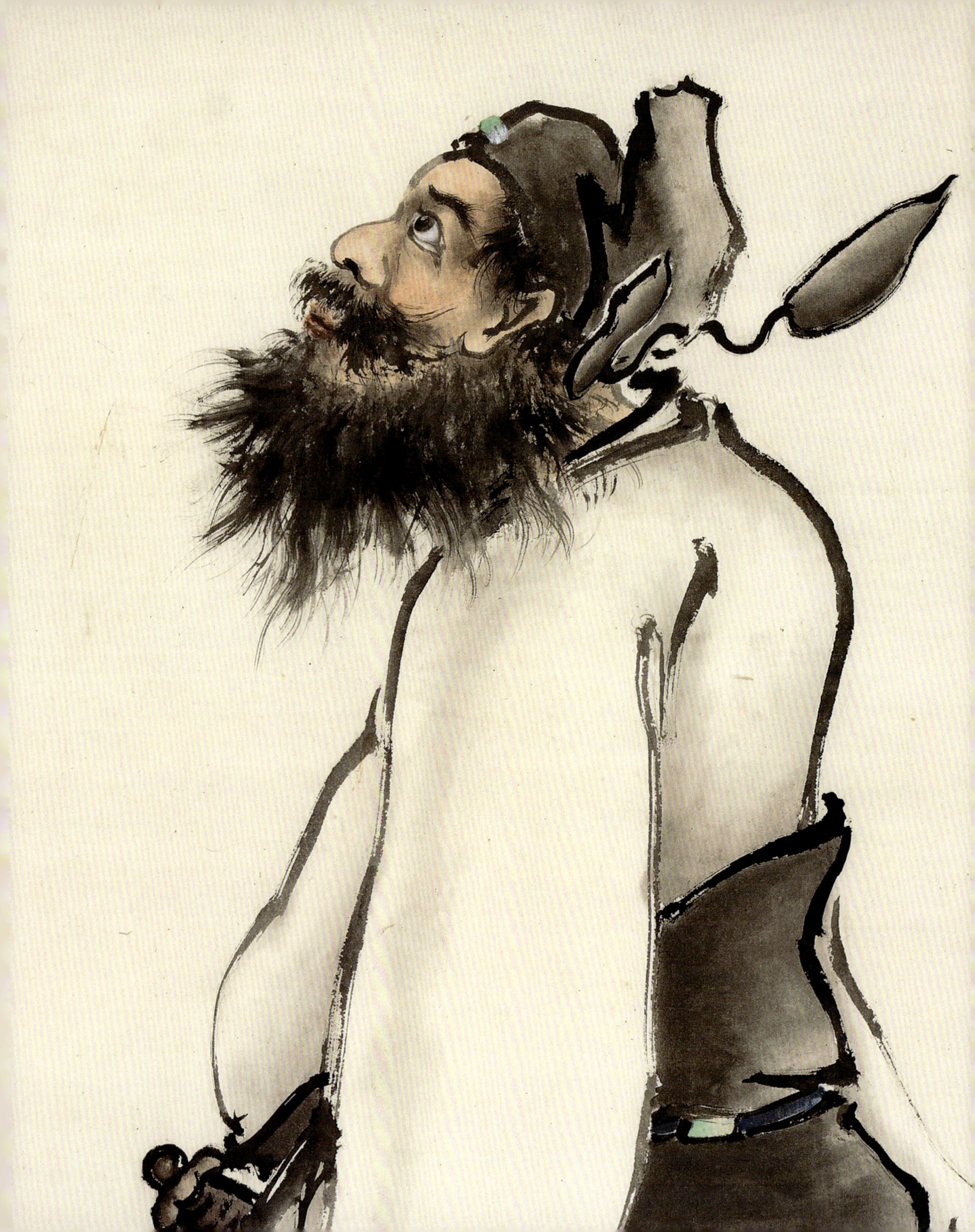

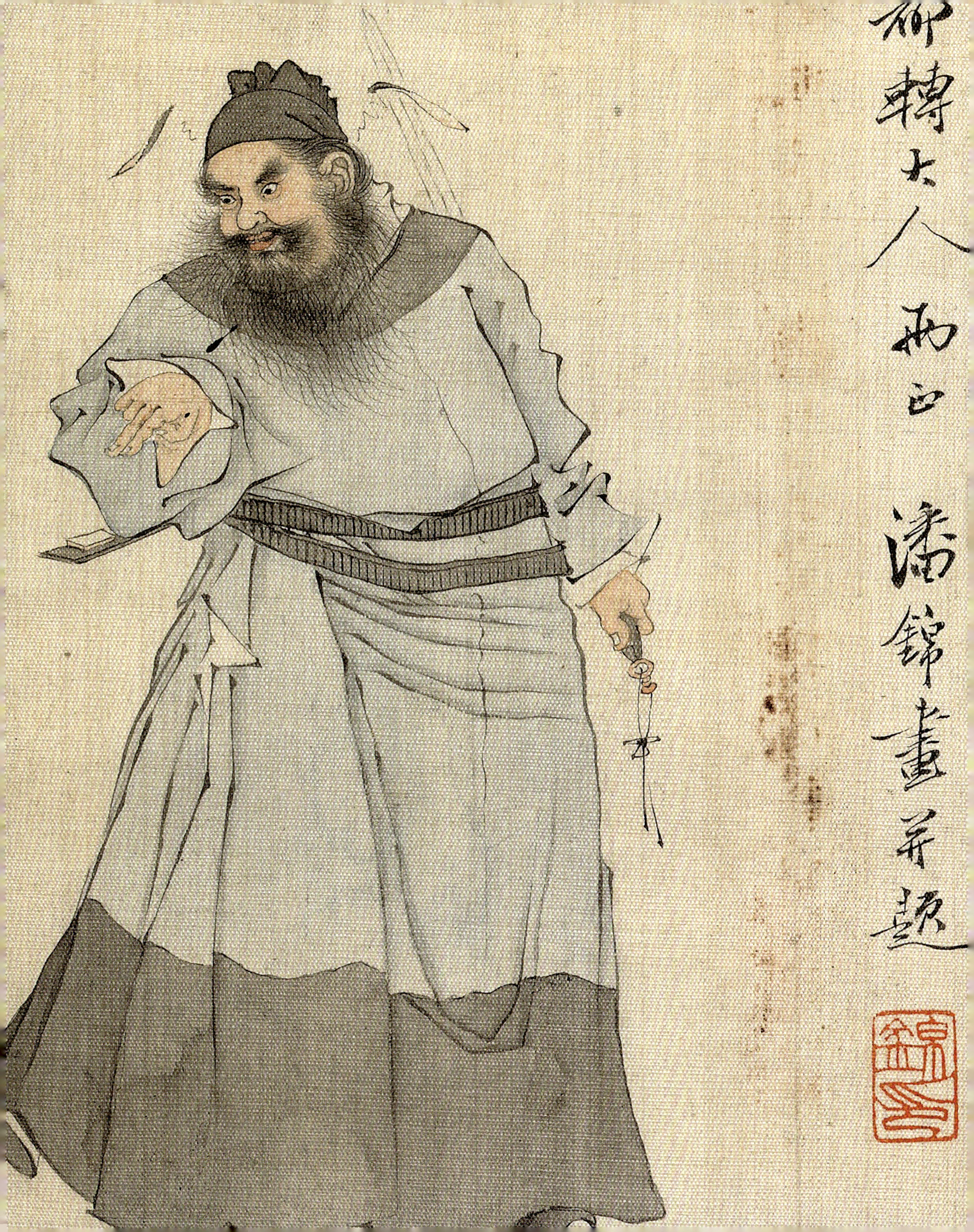
潘錦畫并題

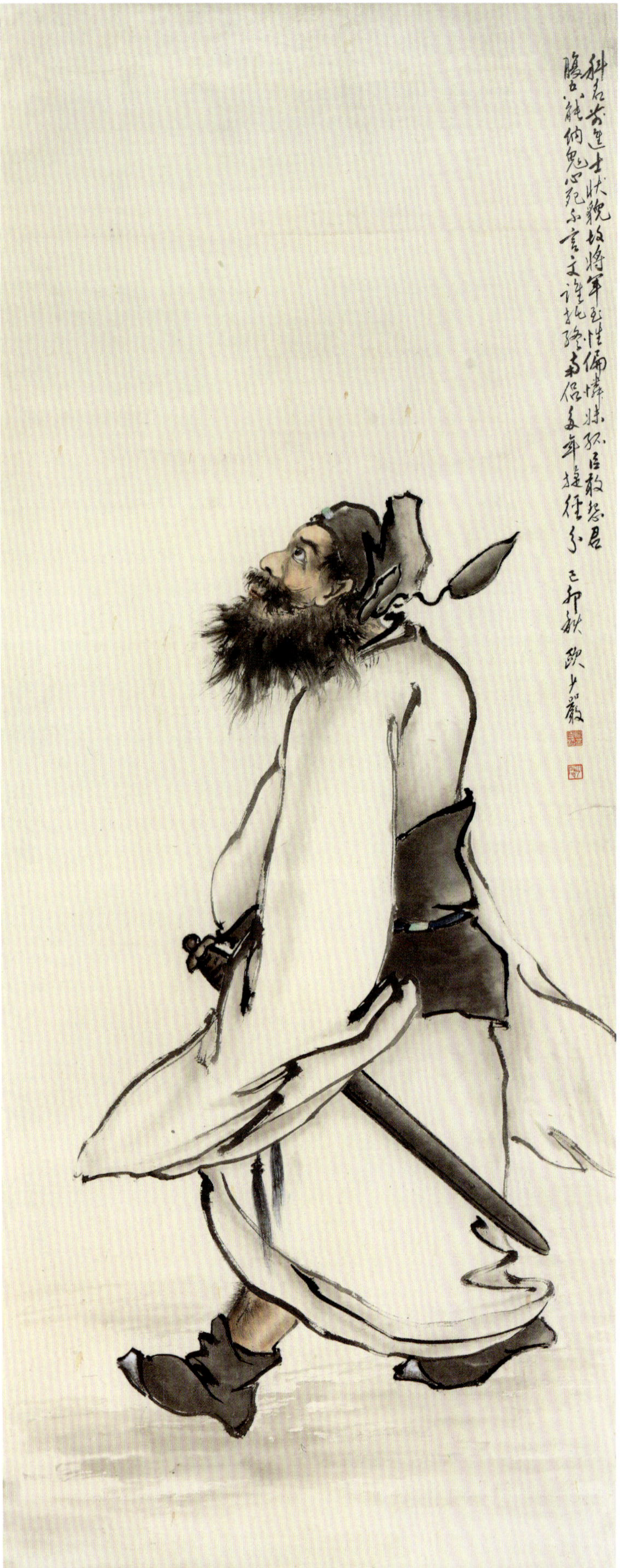

Artist:
Ou Shaoyan

Medium:
Color on paper, Framed piece

Dimensions:
169 cm × 65 cm

The Portrait of Zhong Kui

Inscription:
Foremost in the Juren's scholarly ranks, yet bearing the mien of a general of yore.
His nature so tender towards his sister, how could I, a lone official, the emperor deplore?
With a belly that could entrap specters, his heart dead to the literary lore.
To whom can I entrust the companion of Zhongnan's trails, as years have split the paths we once wore?
Penned in the autumn of the Jimao year by Ou Shaoyan.

Seal:
The Seal of Ou Enzhao, Shaoyan

Ou Shaoyan
A native of Shunde, Guangdong. Studied under the Lingnan school painter Zhao Shao'ang and specialized in the painting of flowers and birds.

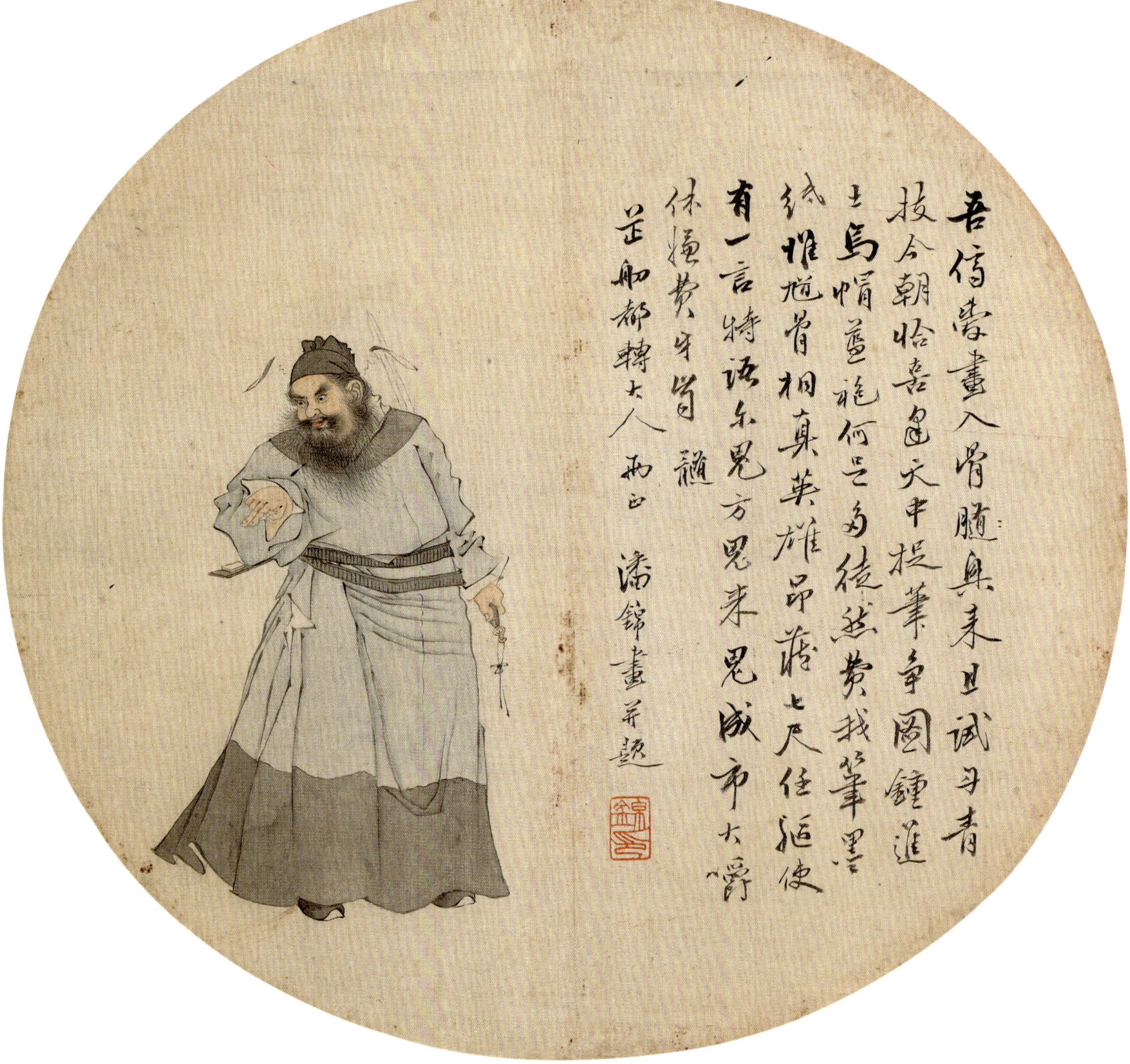

吾信嘗畫入骨髓與來且試丹青
技今朝恰喜逢天中提筆争圖鍾進
士烏帽藍袍何足爲徒然費我筆墨
綫雅髓骨相真英雄昂藏七尺任驅使
有一言特語爾鬼方鬼來鬼成市大爵
休攫費牙齒 髓
芷舫都轉大人两正
潘錦畫并題

Artist:
Pan Jin

Medium:
Color on silk, Round fan, Hanging scroll

Diameter:
26 cm

Jinshi Zhong

Inscription:
Our love for painting pierces deep into the bone, a whim to test the artistry we've known.
This auspicious Mid-Autumn day does bring, the brush in hand to paint Zhong Kui, the Jinshi, in the ring.
Black hats, blue robes, simple in their hue, merely expend my paper and ink anew.
Yet 'tis the heroic form of Kui that stands tall, a true hero, his seven-foot frame I can command at call.
Hear this word I have specially for thee, when ghosts abound as if a market it be, fear not the wear on teeth when you feast heartily.
This painting has been scrupulously examined and approved by the esteemed official Zhishuo, the supervisor, with painting and inscription by Pan Jin.

Seal:
The Seal of Jin

Pan Jin
Pan Jin was a native of Wuxi, Jiangsu Province, known as Ritang, alias Drunken Smoke Taoist. He was good at poetry and calligraphy, and his paintings of landscapes, figures and ladies were all in line with the ancient method, while his flowers were also in good taste.

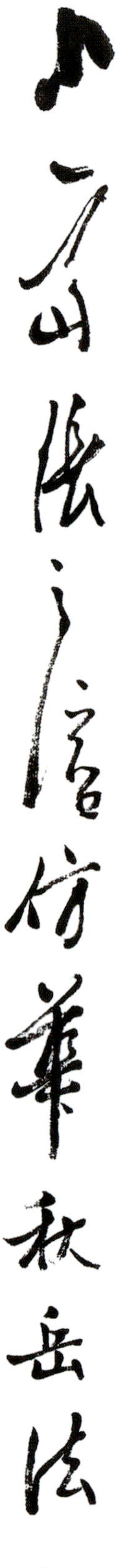

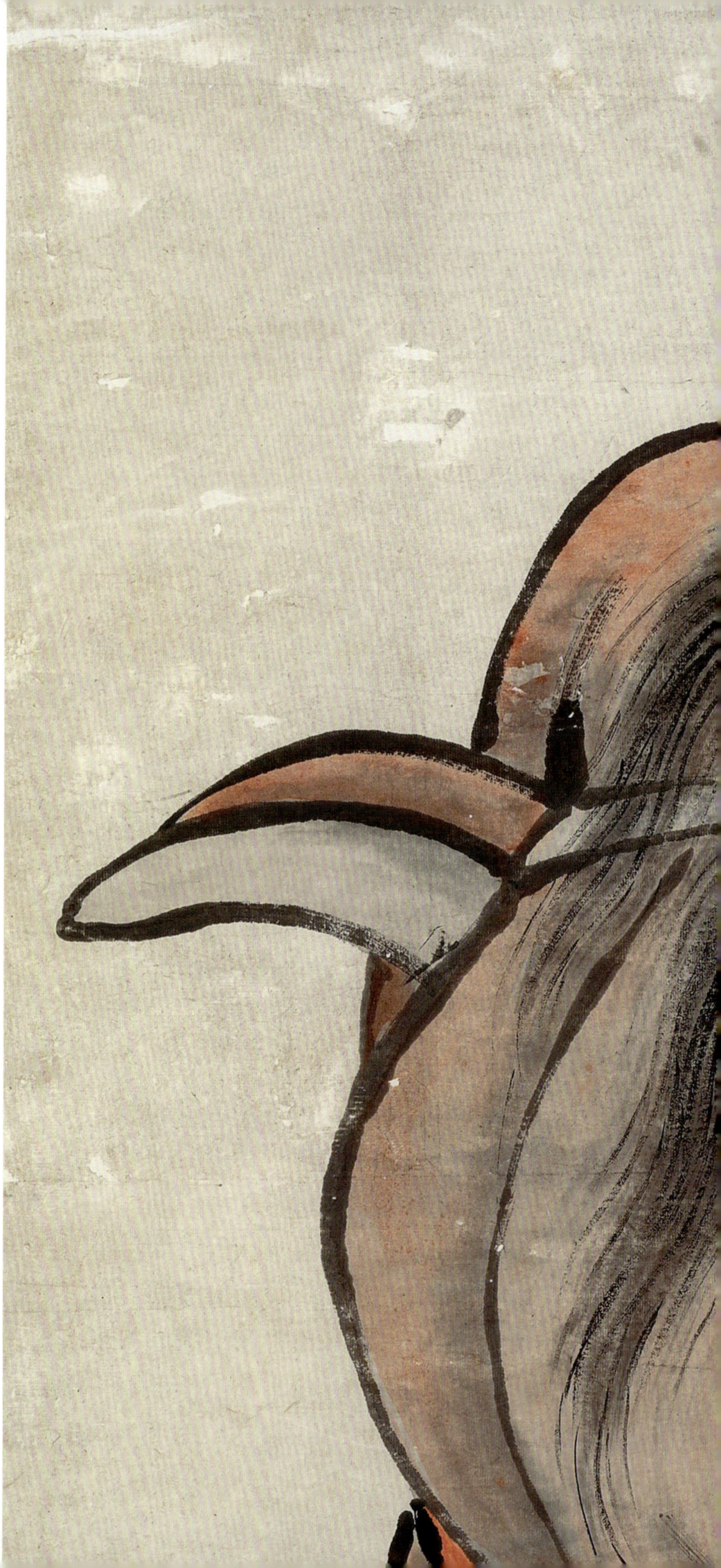

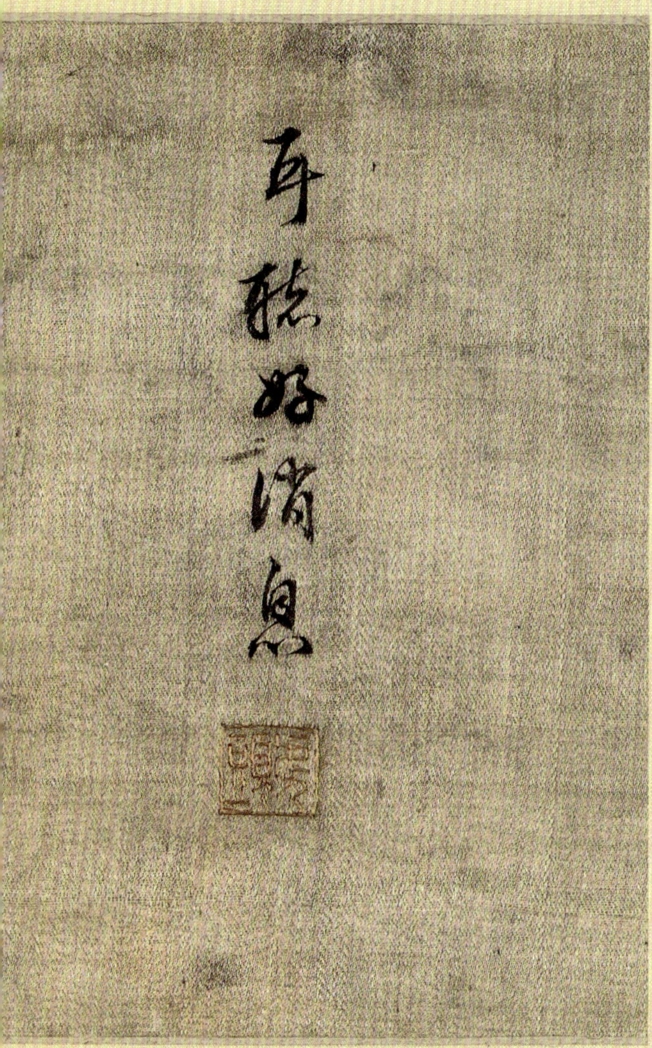
耳聽好消息

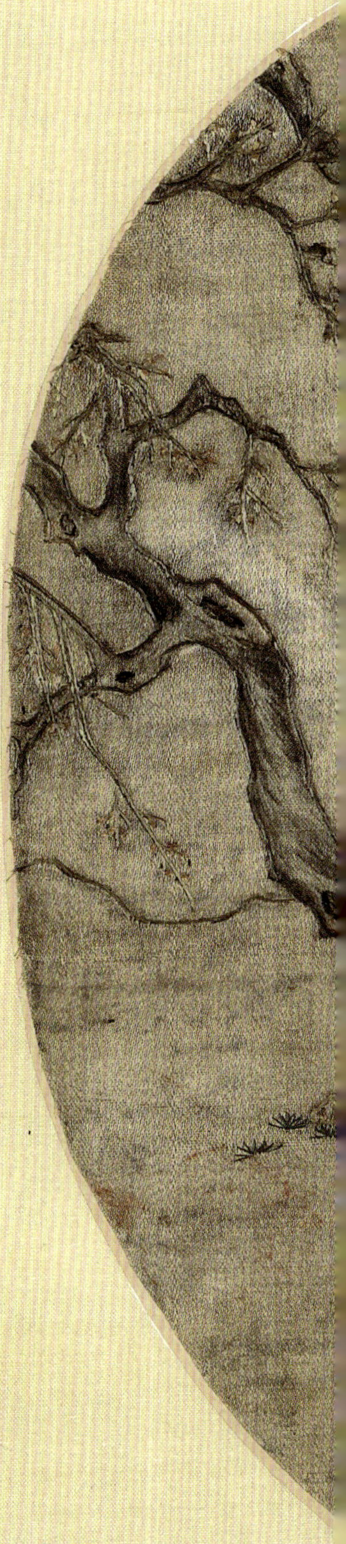

Artist:
Jiang Danxu

Medium:
Color on paper, Hanging scroll

Dimensions:
66 cm × 28 cm

Good Fortune Arrives

Inscription:
On the Double Ninth Festival of the Dingchou year, this piece was penned by Jiang Danxu, Haichang.

Seal:
The seal of subject Danxu

Jiang Danxu
A native of Wuxi, Jiangsu. Styled as Ronghu Historian, he was a painter during the Republic of China period and excelled in landscape painting.

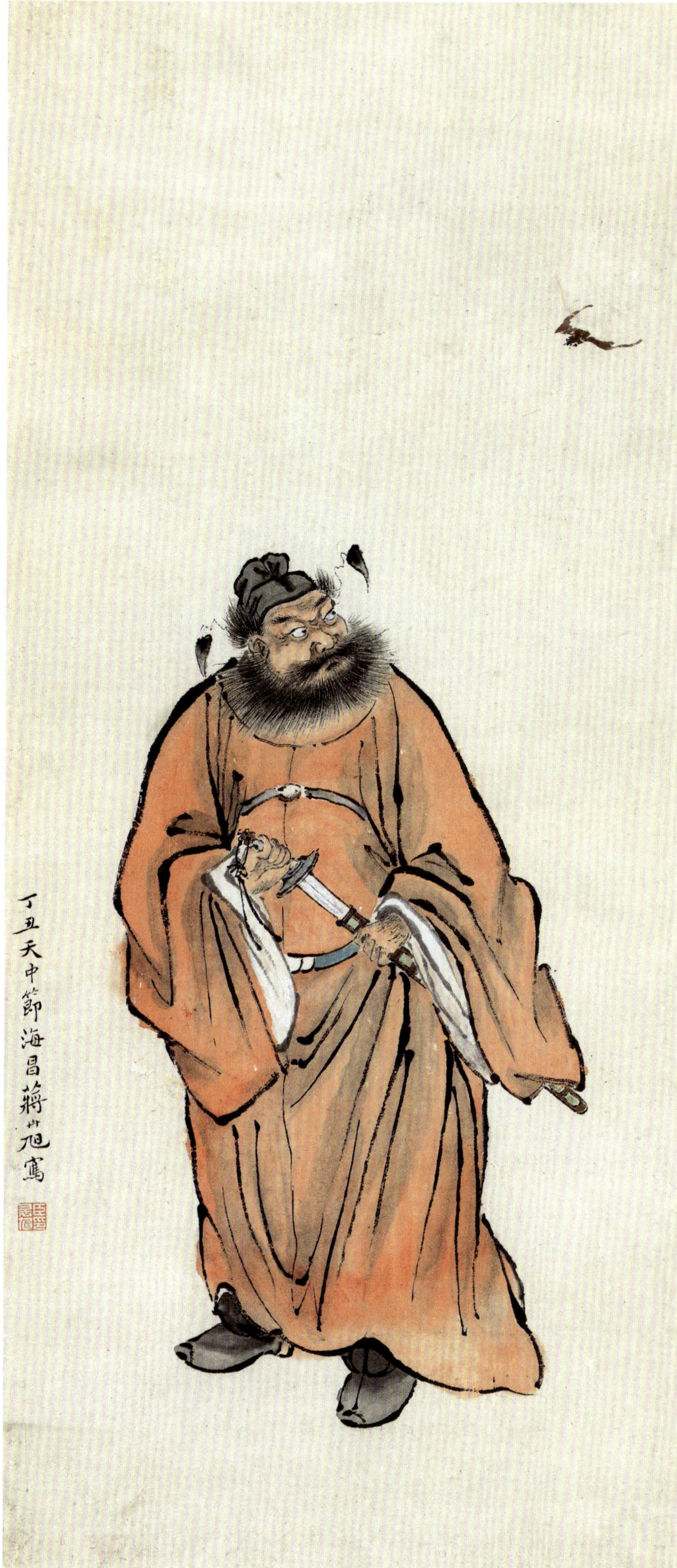
丁丑天中節海昌蔣旭寫

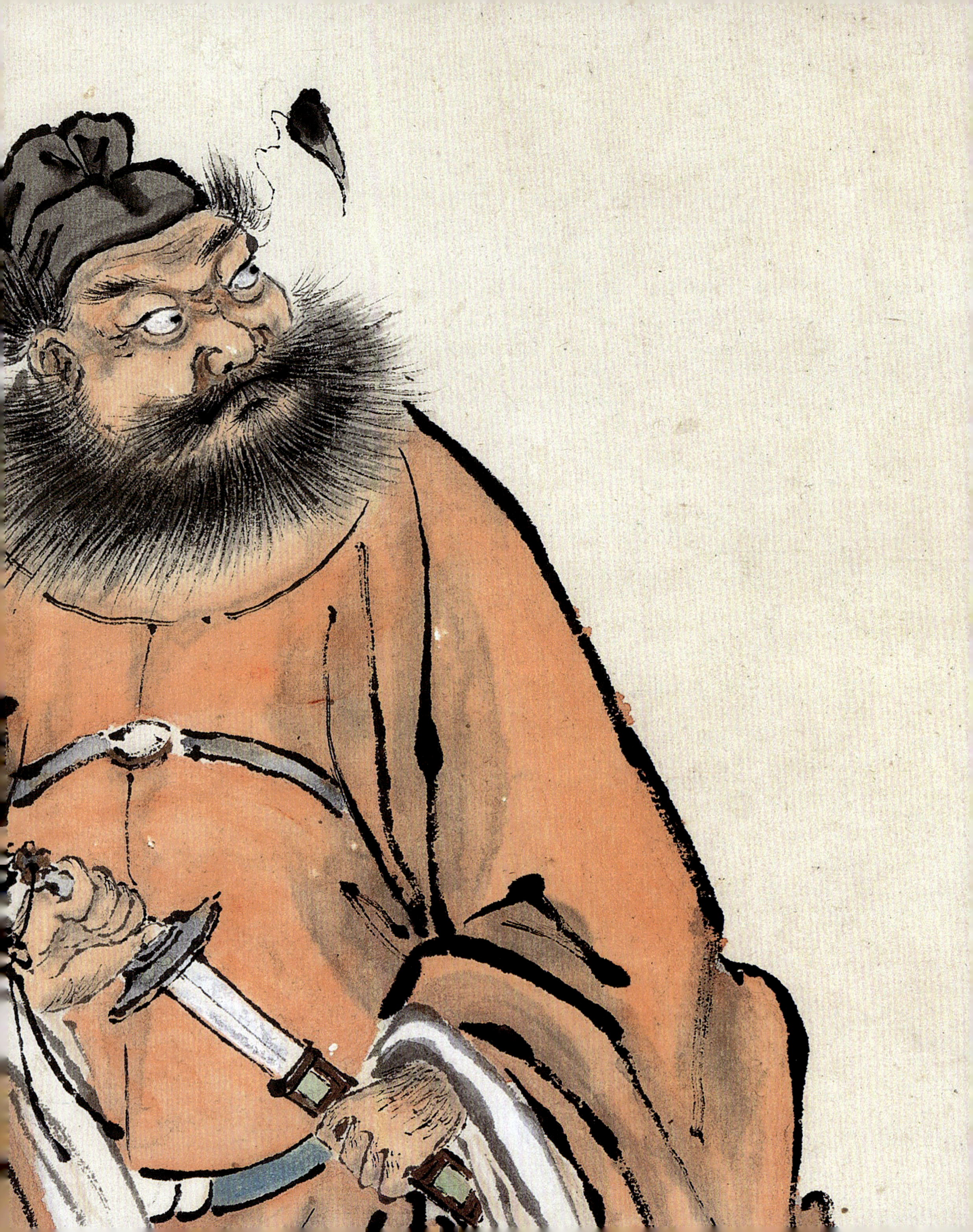

丁丑天中節海昌蔣旭寫

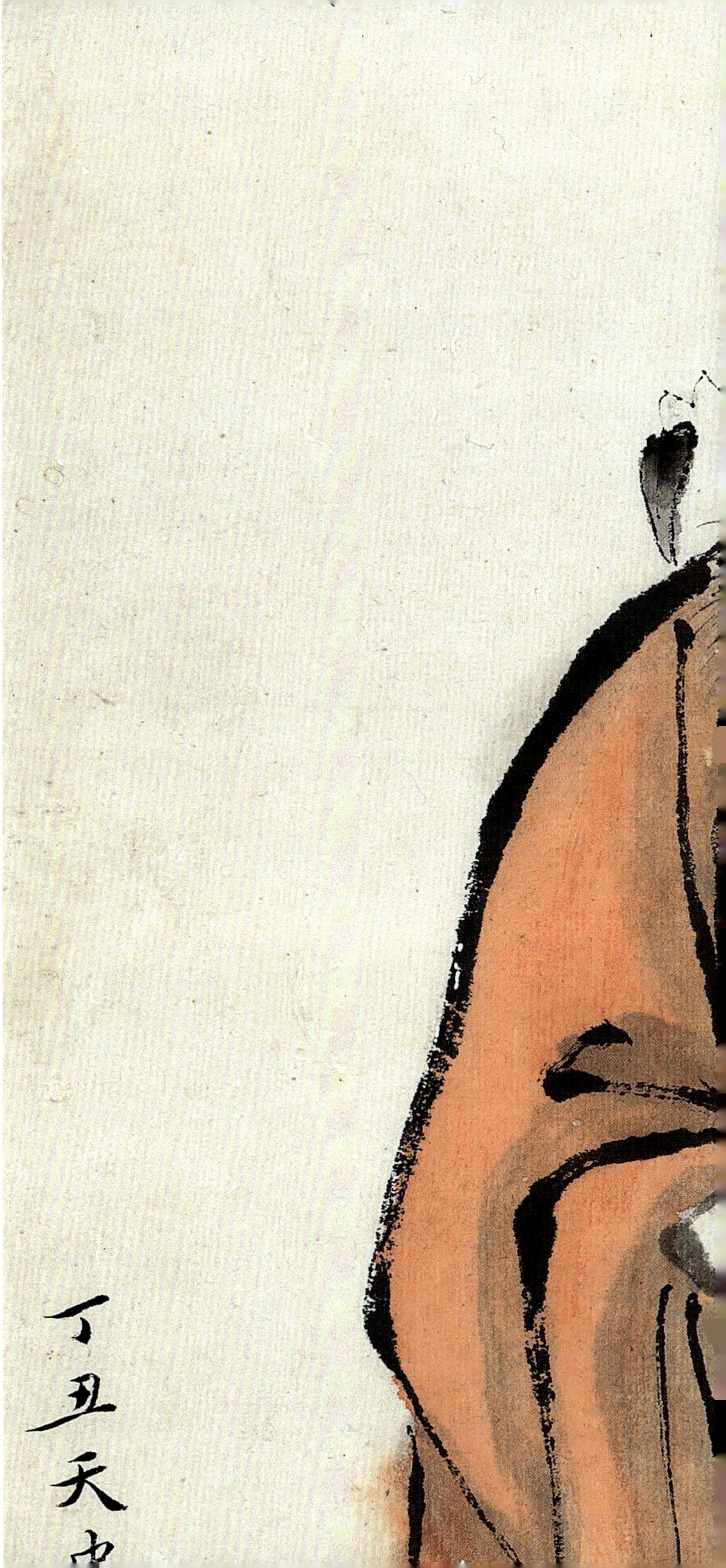

Artist:
Zhang Zhirong

Medium:
Color on paper, Hanging scroll

Dimensions:
139 cm × 71 cm

Zhong Kui

Inscription:
Zhang Zhirong, Xiaozhai, replicated the technique of Hua Qiuyue.

Seal:
The seal of Zhang Zhirong, Works of Xiaozhai after the age of forty

Zhang Zhirong
From Jiangning (present-day Nanjing, Jiangsu). A Qing dynasty painter, styled as Xiaozhai, who excelled in painting flowers, birds, and figures, particularly skilled in depicting horses.

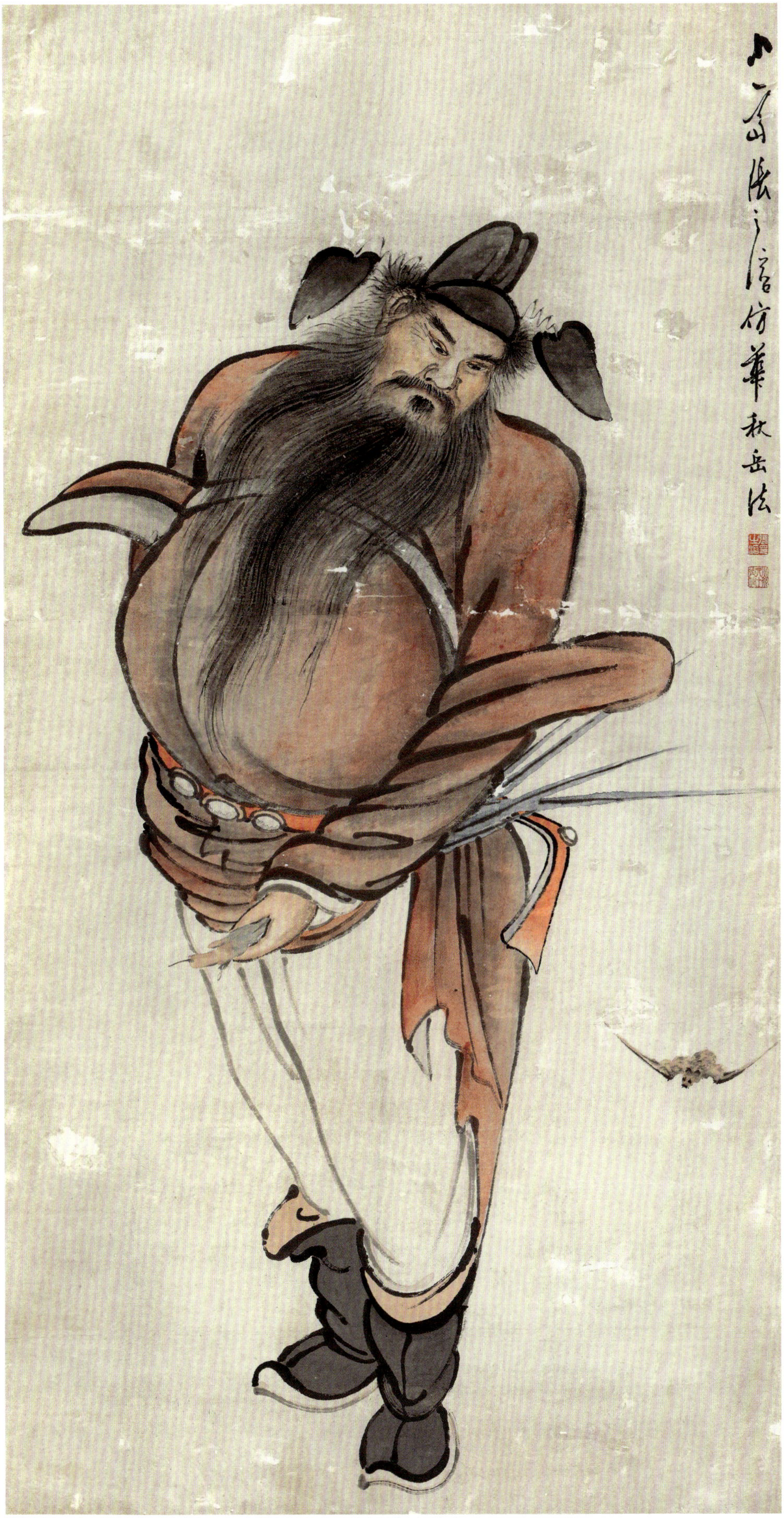

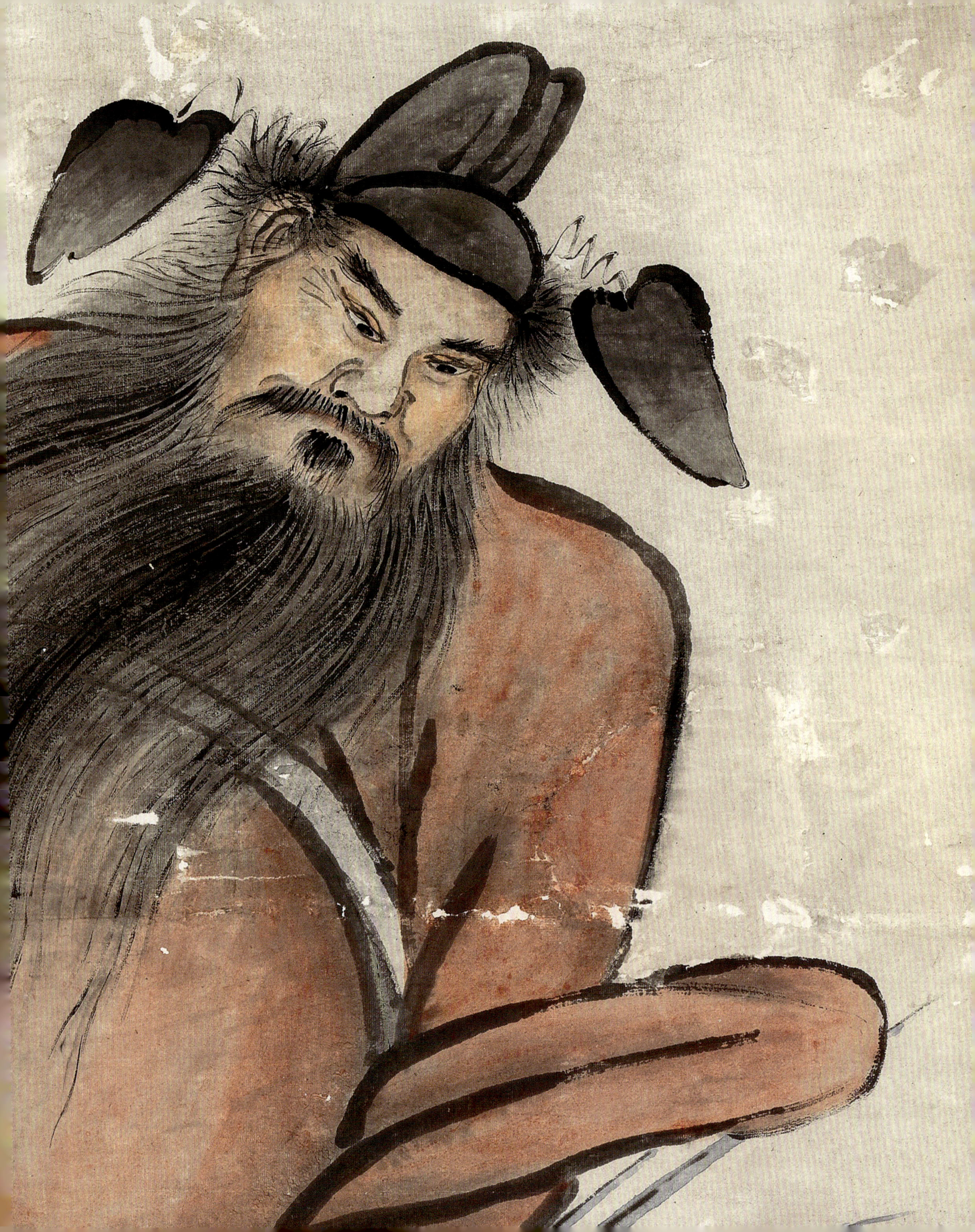

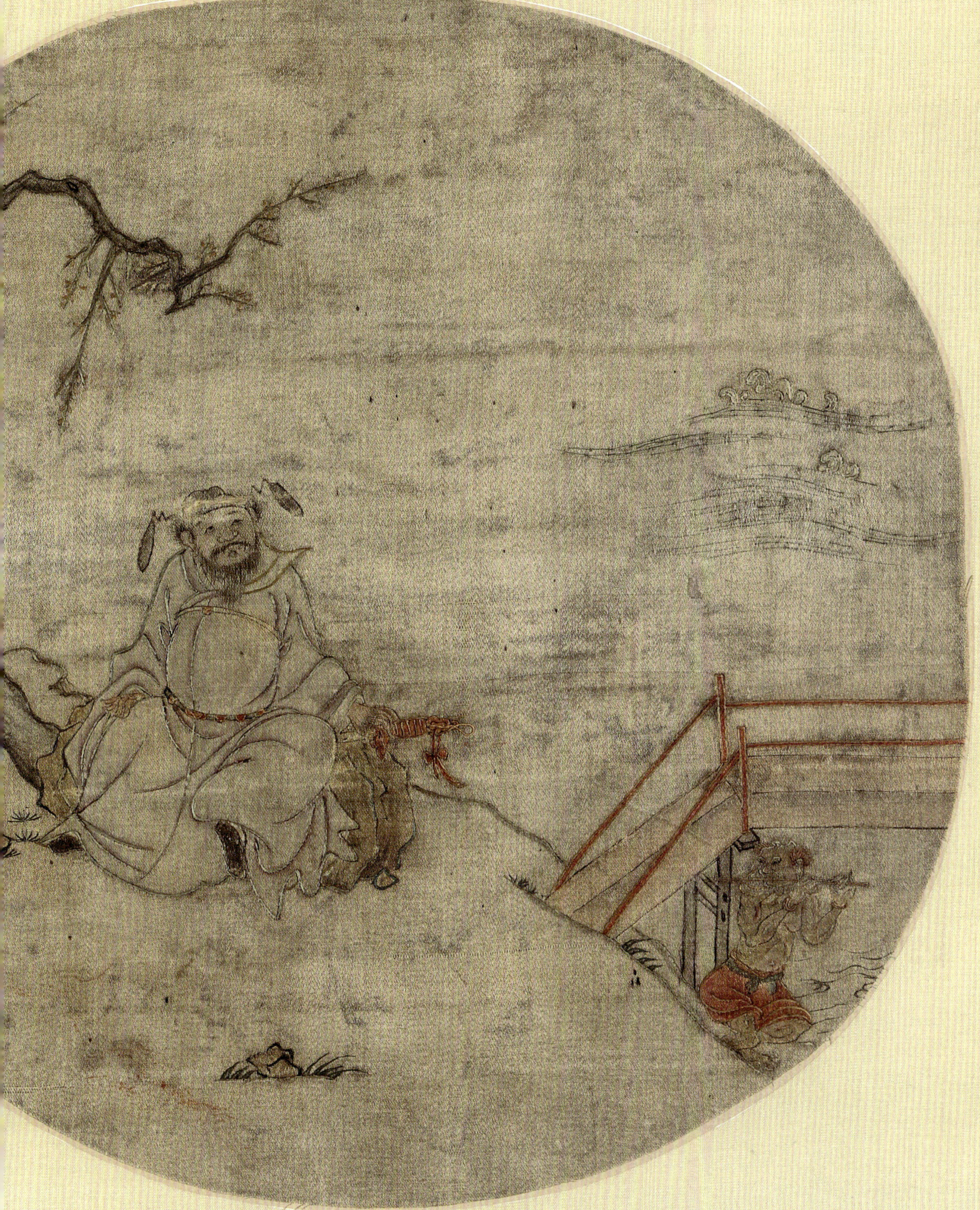

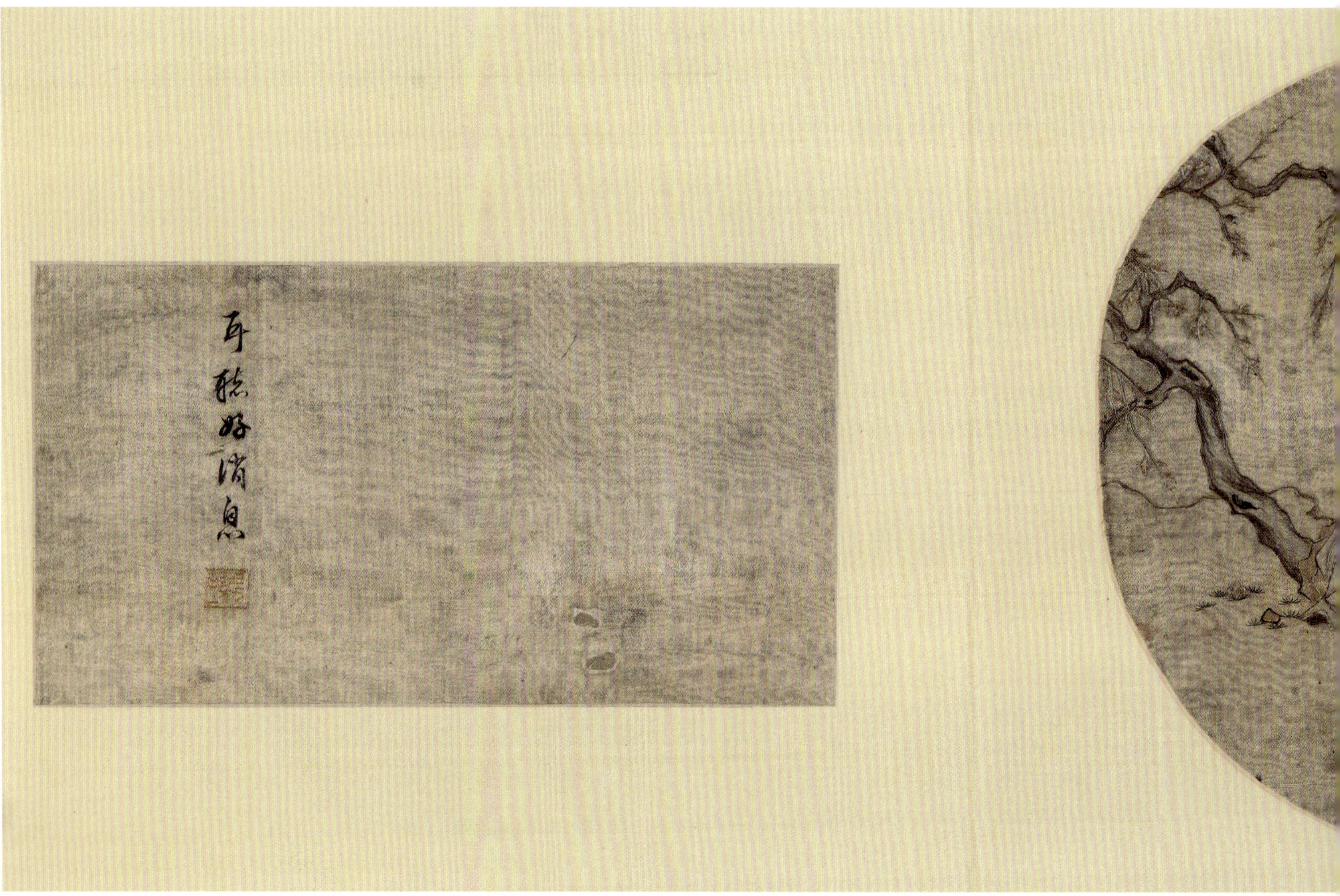
耳聽好消息

Medium:
Qing Dynasty kesi silk tapestry, Framed piece

Dimensions:
12.5 cm × 23 cm; Diameter: 23 cm

Good News Heard

Inscription:
Good news heard

Seal:
Tiger-head

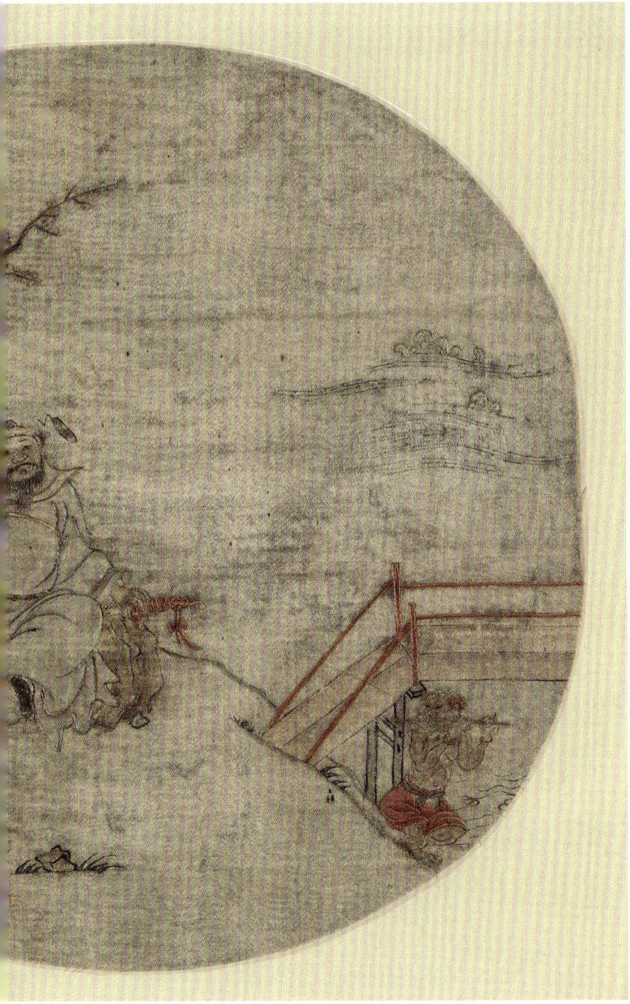

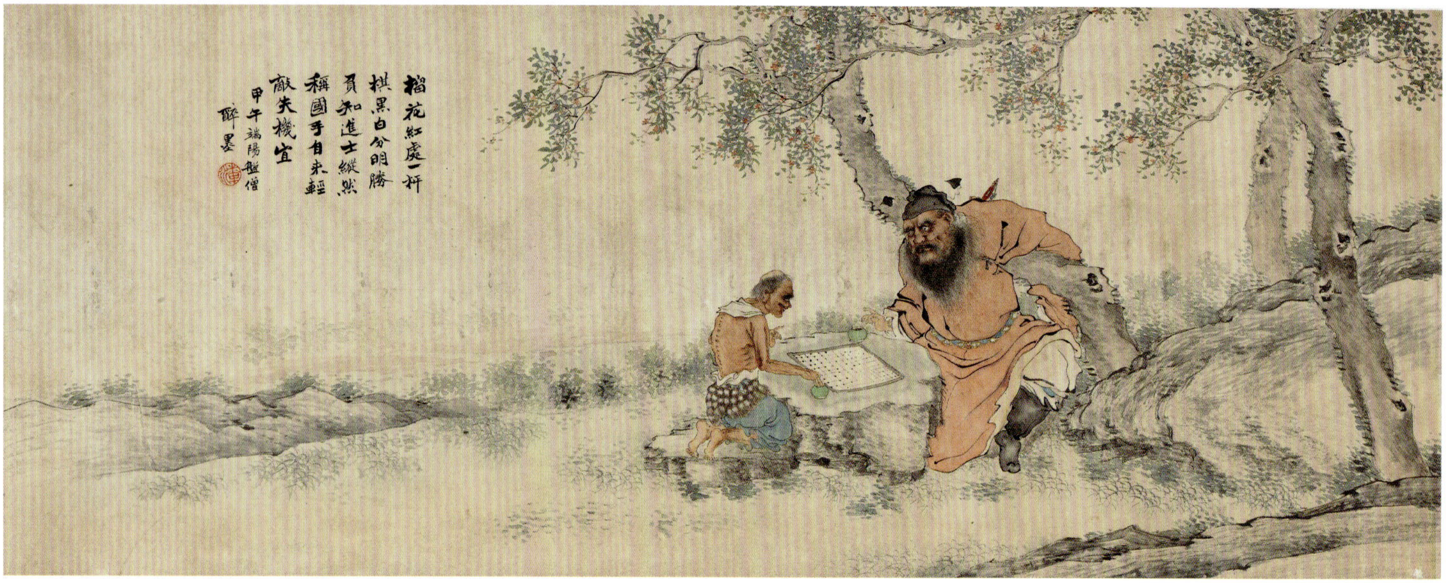
榴花紅處一枰
棋黑白分明勝
負知進士縱然
稱國手自來輕
敵失機宜
甲午端陽盤僧
醉墨

Artist:
Pan Panseng

Medium:
Color on paper, Horizontal scroll

Dimensions:
40.5 cm × 102 cm

Zhong Kui Playing Chess

Inscription:
Where blooms the pomegranate red, lies a chessboard's spread,
Black and white starkly placed, victory and loss readily traced.
Though a Jinshi may claim the nation's best hand,
Complacency to foes can forfeit the upper stand.
On the Dragon Boat Festival of the Jiawu year, Panseng immersed in ink's cheer.

Seal:
Pan Shi

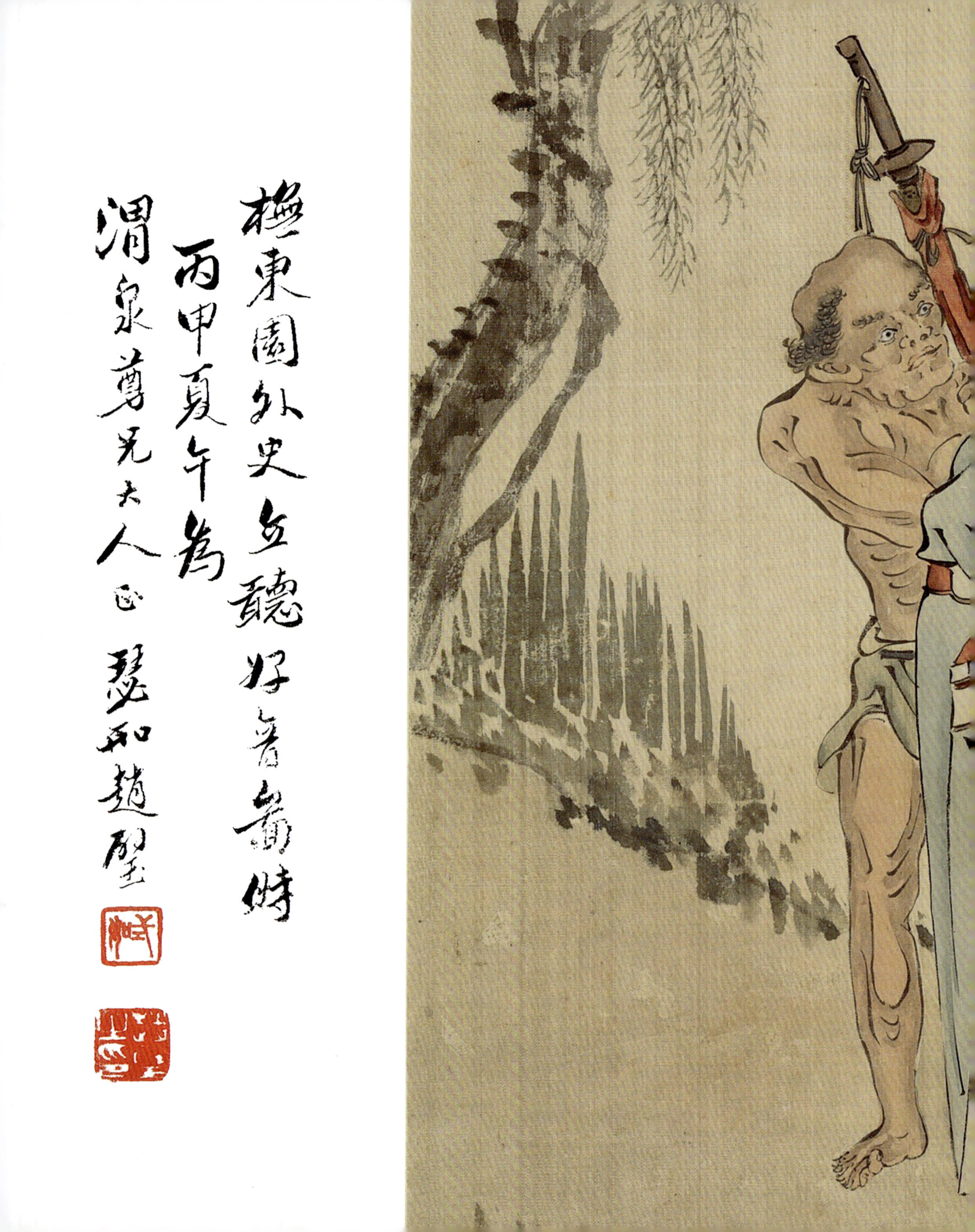
梅東園外史立聽好音鶯時
丙申夏午為
渭泉尊兄大人正
琴和趙

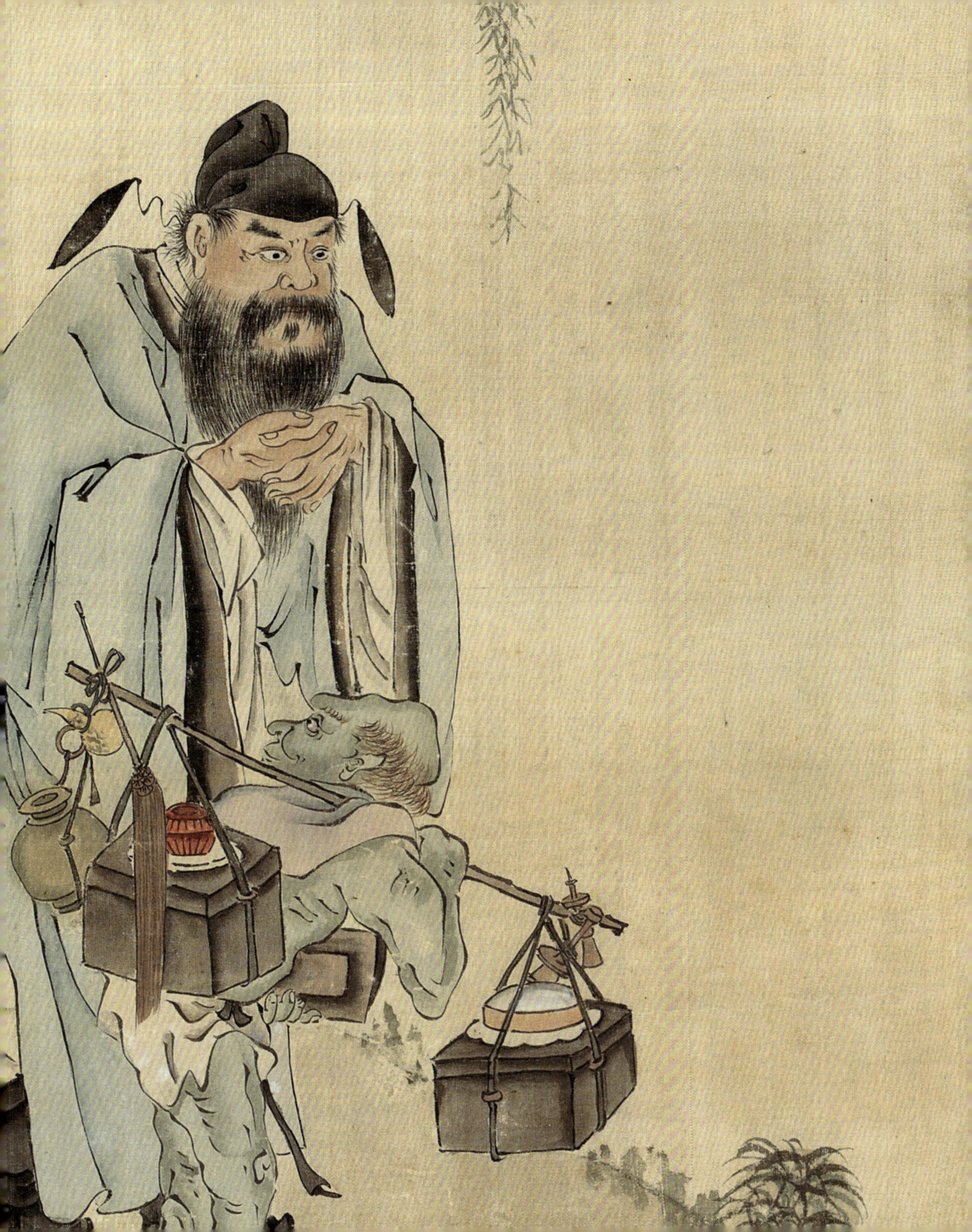

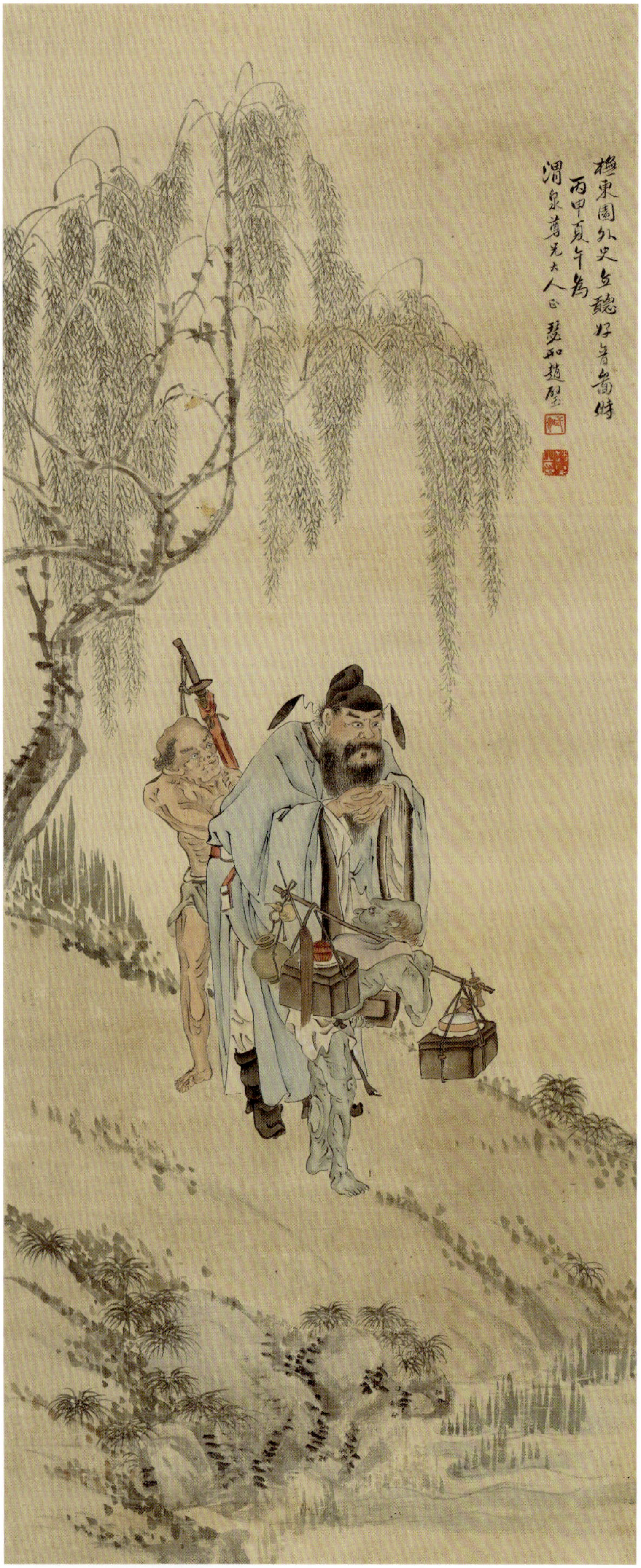

Artist:
Zhao Bi

Medium:
Color on silk, Hanging scroll

Dimensions:
102 cm × 41 cm

Standing to Hear Good Tidings

Inscription:
In the Fudong Garden, the Historian stands, absorbed in sweet sounds. On a summer's noon in the year of Bingshen, the painting was personally refined for the esteemed elder brother from Wei Quan. By Zhao Bi, Seru.

Seal:
Shilu, The seal of Zhao Bi

Zhao Bi
Courtesy name Seru and Shilu, was a painter of the Qing dynasty.

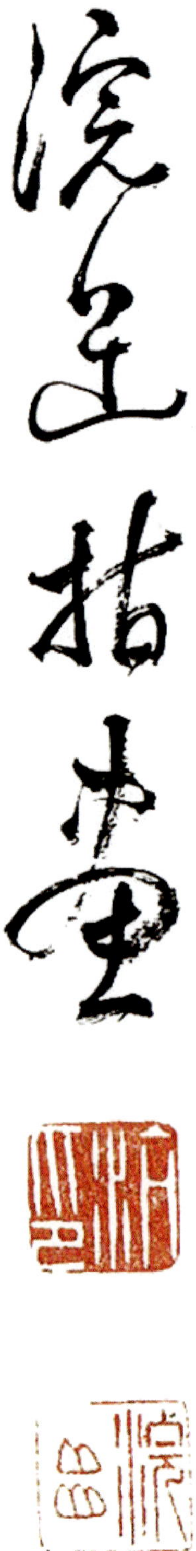

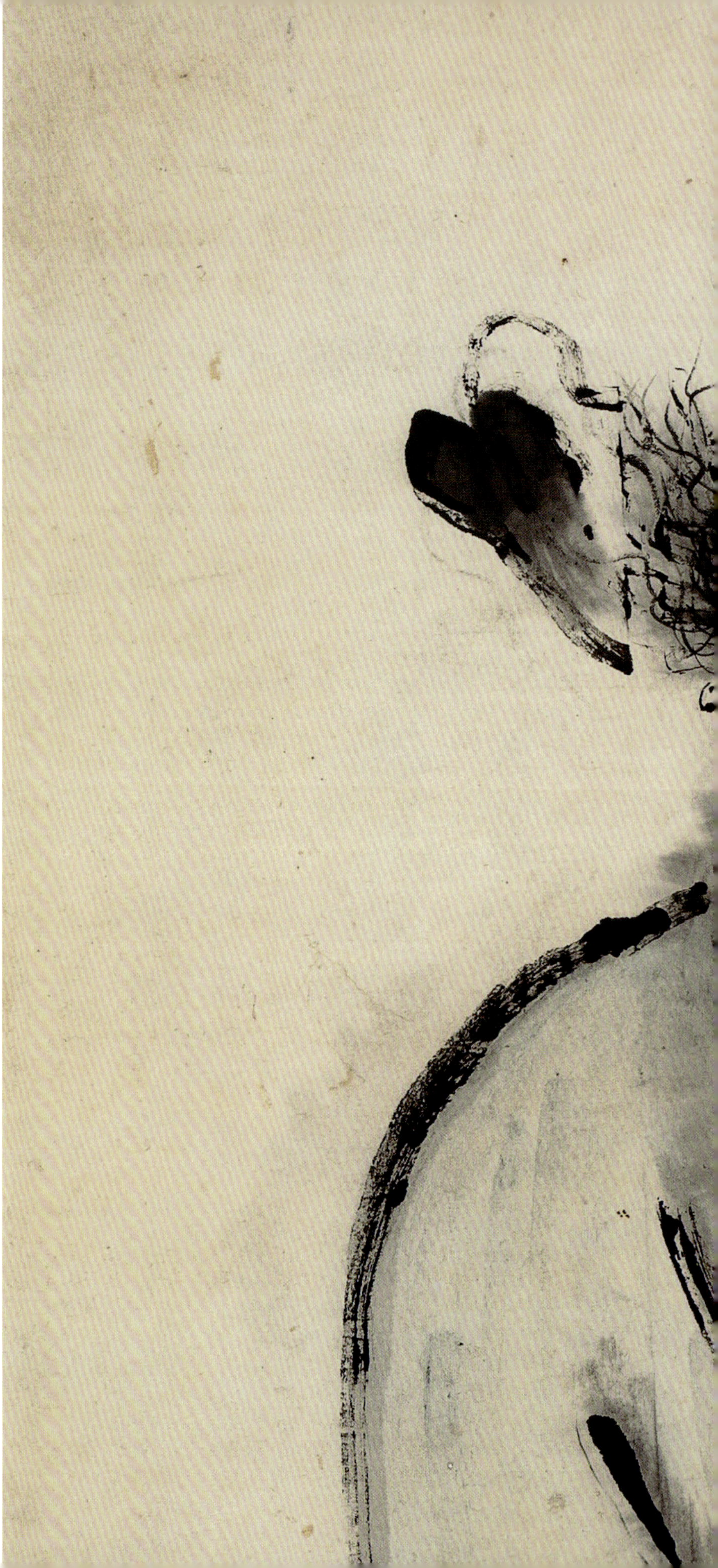

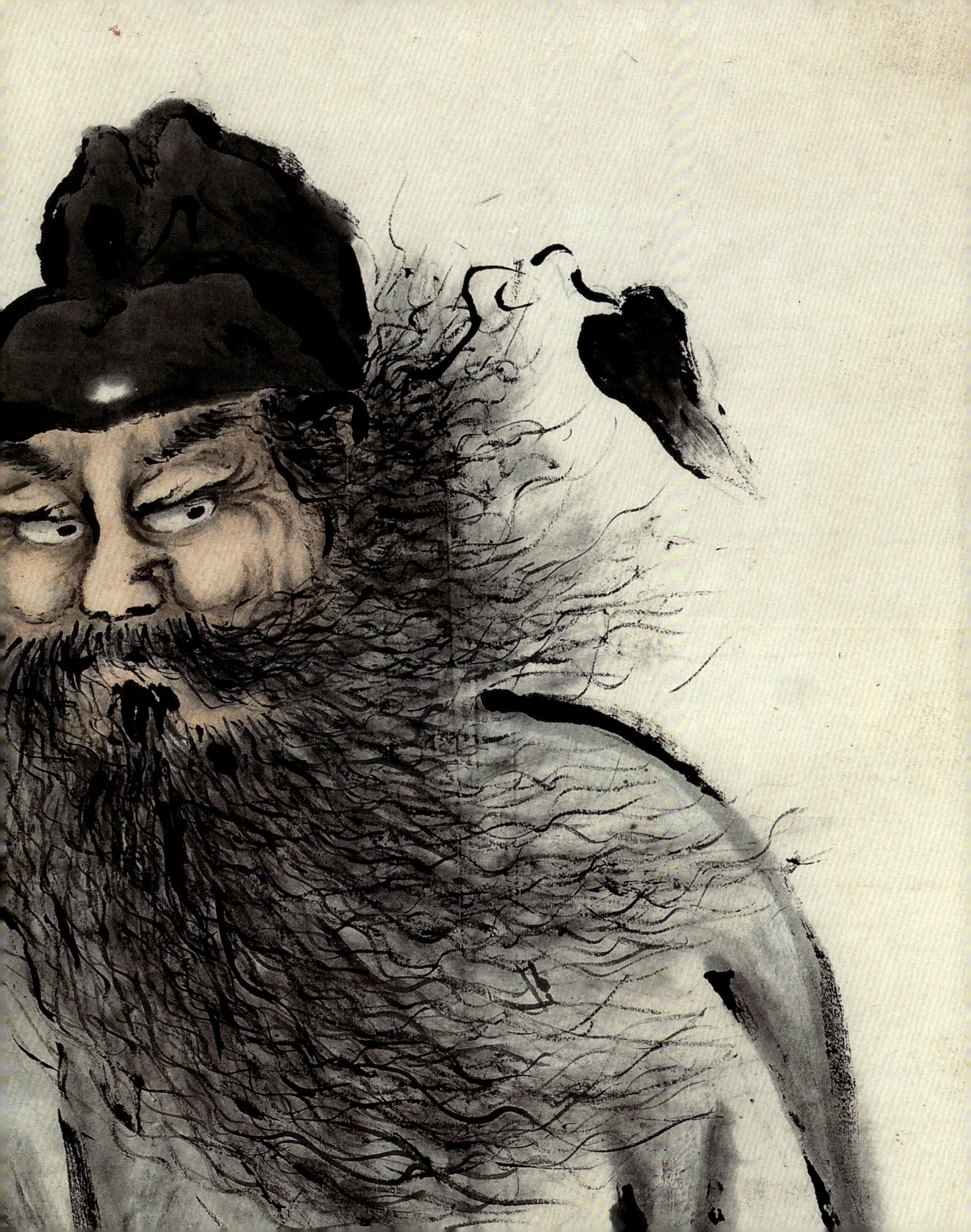

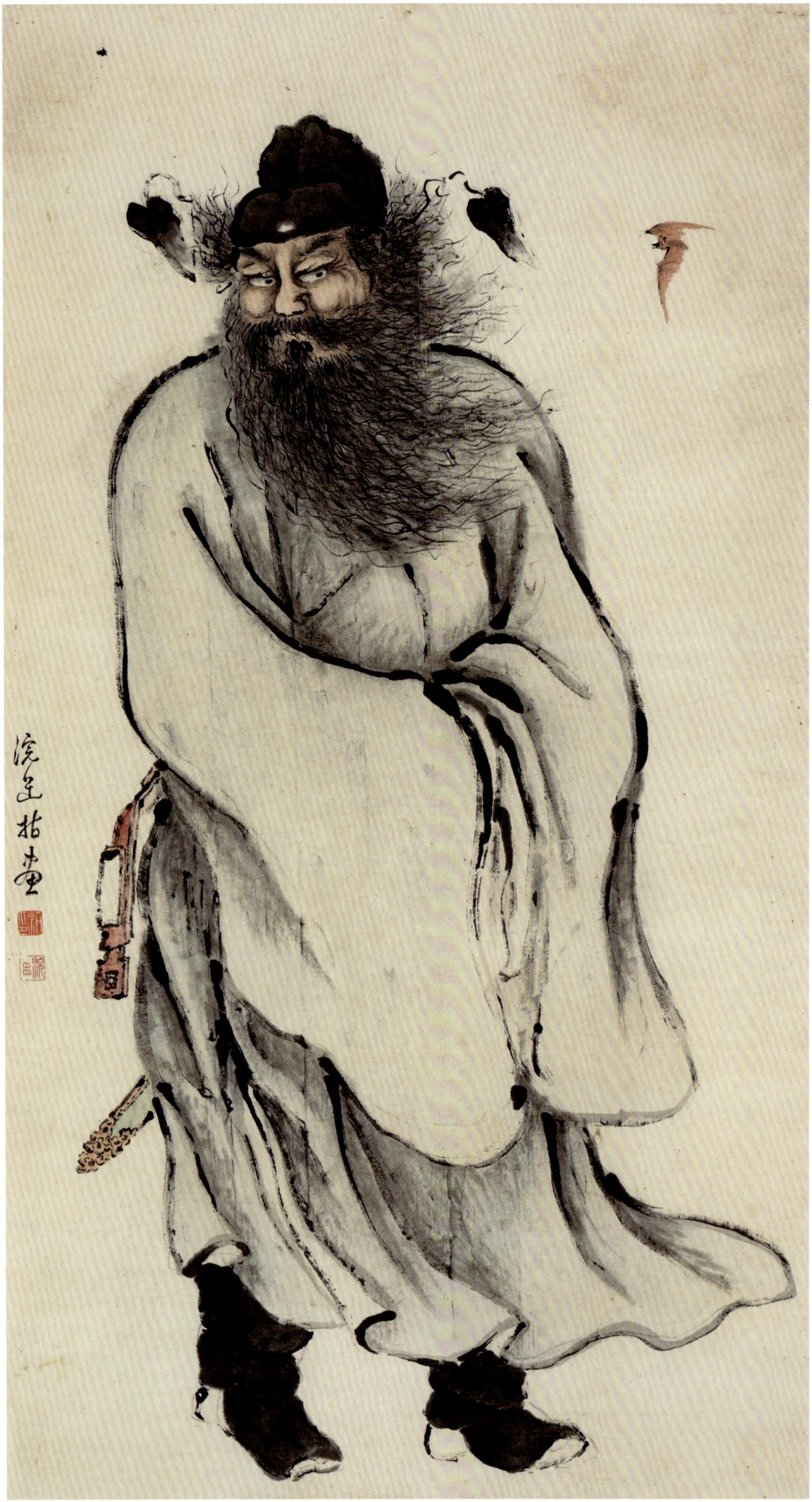

Artist:
Zhu Hang

Medium:
Ink on paper, Hanging scroll

Dimensions:
137 cm × 73.5 cm

Zhong Kui

Inscription:
Finger painting by Huanyue.

Seal:
The seal of Hang, Huanyue

Zhu Hang
Courtesy name Dafu, styled as Huanyue, a native of Shaoxing, Zhejiang. In the twenty-first year of the Daoguang era (1841), he served as the deputy governor of Taizhou in the Lianghuai era. He was known for his unrestrained character and excelled in wild cursive calligraphy. His ink paintings of figures were rich and robust. He passed away in his official residence at the age of over sixty.

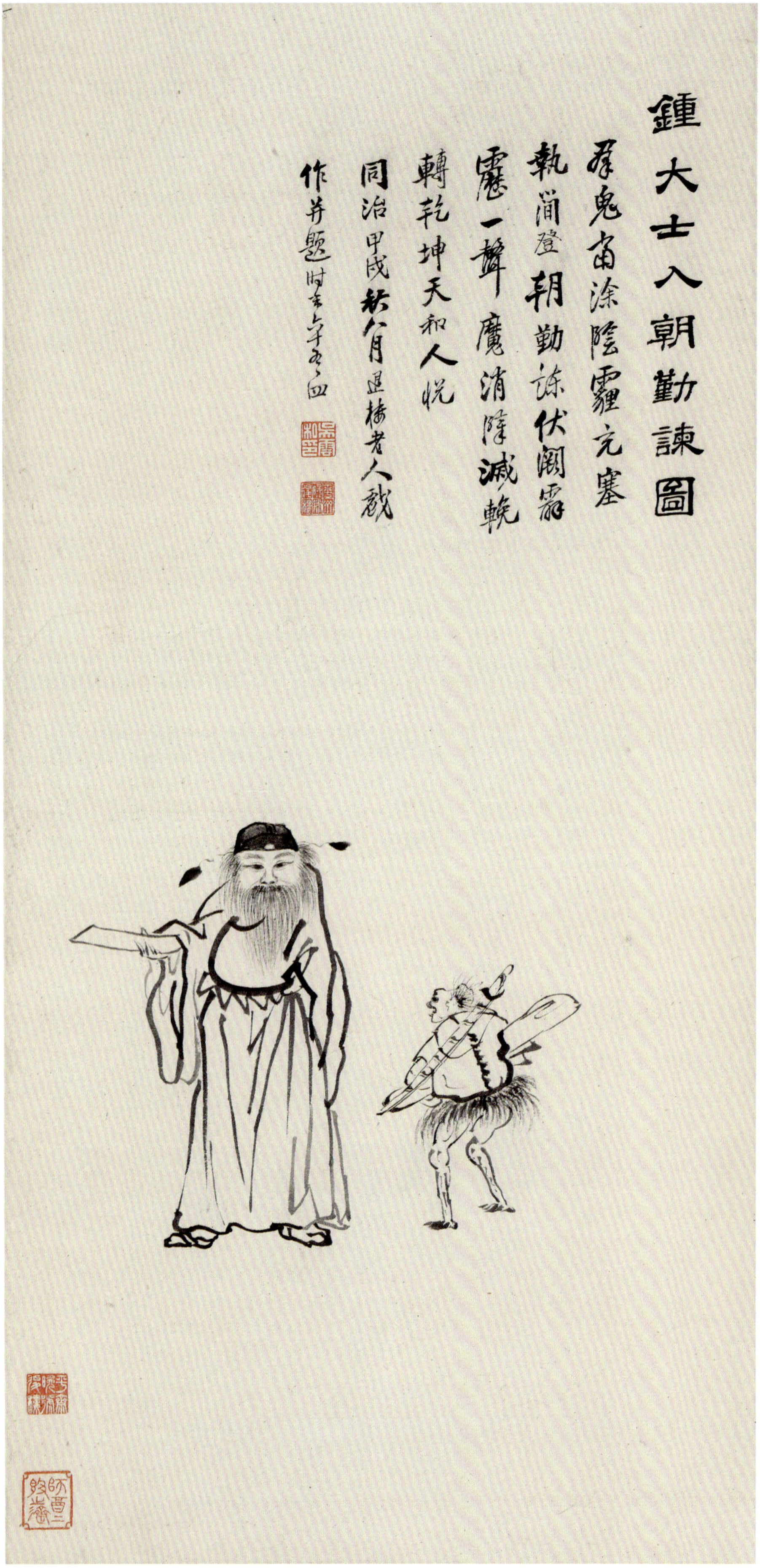
鍾大士入朝勸諫圖
羣鬼當塗陰霾充塞
執簡登朝勸諫伏闕霹
靂一聲魔消降滅斡
轉乾坤天和人悅
同治甲戌秋八月退樓老人戲
作并題時年六十有四

Artist:
Wu Yun

Medium:
Ink on paper, Hanging scroll

Dimensions:
63 cm × 30 cm

The Venerable Zhong Entering the Court to Offer Earnest Admonitions

Inscription:
This is a painting of the venerable Zhong entering the court to offer sincere admonitions. Ghosts obstruct the way, and the air is filled with dark mists. Holding his petition, he goes to the court to advise with dedication. With the sound of thunder, the demons disappear, and obstacles are obliterated. He reverses the order of heaven and earth, bringing clear skies and joy to the people. In the eighth month of autumn, during the Jiawu year of the Tongzhi era, the work was playfully created and inscribed by the elderly Tuilou, who was sixty-four years old.

Seal:
The private seal of Wu Yun, The late style name of Tuilou from Pingzhai, The late style name of Tuilou from Pingzhai, The studio of master Ge Erdun

Wu Yun (1811–1883)
Courtesy name Shaofu, styled as Pingshai, and in his later years known as the Master of Tuilou. A native of Lin'an (present-day Huzhou), Zhejiang, he served as the Prefect of Suzhou. Wu Yun was proficient in appraisal and textual research, skilled in calligraphy, and was also a painter. He occasionally created landscapes, figures, flowers, and birds, applying colors at will, breaking away from the worn path.

福自天降

乙未端陽為

寶笙仁兄大人雅正

海上老夫任伯年寫

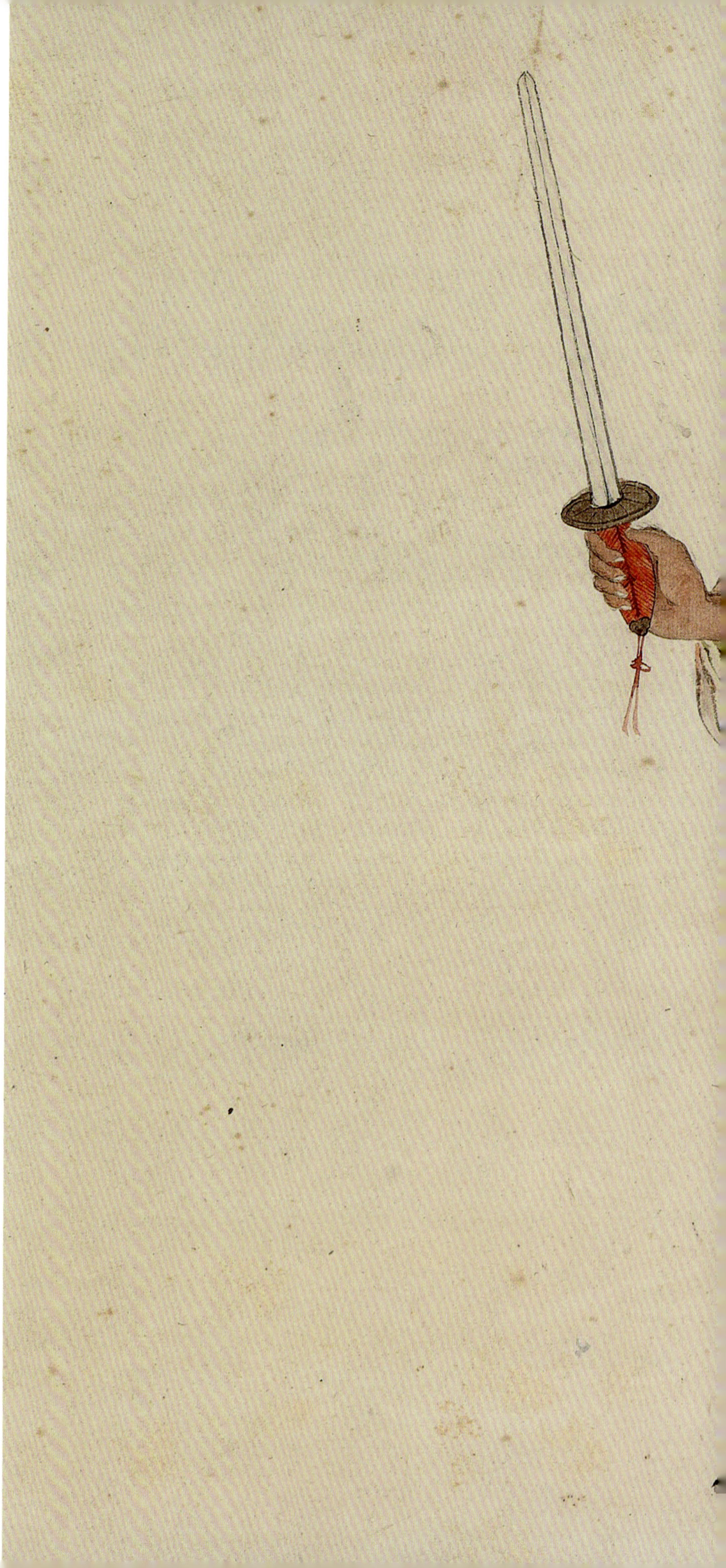

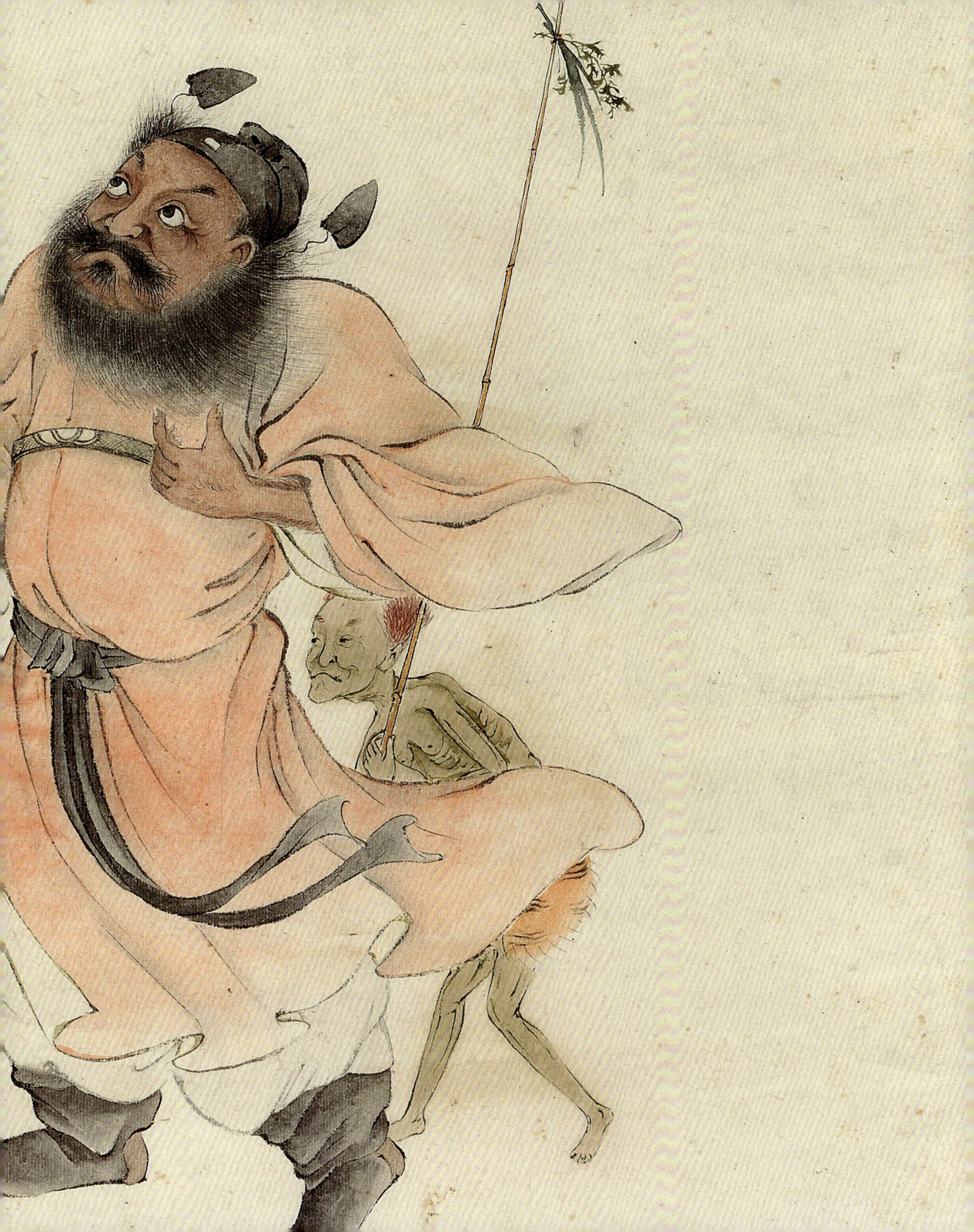

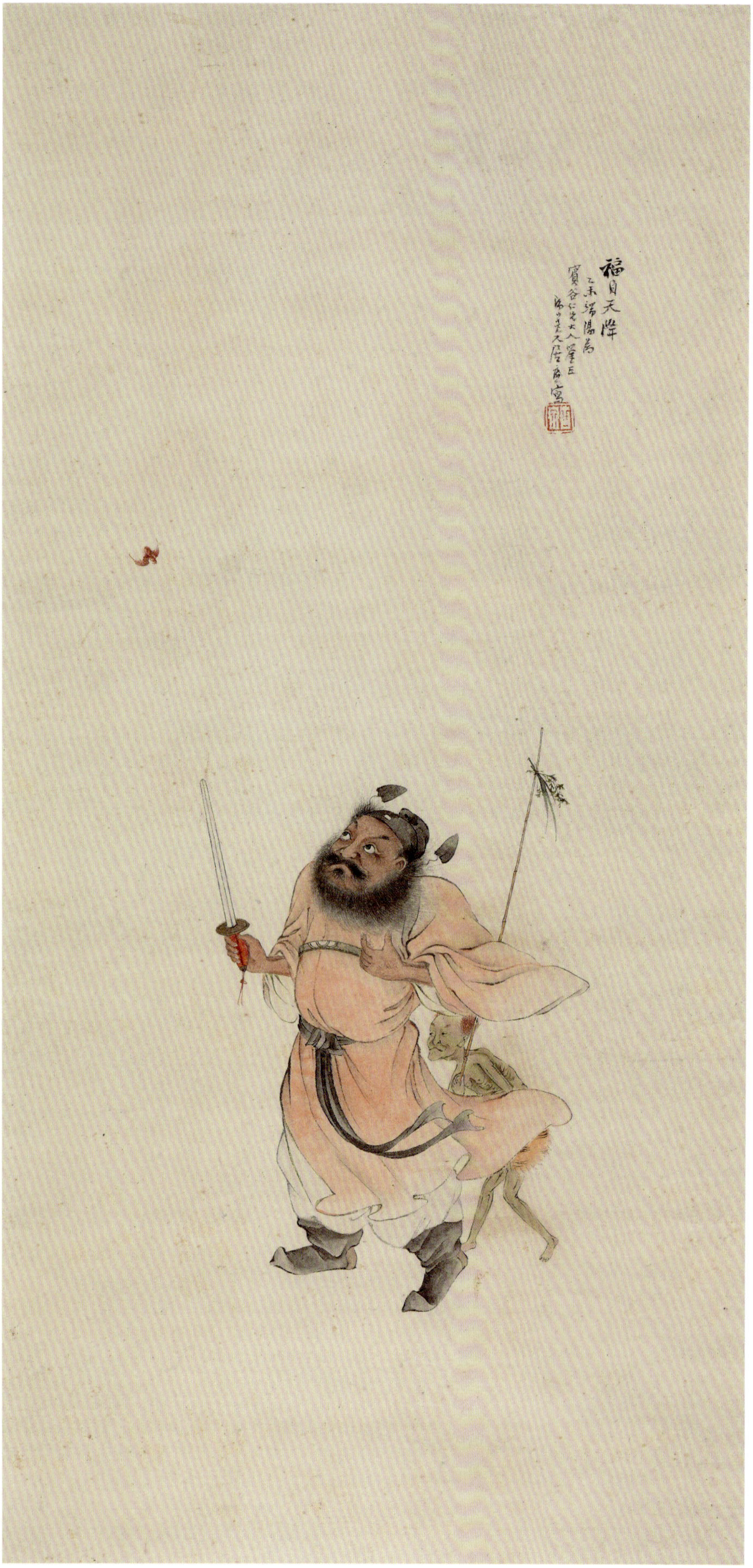
福自天降
乙未端陽為

Artist:
Ju Lian

Medium:
Color on paper, Hanging scroll

Dimensions:
91 cm × 43 cm

Blessings Descend from Heaven

Inscription:
Blessings Descend from Heaven. On the Dragon Boat Festival of the Yiwei year, this was authenticated for the esteemed friend Bingu, inscribed by the Geshan Lay Scholar, Ju Lian.

Seal:
The seal of Guquan

Ju Lian (1828–1904)
Courtesy name Shigang, styled as Guquan, also known as the Geshan Woodcutter and the Wanderer of Luohu, a native of Panyu, Guangdong. A renowned traditional Chinese painter of the Qing Dynasty from Lingnan, he excelled in painting flowers, birds, insects, and figures, especially known for his lifelike depictions. Building upon and advancing Yun Shouping's boneless painting technique, he innovated the methods of "water-penetrating" and "powder-blending," establishing himself as one of the founders of the Lingnan School of painting.

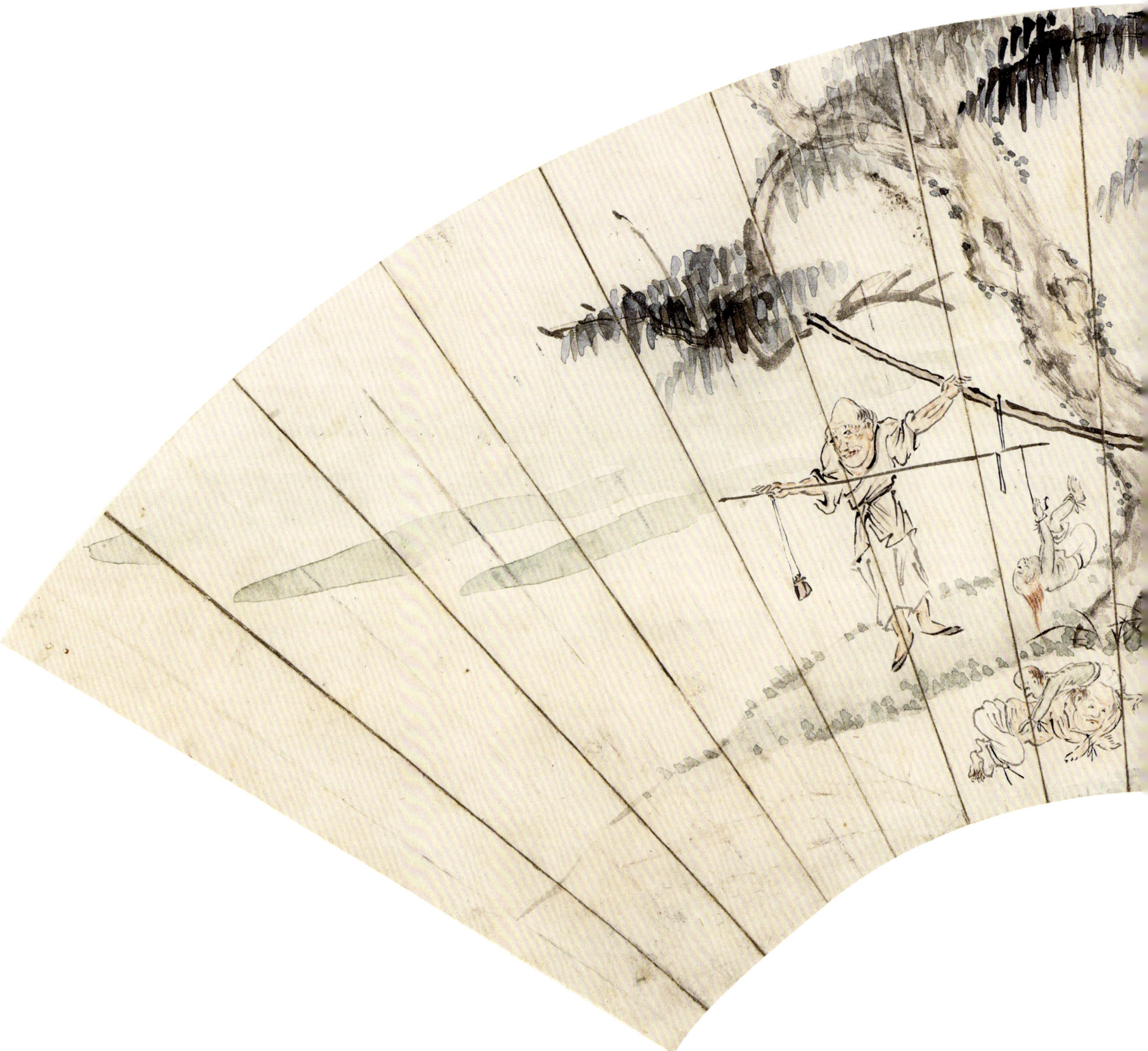

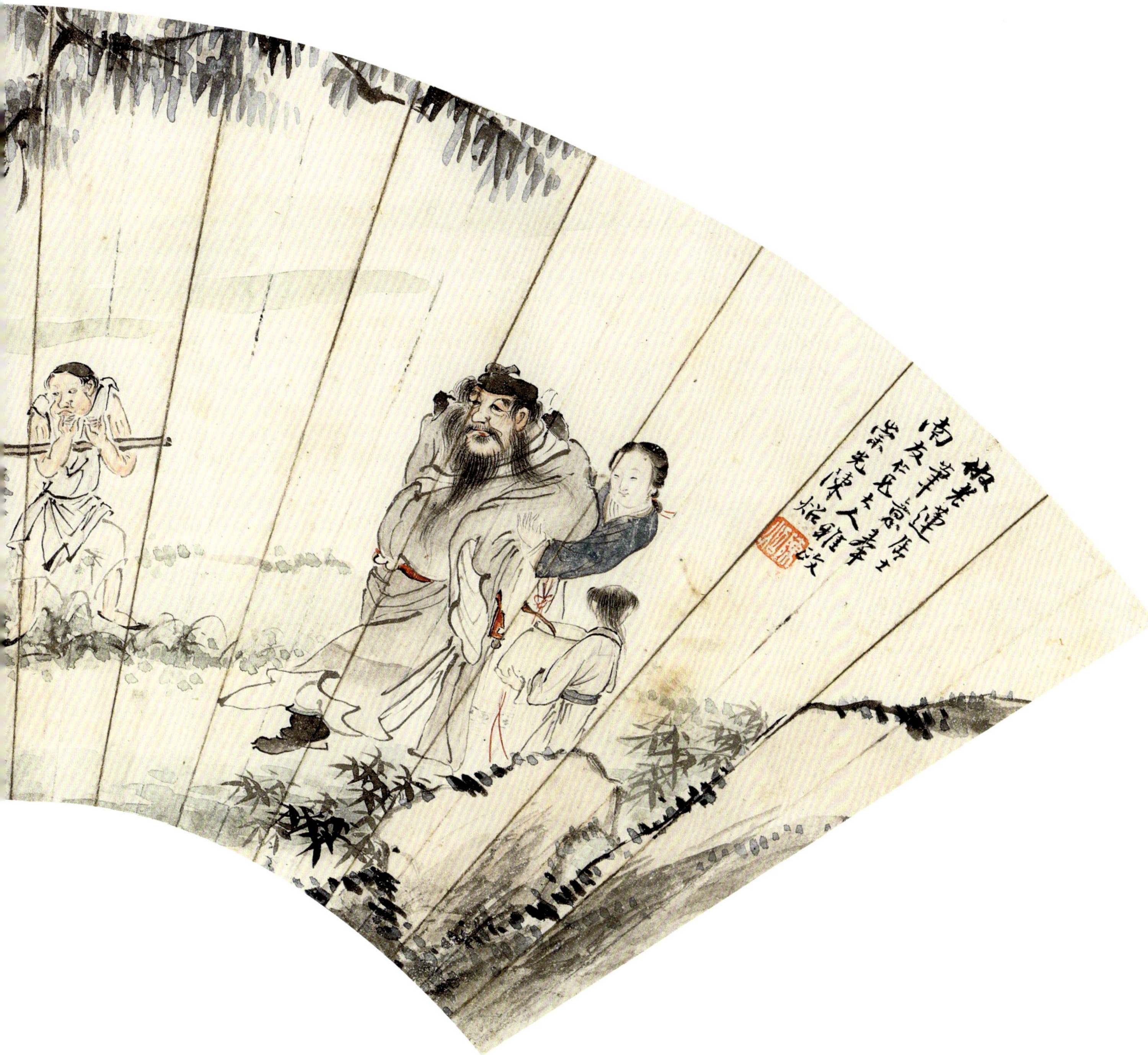

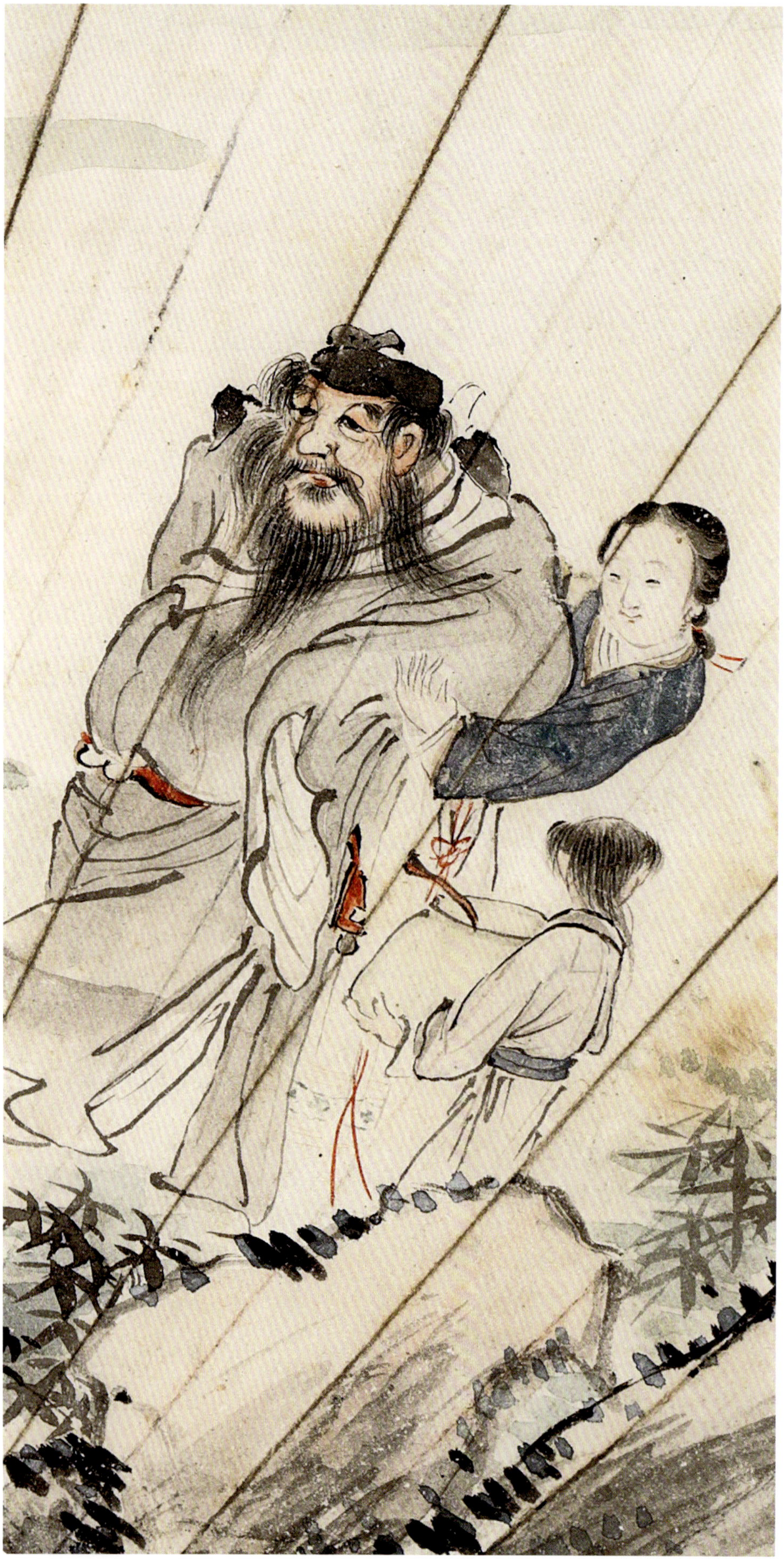

Artist:
Chen Zhao

Medium:
Color on paper, Fan-shaped

Dimensions:
17 cm × 51 cm

Weighing Ghosts

Inscription:
Imitating the brushwork style of the esteemed Lay Scholar Old Lian, this piece is presented for the refined appreciation of dear friend Nanyou. By Chen Zhao, Chongguang.

Seal:
Chen Zhao

Chen Zhao (1838–1896)
Originally named Zhao, his courtesy name was Chongguang, and he was styled as the Pure Taoist, a native of Yangzhou, Jiangsu. Skilled in floral and bird painting, he particularly excelled in the double-hook technique for flowers.

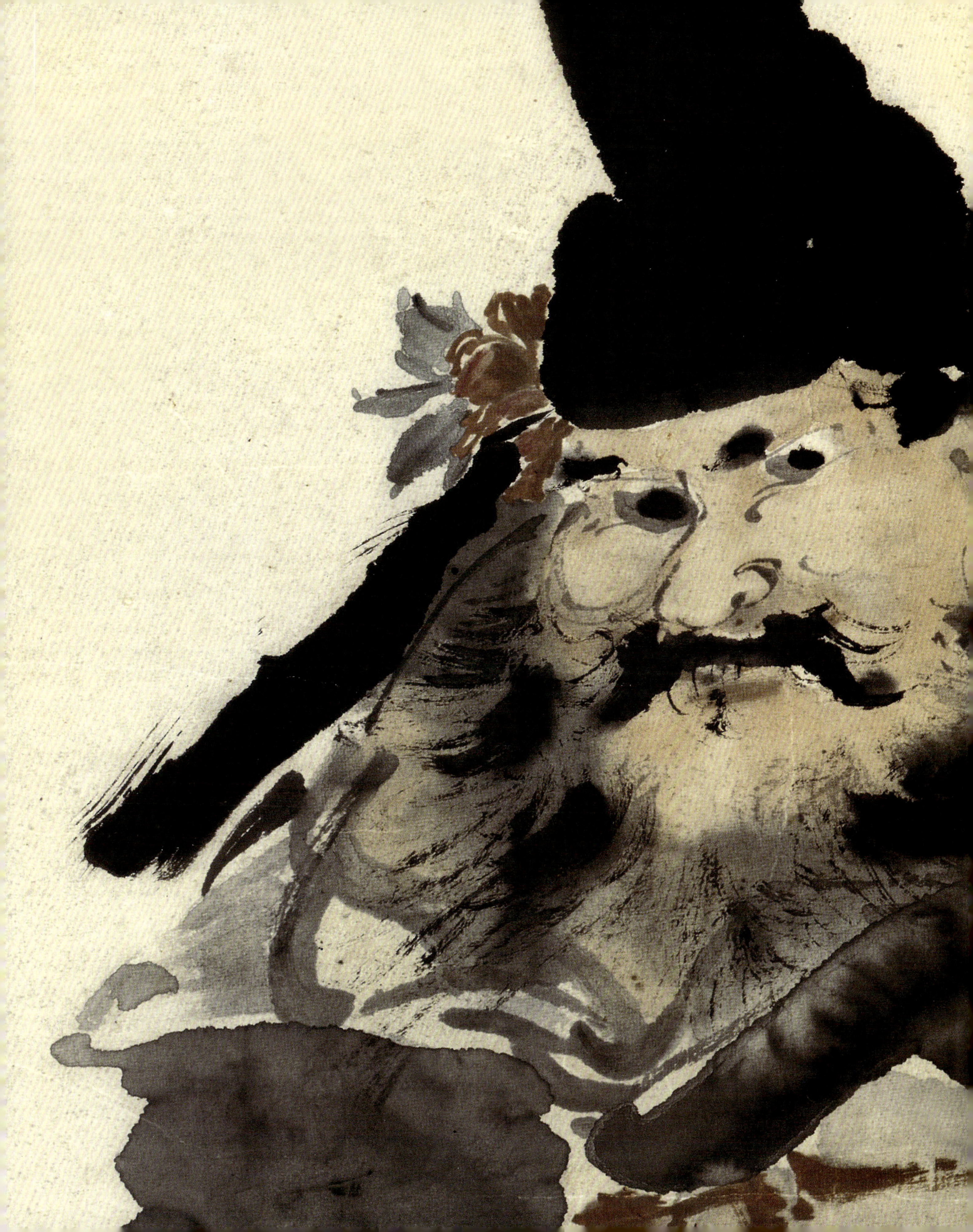

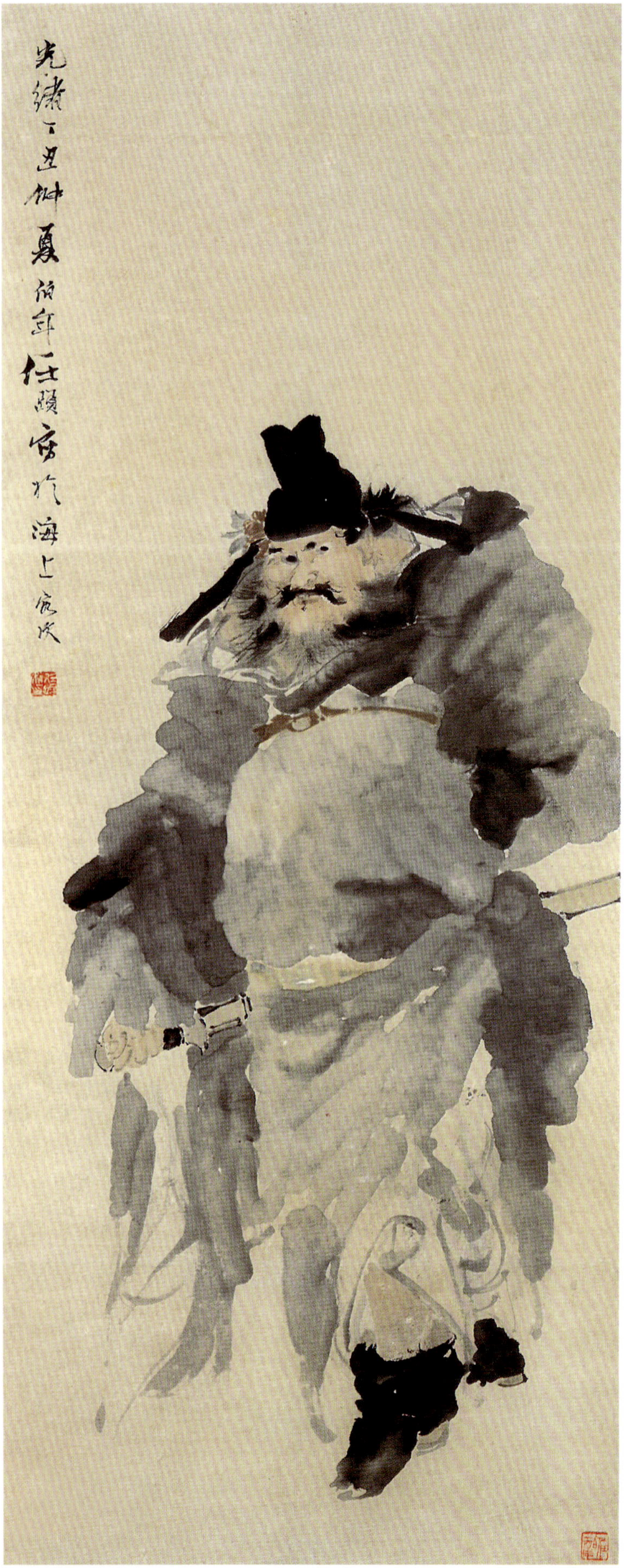
光緒丁丑仲夏伯年任頤寫於海上寓次

Artist:
Ren Bonian

Medium:
Color on paper, Hanging scroll

Dimensions:
136 cm × 54.5 cm

Splashed Ink Zhong Kui

Inscription:

In the midsummer of the Dingchou year during the Guangxu reign, inscribed by Ren Yi, Bonian, while staying as a guest by Shanghai.

Seal:

The private seal of Ren Yi

Ren Bonian (1840–1896)
Originally named Run, with the courtesy name Ciyuan and styled as Xiaolou, he later changed his name to Yi, courtesy name Bonian, and was also known as the Wayfarer of Shanyin and the Longevity Taoist, among others. He was commonly addressed by his courtesy name. A native of Shanyin, Zhejiang (present-day Shaoxing), he was a famous painter of the late Qing Dynasty and a representative artist of the Shanghai School, excelling in paintings of flowers, birds, and figures. Alongside Wu Changshuo, Pu Hua, and Xugu, he was celebrated as one of the "Four Great Masters of the Shanghai School" of the late Qing era.

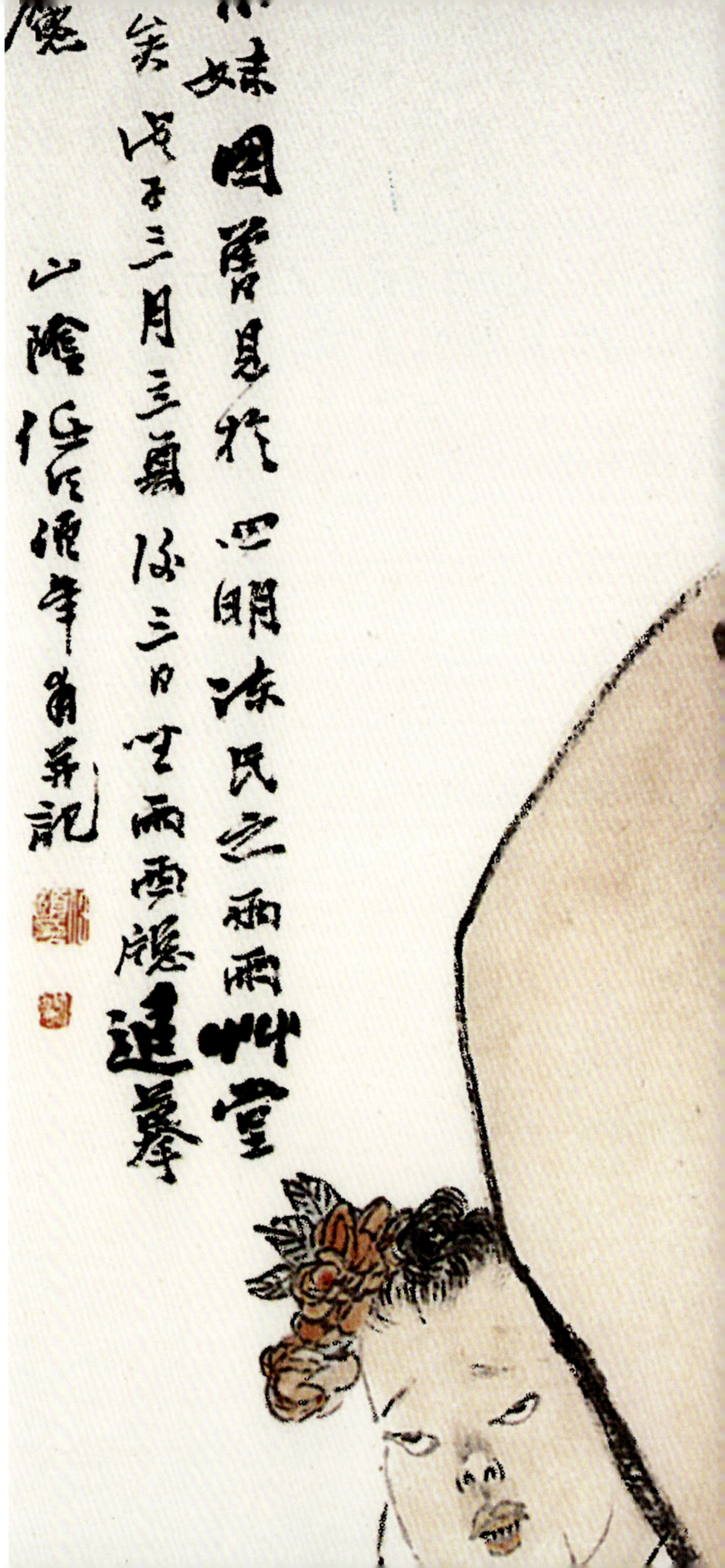

戊子三月三日
山陰任頤伯年甫并記

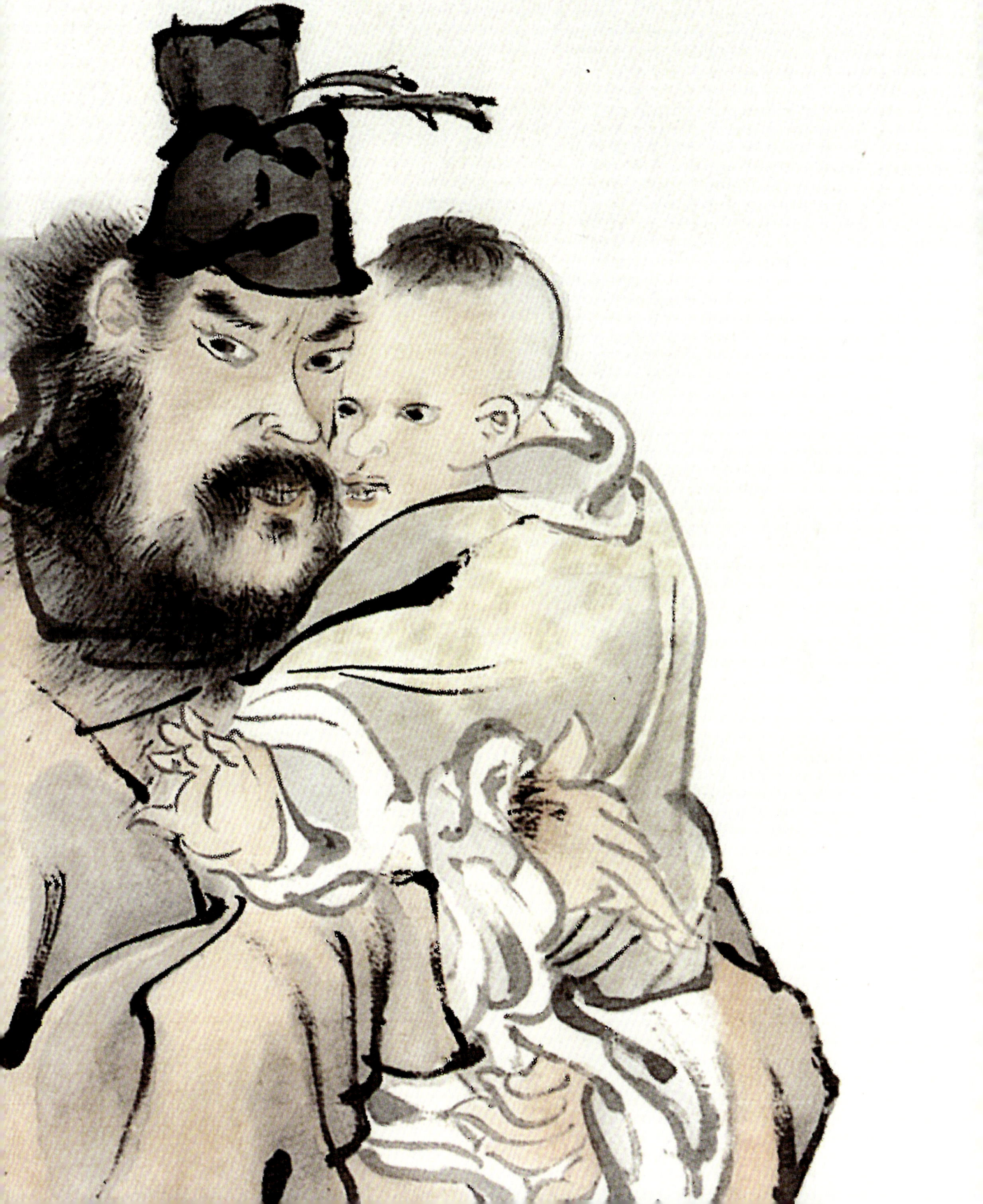

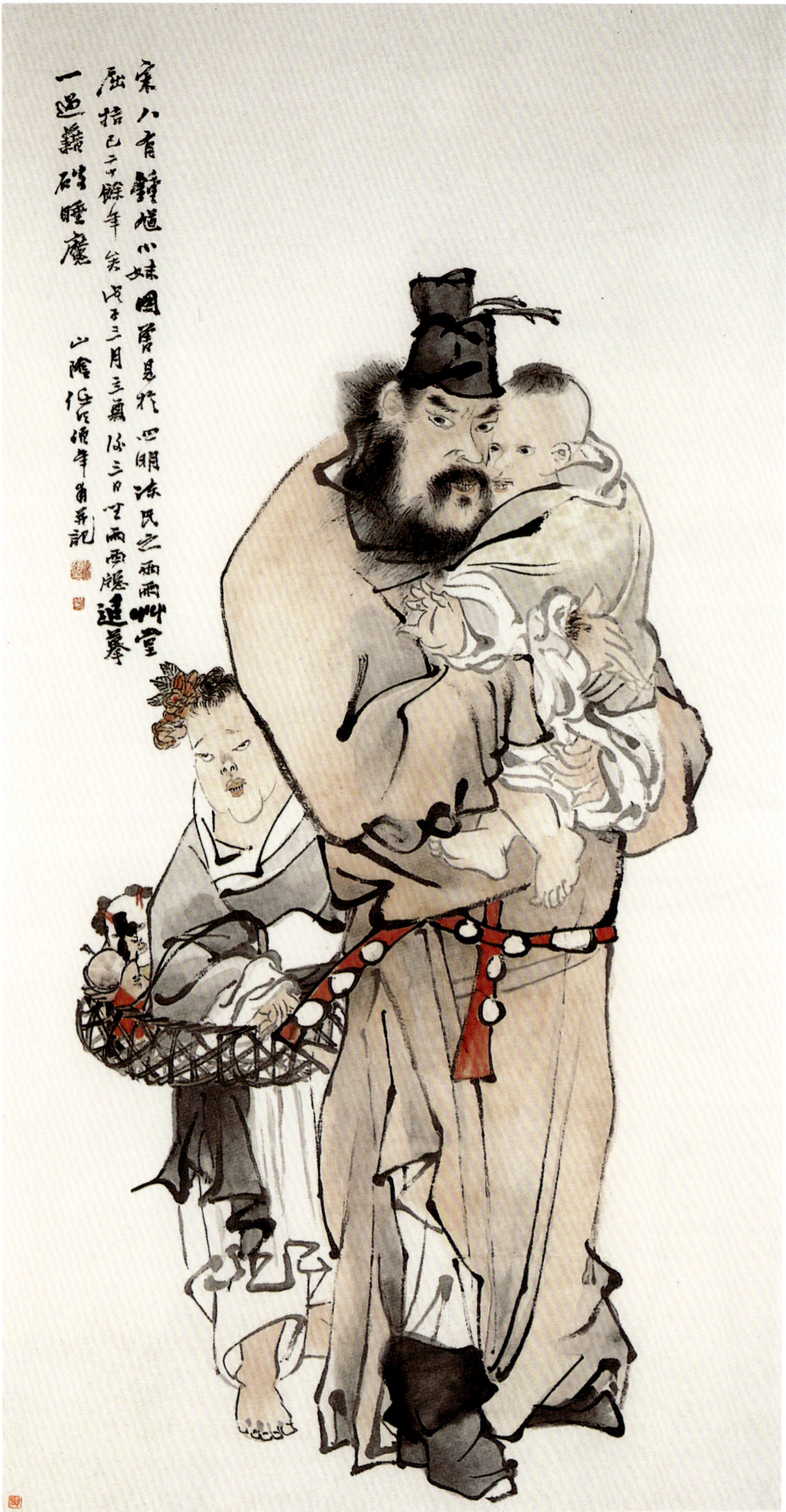

Artist:
Ren Bonian

Medium:
Color on paper, Hanging scroll

Dimensions:
134.5 cm × 68 cm

Zhong Kui's Little Sister

Inscription:
There was a painting of Zhong Kui's sister from the Song dynasty; I once saw it in the Liangyu thatched cottage of Chen Siming, and now more than twenty years have passed. On the third day after the beginning of summer in the Wuzi year, as I sat by the rain-soaked western window, I traced the painting once again to ward off the demon of sleepiness. This was recorded by Ren Yi, Bonian of Shanyin.

Seal:
The seal of Ren Yi, Bonian

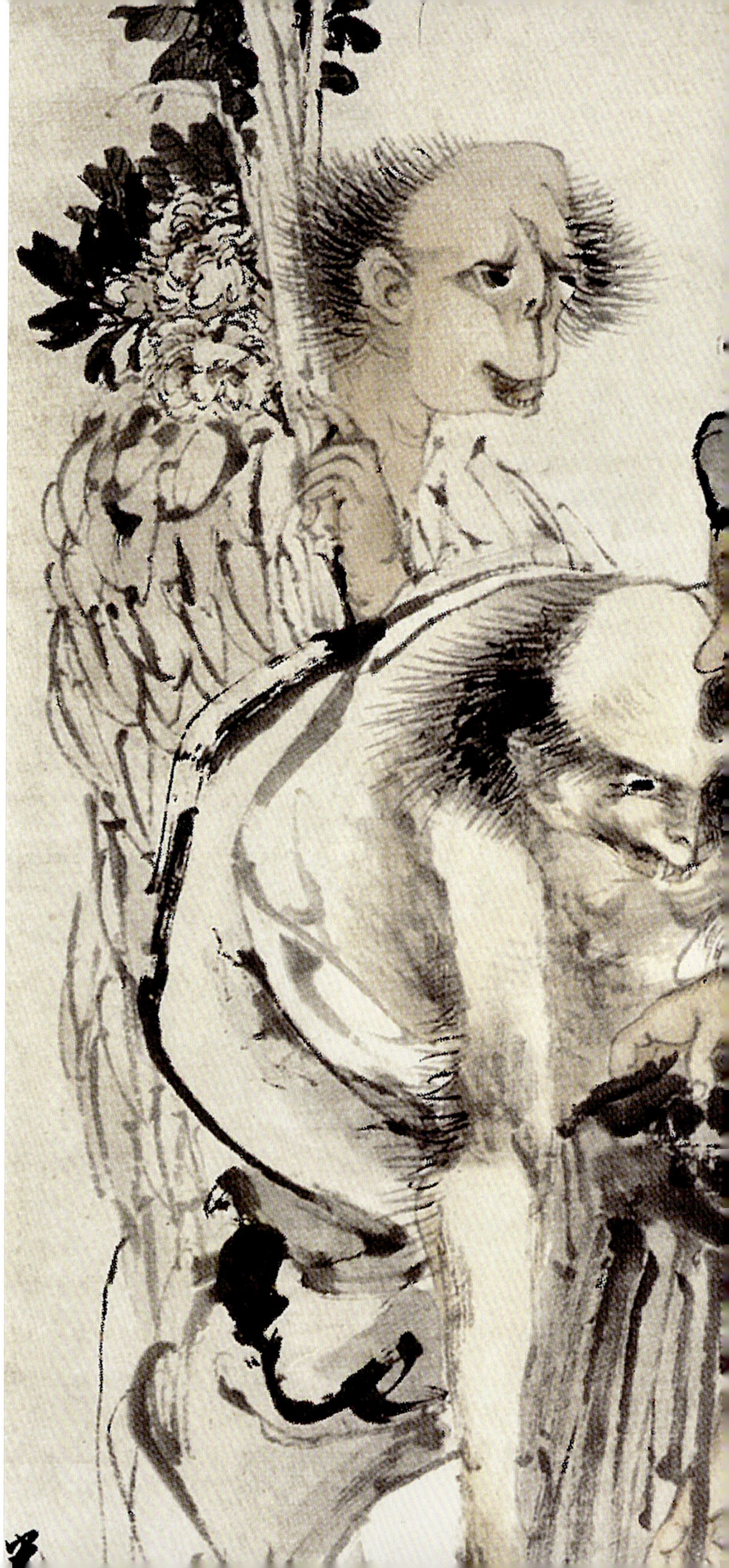

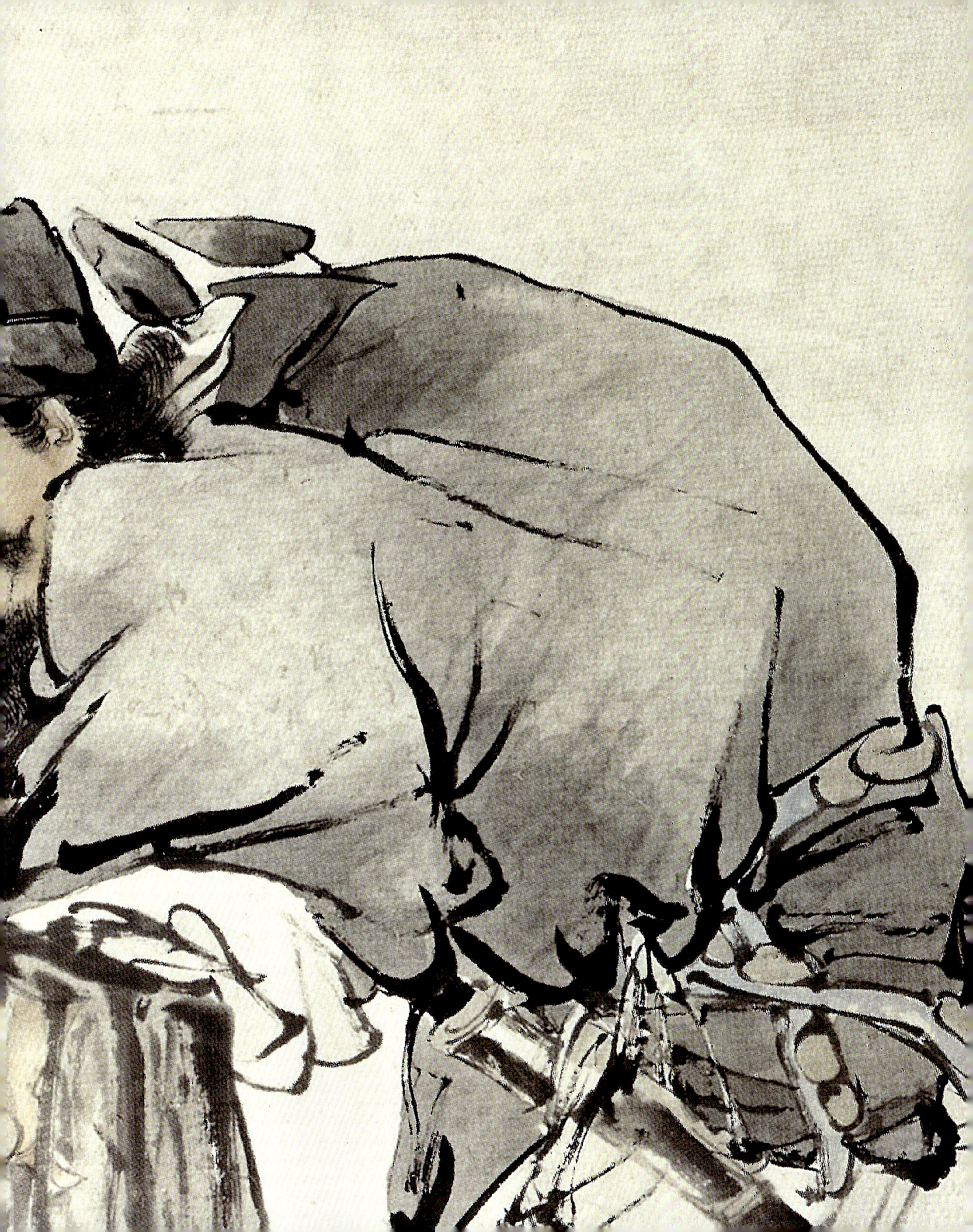

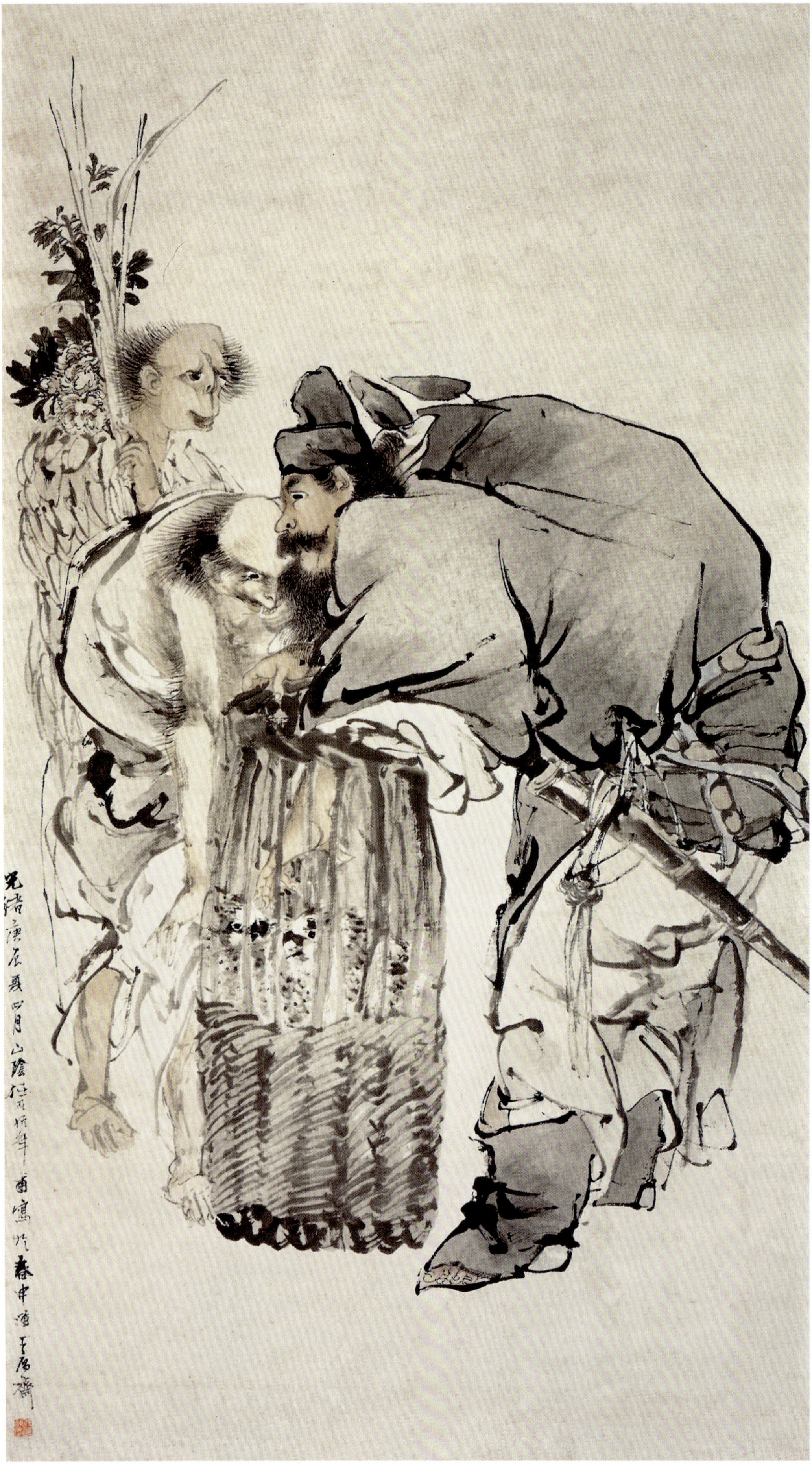
光緒庚辰夏四月山陰任頤伯年甫寫於春申浦寓齋

Artist:
Ren Bonian

Medium:
Color on paper, Hanging scroll

Dimensions:
171 cm × 94 cm

Zhong Kui Capturing Ghosts

Inscription:
In the fourth month of summer in the Gengchen year of the Guangxu reign, this was inscribed by Ren Yi, Bonian of Shanyin, at his studio in Chunshenpu.

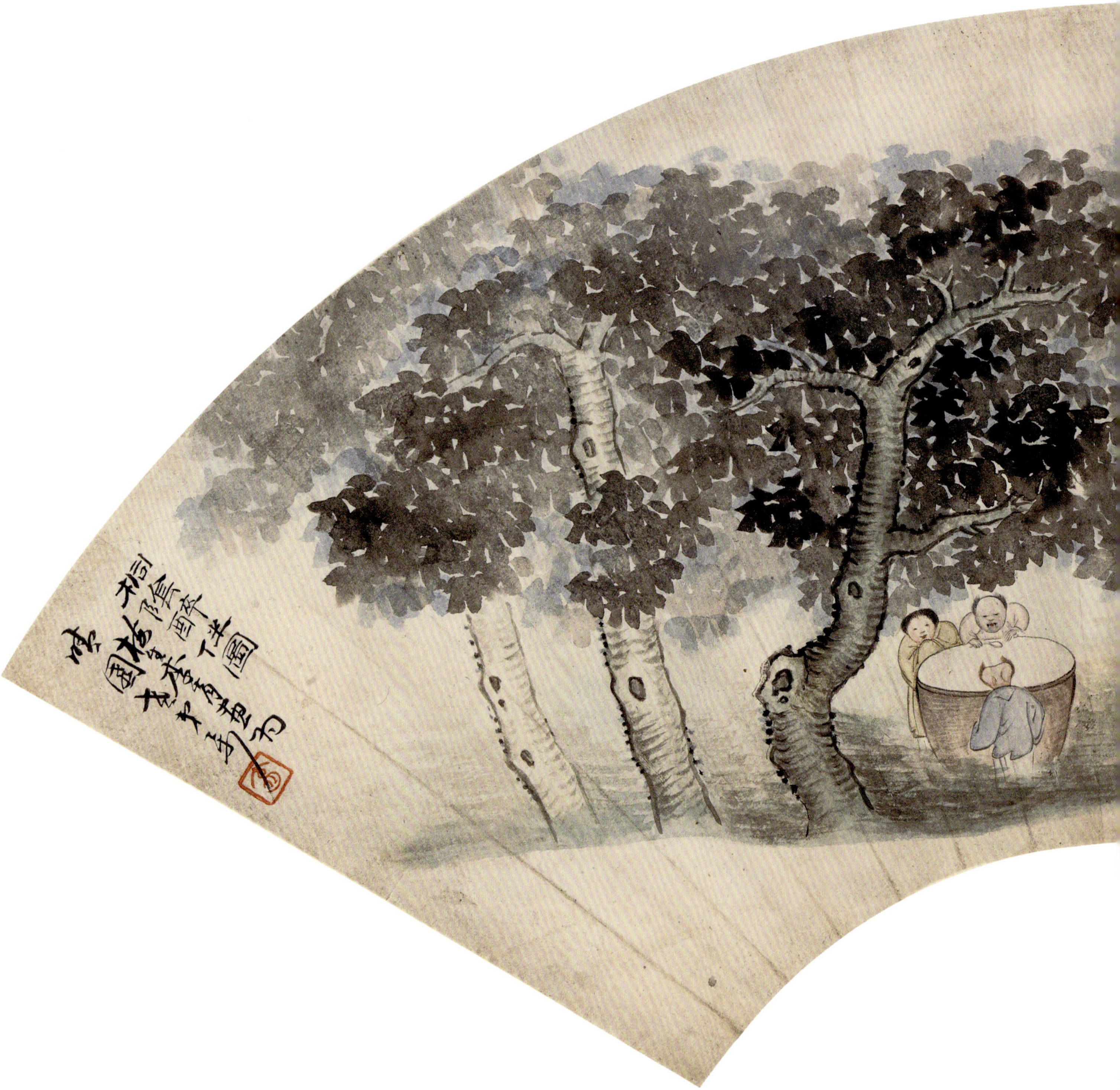

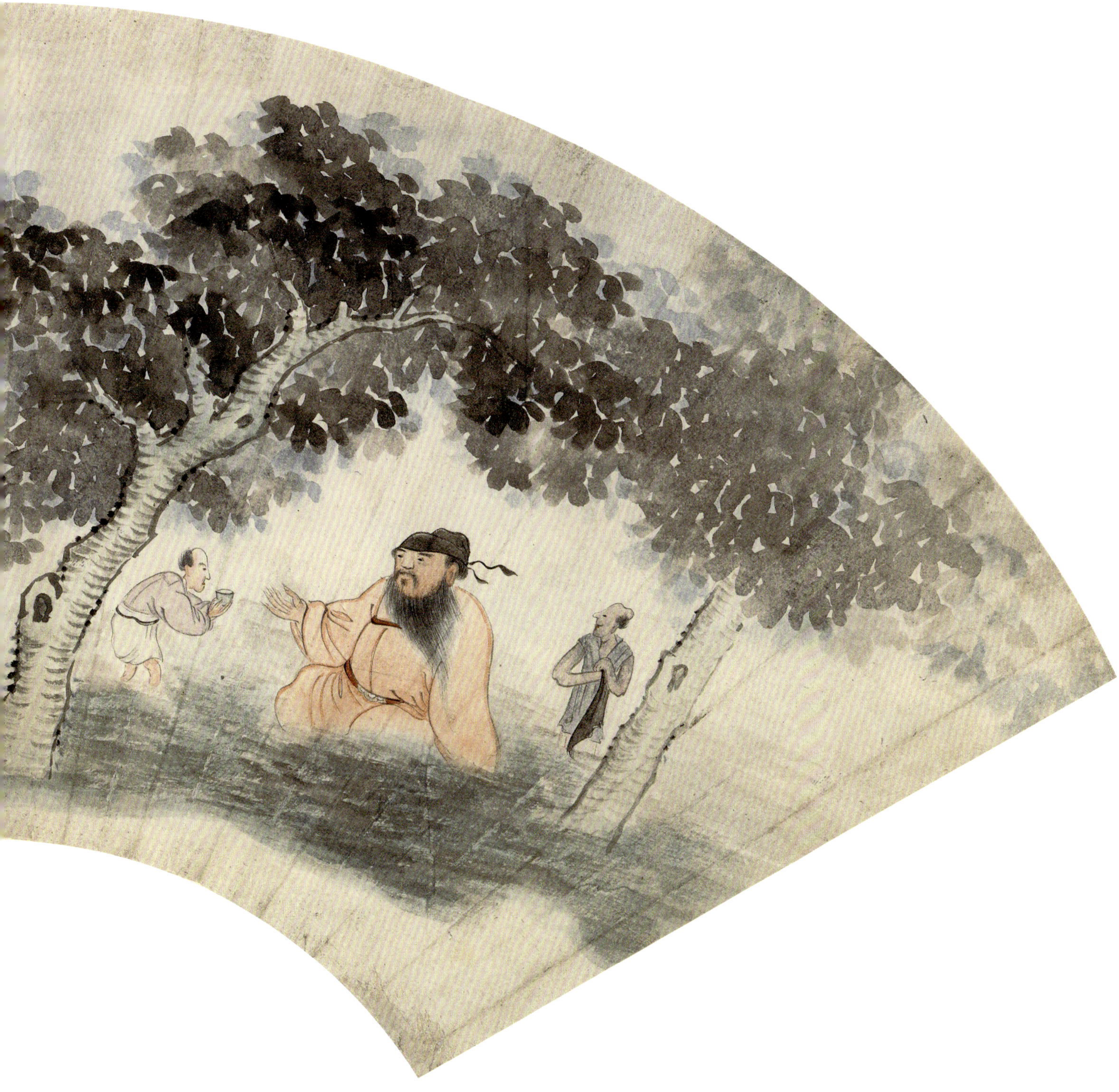

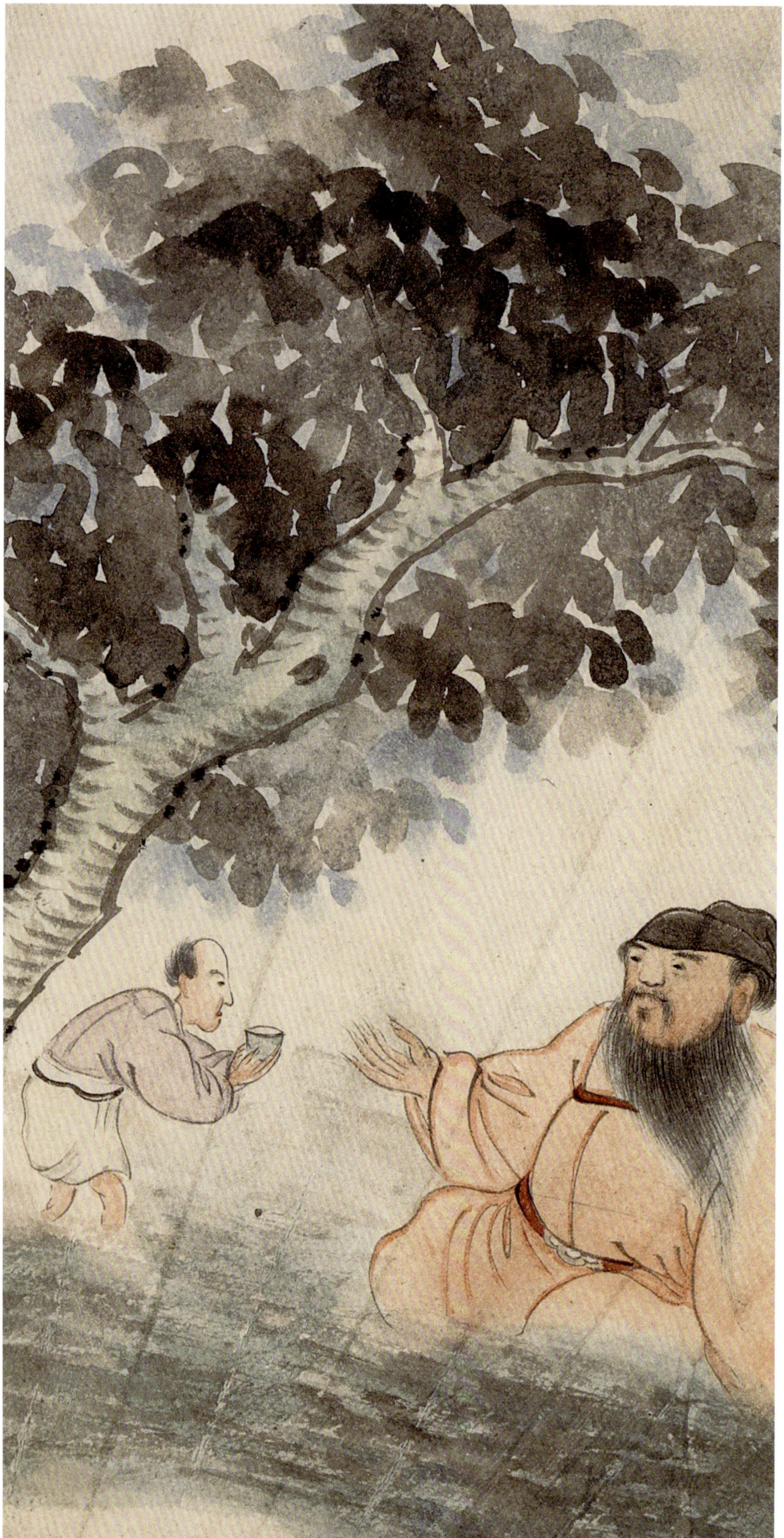

Artist:
Li Yu

Medium:
Color on paper, Fan-shaped

Dimensions:
18.5 cm × 53 cm

Companions Inebriated Beneath the Paulownia Shade

Inscription:
Companions Inebriated Beneath the Paulownia Shade. Painted by Li Yu, Meisheng, for the younger brother of Qingyuan.

Seal:
Yu

Li Yu (1843–unknown)
Courtesy name Meisheng, a native of Ganquan (present-day Yangzhou), excelled in painting figures, flowers, and birds. His freehand depictions of flora and stones combined the strengths of various styles, breaking free from conventional forms. His works, grand yet natural, exhibit a harmony between mind and hand, masterfully blending colors and ink.

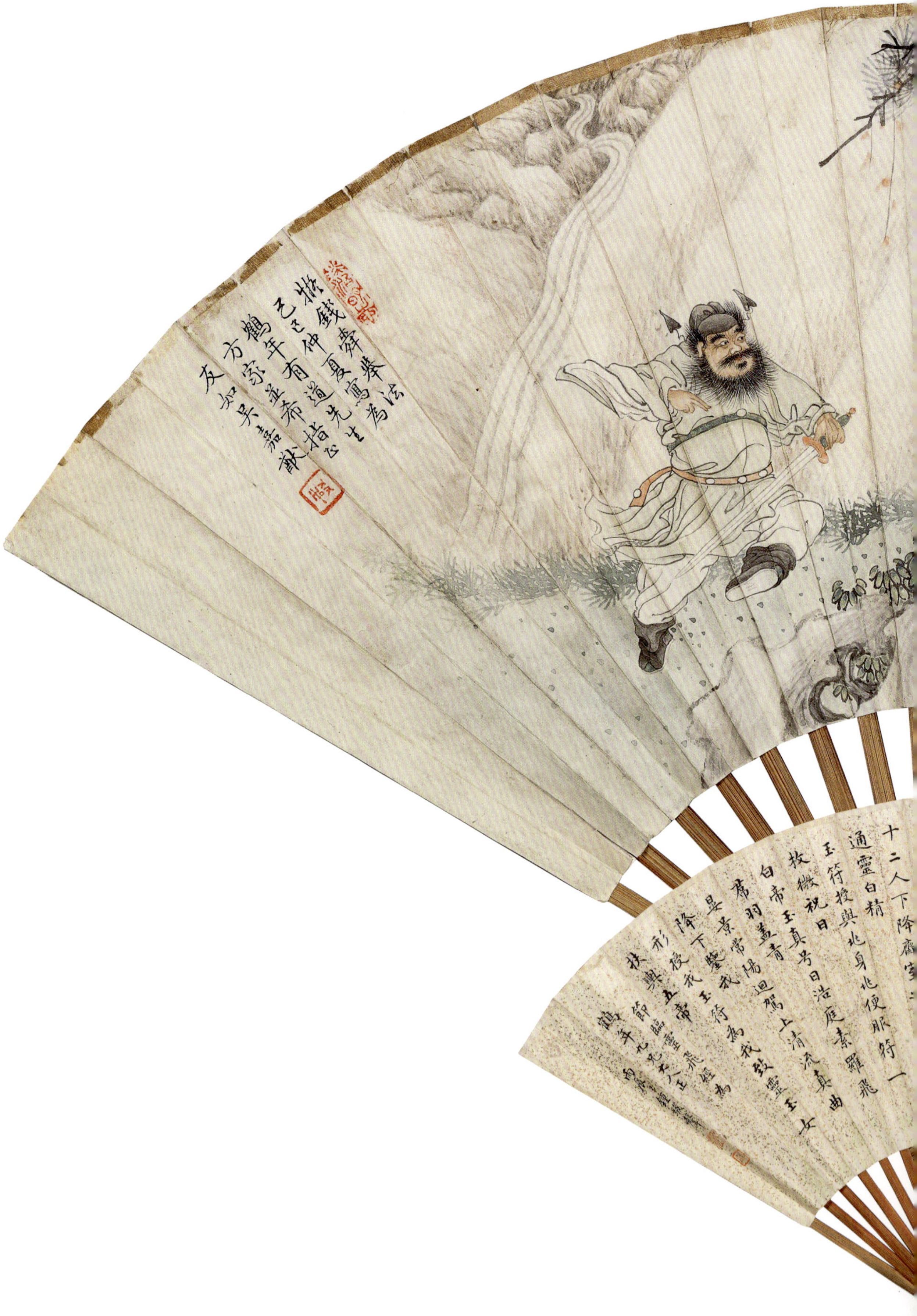

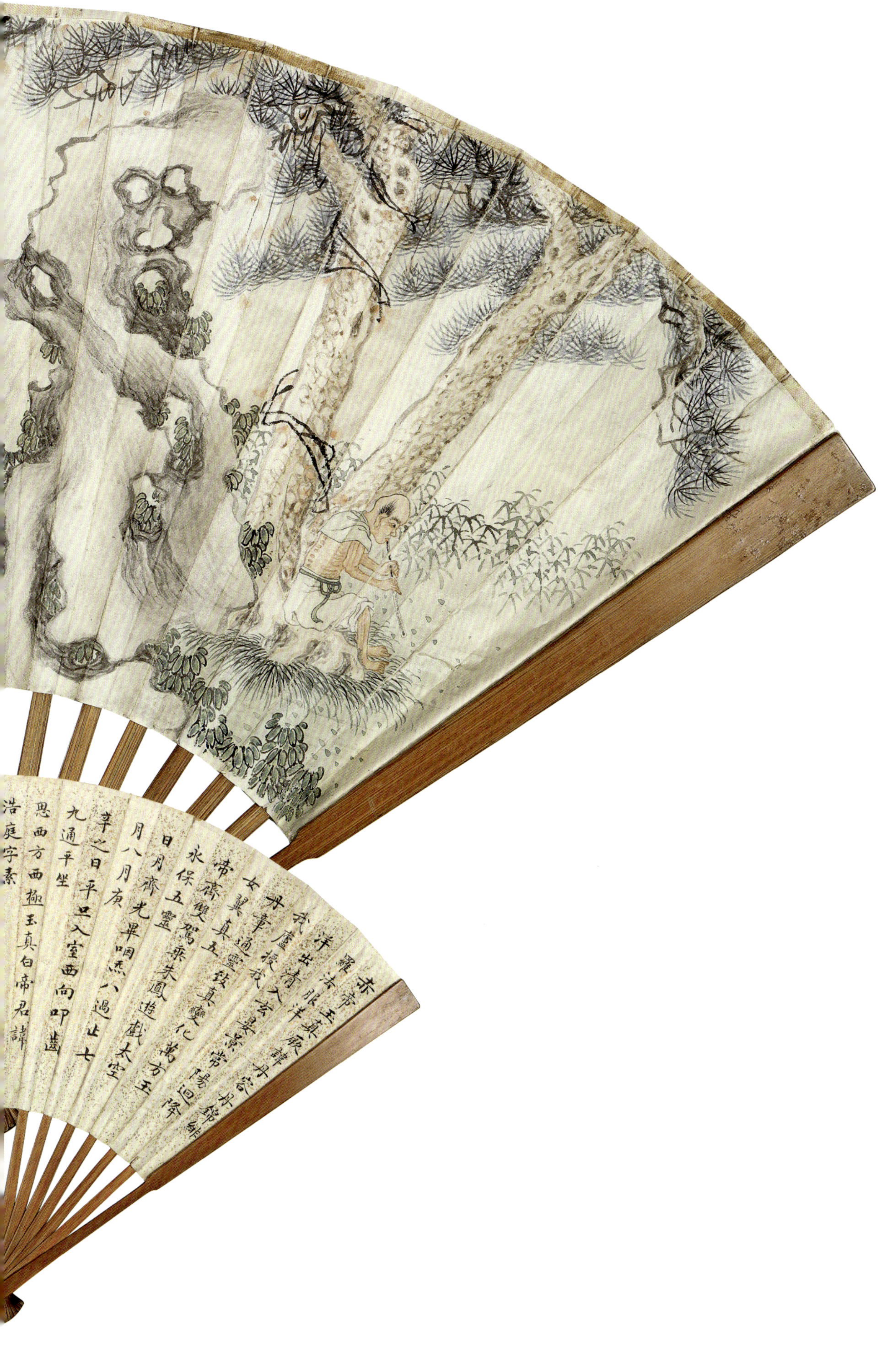

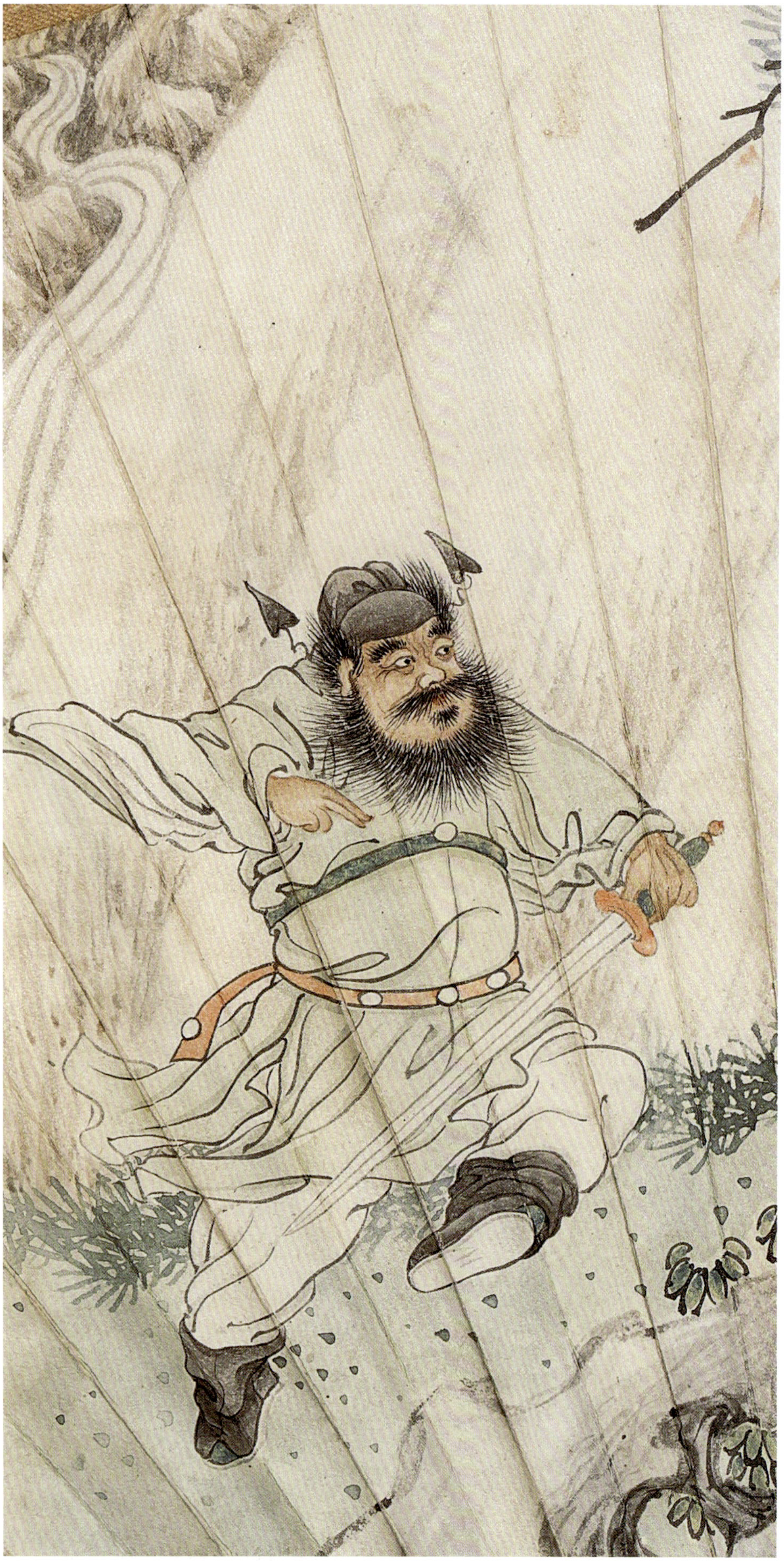

Artists:
Wu Youyu, Zhong Junsheng

Medium:
Color on paper, Completed fan

Dimensions:
19 cm × 49 cm

Zhong Kui Dancing with a Sword

Inscription:
In midsummer of the Jisi year, in imitation of the method of Qian Shunjü, this was painted for Mr. Fang, He Nian, You Dao.

Seal:
You Ru, Aspiring to Clarity

Backside Calligraphy

Inscription:
The Red Emperor, pure as jade, is called Dan Rong,
In his cinnabar robes and wide ceremonial garment, he belongs.
From clarity to the profound, his presence strong,
In lasting sunlight, his tranquil state prolongs.
To my hut he descends, the alchemy truths he confers,
Mystical transformations he masters, the spirit he stirs.
Jade maidens soar, guided by verity's wing,
As the five emperors gather, in celestial harmony they cling.
Astride the vermillion phoenix, through the cosmos they spring,
Forever maintaining the quintessence of five beings. (text abbreviated)
An excerpt from The Scripture of Spiritual Flight, authenticated for the distinguished elder brother, He Nianjiu, by the younger brother, Zhong Junsheng, Yu Chen.

Seal:
The seal of Zhong Junsheng, Yu Chen

Wu Youru (unknown–1894)
Originally named Jiayou, from Yuanhe in the late Qing Dynasty. He once headed the creation of the "Dianshi Studio Pictorial," which was renowned for a time.

Zhong Junsheng (1883–unknown)
Courtesy name Yuchen, styled as Yixi. A native of Renhe (present-day Hangzhou, Zhejiang). He was a Juren during the Xianfeng era of the Qing Dynasty, and he became Zhuangyuan in the tenth year of the Xianfeng reign (1860). Appointed as a compiler in the Hanlin Academy, tasked with editing the national history, he frequently oversaw literary evaluations. In the eleventh year of Xianfeng's reign, he served as an examiner for the provincial examinations in Shuntian (present-day Beijing).

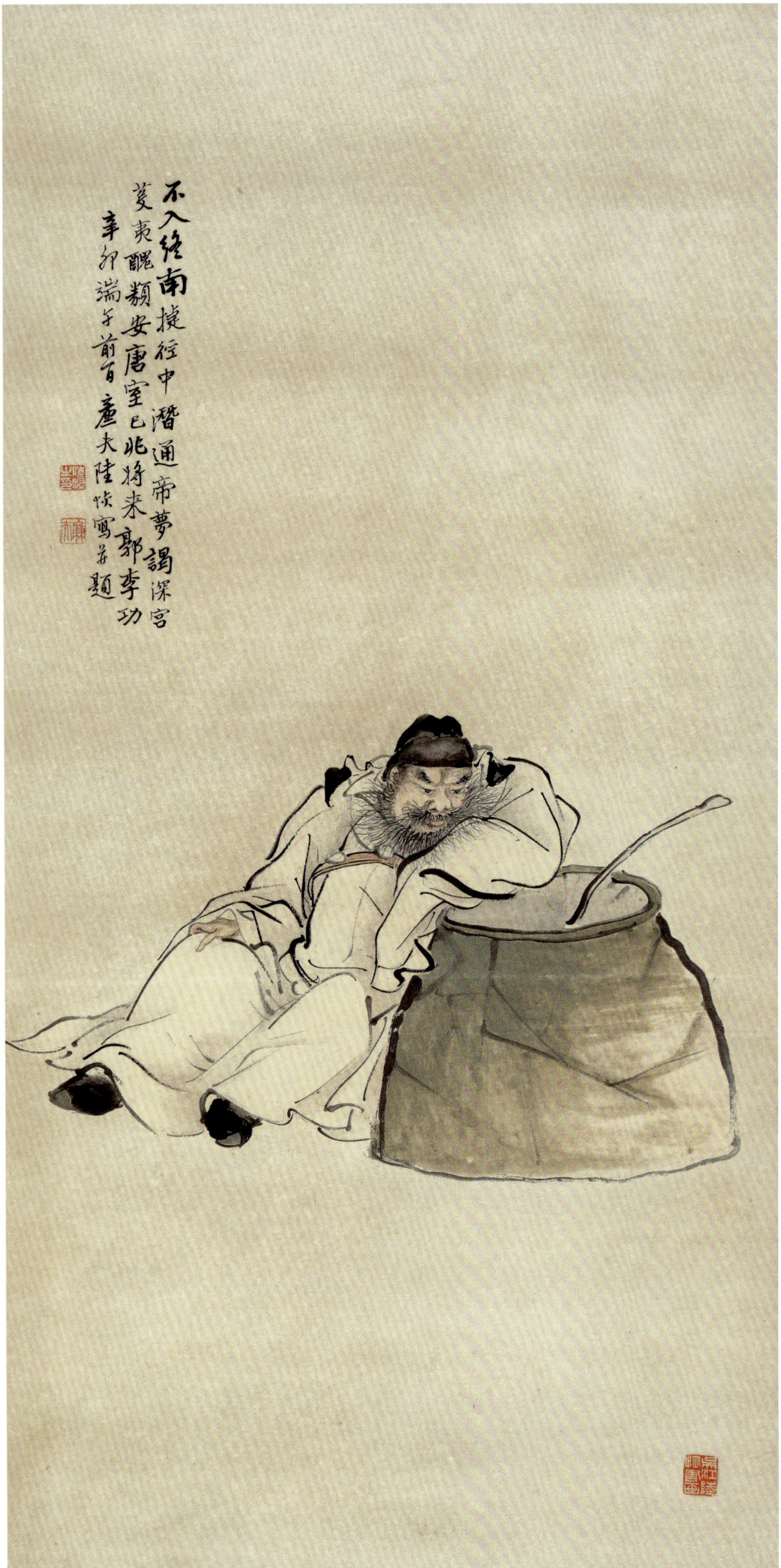
不入終南捷徑中潛通帝夢謁深宮
芟夷醜類安唐室已兆將來郭李功
辛卯端午前日廉夫陸恢寫并題

Artist:
Lu Hui

Medium:
Color on paper, Hanging scroll

Dimensions:
119 cm × 58 cm

Zhong Kui

Inscription:

Without taking shortcuts through Zhongnan's range,
One cannot secretly traverse the emperor's dreams to the palace, so strange.
By cutting down the vile, the Tang House finds peace,
A harbinger of future feats by Guo and Li[2], their fame to increase.
On the day preceding the Dragon Boat Festival in the Xinmao year, this work was inscribed and signed by Lianfu, Lu Hui.

Seal:

The seal of Lu Hui, Lianfu, the calligraphy and paintings of Lu Hui from Wujiang.

Lu Hui (1851–1920)

Originally named Youhui, also known as Hui or Youkui, with the courtesy name Lianfu and styled as Juansou, also known by the Master of the Iconoclastic Teahouse. He was a native of Wujiang, Jiangsu. He excelled in landscape and floral paintings, characterized by elegant brushwork and a spirited, ethereal charm. He once served as an aide to Wu Dacheng.

風動襟裹逸措破須眉鬚魑魅辟頑刻怪君墨法熟氣敵武梁祠力透中原鹿意足不在羣縣辟益驚目
世事可笑人返覆聽謠諑鬼物人邪歟白日肆荼毒老馗怕多事一辭唯裹足進士官不作夫豈畏謗讒請君畫快
劍殺鬼剝皮肉君曰胡劍為鬼怪難盡戮攜此伴行篋嚇鬼當符籙眼張大鬼愁臂攘小鬼哭鬼母與鬼伯伏地求罪
贖此時姑聽之勝把奇書讀旅館風颼颼黃昏飛蝙蝠

康夫老友畫此贈余題詩補空丙戌天中節昌碩道人

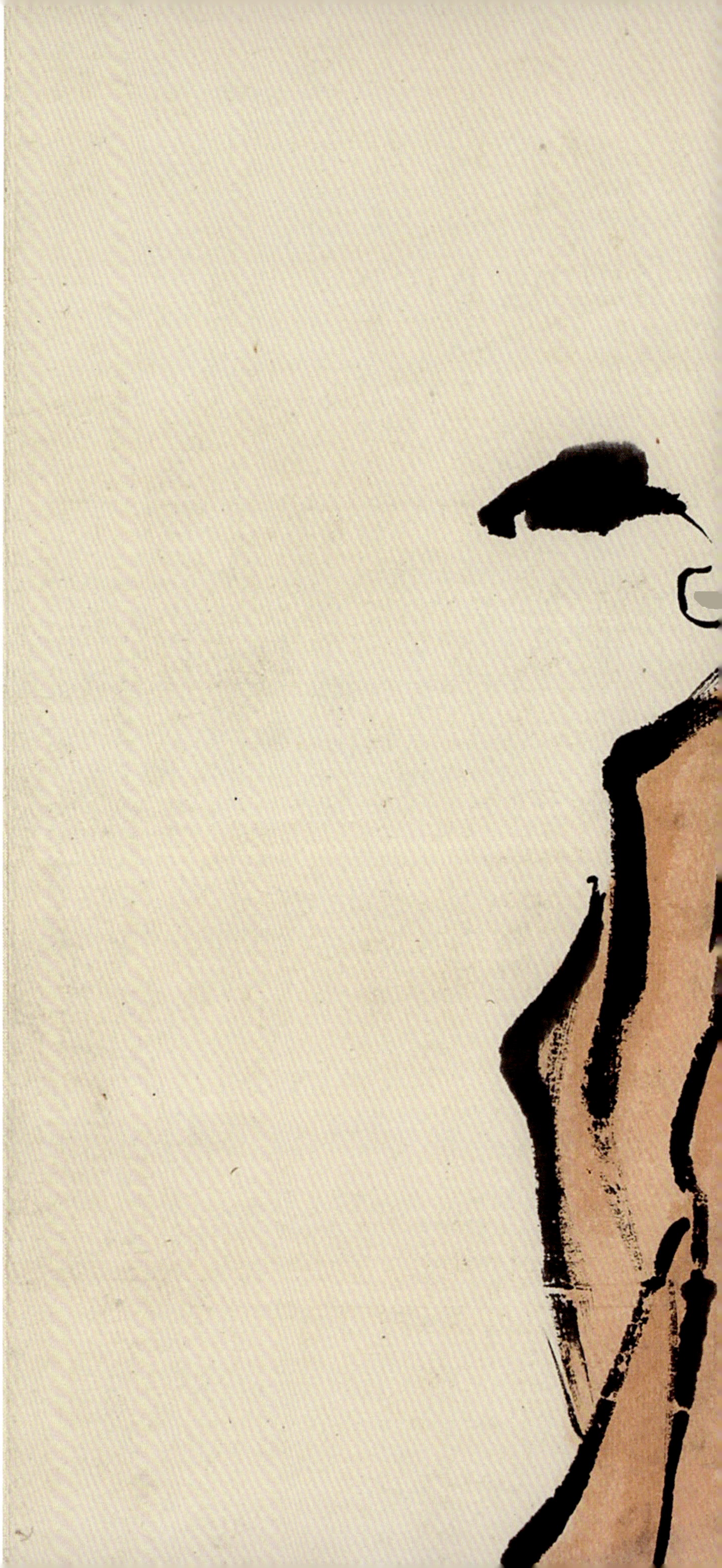

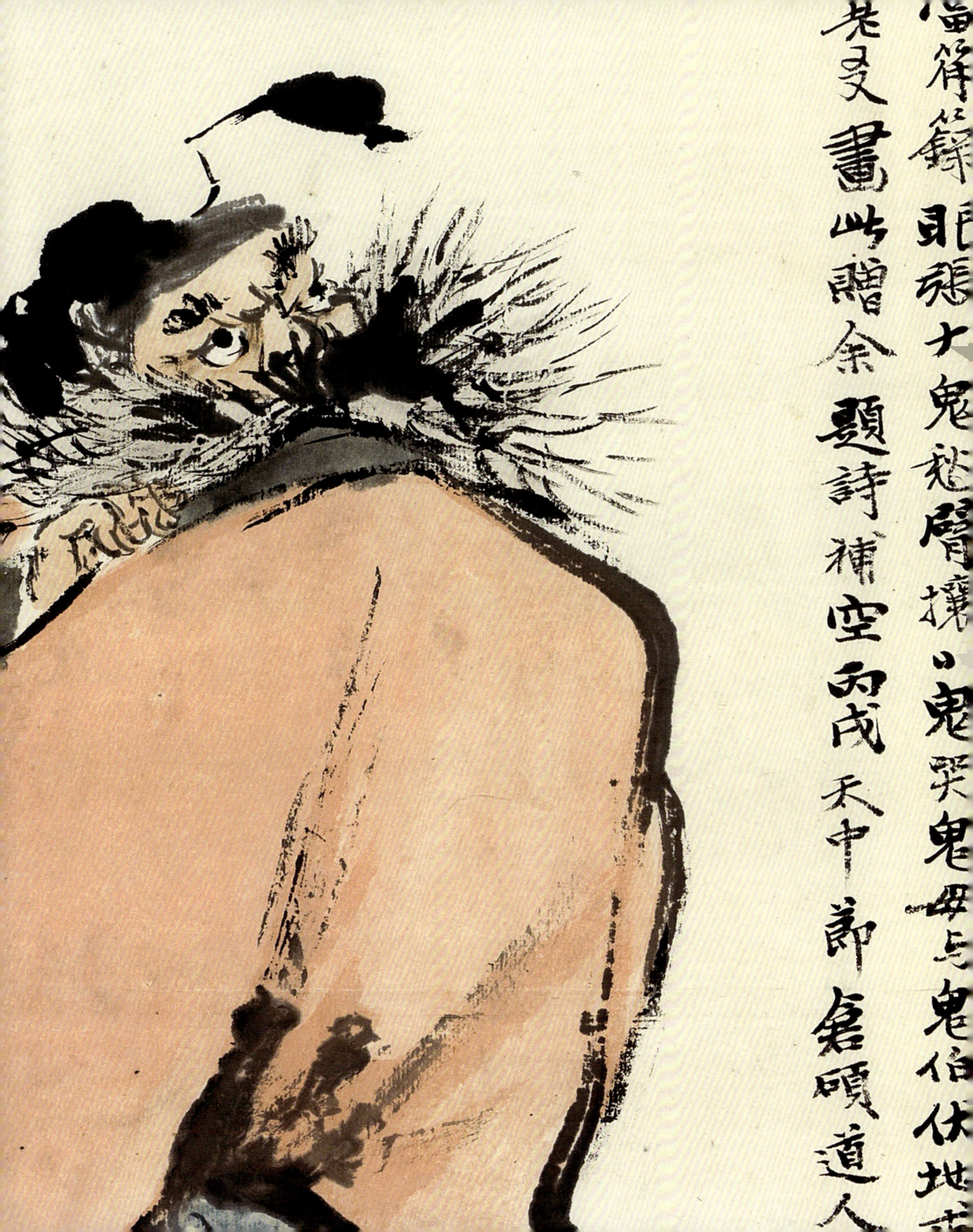
畫此贈余題詩補空丙戌天中節

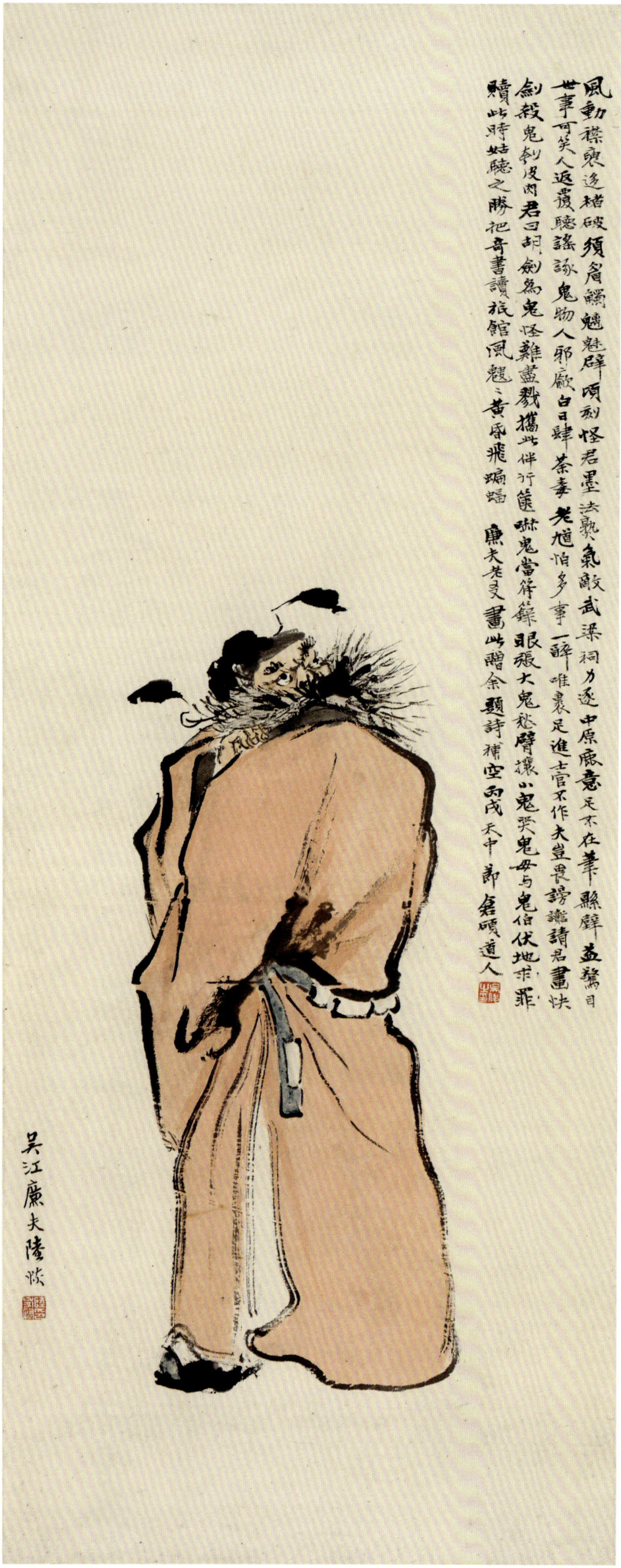
廉夫老友畫此贈余題詩補空丙戌天中節倉碩道人
吳江廉夫陸恢

Artist:
Lu Hui | Inscription by Wu Changshuo

Medium:
Color on paper, Hanging scroll

Dimensions:
109 cm × 42.5 cm

Zhong Kui

Inscription:
Lu Hui, Lianfu, from Wujiang

Seal:
The seal of Lu Youhui

Inscription:
The wind stirs the robes; paper tears meet brow,
Spirits flee in an instant, your ink mastery they allow.
Your vigor rivals the shrines of Wuliang's past,
Your strength chases deer across the Central Plains vast.
Intent not confined to the brush in hand,
Your wall-hung works more startlingly grand.
Worldly affairs, a jest, rumors heard in a loop,
Demons and men alike, in daylight spread dupe.
Old Zhong Kui shuns the overdoer's plight,
In his solitary drunkenness, he wraps his feet tight.
A Jinshi by rank, an official post he forsakes,
Would he fear slanderous talk and its stakes?
Bid the painter a swift sword to wield,
To slay demons, their skins to peel.
"You ask for a Hu blade's art?" says he,
"Ghosts and goblins too numerous to fully flee."
With this painting as part of one's gear,
It scares demons like a charm, never fear.
Wide-eyed, the great ghouls fret,
Small ones weep, their fates met.
The mother of ghosts and their uncle too,
Plead on the ground, their sins to eschew.
For now, grant ear to their pleas, it's best,
It triumphs over reading a tome of the quest.
In the traveler's lodge, the wind whistles through,
As dusk approaches, the bats in flight anew.
My old friend, Lianfu, painted this and gifted it to me, adorning it with a poem to fill the void. Created on the Dragon Boat Festival in the Bingxu year by the Taoist Cangshuo.

Seal:
The seal of Wu Junzhi

Wu Changshuo (1844–1927)
Originally named Jun, with the courtesy name Changshuo, he was known by several pseudonyms, including Cangshuo, Lao Cang, Lao Fou, and Ku Tie, a native of Anji, Zhejiang. A famous painter, calligrapher, and seal engraver of the late Qing and early Republic period. He was a leading figure of the Shanghai School and the inaugural president of the Xiling Seal Art Society.

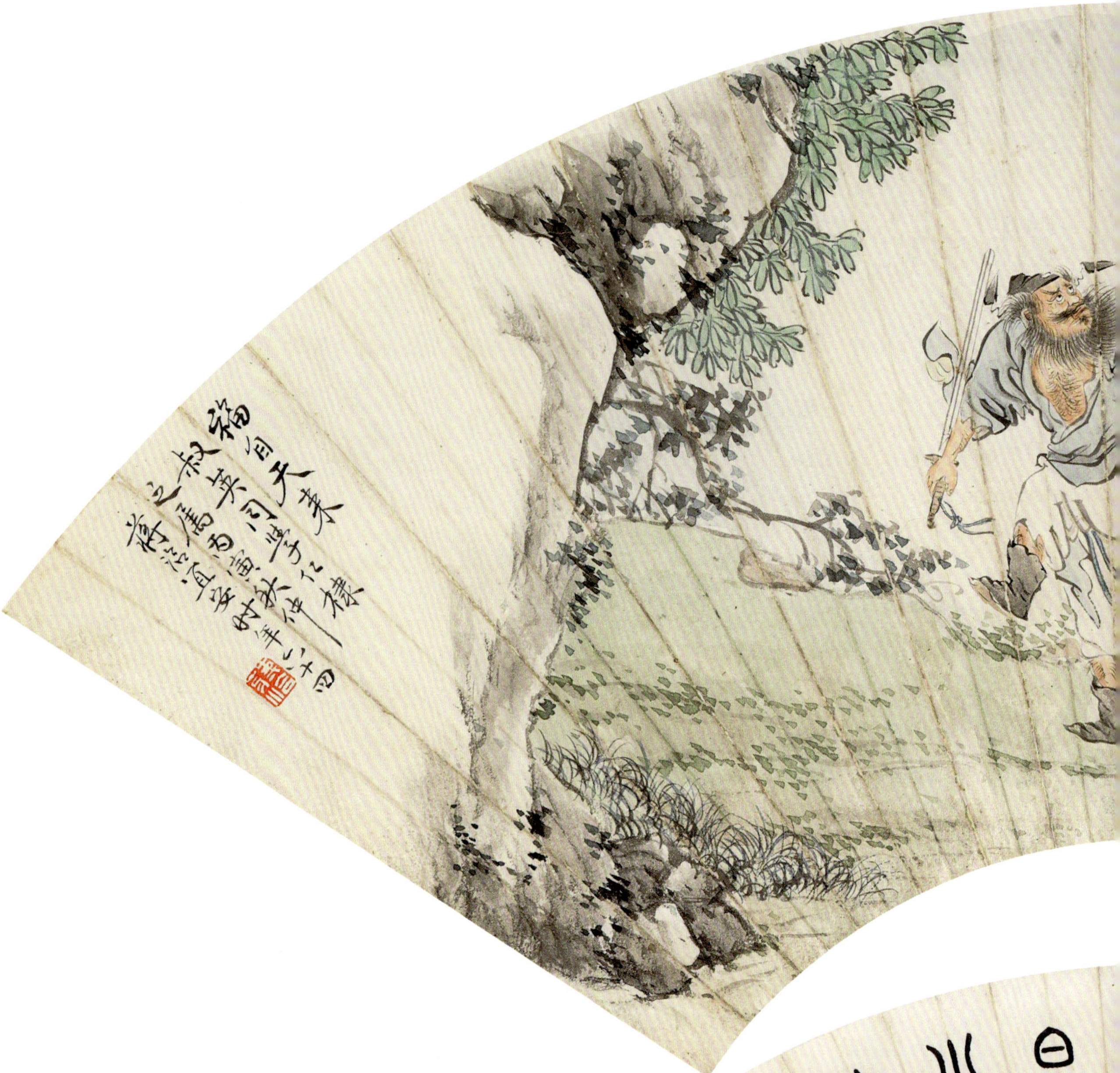
福自天來

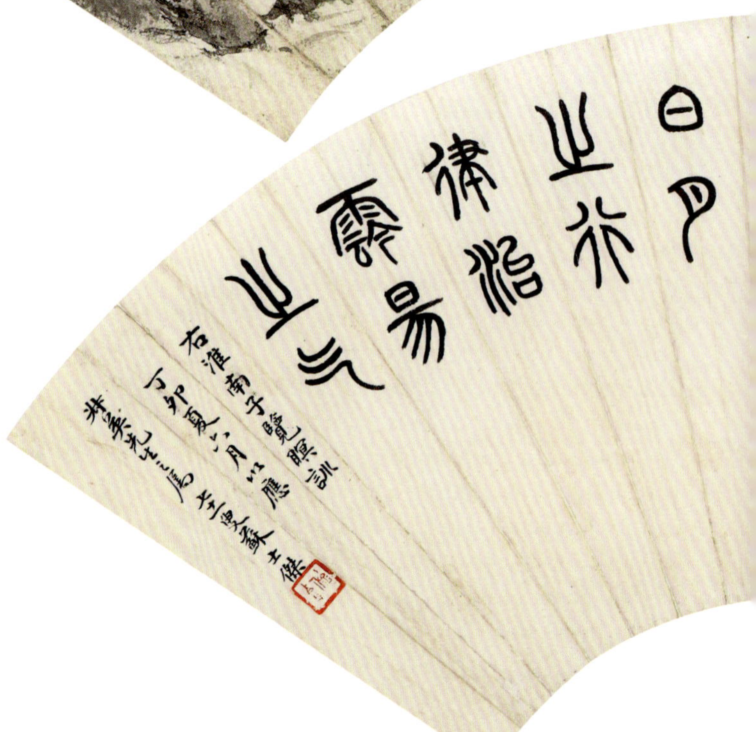
右淮南子覽冥訓
丁卯夏六月以應

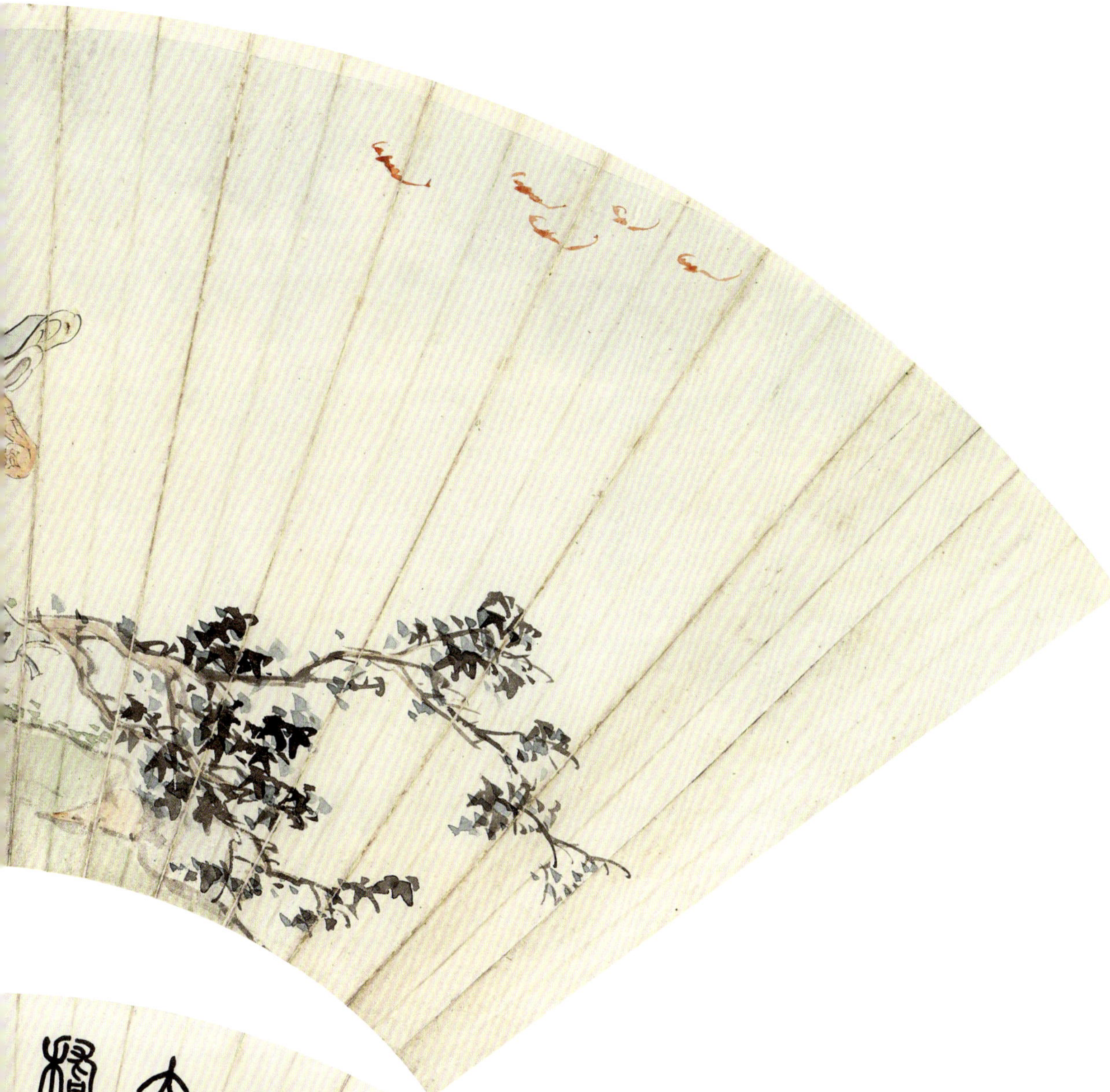

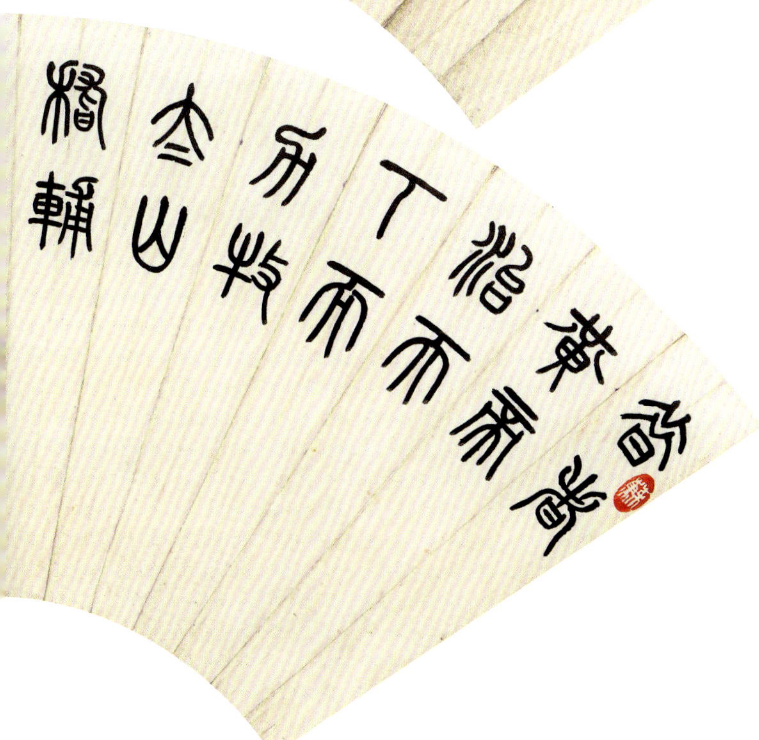

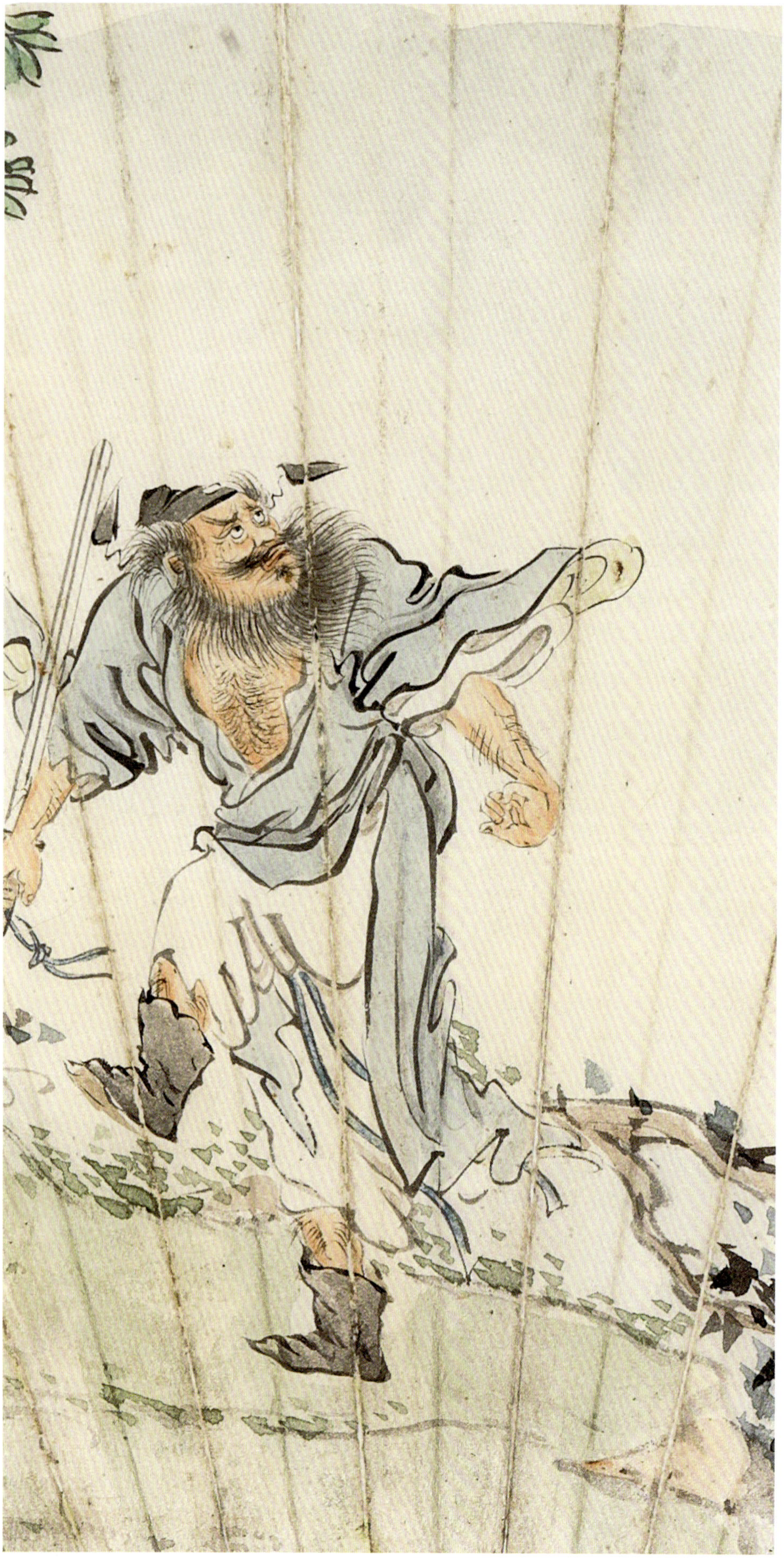

Artists:
Jiang Qia, Su Shijie

Medium:
Color on paper, Fan-shaped

Dimensions:
18 cm × 49 cm

Blessings from Heaven

Inscription:
Blessings from Heaven. For the relative of my classmate Shu Ying, Ren Di, this was inscribed in the autumn of the Bingyin year by Jiang Qia, Yian, at the age of sixty-four.

Seal:
Jiang Qia

Backside Calligraphy

Inscription:
In ancient times, the Yellow Emperor governed all under heaven, assisted by Li Mu and Tai Shan Kui, who, following the movements of the sun and moon, regulated the energies of yin and yang. This is Huainanzi: Exposition on Observing the Hidden, written in the sixth month of summer in the Dingmao year to honor the relative of Mr. Shu Ying, by the seventy-one-year-old Su Shijie.

Seal:
Junbo, Su

Jiang Qia
Styled Yian, commonly known by his courtesy name, also known as the master of Baihua'an, hailing from Suzhou, Jiangsu. He was a direct disciple of Sha Fu, renowned for his portraiture which distinguished the Sha lineage. He was celebrated with accolades such as "Sha Child" and "Sha Family Style" for his eminent works in the genre.

Su Shijie (1857–unknown)
Courtesy name Junbo, a native of Guangdong. He was a calligrapher during the late Qing Dynasty and the Republic of China period.

善禪社長先生屬讚即正 庚申天貺節
馮潤芝鍾馗象容仲生添福弟程景宣題

年〻亦有天中節
今歲君顏不酒紅
想起時清民自樂
告君添福壽〻
鴻如

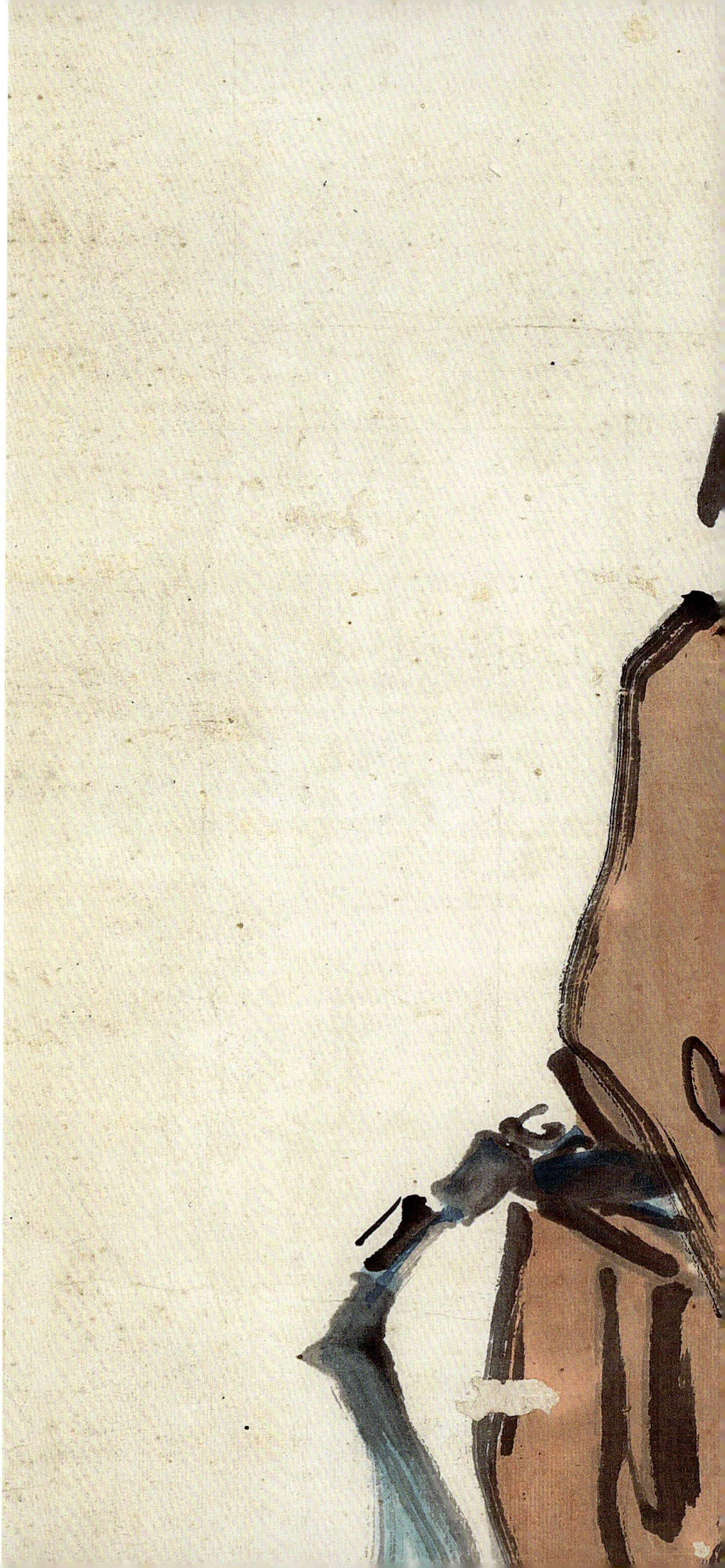

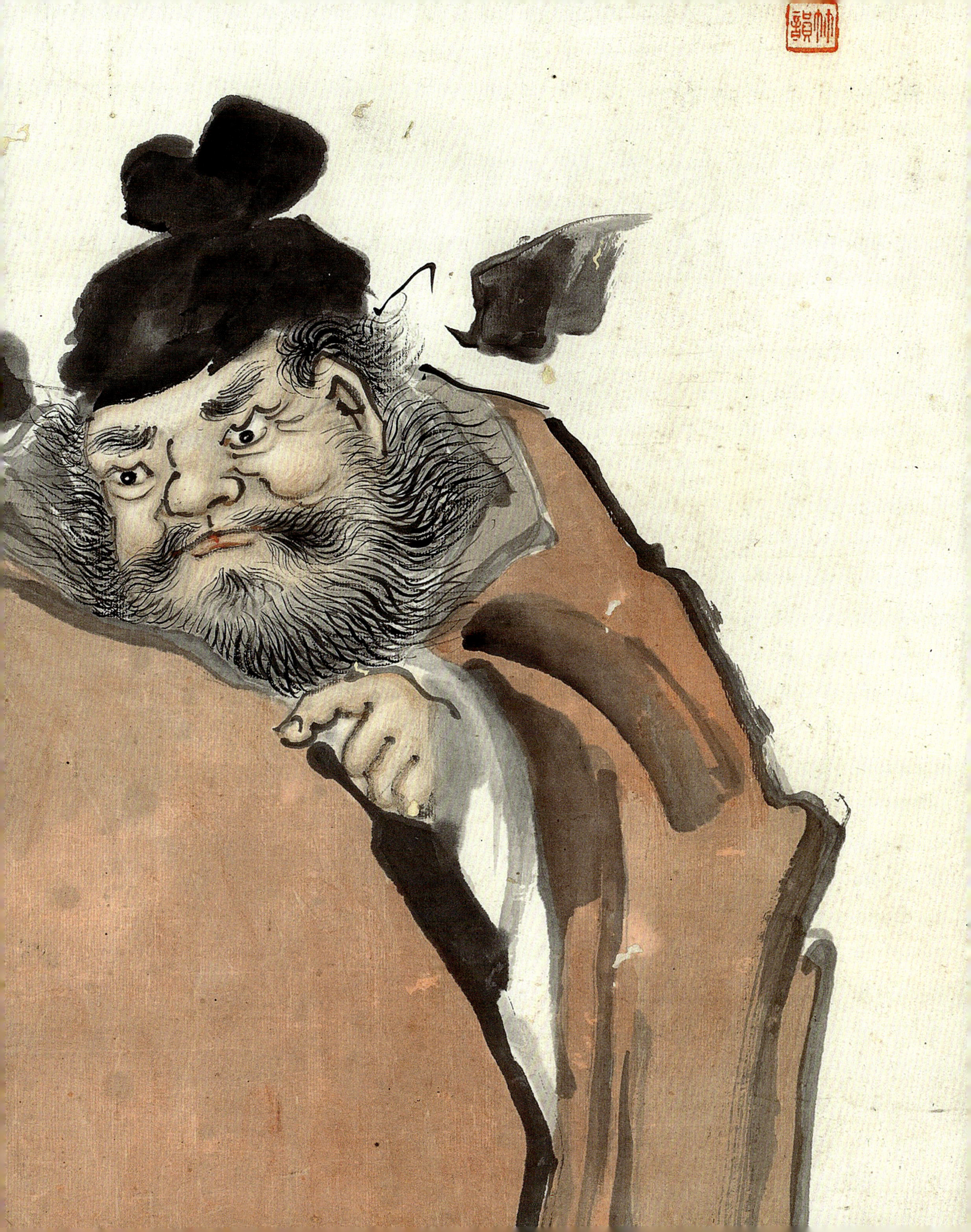

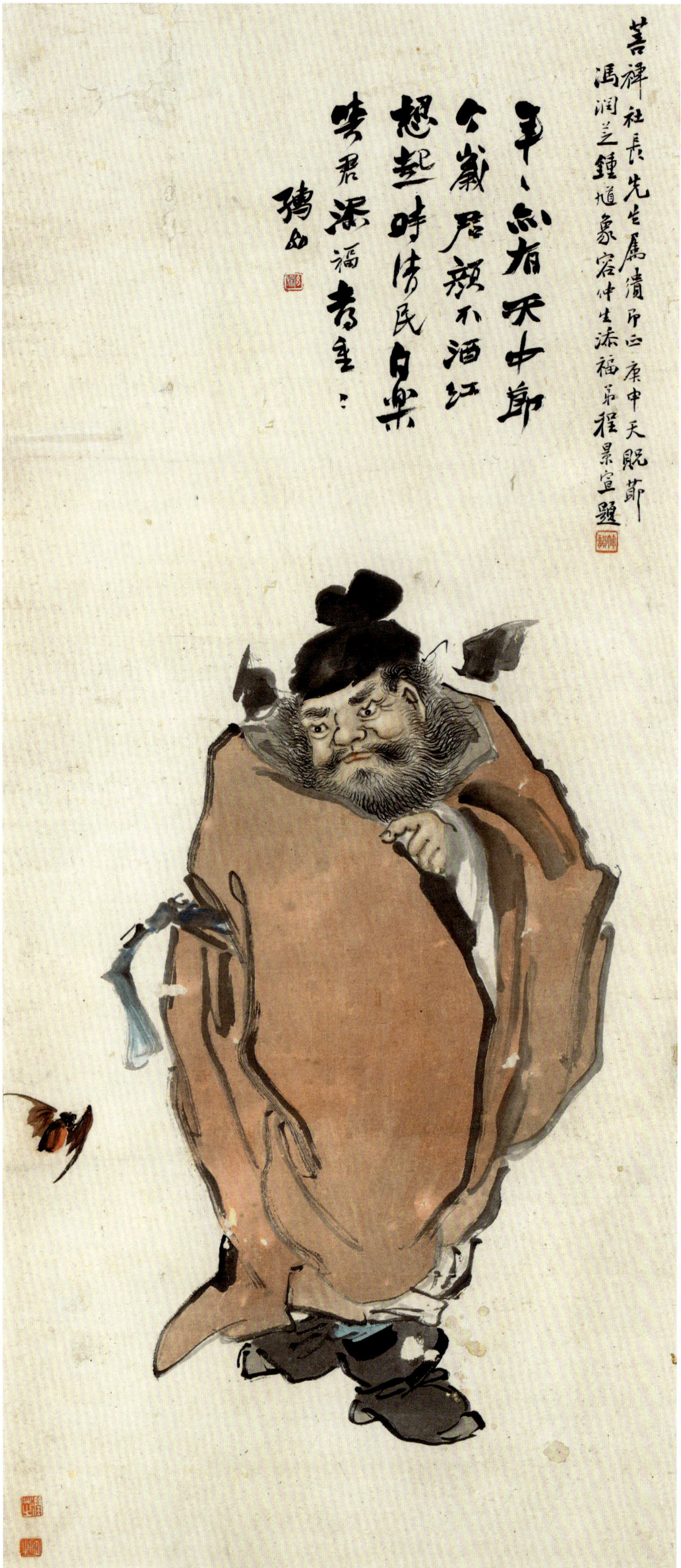

Artists:
Feng Runzhi, Rong Zuchun
Inscription by Cheng Jingxuan,
Yi Dachang

Medium:
Color on paper, Hanging scroll

Dimensions:
107 cm × 46 cm

Zhong Kui Adds Fortune

Inscription:
Commissioned by the esteemed head of the Buddhist Zen society, now duly completed. On the day of the Double Sixth Festival in the Gengshen year, the image of Zhong Kui was painted by Feng Runzhi, with added blessings inscribed by Rong Zhongsheng, and the verse penned by the younger brother, Cheng Jingxuan.

Seal:
Zhuyun, Runzhi, Zhongsheng

Inscription:
Yearly comes the Dragon Boat Festival day,
Yet this year, your cheeks lack the wine's red play.
Recalling times when all found joy in Qingming's light,
With you, I'd share blessings, doubling the delight.

Seal:
Yiru

Feng Runzhi (1852–1937)
Courtesy name Ganlu, also named Lishi, later known as the Old Man of Yu Mountain, a native of Panyu, Guangdong. A renowned figure painter and illustrator in Guangdong during the late Qing period. He was particularly fond of imitating Song and Yuan dynasty paintings, and his depictions of figures were considered exceptional.

Rong Zuchun (1872–1944)
Courtesy name Zhongsheng, styled as Zi'an, and later known as Garden Elder. From Guancheng, Dongguan, he began studying painting with Ju Lian at the age of twelve, excelling in landscapes, figures, flowers, birds, insects, and fish. He gained fame at the age of thirty and joined the Qingyou Society, founded by Chen Shuren and others, in the 1920s. He traveled with Wu Deyi, viewed many paintings, and became skilled in appraisal.

Cheng Jingxuan (1864–1934)
Courtesy name Zhuyun, styled as Elder of Longhu, also known as the master of Zhuanxiang Studio, a native of Foshan, Guangdong. A modern painter and seal carver who excelled in painting landscapes, flowers, birds, insects, and fish, his style was elegant and refined. Skilled in seal script and clerical script, he also used the iron brush. He studied painting with Wang Shigu and Jiang Tingxi. Throughout his life, he devoted himself to art education and creation, establishing the Shangmei Studio in his residence in Xiguan, Guangzhou, where he sold paintings and taught students for over a decade, attracting many learners.

Yi Dachang (1874-1941)
Original name Ting Xi, rotary name Ru, number Dachang, Jifu, Wei Zhai, Wei Zhai, Ru Zhai, Tun Gong, Nian Gong, etc., from Guangdong Heshan. Expertise He was a direct disciple of Chen Lanfu, specialising in calligraphy, painting, seal carving, tablet and tablet rhymes, the origin and flow of characters, and music theory. He was a professor at Jinan University and the National Conservatory of Music, and a technician at the Seal and Casting Bureau.

琳瓊先生指正

癸亥秋容祖椿畫

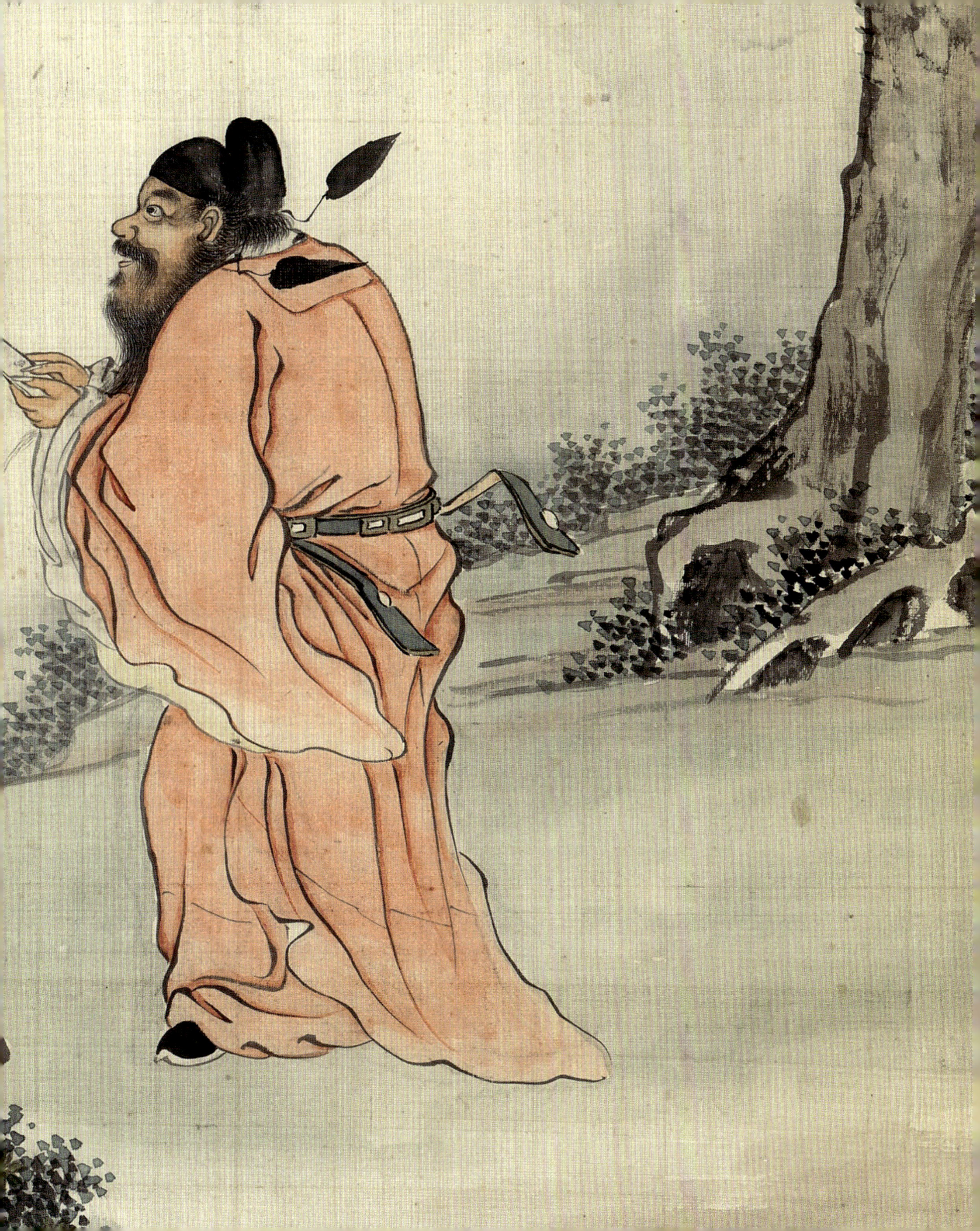

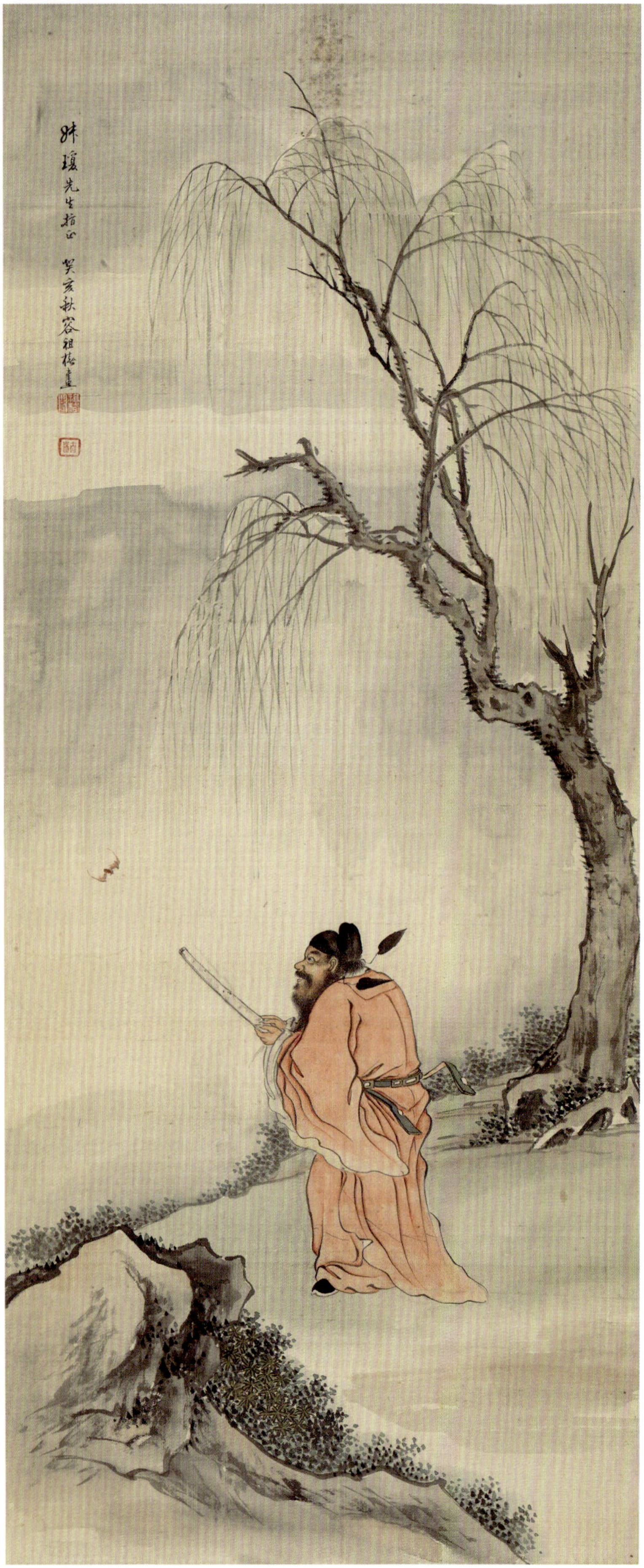
先生指正
癸亥秋容祖椿畫

Artist:
Rong Zuchun

Medium:
Color on silk, Hanging scroll

Dimensions:
100 cm × 40 cm

Blessings from Heaven

Inscription:
In the autumn of the Guihai year, this painting was created by Rong Zuchun, with corrections from Mr. Shu Qiong.

Seal:
The seal of Zuchun, Zi'an

光明正大之謂人闇昧邪僻之謂鬼然鬼不必牛其頭馬其面居枉死城中隸羅剎國內也何也彼牛其頭馬其面居枉死城中隸羅剎國內者猶作冗諸張真人得以驅之鍾進士得以馭之鬼其似人何哉乃今不盡然有人之貌而鬼其行者有名其為人而實為鬼者張真人無如之何鍾進士無如之何崔判官又無如之何於是鬼名鬼姓以相欺矣鬼言鬼語以相惑矣遇微利則鬼張鬼智以謀之見小害則鬼頭鬼腦以避之武所求之必欲得則鬼喊鬼叫不休焉若所求之偶或失則鬼吵鬼鬧不止焉有闖捷而務便者為輕腳鬼有趨炎附勢者為攢天鬼有捕風捉影者為白日鬼有跋前躦後者為冒失鬼其他所謂靈鬼跳鬼酒鬼色鬼病鬼窮鬼醜鬼餓鬼等皆不復論嗚呼人而鬼矣彼何常牛其頭馬其面居枉死城中隸羅剎國內哉當斯時也雖設以鬼門關不得而域之雖壓以鬼畫符不得而制之矣無怪夫張真人之仰天而呼鍾進士之拍手而評崔判官之高枕而臥也歟

陳玉几所寫三不管國列異之錄斯文於上而不知撰者姓名抑其所自撰而托辭以諷與 甲辰秋九月

偉雲吾兄屬臨此本因附記於此 南海潘龢

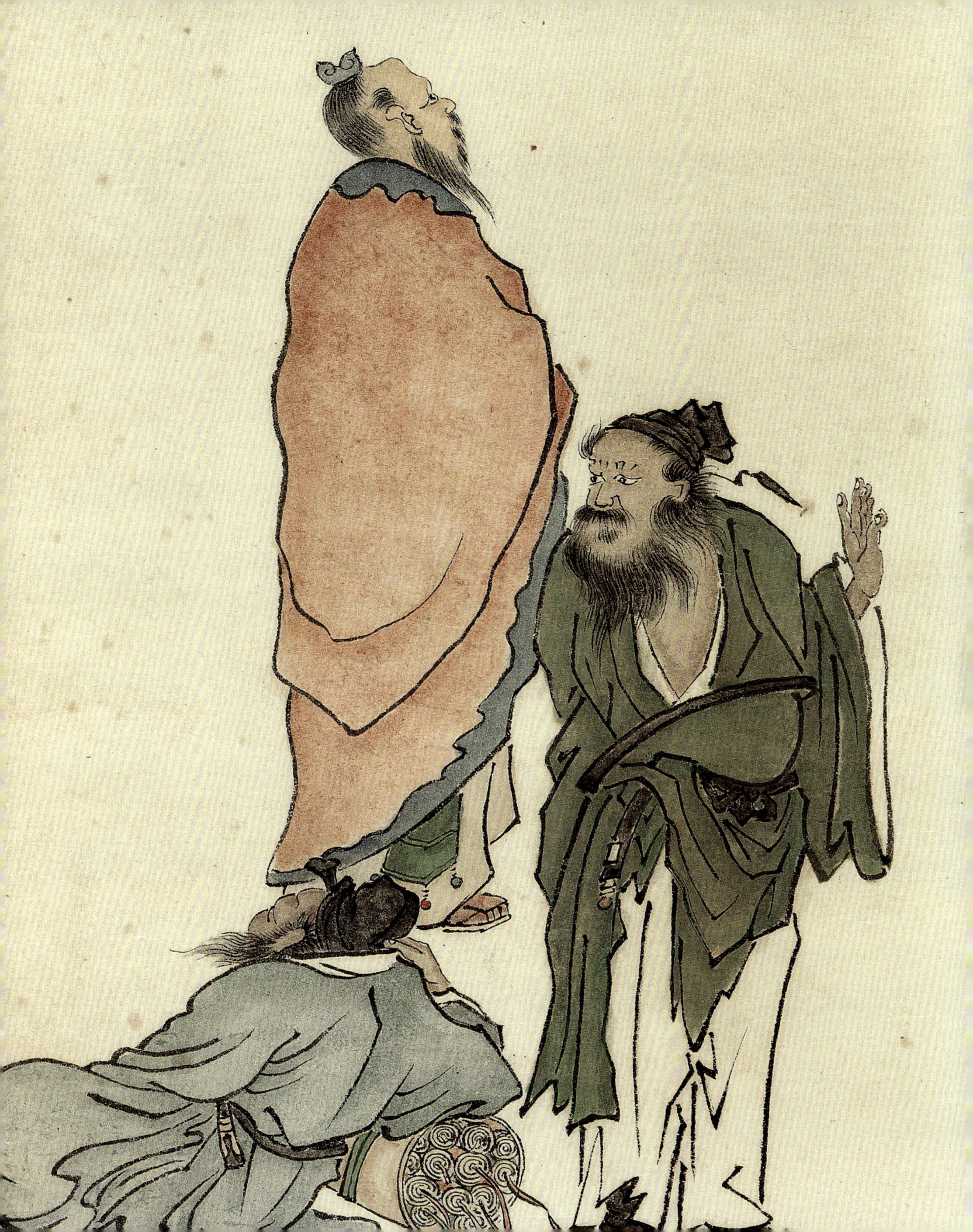

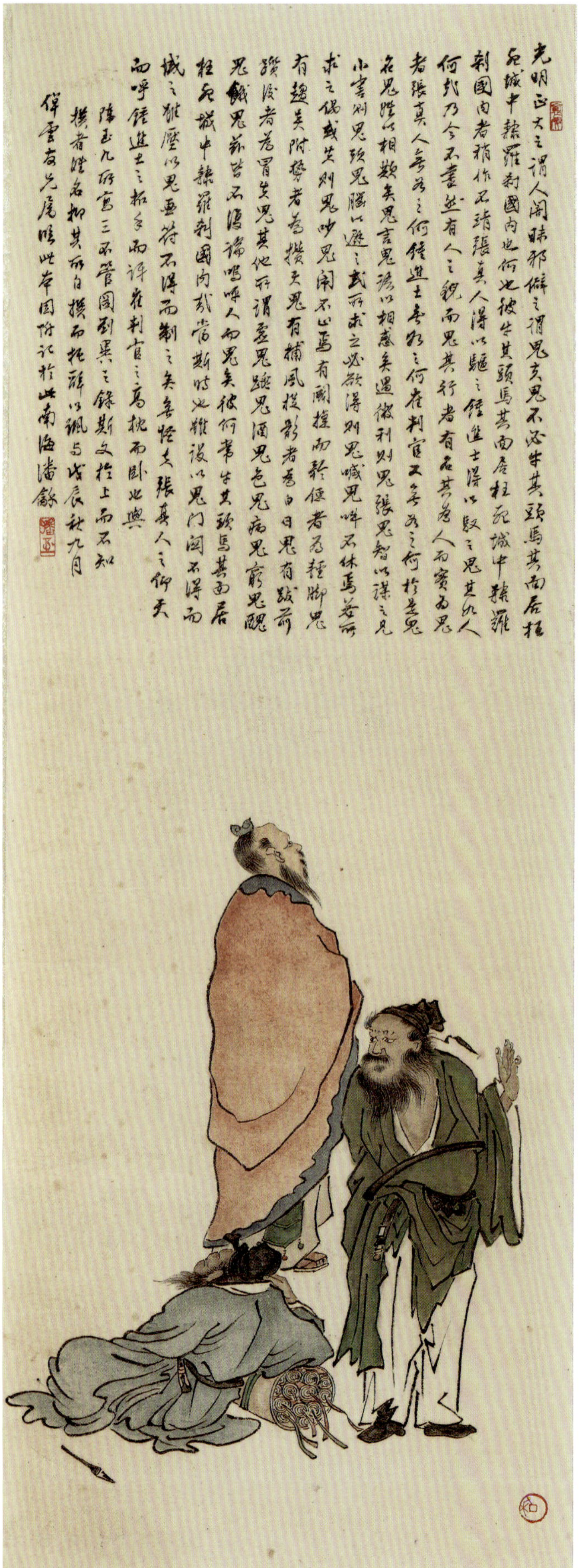
光明正大之謂人閃睒邪僻之謂鬼夫鬼不必牛其頭馬其面居枉
死城中羅剎國內也何也彼牛其頭馬其面居枉死城中羅
剎國內者猶作不靖張真人得以驅之鍾進士得以啖之鬼其人人
何哉乃今不盡然有人之貌而鬼其行者有名其為人而實為鬼
者張真人奈之何鍾進士奈之何崔判官又奈之何於是鬼
名鬼唯以相欺矣鬼言鬼語以相慕矣遇微利則鬼張鬼智以謀之見
小害則鬼頭鬼腦以避之或所求之必欲得則鬼喊鬼叫不休焉若所
求之偶或失則鬼吵鬼鬧不已焉有鬧撞而於便者為種腳鬼
有趨其附勢者為攢尖鬼有捕風捉影者為白日鬼有跋前
躓後者為冒失鬼其他所謂屈死鬼短命鬼酒鬼色鬼病鬼窮鬼醜
鬼餓鬼皆不復論嗚呼人而鬼矣彼何嘗牛其頭馬其面居
枉死城中羅剎國內哉當斯時也雖設以鬼門關不得而
識之雖壓以鬼畫符不得而制之矣吾恐夫張真人之仰天
而呼鍾進士之拊手而評崔判官之高枕而臥也與
陳玉几所寫三不管圖則異之錄斯文於上而不知
撰者姓名抑其所自撰而託辭以諷與戊辰秋九月
偉雲夫子屬賠此本因附記於此南海潘龢

Artist:
Pan He

Medium:
Color on paper, Hanging scroll

Dimensions:
82.5 cm × 29 cm

Three Indifferents

Inscription:
The virtuous by daylight are called humans; the dark and deviant are dubbed ghosts. Not all ghosts bear bovine heads or equine faces, dwelling in twisted death cities, nor are they minions of the Rakshasa realms. Why? Those with the heads of bulls and faces of horses who reside in crooked cities under Rakshasa rule could be easily quelled by Master Zhang or managed by Scholar Zhong. How then could ghosts be likened to humans? But it's not entirely so today. Some appear human but bear the essence of ghosts; some bear human names but act as ghosts. Neither Master Zhang, Scholar Zhong, nor Judge Cui can do anything about them. Hence, ghosts now deceive using human names and surnames; they confound with their spectral speech. Faced with trivial challenges, they plot with ghostly cunning; confronted with minor risks, they dodge with ghostly wit. If they ardently desire something, they wail incessantly like ghosts; if by chance they lose what they seek, they bicker endlessly like ghosts. Those who gloat over minor victories are the frivolous ghosts; those who flatter and cling to power are the sky-clutching ghosts; those who chase rumors are the daylight ghosts; those who stumble in haste are the bumbling ghosts. As for the so-called empty ghosts, leaping ghosts, drunk ghosts, lecherous ghosts, sick ghosts, impoverished ghosts, ugly ghosts, and starving ghosts, these need no further mention. Alas, humans have turned into ghosts. Why bother with those bearing bovine heads and equine faces, residing in crooked death cities, under the rule of Rakshasa? In such times, even the Ghost Gate would fail to contain them, even ghostly talismans would fail to control them. No wonder Master Zhang cries out to the heavens, Scholar Zhong spreads his hands in bewilderment, and Judge Cui lies down to rest. The "Three Indifferents" created by Chen Yujui, with this text inscribed atop by Liu Yi, who knows not the author's name. Could it be that he penned it himself and ascribed it to another for satire? In the ninth month of the Wuchen year, my dear brother Zhuoyun, came to carefully examine this work, prompting me to add this commentary here. Pan He of Nanhai.

Seal:
Pan Ya, Baocan, and He

Pan He (1873–1929)
Courtesy name Zhizhong, styled as Baocan, a native of Nanhai. A well-read individual with a home library known as the Wanjuan Tower. Along with Li Fengting and others, he transformed the Guihai Cooperative Painting Society into the National Painting Research Association. An expert in the appraisal of cultural relics, he was skilled in calligraphy and painting, as well as poetry and prose, and was adept in seal carving.

霏〻梅雨冷橫塘嫁妹舟中對舉觴
離寺經南山已遠計程今日是端陽
甲寅夏四月六日冬心老人筆
心海沈兆涵拜記歲月

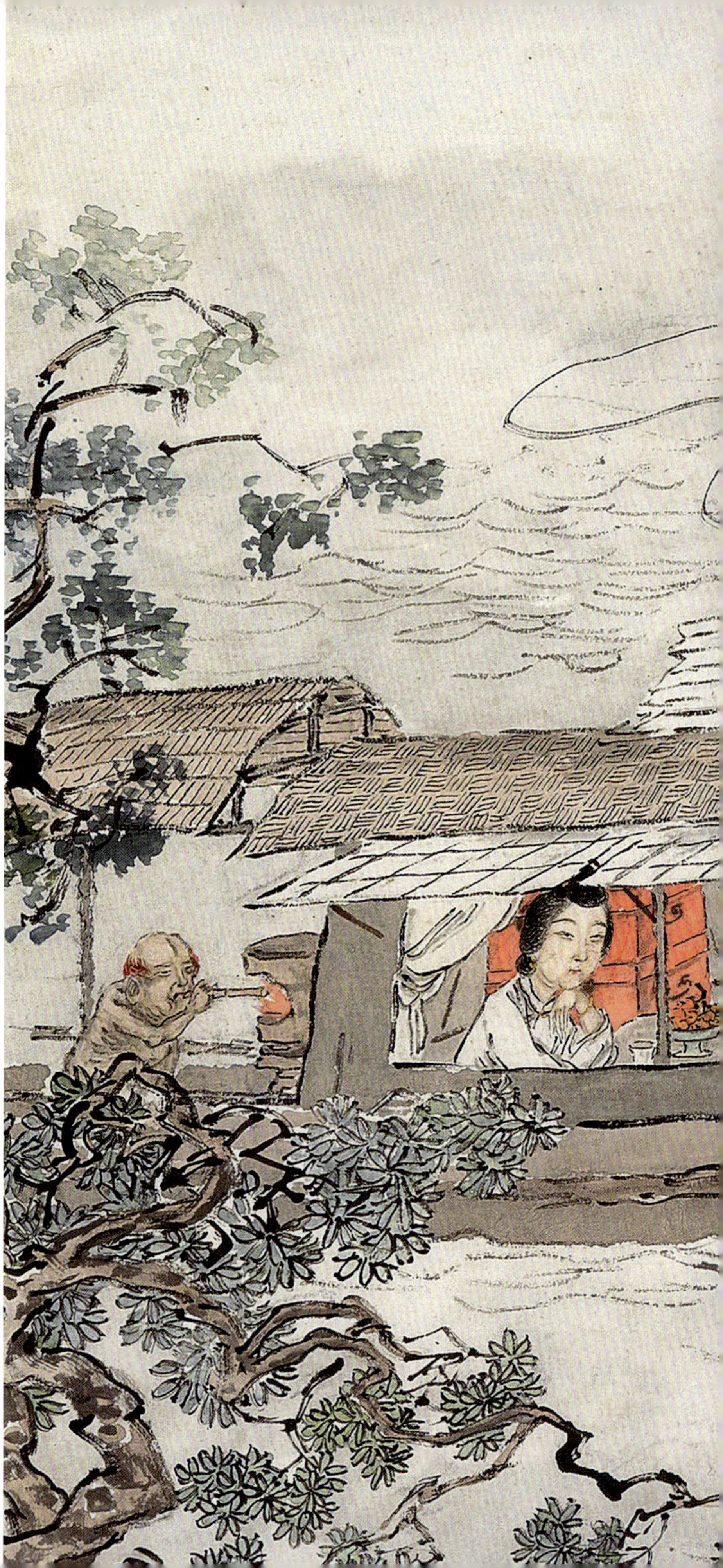

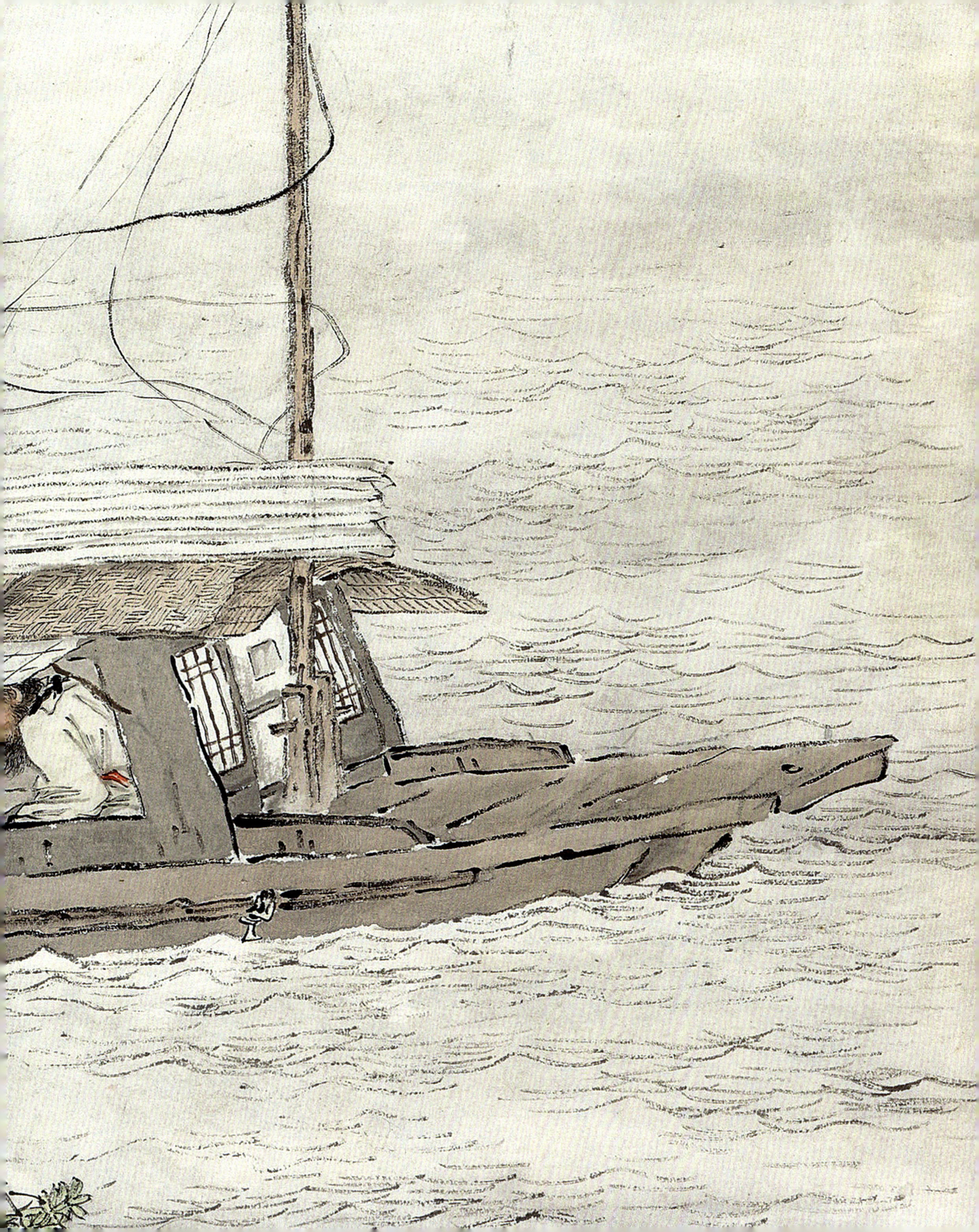

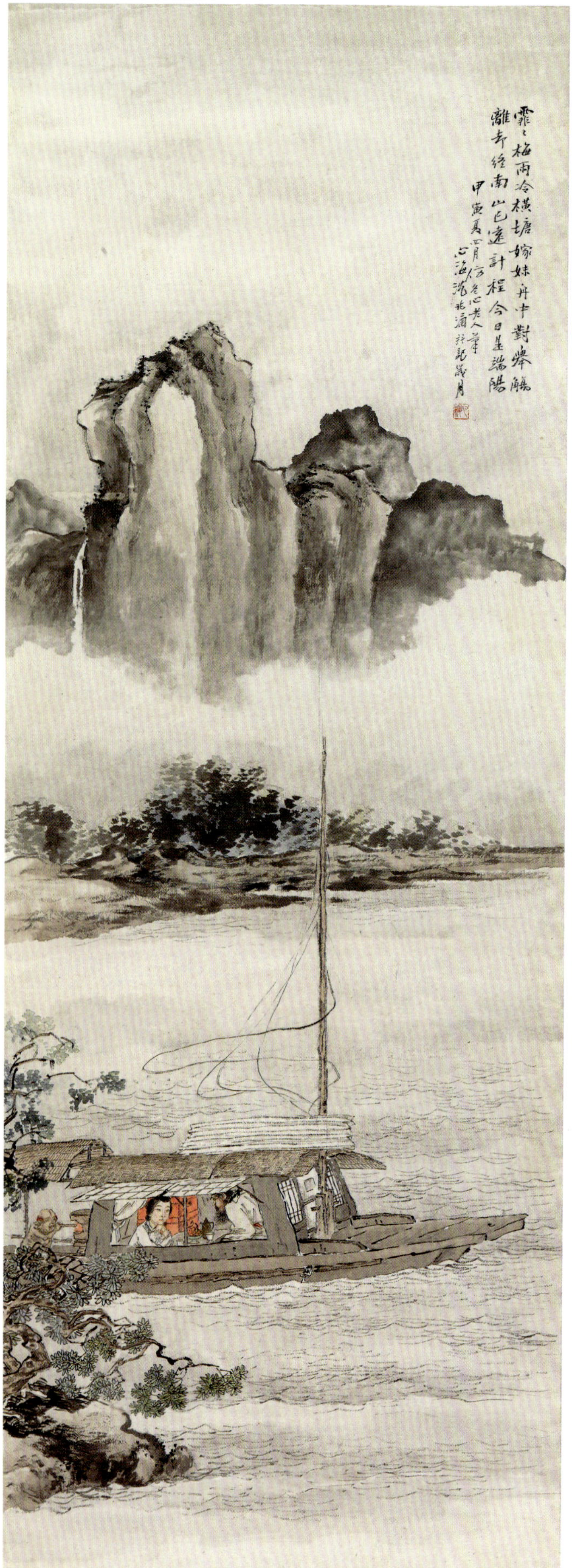
霏霏梅雨冷橫塘嫁妹舟中對嶂觴
離寺經南山已遠計程今日是端陽
甲寅夏四月仿老蓮老人筆
心海沈兆涵

Artist:
Shen Xinhan

Medium:
Color on paper, Hanging scroll

Dimensions:
112 cm × 39 cm

Zhong Kui Marrying Off His Sister

Inscription:

Drizzle swathes the plum rains, chilling Hengtang's expanse,
In a boat, toasting the sister wedded, glasses they advance.
Far from Zhongnan's mount, we've left it way behind,
By the day's journey reckon, it's Dragon Boat Festival we find.
In the fourth month of the summer in the Jia Yin year, imitated the style of the old master Dongxin; recorded by Xinhai, Shen Zhaohan along with the date.

Seal:

Xinhai

Shen Xinhai (1855–1941)

Originally named Han, also known as Zhaohan, a native of Chongming, Shanghai. Skilled in painting flowers, landscapes, and figures, he particularly excelled in painting court ladies. A direct disciple of Qian Hui'an.

鍾進士嫁妹圖

略師金冬心先生筆意 心海沈兆涵

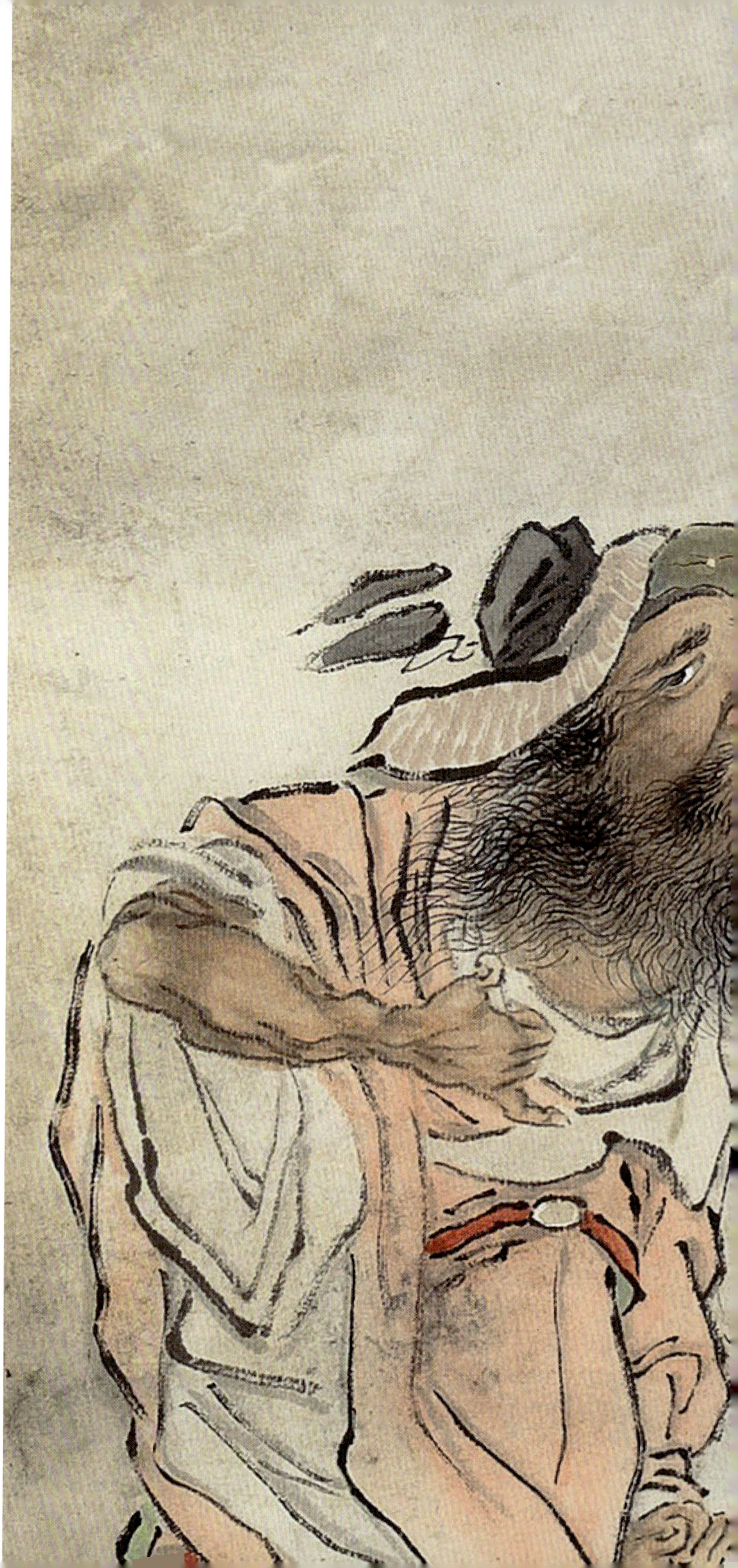

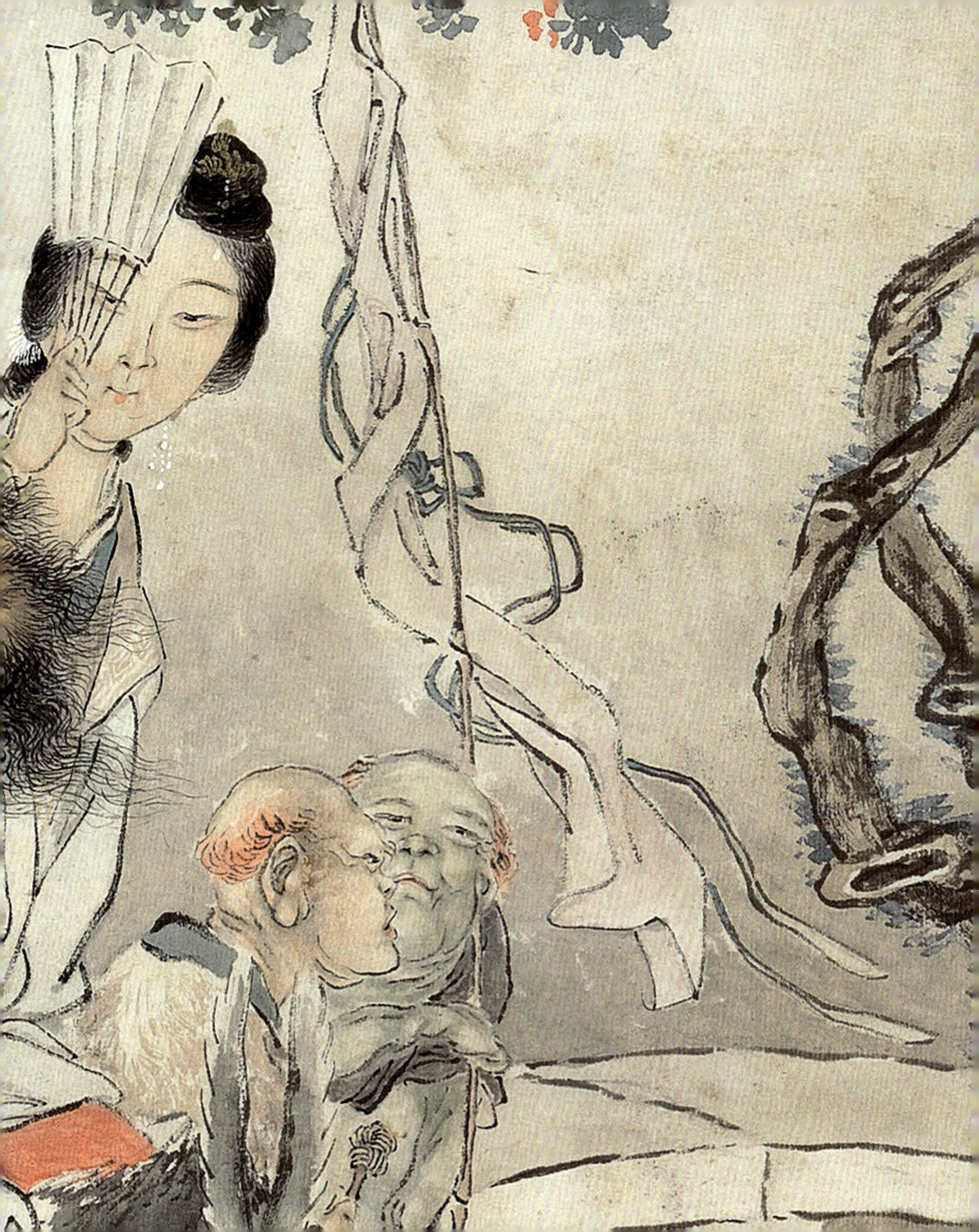

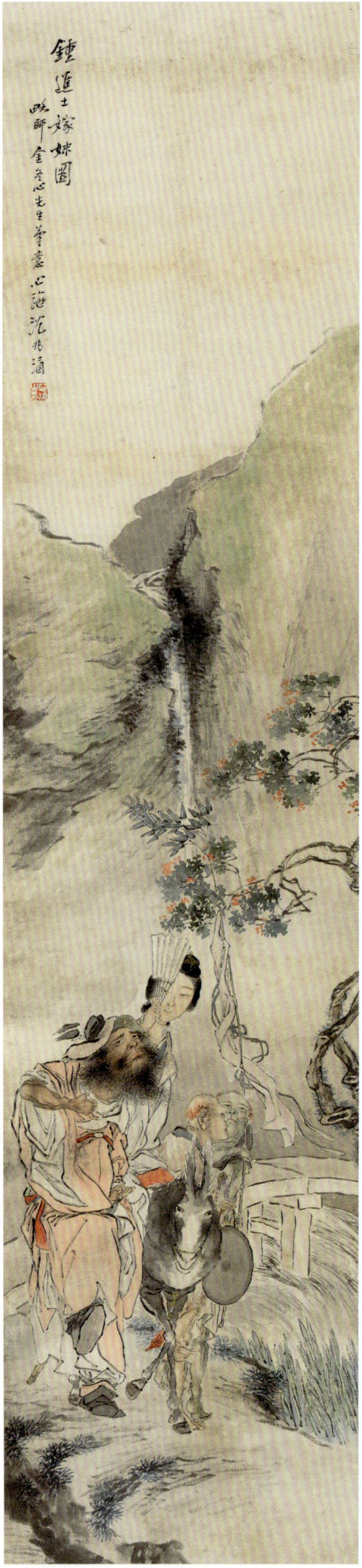
鍾進士嫁妹圖
仿師金冬心先生筆意 上海沈兆涵

Artist:
Shen Xinhan

Medium:
Color on paper, Hanging scroll

Dimensions:
133 cm × 30 cm

Jinshi Zhong Marrying Off His Sister

Inscription:
The "Jinshi Zhong Marrying Off His Sister," subtly follows the brushwork style of Mr. Jin Dongxin, executed by Shen Zhaohan, Xinhai.

Seal:
The seal of Xinhai

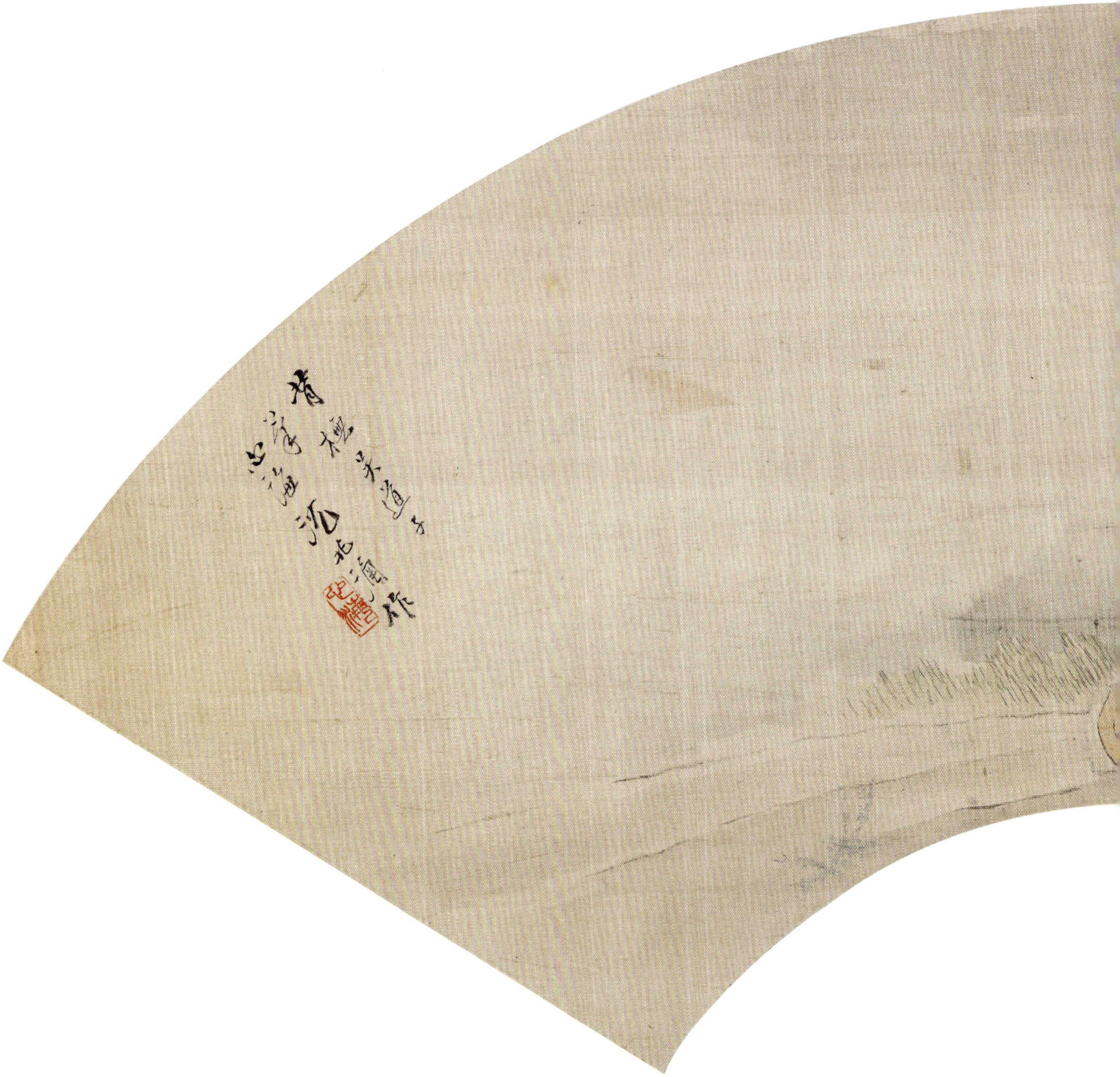

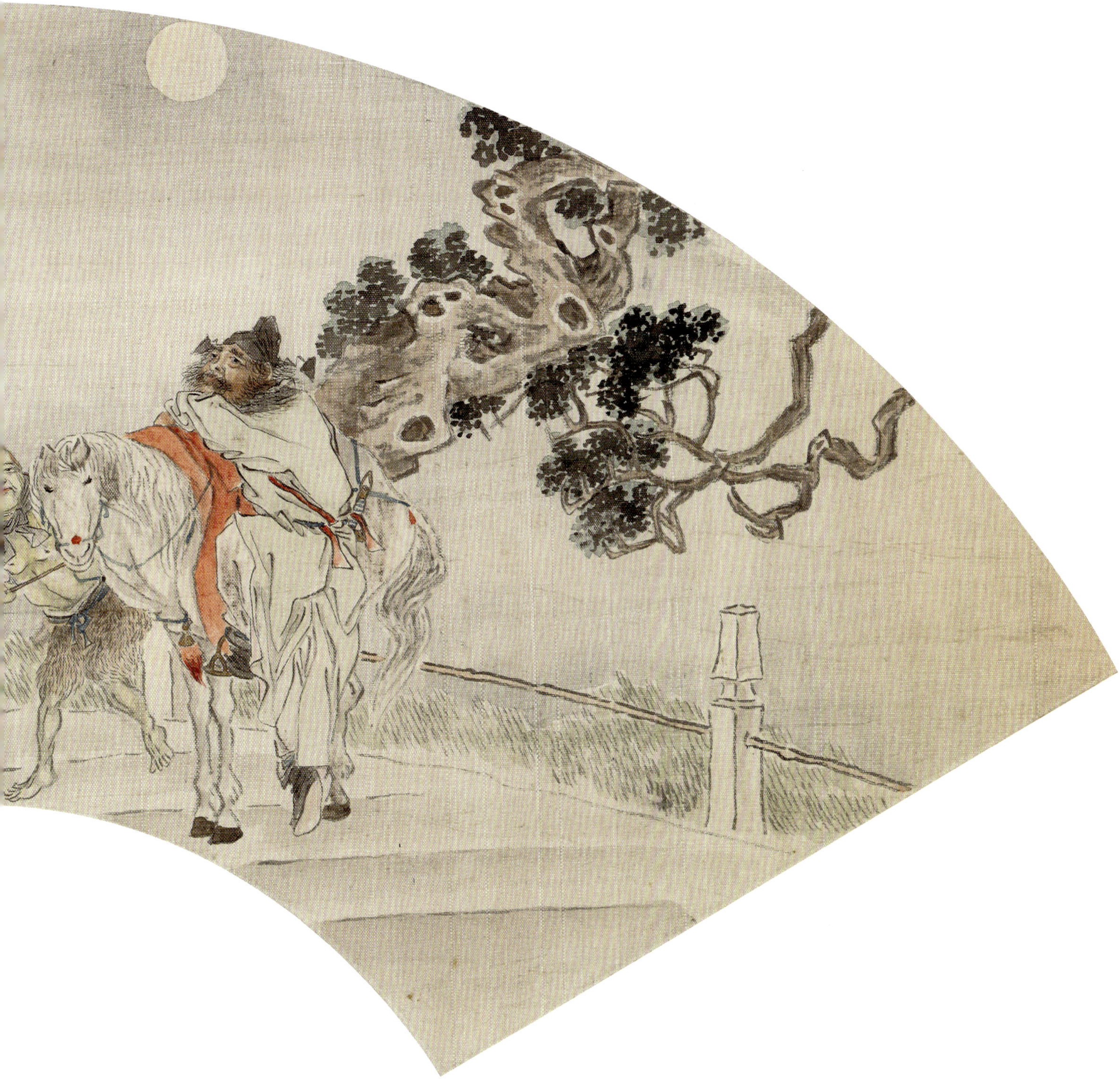

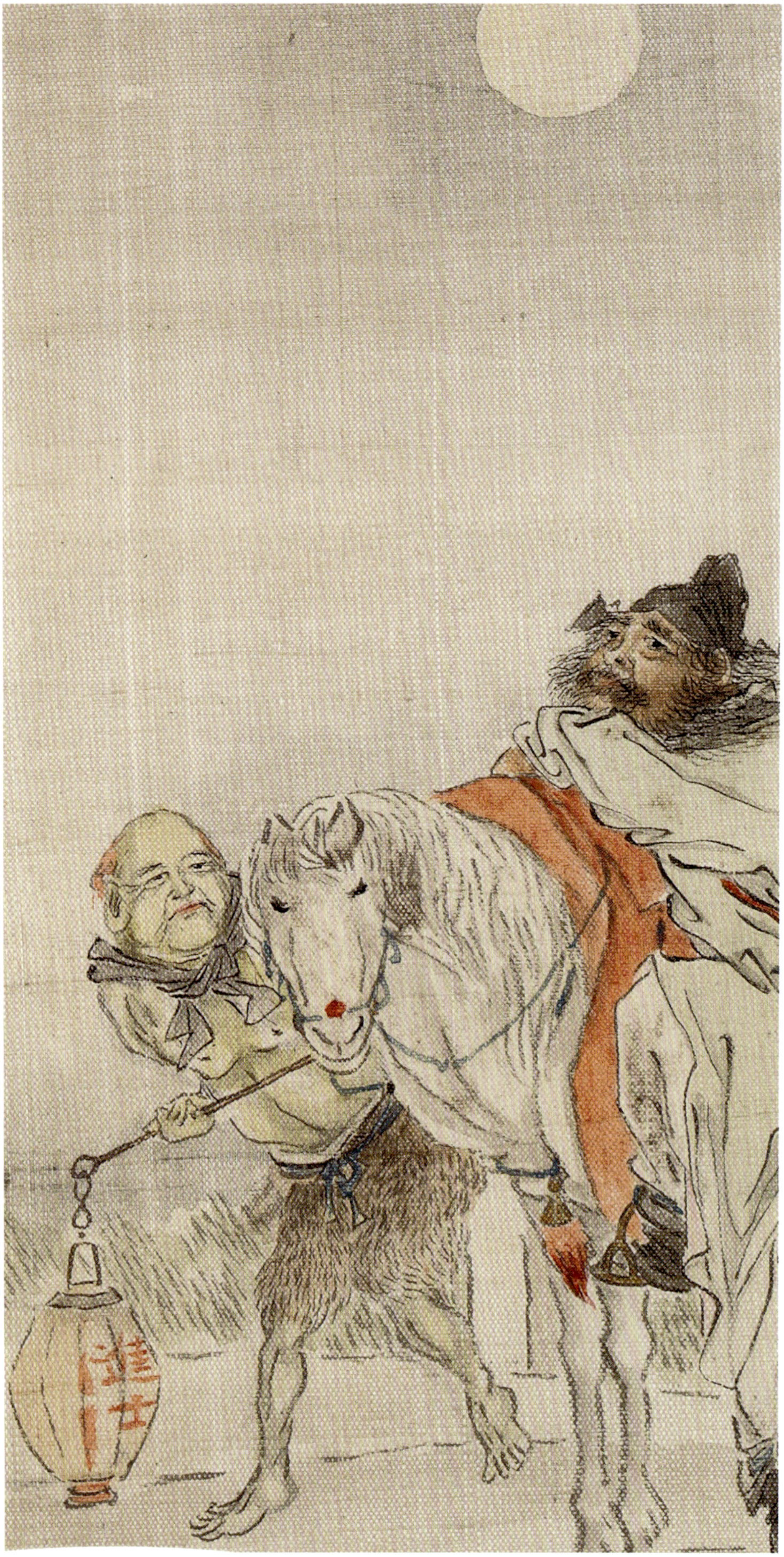

Artist:
Shen Xinhan

Medium:
Color on silk, Fan-shaped

Dimensions:
18 cm × 53 cm

Zhong Kui Returning from the Night Banquet

Inscription:
Embracing the brushwork of Wu Daozi, this piece was created by Shen Zhaohan, Xinhai.

Seal:
The seal of Xinhai

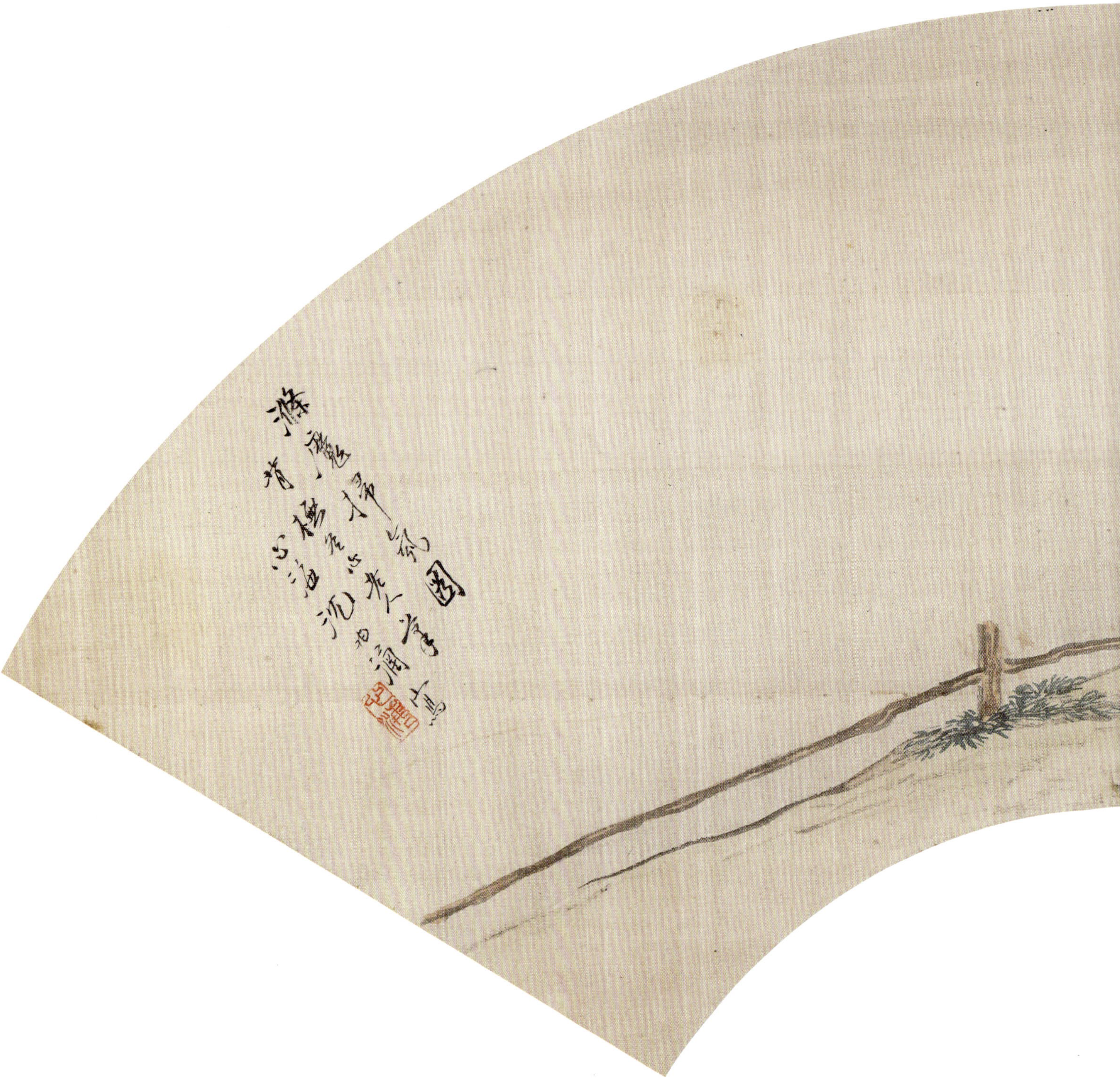

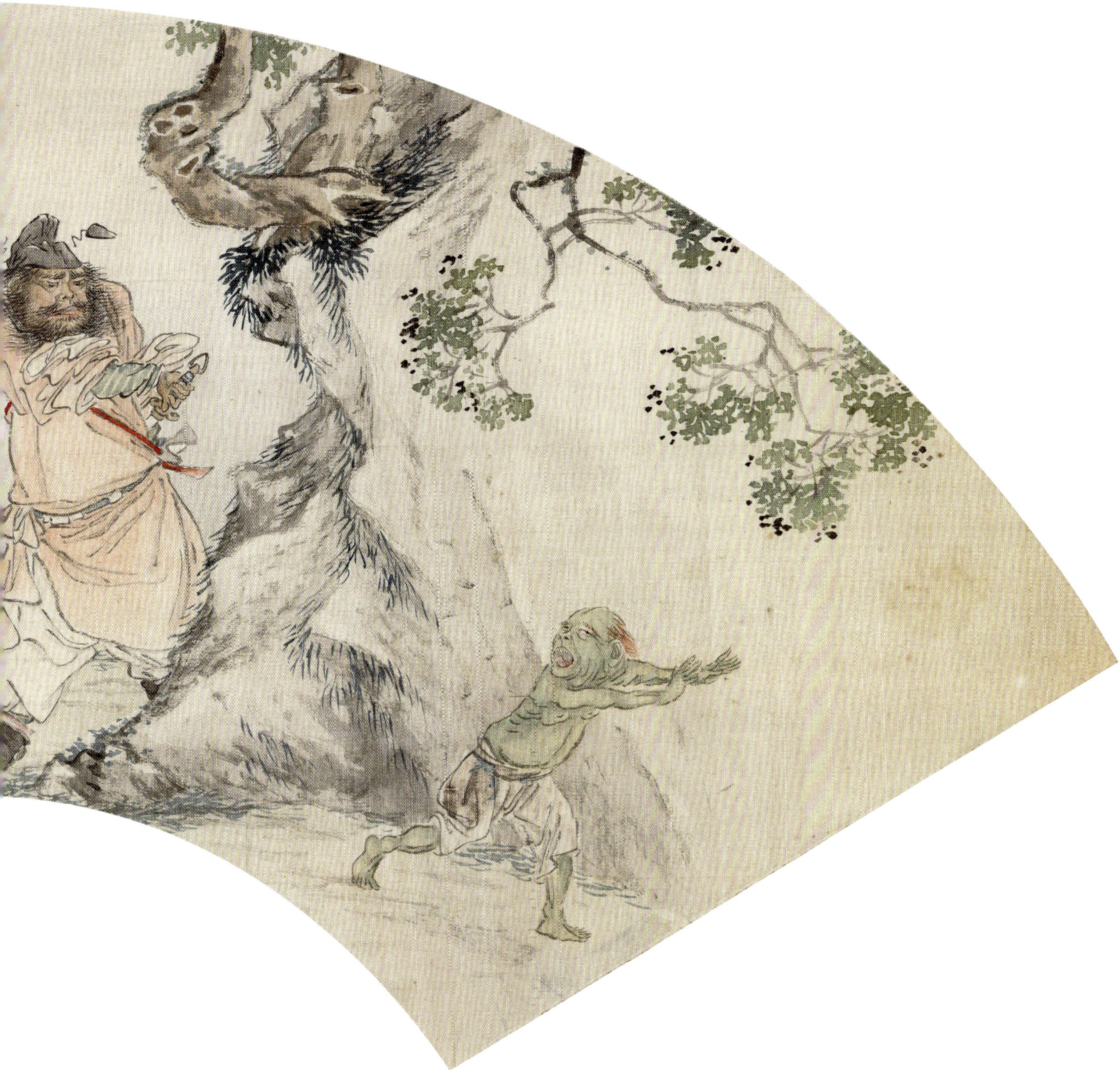

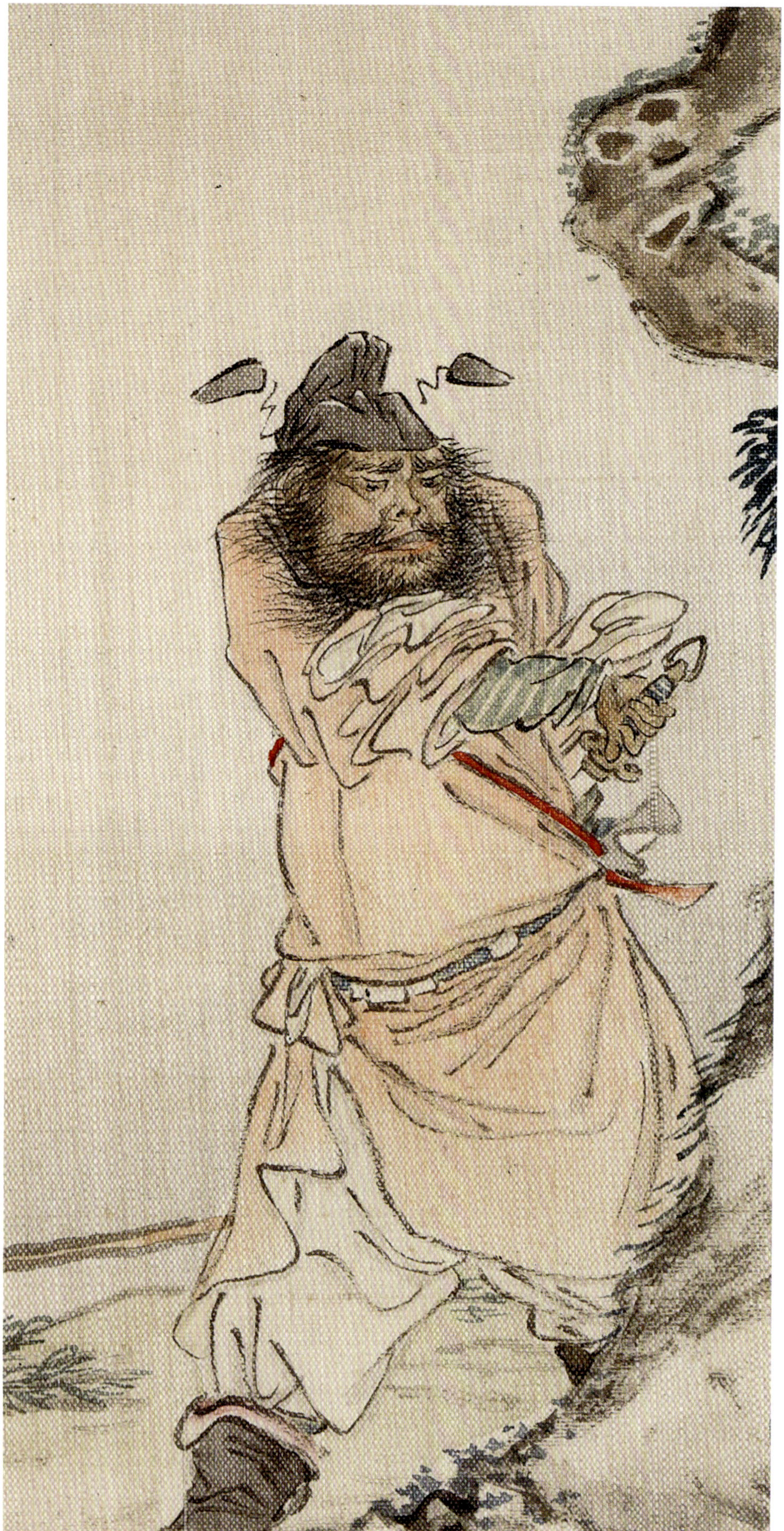

Artist:
Shen Xinhan

Medium:
Color on silk, Fan-shaped

Dimensions:
18 cm × 53 cm

Expelling Evil and Cleansing Aura

Inscription:
Embracing the brushwork of old master Dongxin, this piece was created by Shen Zhaohan, Xinhai.

Seal:
The seal of Xinhai

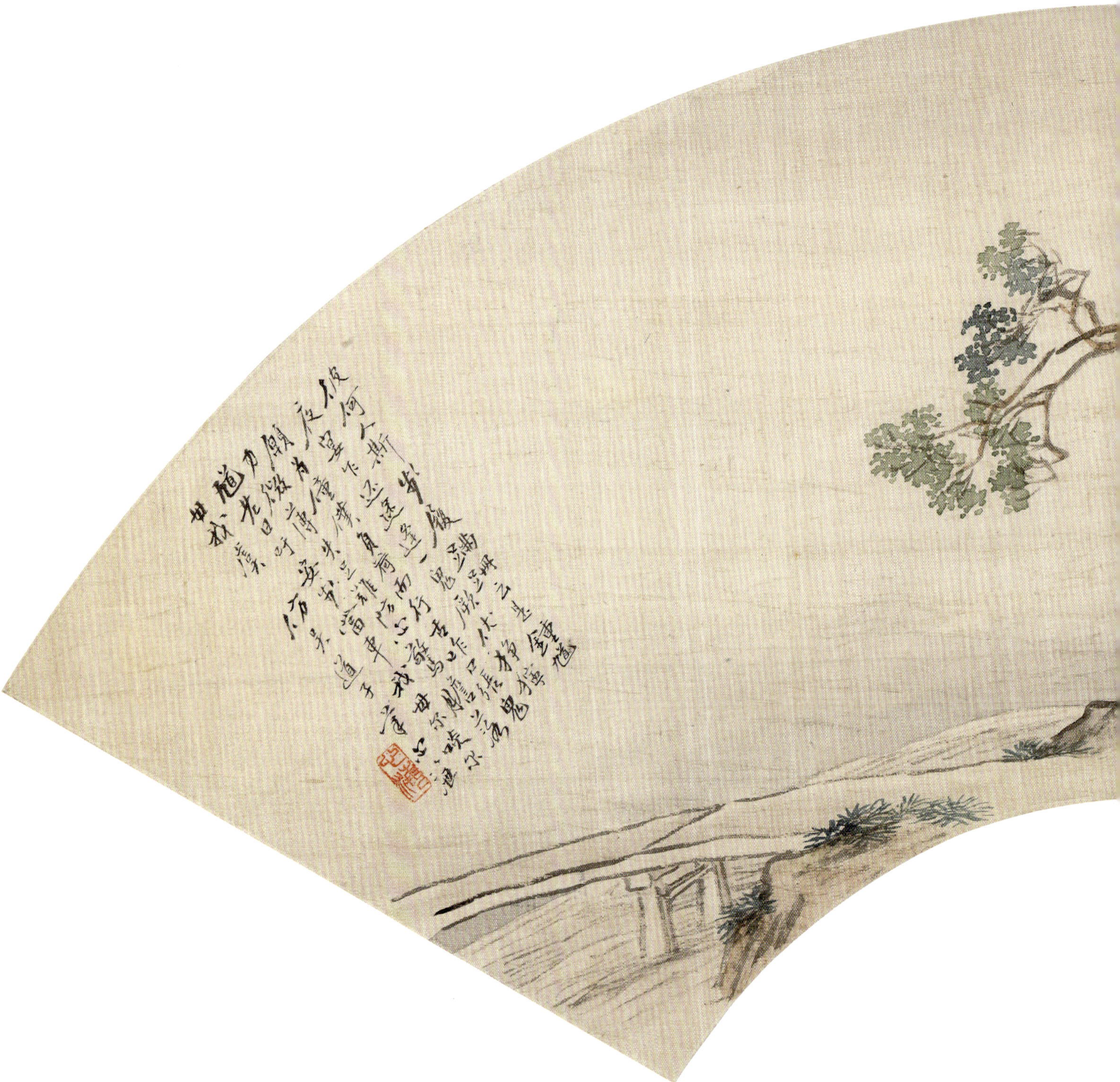

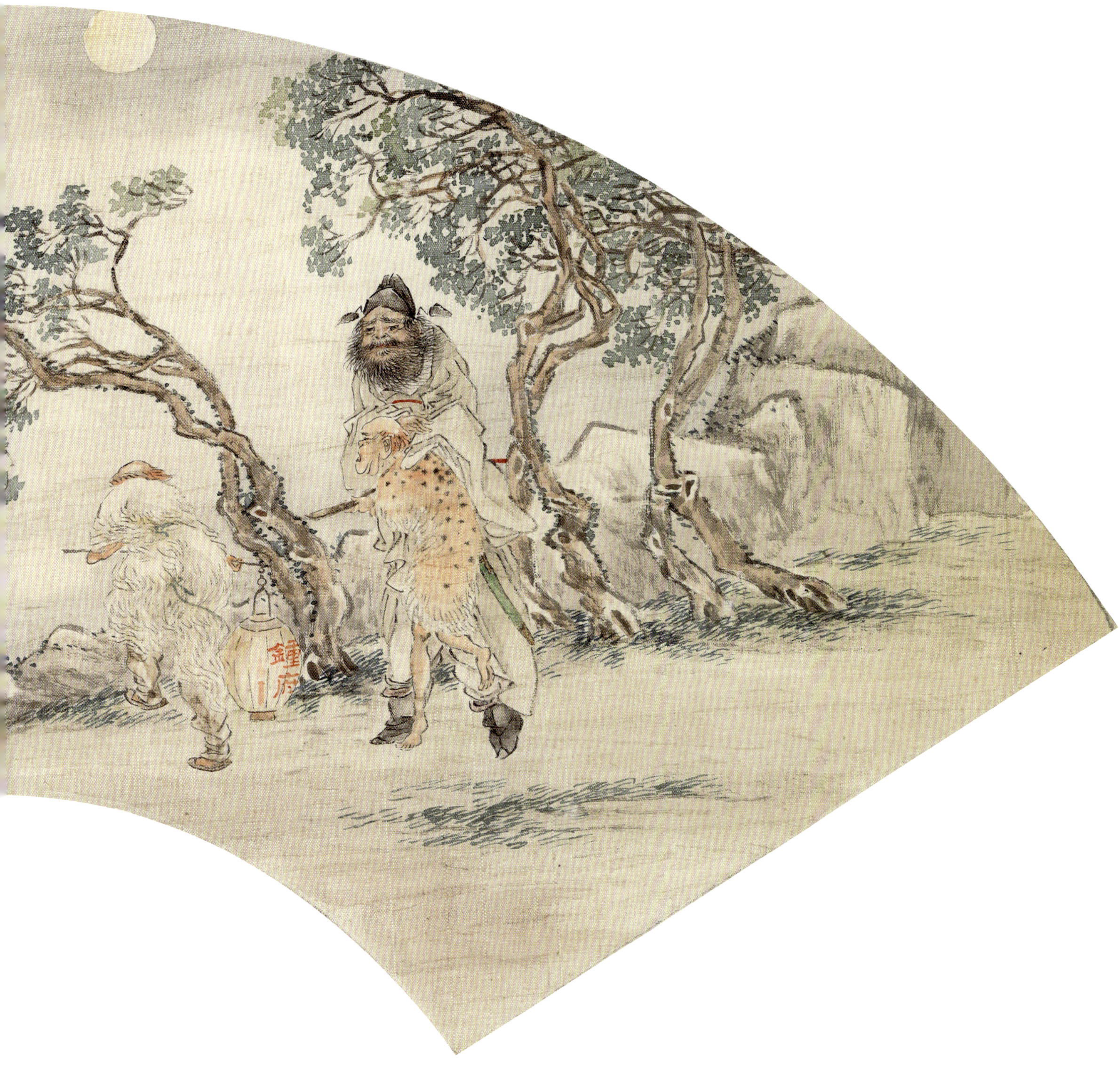
鍾府

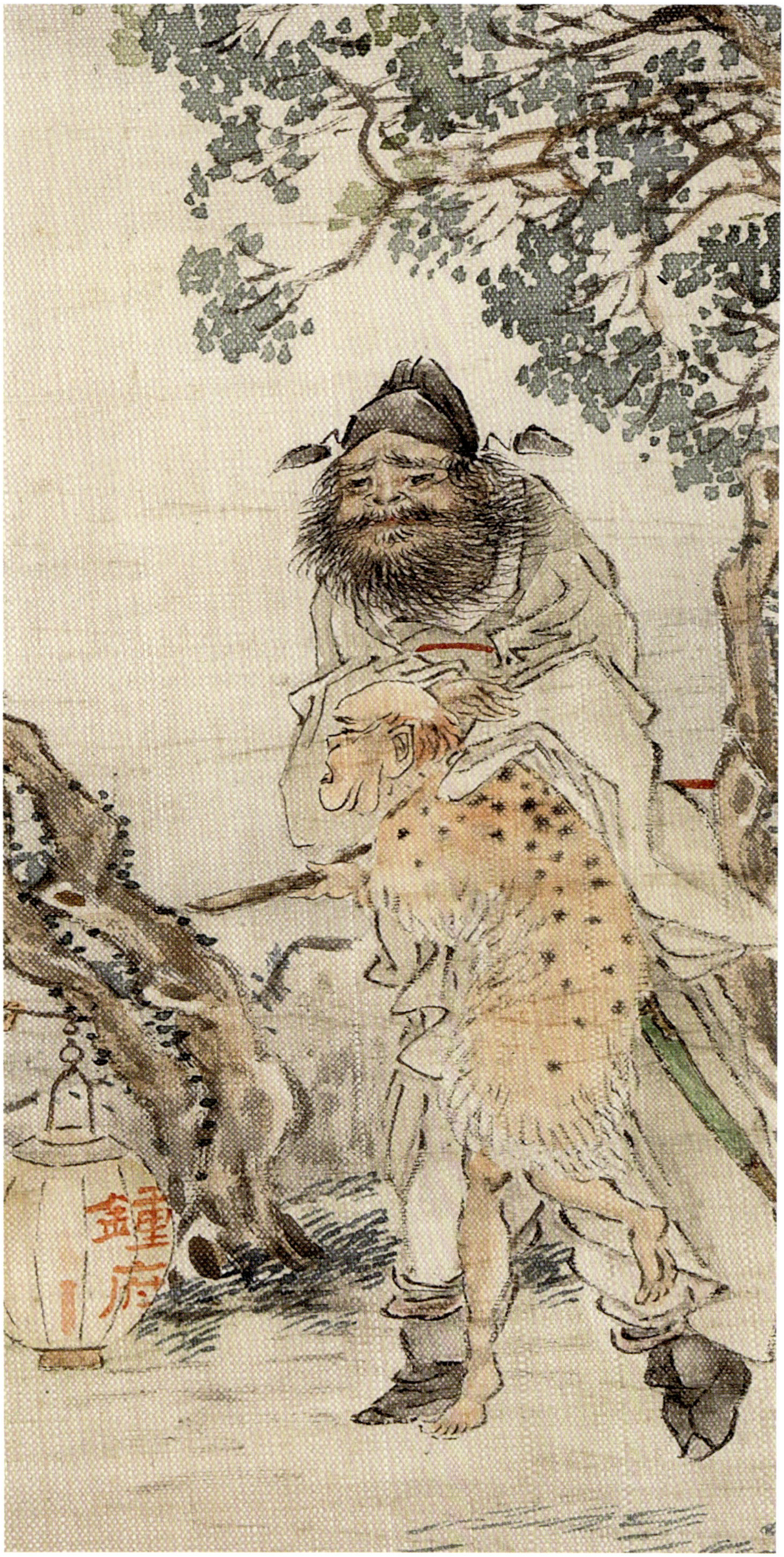
鍾府

Artist:
Shen Xinhan

Medium:
Color on silk, Fan-shaped

Dimensions:
18 cm × 54 cm

Return from the Night Banquet

Inscription:
Imitating the brushwork of Wu Daozi, by Xinhai.
Who is this man, staggering in gait?
'Tis Zhong Kui, from a feast returns late.
On his way, a ghoul he meets, fierce in its sprawl,
Pleads to be his servant, to carry and haul.
With lolling tongue and gaping maw,
The ghost's strength scarce, full of flaw.
A misstep looms, hard to fend,
Heart races, courage tends to bend.
The aged Kui sighs with the sun's fall,
Wishing for a walk tranquil as a carriage's crawl.
"I'll not feast on thee," he avows,
"Nor need you fear my vows."

Seal:
Xinhai

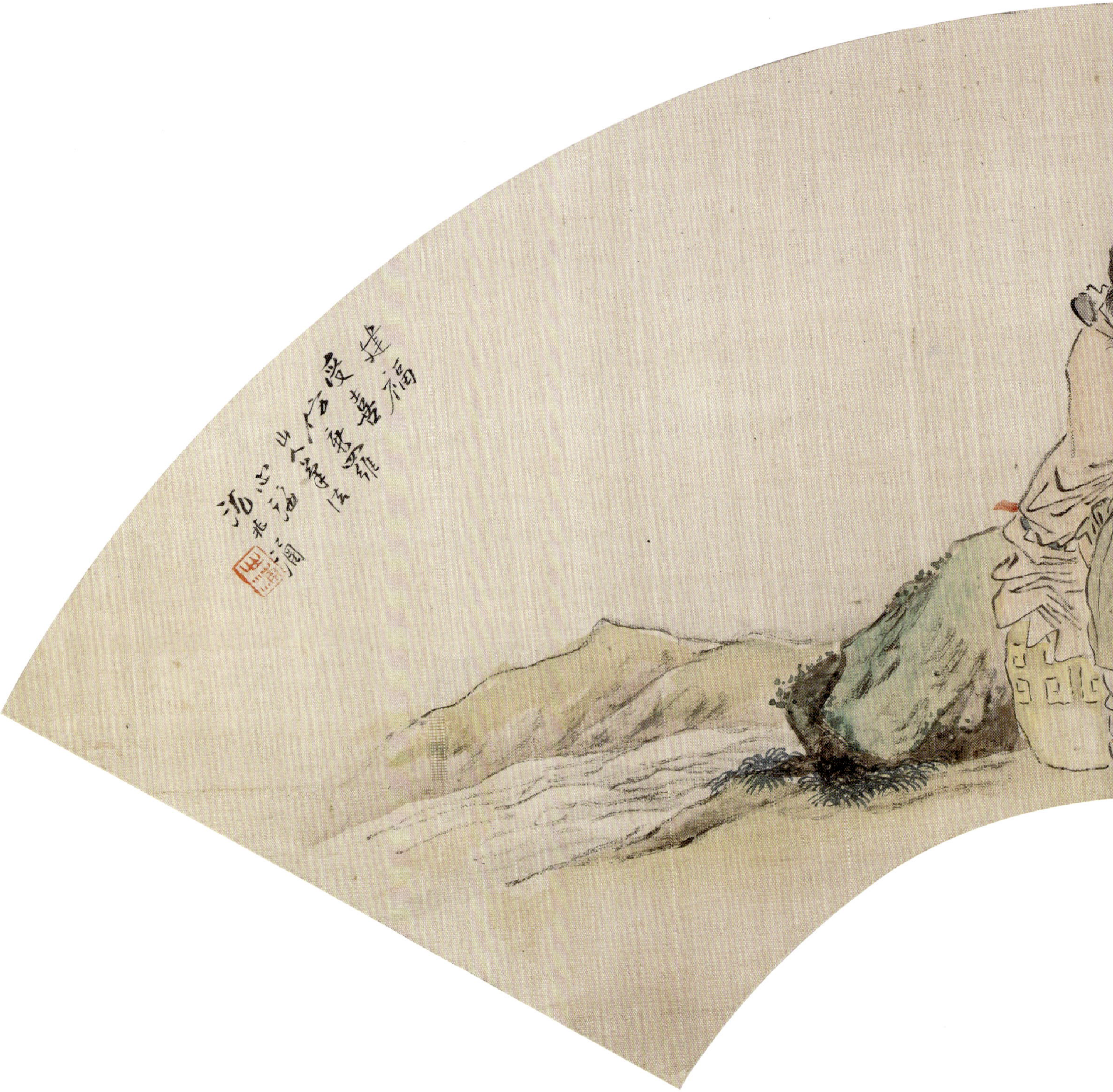

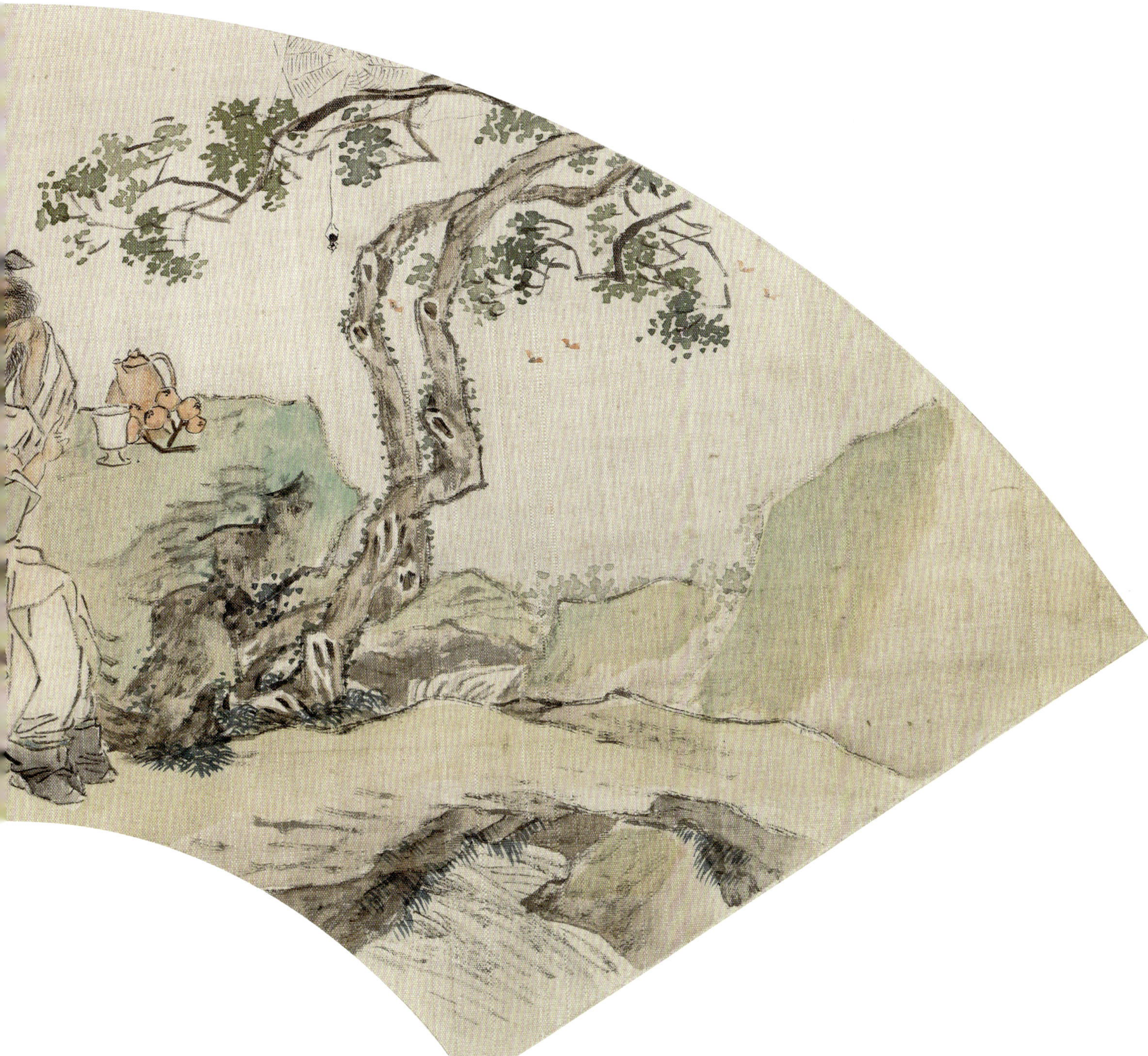

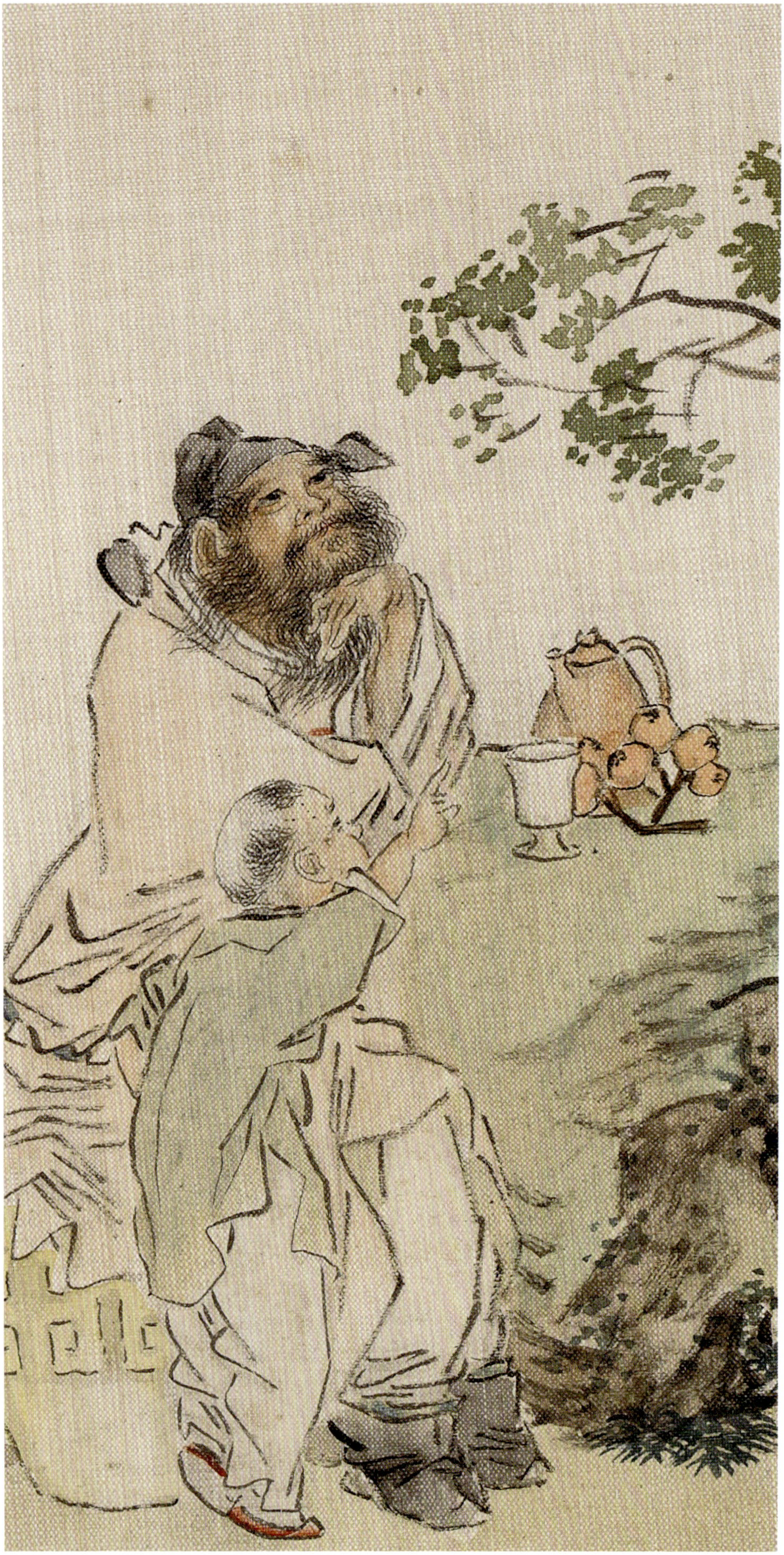

Artist:
Shen Xinhan

Medium:
Color on silk, Fan-shaped

Dimensions:
18 cm × 53 cm

Building Happiness and Receiving Joy

Inscription:
Building Happiness and Receiving Joy. In the style of the hermit of Xinluo mountain, inscribed by Xinhai, Shen Zhaohan.

Seal:
Xinhai

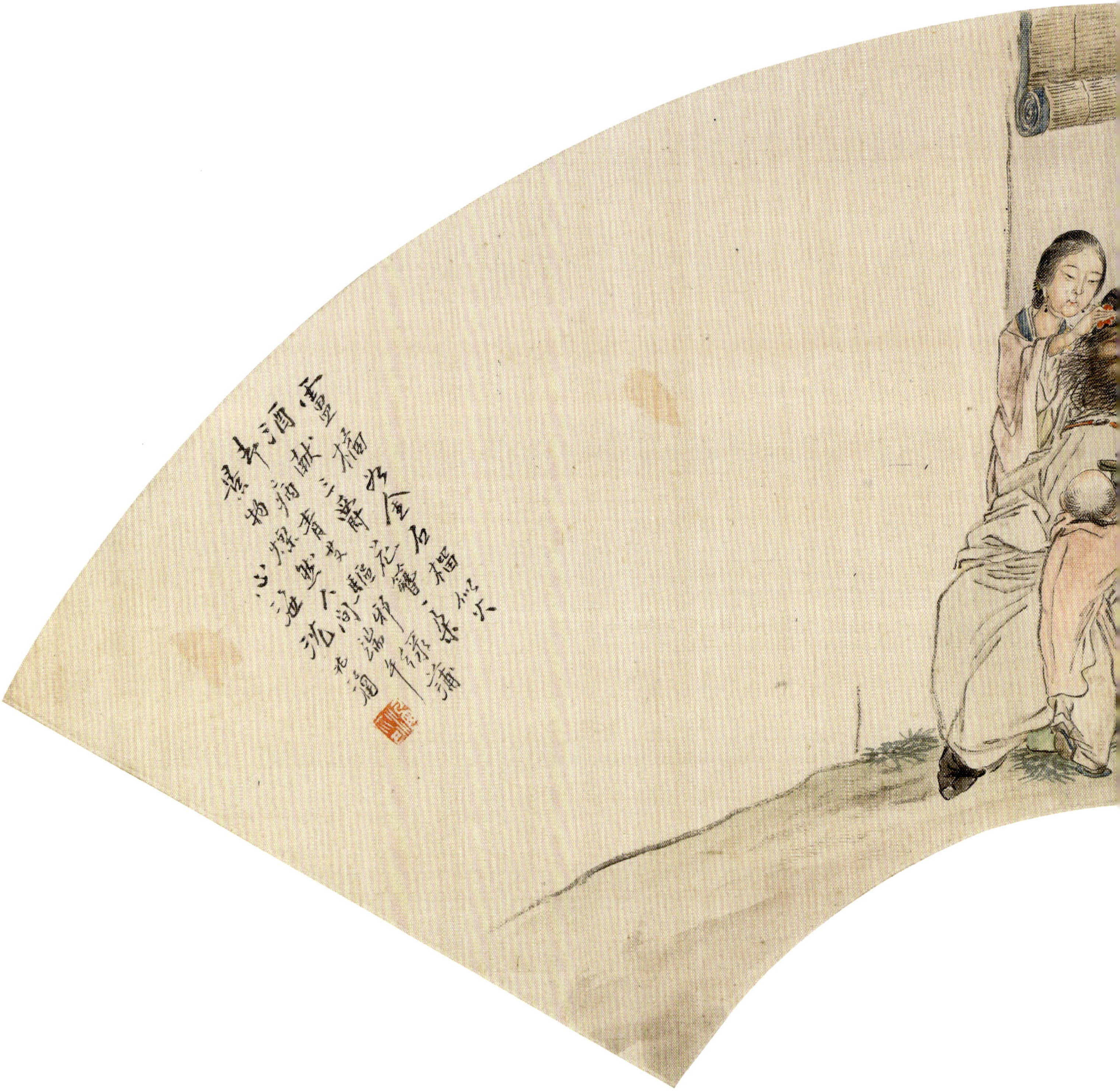

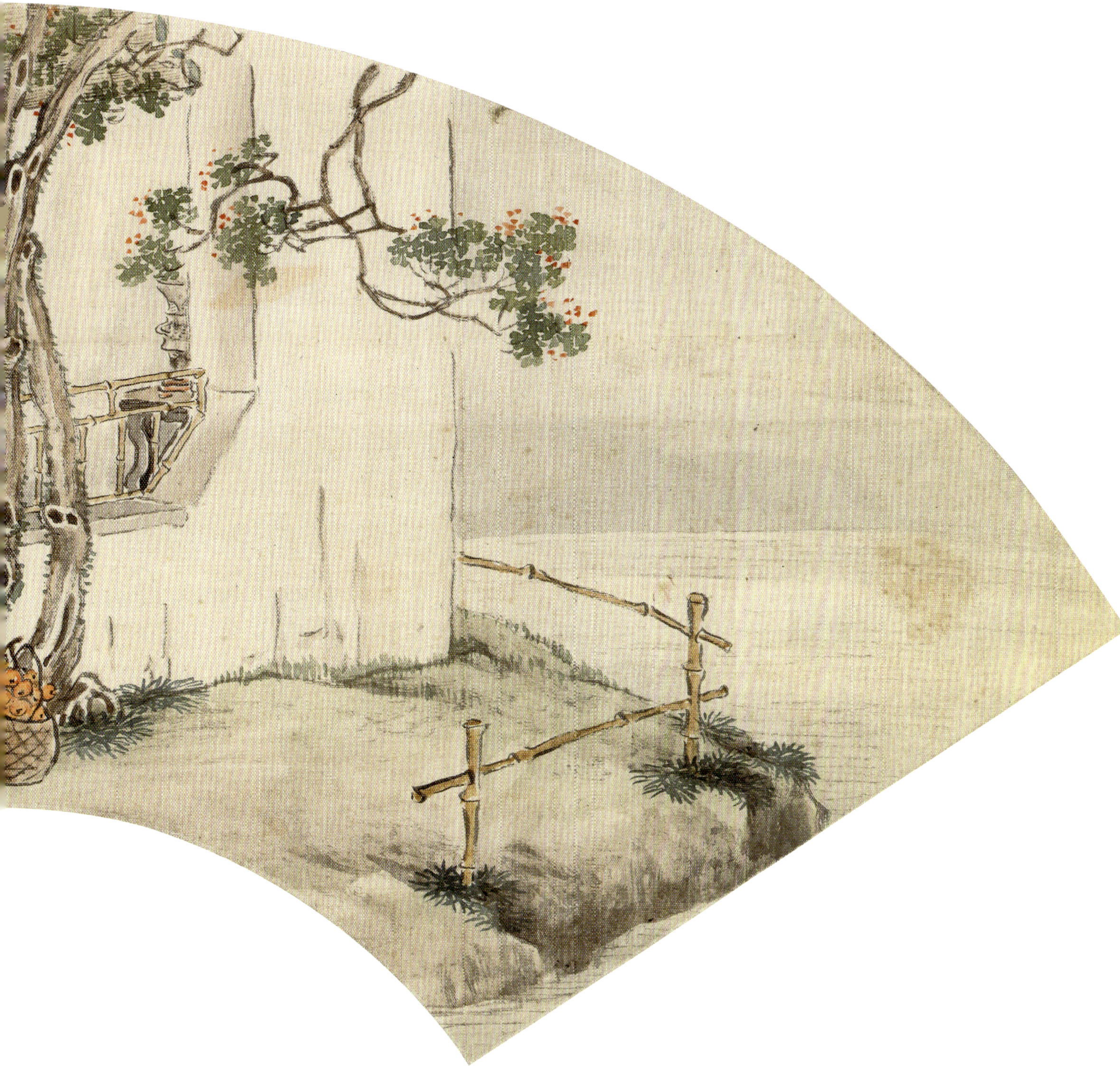

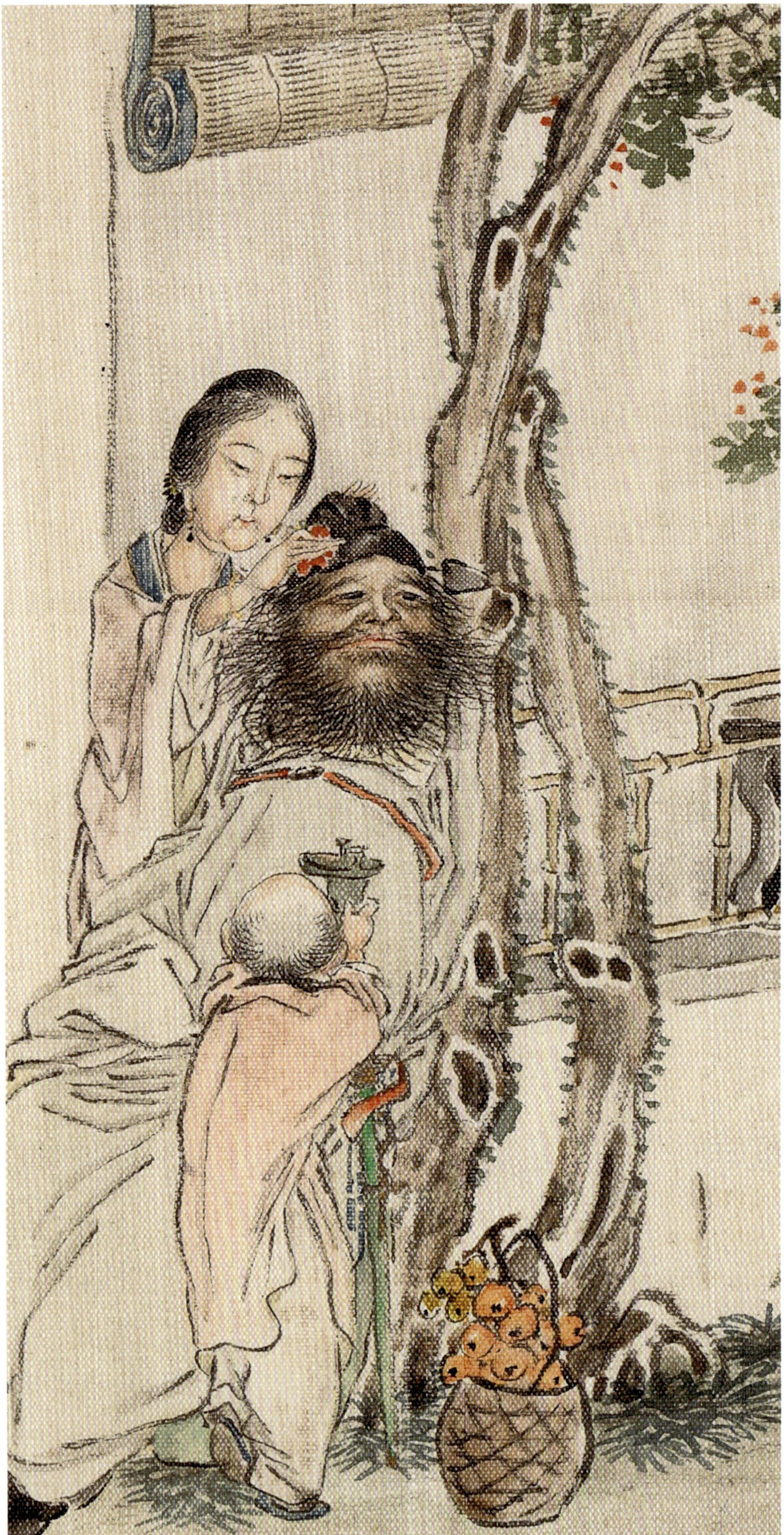

Artist:
Shen Xinhan

Medium:
Color on silk, Fan-shaped

Dimensions:
18 cm × 53 cm

Zhong Kui with a Flower in His Hair

Inscription:
Oranges glow like glinting gold, pomegranates blaze as fire.
Three rounds of wine we offer, a single bloom in hair's attire.
Warding off illness with blue mugwort, expelling evil with green reed,
Splendor abounds all around, Dragon Boat Festival agreed.

Seal:
The seal of Xinhai

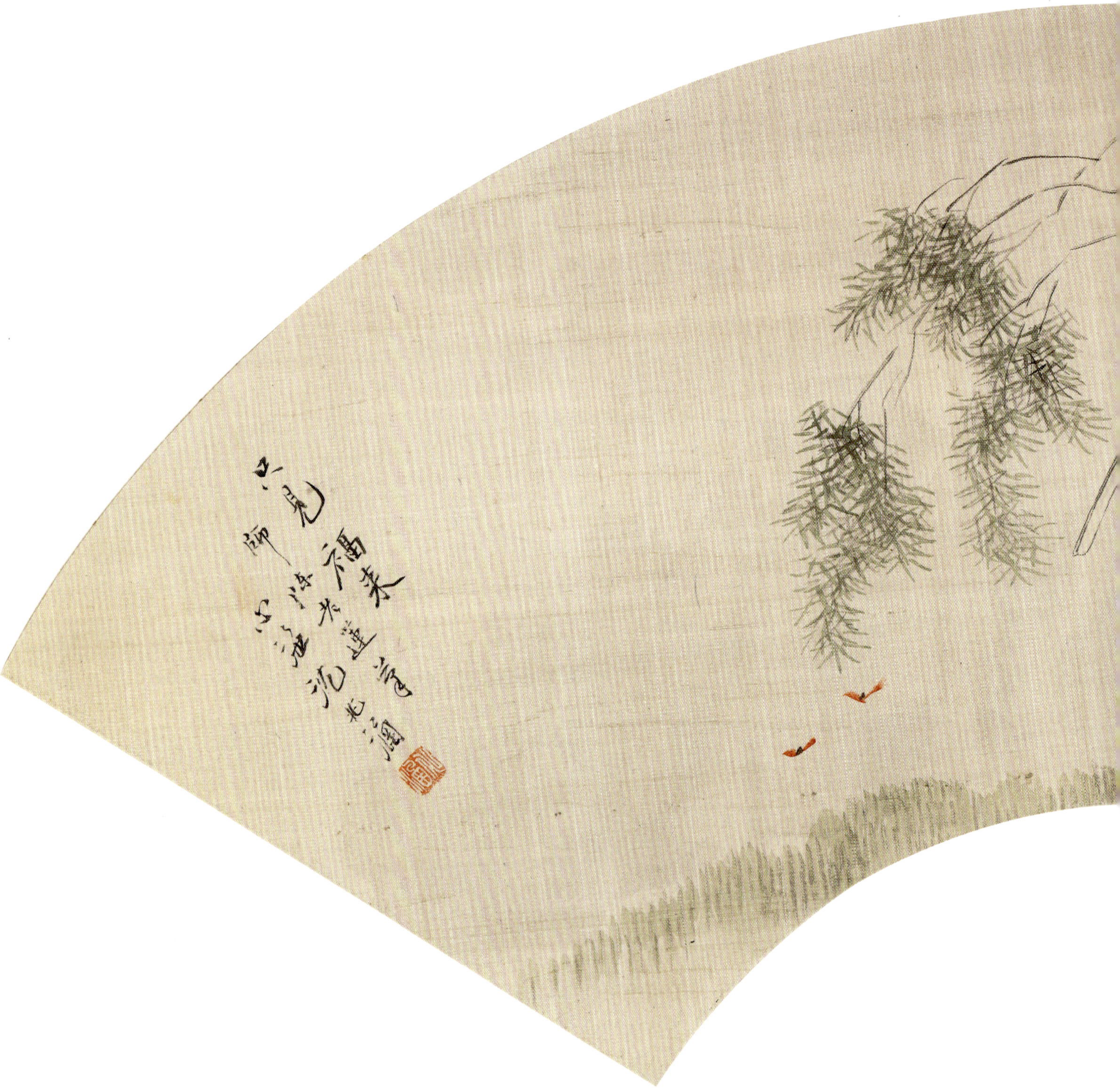

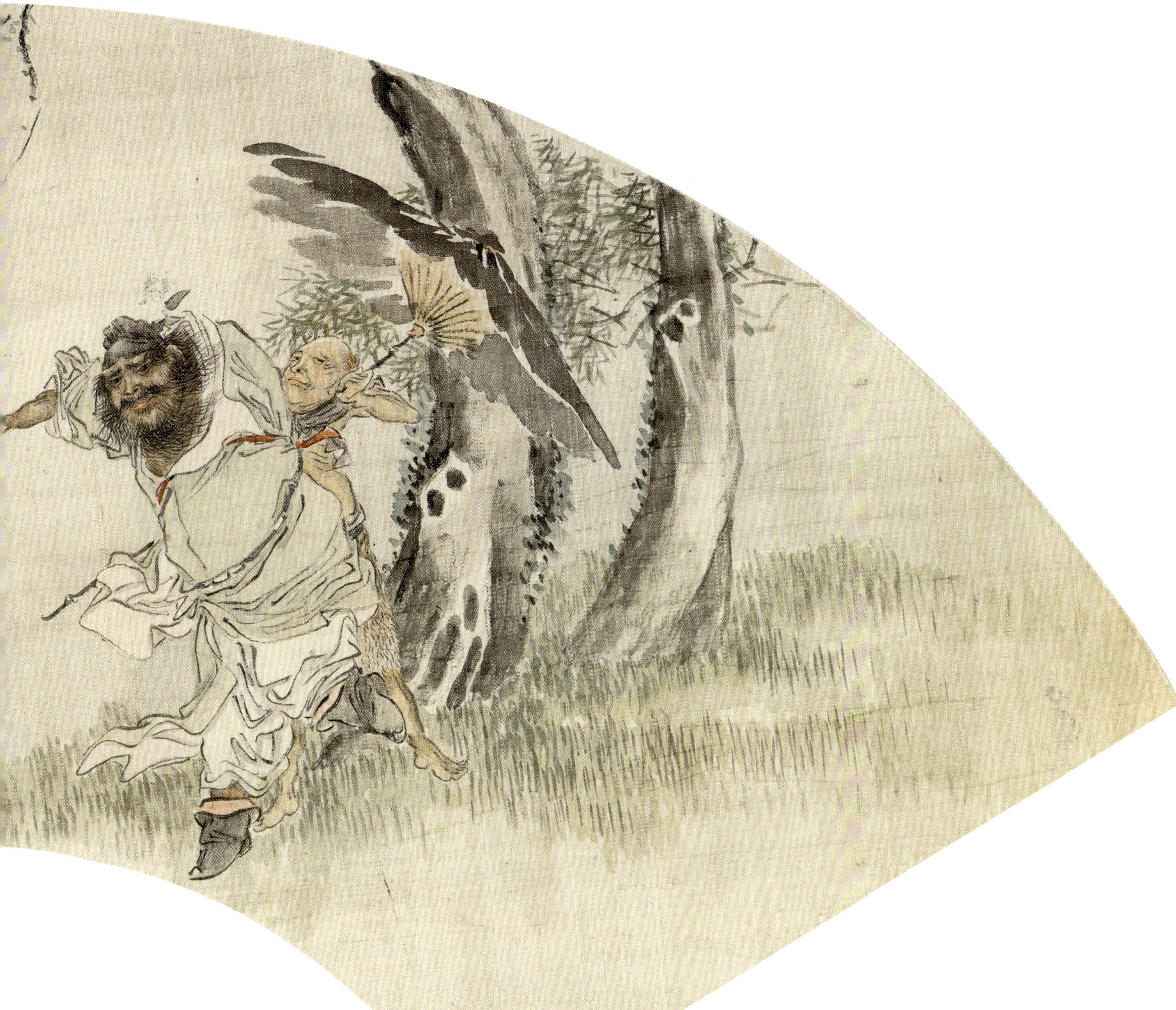

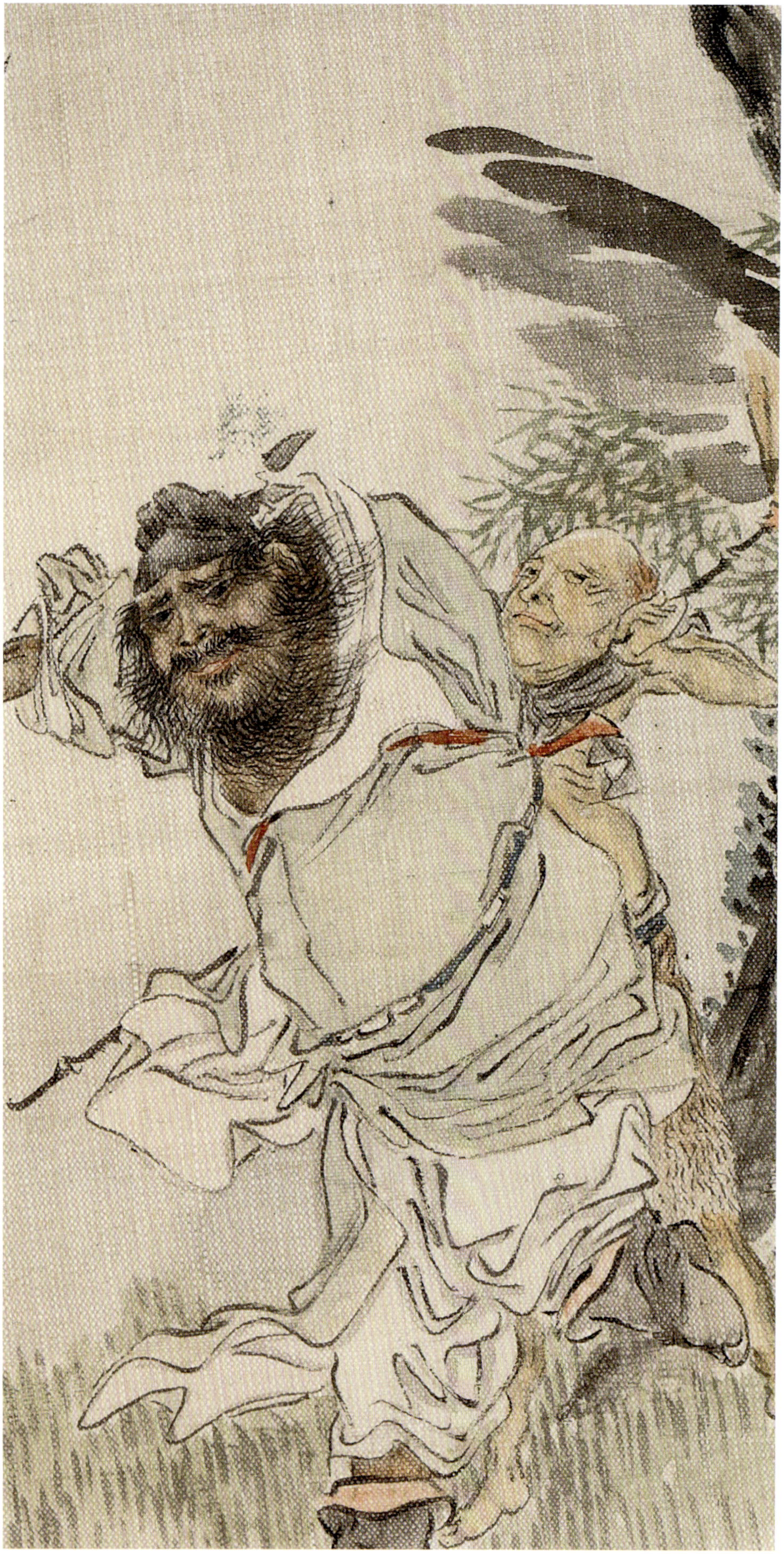

Artist:
Shen Xinhan

Medium:
Color on silk, Fan-shaped

Dimensions:
18 cm × 53 cm

Only Seeing Fortune Arrive

Inscription:
Only Seeing Fortune Arrive. Following the style of Chen Laolian. By Xinhai, Shen Zhaohan.

Seal:
Zhaohan

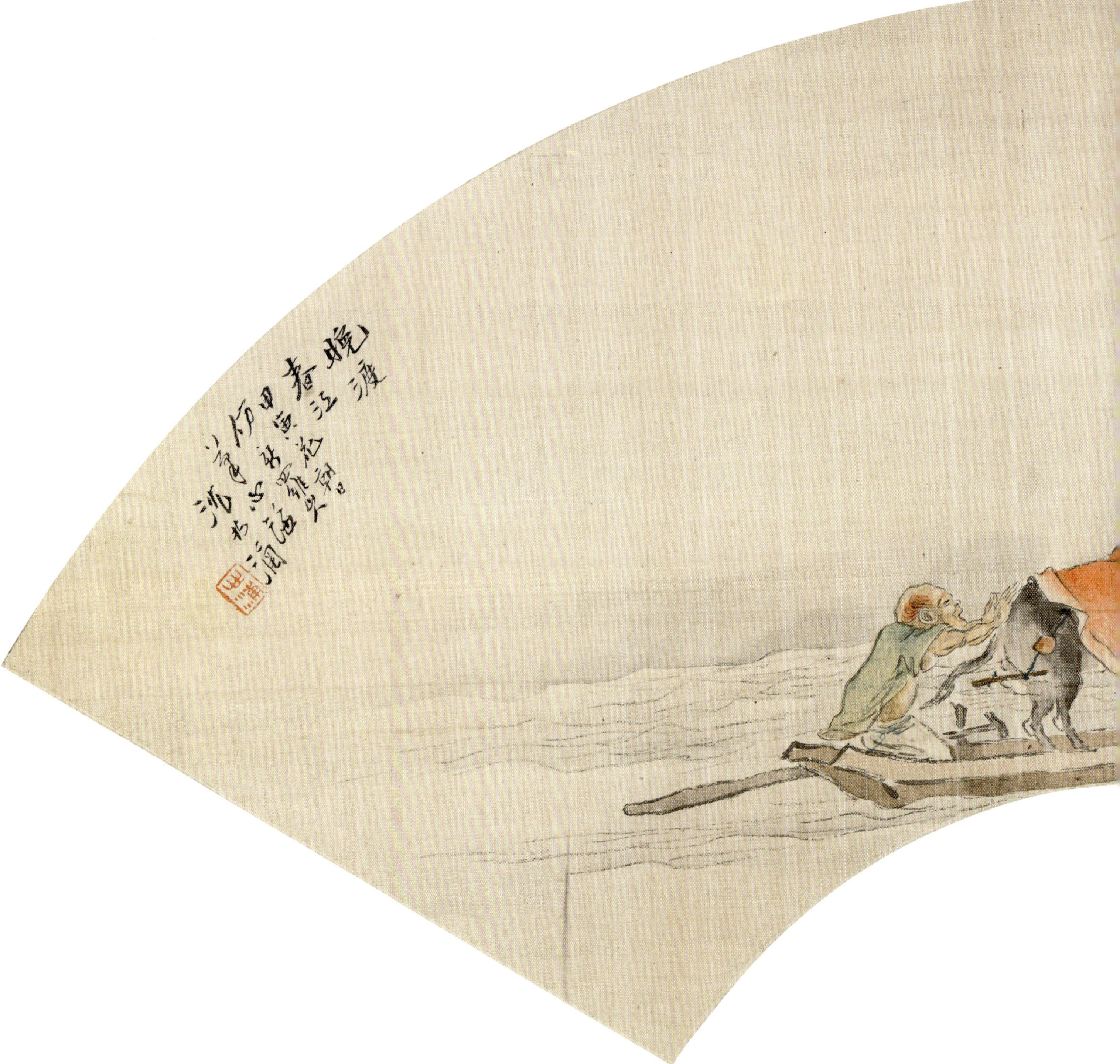
晚渡春江
甲寅花朝

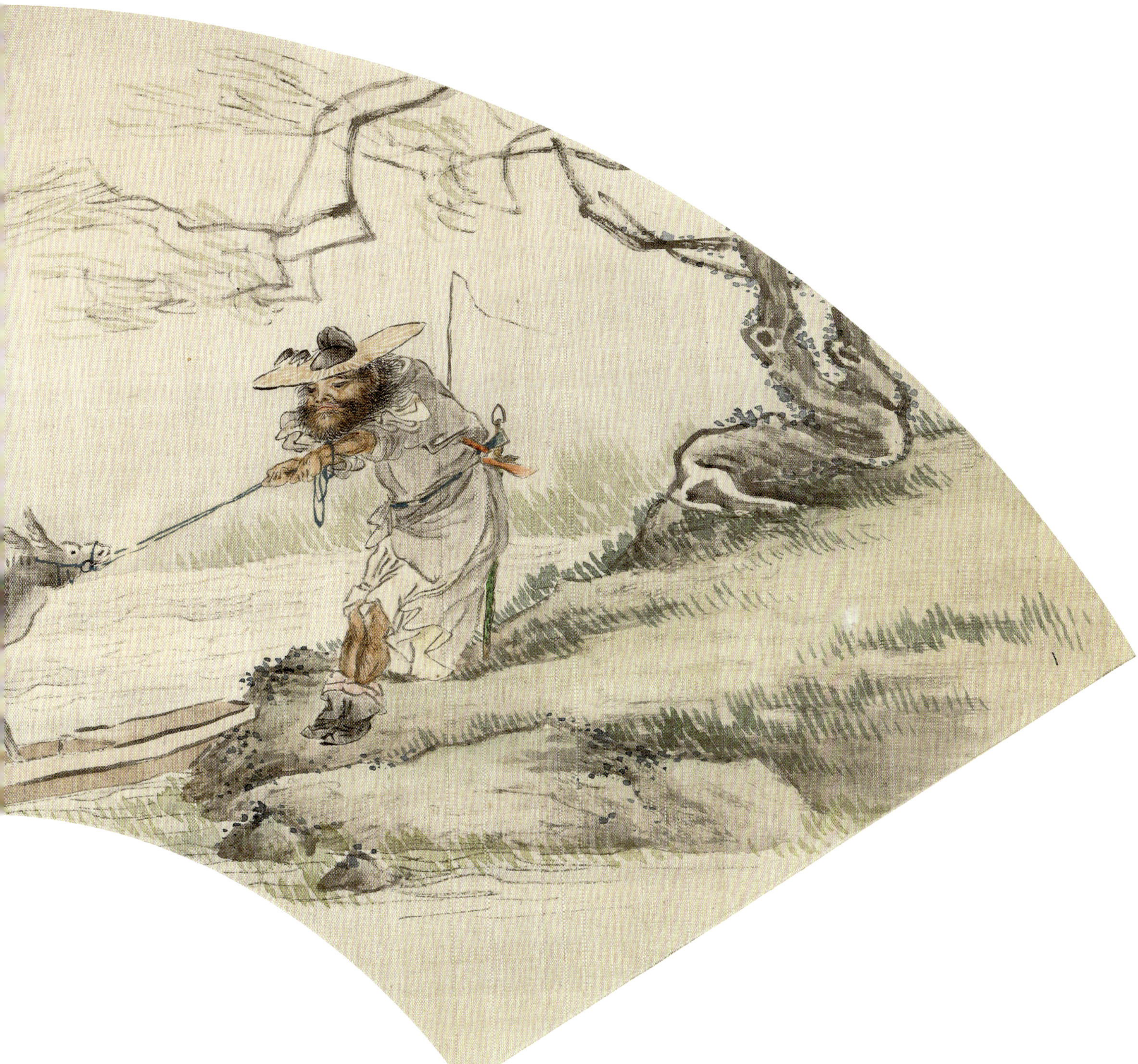

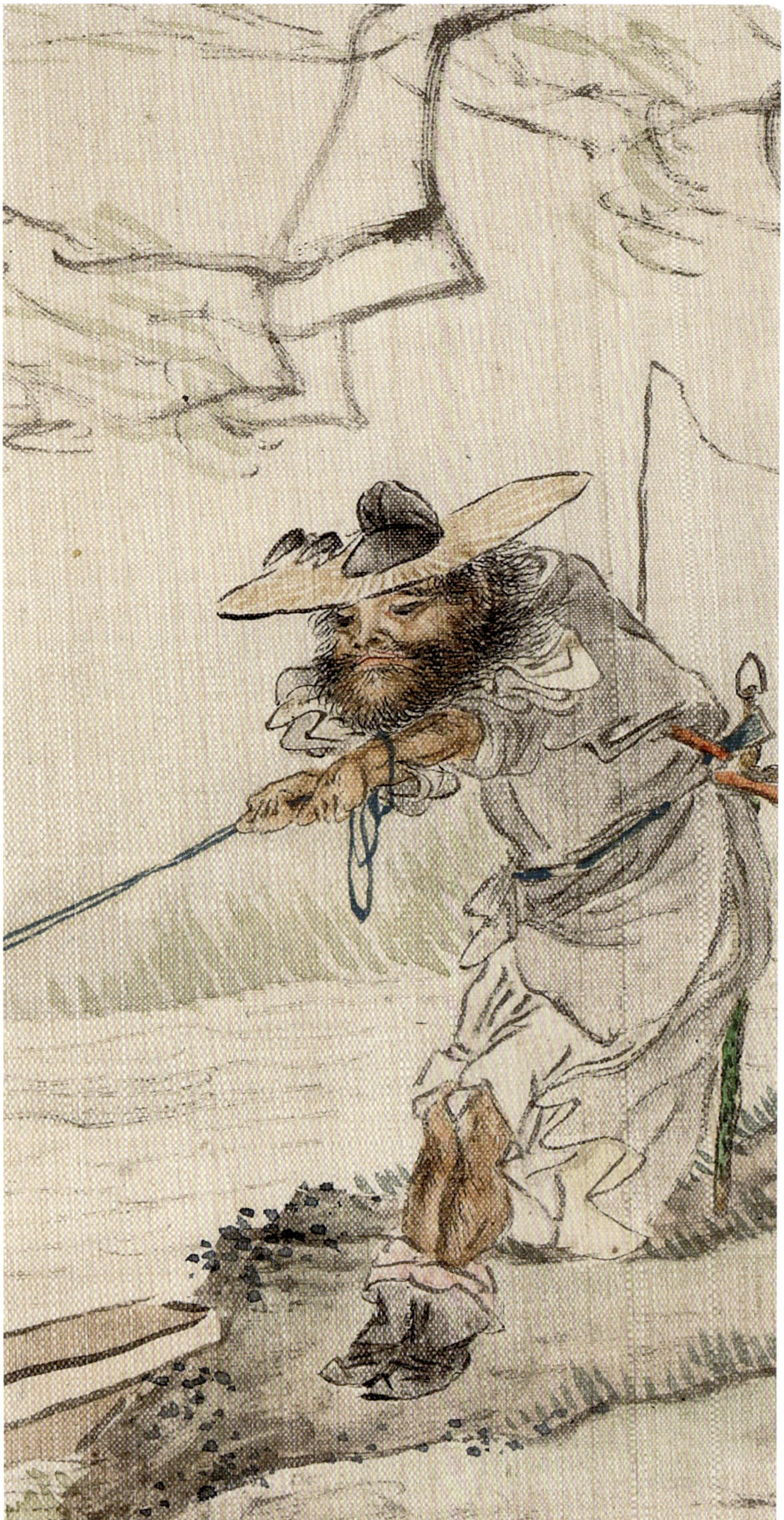

Artist:
Shen Xinhan

Medium:
Color on silk, Fan-shaped

Dimensions:
18 cm × 53.5 cm

Evening Ferry across the Spring River

Inscription:
Evening Ferry across the Spring River. On the day of the Flower Festival in the Jiayin year, imitating the brushwork of the hermit of Xinluo mountain. By Xinhai Shen Zhaohan.

Seal:
Xinhai

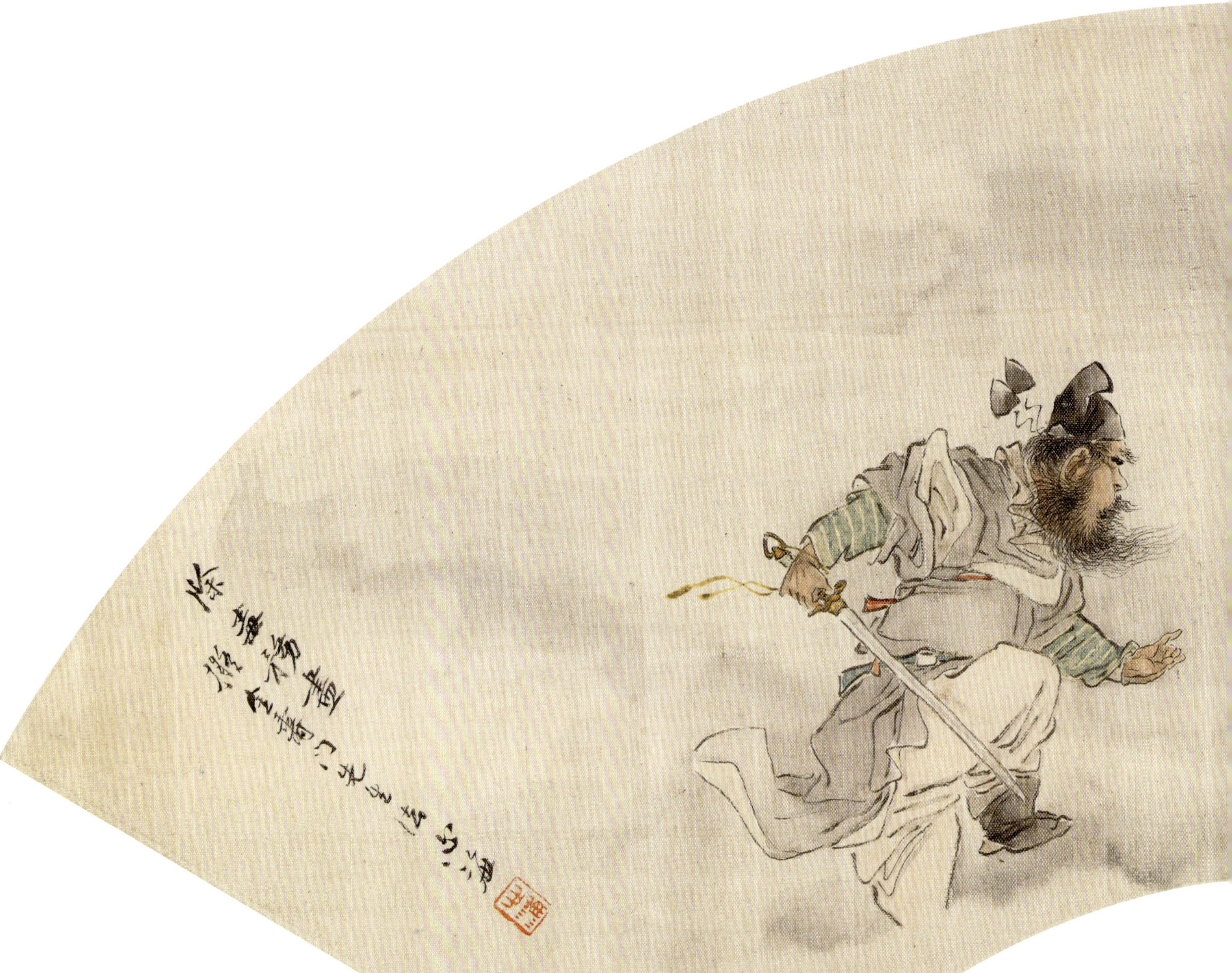

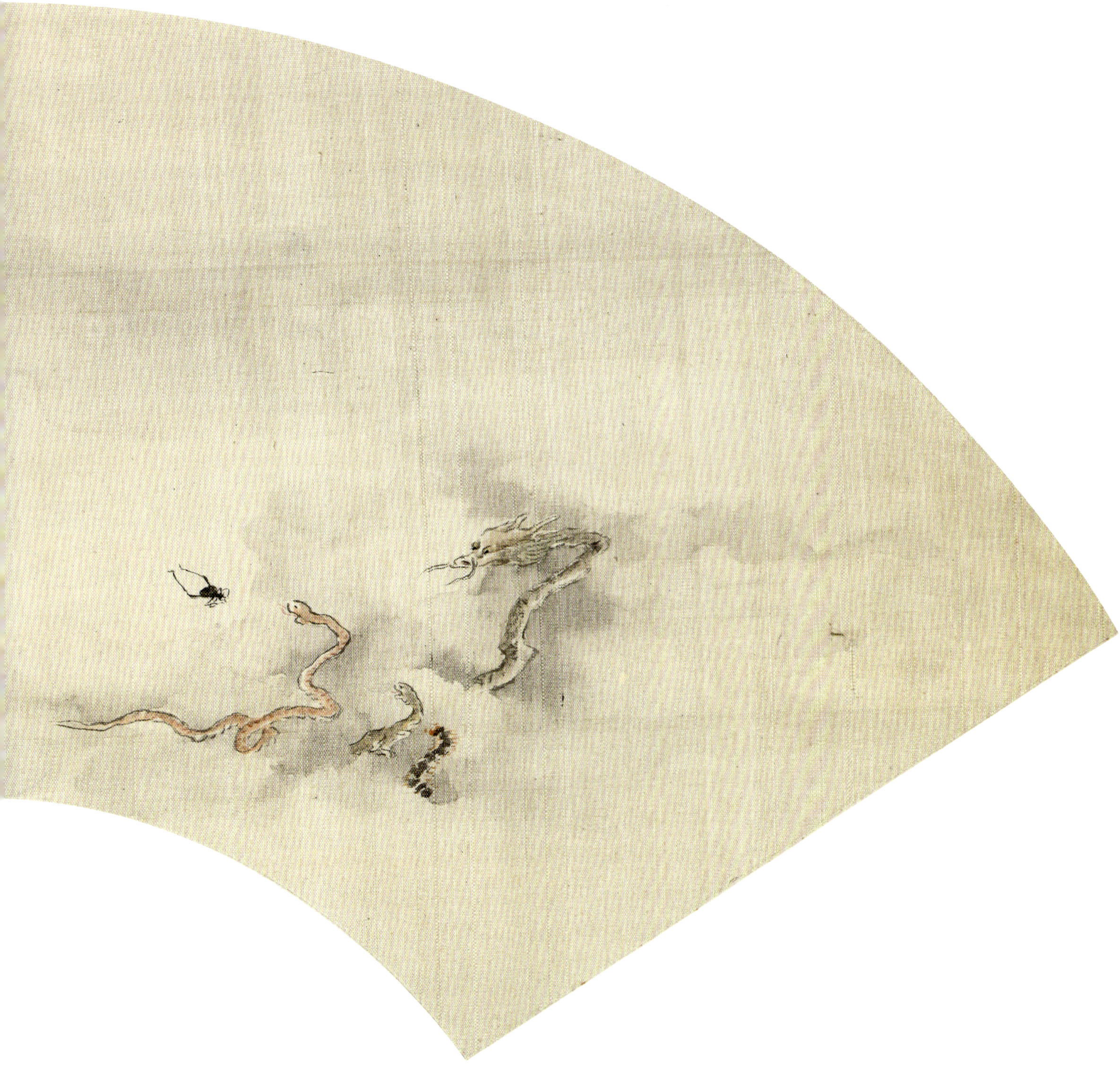

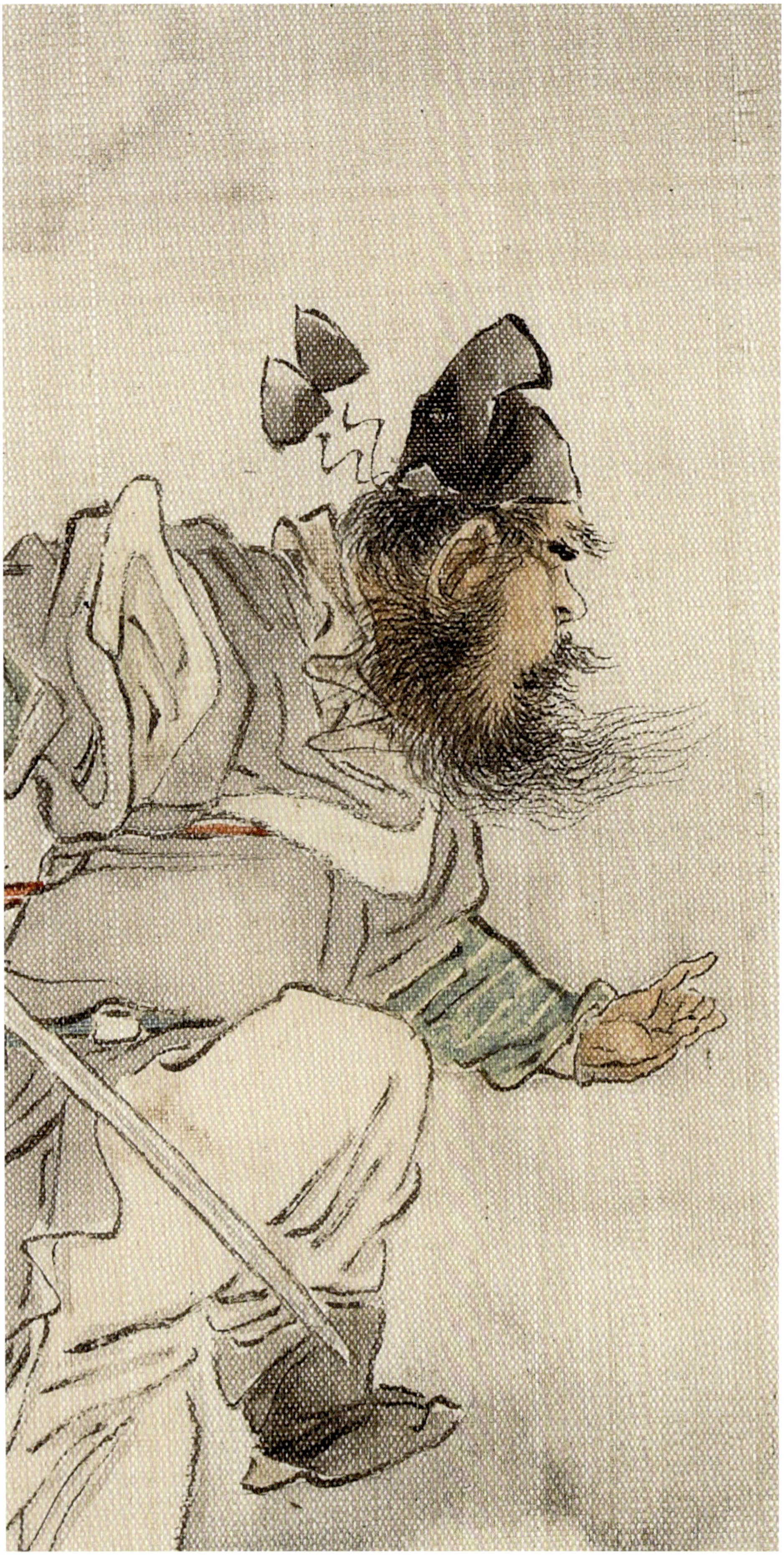

Artist:
Shen Xinhan

Medium:
Color on silk, Fan-shaped

Dimensions:
18 cm × 53 cm

Exhaustively Eliminating Toxins

Inscription:
Exhaustively Eliminating Toxins. Imitating the method of Mr. Jin Shoumen, by Xinhai.

Seal:
Xinhai

只見福來

庚申夏四月仿冬心先生雅屬 心海沈兆涵時年八十有四

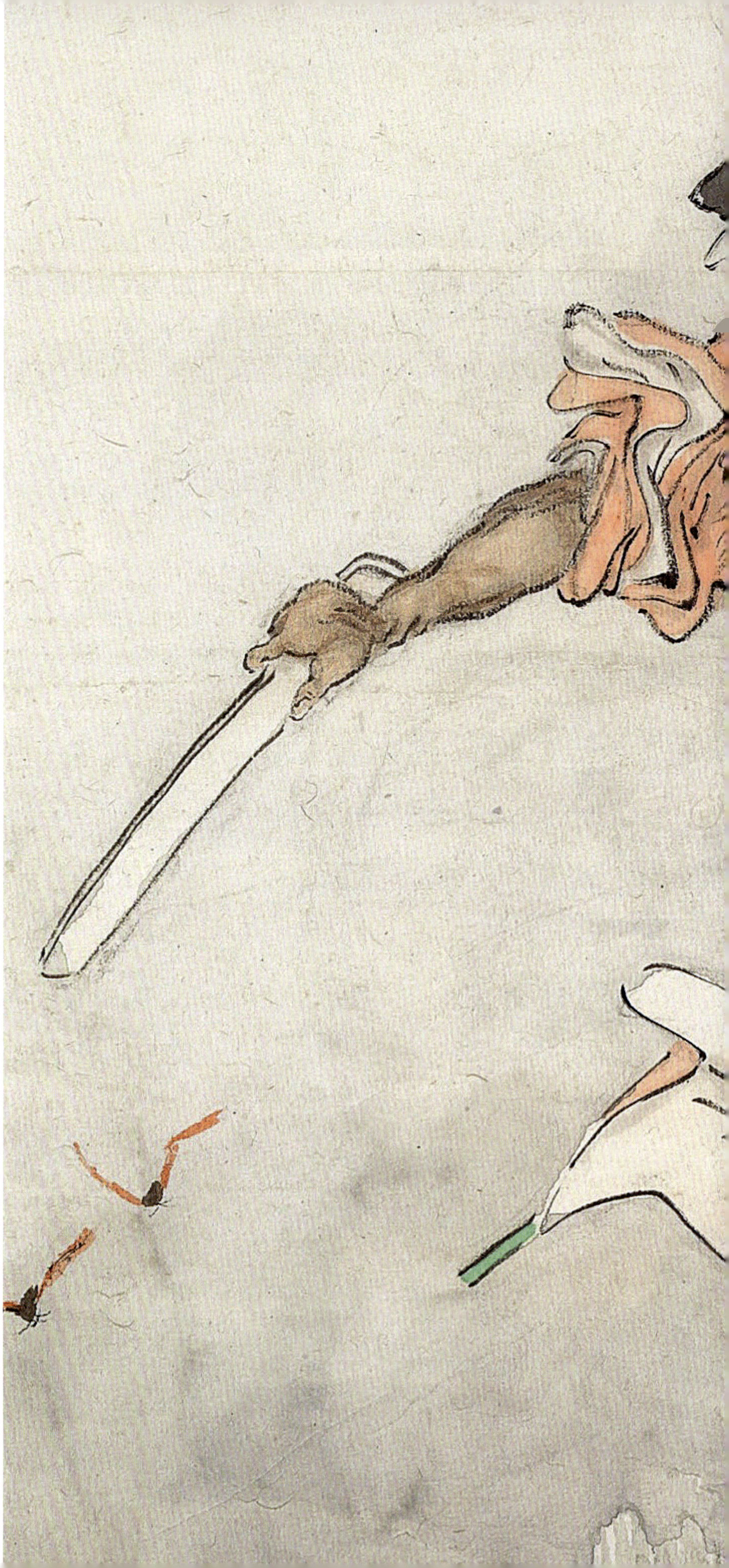

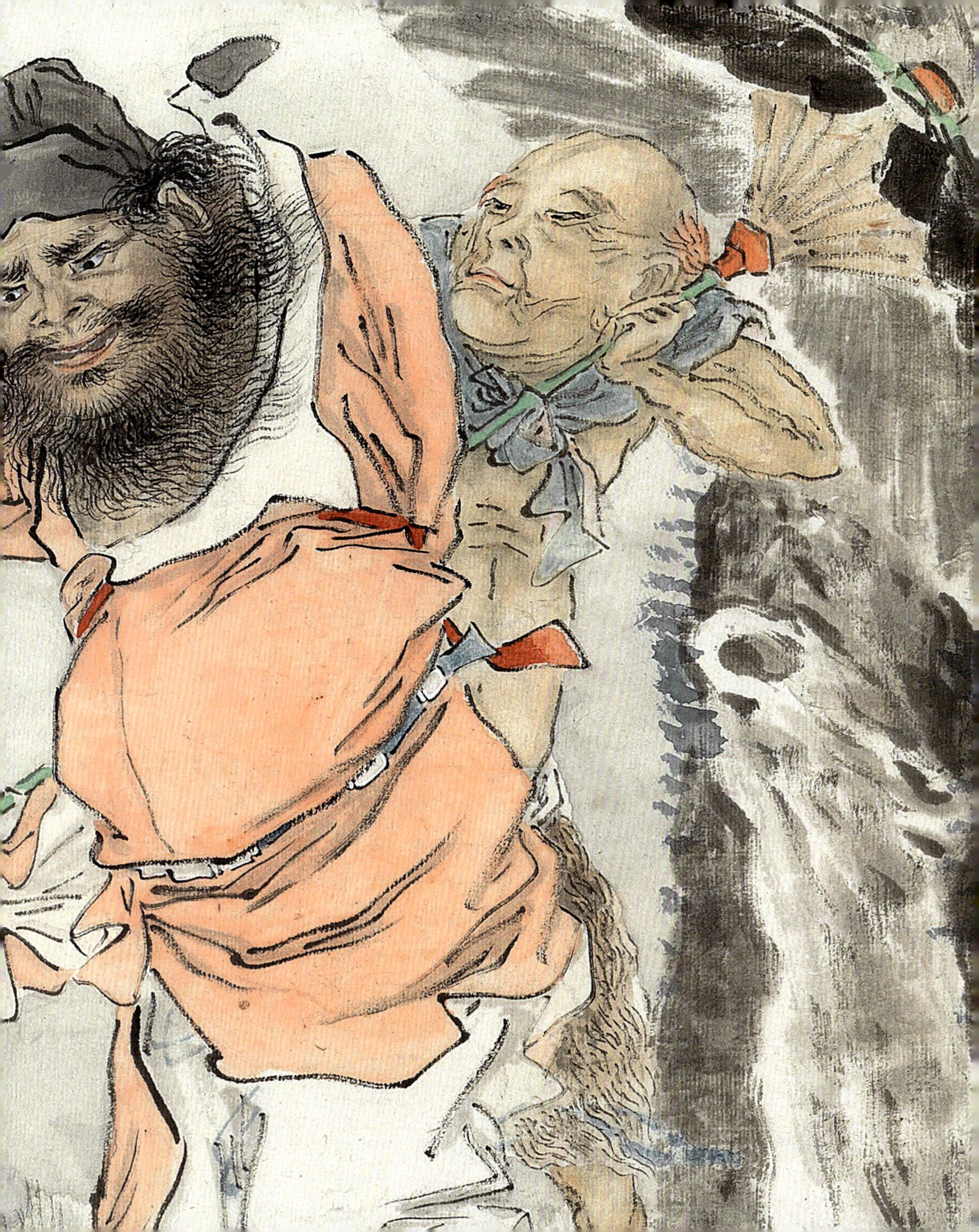

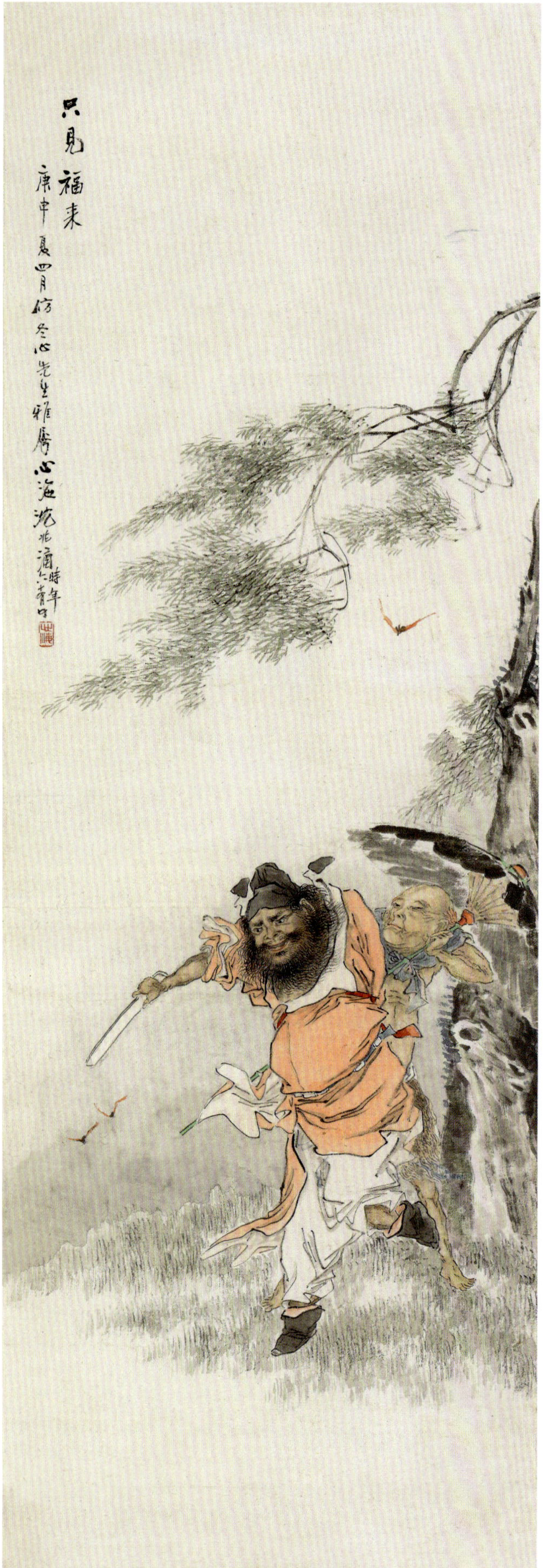
只見福來

Artist:
Shen Xinhan

Medium:
Color on paper, Hanging scroll

Dimensions:
115.5 cm × 39 cm

Only Seeing Fortune Arrive

Inscription:
Only Seeing Fortune Arrive. In the fourth month of the Gengshen summer, emulating the elegant style of Mr. Dongxin, by Xinhai Shen Zhaohan at the age of sixty-five.

Seal:
Xinhai

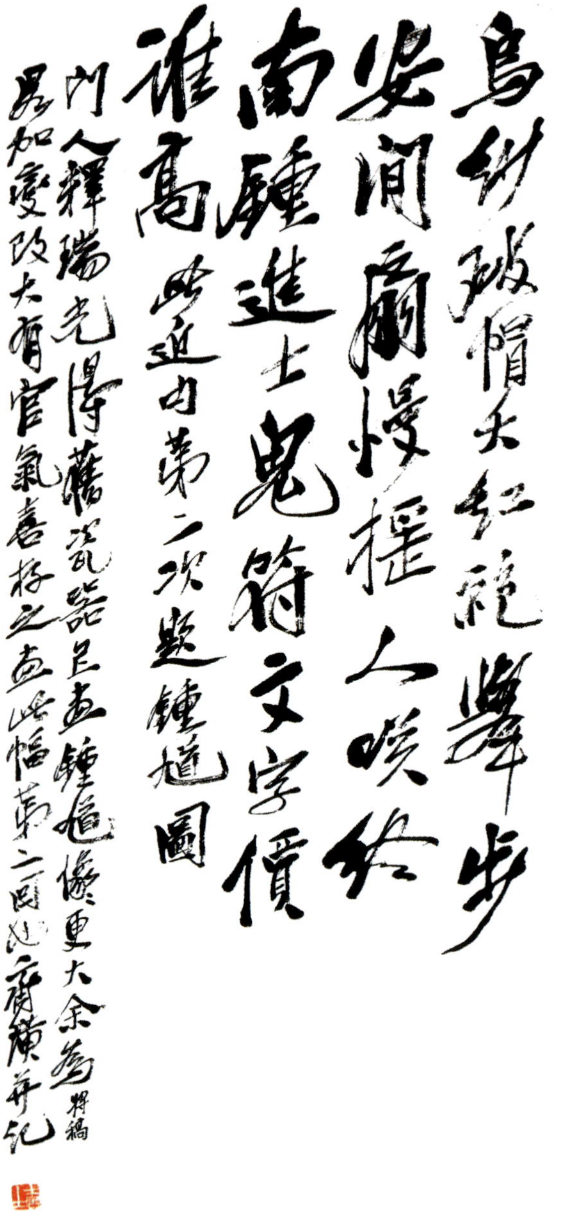
烏紗破帽大紅袍舉步
安閒扇慢搖人笑終
南鍾進士鬼符文字價
誰高

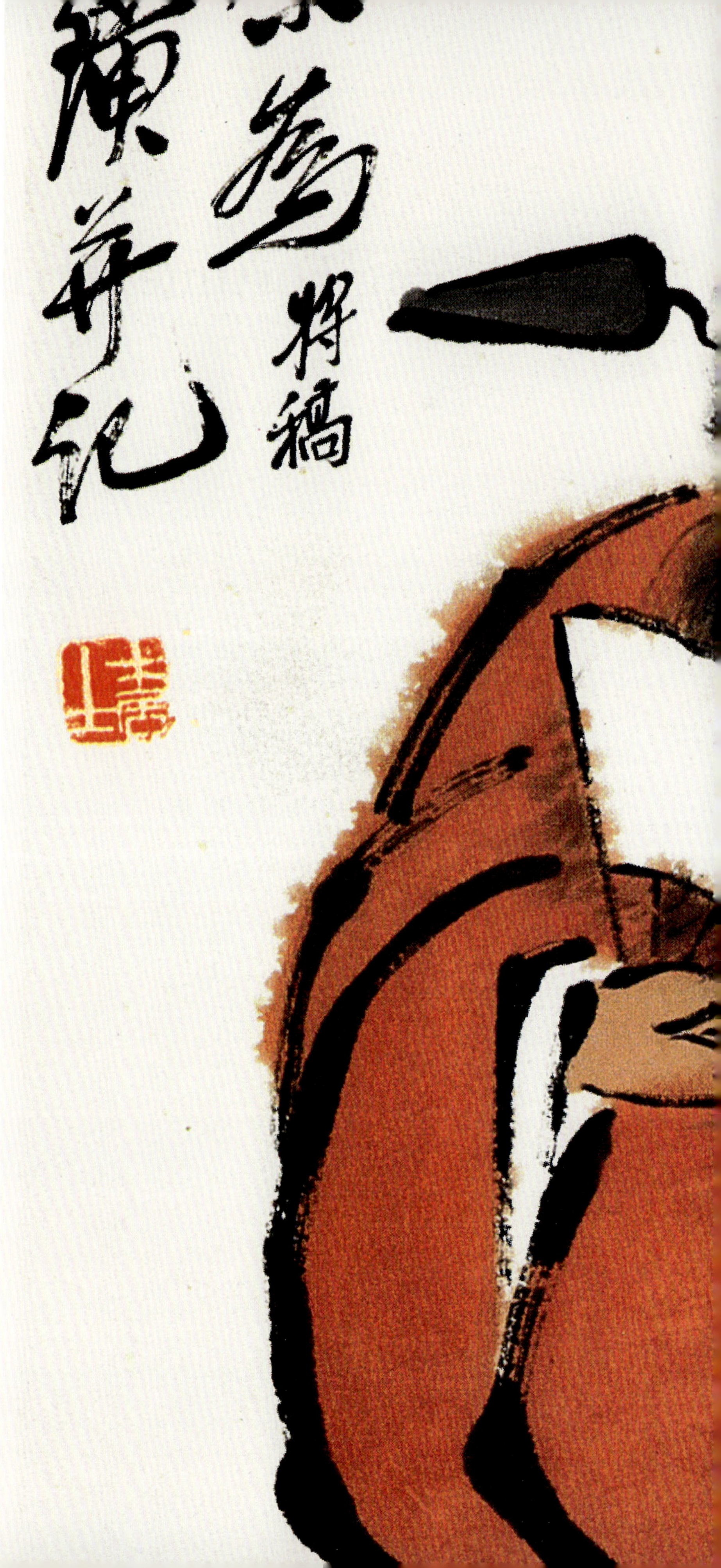
將稿

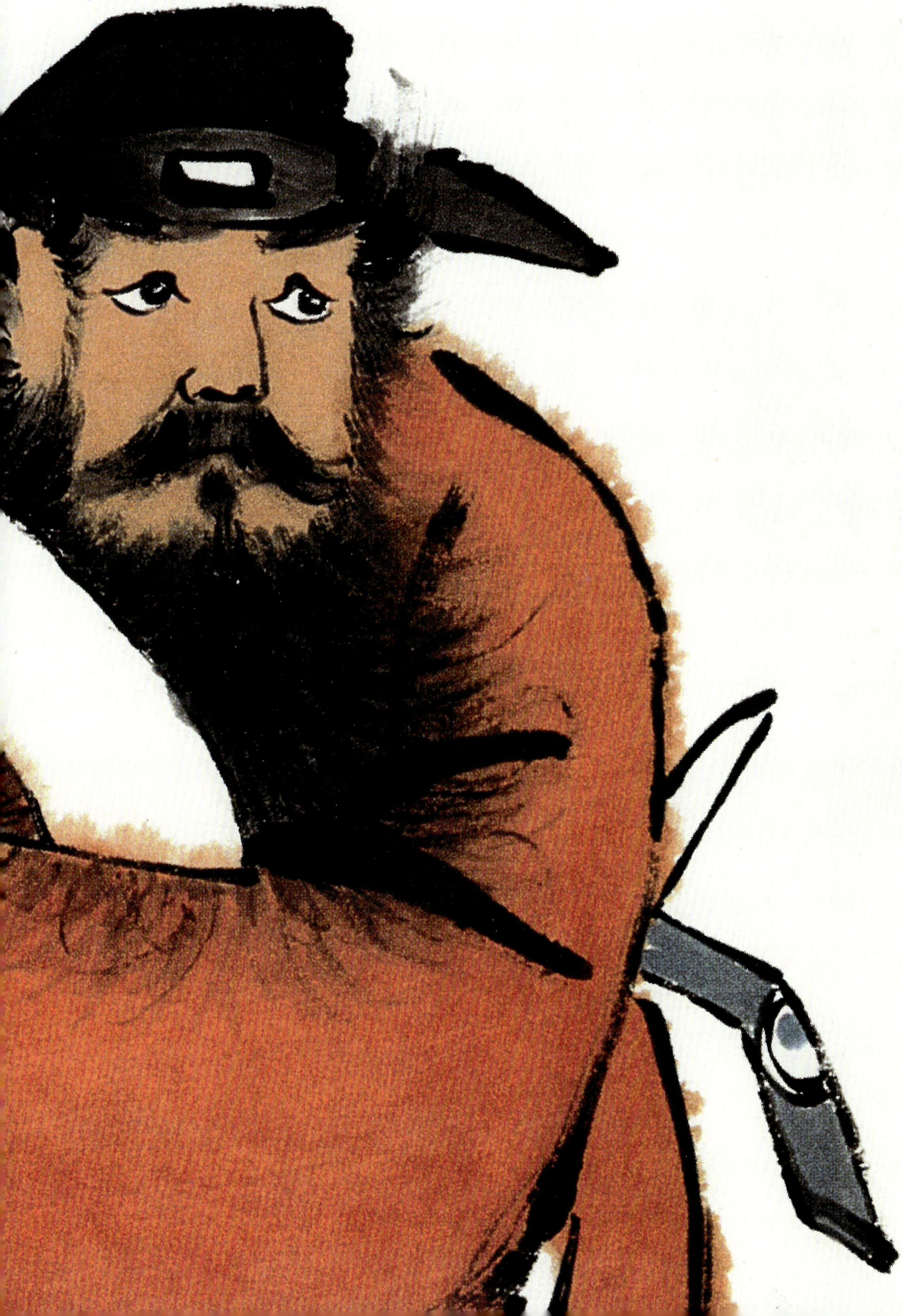

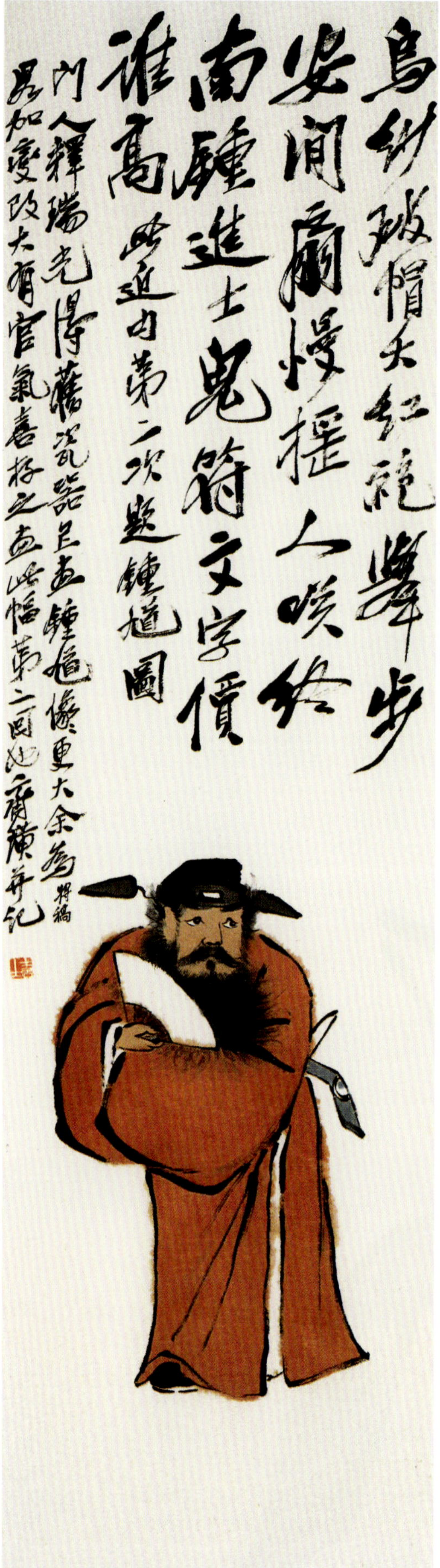
烏紗破帽大紅袍
舉步安閒扇慢搖
人笑終南鍾進士
鬼符文字價誰高
此近日第二次題鍾馗圖

Artist:
Qi Baishi

Medium:
Color on paper, Hanging scroll

Dimensions:
133.4 cm × 36 cm

Jinshi of Zhongnan

Inscription:
This marks the second occasion in recent days that I have painted the figure of Zhong Kui. My disciple Ruiguang made a larger version of the painting of Zhong Kui on an old porcelain piece. I made slight revisions to the original draft, endowing it with a more official air, a change which pleases me greatly. Thus, I have painted this theme for the second time. Recorded by Qi Huang.

Seal:
Lay Scholar Mu

Qi Baishi (1864-1957)
Originally named Chunzhi, with the courtesy name Weiqing and the pseudonym Lanting, he later changed his name to Huang, with the courtesy name Binsheng, and was also known by the aliases Baishi, Elder of Baishi Mountain, Old Ping, the Hungry Elder, Master of Jieshanyin Hall, Old Man of Jiping Hall, and the Three Hundred Stones Wealthy Man, hailing from Xiangtan, Hunan. A master of traditional Chinese painting and a cultural icon globally, he held esteemed positions including Honorary Professor at the Central Academy of Fine Arts and Chairman of the China Artists Association.

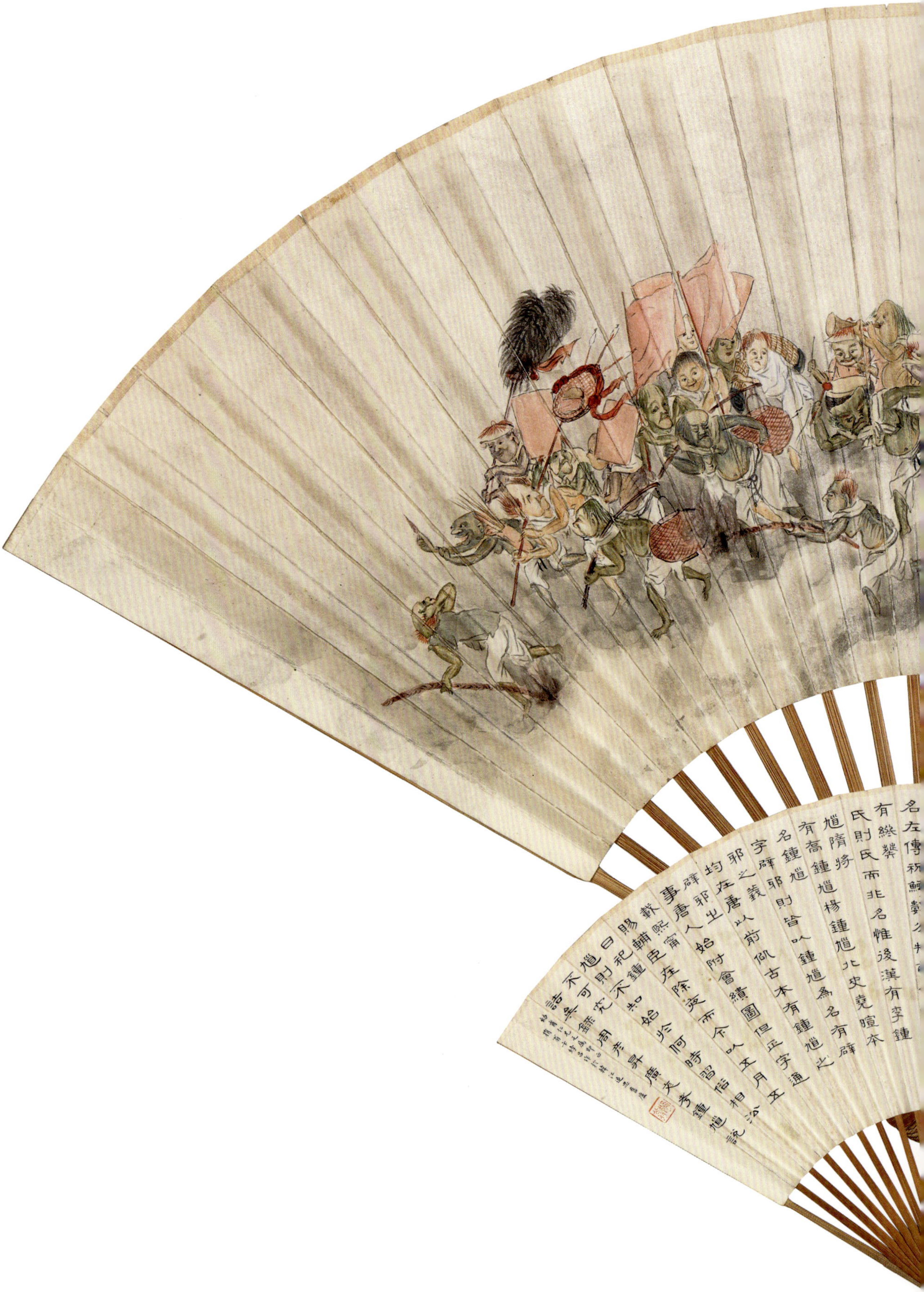

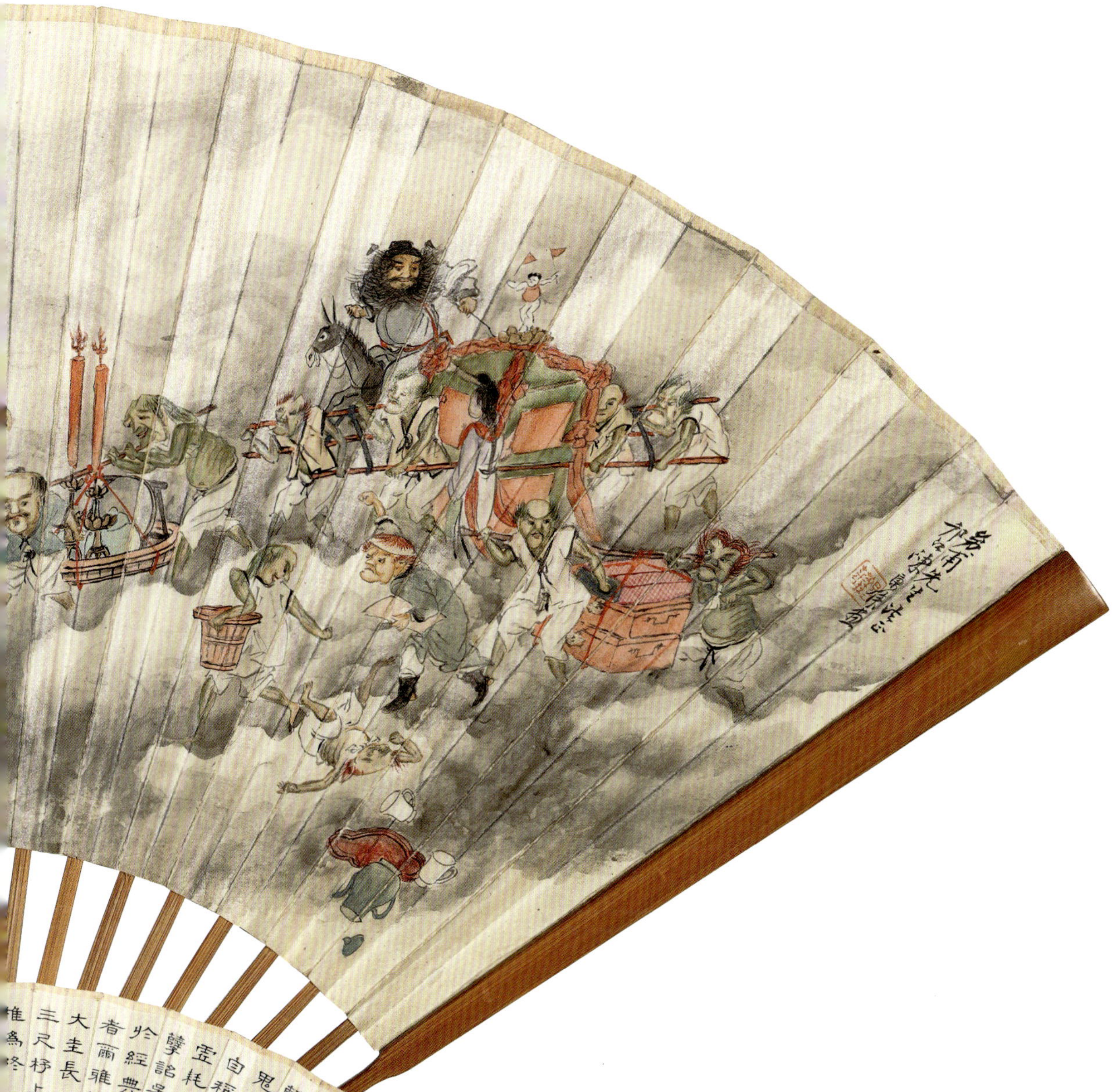

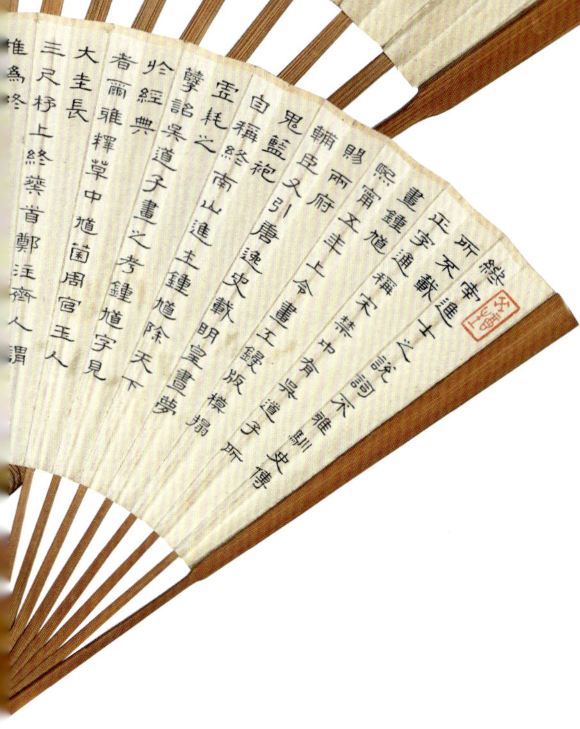

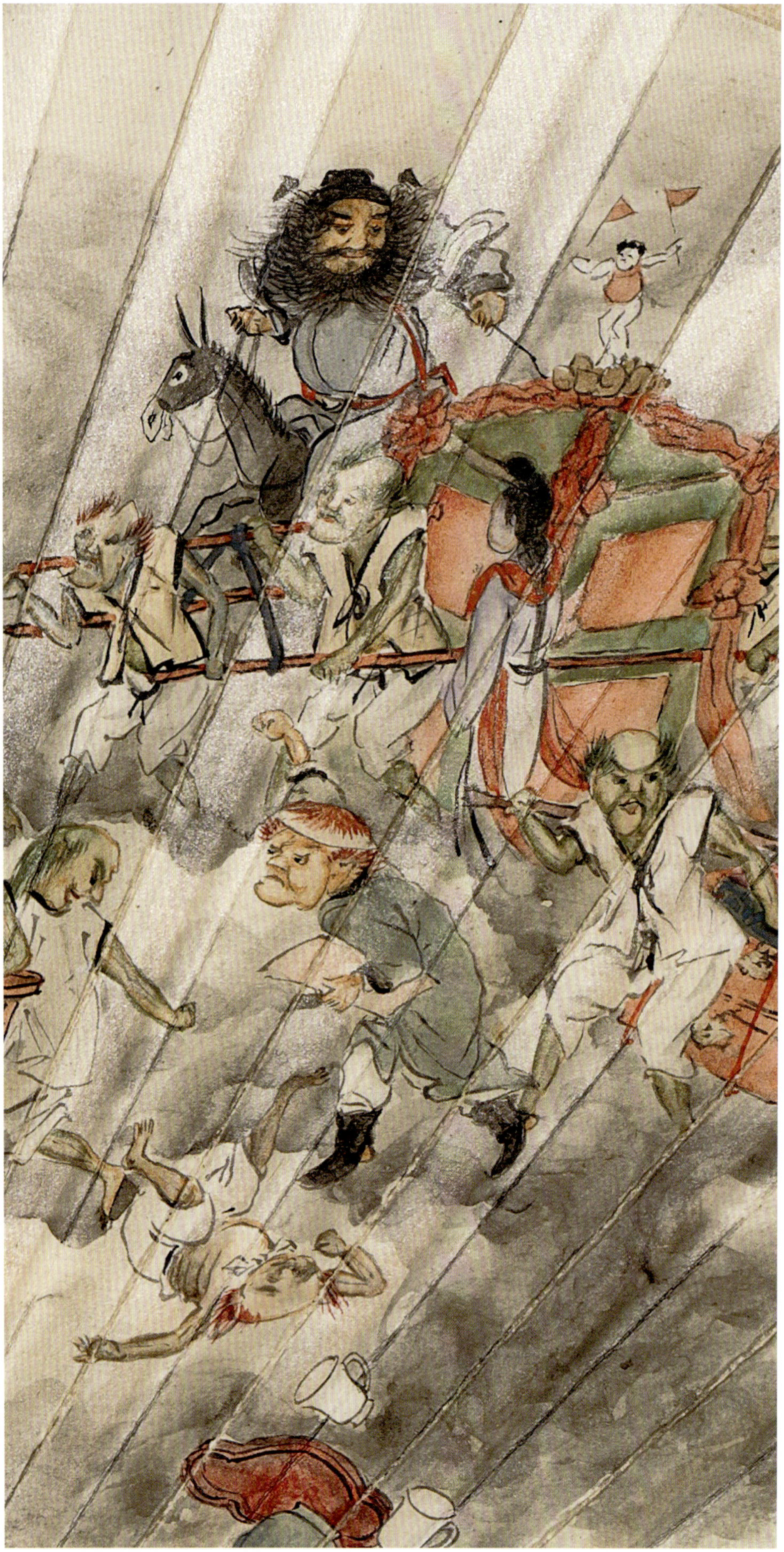

Chen Kanghou (1866–1937)
Courtesy name Xi Fan, a native of Yangzhou, Jiangsu. He was one of the celebrated artists of the Shanghai School, excelled in landscapes, figures, flowers, and birds with a delicate and elegant touch. He was particularly adept at painting insects and grass, often observing the movements of small insects captured in bottles and employing Western perspectives in his work to depict their form and spirit, resulting in vividly lifelike artworks.

Bian Fuchang (1873–1946)
Originally named Lun Chang, styled as Jingfu and later known as Weige, and even later as Xuan An. A native of Yizheng, Jiangsu, born into a bureaucratic family of Yangzhou. He excelled in calligraphy, particularly in the clerical script, with profound and natural strokes full of concealed meaning. He served as a diplomat in Japan for the Qing government and was a son-in-law to Zhang Zhidong. Following the Xinhai Revolution, he opted for seclusion and was an avid collector. He enjoyed drinking, embodying the spirit of the ancient literati figure Wuliu Master.

Artist:
Chen Kanghou, Bian Fuchang

Medium:
Color on paper, Completed fan

Dimensions:
18 cm × 49 cm

Zhong Kui Marrying Off His Sister

Inscription:
The notion of a Jinshi from Zhongnan Mountain is not commonly found in historical records and lacks elegance. As mentioned in *Zhengzitong*, during the Song Dynasty, there existed a painting of Zhong Kui (钟馗) by Wu Daozi in the imperial palace. In the fifth year of Xining, the Emperor ordered the painting to be replicated and engraved on printing plates, and printed copies were bestowed upon each of the ministers of the two bureaus. *The Unofficial History of Tang* recounts that Emperor Xuanzong of Tang once dreamt of a blue-robed ghost, who claimed to be Zhong Kui (钟馗), a Jinshi from Zhongnan Mountain, dedicated to eradicating evil spirits from the world. Consequently, Emperor Xuanzong commissioned Wu Daozi to depict this figure. The name Zhong Kui appears in ancient texts; *Erya, Shicao* describes Zhong Kui (中馗) as a type of fungus, and *Rites of Zhou, Office of Winter, Yuren* mentions a Da Kui (大圭) is recorded to be three chi long, with a Zhong Kui (终葵) at its shuttle's end. Zheng's note: people from Qi referred to a mallet as Zhong Kui (钟馗). "Zhong(中)" and "Zhong(终)" both refer to "Zhong(钟)", and "Kui (葵)" is a phonetic loan for the homophone, none of which denote a personal name. In *Zuo Zhuan*, Zhutuo categorized merchants into seven clans based on the goods they traded, among which was the Zhong Kui (终葵) clan, denoting a family name rather than an individual's. It was only during the Later Han that individuals bore the name, such as Li Zhongkui (钟馗), and in the Sui Dynasty, there were generals named Gao Zhongkui (钟馗) and Yang Zhongkui (钟馗). 《*History of the Northern Dynasties*》 records that Yao Xuan's original name was Zhong Kui (钟馗), courtesy name Bi Xie, signifying a talisman against evil. These instances suggest that tales of Zhong Kui (钟馗) warding off evil predate the Tang Dynasty, which later incorporated these legends into paintings. However, as "Zhengzitong" notes, the Zhong Kui (钟馗) paintings gifted to senior officials during Xining were associated with New Year's Eve, whereas the current custom is to worship Zhong Kui (钟馗) on the fifth day of the fifth month, with the origins of this practice unknown. Zhou Yansheng recorded this in Extensive Discourses on Literature: Treatise on Zhong Kui. The friend Youfu has completed the revisions, and the work was crafted authored by Bian Xuchang, known as the Uncompromising Elder, at his Old Lodge of Contemplation by the Han River.

Seal:
Xifan

丙子午月竹人王雲寫

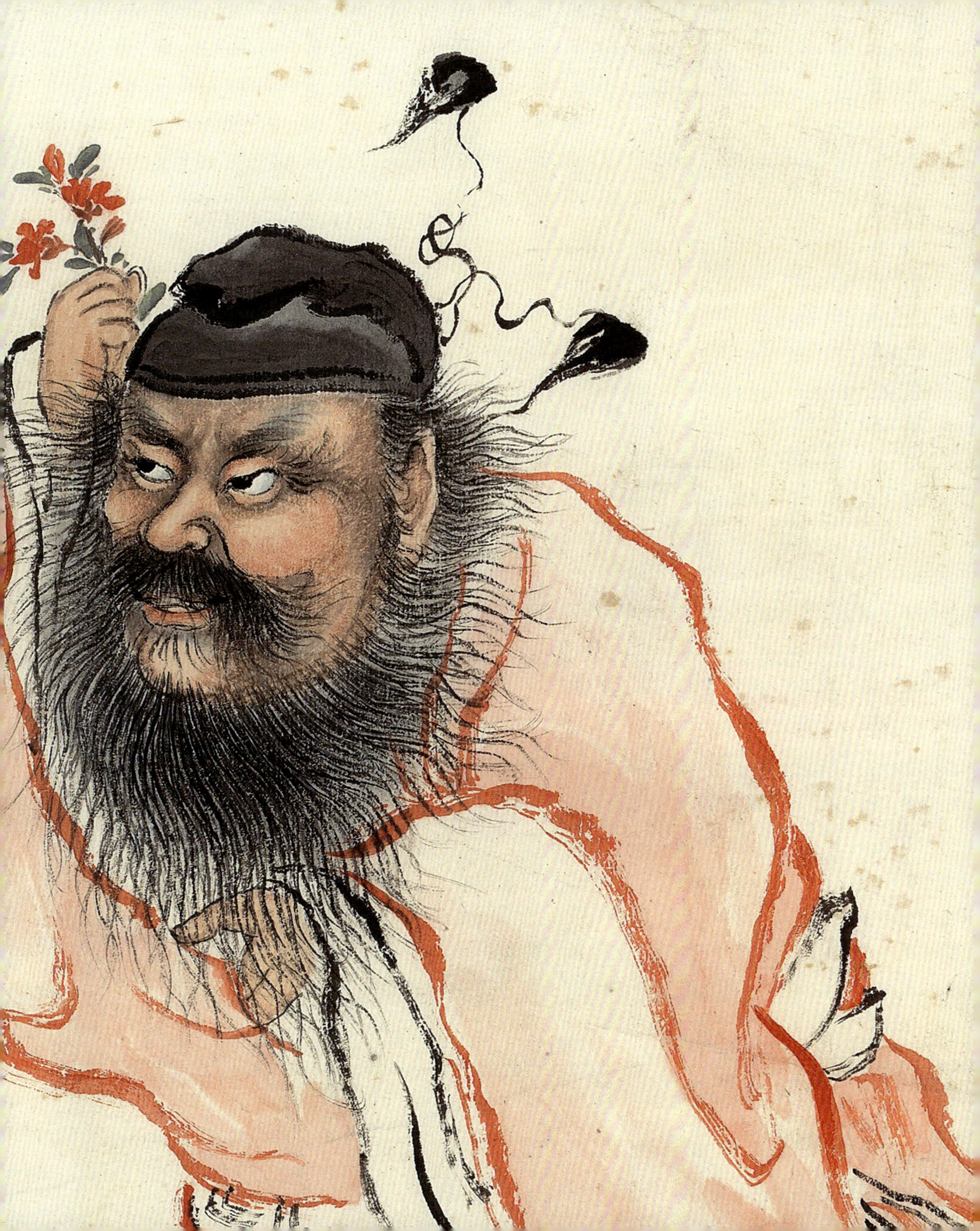

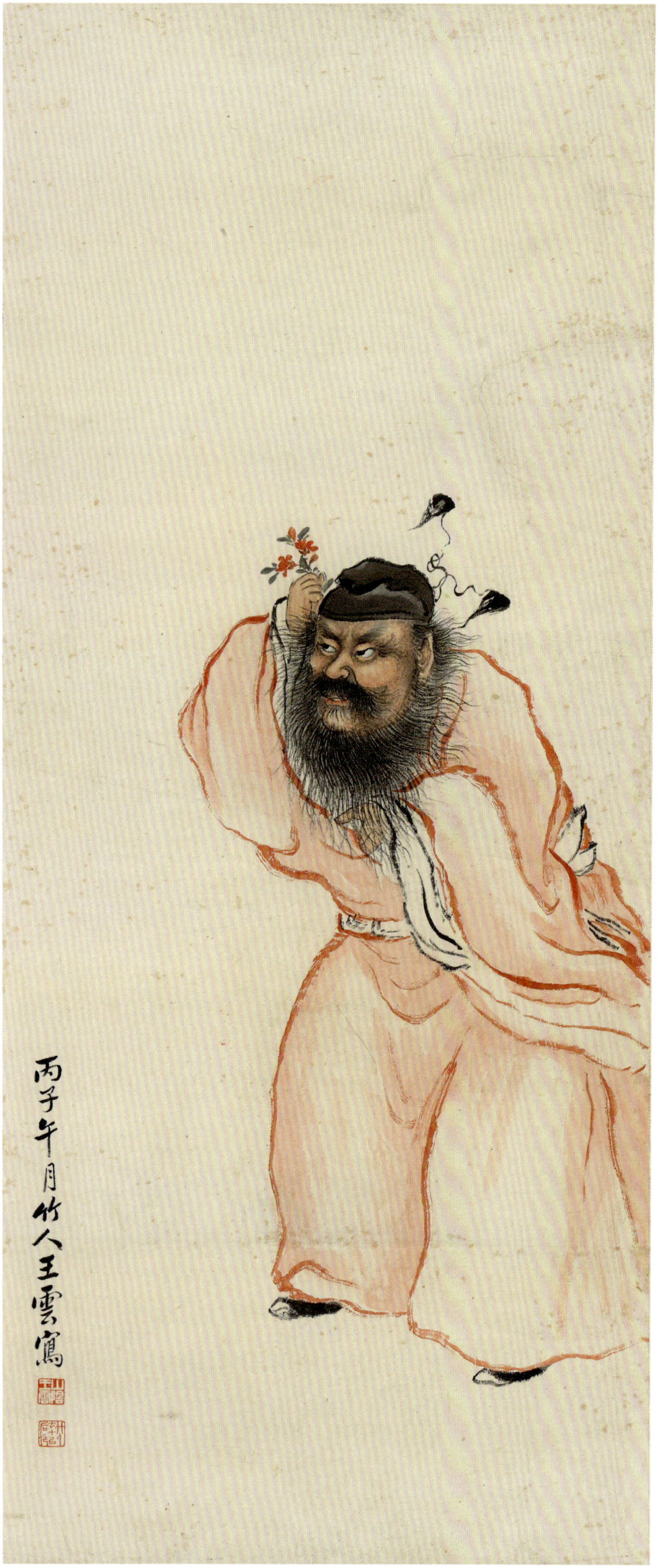
丙子午月竹人王雲寫

Artist:
Wang Yun

Medium:
Color on paper, Hanging scroll

Dimensions:
81 cm × 33 cm

Flower Hairpin

Inscription:
In the month of Wu, of the Bingzi year, this inscription was written by Wang Yun.

Seal:
Wang Yun of Shanyin, Zhuren's work after the age of seventy

Wang Yun (1866 –1950)
A native of Hangzhou, known by his courtesy name Zhuren, he was recognized by this name. His study was named Yunqiao Mountain Villa. His father, Yuan, excelled in painting portraits that were remarkably vivid, earning an artistic reputation. Yun inherited his father's skills and followed the painting methods of Fei Danxu. In calligraphy, his clerical and seal scripts were particularly admirable, though his running and regular scripts were also exquisite. In seal carving, he most admired the techniques of Zhao Zhichen, and although he studied under many masters, his style remained characteristic of Zhejiang artists. He was skilled in crafting jade seals, especially in smaller sizes, with meticulous workmanship. He had close associations with Zhong Yijing, Ding Fuzhi, Wu Yin, and Ye Weiming, among others. He also set up an inkstone at the Xiling Seal Art Society. Additionally, he was adept at carving bamboo and had a special fondness for gardening. He was an early member of the Xiling Seal Art Society.

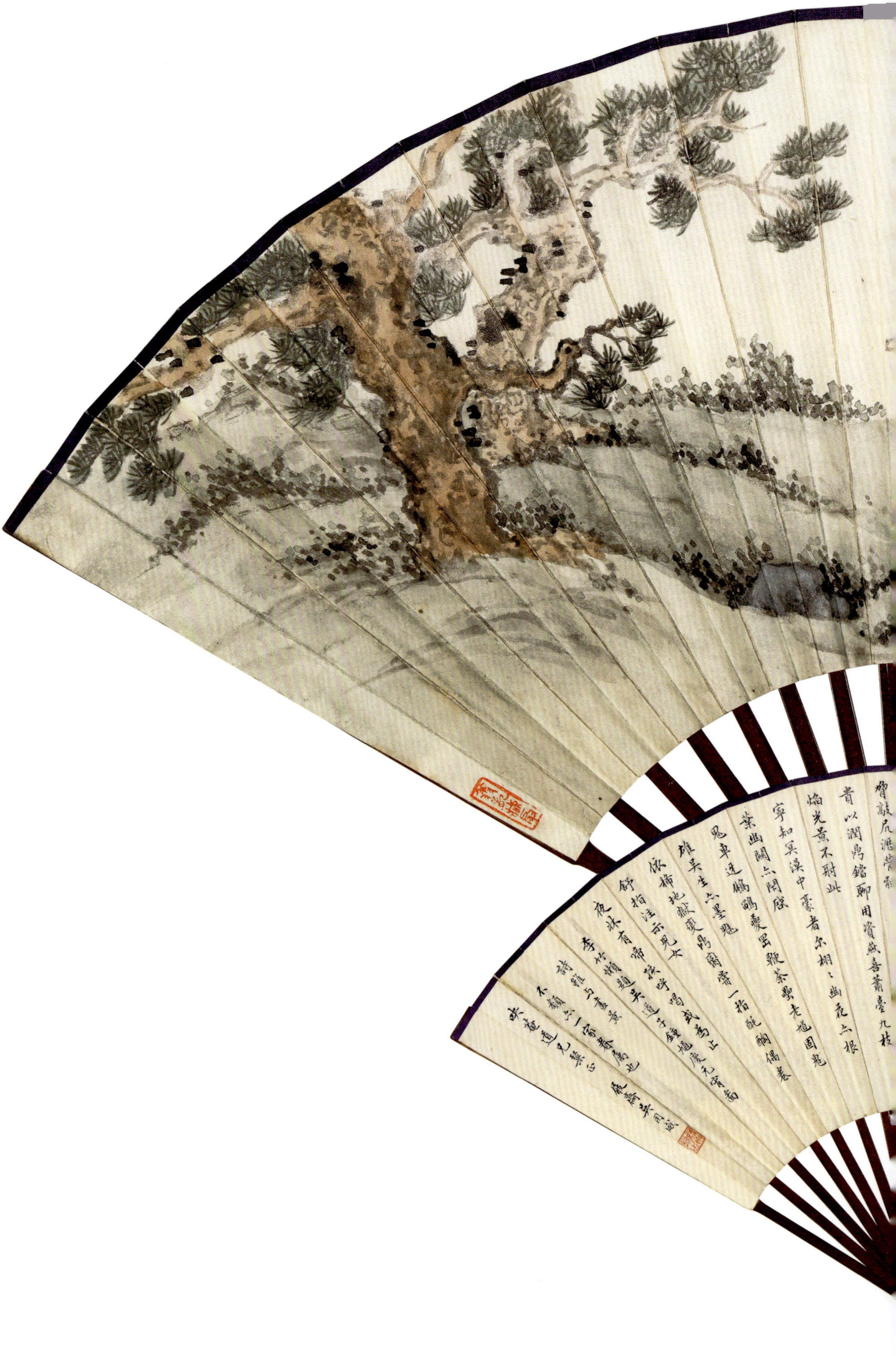

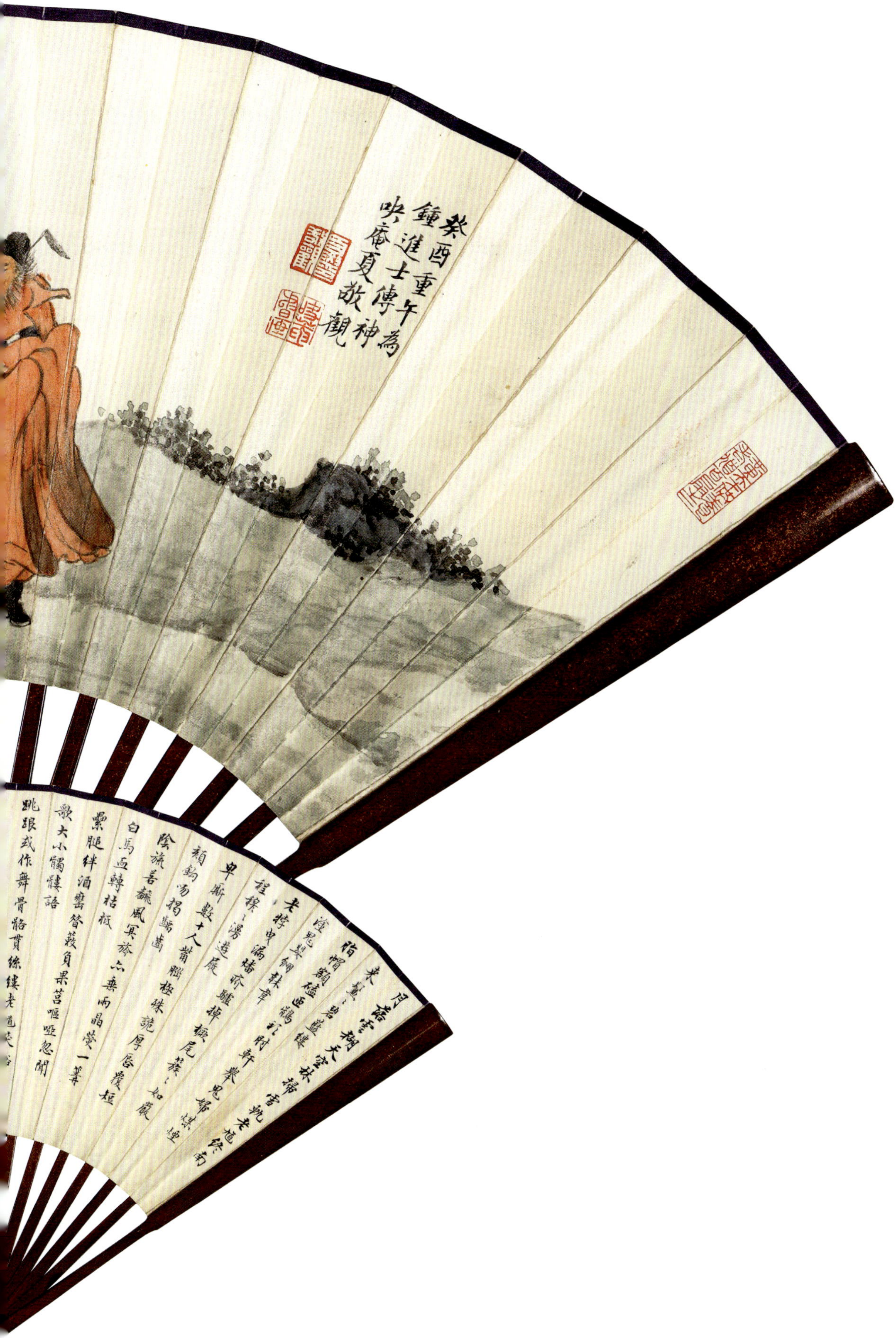
癸酉重午為
鍾進士傳神
吷庵夏敬觀

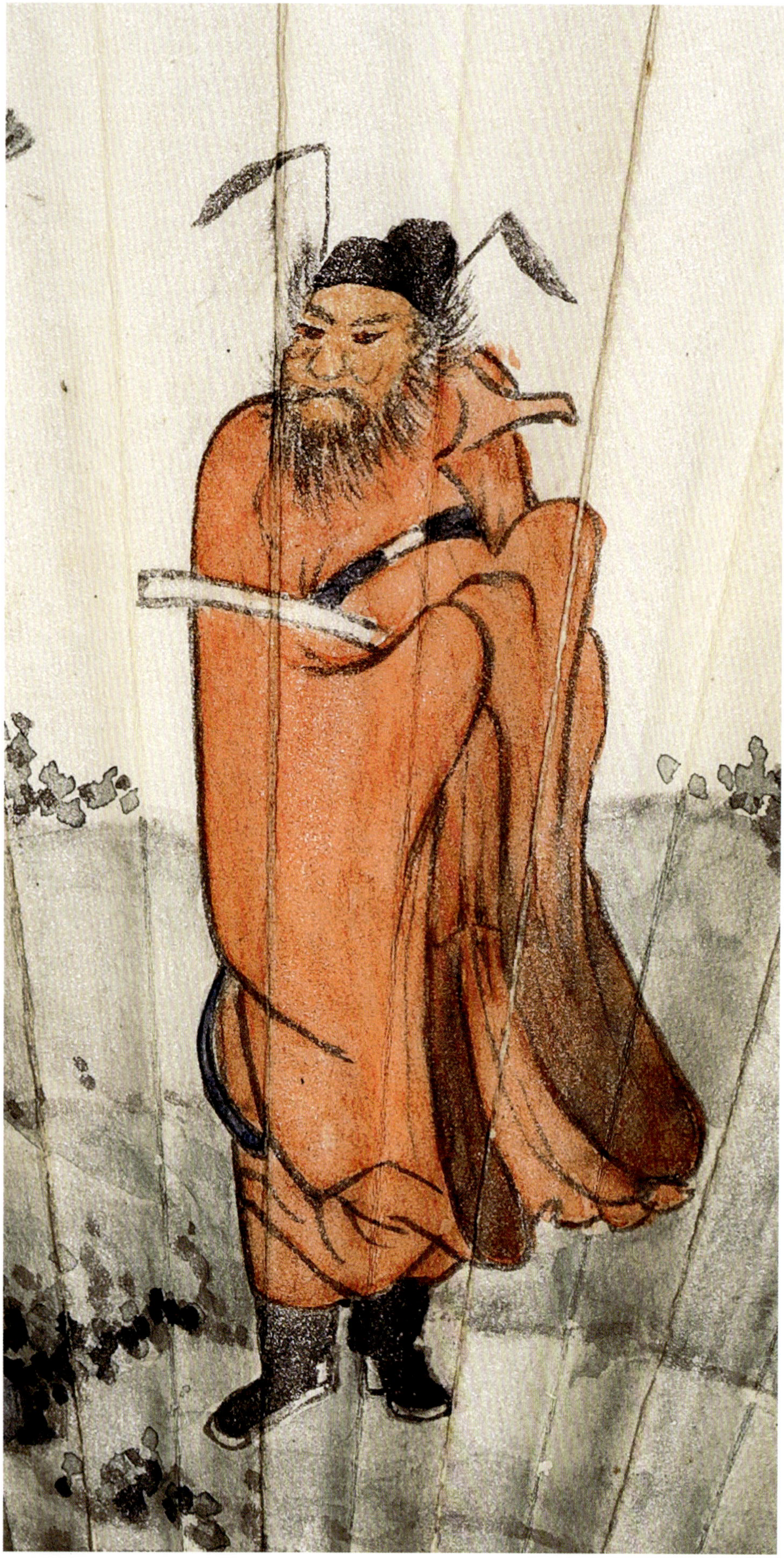

Xia Jingguan (1875–1953)
Courtesy name Jiancheng, also known as Guanren and Jiansai, styled as Xia'an in his later years, with alternate names Xuanxiu and Niulin Elder. A native of Changsha, who later settled in Shanghai. A modern lyricist and painter of the Jiangxi school, he excelled in landscapes and also delved into florals. Achieved the rank of Juren in the twentieth year of the Guangxu era and was celebrated for his poetry throughout the south and north. He once served in Zhang Zhidong's office, managed the Normal School of both Jiangs, held the post of Educational Commissioner of Jiangsu, overseeing institutions like Fudan University and China Public School. In 1919, he was appointed as the Director of the Education Department of Zhejiang Province.

Wu Yongwei (1873–1941)
Courtesy name Dongqing, styled as Jizhai, a native of Yangzhou.

Artist:
Xia Jingguan, Wu Yongwei

Medium:
Color on paper, Completed fan

Dimensions:
18 cm × 47 cm

Zhong Kui

Inscription:
In the the fifth day of the fifth month of the Guiyou year, Xia'an, Xia Jingguan, animated the portrait of Jinshi Zhong.

Seal:
The seal of Xia Jingguan, calligraphy and paintings of Xia'an

Backside Calligraphy

Inscription:
The moon descends, clouds blur the sky,
In silent woods, the snow tracks swept aside.
From Zhongnan comes the venerable Zhong Kui,
His azure garb edged sharp as lapis.
His glossy cap grazes his brow,
A hawk's plumage lifts at the elbow's throw.
Demoness faces smeared with soot,
Demon children bound in leather boot.
An old wolf drags a leaking pyre,
Scabbed donkeys flick their pegged desire.
Ghosts muster close in solemn stance,
Meandering in boots, a somber dance.
Base servants, a dozen in their guise,
Faces contorted, a sight for surprise.
Thick lips mask a chin so slight,
Hooked mouths reveal teeth blighted by blight.
Shadowy banners seem to billow like the wind,
Obscure standards too, as if rain's pinned.
Crystal sparks over a basket of white coal,
Horse blood rejuvenates a withered bole.
Stumbling legs entangled by a wine jar's cling,
Once carrying baskets, now fruitless, they bring.
A sudden song amidst retching, loud,
Skulls of all sizes speak in shroud.
Leaping and lurching as if to dance,
Bones threaded through with silk, by chance.
Zhong Kui laughs, his wide mouth bared,
Cheek bristles measuring an inch, unpared.
Hoarse ghosts gather, to you I'll not fail,
He splits carcasses, marrow tapped, blood to scale.
Esteemed for greasing the pot's ringing clang,
A trifle to fuel the swallow's merry twang.
On Xiao's platform, nine flames burn bright,
Their light and scene do not reach this night.
How could it be known in the dark so vast,
That noble spirits, too, seem vividly cast?
Hidden flowers have roots and leaves to show,
Secret gates also open and close.
Ghostly carriages escort the owl,
On Kui's slopes, whips lash the bitter toul.
Zhong Kui, the ghostly hero stands,
And Wu, alive in inky spectral lands.
Dimly the underworld seems to shift,
A stew's morsel, with a single whiff.
Drunkards roll and unfurl at whim,
Fingers pointing, a lesson to kin.
Cries from a bed, a child in the night,
Shouts, perhaps, to halt their fright.
Li Zhulan inscribed a poem on Wu Daozi's painting of Zhong Kui celebrating the Lantern Festival. Although the poem differs from the painting's scene, it belongs to the same discourse. Friend Xia'an has executed the work with splendid precision, and the work is by Jizhai, Wu Yongwei.

Seal:
Crafted by Jizhai

Collector's Seal:
Weng Long's collection of fans

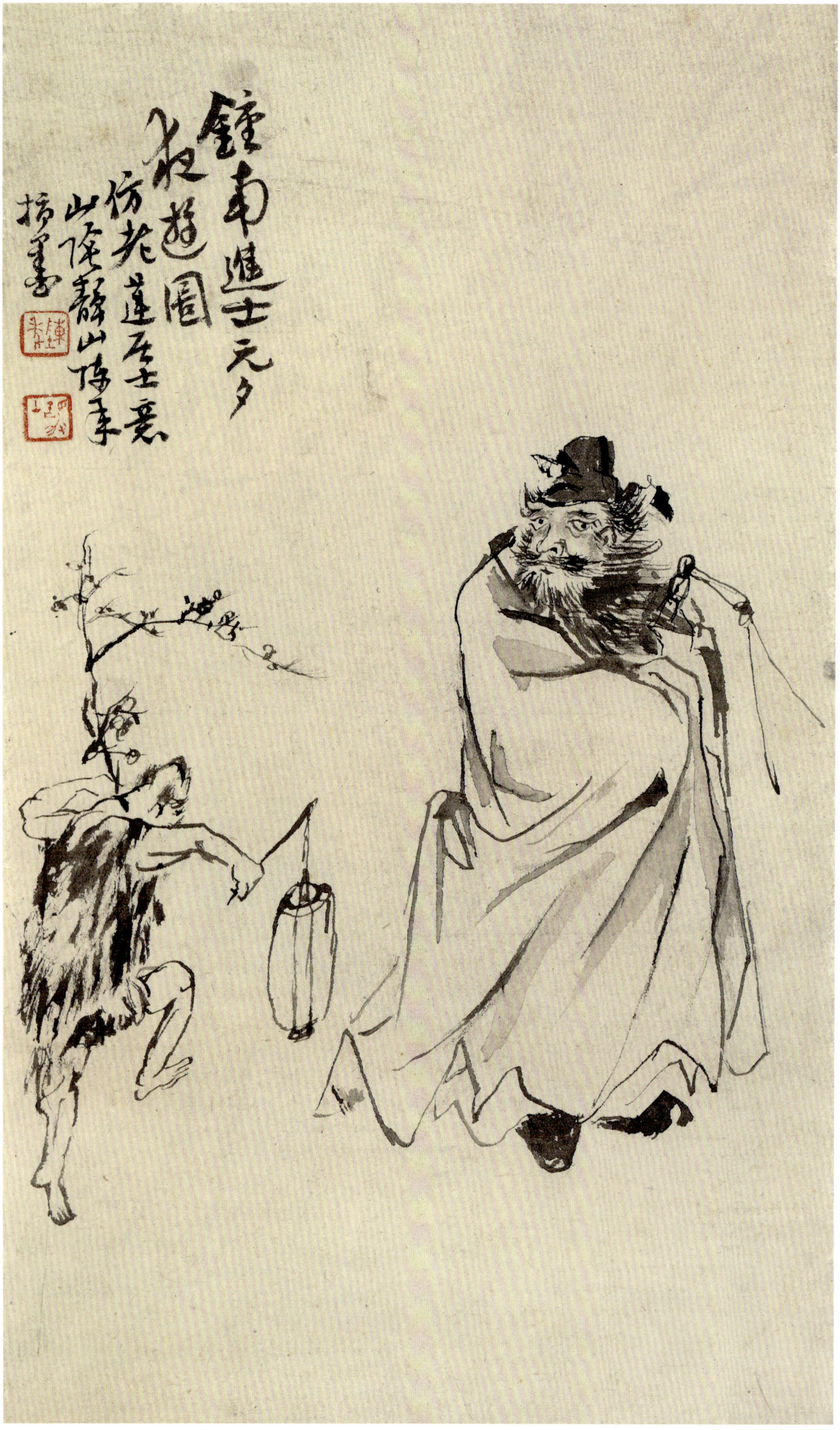
鍾南進士元夕
夜遊圖
仿老蓮居士意

Artist:
Chen Banding

Medium:
Ink on paper, Hanging scroll

Dimensions:
33 cm × 20 cm

Zhong Kui's Nightly Patrol

Inscription:
The New Year's Eve Excursion of Zhong Kui. Created in the spirit of the venerable Lay Scholar Laolian, the work was painted with ink-dipped fingers of Jingshan, Chen Nian of Shanyin.

Seal:
Chen Nian, Jingshan

Chen Banding (1876–1970)
Also known as Chen Nian, courtesy name Banding, a native of Shanyin, Zhejiang. He was a painter, excelled in the art of flowers and landscapes, and was also adept at calligraphy and seal carving. From an early age, he pursued the study of poetry, literature, and painting, later becoming a direct disciple of Wu Changshuo. He held prestigious roles including as a council member of the China Artists Association, vice-president of the Beijing Painting Studio, and president of the Chinese Painting Research Society.

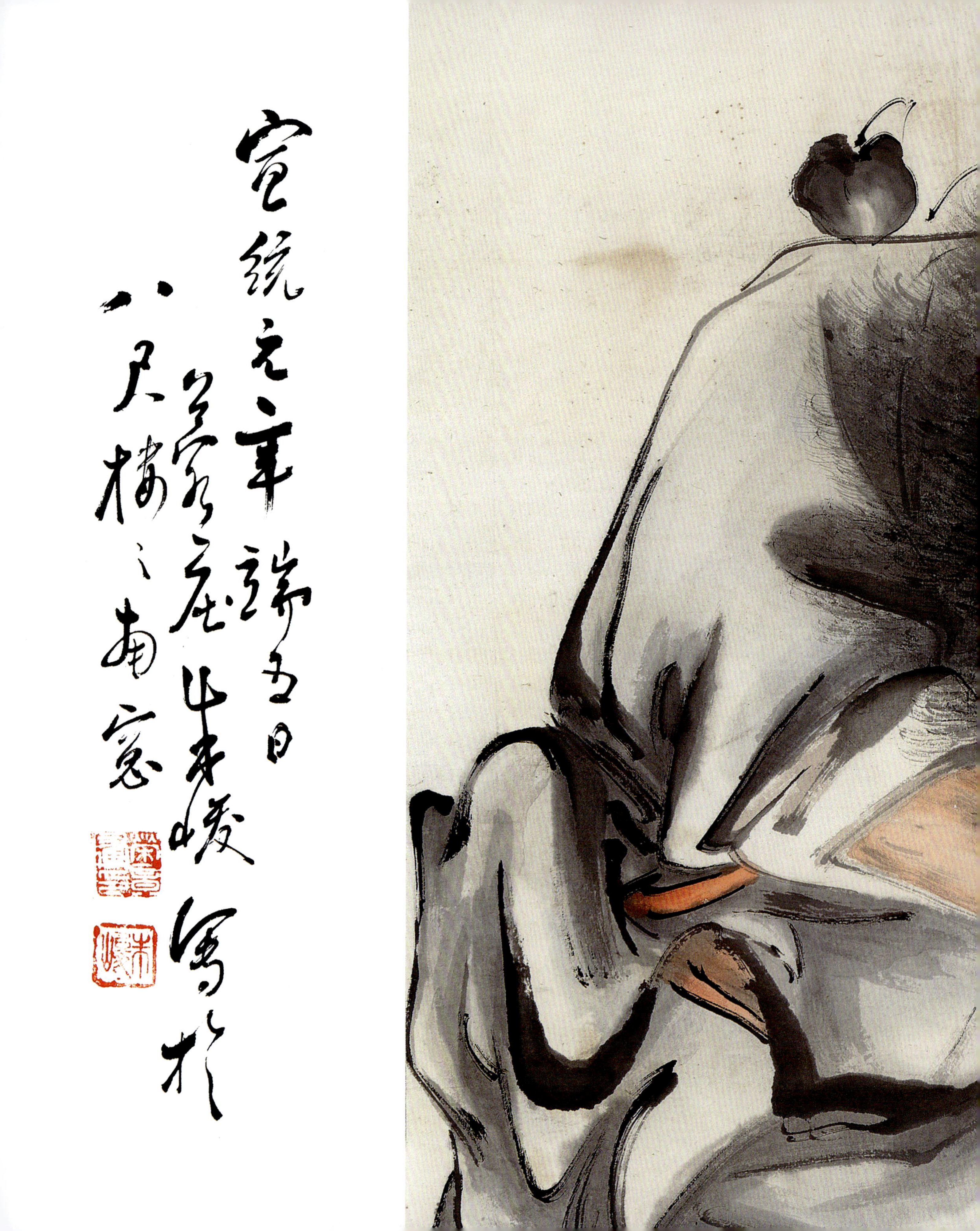
宣統元年端午日
八尺樓之南窗

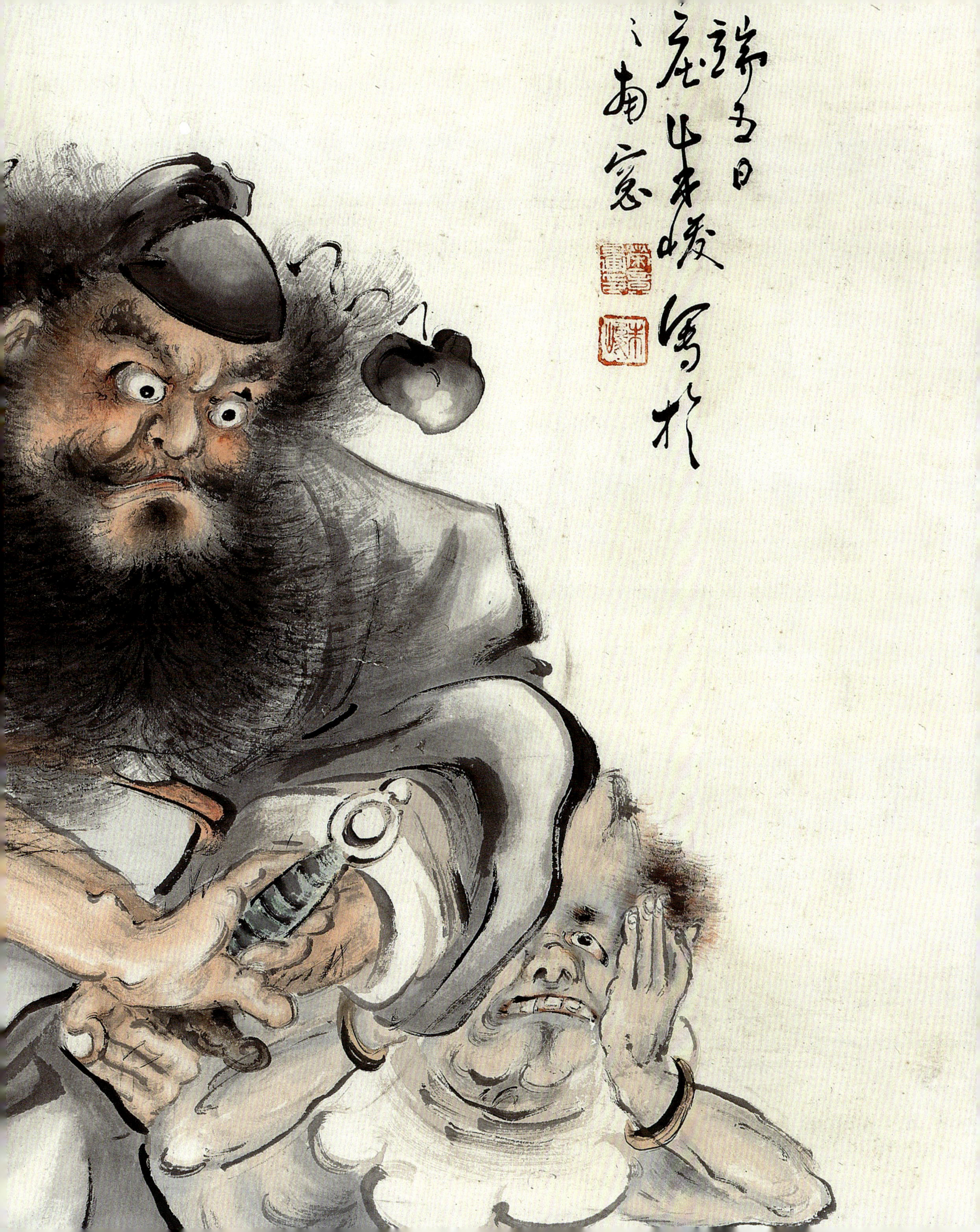

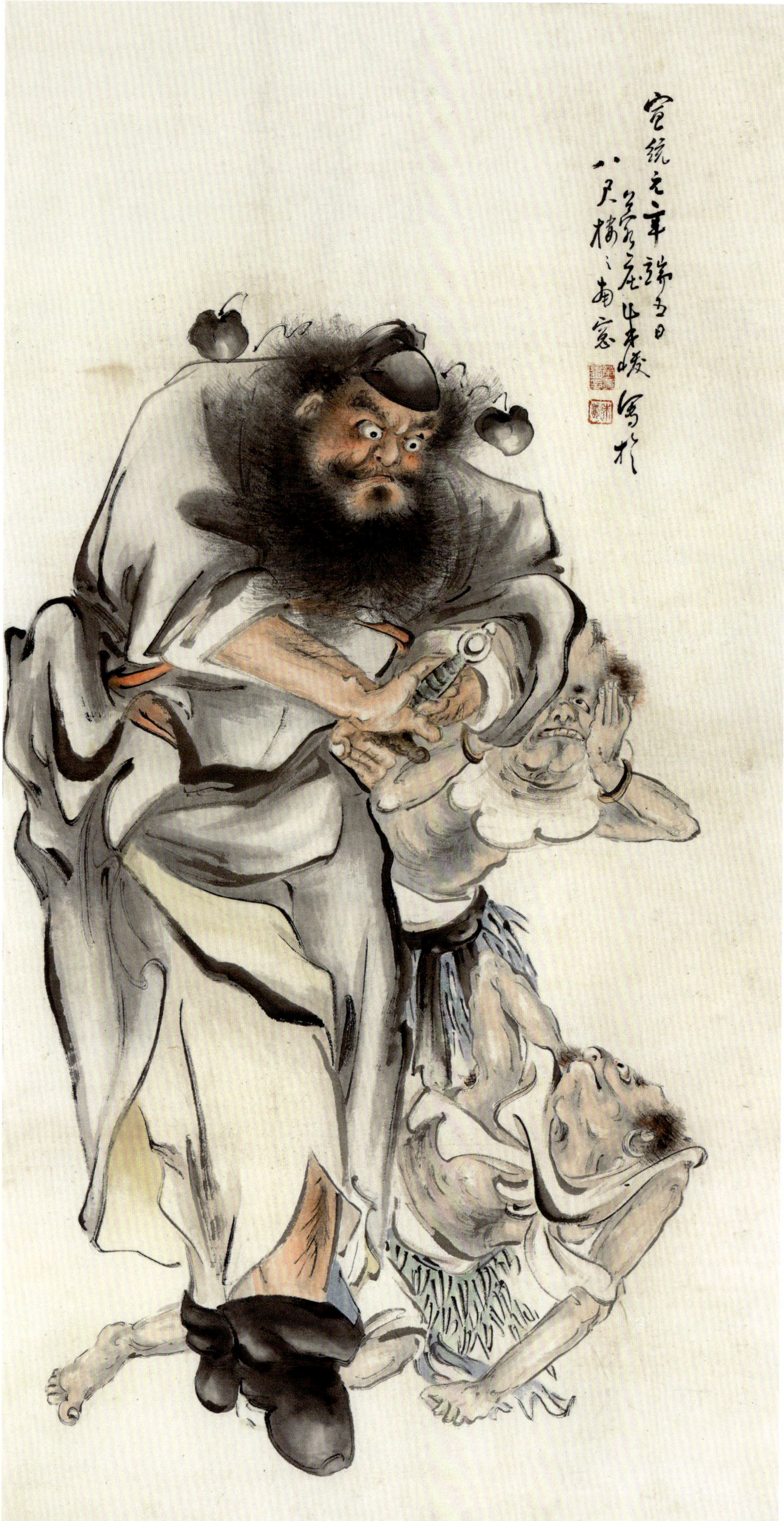

Artist:
Zhu Jun

Medium:
Color on paper, Hanging scroll

Dimensions:
140 cm × 72.5 cm

Zhong Kui Suppressing Evil

Inscription:
On the Dragon Boat Festival of the first year of the Xuantong era, Mengzhuang, Zhu Jun, penned this inscription by the south window of the Bachi Tower.

Seal:
The painting seal of Rongyi, Zhu Jun

Zhu Jun
Styled as Mengzhuang, he was a calligrapher and painter during the late Qing Dynasty and the Republic of China period.

鍾馗嫁妹

丁丑季春仿老蓮居士筆法 芳園書閒

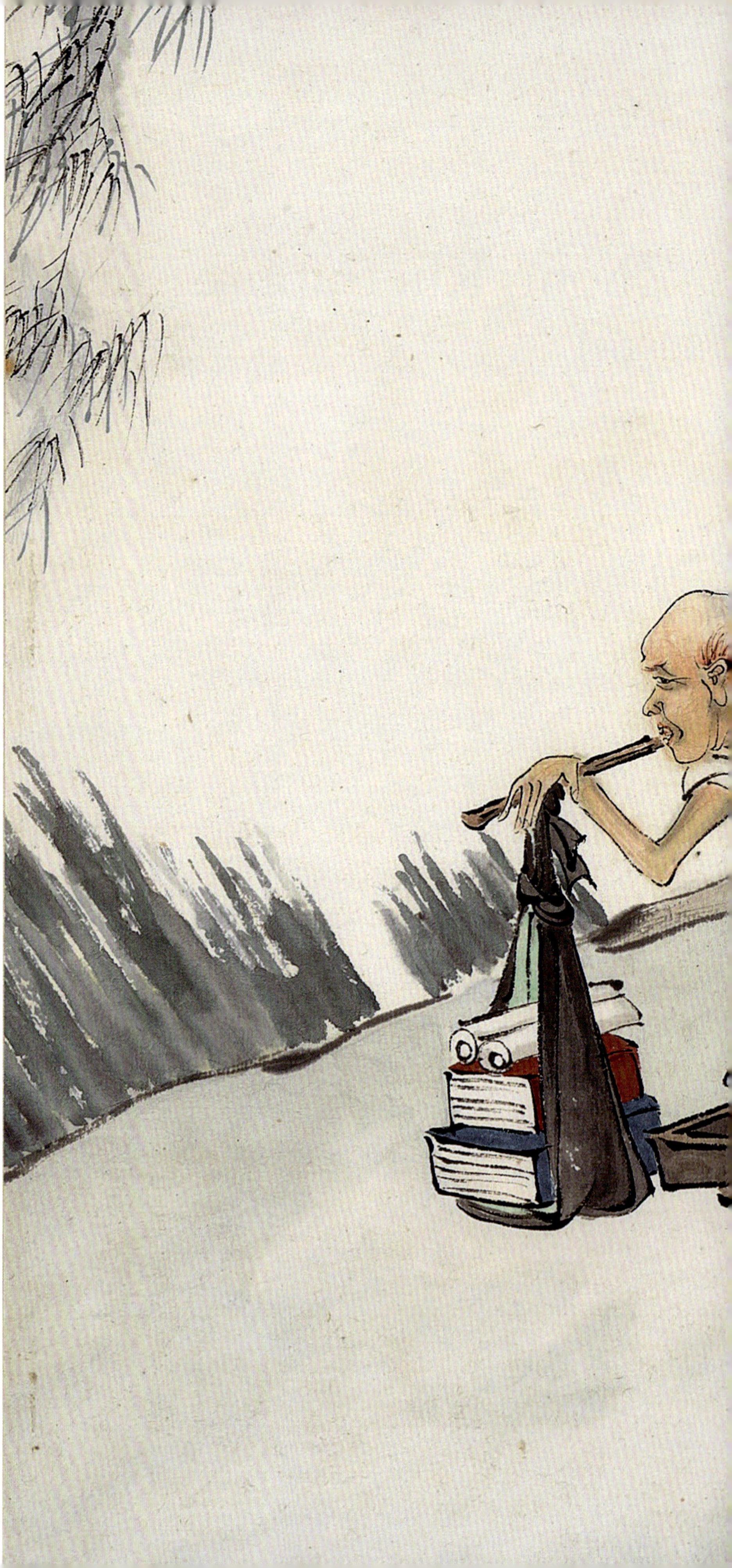

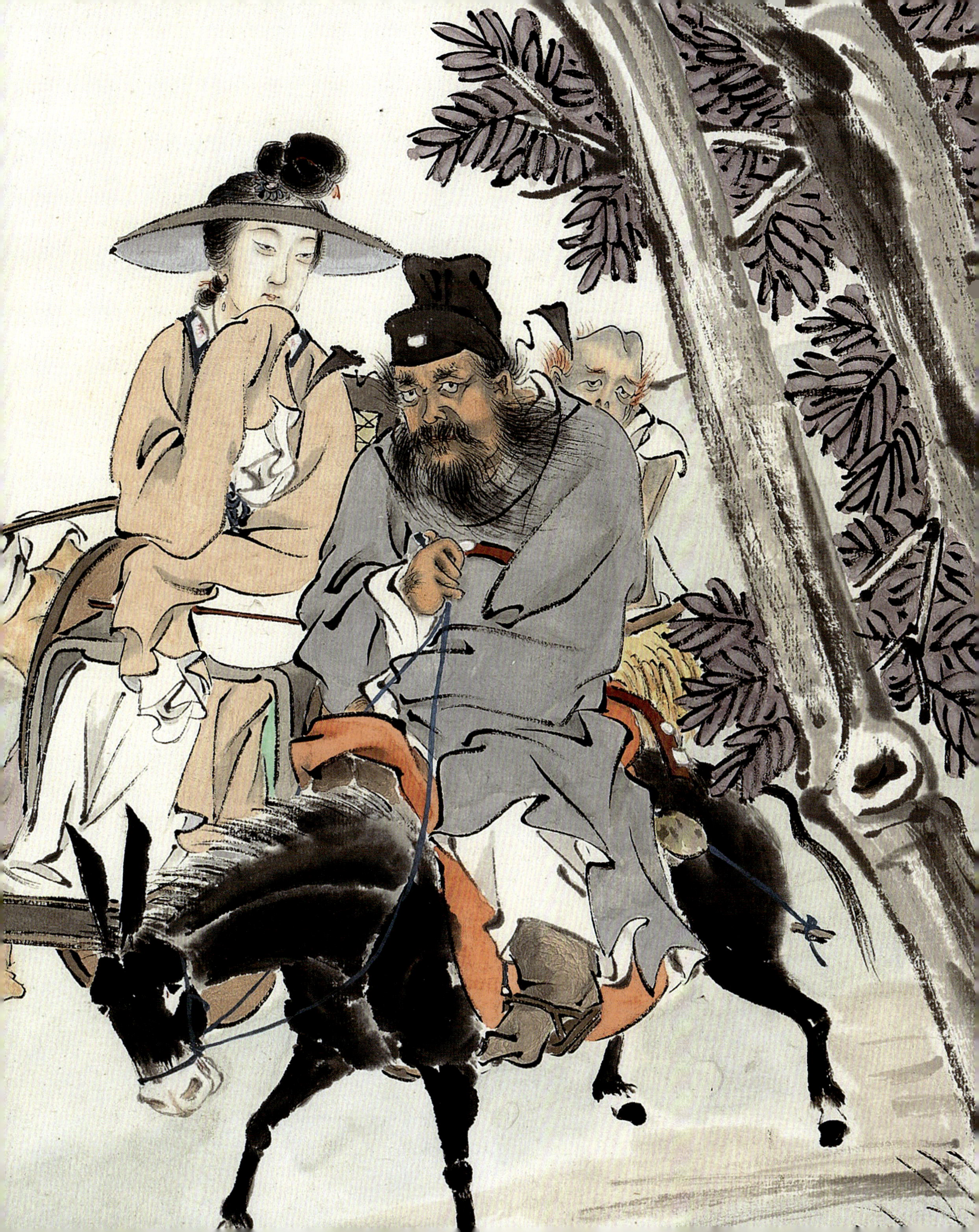

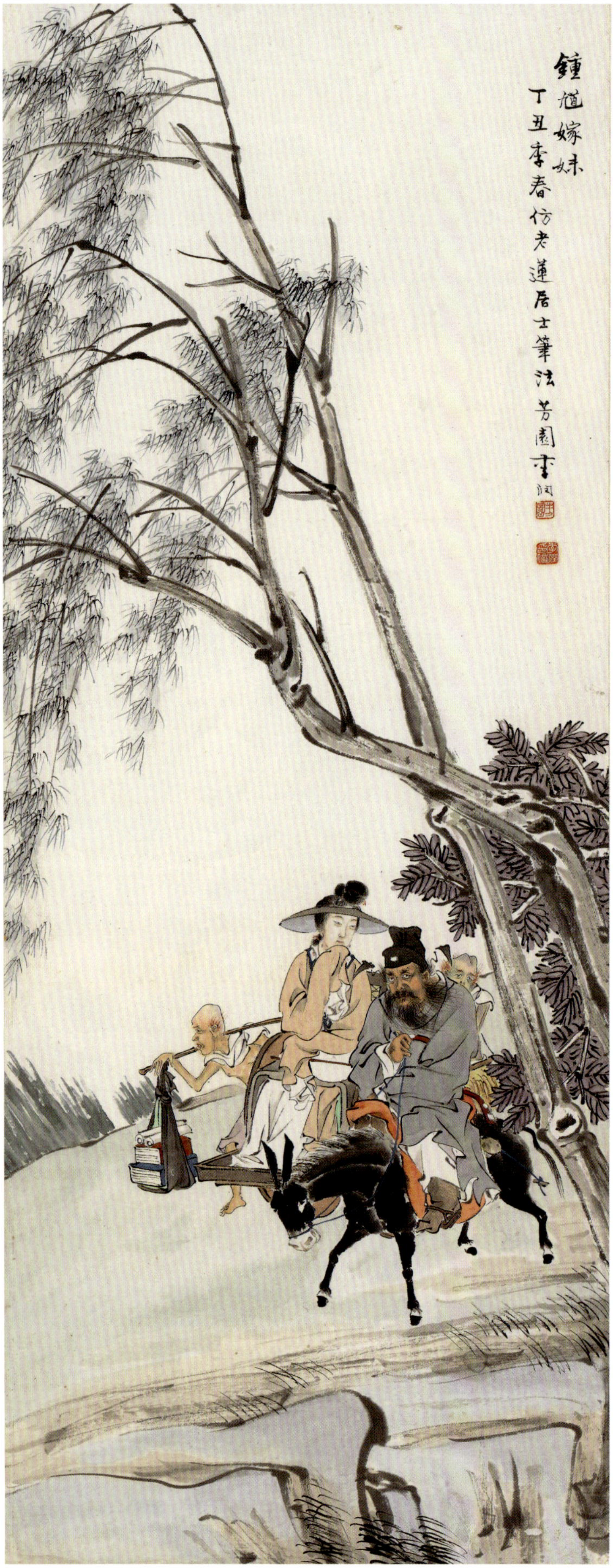
鍾馗嫁妹
丁丑季春仿老蓮居士筆法 芳園李潤

Artist:
Li Fangyuan

Medium:
Color on paper, Hanging scroll

Dimensions:
97 cm × 37 cm

Zhong Kui Marrying Off His Sister

Inscription:
In the late spring of the Dingchou year, the brushwork inspired by the venerable Lay Scholar Laolian was rendered by Fangyuan, Li Run.

Seal:
Fangyuan, the signature seal of Li Run

Li Fangyuan (1883–1947)
A native of Shanghai. Influenced by Ren Yi, he excelled in painting figures and animals and served as a teacher at institutions such as the Shanghai Academy of Fine Arts and Xinhua Art College.

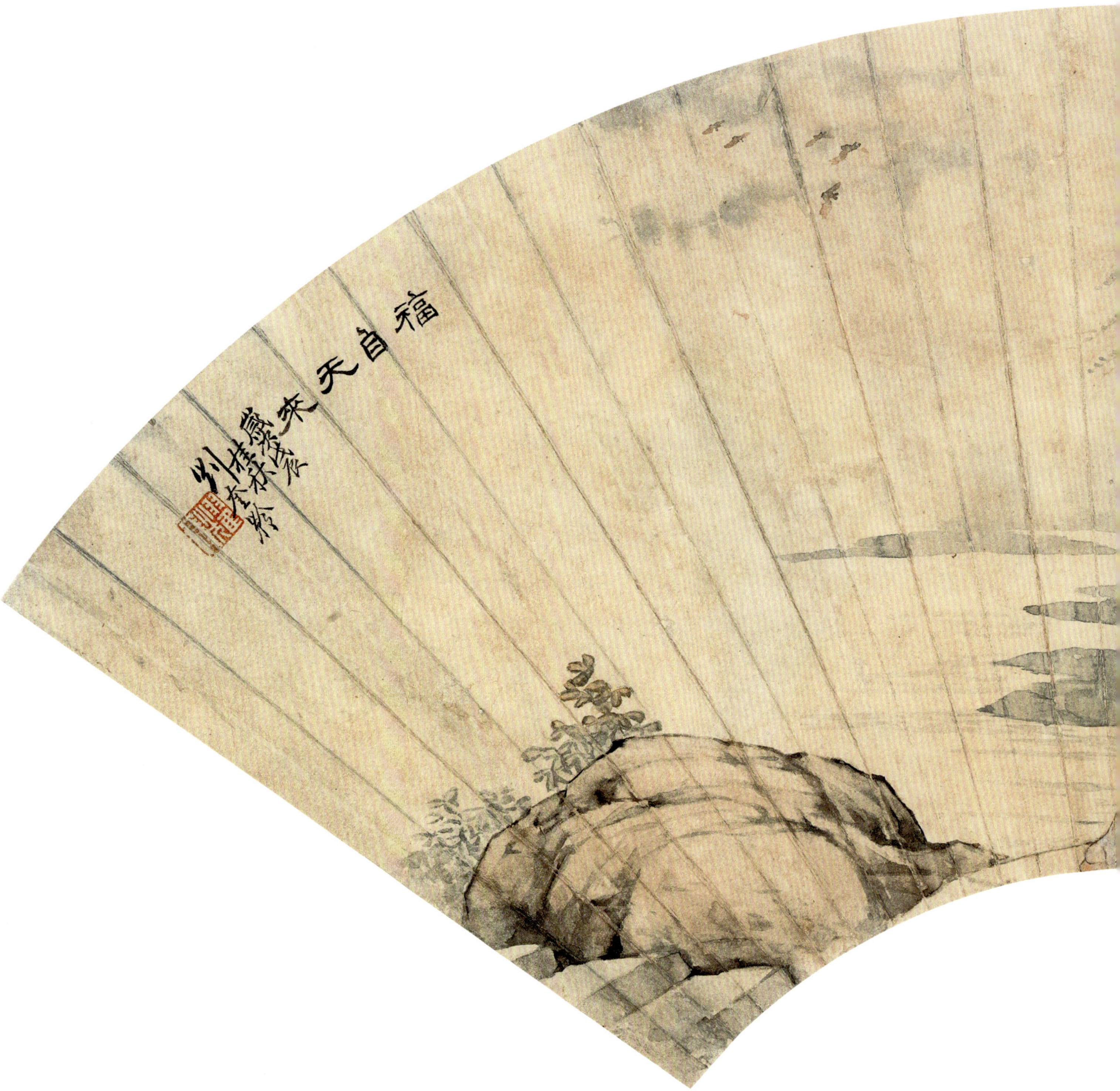
福自天來

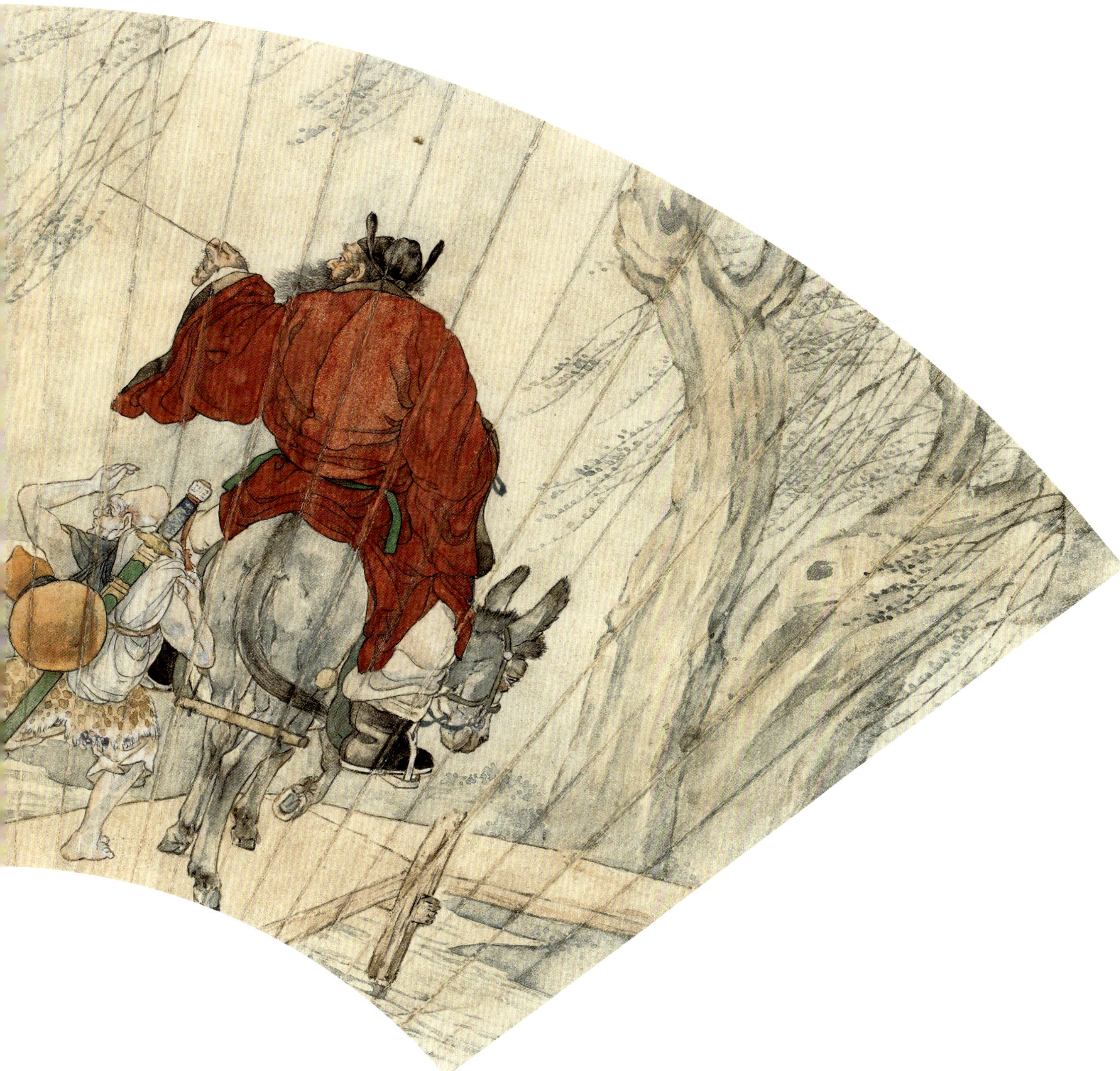

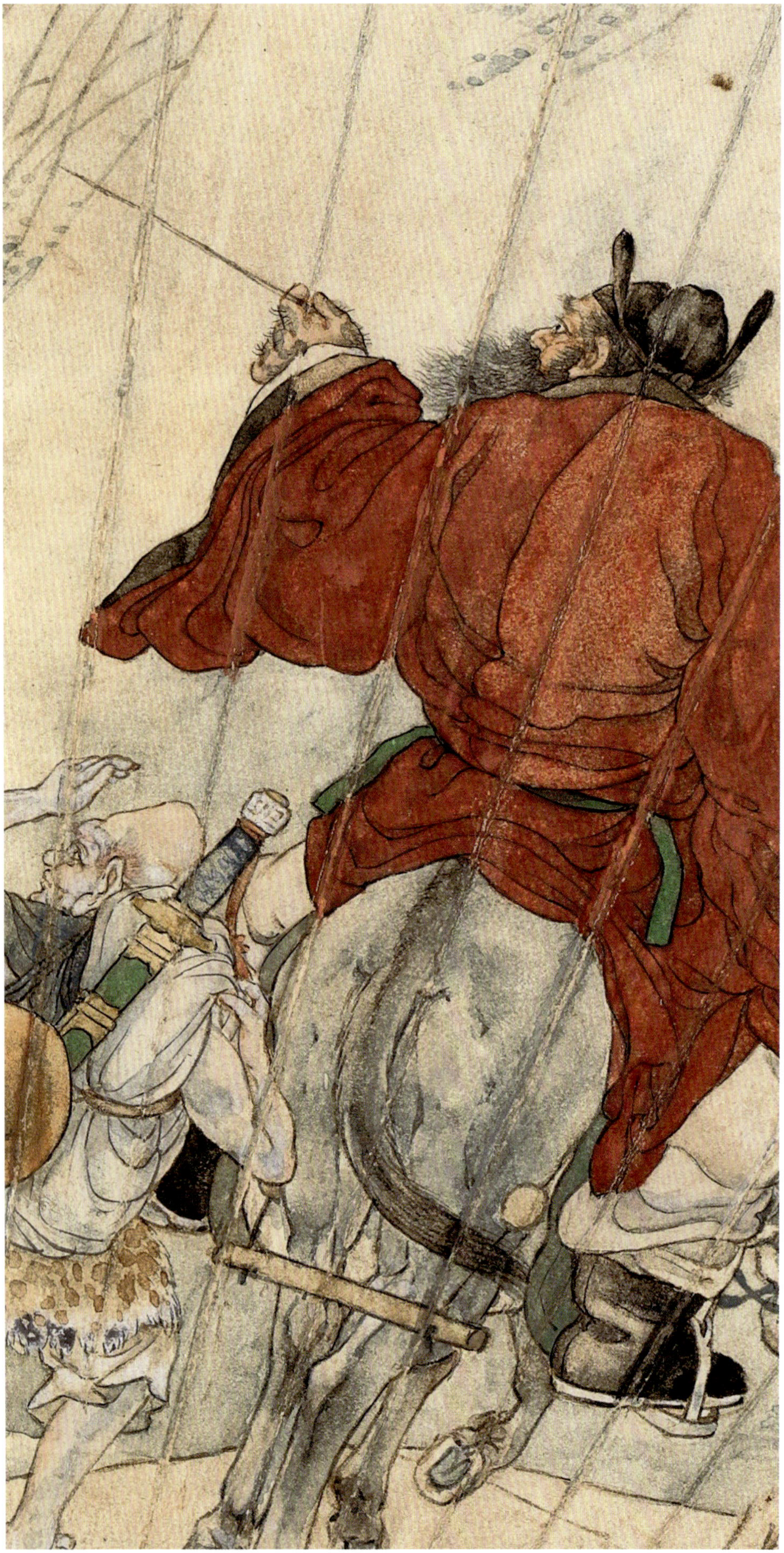

Artist:
Liu Kuiling

Medium:
Color on paper, Framed piece

Dimensions:
18 cm × 48.5cm

Blessings from Heaven

Inscription:
In the osmanthus autumn of the year Wuchen, completed by Liu Kuiling.

Seal:
Yaochen

Liu Kuiling (1885–1967)
Courtesy name Yaochen, styled as Dieyin, self-titled as the Master of the Ink Garden Hermitage, a native of Tianjin. He was a calligrapher and painter.

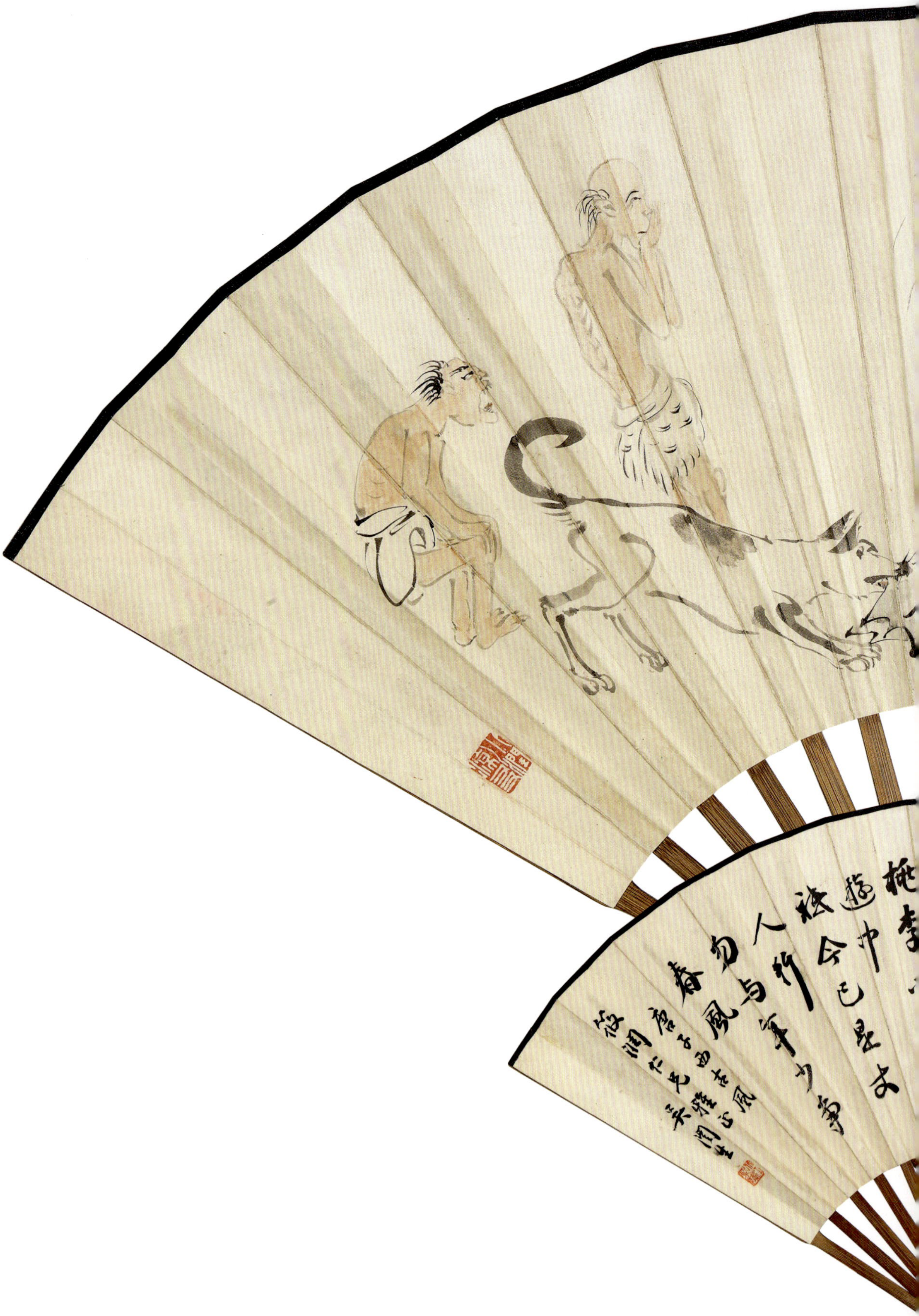

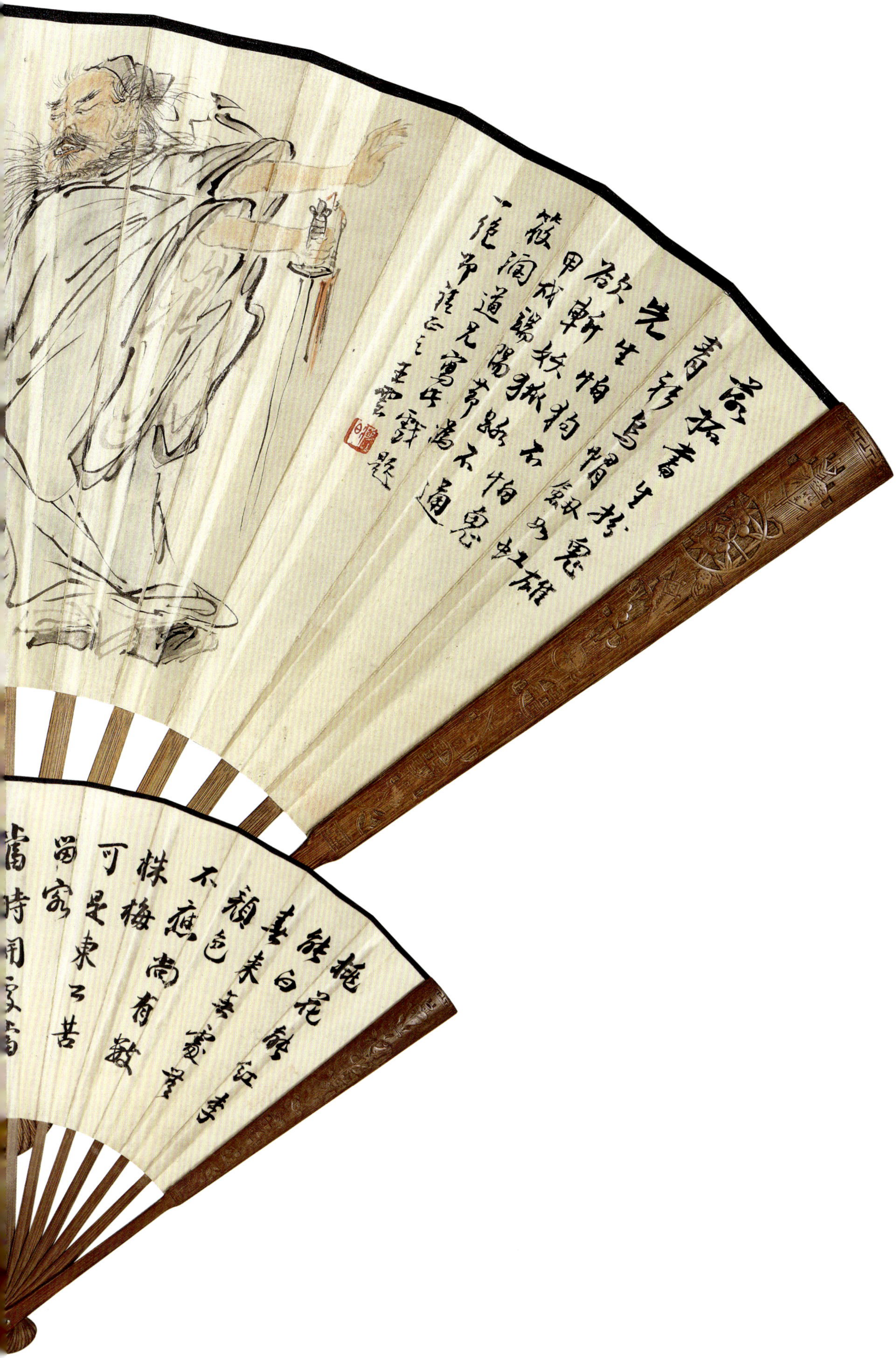

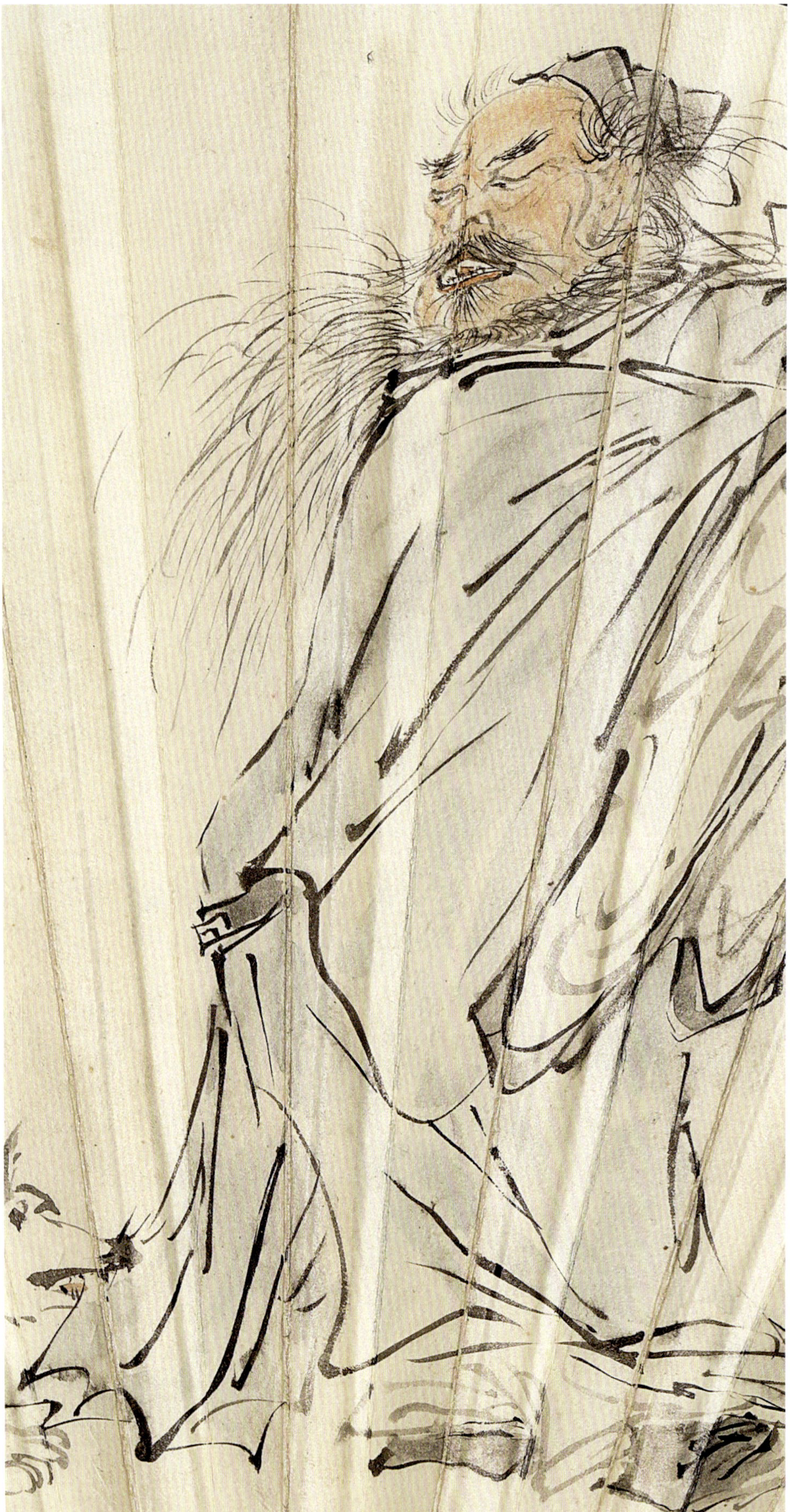

Artist:
Wang Mengbai, Wu Kaisheng

Medium:
Color on paper, Completed fan

Dimensions:
20 cm × 52 cm

Zhong Kui Fearing Dog

Inscription:
A carefree scholar takes on the guise of a ghostly knight,
In his blue robe and black hat, his sword shines bright like light.
Though ghosts don't scare this man, he's wary of hound's bark,
He aims to cut down demon foxes, but finds no path through the dark.
On the Dragon Boat Festival of the Jiaxu year, I composed this playful verse for friend Xiaorun. Please promptly correct any errors. Wang Yun.

Seal:
Mengbai, Shuirun Liangyou

Backside Calligraphy

Inscription:
Peach blossoms flaunt a vibrant red, plum flowers a pristine white,
With spring's arrival, every place is drenched in colorful light.
Yet, there should be more than just a few plum trees in bloom,
But the old neighbor to the east delights in keeping guests in his room.
When the plums first blossomed, it was the deep of winter's chill,
Peach and plum had not yet joined in the season's festive thrill.
Now, as I walk the path of an elder, no longer youthful and free,
I shall not contend with the young for the spring's fickle glee.

Seal:
Beijiang Ranhan

Wang Mengbai (1888–1934)
Named Yun, with the courtesy name Mengbai, styled as the Master of Po Zhai, also known as San Dao Ren, a native of Fengcheng, Jiangxi. He studied the painting style of Ren Yi and was guided by Wu Changshuo.

Wu Kaisheng (1877–1950)
Styled as Beijiang, respectfully known as Mr. Beijiang, the son of Wu Rulun. A native of Zongyang, Anhui, he studied in Japan. During the late Qing dynasty, he served as the chief officer of the Finance Department of the Board of Revenue. In the era of the Beiyang Government, he served as the Vice Minister of Education and a Councilor of the State Council. After 1928, he held positions as a professor at the Cuisheng Academy in Fengtian and as a literary researcher at the Beijing Ancient Academy. His works include five volumes of Mr. *Beijiang's Collection of Poems*, twelve volumes of *Commentary of Zuo Zhuan*, and seven volumes of Mr. *Beijiang's Collection of Essays.*

菊蔚先生大雅并正

山林豪客

癸未夏日画於大佛古寺 [illegible]天

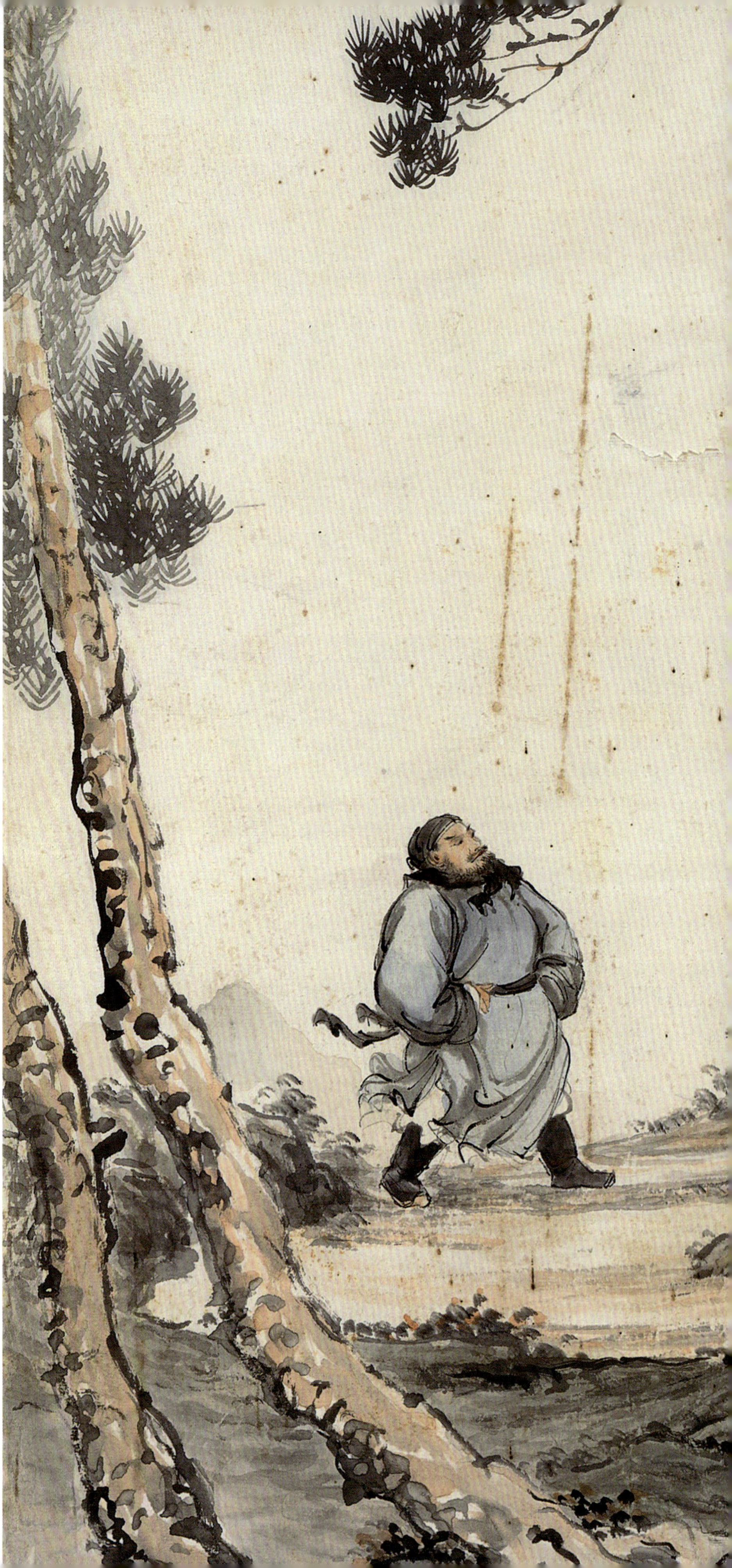

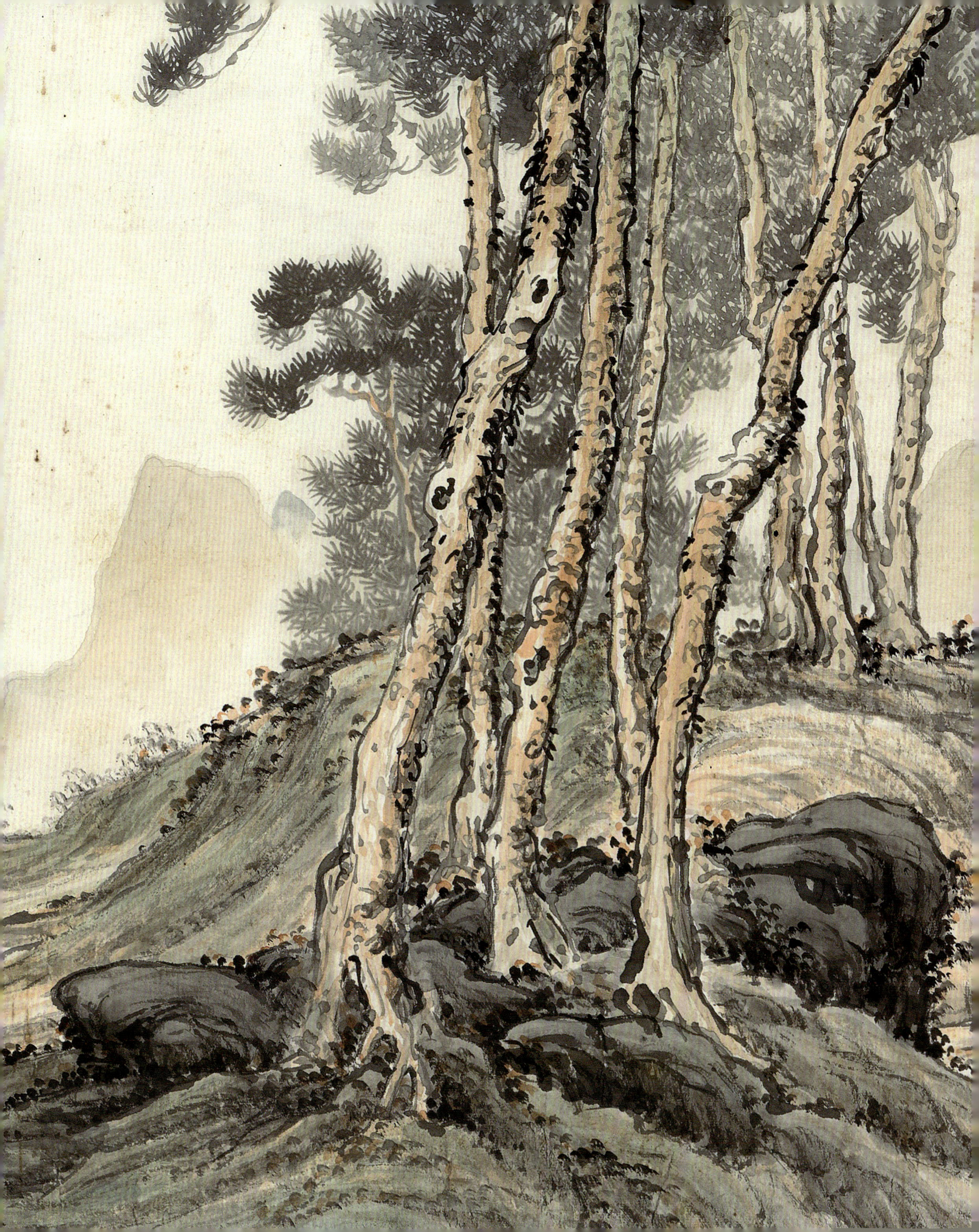

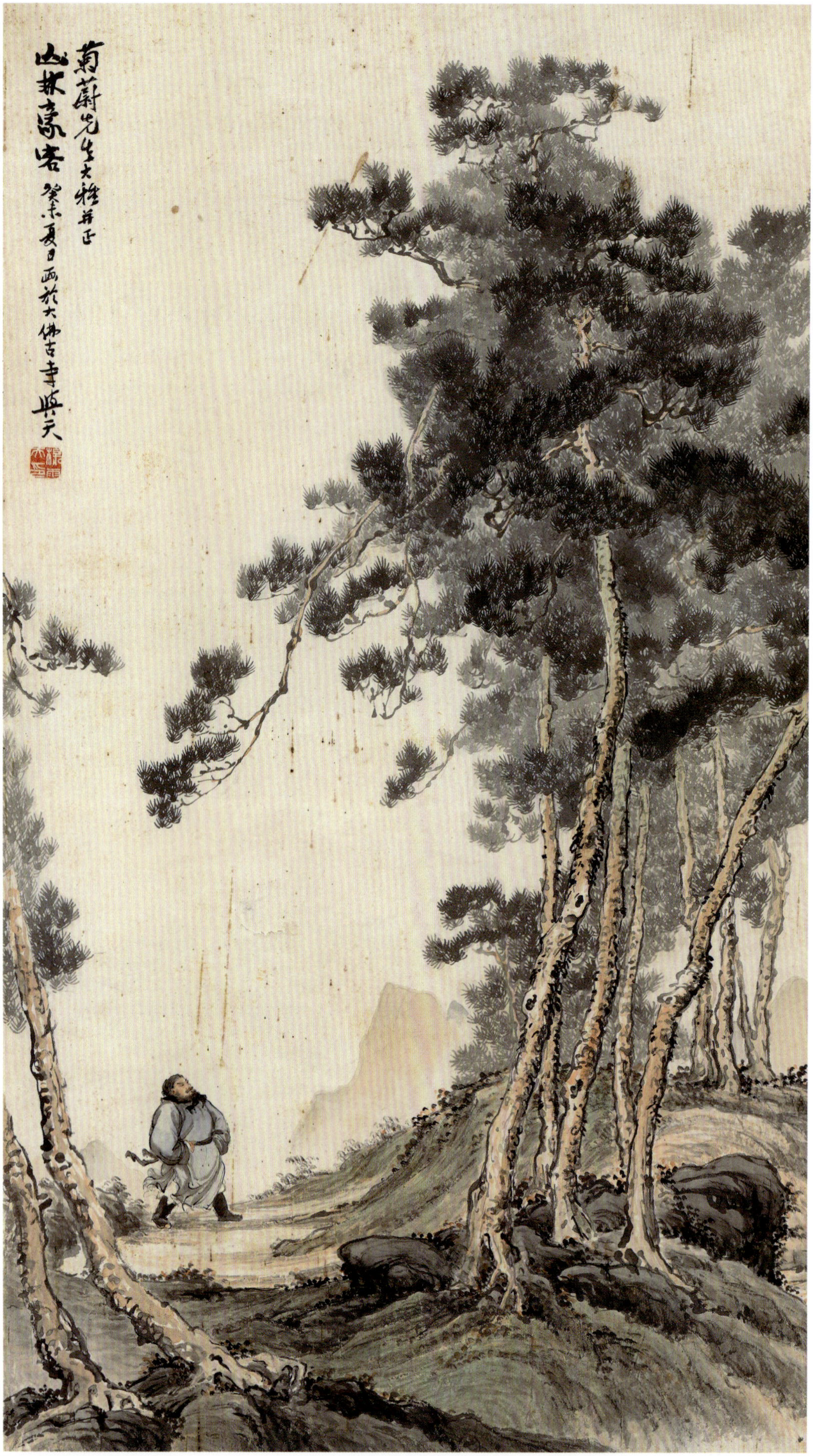
山林豪客

Artist:
Mei Yutian

Medium:
Color on paper, Completed fan

Dimensions:
94 cm × 51.5 cm

Mountain Forest Noble Guest

Inscription:
Mountain Forest Noble Guest. On the summer day of the Guiwei year, I painted at the ancient temple of the Great Buddha, Yutian. Mr. Juwei's work is of great elegance and correctness.

Seal:
The seal of Mei Yutian

Mei Yutian (1891–unknown)
A native of Shunde, Guangdong, he was a painter and an art educator. He served as a teacher at several art schools in Guangzhou and Hong Kong. Adept in Western painting, he relocated to Hong Kong after the war and settled in Honolulu, United States, in the 1960s.

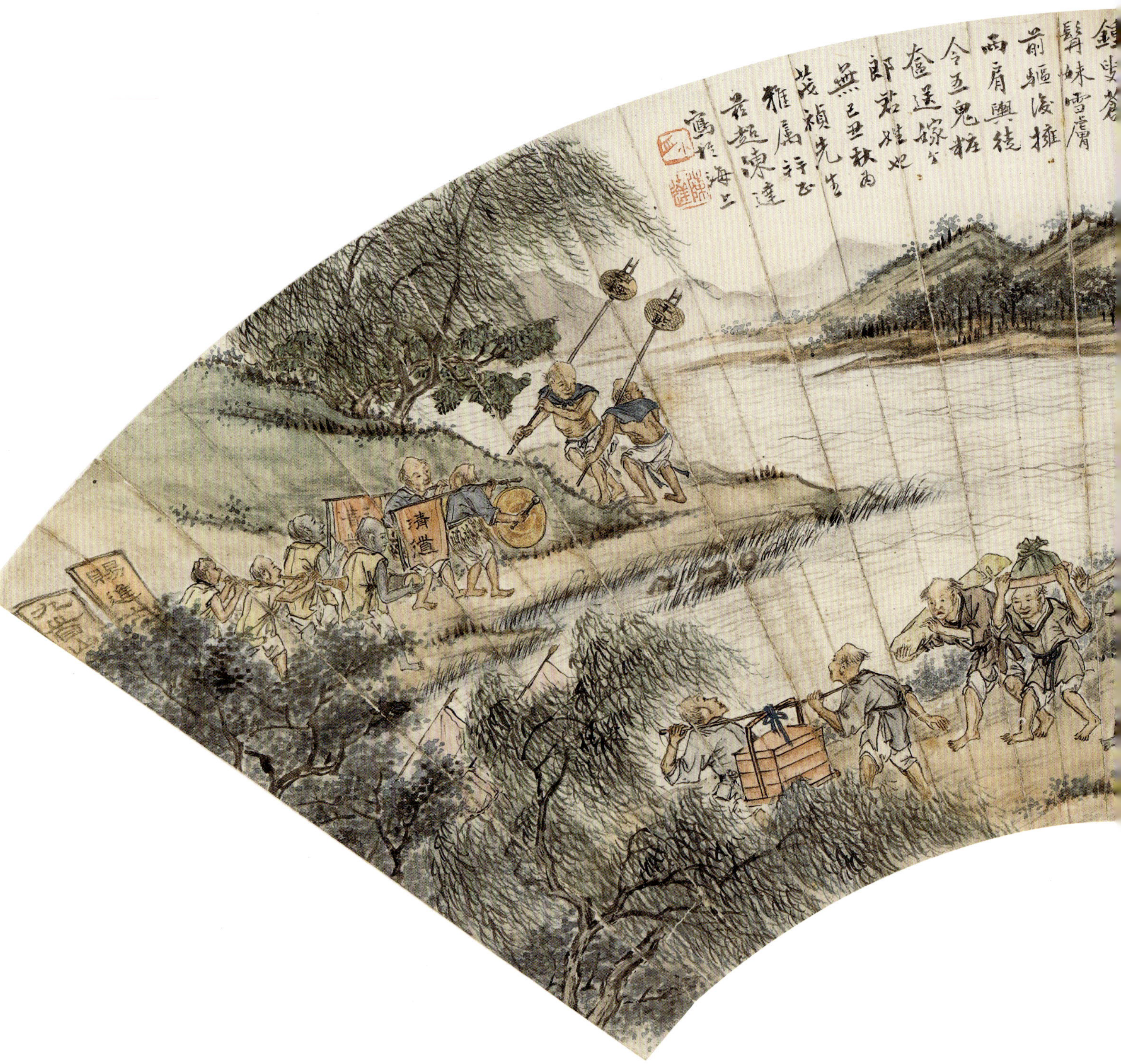
寫於海上
清道
賜進士

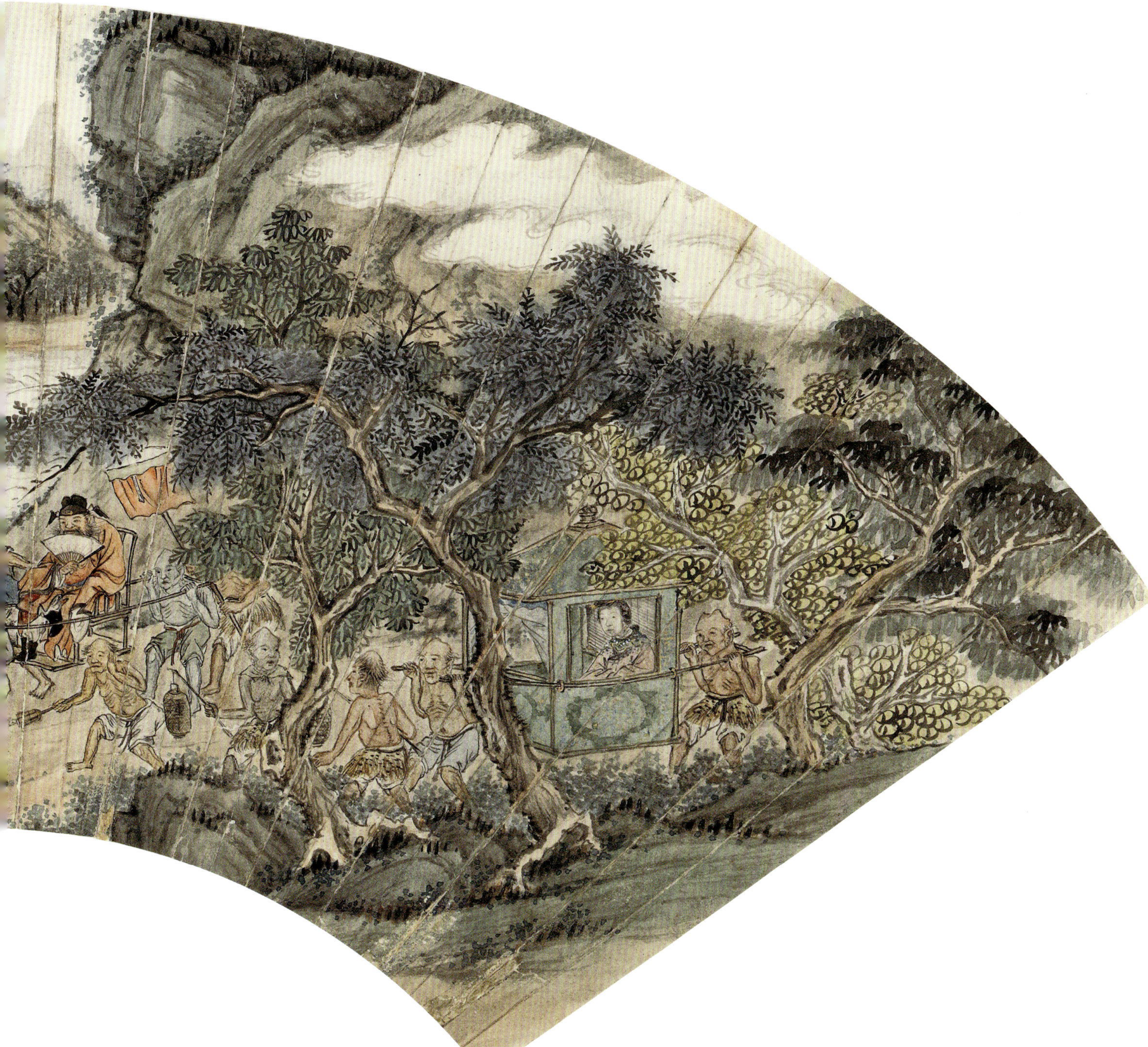

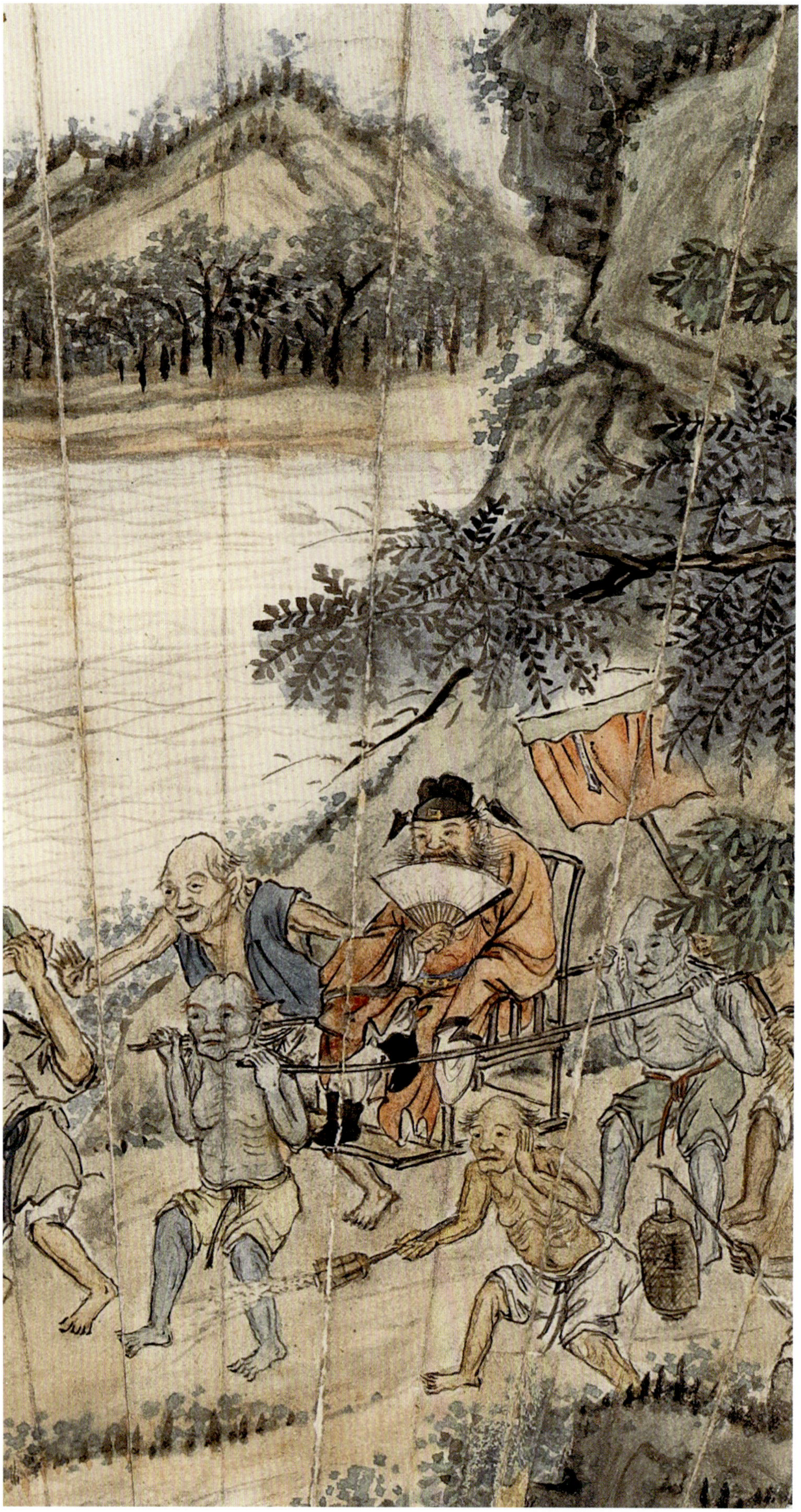

Artist:
Chen Da

Medium:
Color on paper, Fan-shaped

Dimensions:
18 cm × 51 cm

Zhong Kui Marrying Off His Sister

Inscription:
An elder with silver beard, a maid with skin like snow,
A procession leads and follows the bridal palanquin's slow tow.
In vain do five ghosts deck the bridal box to send,
For she's wed to a groom without a name.
In the autumn of the Jichou year, I made revisions and corrections to the elegant section belonging to Mr. Mao Zhen. This task was completed by Zi Chao, Chen Da, in Shanghai.

Seal:
Xiaozhou, Chen Da, Chengxing

Chen Da (1892–1975)
A native of Changshu, Jiangsu, with the courtesy name Xiaozhou, was a landscape painter during the Republic of China period.

初三月好落黃浮玉篴江城五月秋扶
醉踈來香攤袖幾回含笑看吳鉤
筱嵒寫 壺巢題 己丑天中

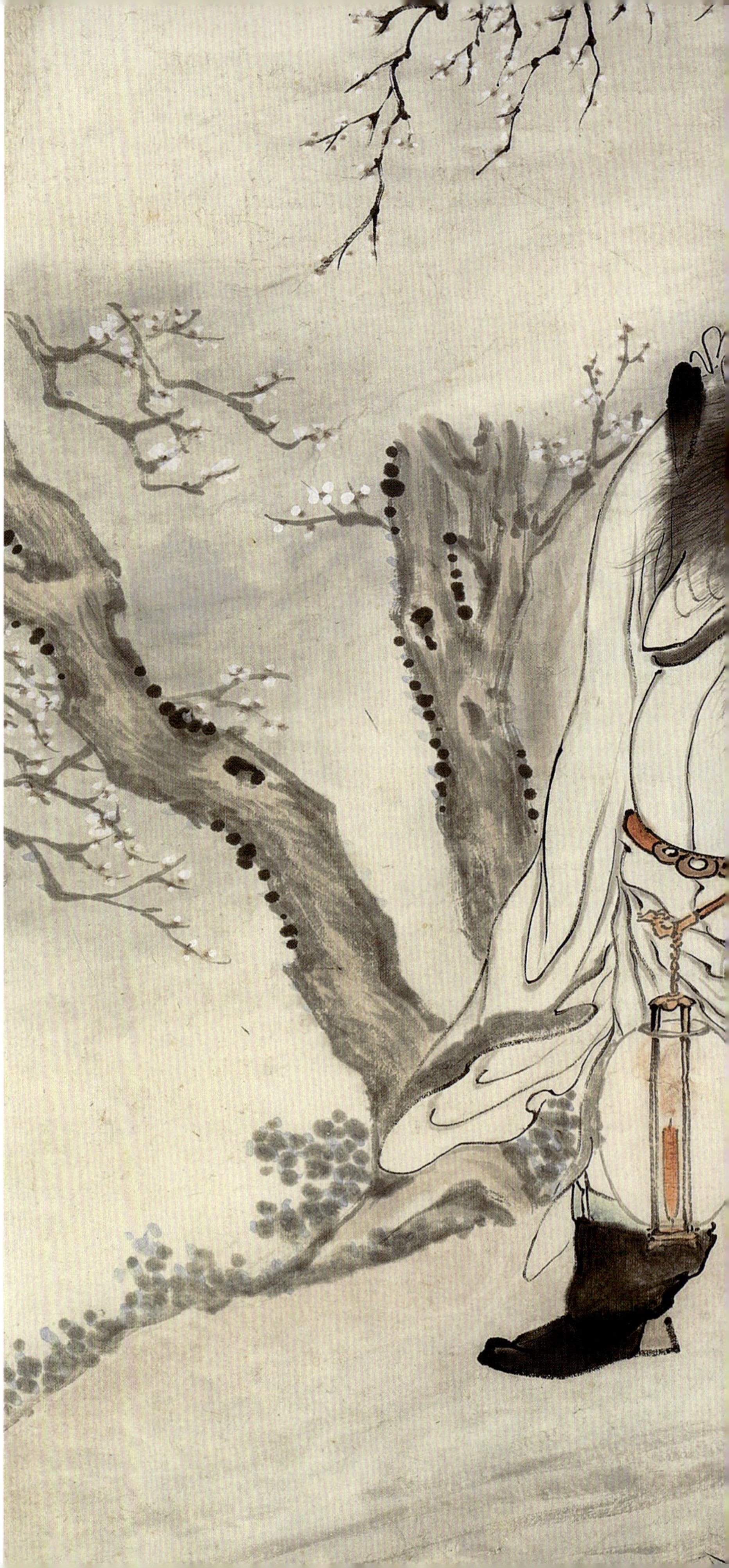

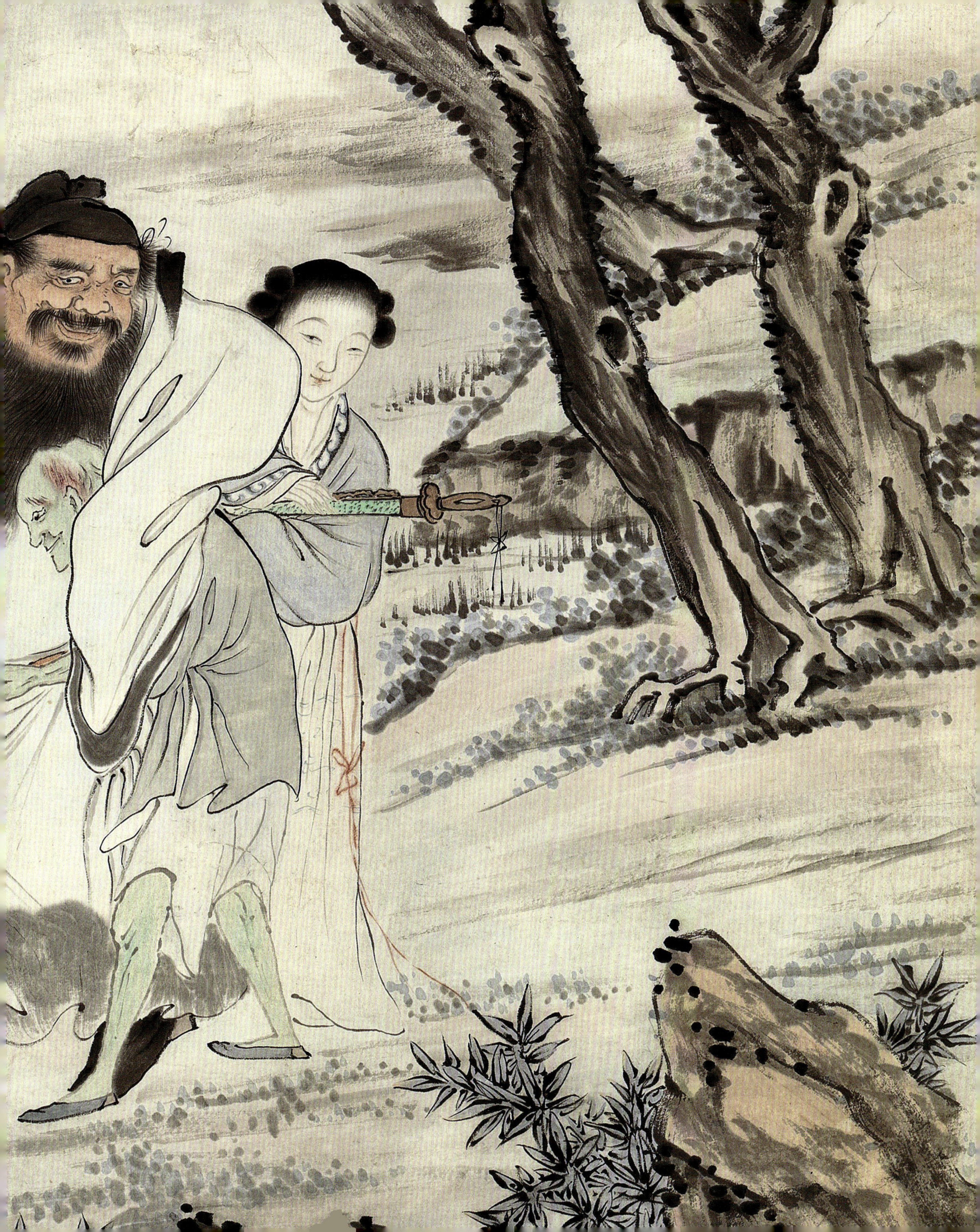

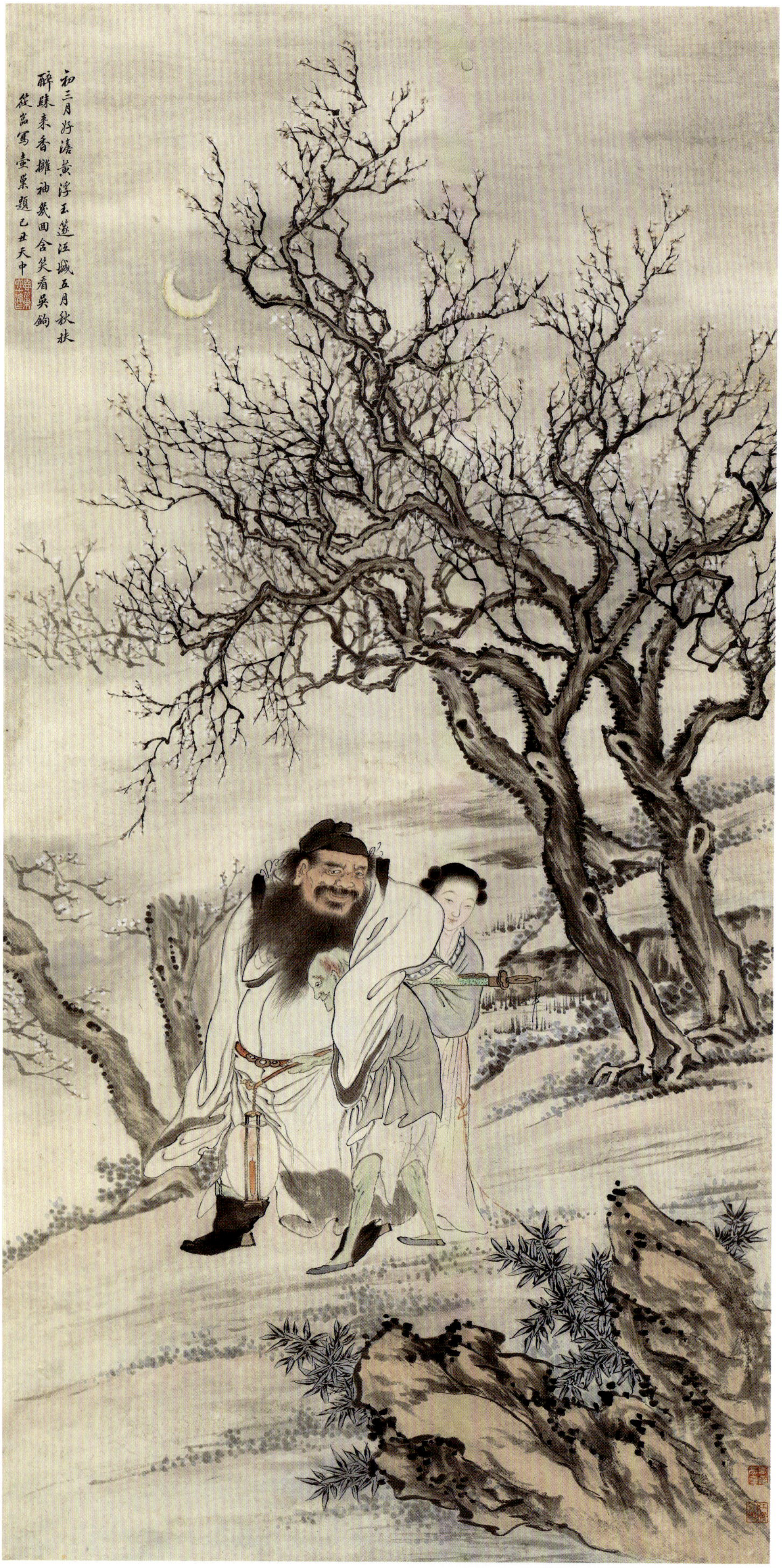
初三月好濤黄浮玉蕊江城五月秋扶
醉踈来香攤袖幾回含笑看吳鈎
筱㟁寫壷巣題乙丑天中

Artist:
Gu Xiaoyan

Medium:
Color on paper, Hanging scroll

Dimensions:
133 cm × 65 cm

Zhong Kui Marrying Off His Sister

Inscription:
In early March, the gentle yellow catkins drift,
While the jade flute in the river city hints of May's autumn shift.
Steadied from my tipsy return, fragrance clings to my sleeve,
Often with a smile, I gaze back at the sword, so naive.
Written by Xiaoyan, inscribed by Huchao, on Tianzhong Festival in the Jichou year.

Seal:
Works of Huchao post-sixty, the seal of Li Yankui, Historian of Hongqiao

Gu Xiaoyan (1892–1968)
A native of Pudong, Shanghai, originally named Hongxian, he studied medicine from an early age under his father Yunyan and brother Xiaoyun. He was acclaimed as one of the "Three Xiaos of Shanghai"along with the renowned orthopedist Shi Xiaoshan and the famed gynecologist Chen Xiaobao. In 1948, he relocated to Hong Kong and practiced medicine in Kowloon. In 1956, he was among the first to return to Shanghai, taking a post at the Shanghai Institute of Traditional Chinese Medicine Literature, where he devoted himself to writing. He was also skilled in calligraphy and painting and had an extensive collection.

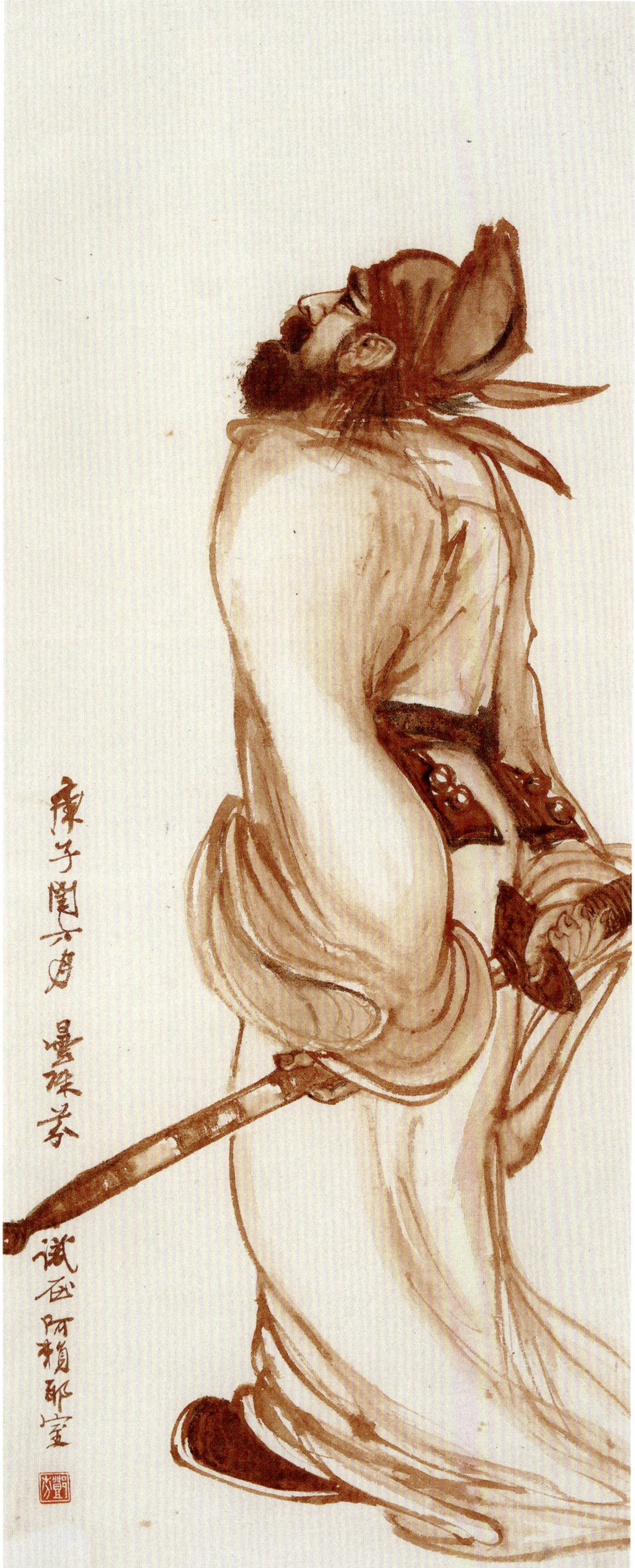

Artist:
Deng Fen

Medium:
Color on paper, Hanging scroll

Dimensions:
84 cm × 33 cm

Cinnabar Zhong Kui

Inscription:
In the intercalary sixth month of the Gengzi year, Tanshu, Deng Fen made an inscription within the ālaya-vijñāna.

Seal:
Deng Fen

Deng Fen (1894–1964)
Courtesy name Songxian, styled as Tanshu, and also known as Mr. Congxin, was a native of Nanhai, Guangdong. A modern painter of the Lingnan school, he was exceptionally intelligent from a young age, excelling in calligraphy, painting, seal carving, poetry, and music.

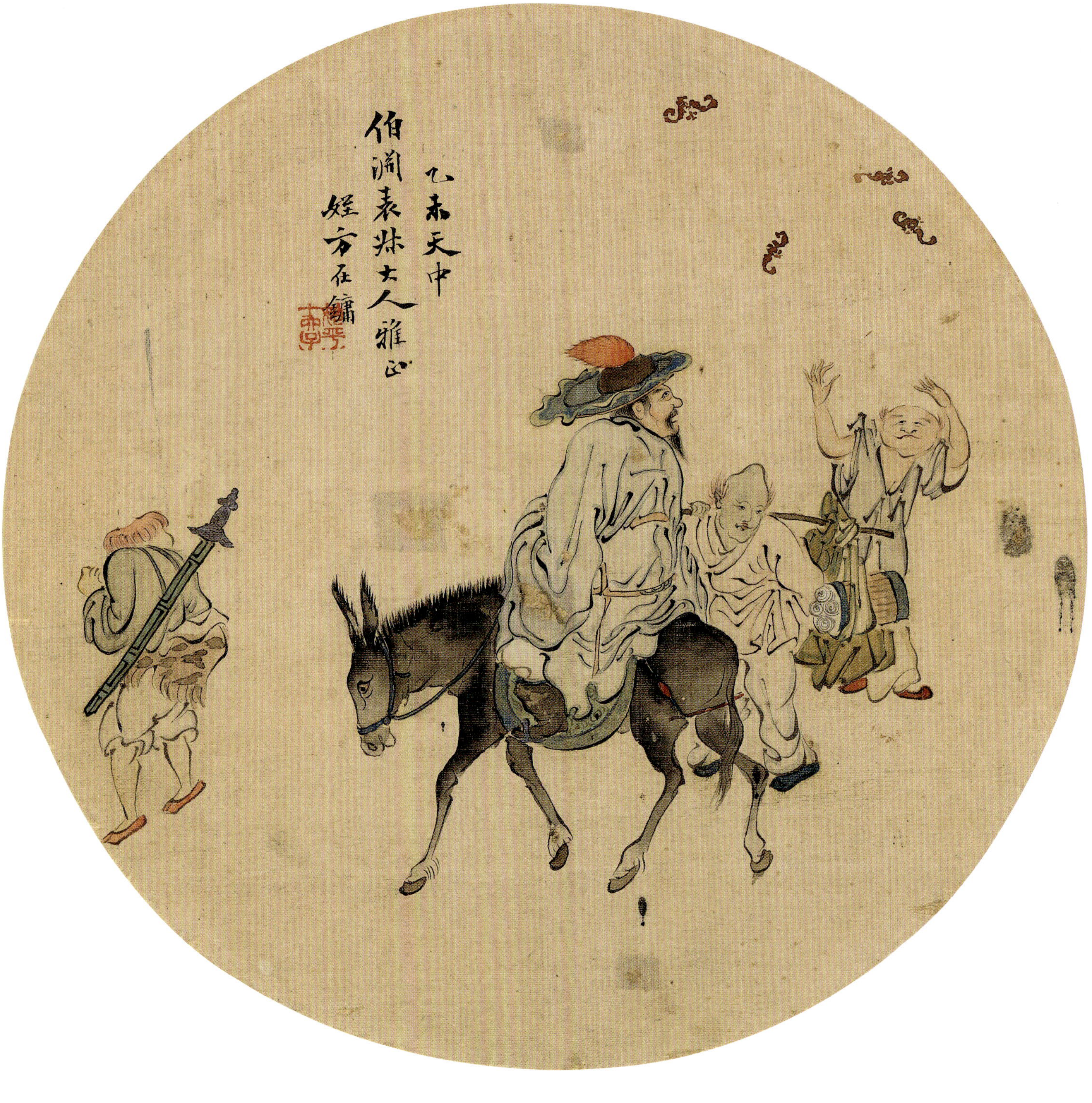
乙未天中
伯淵表妹大人雅正
姪方在鏞

Artist:
Fang Zaiyong

Medium:
Color on silk, Framed piece

Dimensions:
24 cm

Blessings from Heaven

Inscription:
On the Tianzhong Festival of the Yiwei year, my uncle Boyuan meticulously corrected this work, Fang Zaiyong.

Seal:
Yaoping's sixteenth son

Fang Zaiyong
He served as a local official in the northern Jiangsu region during the late Qing and early Republic of China periods, with little detail known about his life.

終南捷徑

著雍攝提格又相月 張侶笙繪 袁希廉題

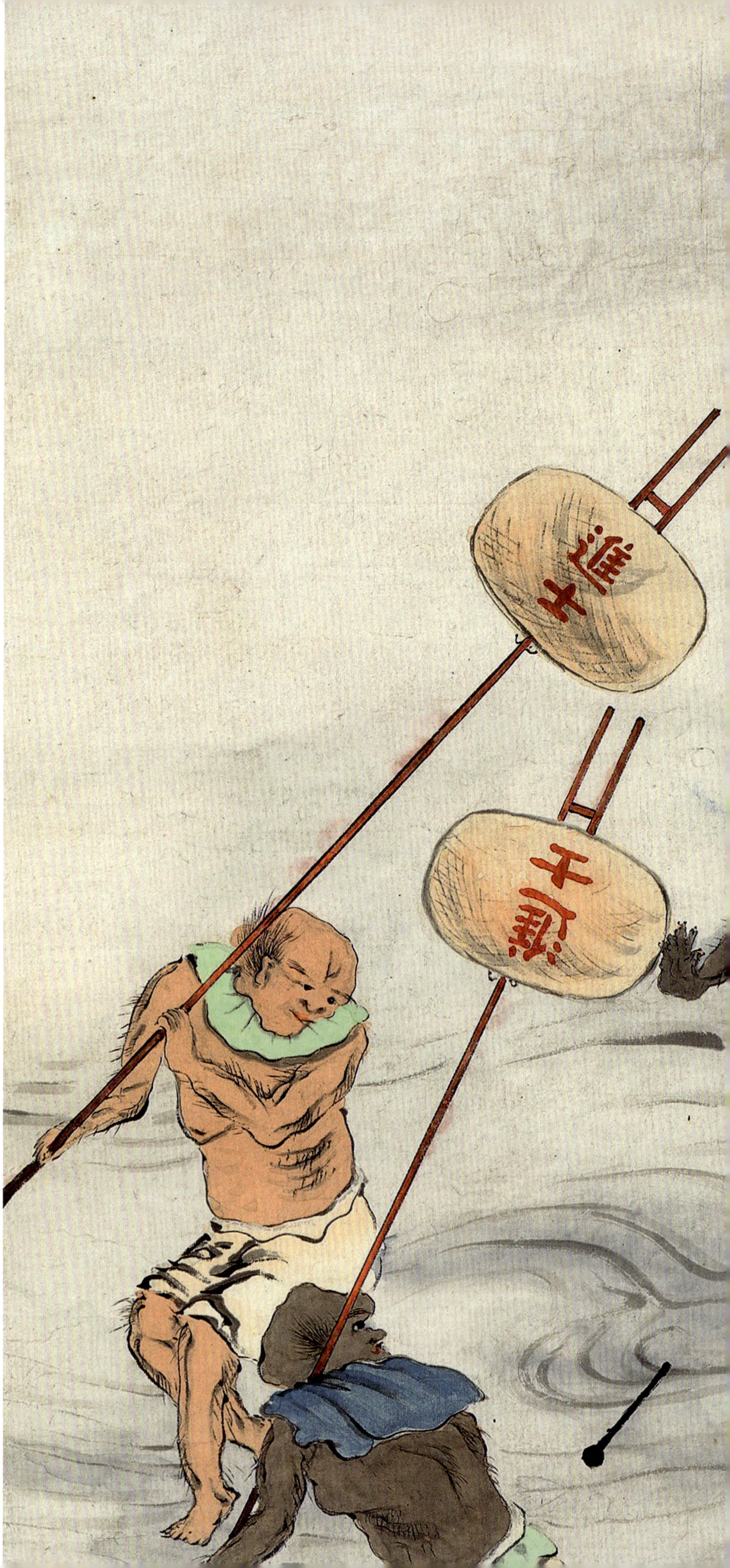

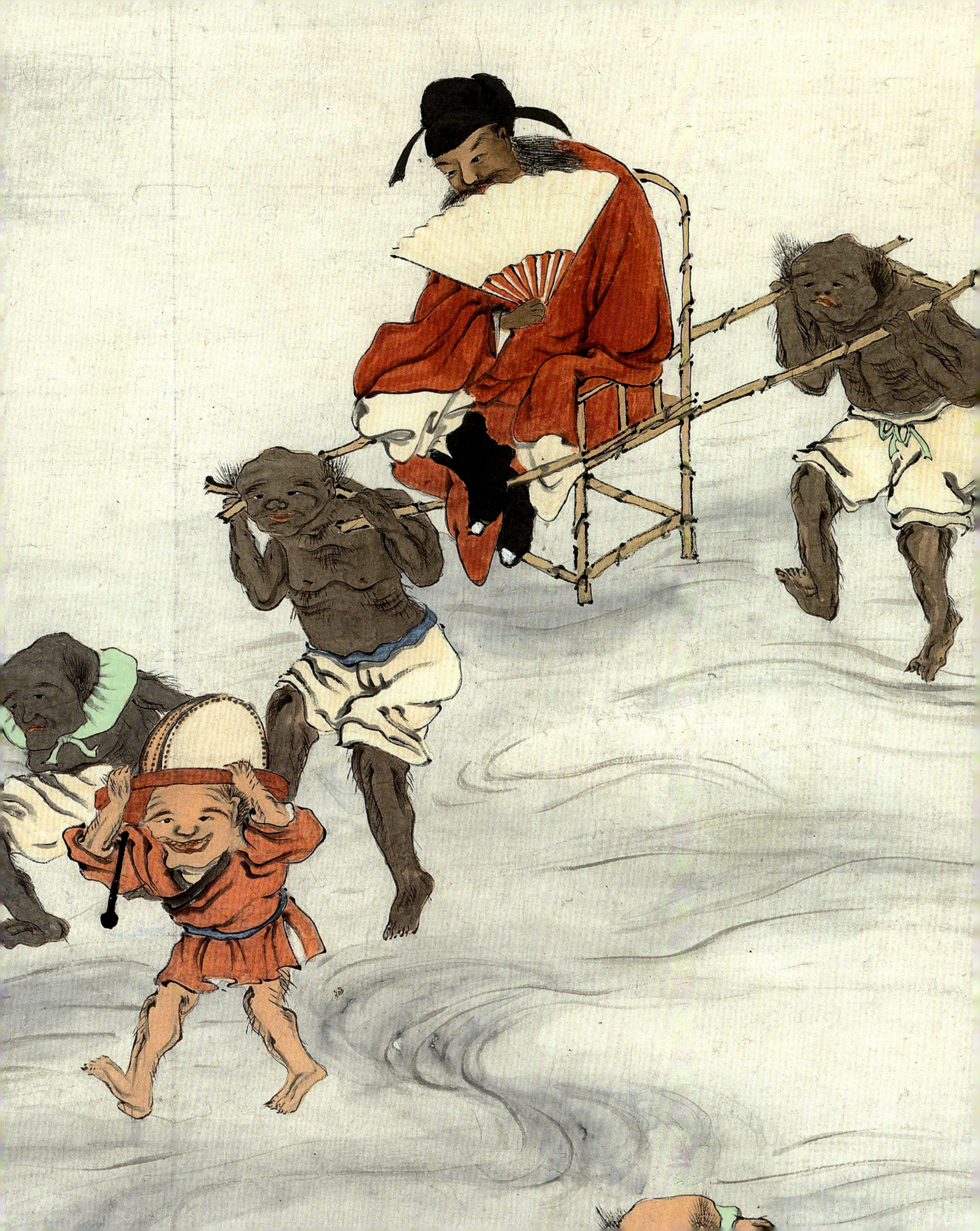

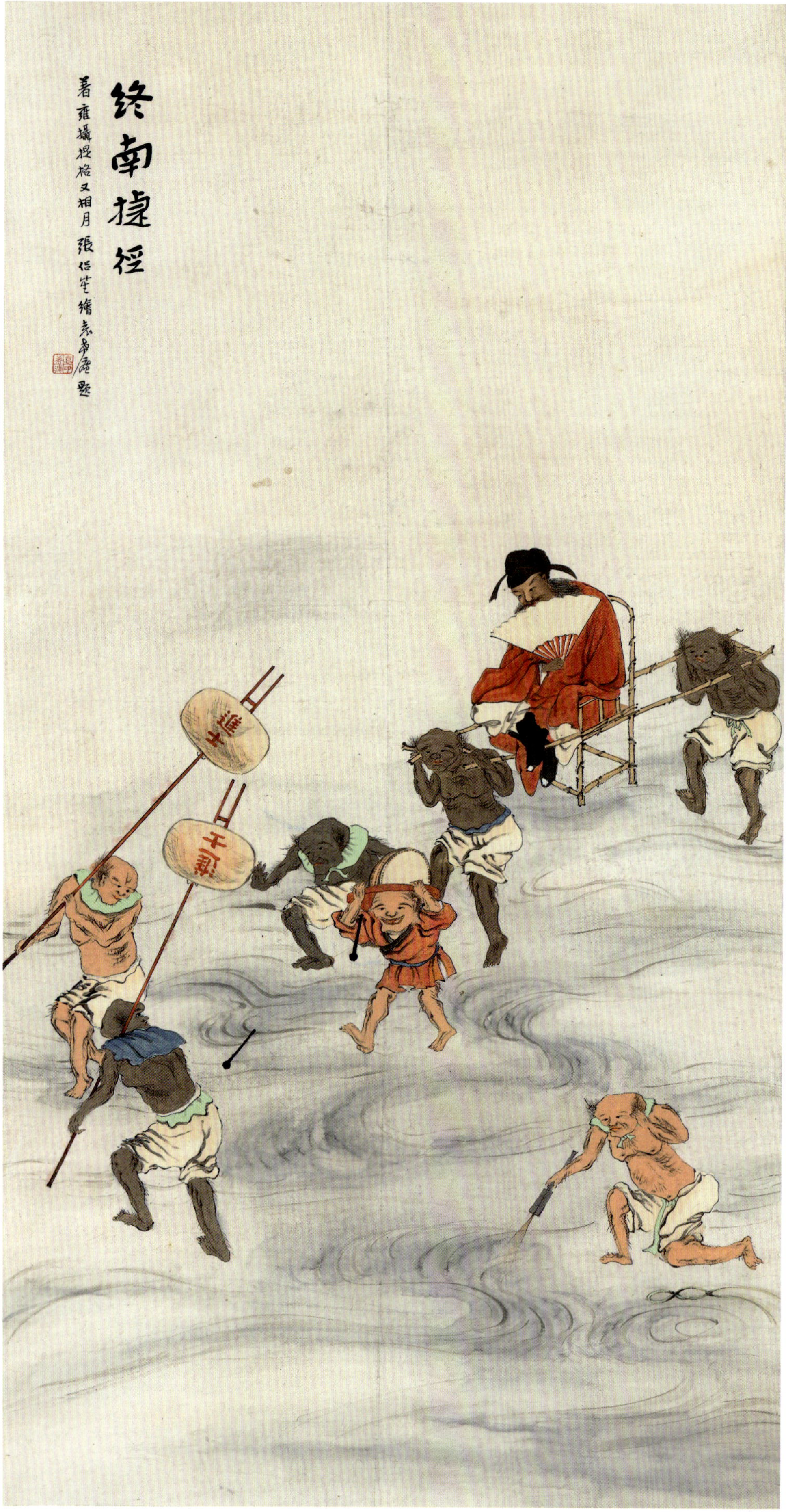
終南捷徑
著雍攝提格又相月張信笙繪袁希廉題

Artist:
Zhang Lusheng, Yuan Xilian

Medium:
Color on paper, Hanging scroll

Dimensions:
134 cm × 69 cm

Shortcut to Zhongnan

Inscription:
In the Yongzheng era, under the Sheti Ge[3], the moon was beheld anew; the painting executed by Zhang Lusheng, with an inscription by Yuan Xilian.

Seal:
The seal of Yuan Xilian

Zhang Lusheng (1897–1949)
Originally named Shengyong, courtesy name Huian, styled as Lusheng, hailing from Yinxian (now Ningbo City). He delighted in painting bamboo, rocks, and flowers, using vivid colors that brimmed with vitality. Equally skilled in landscapes and figures, his depictions of Mount Huang were so lifelike they could be mistaken for the real thing. He was also proficient in calligraphy. In 1945, he relocated to Shanghai, sustaining himself with his paintings. His brother Shenghao was also adept in calligraphy and excelled in floral paintings, sharing a similar artistic style with his brother.

Yuan Xilian (unknown–1950)
Courtesy name Zhonglian, from Baoshan, Jiangsu, known along with his brothers Yuan Xiluo and Yuan Xitao as the "Three Yuans of Baoshan." He studied at the Longmen Academy in Shanghai during the reign of Emperor Guangxu. After returning to China in the year of Xinhai (1911), he served as a judge in Tianjin. He formed a close bond with Li Shutong, Cai Xiaoxiang, Zhang Xiaolou, and Xu Huanyuan, known collectively as the "Five Friends of Tianya." He was also involved in organizing the Shanghai Calligraphy and Painting Association.

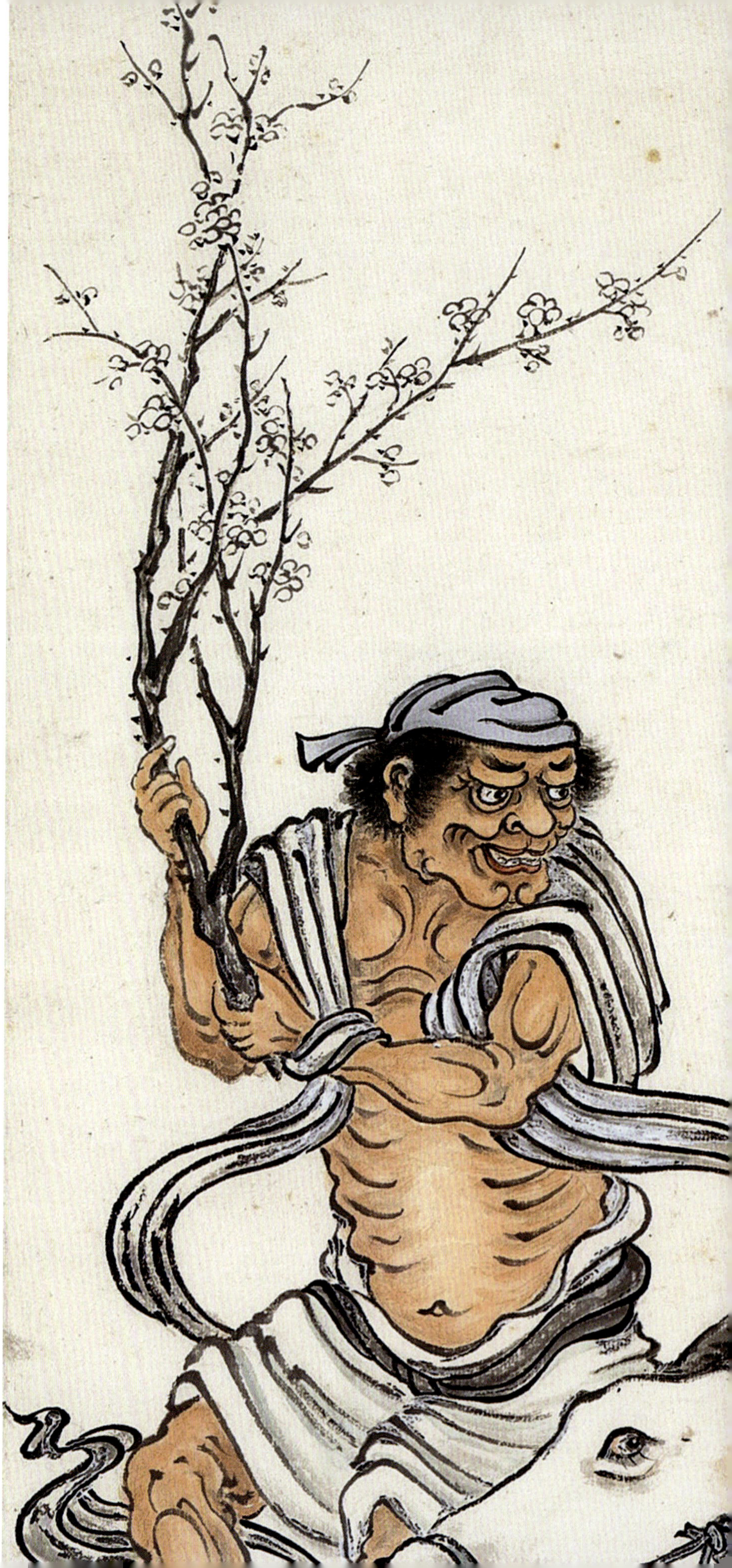

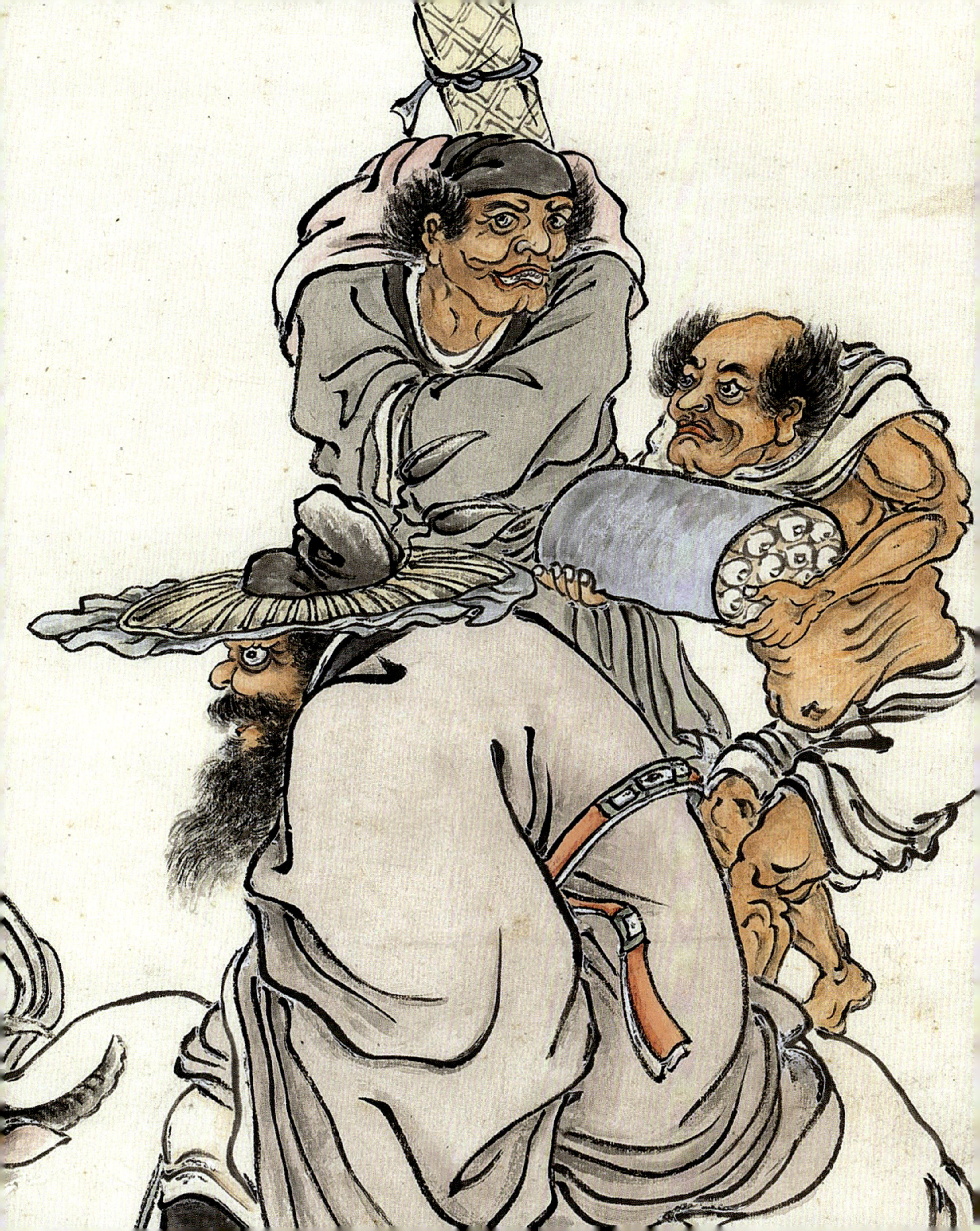

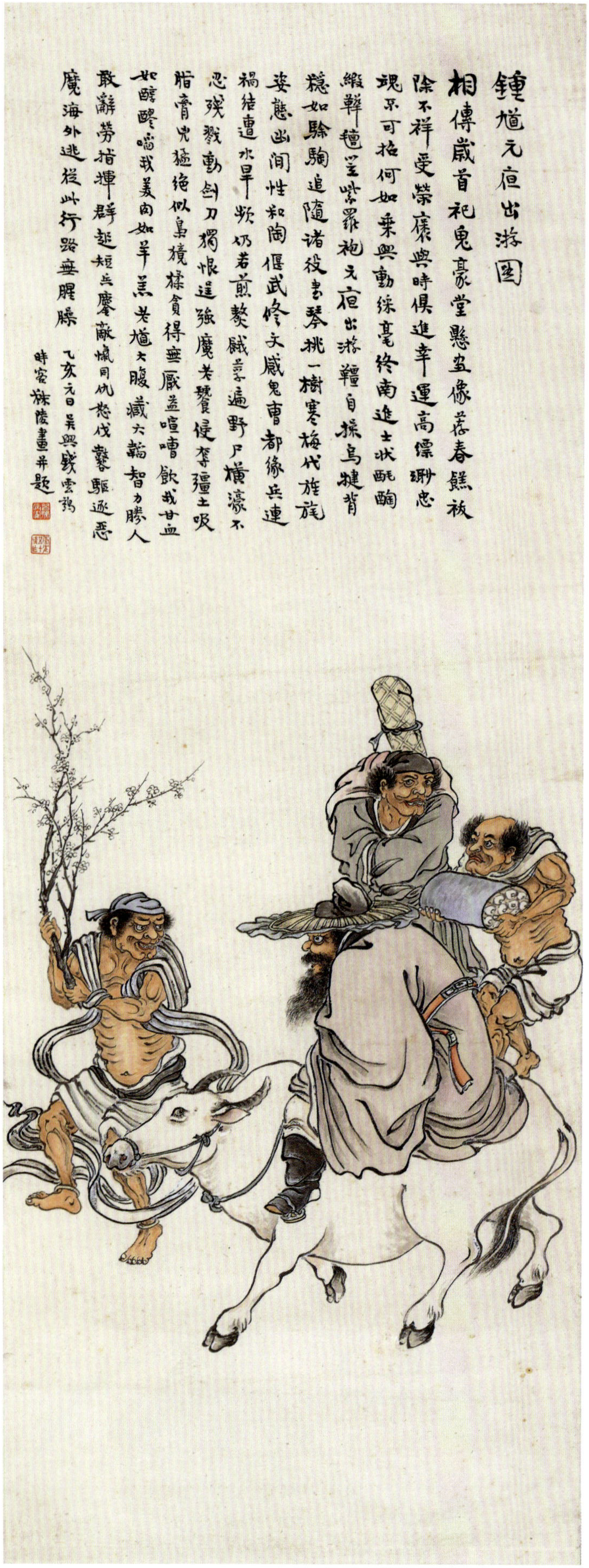
鍾馗元宵出游圖
相傳歲首祀鬼豪堂懸畫像荐春餻祓
除不祥受禁褒與時俱進幸運高標聯忠
魂不可招何如乘輿動絲毫終南進士狀酕醄
緞鞾氈笠紫羅袍元宵出游韉自操烏犍背
穩如騄駒追隨諸役書琴挑一樹寒梅代旌旗
姿態幽閒性和陶偃武修文感鬼曹都緣兵連
禍結遭水旱粃仍若煎熬賊寇遍野尸橫濠不
忍殘殺動劍刀獨恨暹強魔羌饕侵奪疆土吸
脂膏兇猛絕似梟獍棣貪得無厭益喧嘈飲我甘血
如醇醪噉我美肉如羊羔老馗大腹藏六韜智力勝人
敢辭勞指揮群鬼短兵鏖敵愾同仇怒伐鼛驅逐惡
魔海外逃從此行路無腥臊
乙亥元日吳興錢雲鶴
時客秣陵畫并題

Artist:
Qian Yunhe

Medium:
Color on paper, Hanging scroll

Dimensions:
108 cm × 40 cm

The New Year's Eve Excursion of Zhong Kui

Inscription:
The New Year's Eve Excursion of Zhong Kui.
It's said at the year's start heroes' spirits are revered,
With portraits hung and spring cakes offered, auspiciousness endeared.
Such rituals are to dispel misfortune, hoping for fame and luck to accrue,
But the loyal souls of yore are beyond summoning, this much is true.
Instead, in a joyous mood, why not let the colorful brush freely sway,
As those who passed the imperial exams at Zhongnan in their drunken play.
On Lantern Festival's eve, one takes the reins alone, content to roam,
The steadfast black ox steady as the tried and true at home.
Servants in tow with books and qin, as a lone plum tree stands for the army's guide,
Leisurely and content in demeanor, by the spirits' grace, they abide.
But war's relentless spread, calamity upon calamity, the land does scorch,
With famine-stricken bodies strewn across fields, a massacre's grim porch.
Unable to bear further slaughter, the sword laid to rest, its duty done,
Cursing those whose strength is spent in greed, their voracious hunger never shun.
They ravage lands, their ferocity unmatched, their clamor loud and coarse,
Drinking our blood as if fine ale, devouring our flesh without remorse.
Yet Zhong Kui, with belly vast, harbors grand strategies bold,
Wise beyond measure, unafraid of labor, his valor unfolds.
Commanding the troops, short weapons clashing, united in wrathful tide,
Driving demons to distant shores, purging the path of their rank hide.

Seal:
Formerly styled as Binghe, Works of Yunhe after Fifty

Qian Yunhe (1878–unknown)
Also known as Binghe, with the given name Xin, courtesy name Weixin, Minyou. A native of Huzhou, Zhejiang. He excelled in landscape painting and was well-known in Shanghai where he sold his paintings between 1912 and 1927.

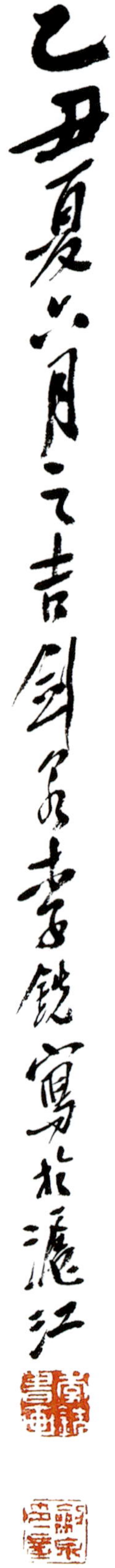
乙丑夏六月之吉劍客李銳寫於滬江
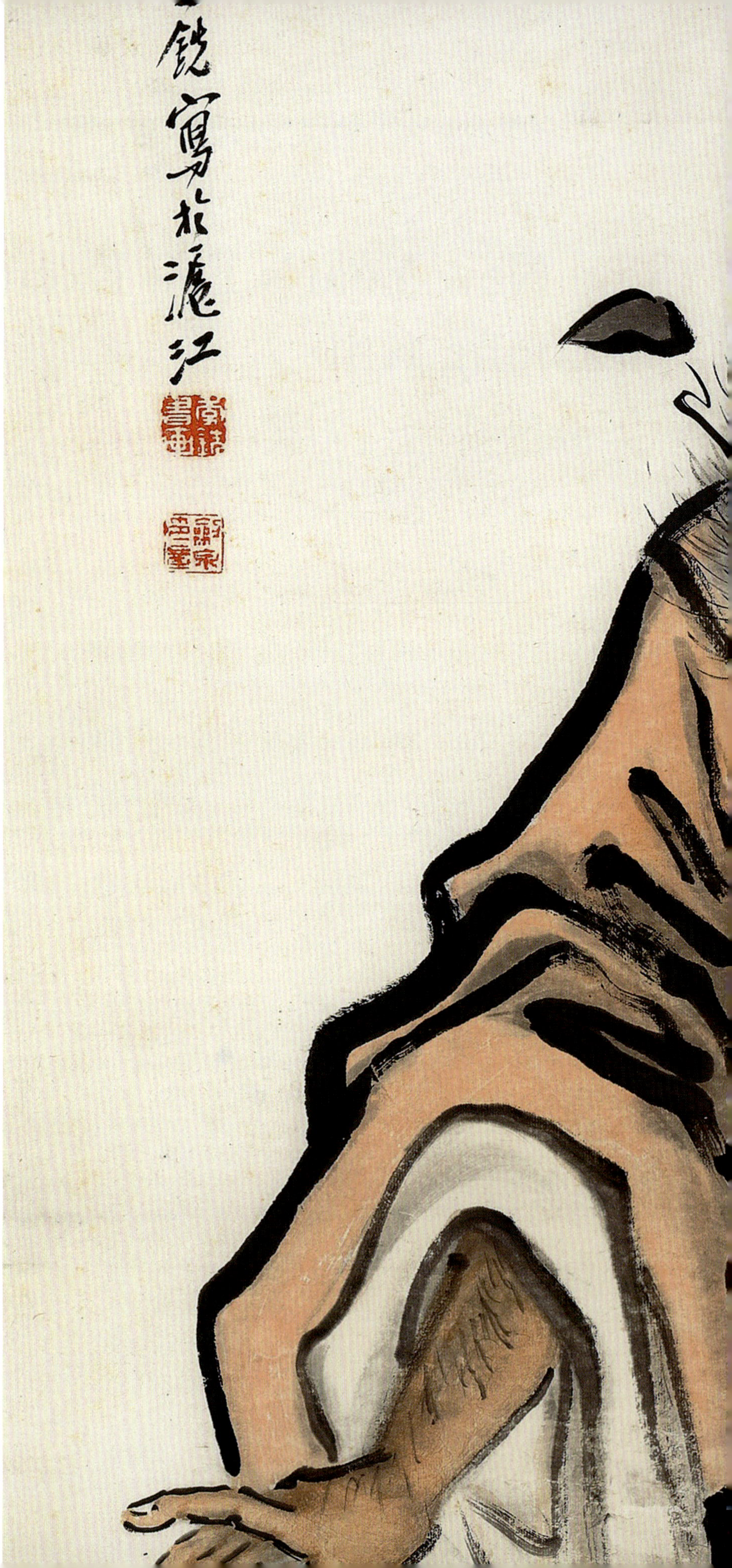
銳寫於滬江

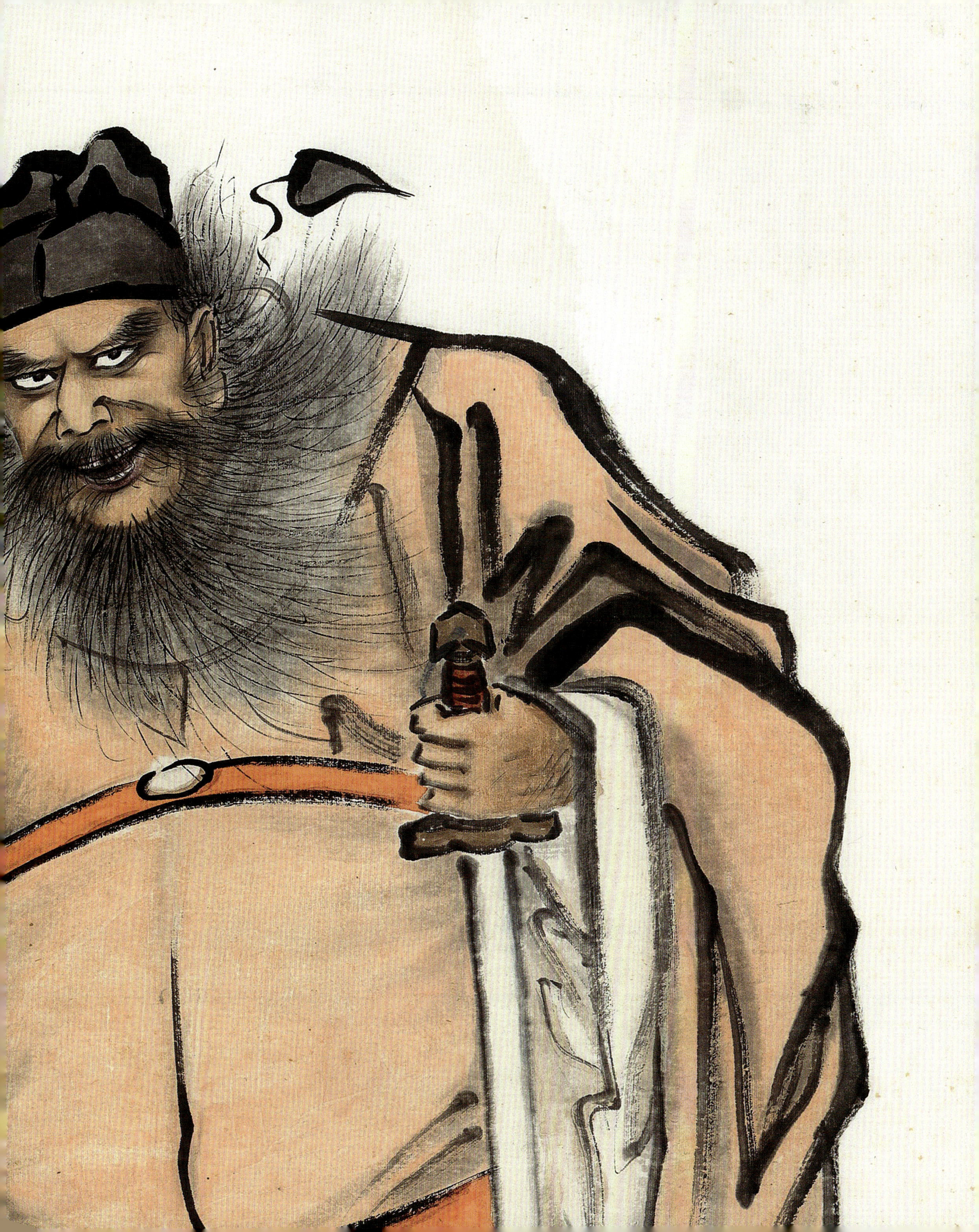

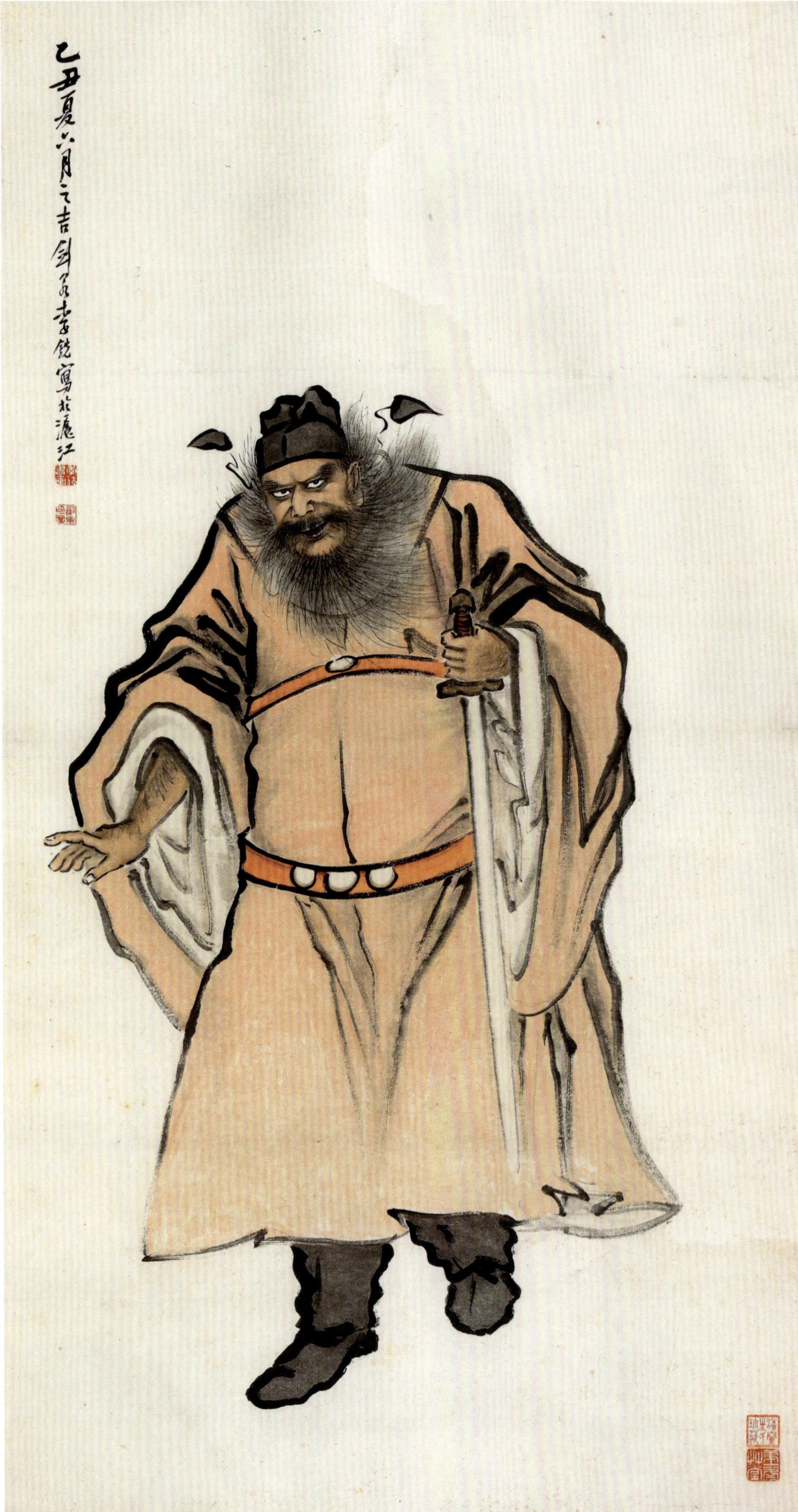

Artist:
Li Xian

Medium:
Color on paper, Hanging scroll

Dimensions:
147 cm × 78 cm

Zhong Kui

Inscription:
On an auspicious day in the sixth month of the summer of the Yichou year, Jianquan, Li Xian, wrote this in Shanghai.

Seals:
Li Xian's calligraphy and painting, the seal of Jianquan

Collector's Seal:
Treasured by Mr. Pan Lansheng, Thatched Cottage of the Premier Peak

Li Xian
Styled Jianquan, a native of Hangzhou. He was a painter during the Republic of China era, skilled in depicting plum blossoms and figures.

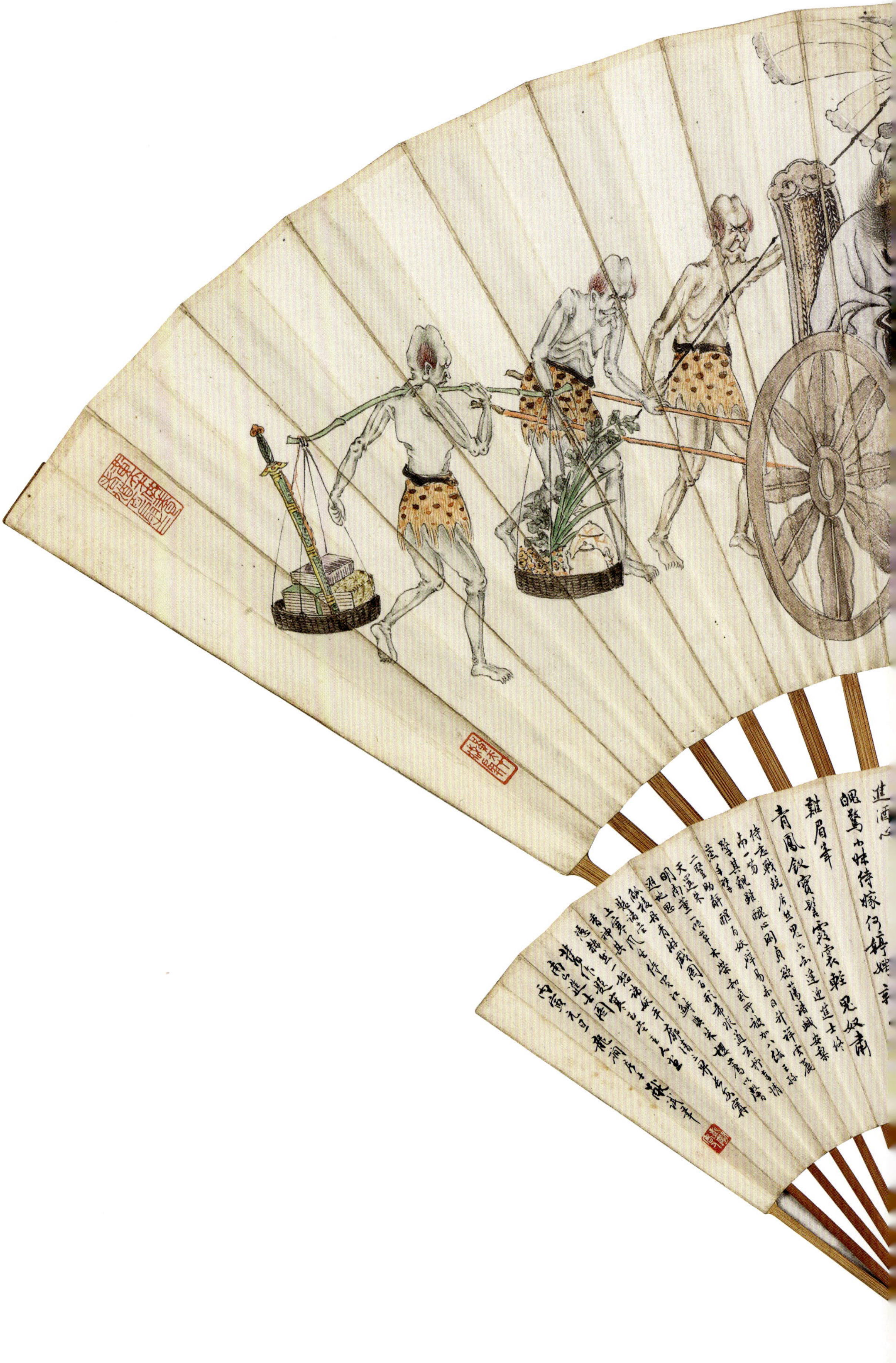

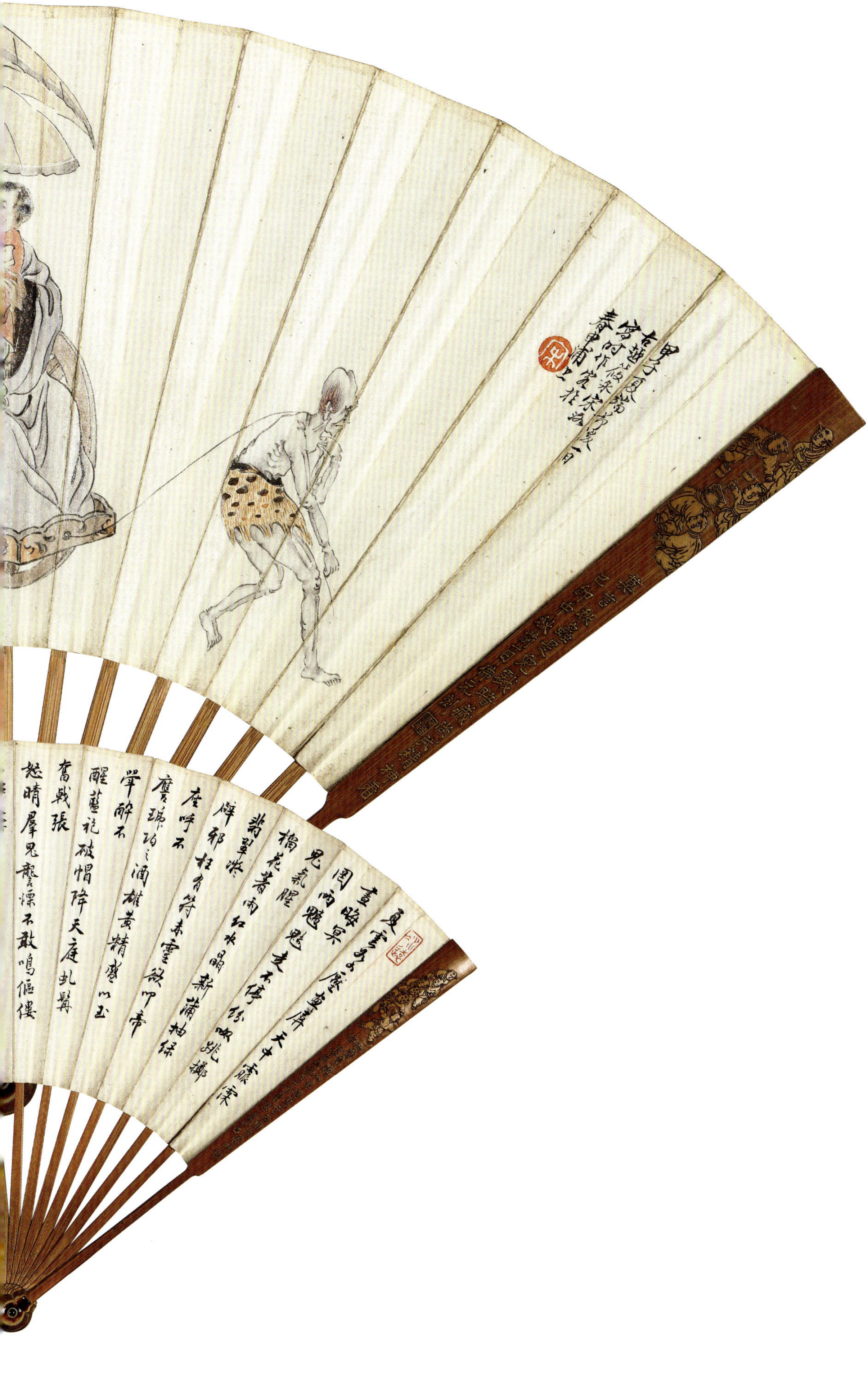

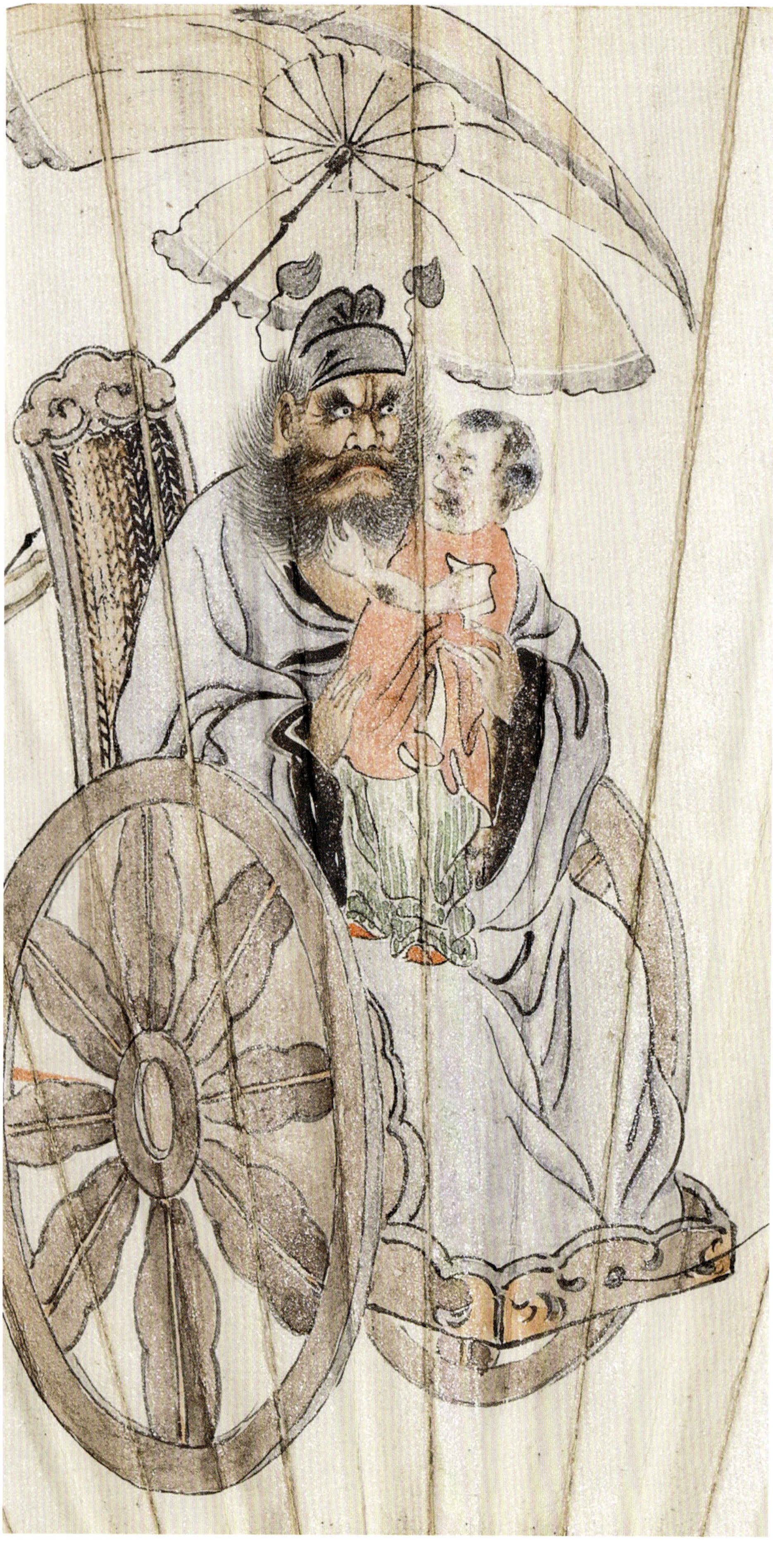

Song Luo
Styled Xiaochuan, a painter from Zhejiang.

Li You
Styled Jiayou, a calligrapher from Changshu, Jiangsu, active in modern times.

Artist:
Song Luo, Li You

Medium:
Color on paper, Completed fan

Dimensions:
18 cm × 46 cm

Zhong Kui's Outing

Inscription:
The day after the Dragon Boat Festival in the Jiazi summer, this was penned by Guyue, Xiaochuan, Song Luo, while sojourning by the banks of the Huangpu River.

Seal:
Song

Backside Calligraphy

Inscription:
Summer clouds press down like mountains, darkening the day,
Amidst mid-heaven's drizzle, the noon turns dim and gray.
Restless spirits and demons scurry, their presence never still,
Their raucous shouts and foul stench the air do fill.
The rain-drenched pomegranate blossoms shine like rubies bright,
New reeds shoot up in emerald splendor, a jade-like sight.
All the talismans and charms seem powerless to protect,
Calls to the divine throne go unanswered, ignored with neglect.
Amber wine, infused with realgar's spirit, fills the cup,
Even in drunken stupor, awareness does not give up.
Zhong Kui, in his tattered blue robe and hat, descends from the skies,
His fierce beard brandishing a halberd clears the stormy cries.
Ghosts in throngs dare not utter, silenced by the sight,
A hunched elder dances alone, his spirit light.
With a gourd of wine overturned, the strong liquor flows,
Kneeling guests bring forth the drinks, a chilling awe it bestows.
A young maiden yet to be wed, in grace she does inquire,
Challenges her brother with a frown, her eyebrows knit in dire.
Her phoenix hairpin and jeweled bun, her rosy garments sway,
Attended by cautious specters, their dread on display.
Even the ghosts seem to understand the need to greet,
The Jinshi of Zhongnan holds his tablet up, a feat.
Though his visage may be grotesque, his heart remains pure,
Intent on clearing the realm of all vile creatures, his aim sure.
Splitting his eyes wide open with his hands, to awaken the mind,
The rising sun dispels the horde, leaving darkness behind.
Auspicious clouds adorn the sky, the sun regains its blaze,
As the southern breeze revives the land, all nature sings in praise.
Harmony spreads, joy abounds, even nobles seek reprieve,
Avoiding the haunts of devils, in tranquil respite believe.
In paintings, a hundred forms are depicted,
Daoist wonders unfurled,
The desire for the mysterious voiced, the odd
sentiments of the world.
Hung high in the hall where cold breezes stir,
Awaiting the purchase of fish and crimson
cherries to occur.
With fragrant offerings, the gods do rely,
With righteous fury, all demons are quelled,
peace restored under the sky,
Clearing the three realms, bringing tranquility
to all of Chang'an's ring.

Seal:
Elder of Longkan, Bingyuan

Inscription:
A painting inspired by the "Hundred Children" from the Feiying Pavilion, created by Bo Yu.

Carved seal:
Yu

Inscription:
Carved by Fo Yuan on the day before the Mid-Autumn Festival of the Jimao year.

Carved seal:
Work of Fo Yuan

Collector's Seal:
Huang Tiancai, the custodian of the Hundred Fans of Old Zhong Kui, the fan collection of Huang Tiancai

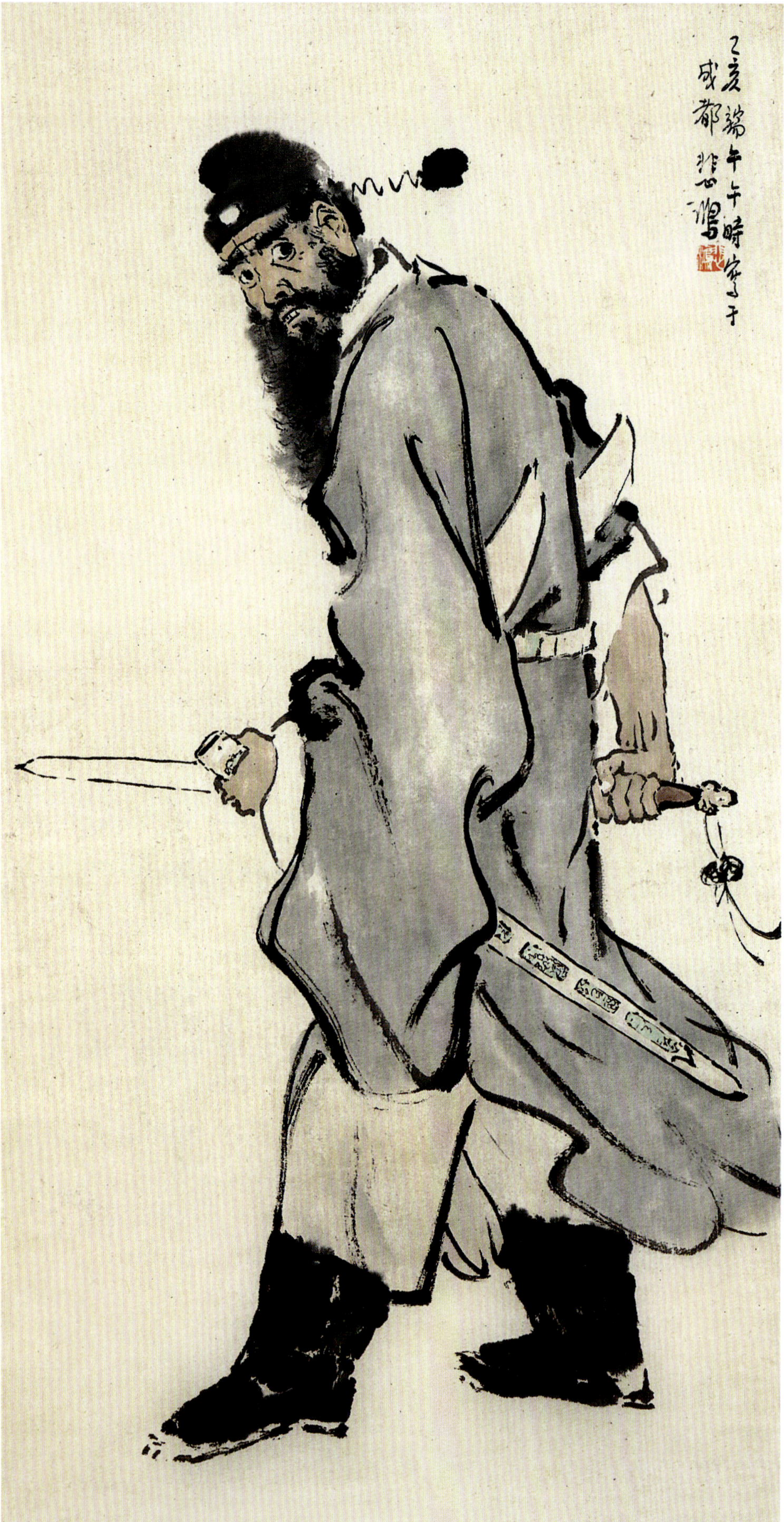
乙亥端午午時寫于
成都悲鴻

Artist:
Xu Beihong

Medium:
Color on paper, Hanging scroll

Dimensions:
106 cm × 54 cm

Zhong Kui

Inscription:
On the day of the Dragon Boat Festival in the Yihai year, written in Chengdu, by Beihong.

Seal:
Beihong

Xu Beihong (1895–1953)
Originally named Xu Shoukang, a native of Yixing, Jiangsu. He studied Western art in France and devoted himself to art education upon his return to China. He taught at the National Central University's Department of Art, Beiping University's College of Art, and Beiping Art School, and later served as the president of the Central Academy of Fine Arts after the founding of the People's Republic of China. His Chinese paintings, especially those depicting horses, are noted for their vibrant colors and complete composition, earning him international fame.

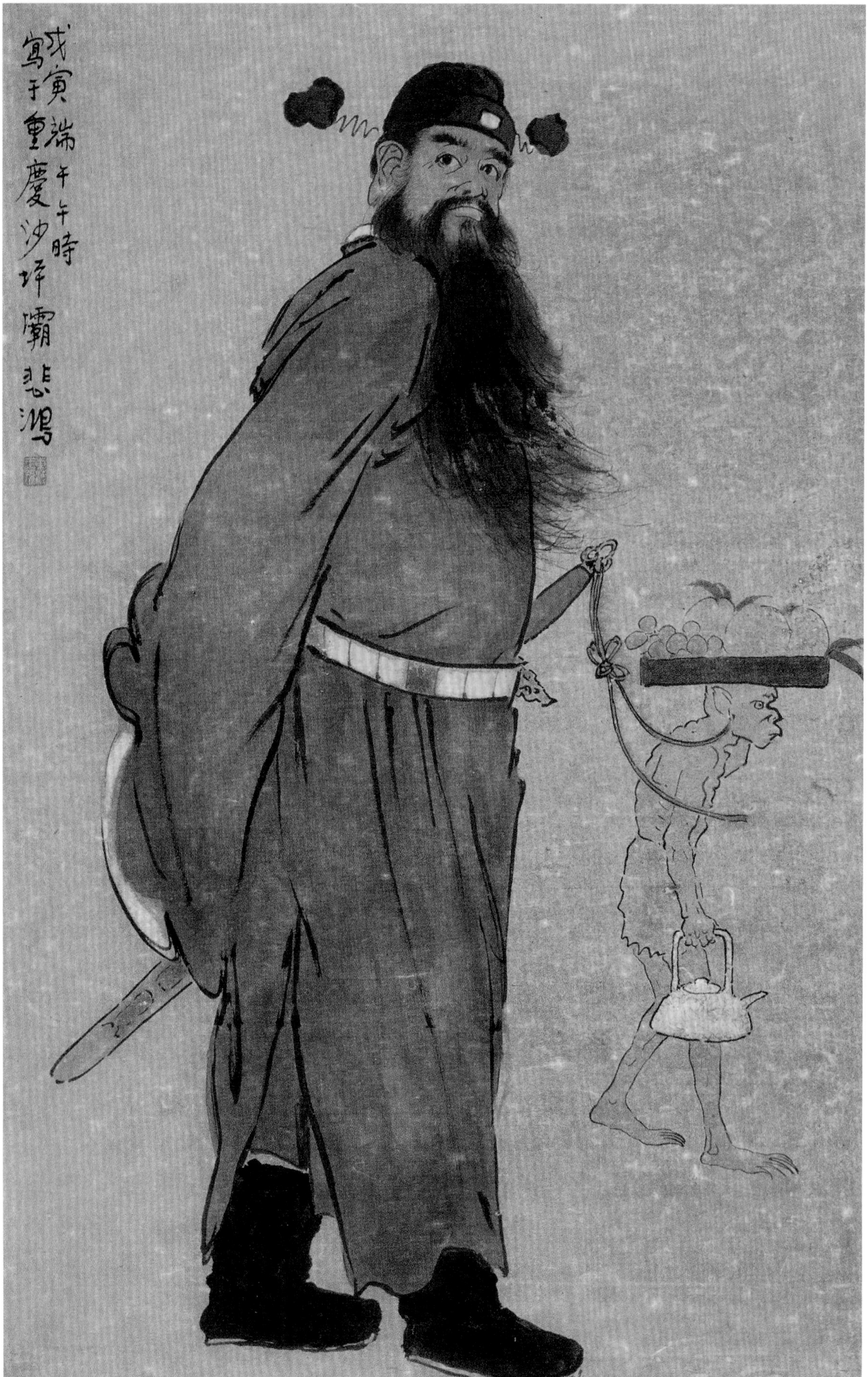
戊寅端午午時
寫于重慶沙坪壩悲鴻

Artist:
Xu Beihong

Medium:
Color on paper, Hanging scroll

Dimensions:
100 cm × 62 cm

Zhong Kui and the Little Ghosts

Inscription:
At noon on the Dragon Boat Festival in the Wuyin year, written in Shapingba, Chongqing, by Beihong.

Seal:
Scion of the Eastern Sea

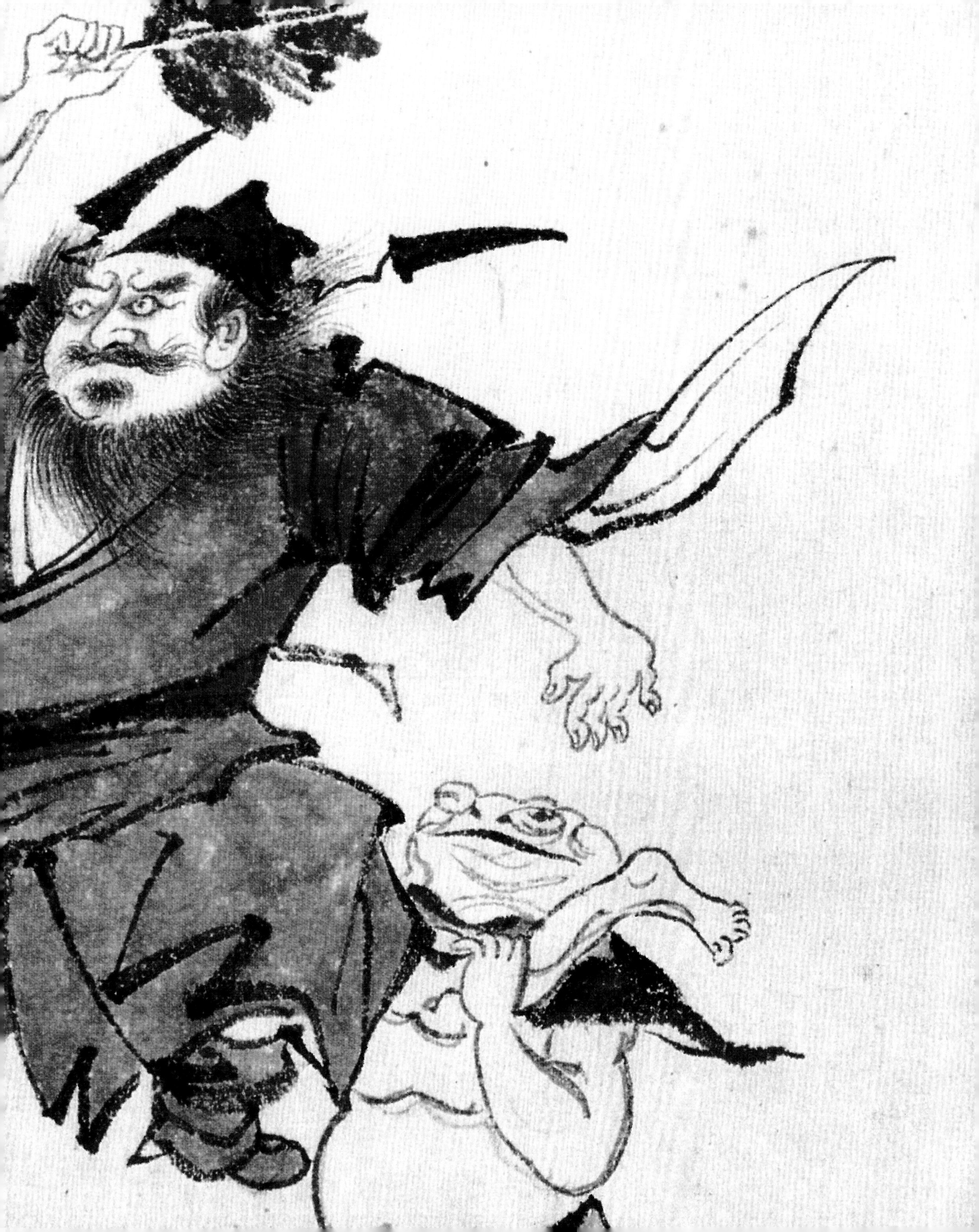

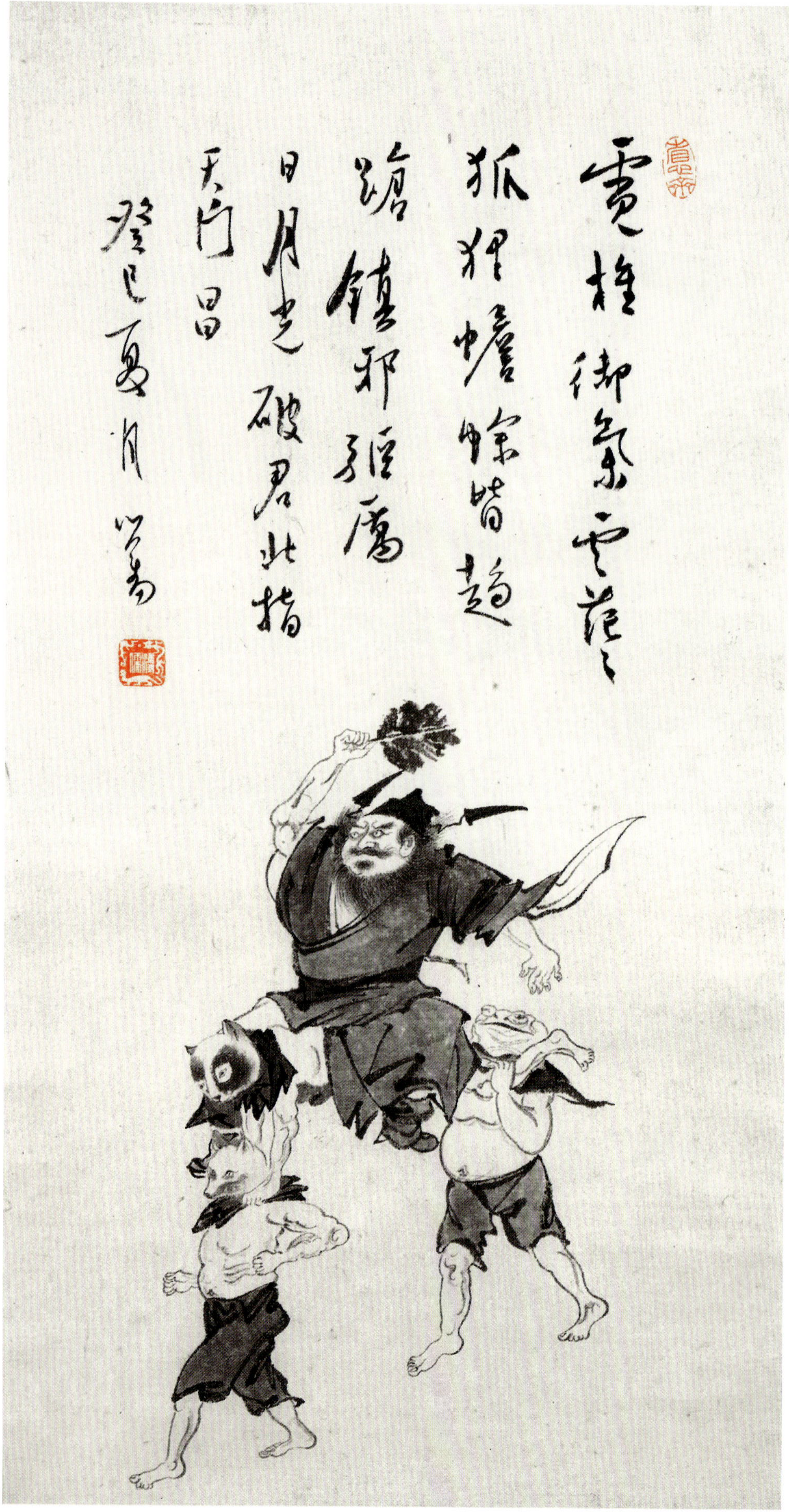

Artist:
Pu Ru

Medium:
Color on paper, Hanging scroll

Dimensions:
57 cm × 30 cm

Zhong Kui Expelling Malevolence

Inscription:
Rainbows arch with celestial qi amidst boundless mists,
Foxes and toads alike stumble and falter in their midst.
It suppresses the evil, banishes the vicious, letting sun and moon gleam bright,
Shatters the northern darkness, pointing towards the heavenly gate's light.
In the summer month of the Guisi year, Xinyu.

Seal:
Pu Ru

Pu Ru (1896–1963)
Originally named Aisin Gioro Pu Ru, initially styled Zhongheng, later known as Xinyu. He styled himself as the "Hermit of the Western Hills" and "Descendant of the Yellow Emperor," and was the grandson of Prince Gong Yixin of the Qing dynasty. A devotee of poetry, calligraphy, and painting, he achieved distinction in his artistic endeavors, especially in landscape, figures, flowers, as well as in the art of calligraphy.

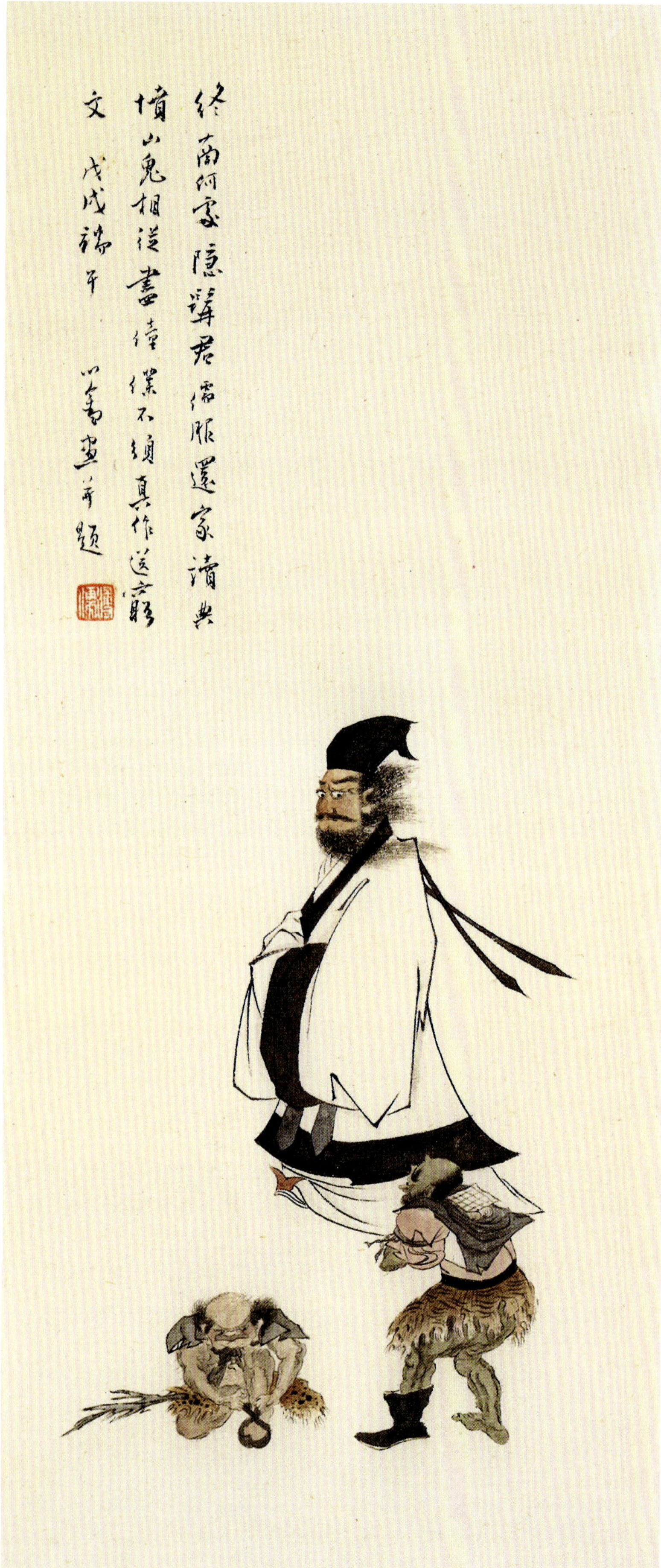
終南何處隱髯君儒服還家讀典
墳山鬼相從畫僮僕不須真作送窮
文　戊戌端午
心畬畫并題

Artist:
Pu Ru

Medium:
Color on paper, Hanging scroll

Dimensions:
38.5 cm × 16.3 cm

Jinshi Zhong

Inscription:
Where in Zhongnan hides the bearded sage, in scholar's garb, he returns to his hermitage.
To study the ancient texts, he withdraws to his home, while mountain spirits attend him, no longer alone.
No need for real letters of solace to pen, for in his service, the ghosts are now his men.
On the Dragon Boat Festival of the Wuxu year, Pu Xinyu painted and inscribed this himself.

Seal:
Pu Ru

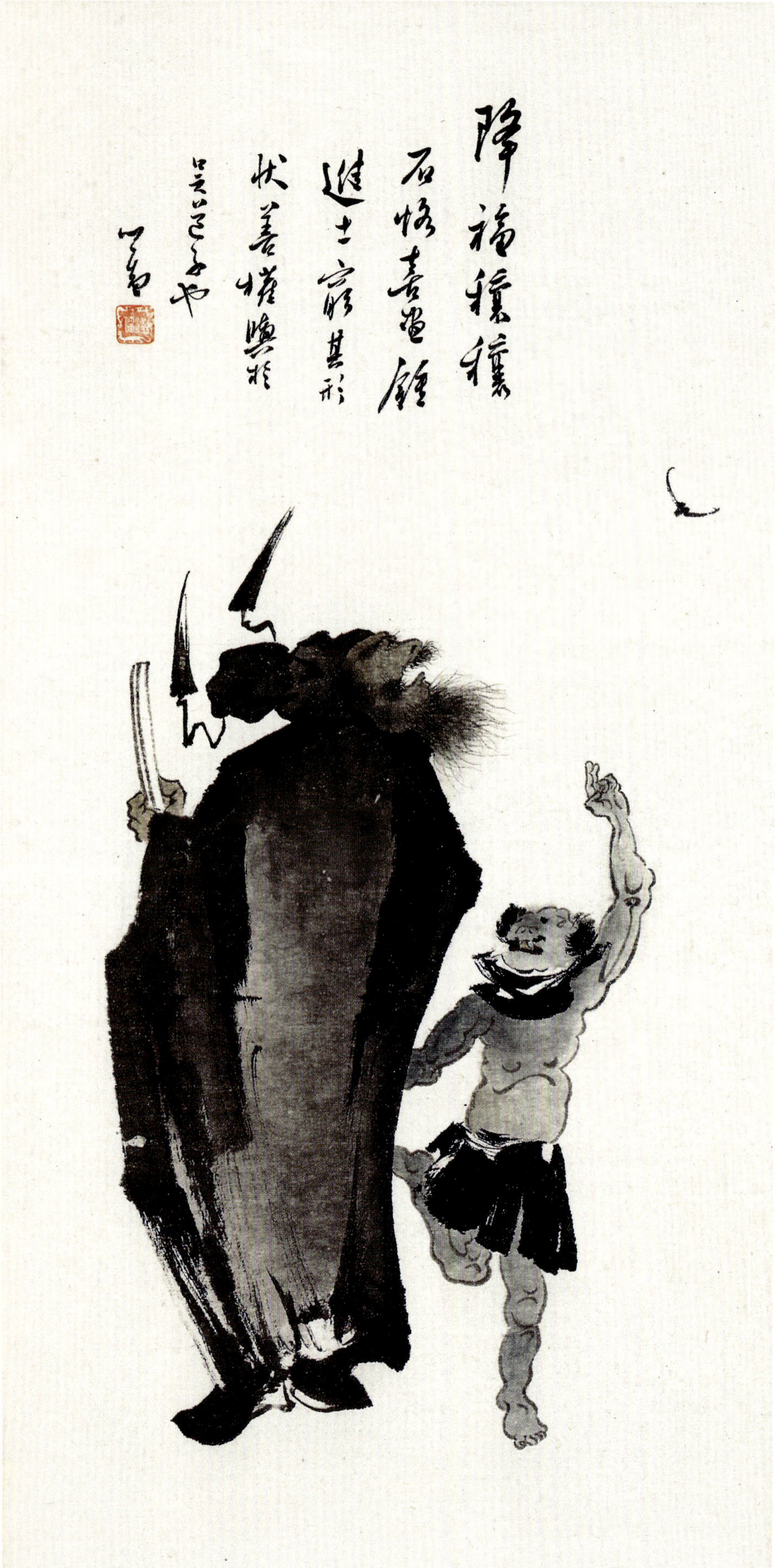

Artist:
Pu Ru

Medium:
Color on paper, Hanging scroll

Dimensions:
74.5 cm × 36.5 cm

Blessings Abundant

Inscription:
Blessings Abundant. Shi Ke took great pleasure in painting Zhong Kui, striving to capture his likeness and exhibiting a mastery of balance in his style comparable to that of Wu Daozi. Xinyu.

Seal:
Pu Ru

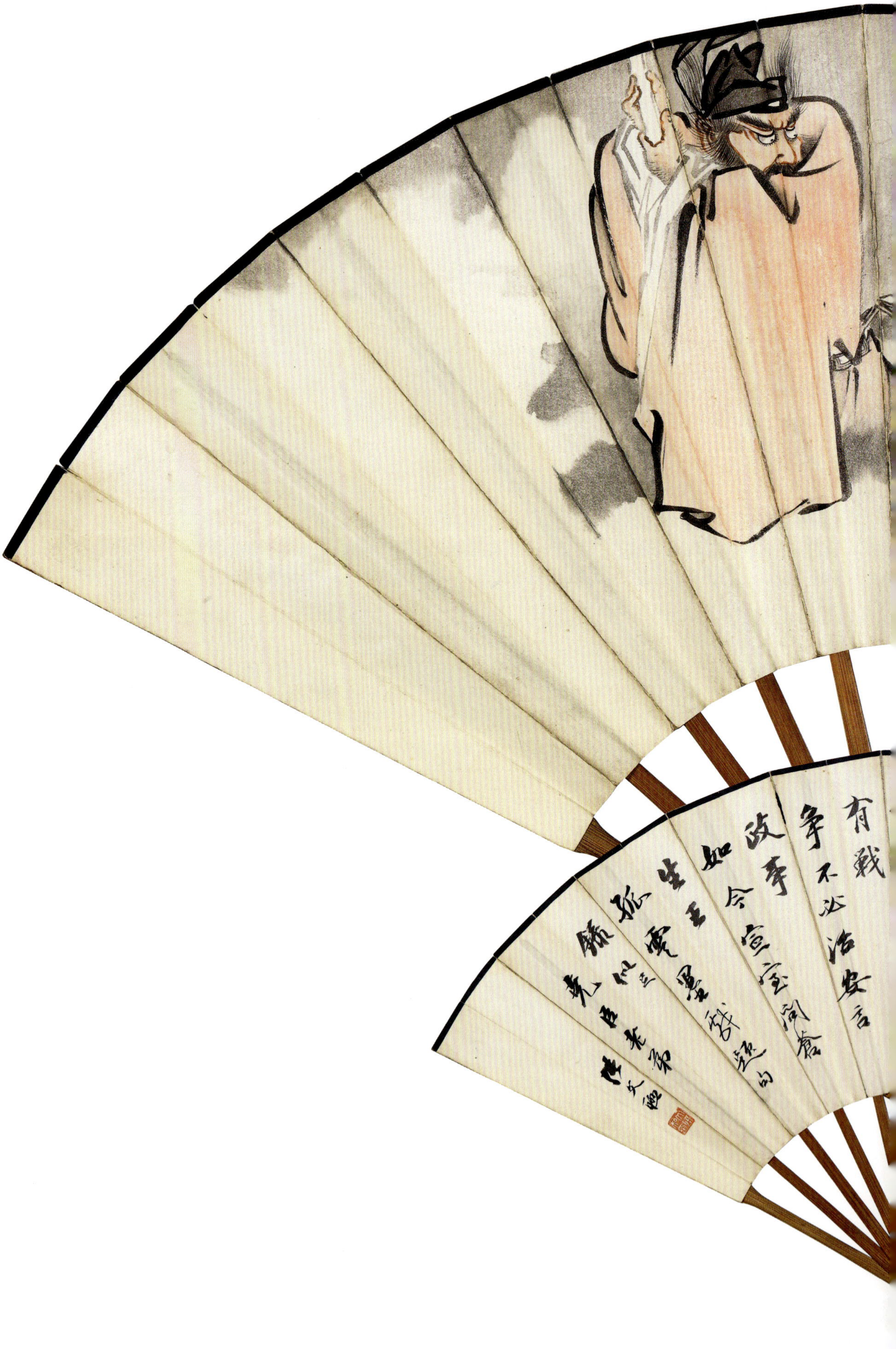

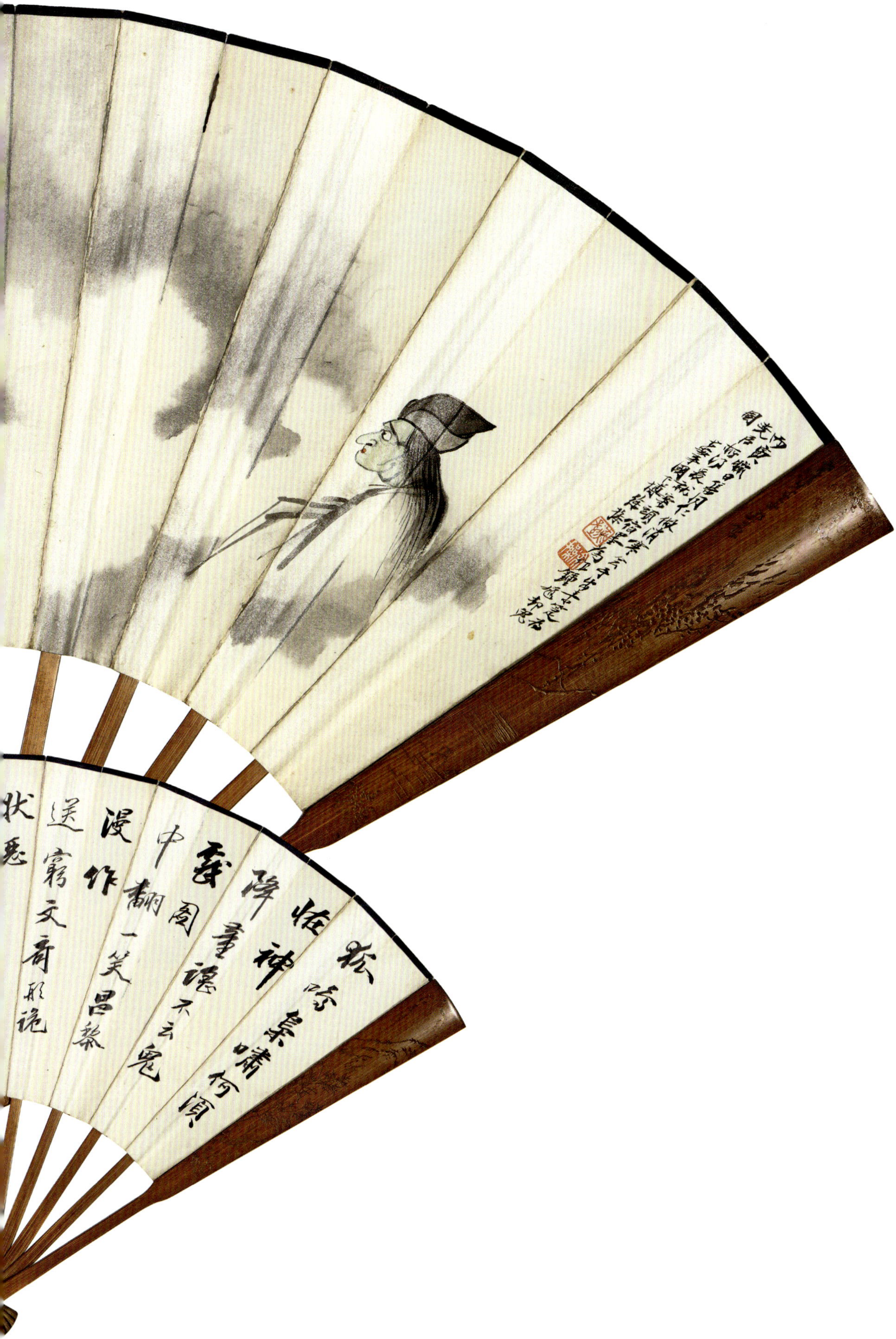

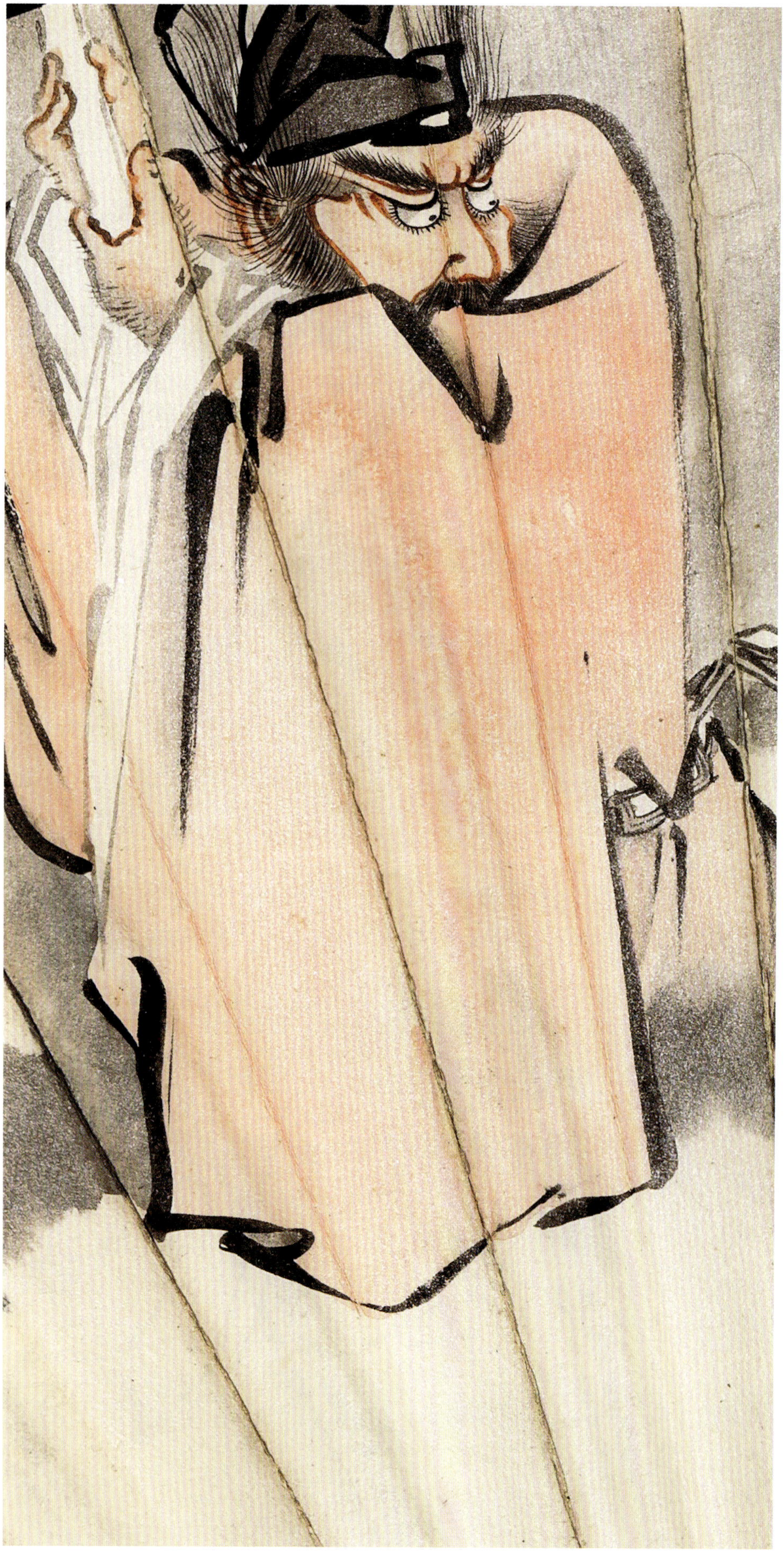

Artist:
Xu Cao, Zhang Wenlian

Medium:
Color on paper, Completed fan

Dimensions:
19 cm × 52 cm

Zhong Kui Repelling Ghosts

Inscription:
On the last day of the twelfth lunar month in the year of Bing Yin, we held a gathering to ward off the cold. I presented a plain fan, which was later acquired by Yao Chen. Consequently, I used the remaining ink at my desk to create an image of Zhong Kui expelling demons. Xu Cao, a learned man from Anping.

Seal:
Yansun, Xu Cao

Backside Calligraphy

Inscription:
Why marvel at the fox's cry and the owl's fierce screech?
Divine descent and children's rhymes are beyond ordinary speech.
A mere smile flips the script in this playful ghostly art,
Changli (Han Yu) pens casual verses to soothe the poor's heart.
Bizarre and eerie shapes, these demons seem so wild,
Yet they're no more dreadful than warring tribes, meek and mild.
No need for concern over governance and state affairs,
It's time the Emperor's chamber inquires into the commoners' cares.
Wang Guyun playfully inscribed a few lines as if they were recorded by brother Yaochen. Zhang Wenlian.

Seal:
The personal seal of Wenlian

Xu Cao (1899–1961)
Originally named Cunzhao, styled Yansun, also known as the Master of Shuanghong Tower, and alternatively titled the Keeper of Shuanghong Niche and "Born in the Mid-Autumn", with studio names including Shuanghong Lou, Hanshui Tang, and Guiyan Lou, from Beijing. He was a renowned painter of figures.

Zhang Wenlian
Active during the late Qing and Republic of China period, little is known of his life.

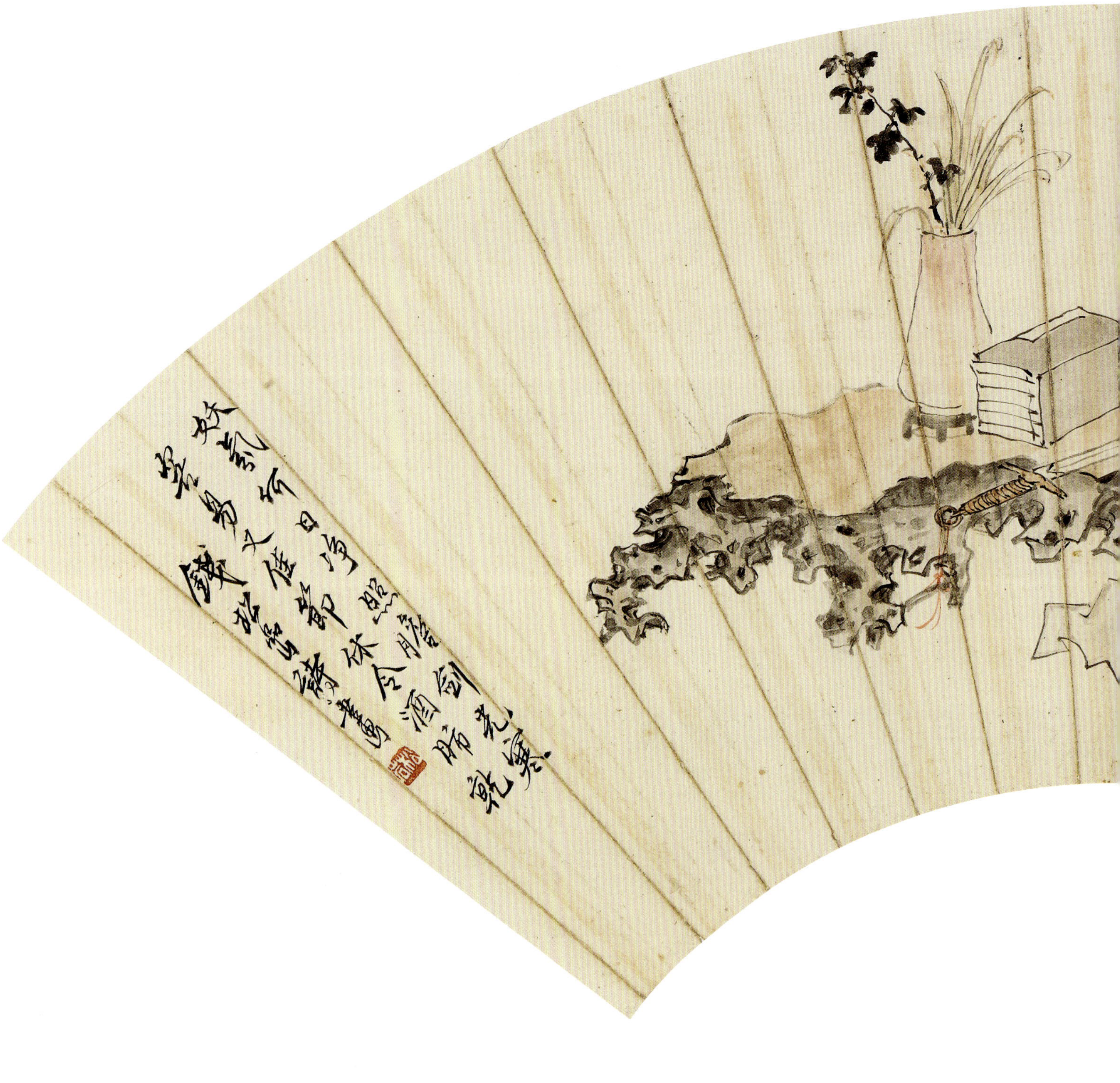

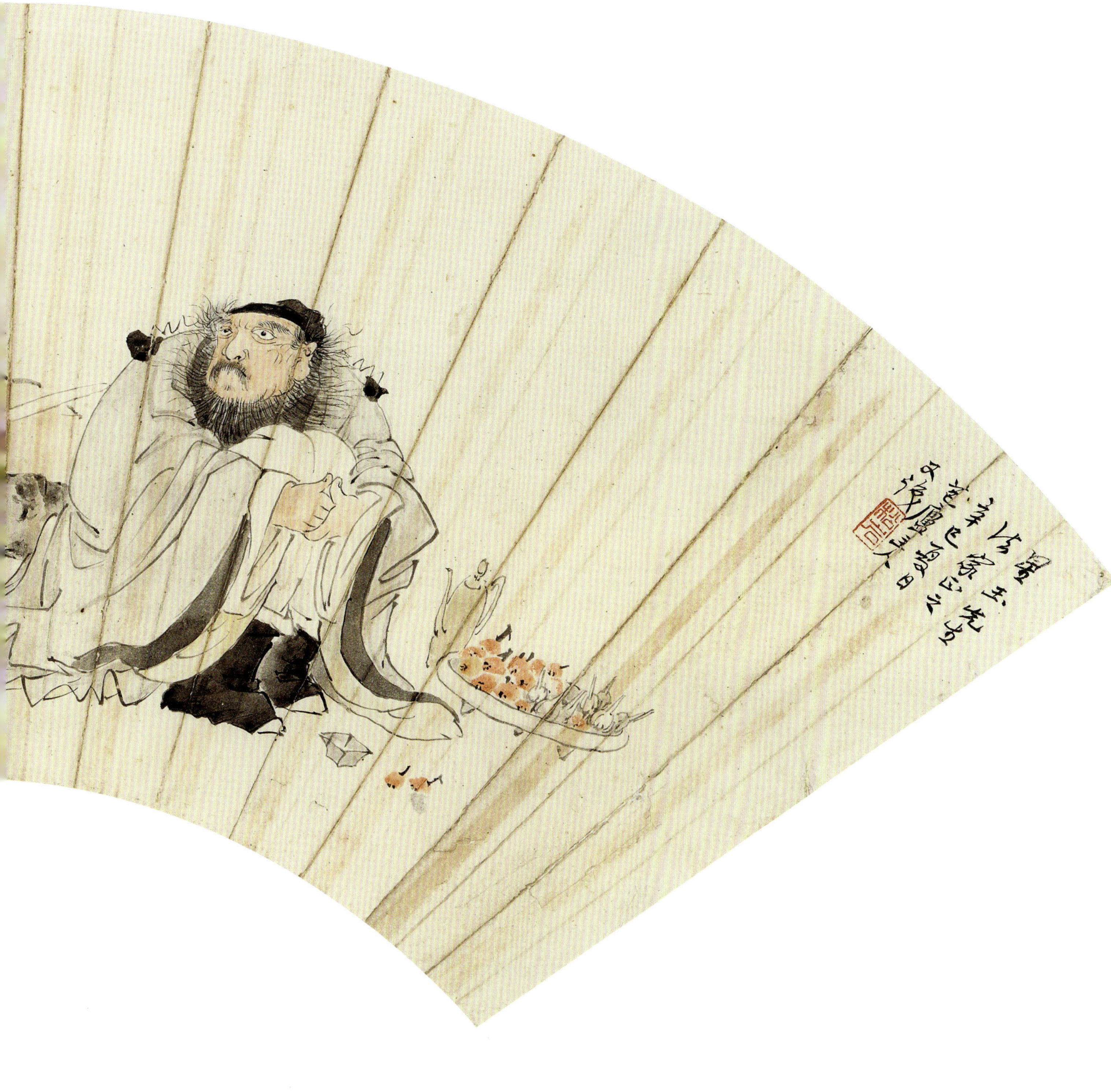

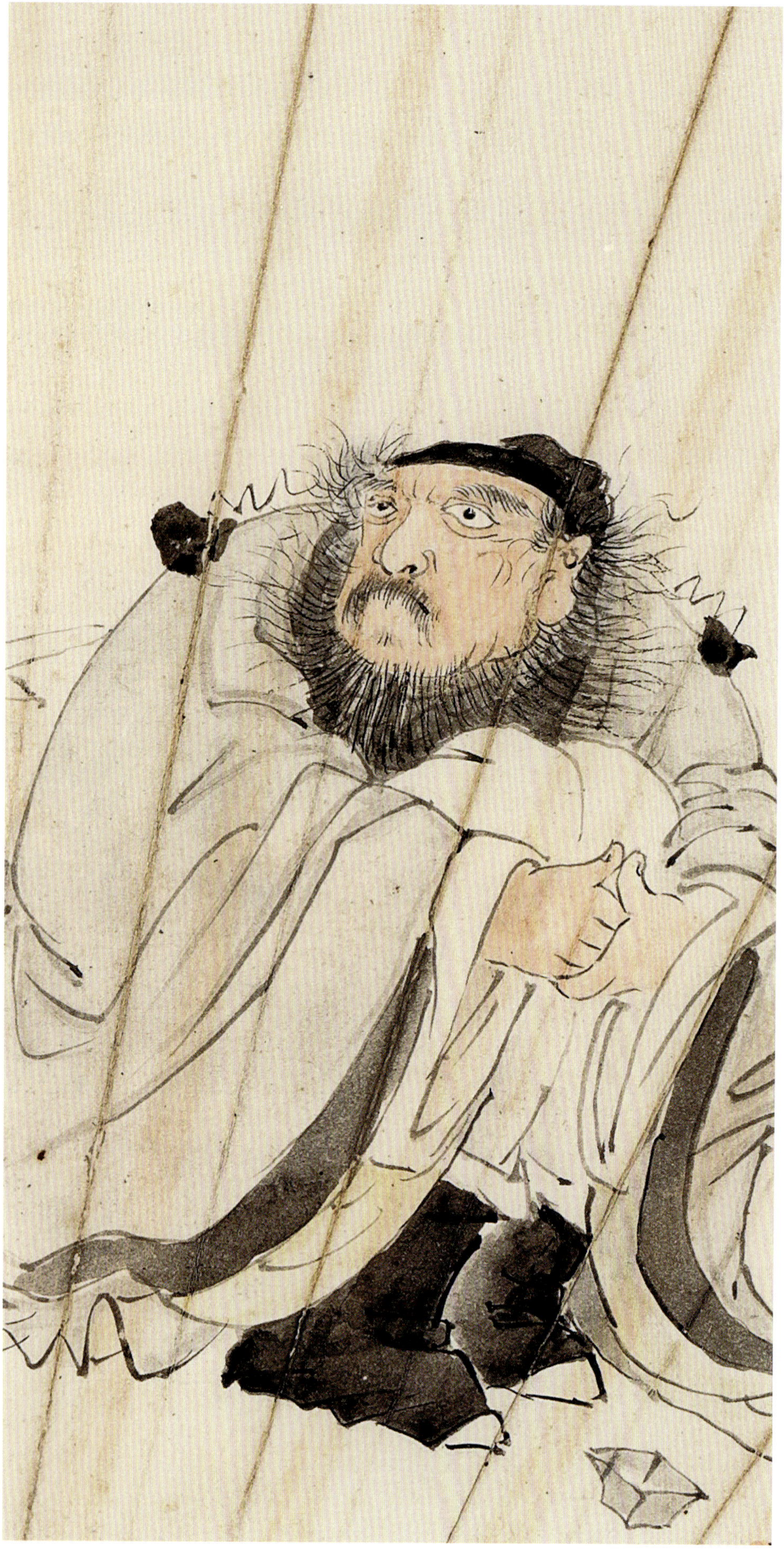

Artist:
Qian Songyan

Medium:
Color on paper, Fan-shaped

Dimensions:
17.5 cm × 50.4 cm

Zhong Kui

Inscription:
First,
When will the malevolent mists be purged from our days,
The sword's chill light gleaming, daunting the brave heart's gaze?
Easily arrives another splendid festival's cheer,
Let not wine dry out the lungs, nor spirit's warmth disappear.
The poetry and painting of Qian Songyan.
Second, corrected according to the legalist tradition by Mr. Xingyu, and once again acknowledged in the summer of the Xinsi year by the master of Qilu.

Seal:
Songyan

Qian Songyan (1899–1985)
A native of Yixing, Jiangsu, was a painter. He served as the president of the Jiangsu Provincial Academy of Chinese Painting, chairman of the Jiangsu Artists Association, and was a standing director and advisor of the China Artists Association.

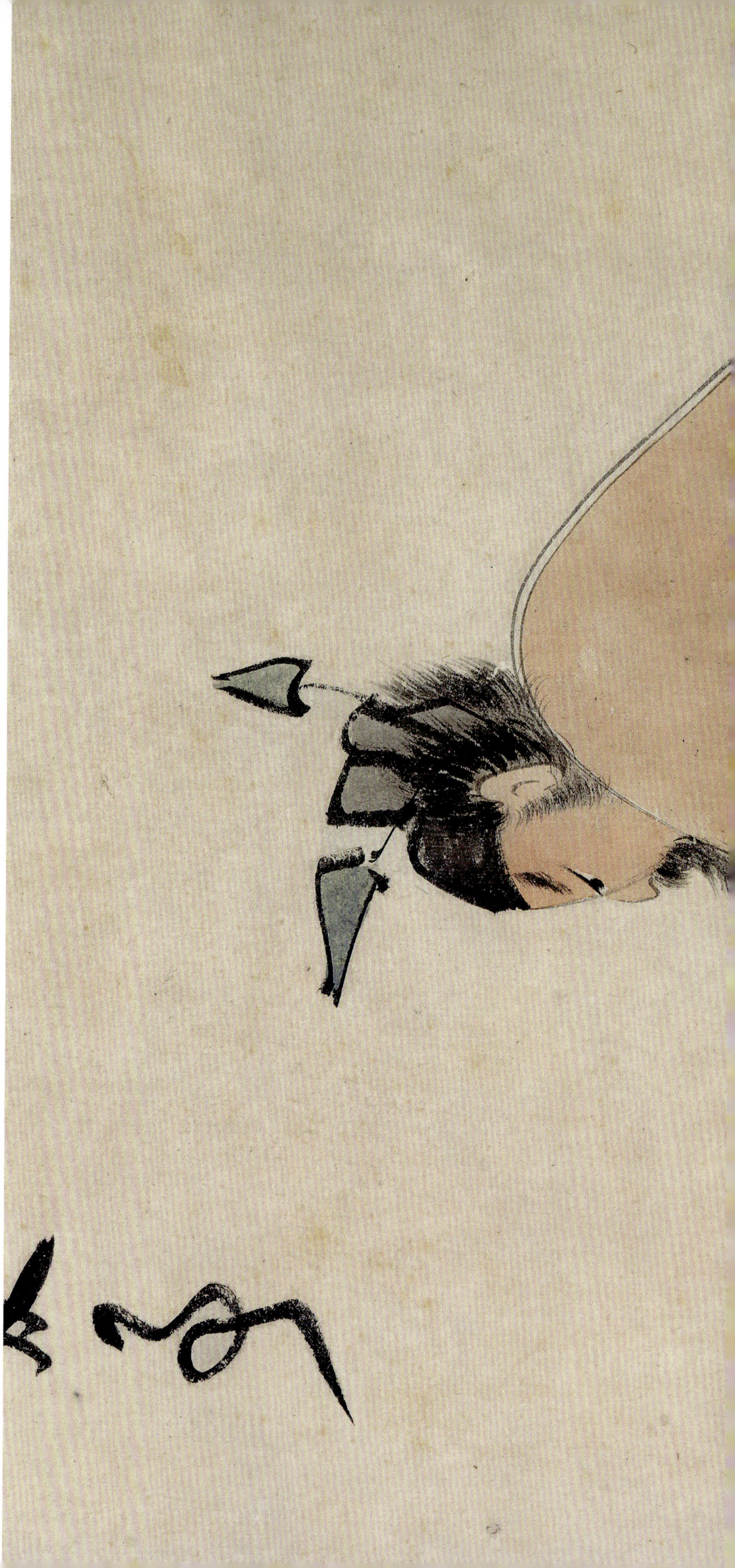

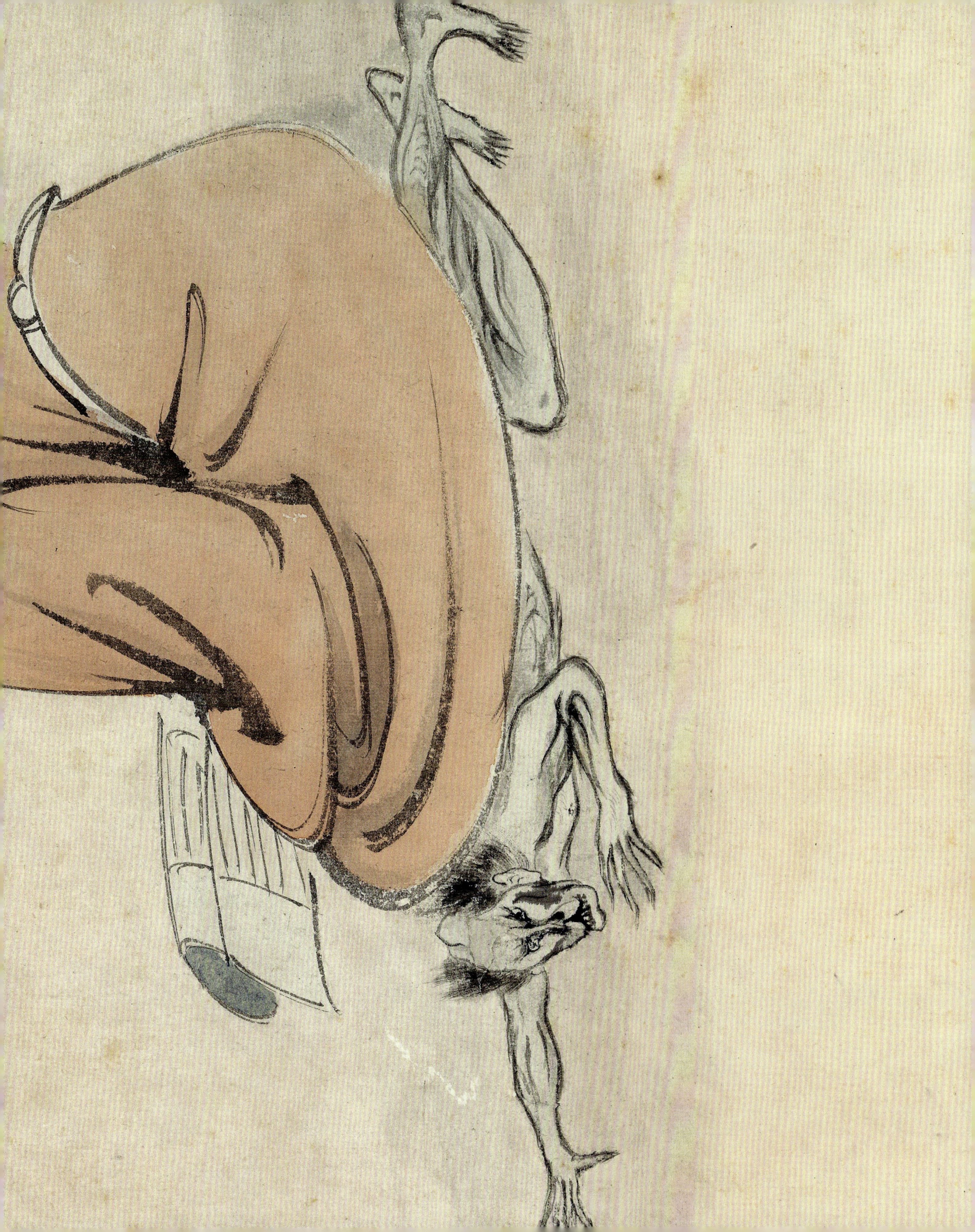

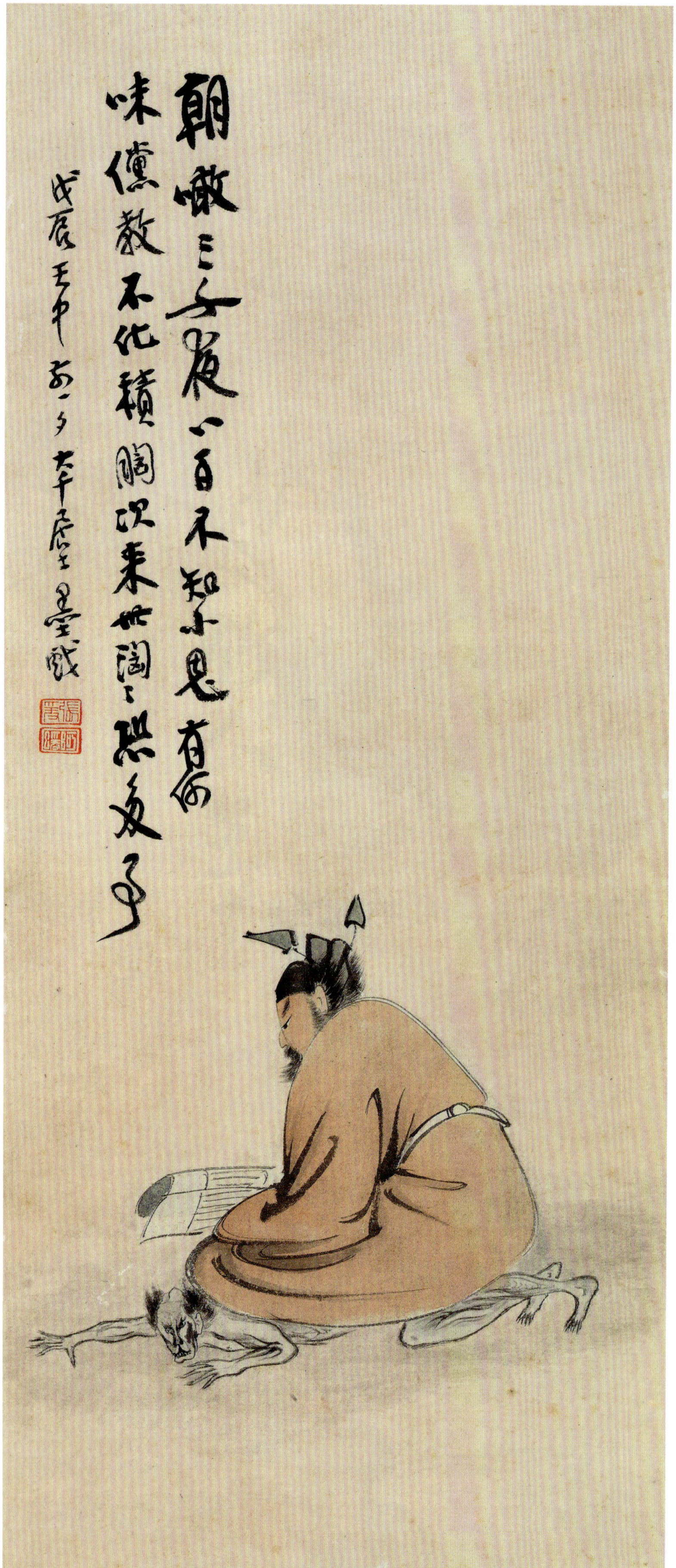

Artist:
Zhang Daqian

Medium:
Color on paper, Hanging scroll

Dimensions:
90 cm × 37 cm

Zhong Kui Reading

Inscription:
Each morn I devour three thousand, and eight hundred more come night, yet the flavor of these tiny demons eludes me quite.
Should they learn not to haunt the recesses of my chest, the next life may hold fewer troubles, granting more rest.
On the eve of Tianzhong Festival in the year of Wuchen, Lay Scholar Daqian indulged in playful ink doodles.

Seal:
Zhang Yuan, Yuan

Zhang Daqian (1899–1983)
A legendary figure from Neijiang, Sichuan, was a grandmaster of traditional Chinese painting and a calligrapher. Proficient in painting, calligraphy, seal carving, and poetry, his style synthesized meticulous brushwork with freehand techniques. Later, he pioneered a new artistic style of splash ink and color, earning acclaim in the Western art world as "the Oriental Brush." He and his elder brother, Zhang Shanzi, founded the influential "Da Feng Tang School."

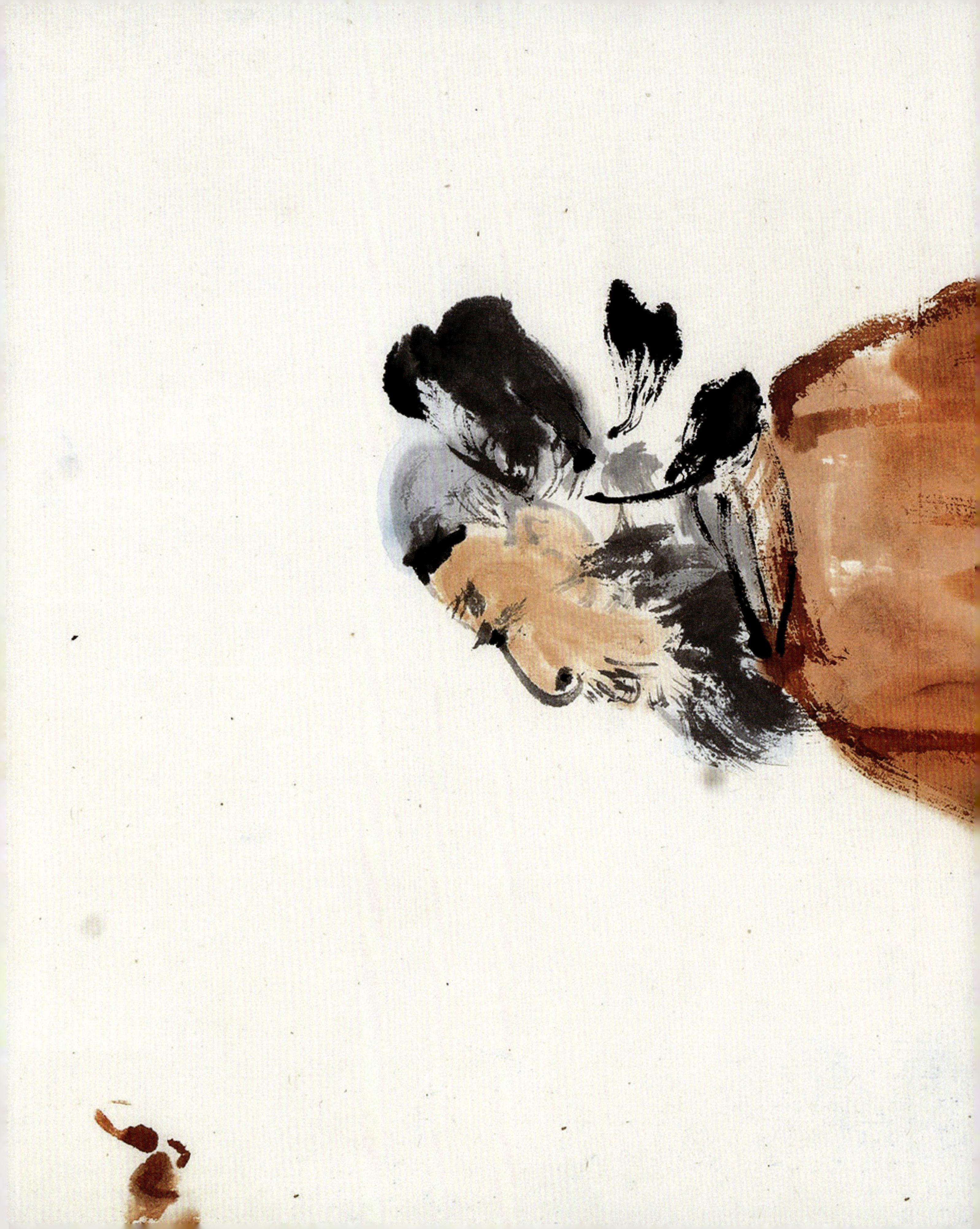

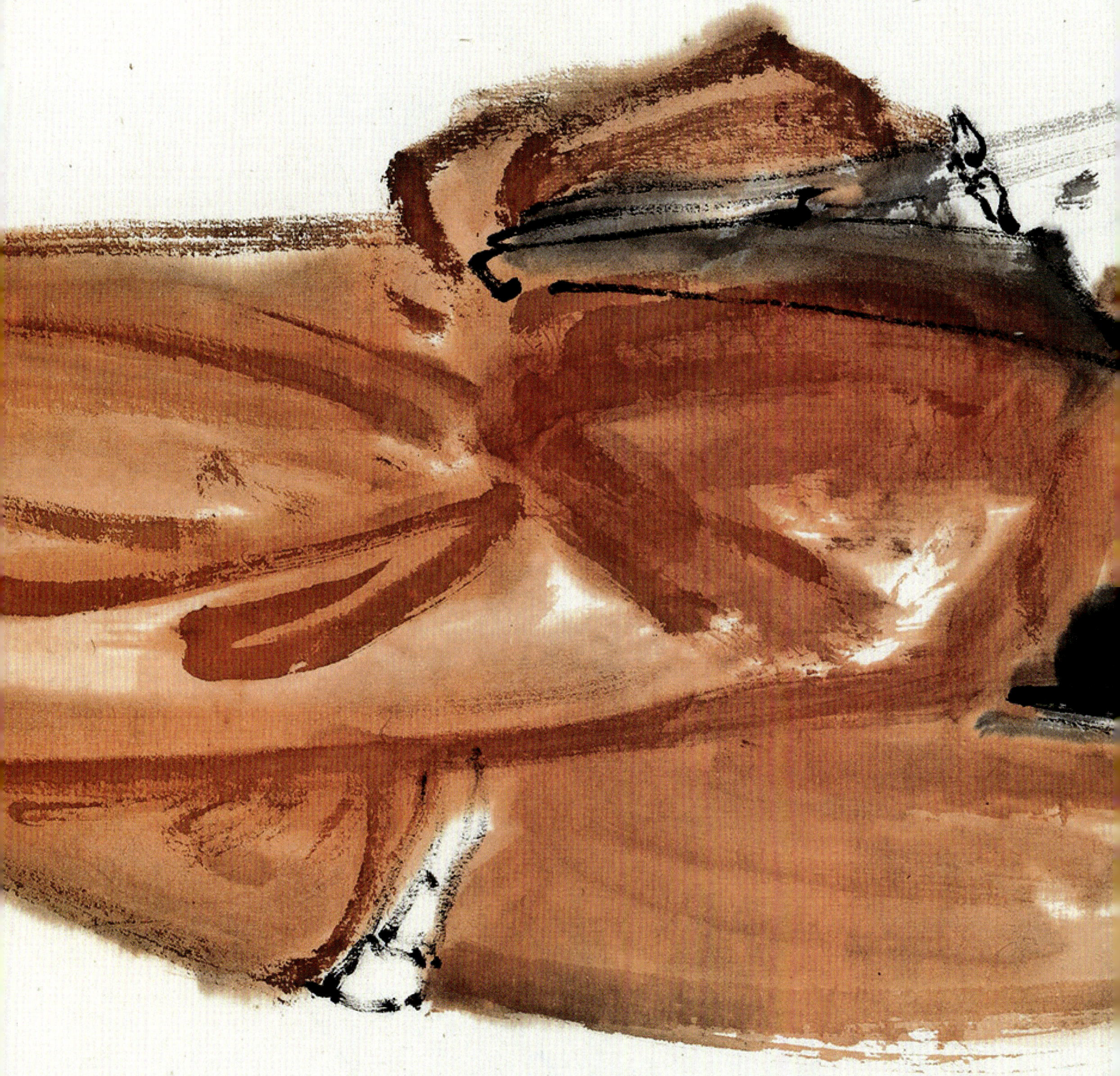

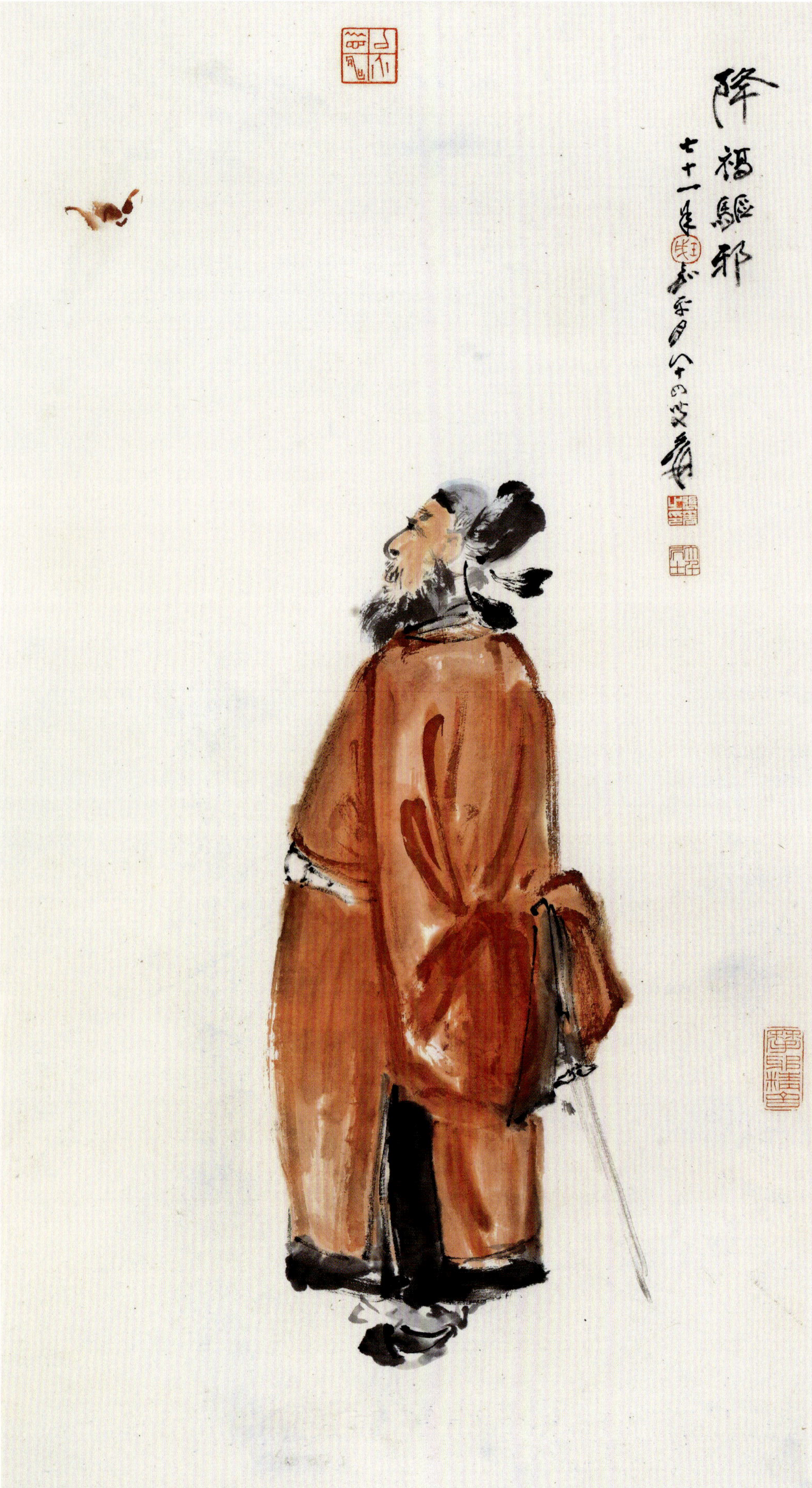
降福驅邪

Artist:
Zhang Daqian

Medium:
Color on paper, Hanging scroll

Dimensions:
100 cm × 54.5 cm

Descending Blessings and Banishing Evil

Inscription:
Descending Blessings and Banishing Evil. In the seventy-first year of the Jiaping period, an elder aged eighty-four inscribed. Yuan.

Seal:
The seal of Zhang Yuan, Lay Scholar Daqian, Yijie Mei Shou, Maya Jingshe, Renxu

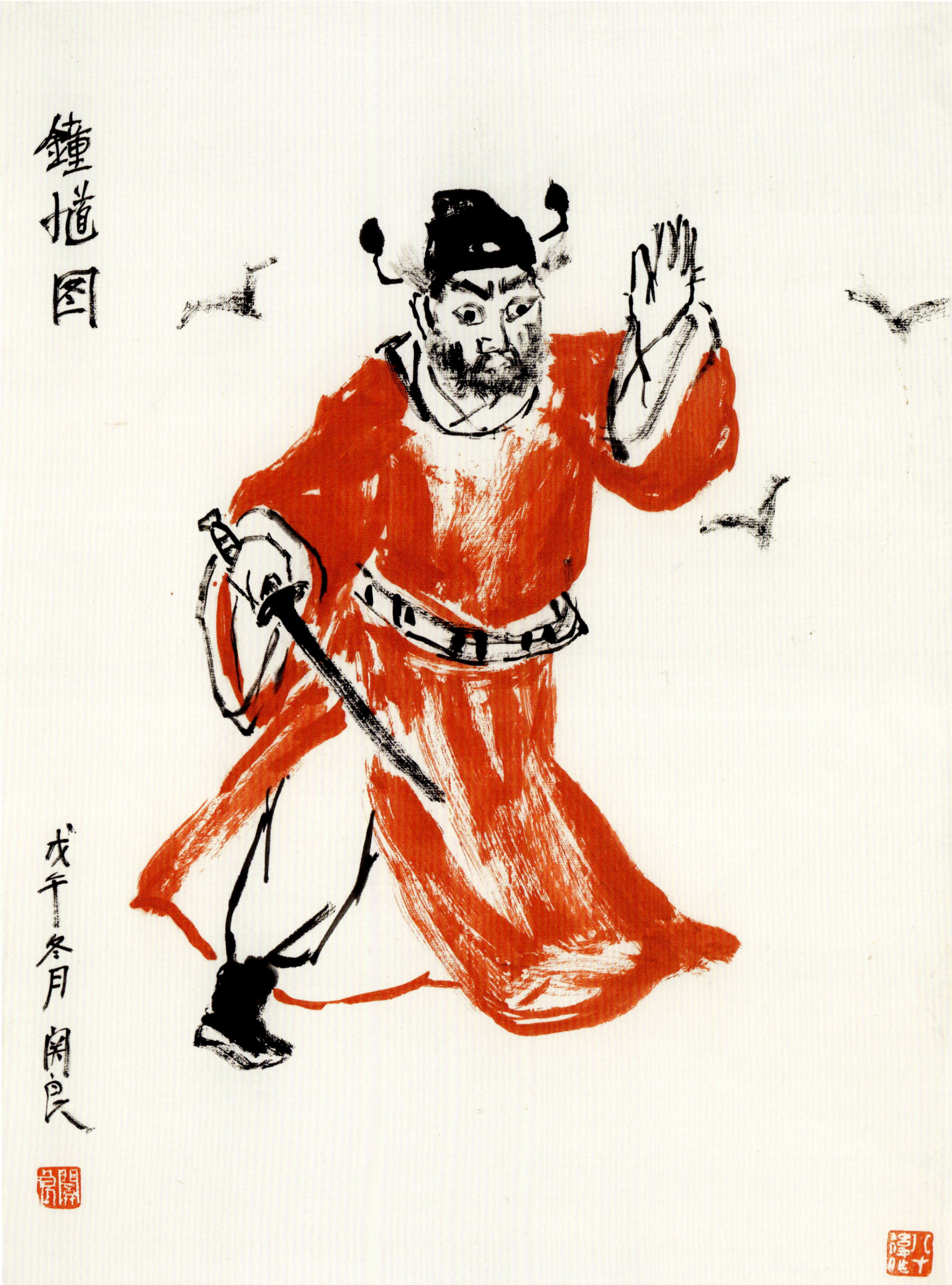
鍾馗图
戊午冬月 関良

Artist:
Guan Liang

Medium:
Color on paper, Framed piece

Dimensions:
64 cm × 47.5 cm

Zhong Kui

Inscription:
A painting of Zhong Kui, created in the winter month of the Wuwu year, by Guan Liang.

Seal:
Guan Liang, Work after Eighty

Guan Liang (1900–1986)
Styled Lianggong, he hailed from Panyu, Guangdong. A renowned painter proficient in Chinese ink painting and oil painting, he was especially noted for his depictions of theatrical figures. Guan Liang served as a professor at the Zhejiang Academy of Fine Arts and as a painter at the Shanghai Academy of Chinese Paintings.

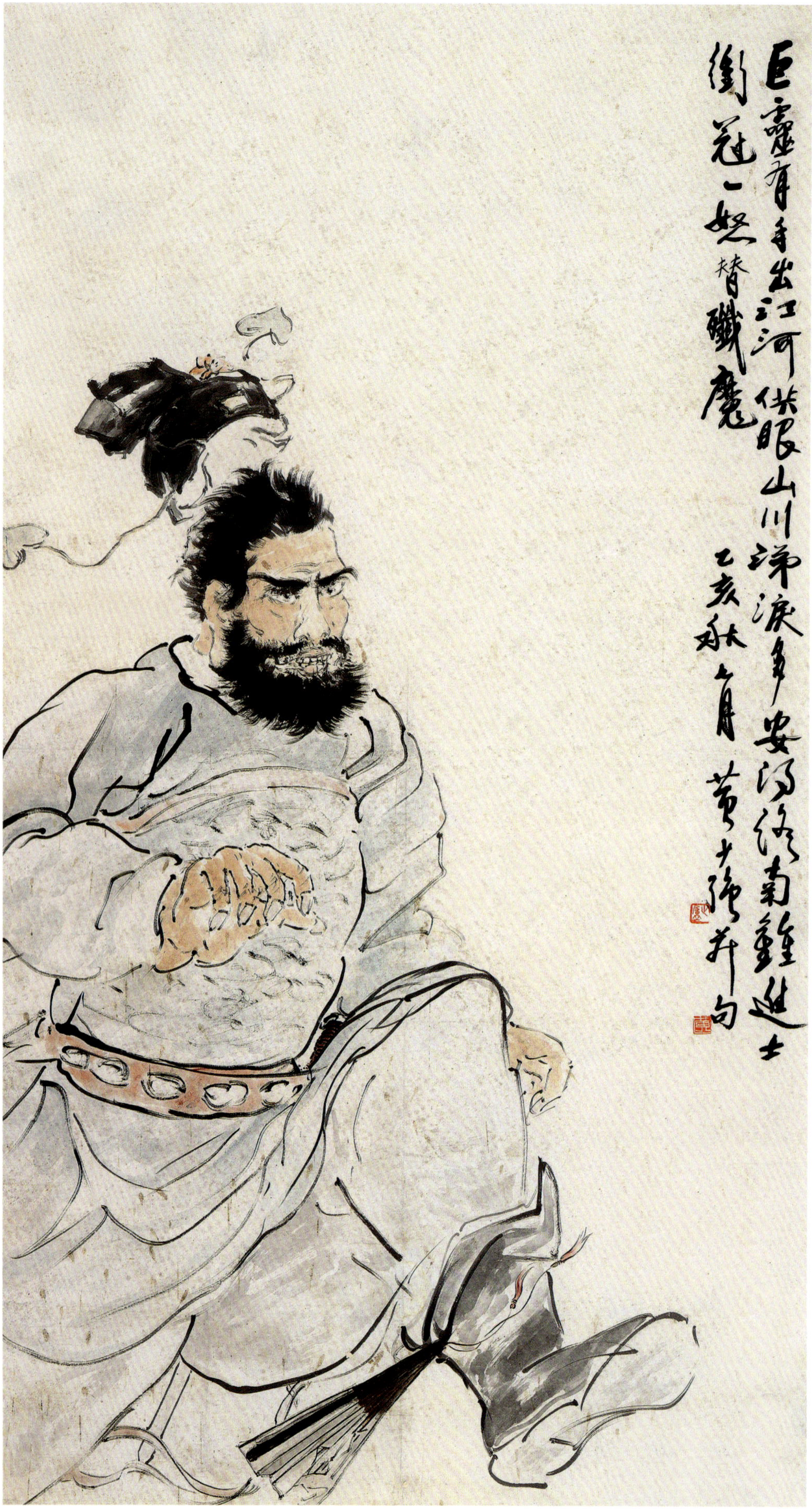
巨靈有手出江河供眼山川涕淚多安得終南鍾進士
衝冠一怒替殲魔
乙亥秋月

Artist:
Huang Shaoqiang

Medium:
Color on paper, Hanging scroll

Dimensions:
170 cm × 91 cm

Zhong Kui

Inscription:
The giant spirit reaches out his hands, drawing from the rivers and the streams,
Before mountains and rivers, his emotions overflow, shedding tears it seems.
Oh, to summon Zhong Kui from Zhongnan's heights,
With a wrathful rise, he'd vanquish fiends, setting to rights all plights.
In the seventh month of the autumn of the Yihai year,
Huang Shaoqiang composed these lines.

Seal:
Zhilu, Huang

Huang Shaoqiang (1901–1942)
Originally named Yishi, styled Shaoqiang, also known as Zhilu, was a painter. He initially studied under Gao Qifeng and Gao Jianfu, and later continued his studies in painting under Liu Haisu at the Shanghai Art School.

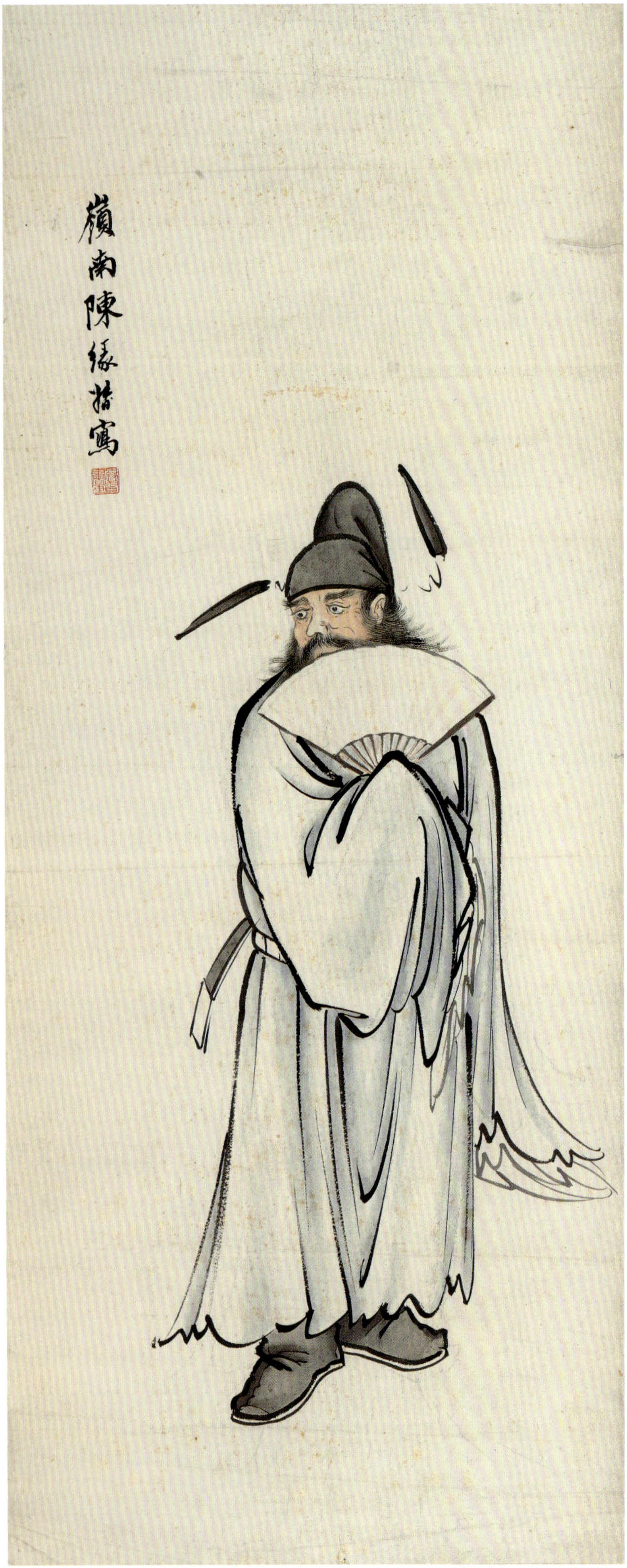
嶺南陳緣措寫

Artist:
Chen Yuandu

Medium:
Color on paper, Hanging scroll

Dimensions:
84 cm × 33 cm

Zhong Kui

Inscription:
Written by Chen Yuandu of Lingnan.

Seal:
Yuandu's Calligraphy and Painting

Chen Yuandu (1902–1967)
Originally named Chen Xu, styled Yuandu, also known as Meihu, was from Meixian, Guangdong. He held teaching positions at the National Beiping School of Fine Arts, Jinghua School of Fine Arts, Fu Jen Catholic University Department of Fine Arts, Beijing Art Normal College, and the Central Academy of Arts and Crafts. He also served as the vice-chairman of the New Chinese Painting Research Association in Beijing and was an executive director of the Chinese Painting Research Society.

鍾進士戲嬰圖

辛巳五月陳緣督

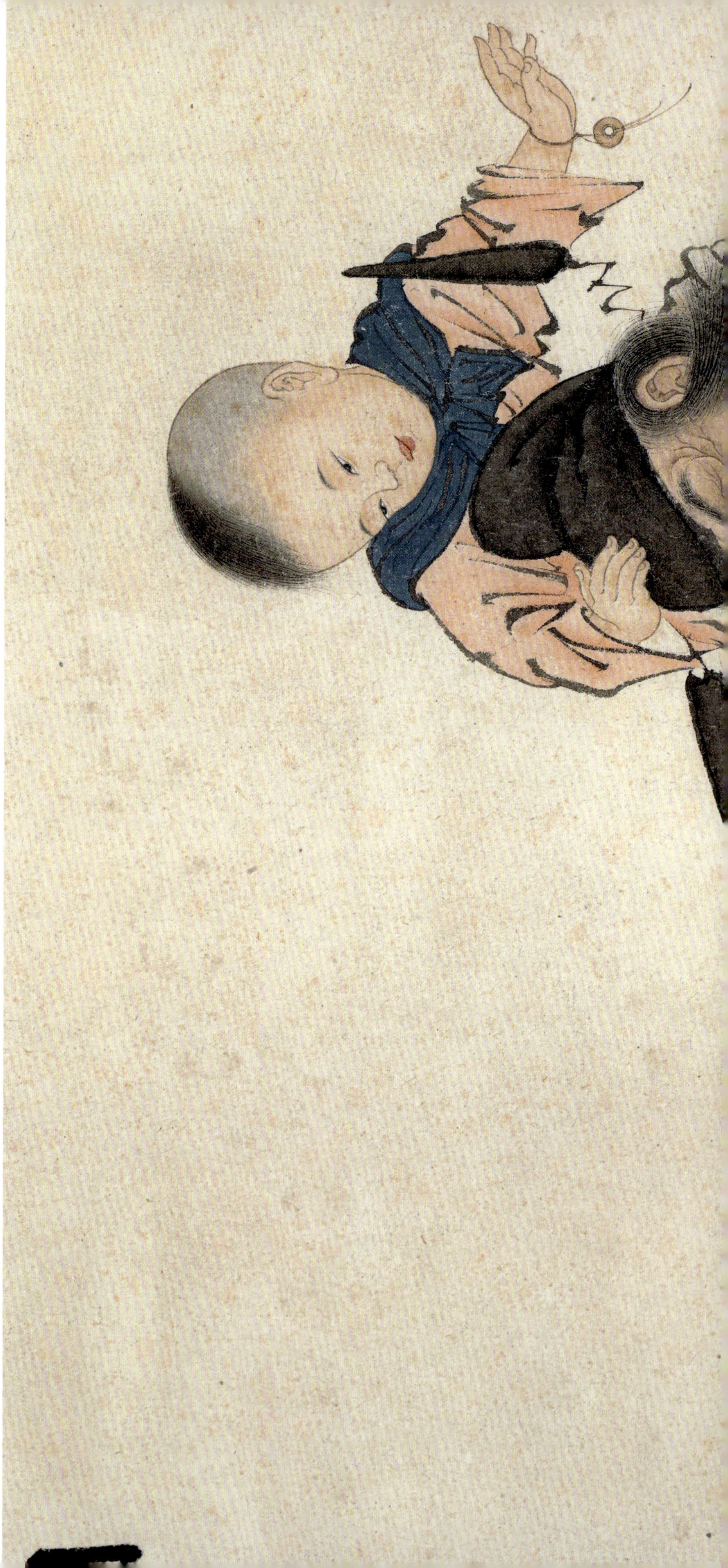

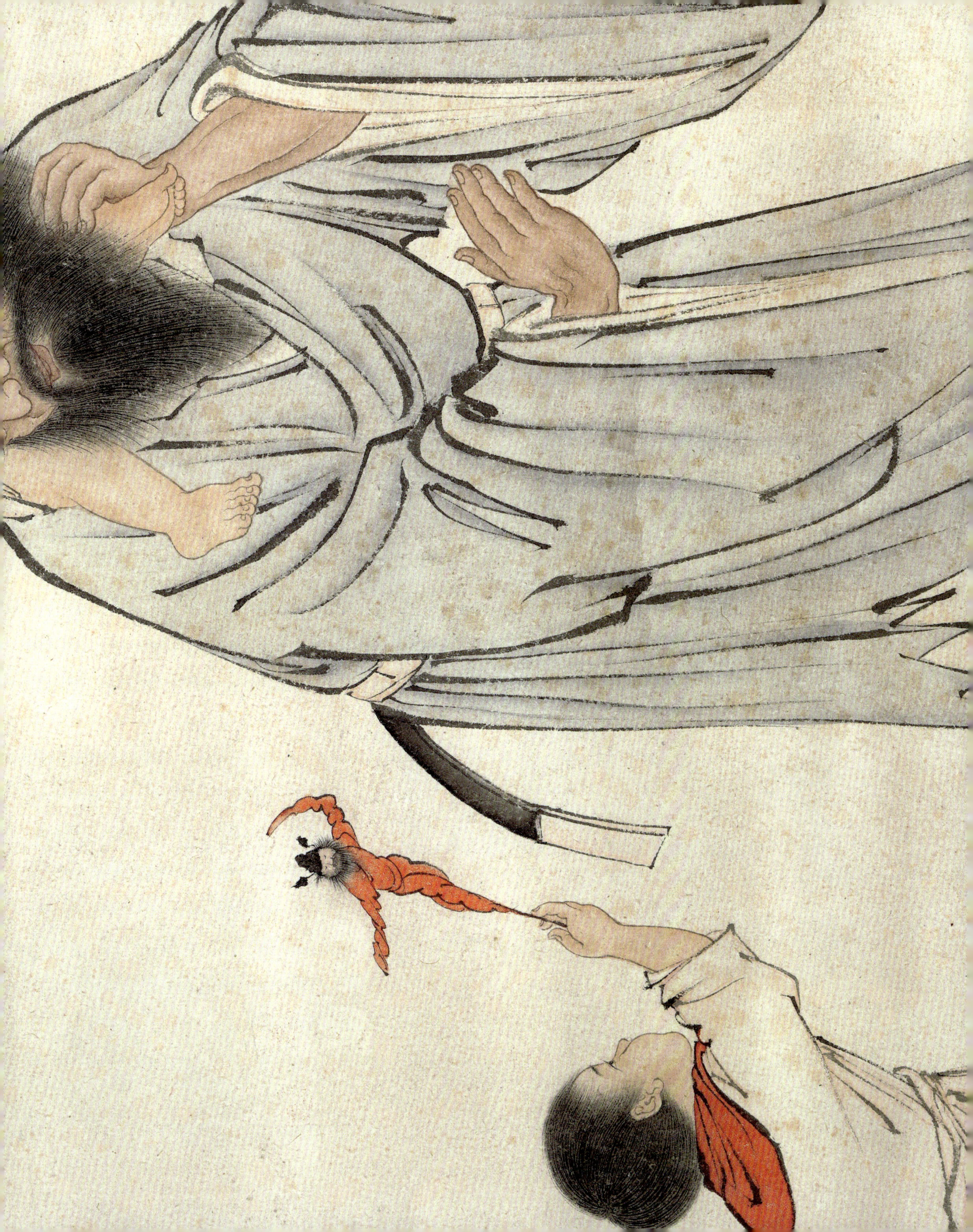

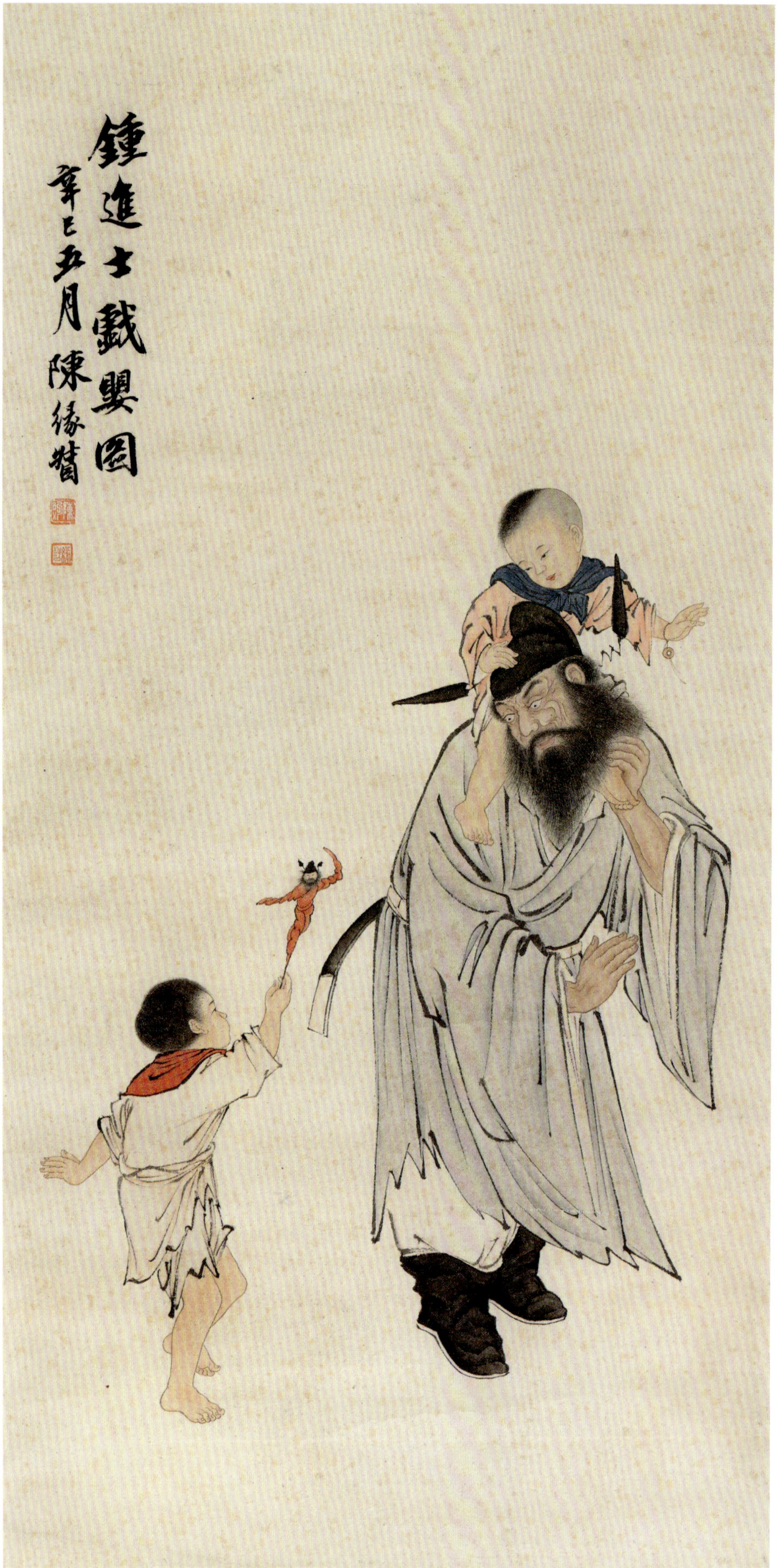
鍾進士戲嬰图
辛巳五月陳緣督

Artist:
Chen Yuandu

Medium:
Color on paper, Hanging scroll

Dimensions:
91.5 cm × 45 cm

Jinshi Zhong Playing with Children

Inscription:
Jinshi Zhong Playing with Children. Created in the fifth month of the year Xinsi by Chen Yuandu.

Seal:
Chen Xu, Yuandu

甲子端陽子丞戲圖于

聽蛙館

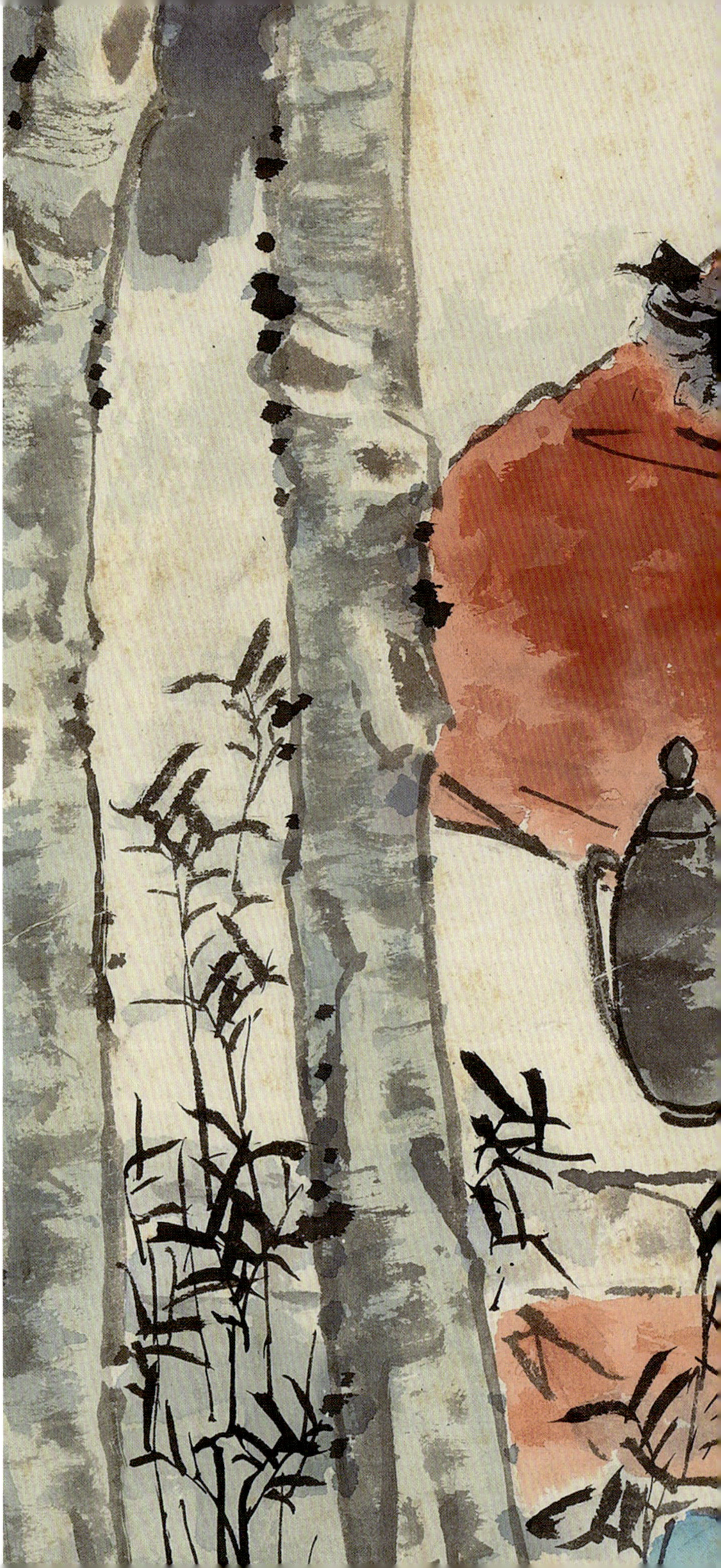

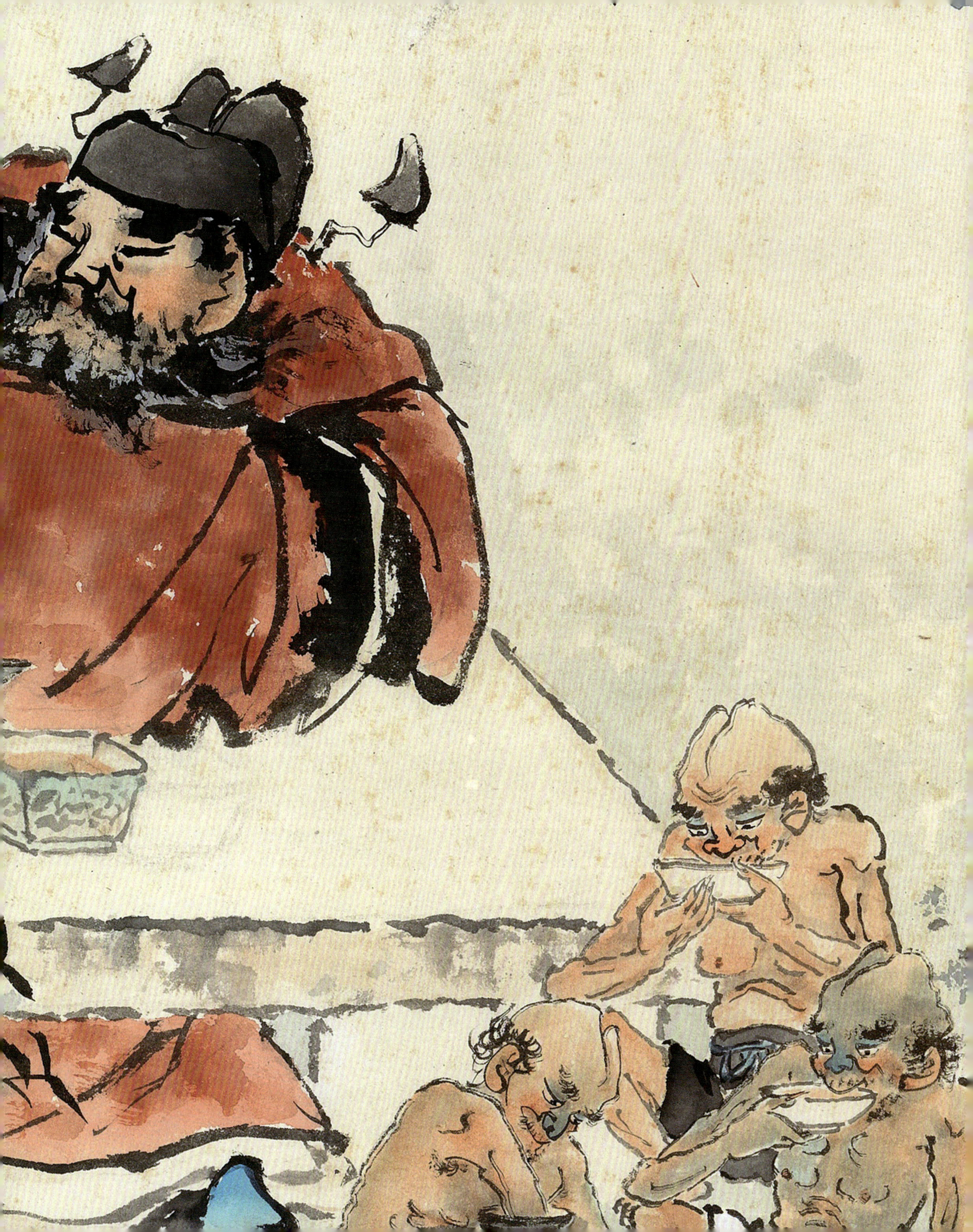

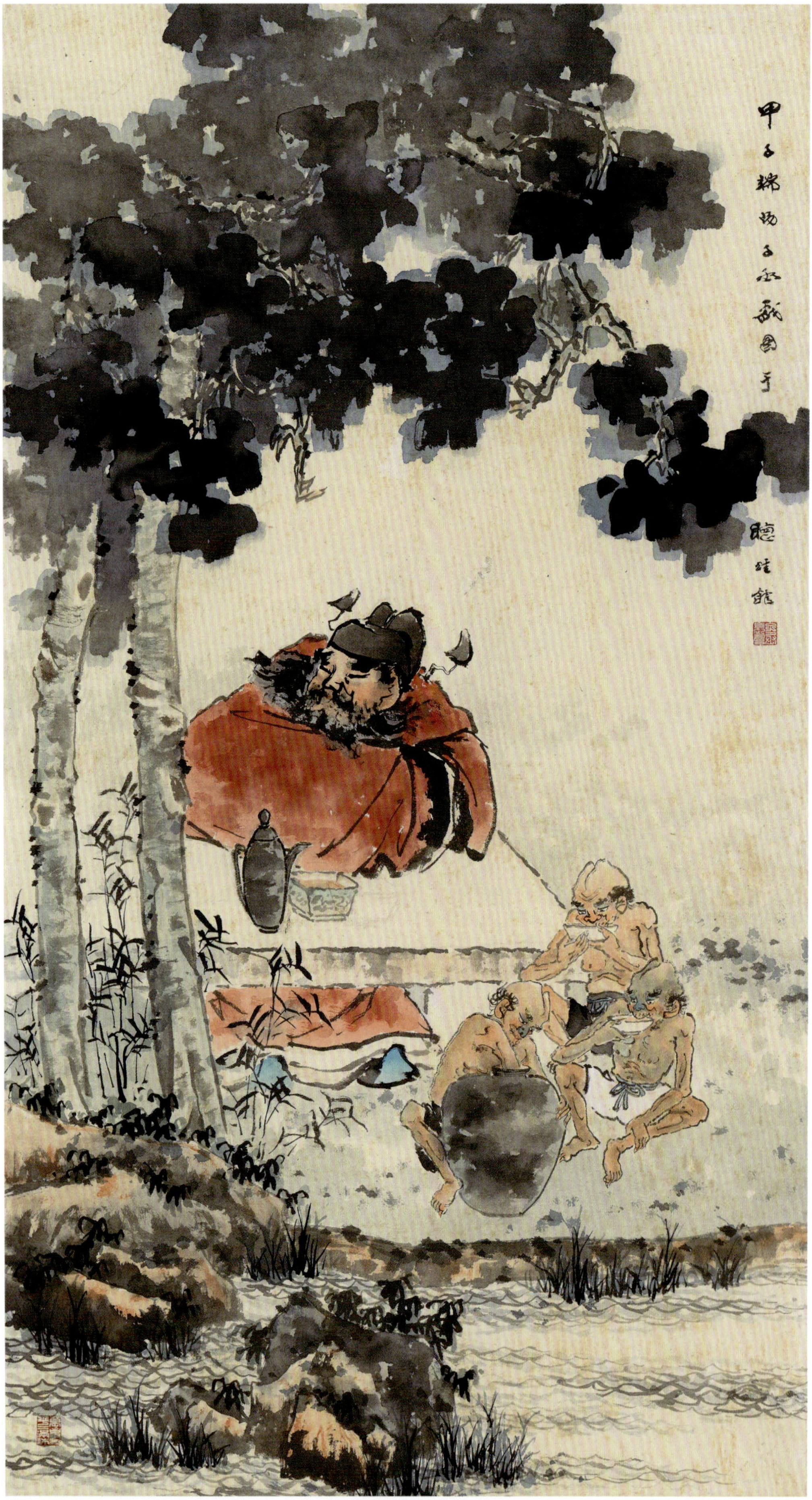

Artist:
Shen Zicheng

Medium:
Color on paper, Hanging scroll

Dimensions:
127.5 cm × 68 cm

Zhong Kui Drunk

Inscription:
On the Dragon Boat Festival of the Jiazi year, Shen Zicheng whimsically painted at the Pavilion of Tingwa.

Seal:
Zicheng Longevity, Everything Is Twice Settled and Thrice Even

Shen Zicheng (1904–1996)
Originally named Dejian, also known as Zhichun, styled the Old Man of Listening to Frogs, from Jiaxing, Zhejiang. He excelled in painting figures and landscapes and served as a researcher at the Shanghai Municipal Institute of Culture and History and as a painter at the Shanghai Chinese Painting Institute.

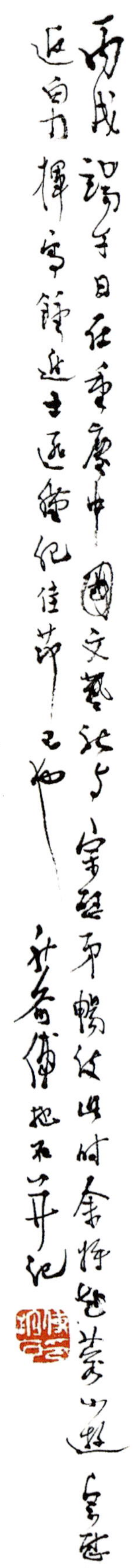

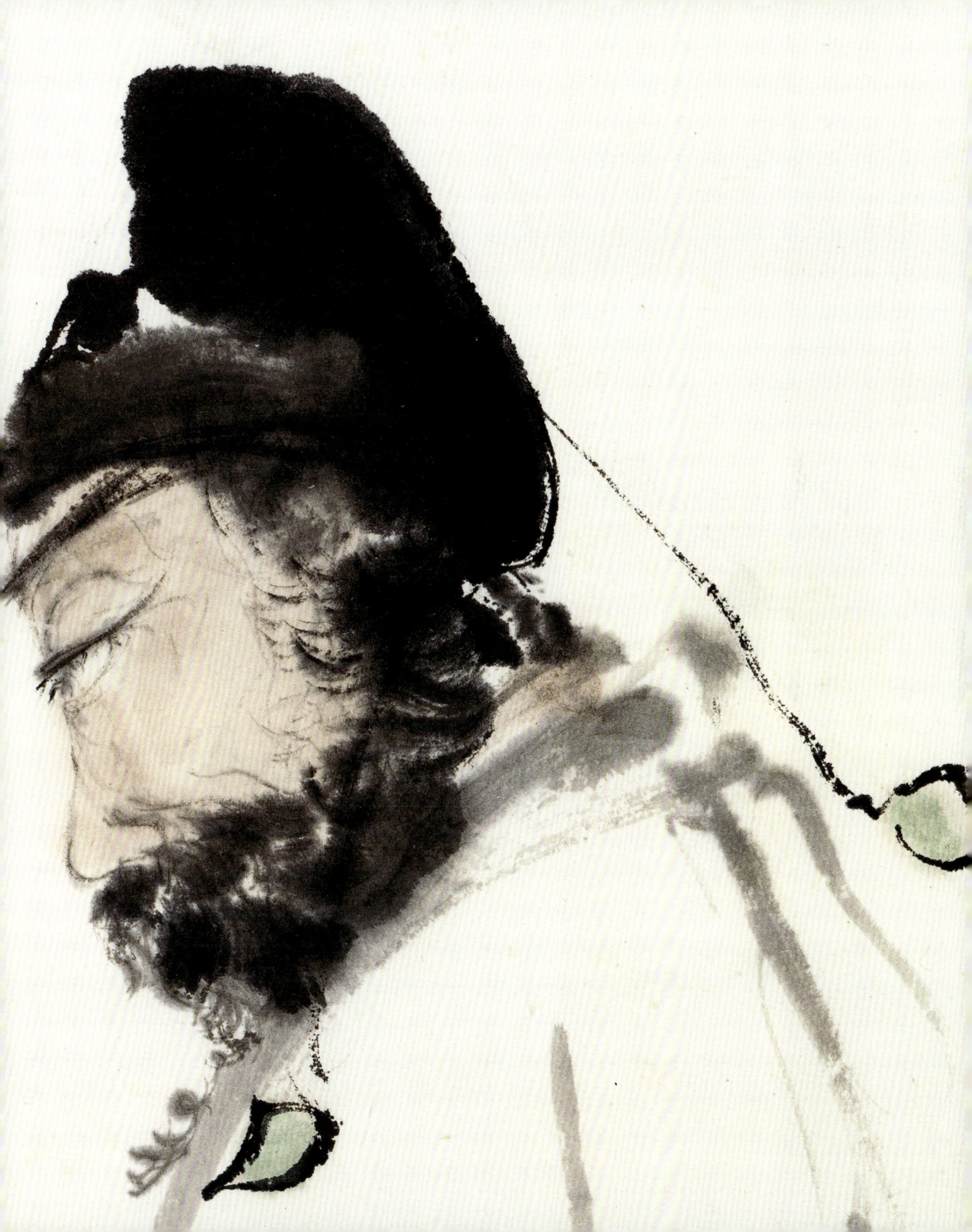

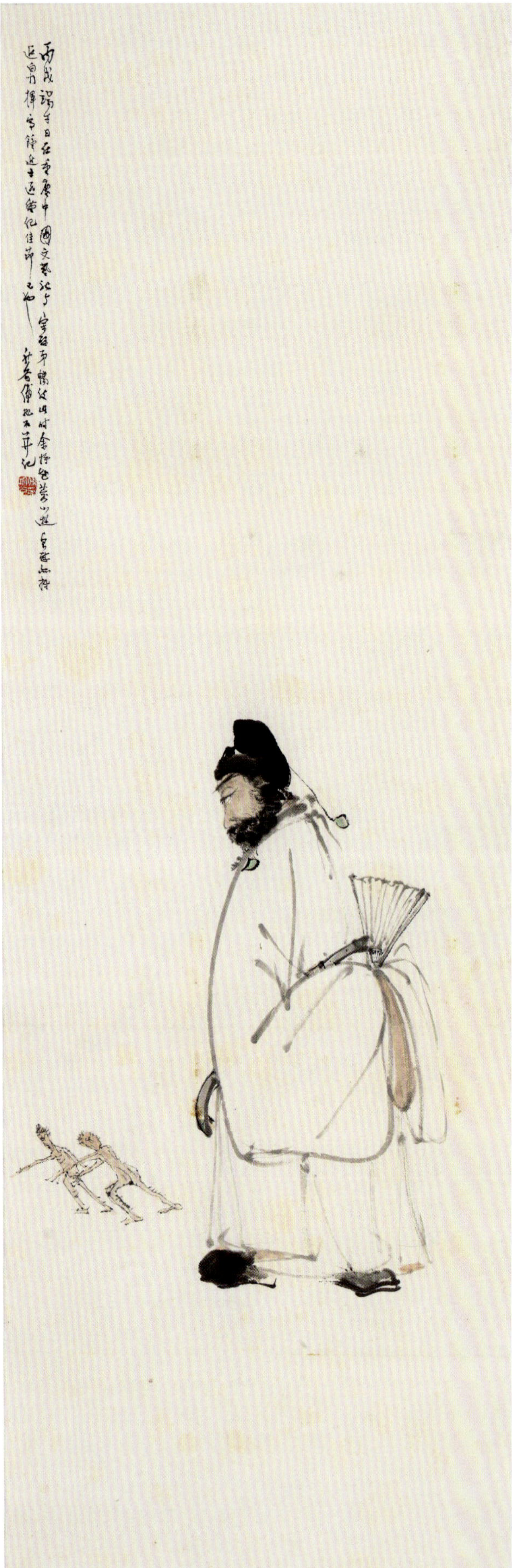

Artist:
Fu Baoshi

Medium:
Color on paper, Hanging scroll

Dimensions:
104.5 cm × 34 cm

Jinshi Zhong

Inscription:
On the Dragon Boat Festival of the Bingxu year, I engaged in a delightful conversation with my brother Zong Wei at the China Art and Literature Society in Chongqing. As I was about to embark on a brief visit to Chengdu and Zong Wei was set to return to Baicheng, I briskly penned a depiction of Zhong Kui. This was not merely to commemorate the festive day but also to symbolize a new chapter. By Fu Baoshi.

Seal:
The seal of Fu Baoshi

Fu Baoshi (1904–1965)
Originally named Changsheng, also known as Ruilin and styled the Master of Baoshi Studio, was from Jiangxi. A modern painter renowned for his landscapes, he developed the distinctive "Baoshi texture strokes" in his middle years. He held positions such as the vice-chairman of the China Artists Association, chairman of the Jiangsu branch of the Artists Association, and president of the Jiangsu Chinese Painting Institute.

風吹胡沙目欲迷官柳樣全梅綻蕊終南進士屹然把笏束藍袍辮霧趾
手執硬黃青紙義曰上帝錫爾祉蝟磔子思含者盡順指守門荼與壘肯放
孫狐樣九尾一聲爆竹人安靡明日春光萬斛里

戊寅元旦題終南進士早朝圖 貞白時寓東江之五月壬

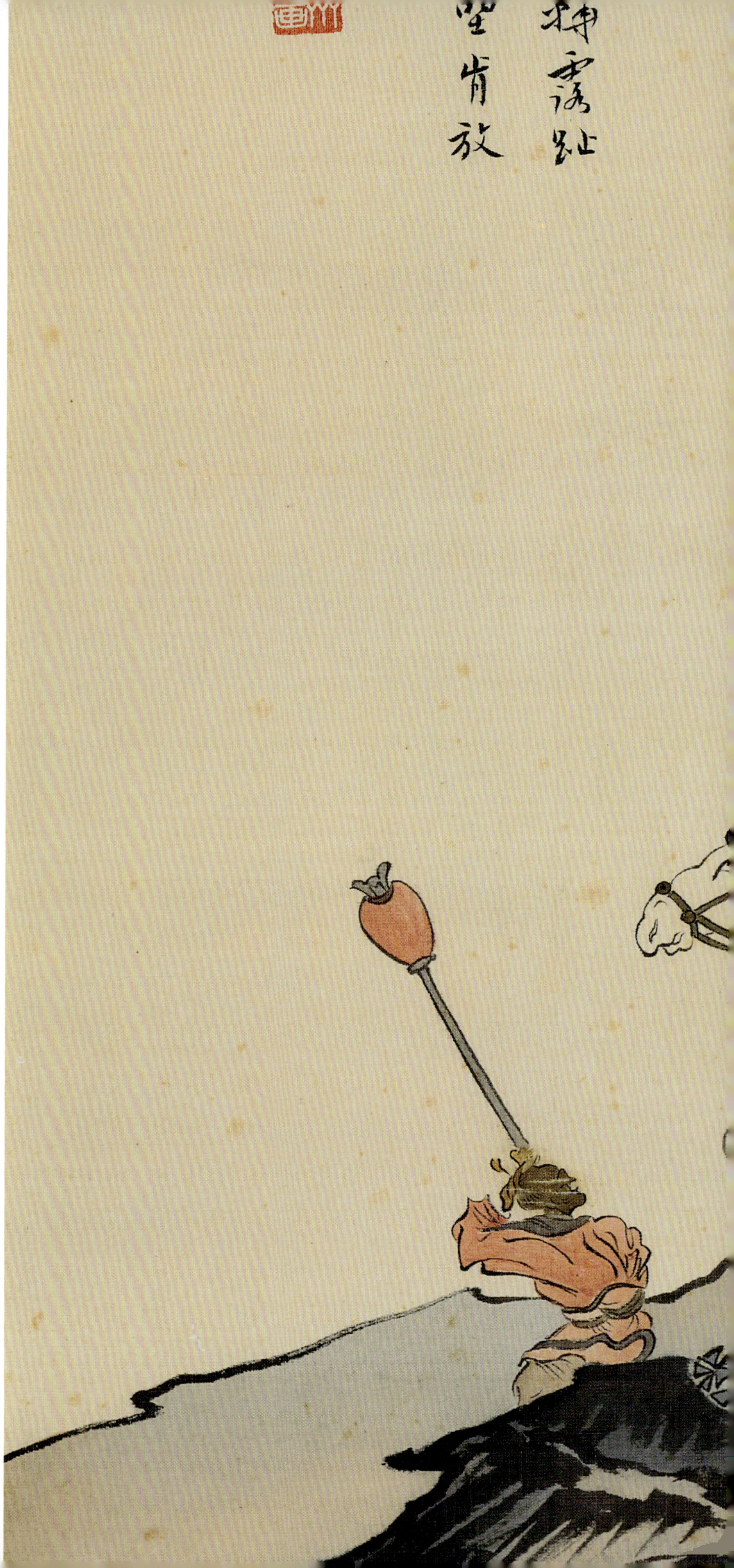

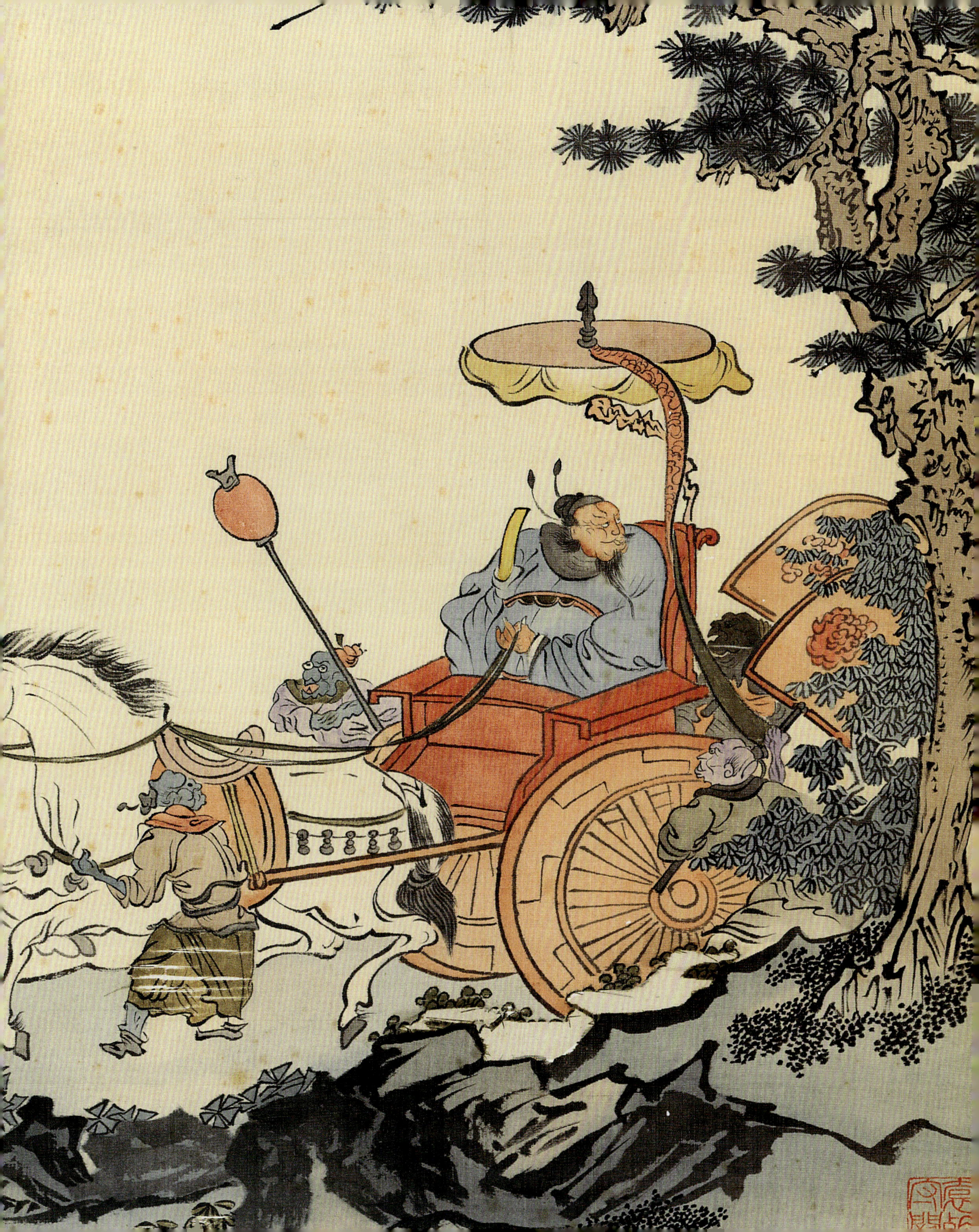

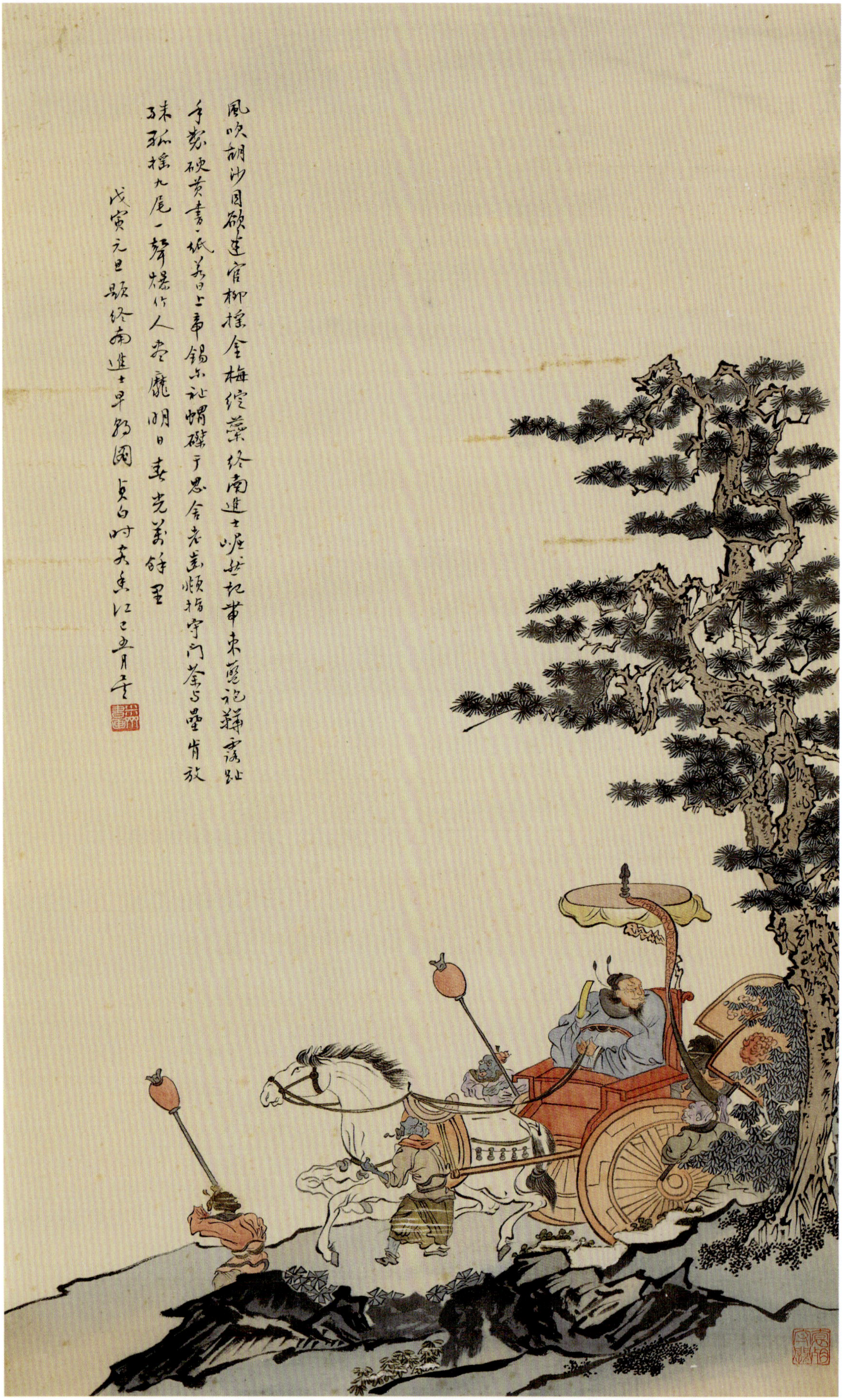

Artist:
Gao Zhenbai

Medium:
Color on paper, Hanging scroll

Dimensions:
73 cm × 44 cm

Zhong Kui Attending the Morning Court

Inscription:
The wind whips up the desert sands, nearly blinding the eye,
Yet willow branches by the office sway in gold, as plum blossoms open nigh.
Suddenly, the Jinshi from Zhongnan stands, his blue robe loosely tied, his boots revealing toes,
A sheet of stiff yellow in his hand, as though from God, fortune flows.
The hedgehog is bound at his abode, its aged teeth worn away, pointing to the bitter herbs and stones at the gate it showed.
He refuses to release the odd foxes with their nine tails swaying; with a burst of firecrackers, all scatter away,
For tomorrow, spring's light shall shine over a myriad miles in its play.
On New Year's Day of the Wuyin year, I inscribed the "Zhong Kui Attending the Morning Court", by Zhen Bai. At that time, I had already been a visitor in Hong Kong for five months.

Seal:
Calligraphies and paintings of Mi Zhai, Preserving despite imperfections

Gao Zhenbai (1906–1992)
Originally named Bingyin, also known as Boyu, from Chenghai, Guangdong. He studied painting under Pu Ru and seal carving under Yang Qianli in his early years. He pursued his education in English literature in the United Kingdom and traveled throughout Europe. Upon returning to China, he worked at the Bank of China in Shanghai, the Foreign Affairs Department in Nanjing, and other institutions. Later, he moved to Hong Kong and earned his living as a writer, becoming a renowned modern raconteur with works such as Random Notes from the Tingyu Pavilion.

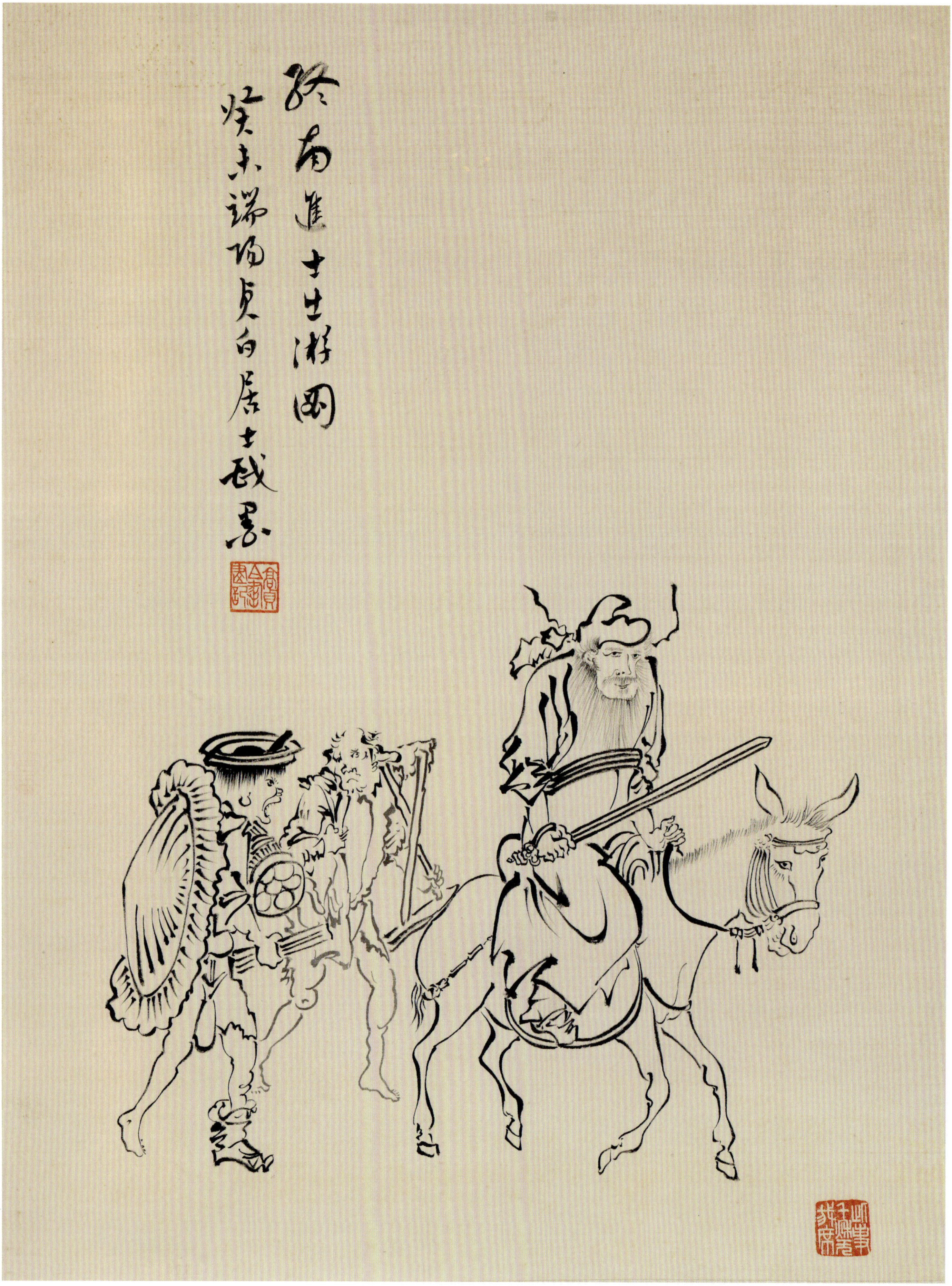
終南進士出游圖
癸未端陽貞白居士戲墨

Artist:
Gao Zhenbai

Medium:
Color on paper, Hanging scroll

Dimensions:
53 cm × 39 cm

Zhong Kui's Outing

Inscription:
A depiction of Zhongnan's Jinshi on an excursion. On the Dragon Boat Festival of the Guiwei year, Lay Scholar Zhenbai dabbled in ink.

Seal:
The calligraphy and paintings record of Gao Zhenbai, No Seat for Me in Thousand Autumns

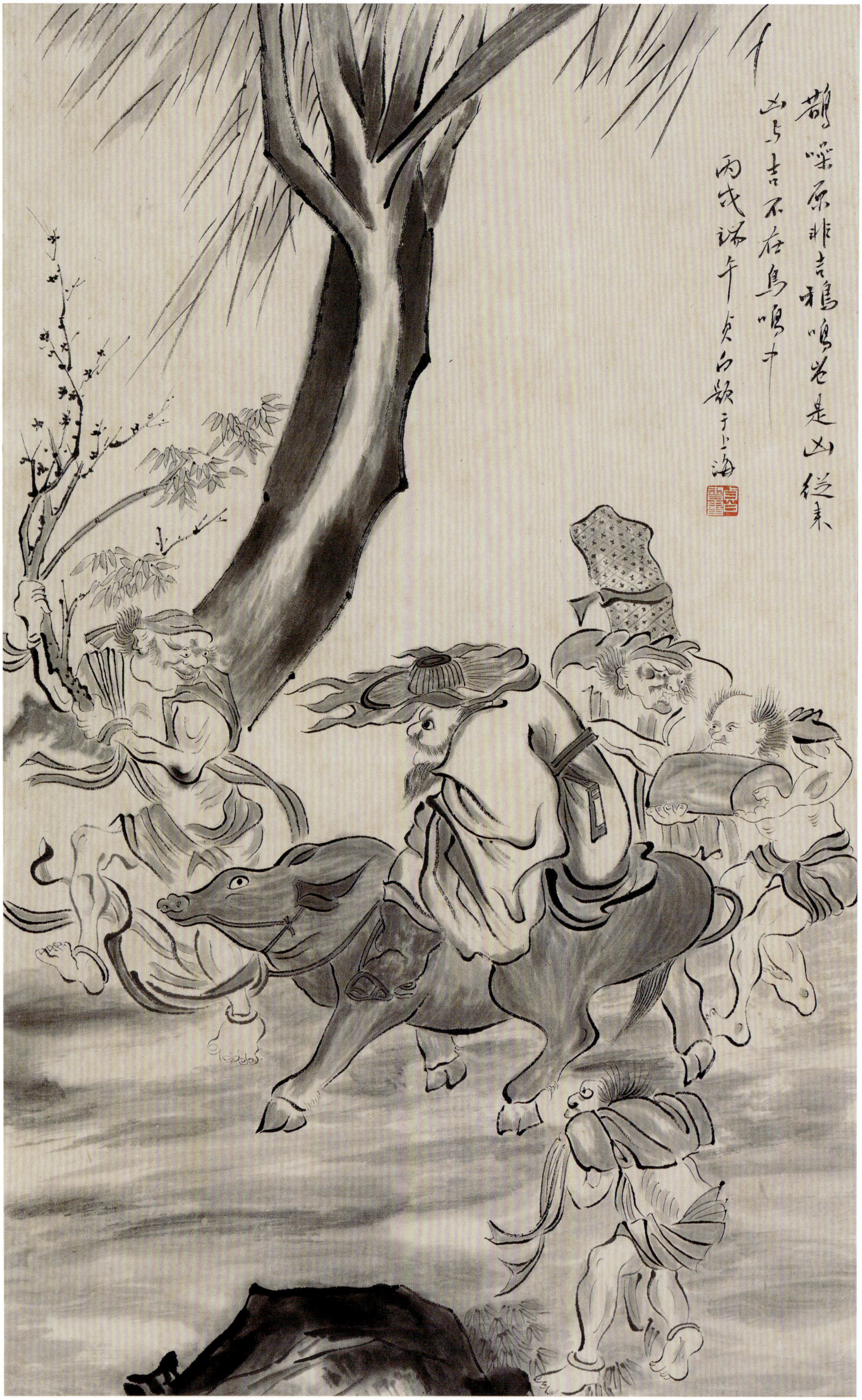
鵲噪原非吉鴉鳴豈是凶從來
凶与吉不在鳥鳴中
丙戌端午貞白題于上海

Artist:
Gao Zhenbai

Medium:
Ink on paper, Hanging scroll

Dimensions:
67 cm × 40 cm

Zhongnan's Jinshi Welcoming Spring

Inscription:
The magpie's chatter does not always herald good fortune, nor does the crow's caw surely portend disaster. Since ancient times, omens of luck and misfortune have never been found in the calls of birds.

On the Dragon Boat Festival of the Bingxu year, Zhenbai inscribed this in Shanghai.

Seal:
The calligraphy and paintings of Zhenbai

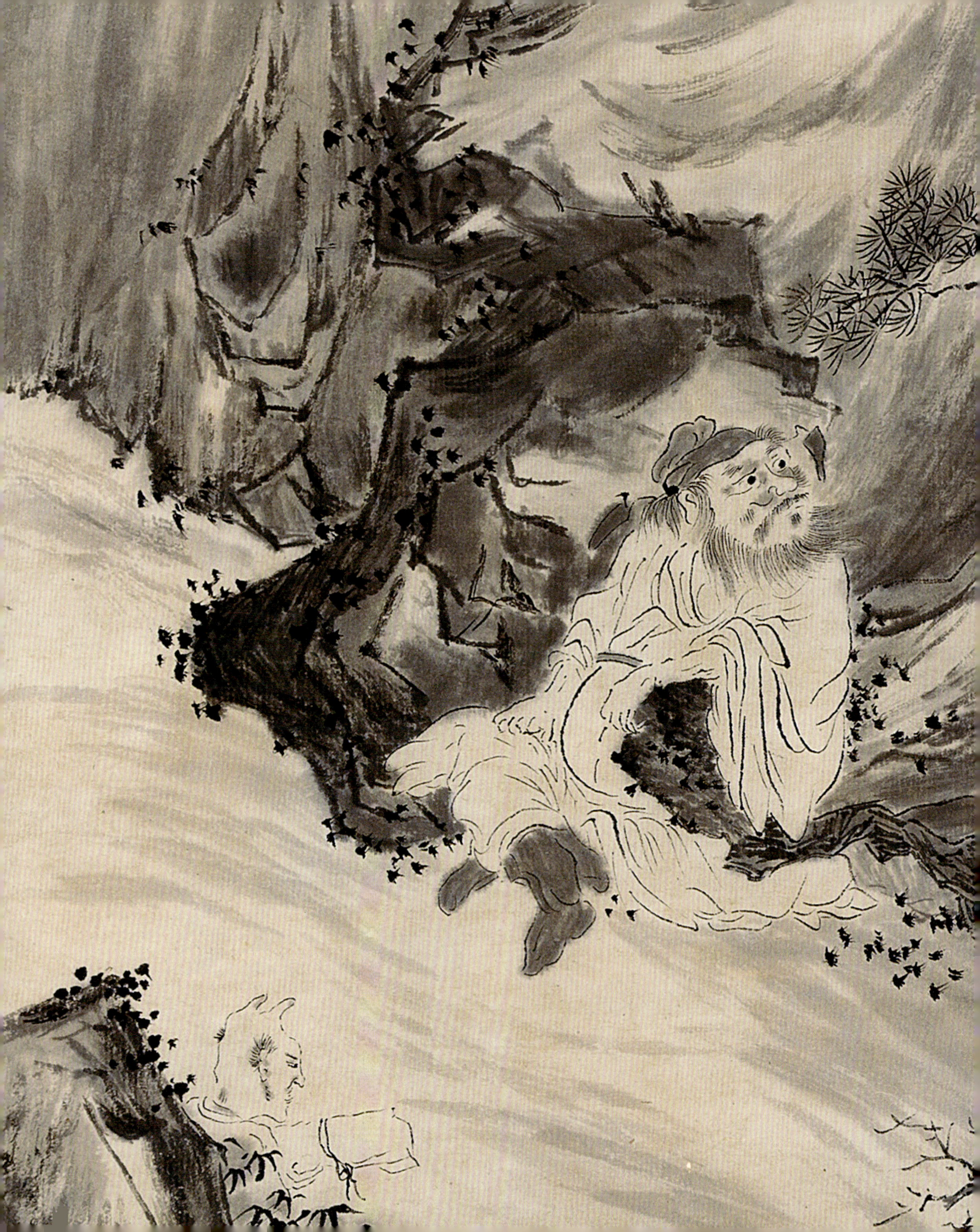

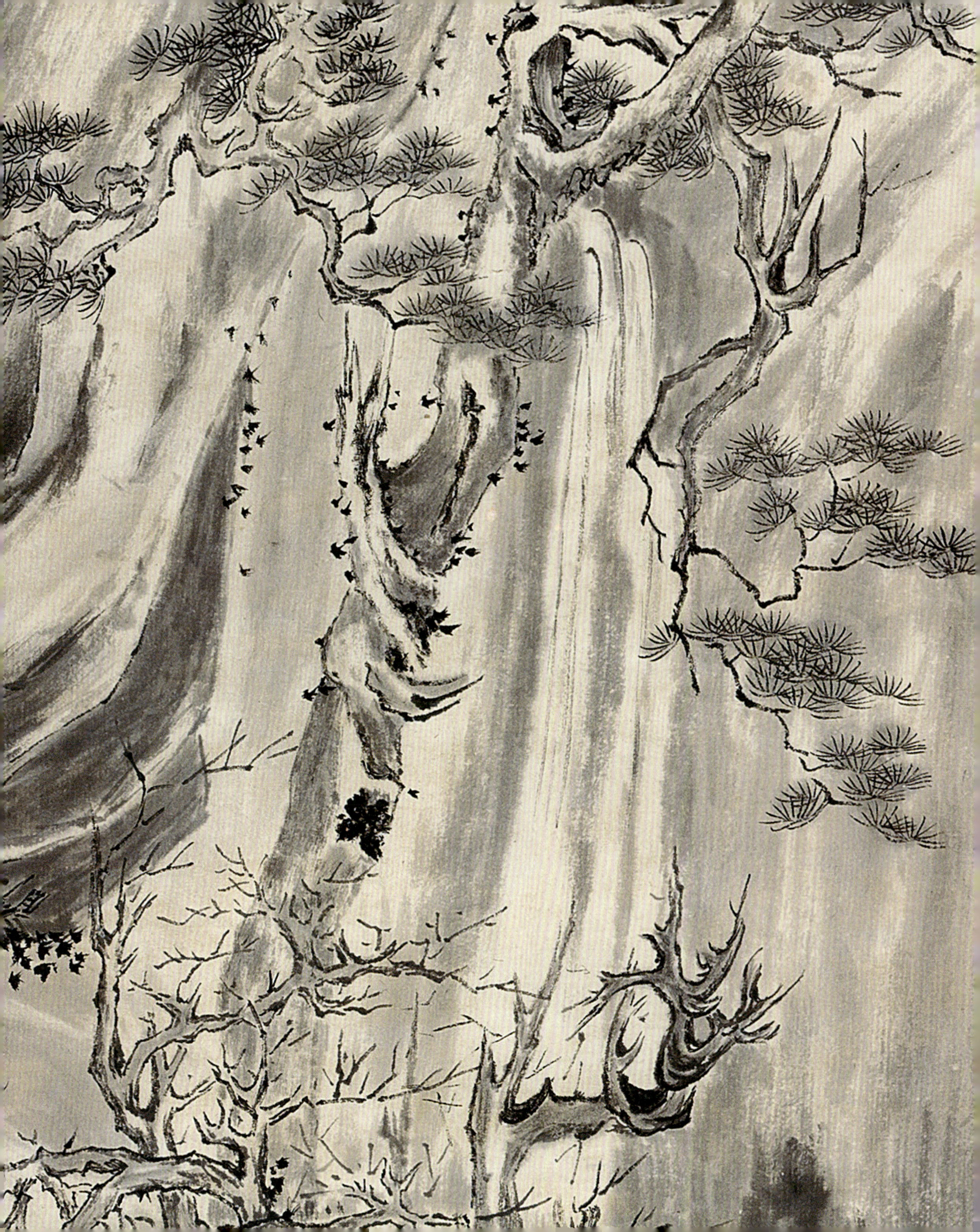

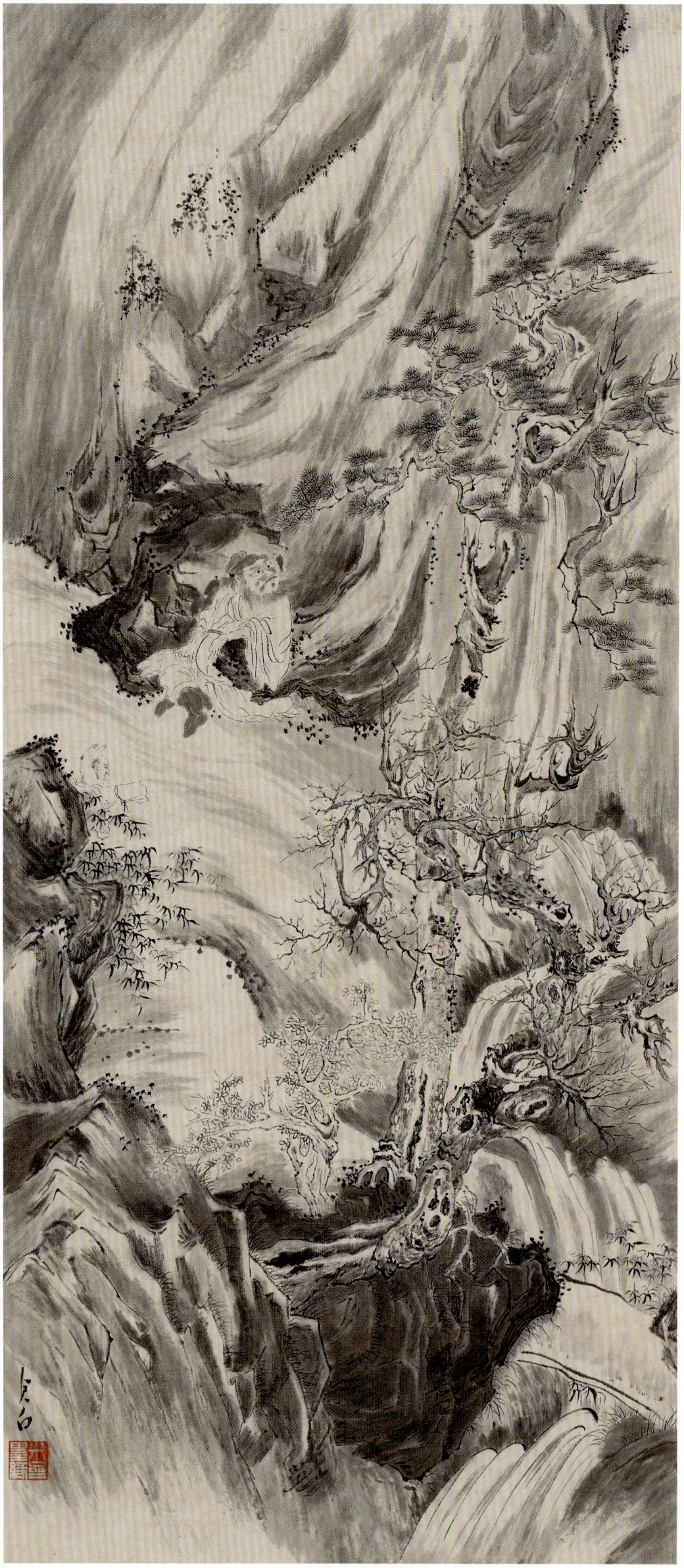

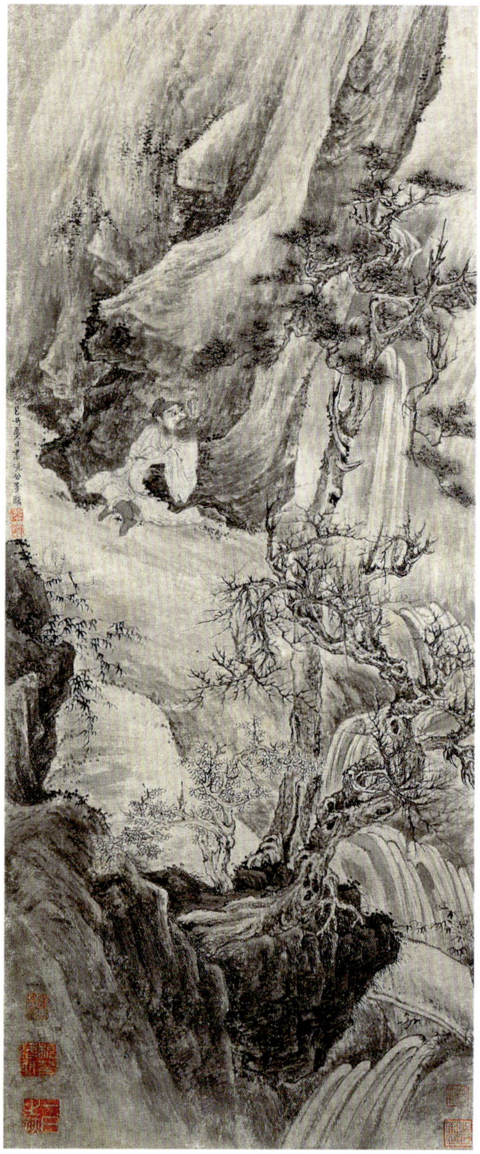

Zhong Kui in the Chilly Woods

Artist: Li Lin (Ming Dynasty)
Medium: Ink on paper, Hanging scroll

Artist:
Gao Zhenbai

Medium:
Ink on paper, Hanging scroll

Dimensions:
79 cm × 34 cm

Zhong Kui in the Chilly Woods

Inscription:
Zhenbai

Seal:
Ink Affinity of Mi Zhai

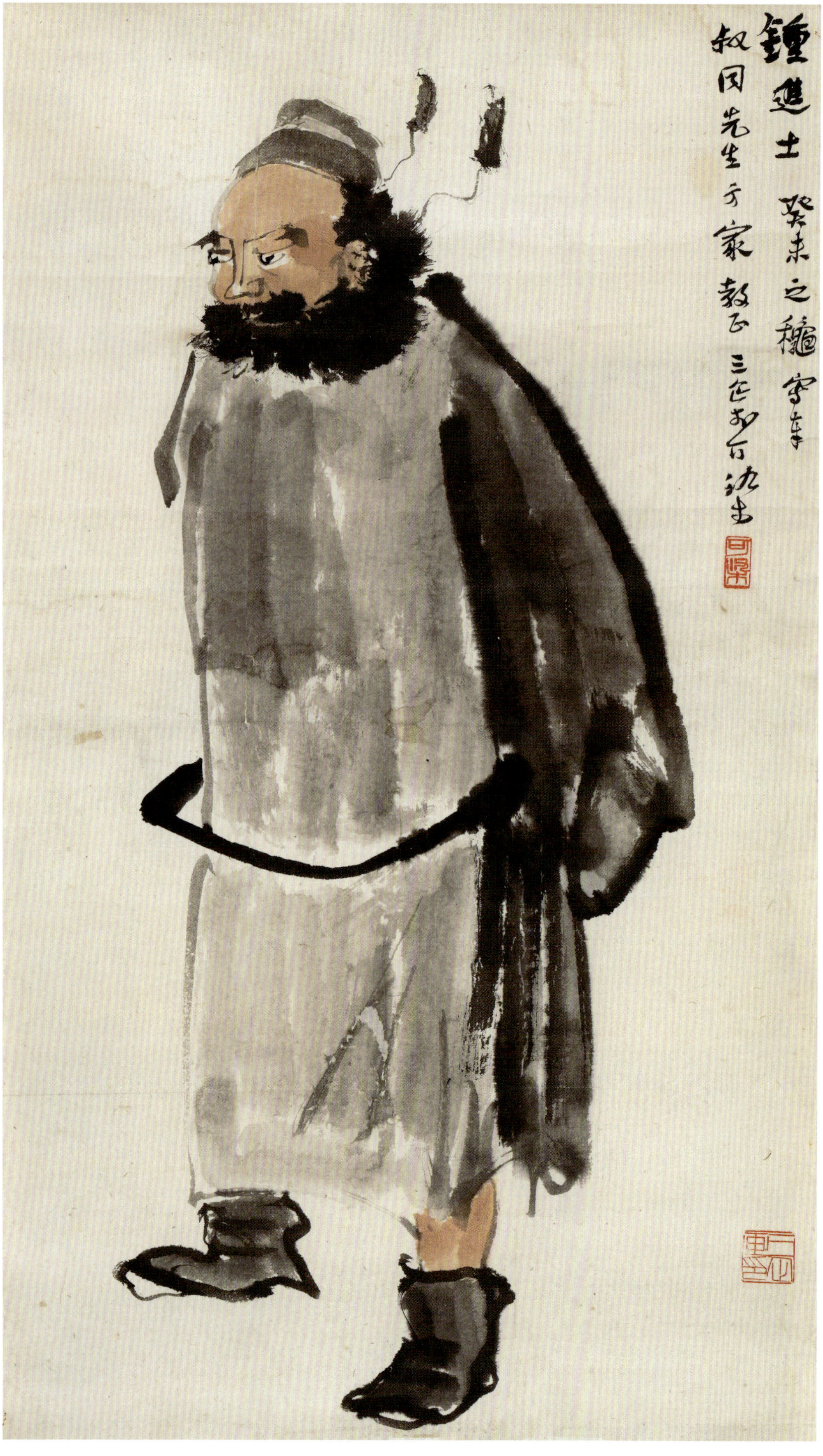
鍾進士

Artist:
Li Keran

Medium:
Color on paper, Framed piece

Dimensions:
65.5 cm × 37 cm

Jinshi Zhong

Inscription:
Jinshi Zhong. In the autumn of the Guiwei year, this was painted in respect for the family instruction of Mr. Shu Tong, by Sanqi, Li Keran.

Seal:
Keran, The painting seal of Sanqi

Li Keran (1907–1989)
An outstanding modern painter and poet, who was a disciple of Qi Baishi. He served as a professor at the Central Academy of Fine Arts, vice-chairman of the China Artists Association, and president of the Chinese Painting Institute.

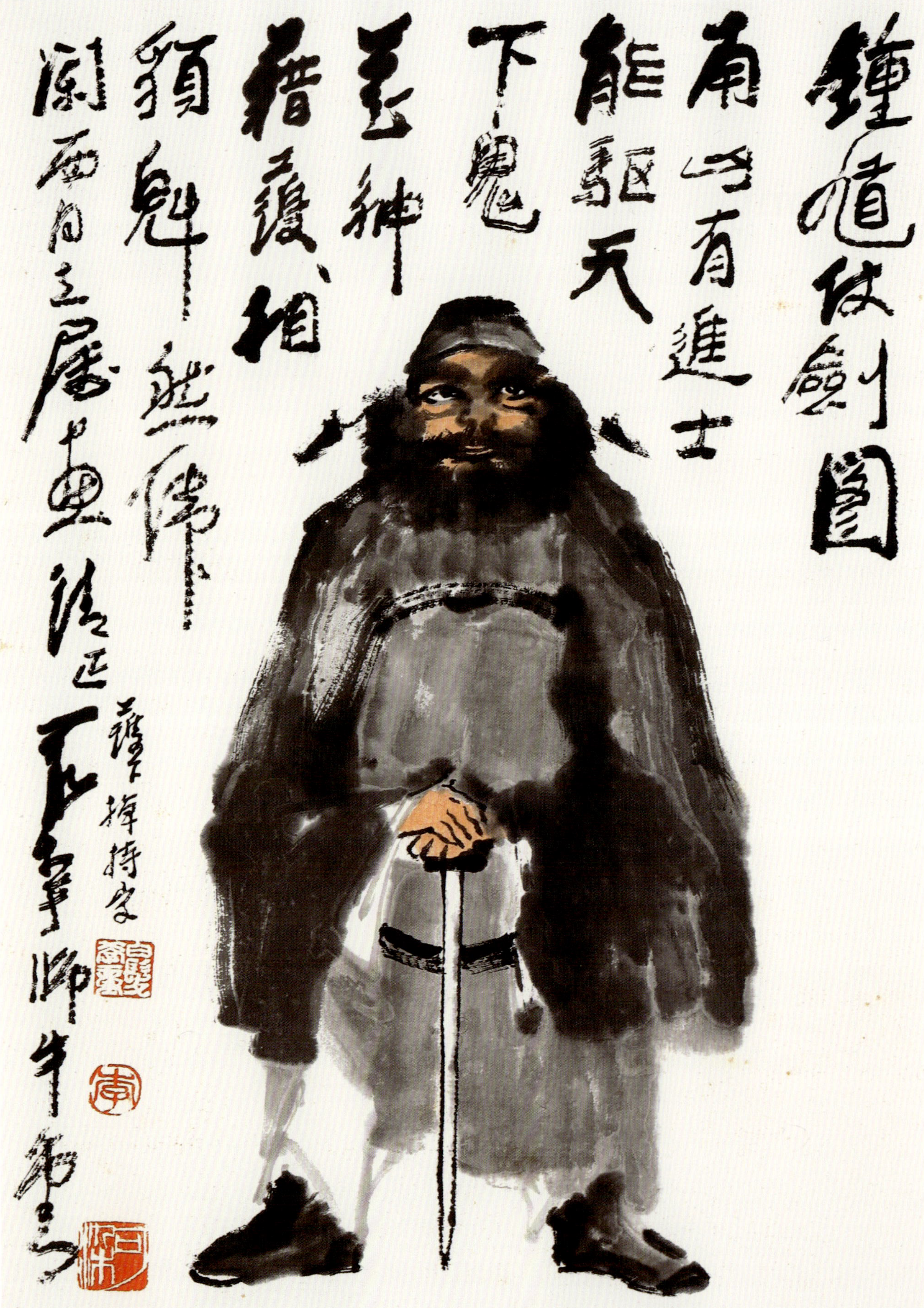
鍾馗仗劍圖
南山有進士
能驅天下鬼

Artist:
Li Keran

Medium:
Color on paper, Hanging scroll

Dimensions:
59 cm × 41 cm

Zhong Kui Wielding a Sword

Inscription:
Zhong Kui Wielding a Sword. In the Southern Hills, a Jinshi resides; with power to banish ghosts far and wide. Guarded by the deity of flowers bright; his visage majestic, a grandiose sight. This painting, commissioned by Comrade Lanxi, awaits correction. By Keran at Shiniu Cottage.

Seal:
White-haired student, Li, Keran

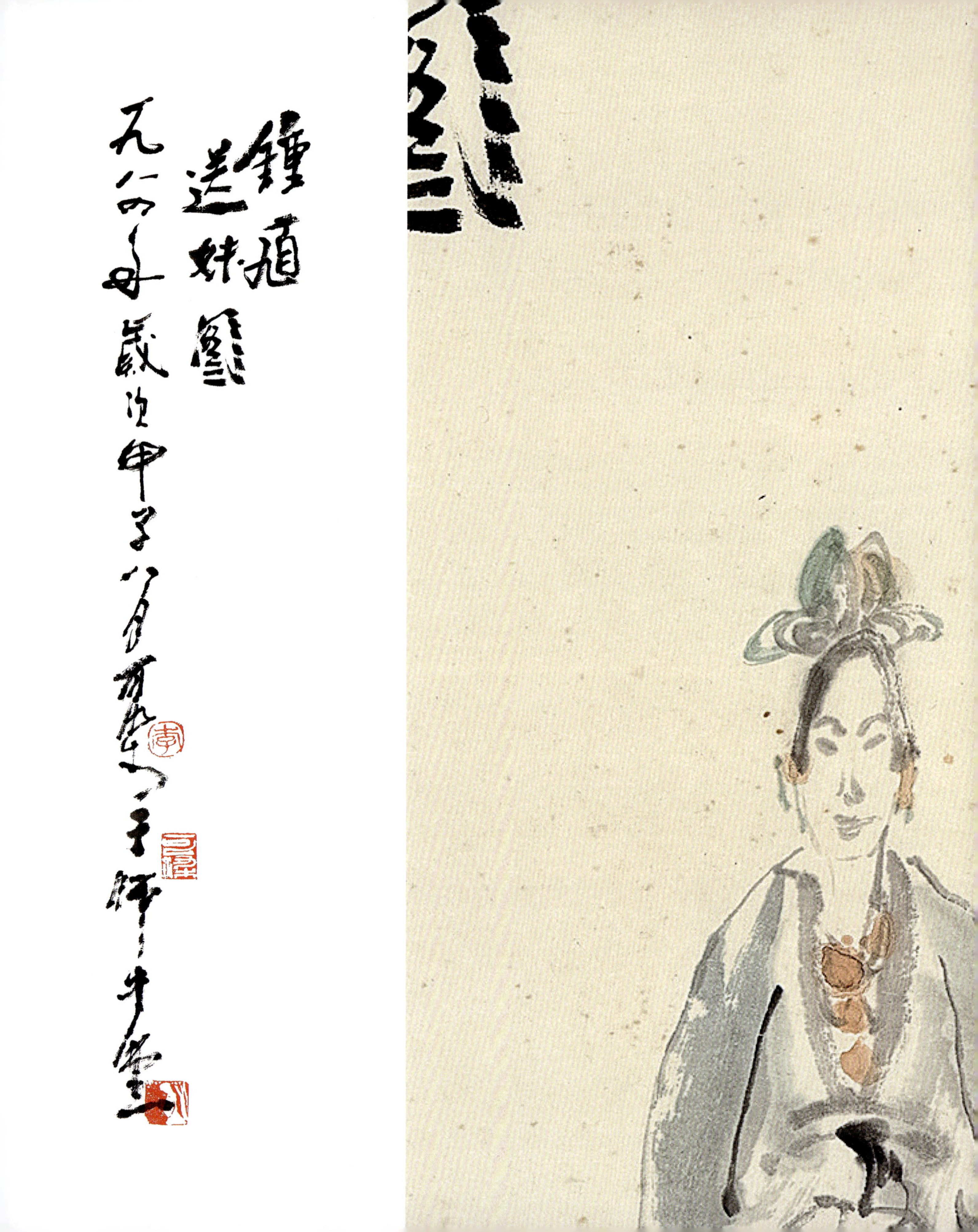
鍾馗送妹圖

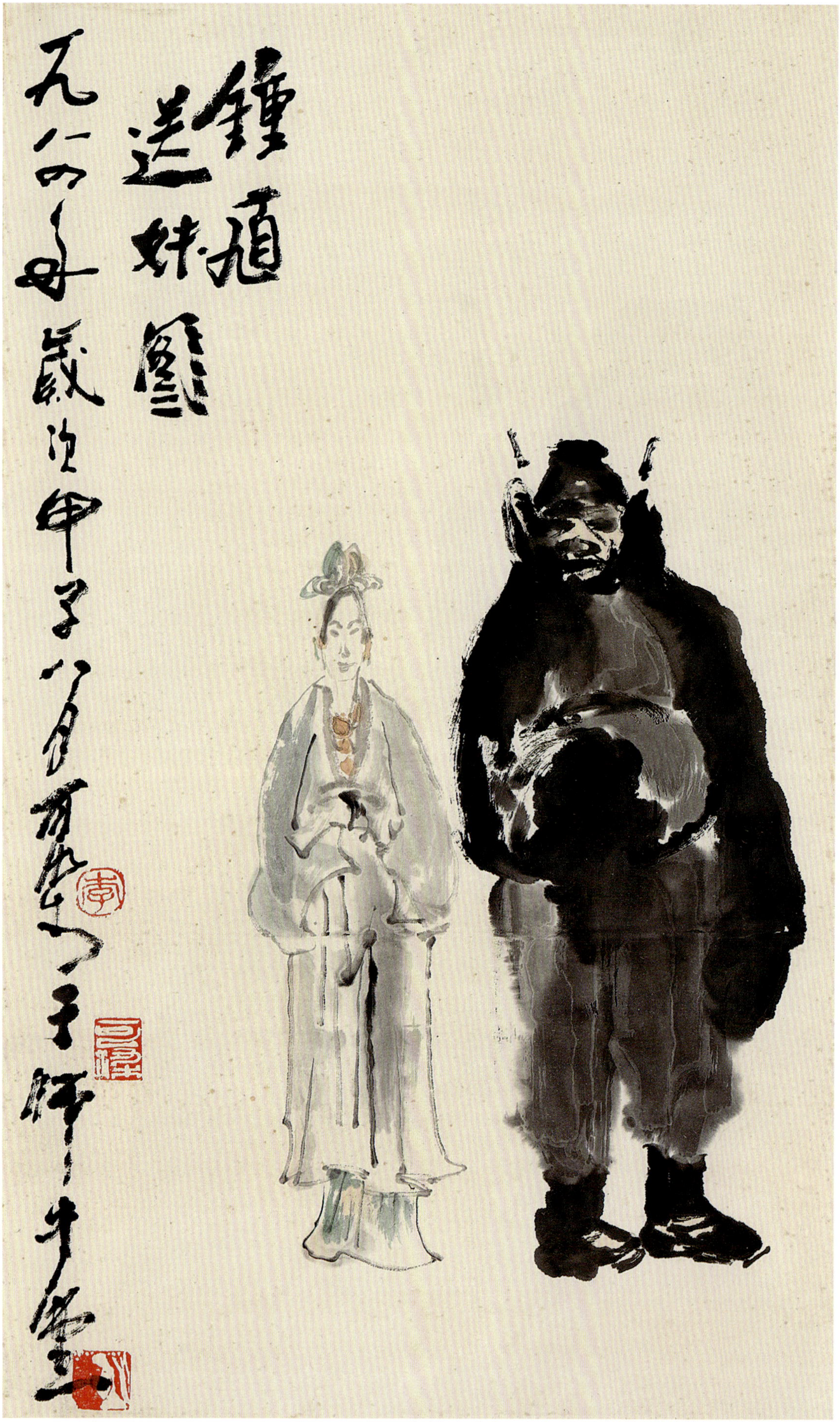
鍾馗送妹圖

Artist:
Li Keran

Medium:
Color on paper, Framed piece

Dimensions:
65.5 cm × 37 cm

Zhong Kui Giving His Sister Away in Marriage

Inscription:
Zhong Kui Giving His Sister Away in Marriage. In August of the year 1984, during the cyclical year of Jiazi, painted by Keran in the Shiniu Hall.

Seal:
Li, Keran

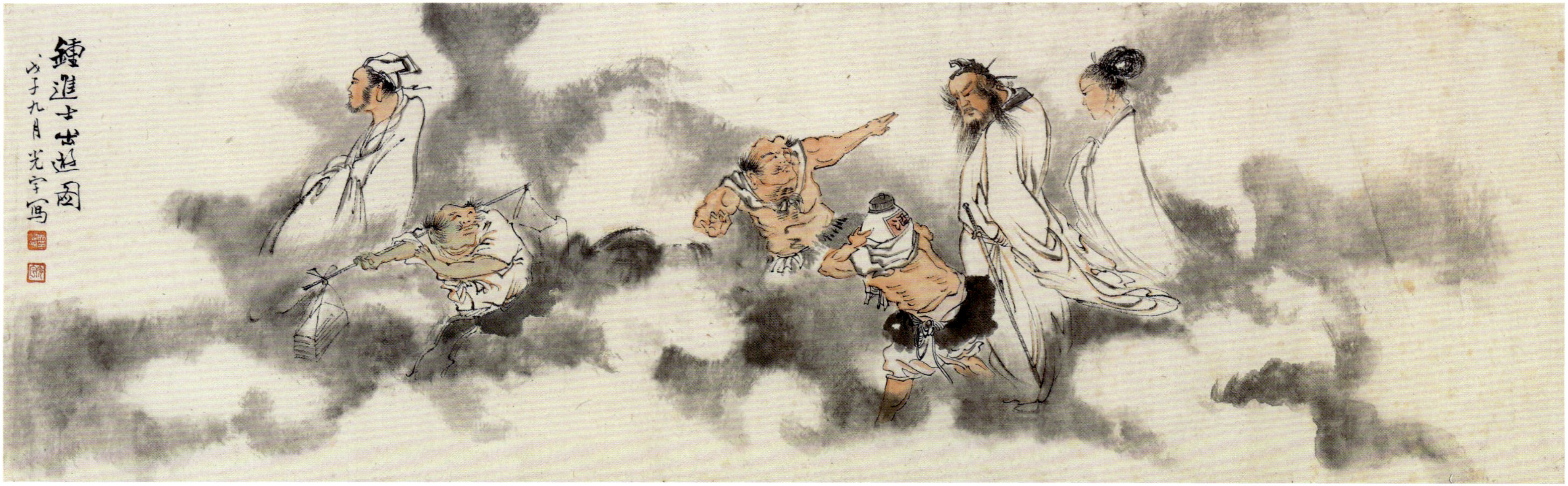
鍾進士出遊圖
戊子九月 光宇寫

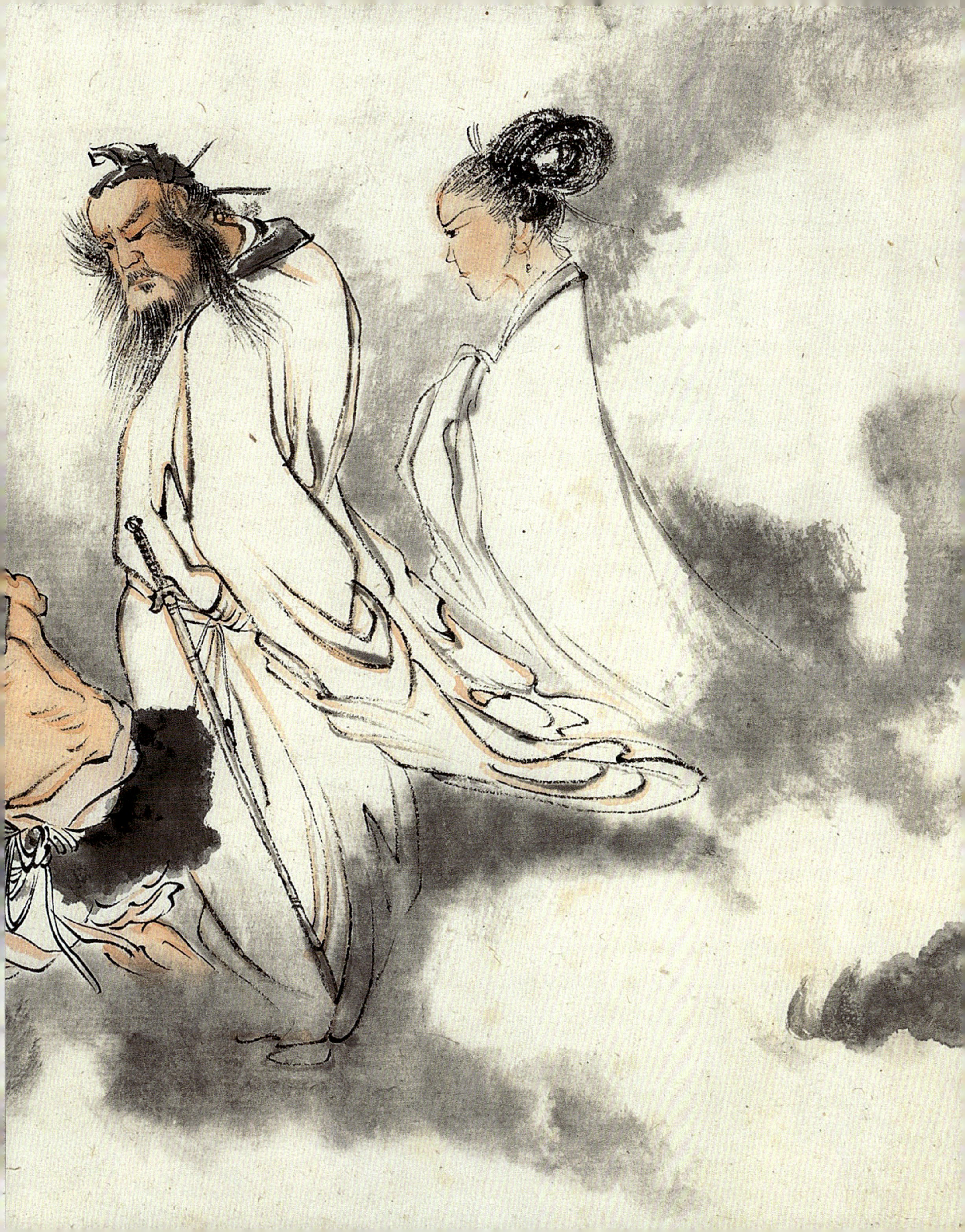

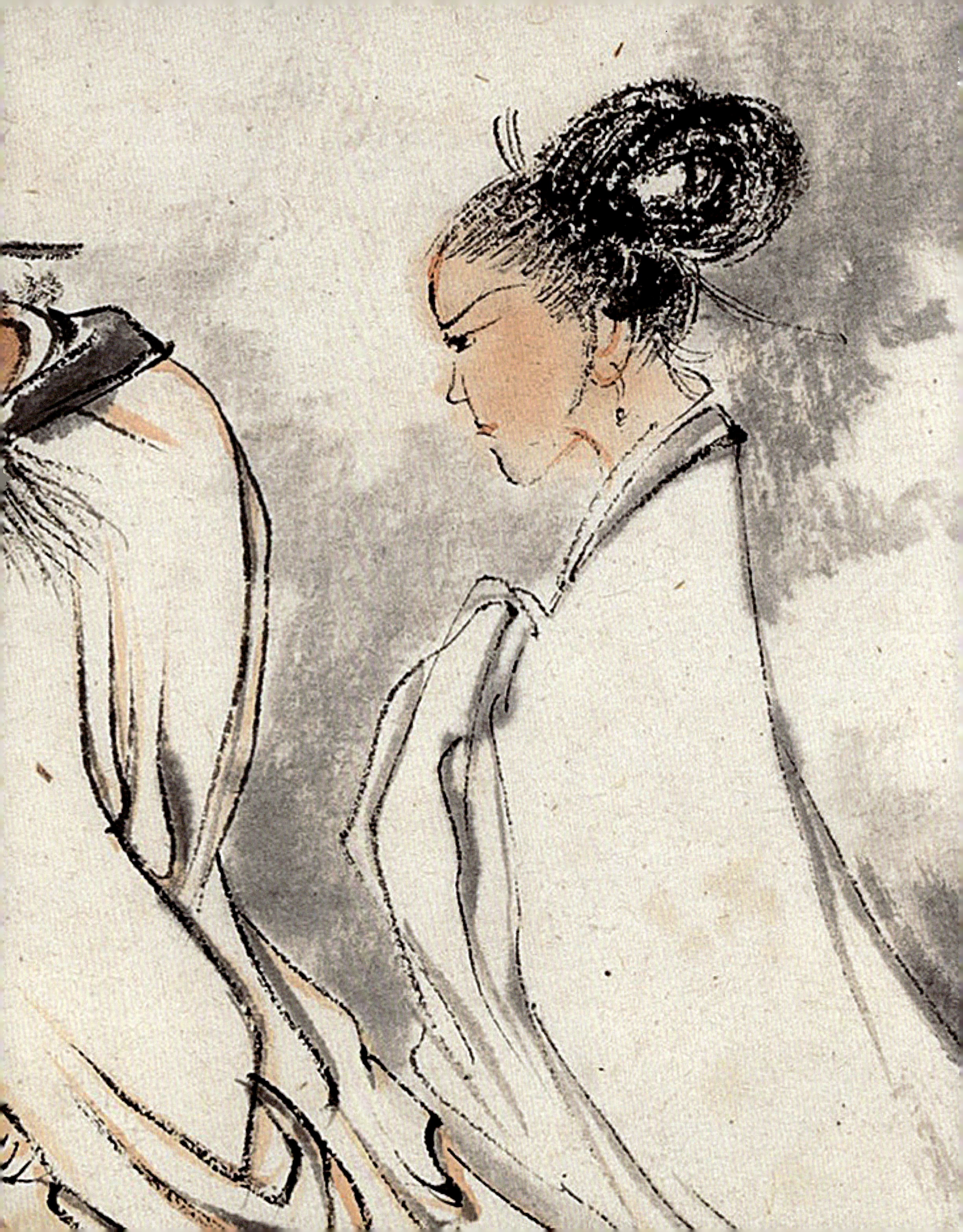

Artist:
Wu Guangyu

Medium:
Color on paper, Framed piece

Dimensions:
16.5 cm × 54.5 cm

Jinshi Zhong's Outing

Inscription:
Jinshi Zhong's Outing. Painted in September of the Wuzi year by Guangyu.

Seal:
The seal of Wu Xianzeng, Guangyu

Wu Guangyu (1908–1970)
Originally named Xianzeng, commonly known by his courtesy name, from Shaoxing, Zhejiang. He had a passion for painting since childhood and studied under Xu Yansun. He taught at the National Art School of Beiping and the Jinghua Art Academy. After 1949, he engaged in professional creation at the Beijing Painting Academy and held joint exhibitions with his brother Wu Jingting in Beijing and other locations.

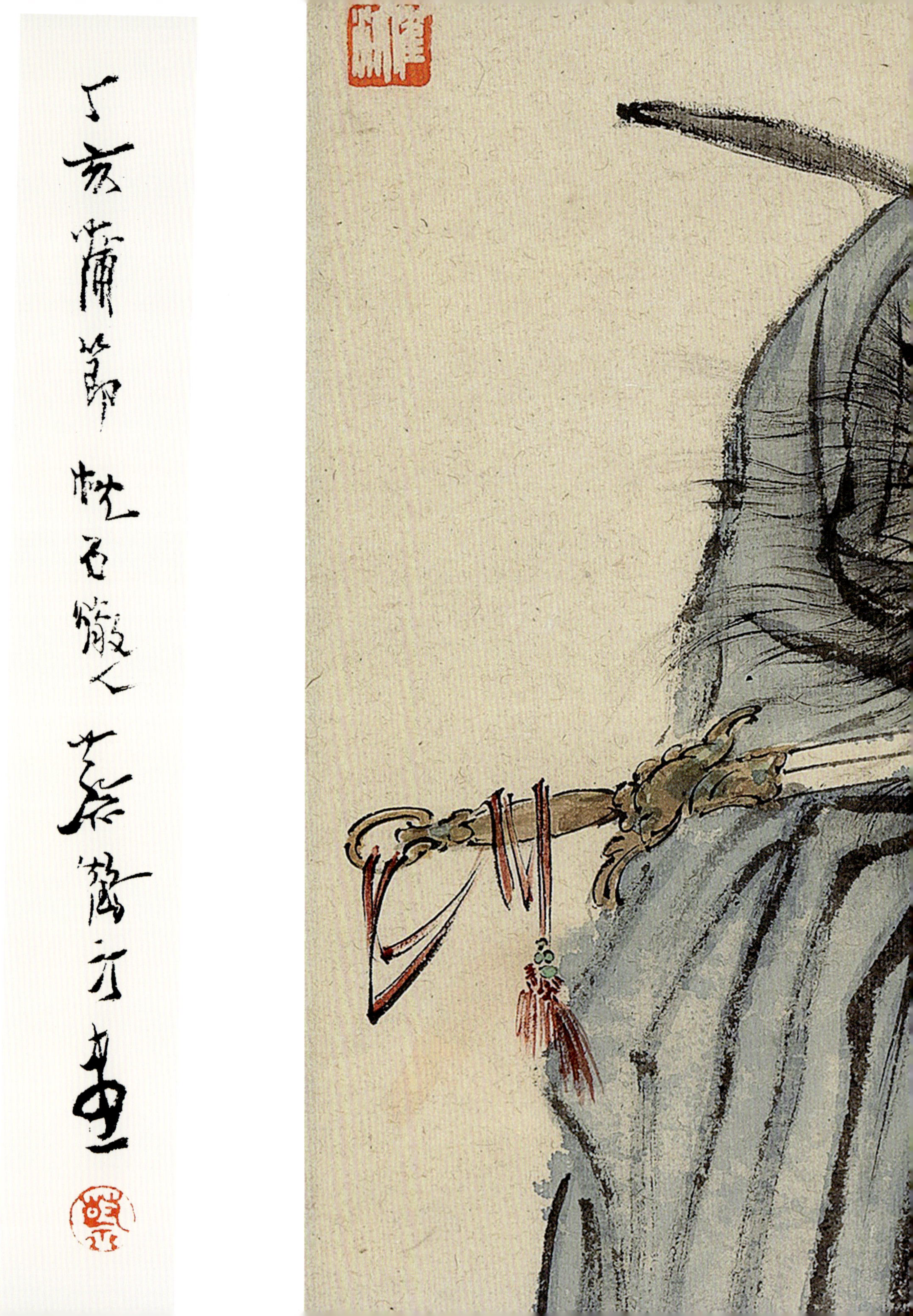
丁亥蒲節
大千張爰畫

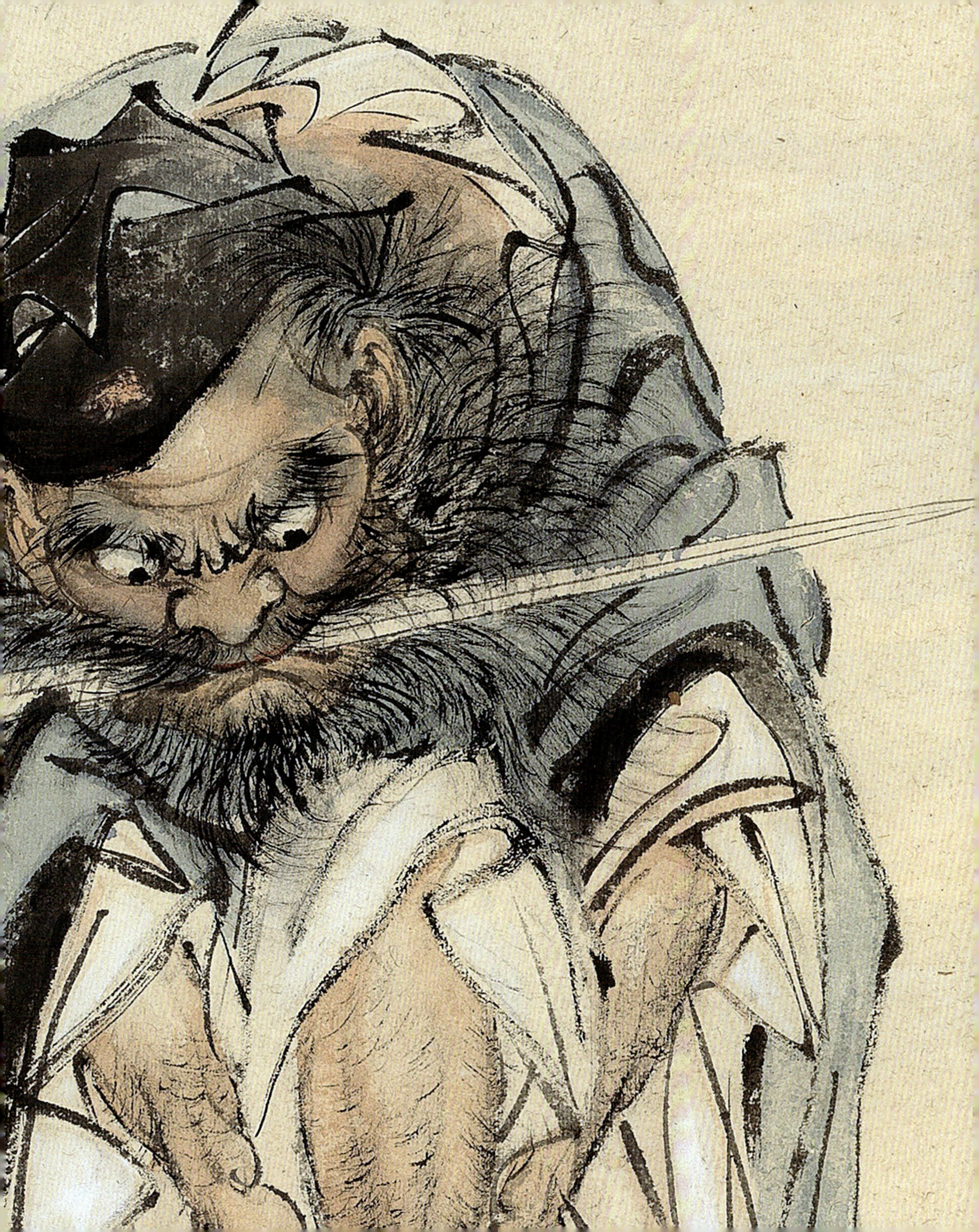

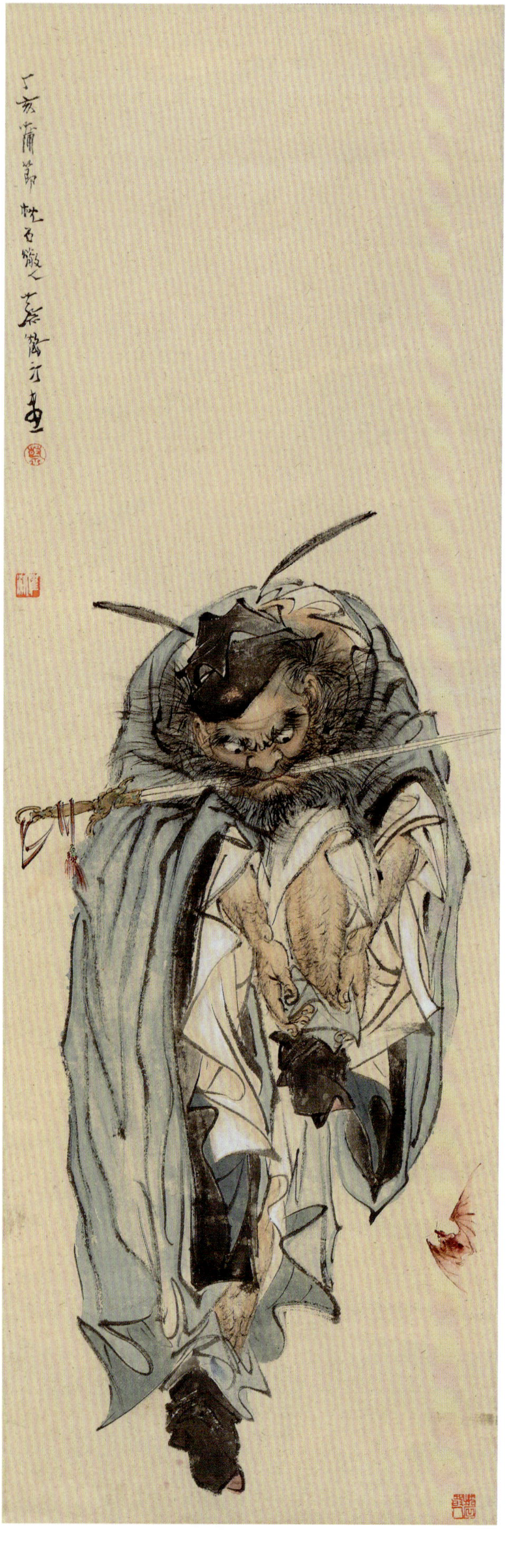

Artist:
Cai Heting

Medium:
Color on paper, Framed piece

Dimensions:
100 cm × 32.5 cm

Zhong Kui

Inscription:
On the Dragon Boat Festival of the Dinghai year, the Zhenshi hermit Cai Heting painted this.

Seal:
Cai, Heting

Cai Heting (1909–1976)
Styled Yiyuan, known as the Zhenshi hermit. A native of Taijiang, Fuzhou, he excelled in paintings of birds, feathers, beasts, and court ladies. He was a member of the China Artists Association, a standing director of its Shaanxi branch, a member of the Xi'an Political Consultative Conference, and a representative of the Xi'an People's Congress.

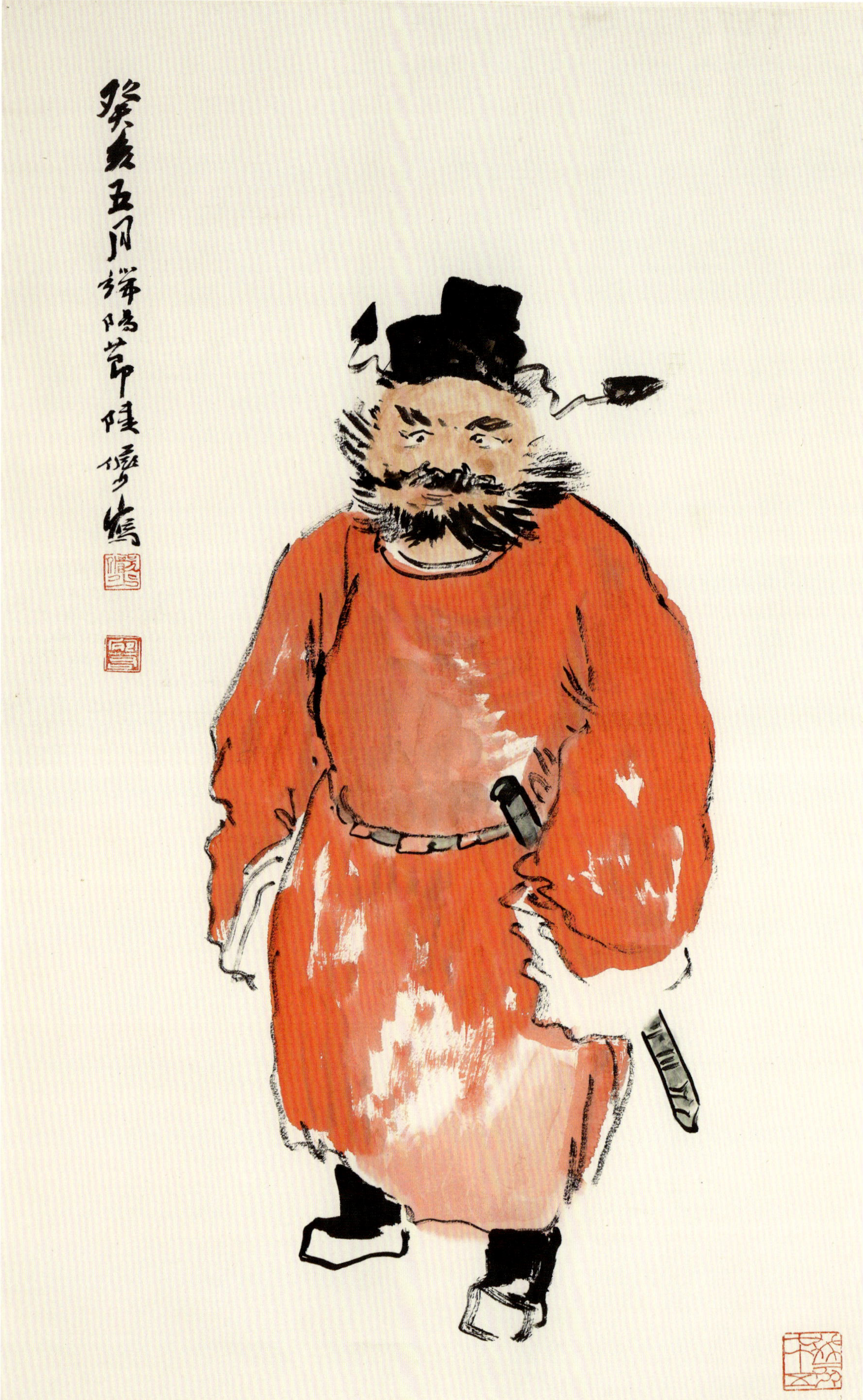

Artist:
Lu Yanshao

Medium:
Color on paper, Framed piece

Dimensions:
96 cm × 59 cm

Red-Robed Zhong Kui

Inscription:
On the Dragon Boat Festival of the Guihai year, written by Lu Yanshao.

Seal:
Yanshao, Wanruo, Seventy-five in Guihai

Lu Yanshao (1909–1993)
Also known as Di, styled Wanruo, was a native of Nanxiang Town, Jiading County, Shanghai. In 1926, he was admitted to the Wuxi School of Fine Arts and began his formal studies in Wuxi the following year. In the same year, he studied poetry, calligraphy, and literature under Wang Tongyu, and painting under Feng Chaoran the next year, where he also met Wu Hufan and traveled extensively across the scenic landscapes of North and South China. In 1956, he became a painter at the Shanghai Chinese Painting Academy. Starting in 1962, he also taught at the Zhejiang Academy of Fine Arts and officially joined its faculty in 1980, serving as the president of the Zhejiang Painting Academy. He excelled in landscape painting.

七十斤甕空進士頭六重眼睛只賸一條縫小兒哈哈無驚恐雲間先生一愰杖扶頭為廣酒德頌

梁俊青寫白蕉題句

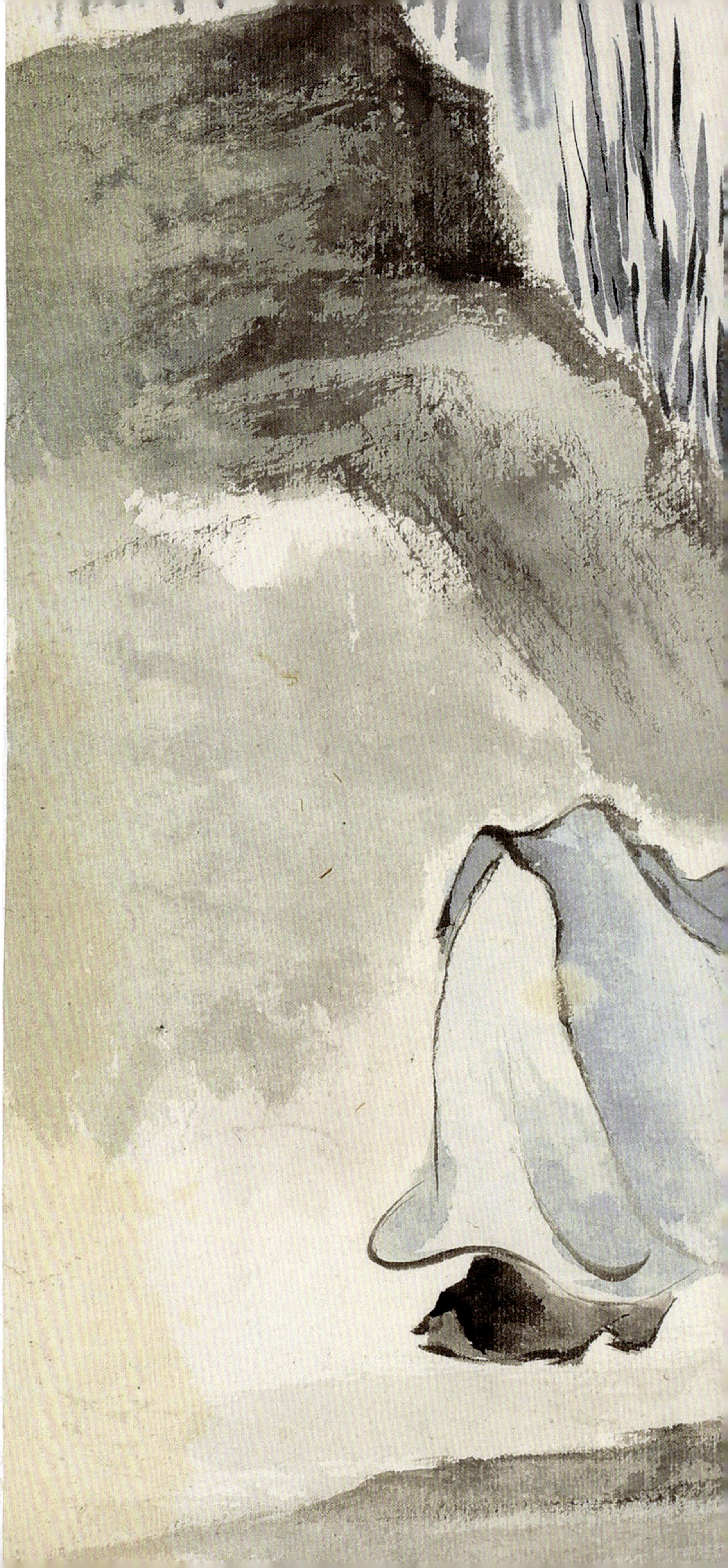

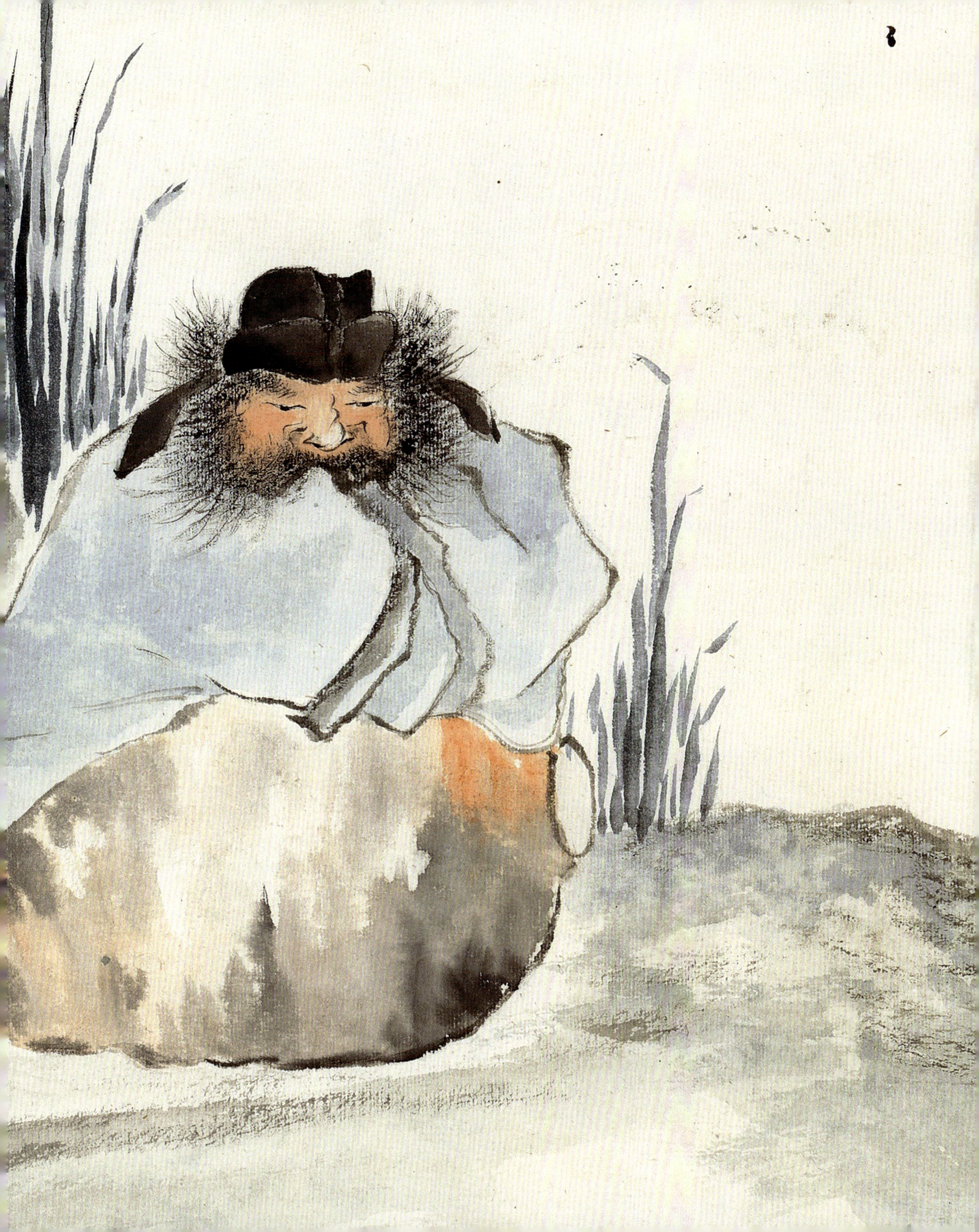

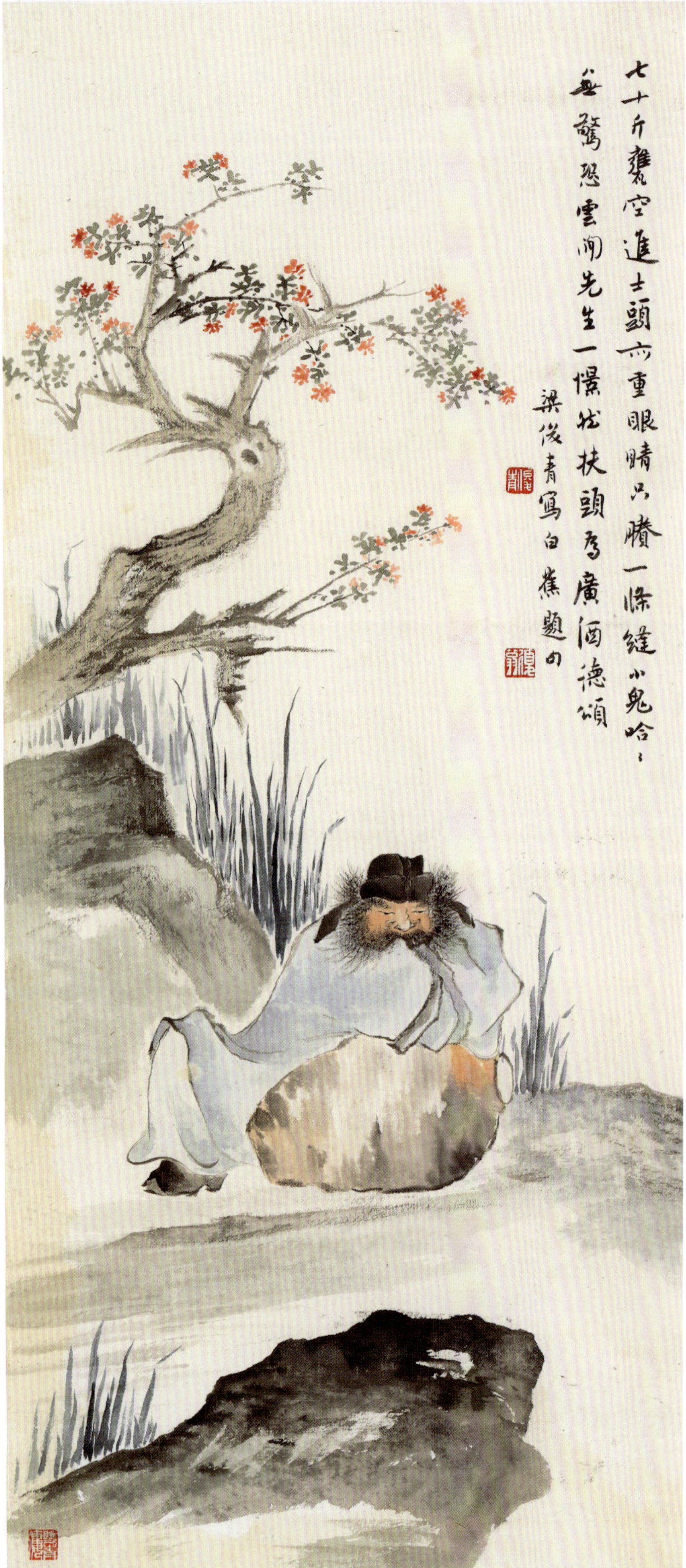
七十斤甕空進士頭六重眼睛只賸一條縫小鬼哈哈
梁俊青寫白蕉題句

Artist:
Liang Junqing | Inscribed by Bai Jiao

Medium:
Color on paper, Hanging scroll

Dimensions:
77 cm × 33 cm

Zhong Kui Drunk

Inscription:
The seventy-jin jar stands empty, the Jinshi's head weighs heavy, and his eyes are but slits. The little demons laugh without fear, as the master among the clouds reflects deeply, steadying his head to sing the praises of wine's virtue. Written by Liang Junqing, with an inscription by Bai Jiao.

Seal:
Junqing, Fuweng, Shuangqing Lou

Liang Junqing
A renowned Western physician in Shanghai during the Republic of China era, he was also skilled in calligraphy and painting.

Bai Jiao (1907–1969)
A native of Jinshan, Shanghai. Originally named He Fu with the courtesy name Yuanyang and styled Xuru, he later changed his name and surname to Bai Jiao. Also known as the Lay Scholar Among the Clouds, Bai Jiao from "Among the Clouds", and Fuweng, he held positions including committee member and deputy director of the secretariat at the preparatory committee of the Shanghai Chinese Painting Academy, member of the Shanghai branch of the China Artists Association, and member of the Shanghai Chinese Calligraphy and Seal Carving Research Association. He served as a calligrapher and painter at the Shanghai Chinese Painting Academy. Bai Jiao was the chief editor of *Humanity (Monthly)* and authored works such as *Talk on Art Among the Clouds, Ji Lu Poetry Draft, Guest Departure Records, Ten Lectures on Calligraphy*, and *Discourses on Learning Calligraphy.*

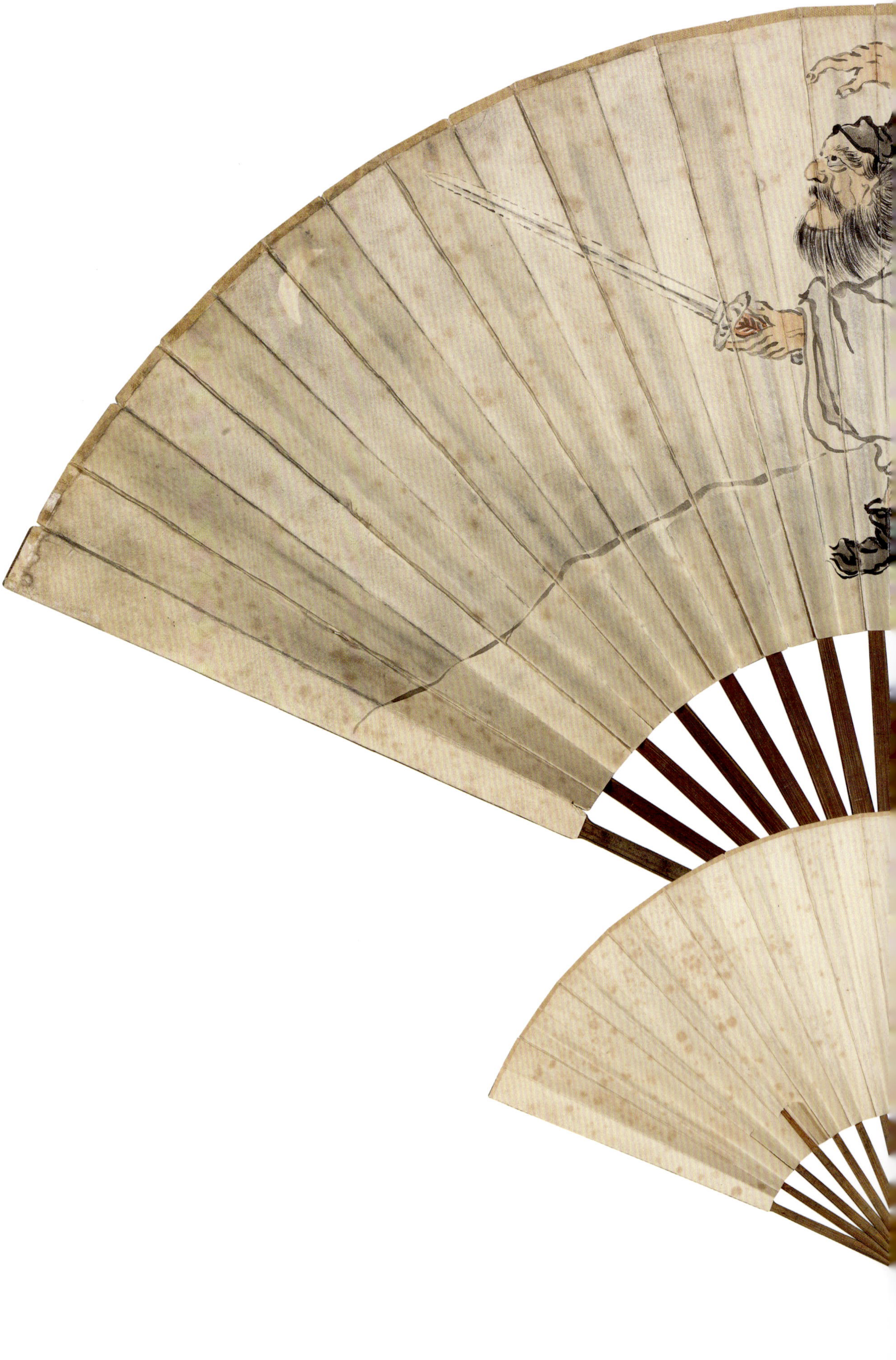

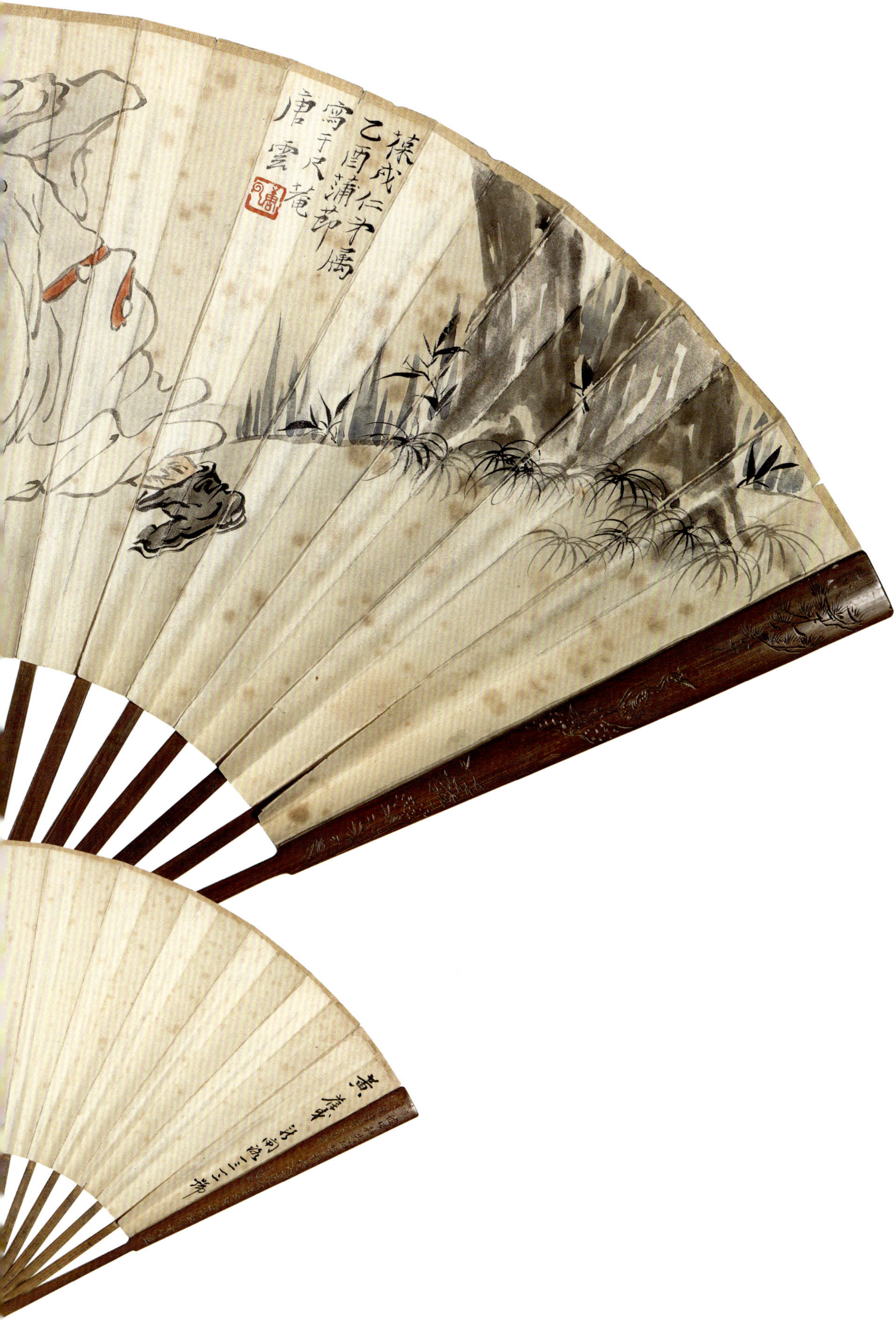
葆成仁兄大屬
乙酉蒲節
寫于尺菴
唐雲

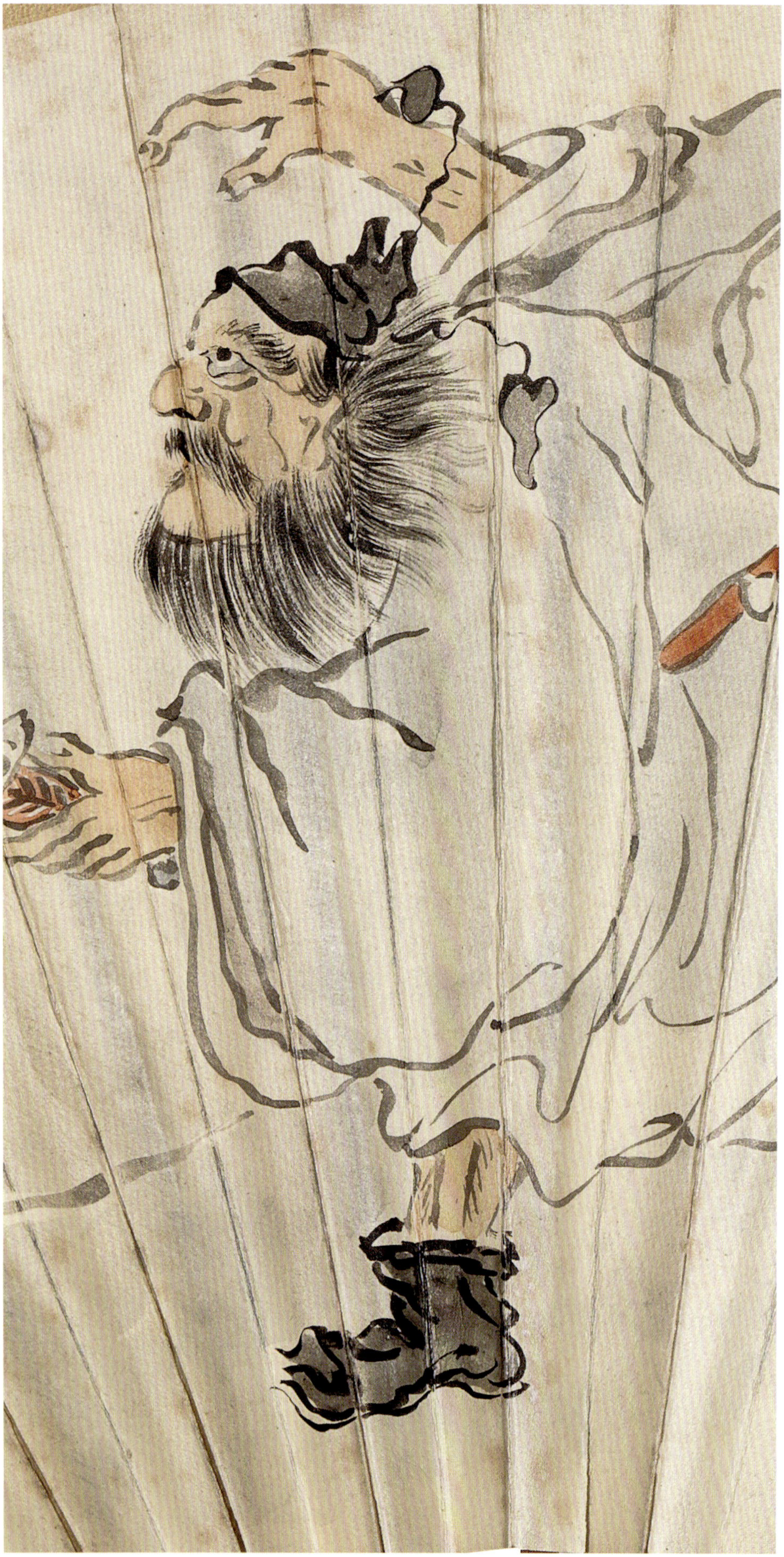

Artist:
Tang Yun

Medium:
Color on paper, Completed fan

Dimensions:
18 cm × 49.5 cm

Zhong Kui Under the Moon

Inscription:
Commissioned by brother Baoshu, written by Tang Yun on the Dragon Boat Festival of the Yiyou year at Chi'an, Tang Yun.

Seal:
Tang Yun

Tang Yun (1910–1993)
Styled Xiachen, also known by various sobriquets such as Yaocheng, Yaochen, Yaoweng, Laoyao, Dasheng, and Dashiweng, with his studios named "Dashizhai" and "Shanleixuan," he was a native of Hangzhou, Zhejiang. He served as a director of the China Artists Association, vice-chairman of the Shanghai branch of the China Artists Association, a committee member of the affairs at the Chinese Painting Research Institute, and held positions including the vice-president, acting president, and honorary president of the Shanghai Chinese Painting Academy.

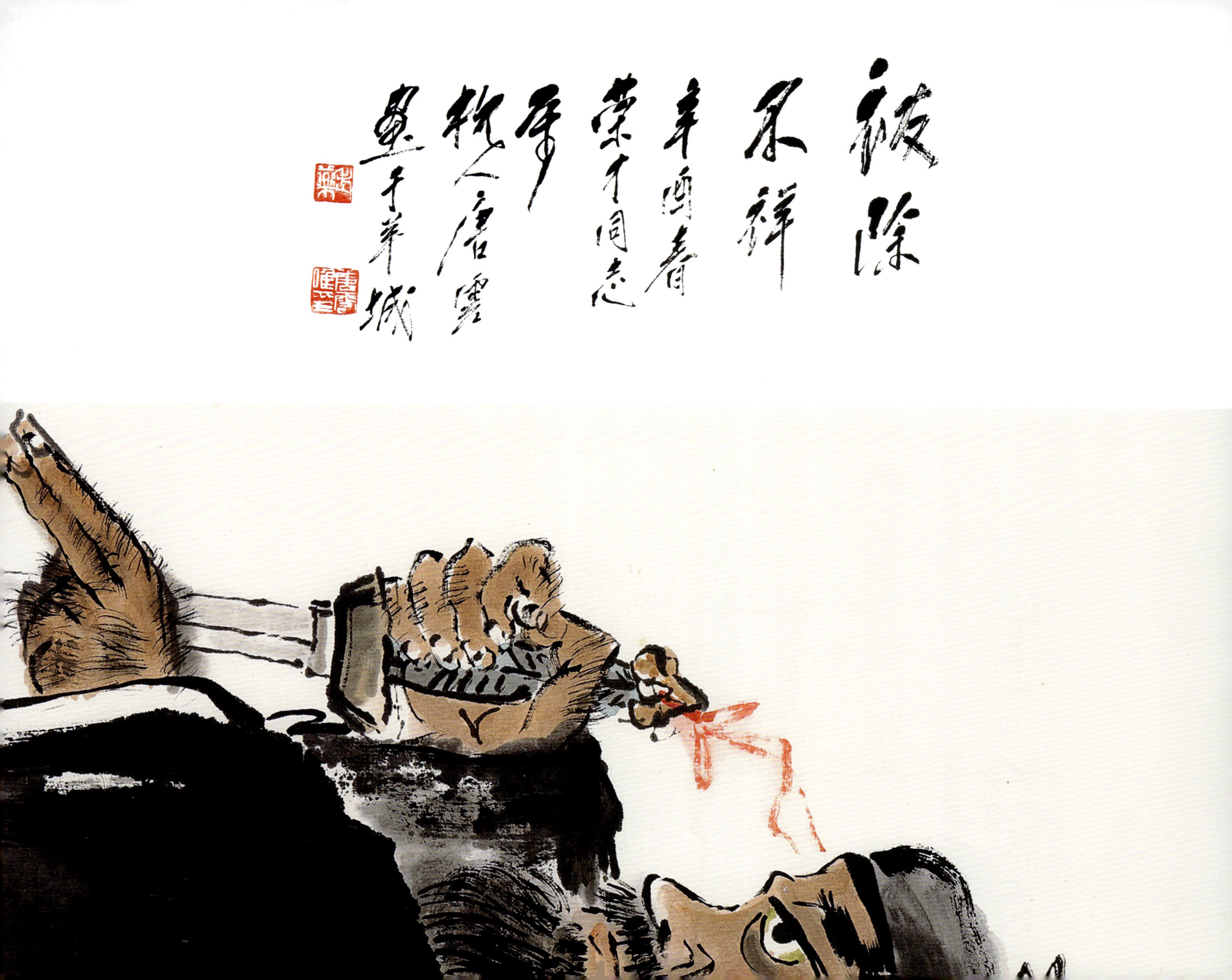
祓除不祥
辛酉春
榮才同志屬
牧之唐雲
畫于羊城

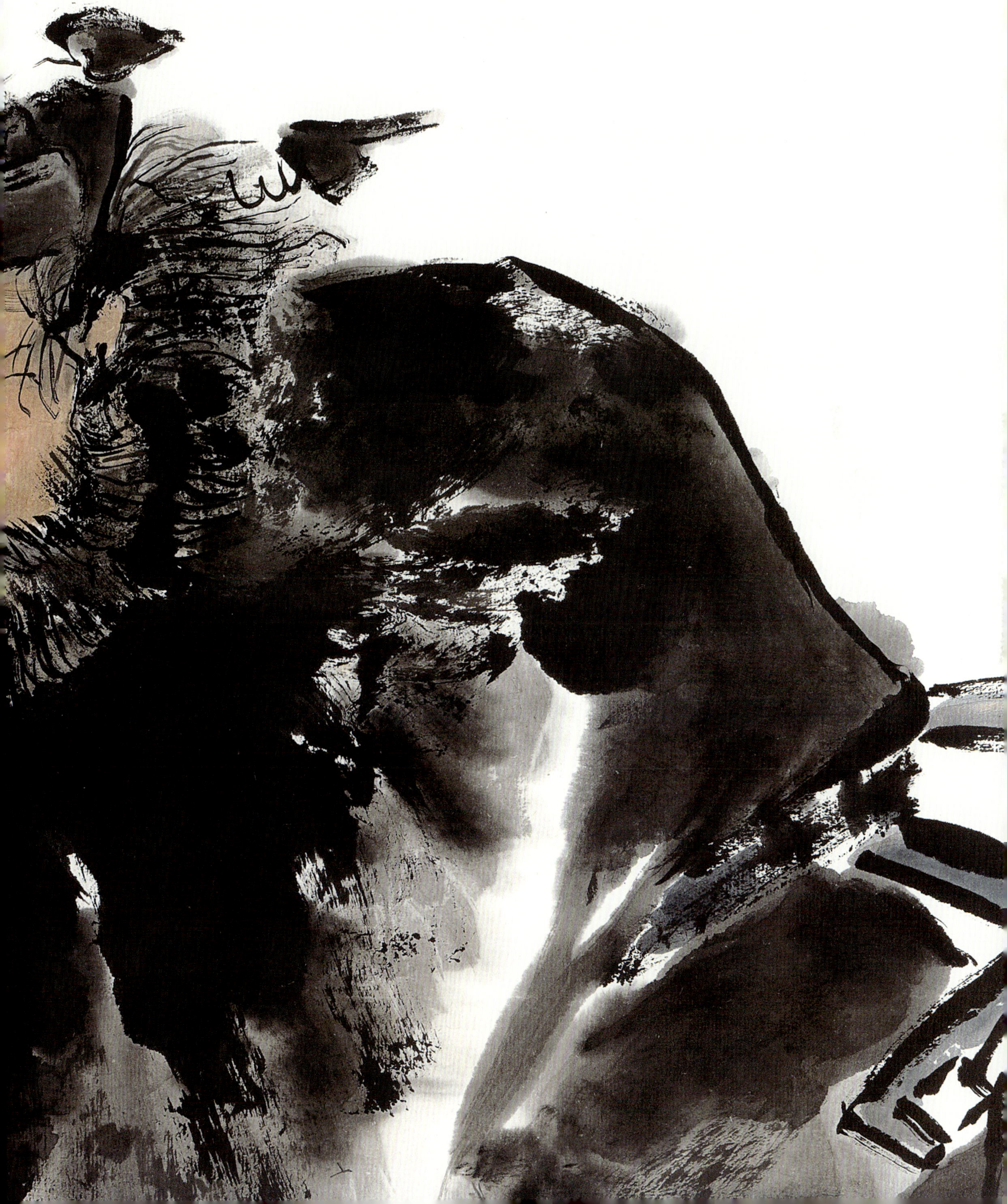

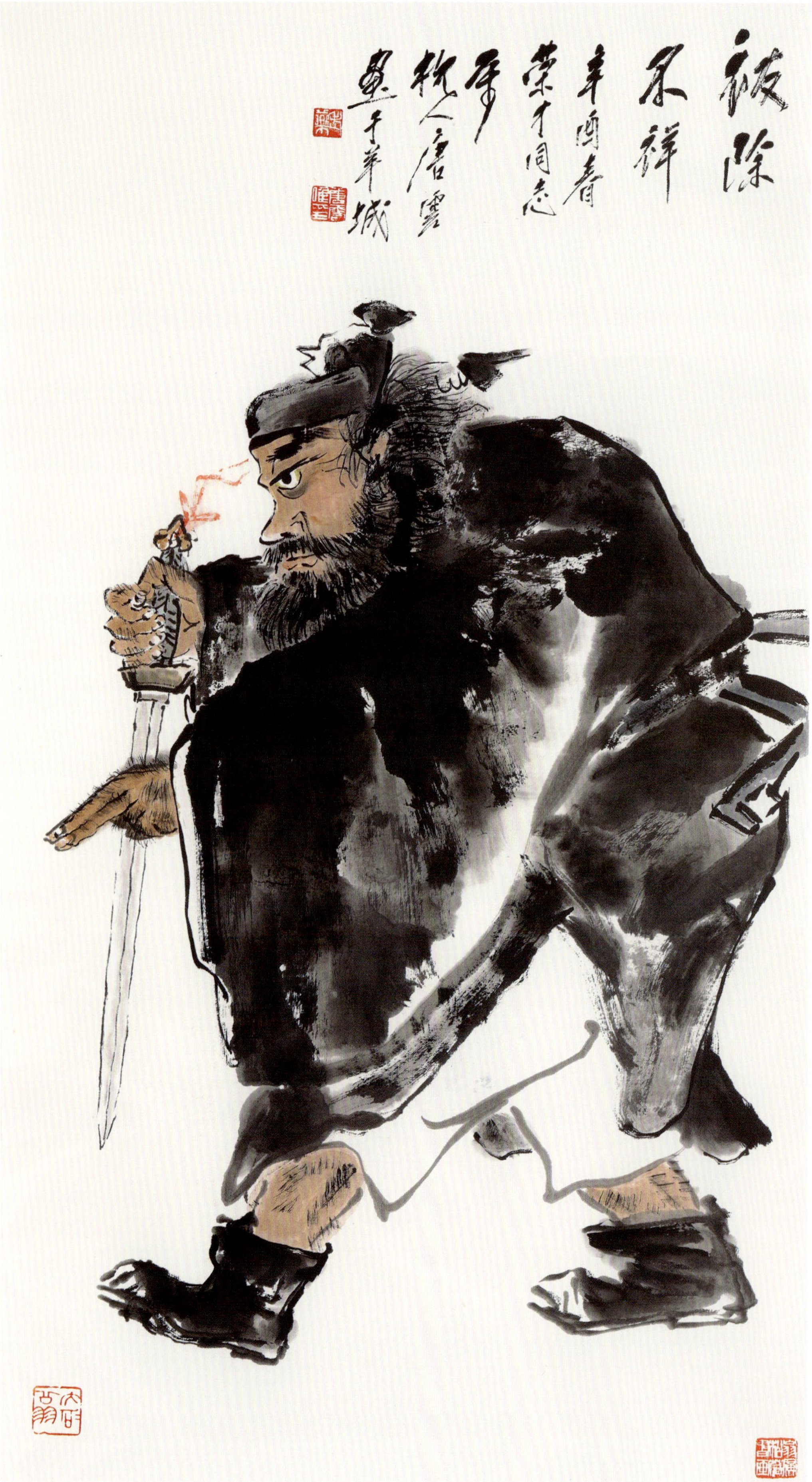
祓除不祥
辛酉春
杭人唐雲畫于羊城

Artist:
Tang Yun

Medium:
Color on paper, Hanging scroll

Dimensions:
90 cm × 49 cm

Exorcising Misfortune

Inscription:
Exorcising Misfortune. Commissioned by Comrade Rongcai in the spring of the Xinyou year, painted by Tang Yun of Hangzhou in Yangcheng.

Seal:
Laoyao, The only seal of Tang Yun

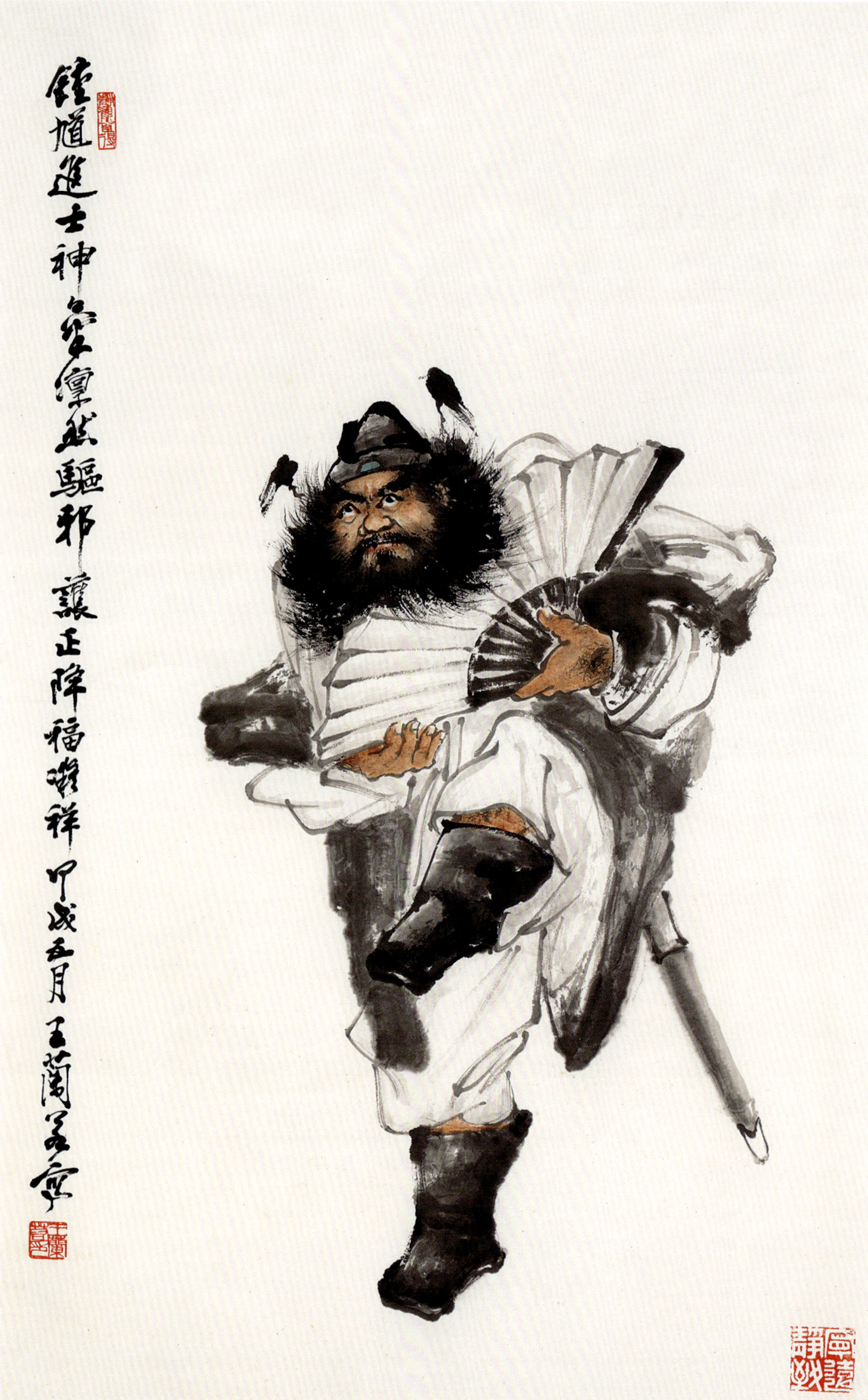
甲戌五月 王蘭若寫

Artist:
Wang Lanruo

Medium:
Color on paper, Framed piece

Dimensions:
111 cm × 68 cm

Dispelling Evil and Condensing Auspiciousness

Inscription:
Zhong Kui, the Jinshi, his aura stern and commanding, dispels evil and protects the righteous, bestowing blessings and grace. Written by Wang Lanruo in May of the Jiaxu year.

Seal:
The seal of Wang Lanruo, Stillness brings depth, Quietness yields insight

Wang Lanruo (1911–2015)
Originally named Xunlue, also known as the Master of the Ailü Thatched Cottage, was a native of Jieyang, Guangdong. He held various positions including professional painter at the Shantou City Arts and Crafts Research Institute, and served as the vice-president and honorary president of the Shantou Painting Academy.

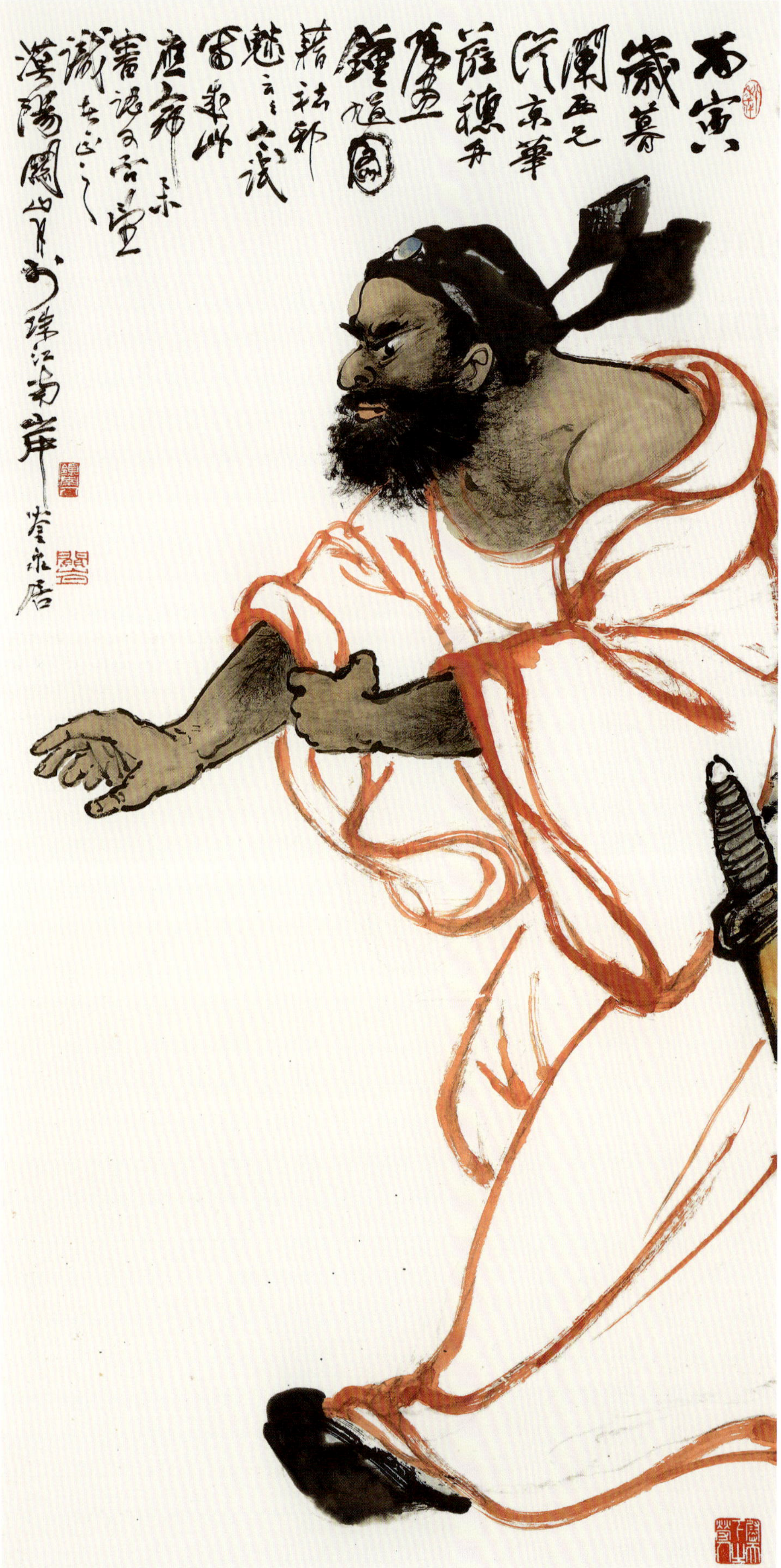

Artist:
Guan Shanyue

Medium:
Color on paper, Hanging scroll

Dimensions:
138 cm × 68 cm

Righteousness Prevails in the Human World

Inscription:
As the year of Bingyin drew to a close, friend Lanxi came from the capital to Guangzhou, entrusting me with the task of painting Zhong Kui to dispel evil spirits and such. Now, in an attempt to fulfill this request, I have composed this work. Whether it meets approval remains uncertain. I look forward to corrections from those knowledgeable. Written by Guan Shanyue of Moyang at Jianquan Stuido, south of the Pearl River.

Seal:
Person of Lingnan, Guan Shanyue, The Eighties, Comforting the weary of the world

Guan Shanyue (1912–2000)
Originally named Guan Zepei, Guan Shanyue was a native of Yangjiang, Guangdong. He was one of the representative figures of the Lingnan School of painting, known as one of the "Four Masters of the Second Generation of the Lingnan School" alongside Zhao Shao'ang, Li Xiongcai, and Yang Shanshen. Guan specialized in landscapes, figures, and flowers-and-birds paintings, particularly renowned for his plum blossom paintings. To honor Guan Shanyue's artistic achievements, the Guan Shanyue Art Museum was established at the foot of Lianhua Mountain in Futian District, Shenzhen.

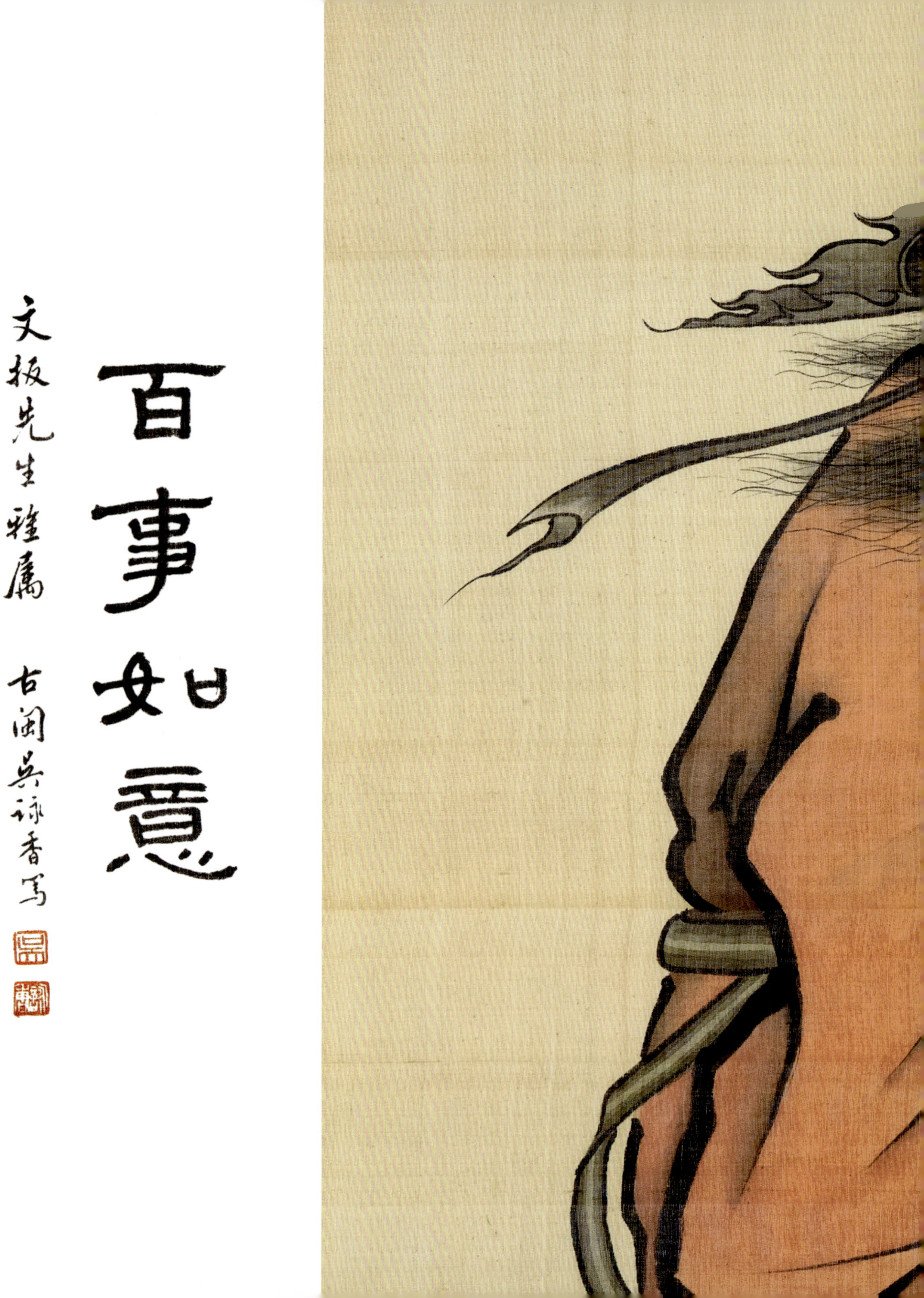
百事如意
文叔先生雅屬
古閩吳詠香寫

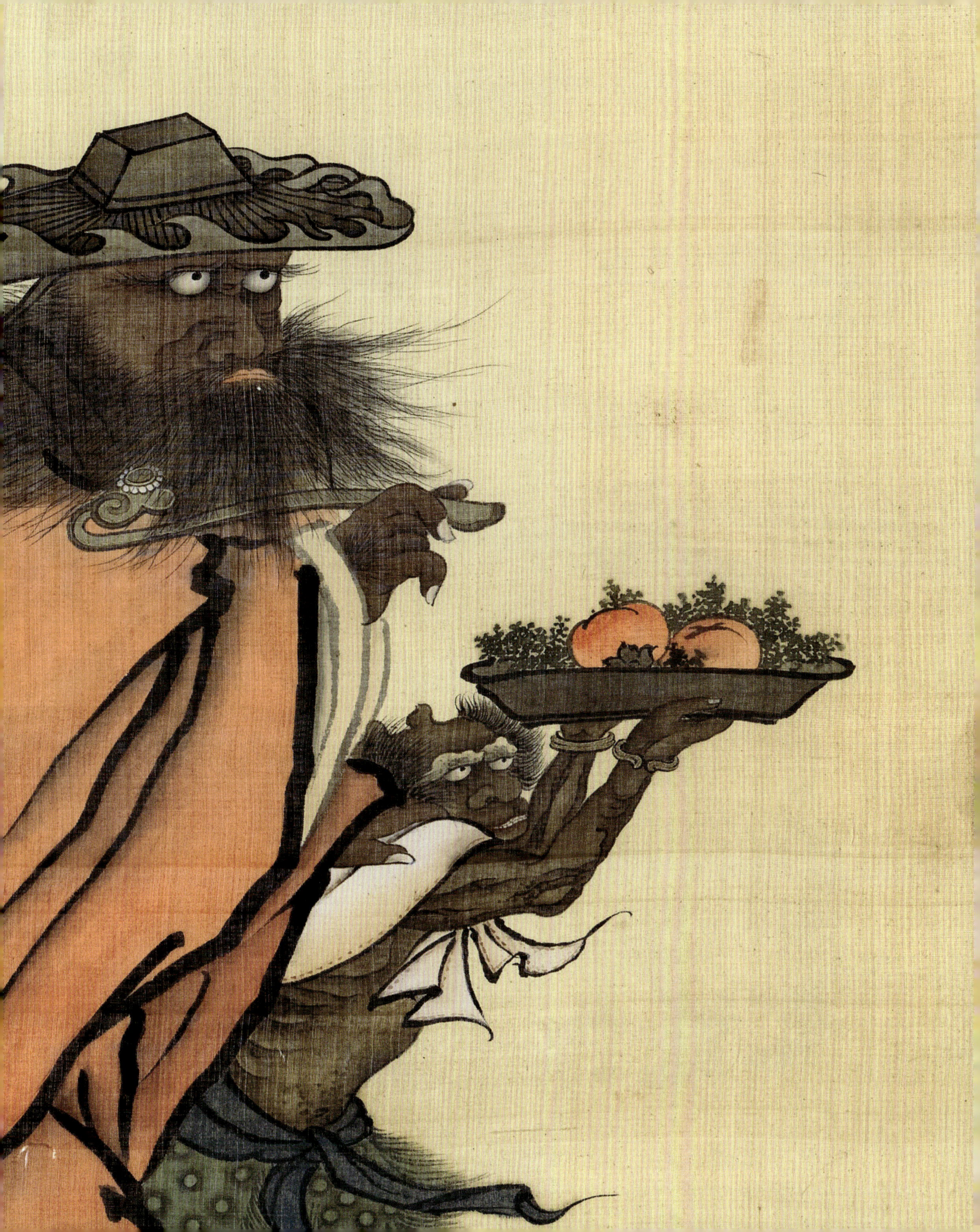

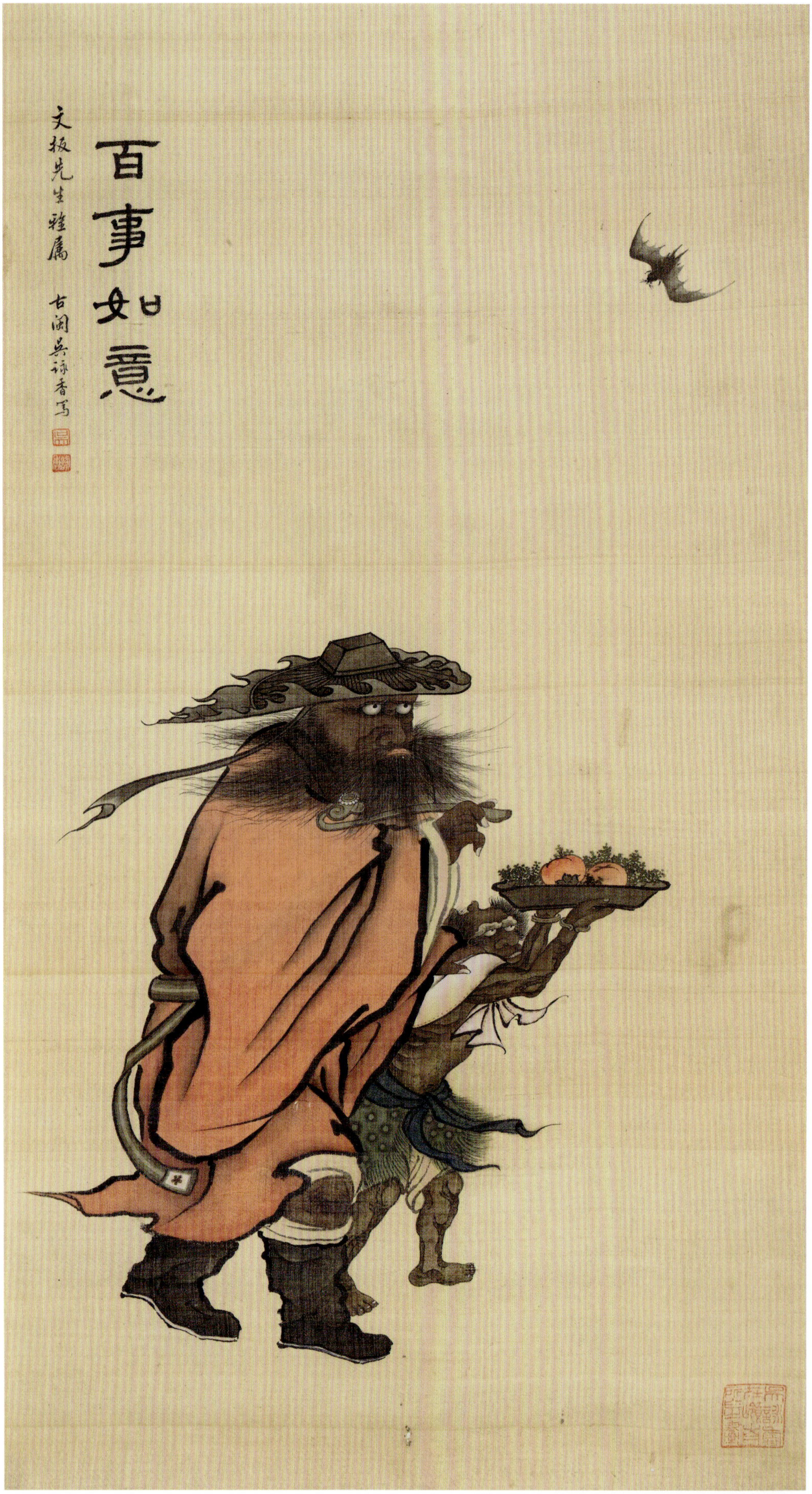

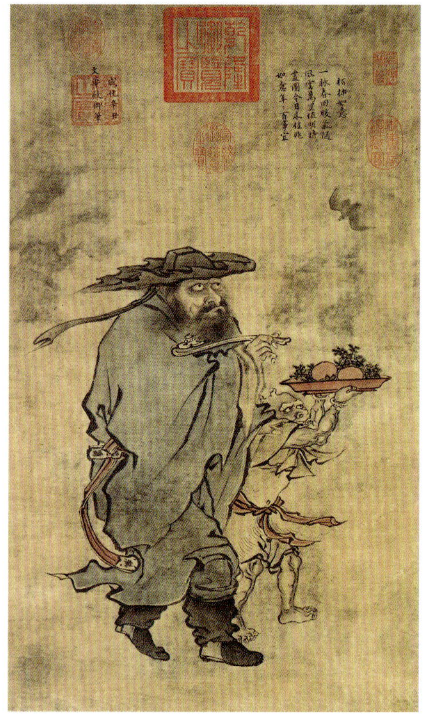

Welcoming Blessings of Good Fortune

Artist: Zhu Jianshen
(Emperor Xianzong, Ming Dynasty)

The Palace Museum Collection

Artist:
Wu Yongxiang

Medium:
Color on silk, Framed piece

Dimensions:
89.5 cm × 48 cm

Everything Goes Well

Inscription:
May all things be as you wish. Commissioned by Mr. Wen Ban, written by Wu Yongxiang of ancient Min.

Seal:
Wu, Yongxiang, Paintings by Wu Yongxiang created in Lingnan

Wu Yongxiang (1913–1970)
A native of Minhou, Fujian. He graduated from the National Beiping Art School, where he was enlightened by Qi Baishi and Pu Xinyu. He studied for three years at the Chinese Painting Research Institute of the Beiping Antiquities Museum, delving into the essence of the Song and Yuan dynasties, and became a distinguished figure in the field. Later, he became a disciple of Huang Binhong, which further sharpened his style. Pu Xinyu titled one of his studios "Ou Bo Pavilion," evoking the companions of the immortal Zhao Guan. Wu later served as a lecturer and professor in the Art Department at Taiwan Normal University.

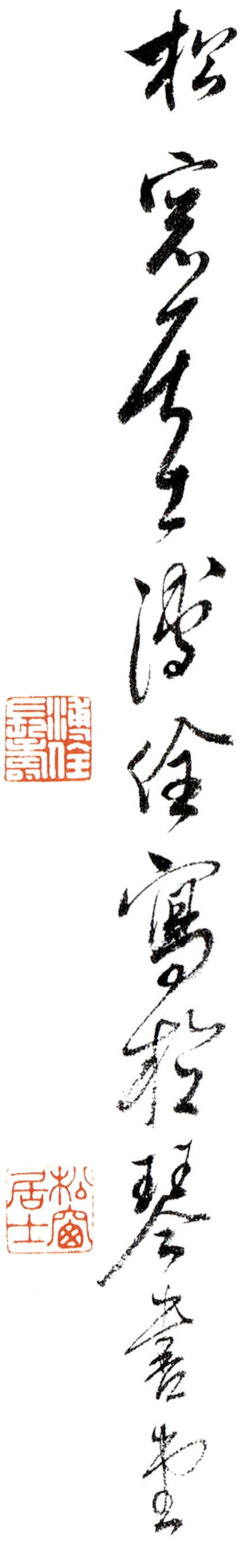

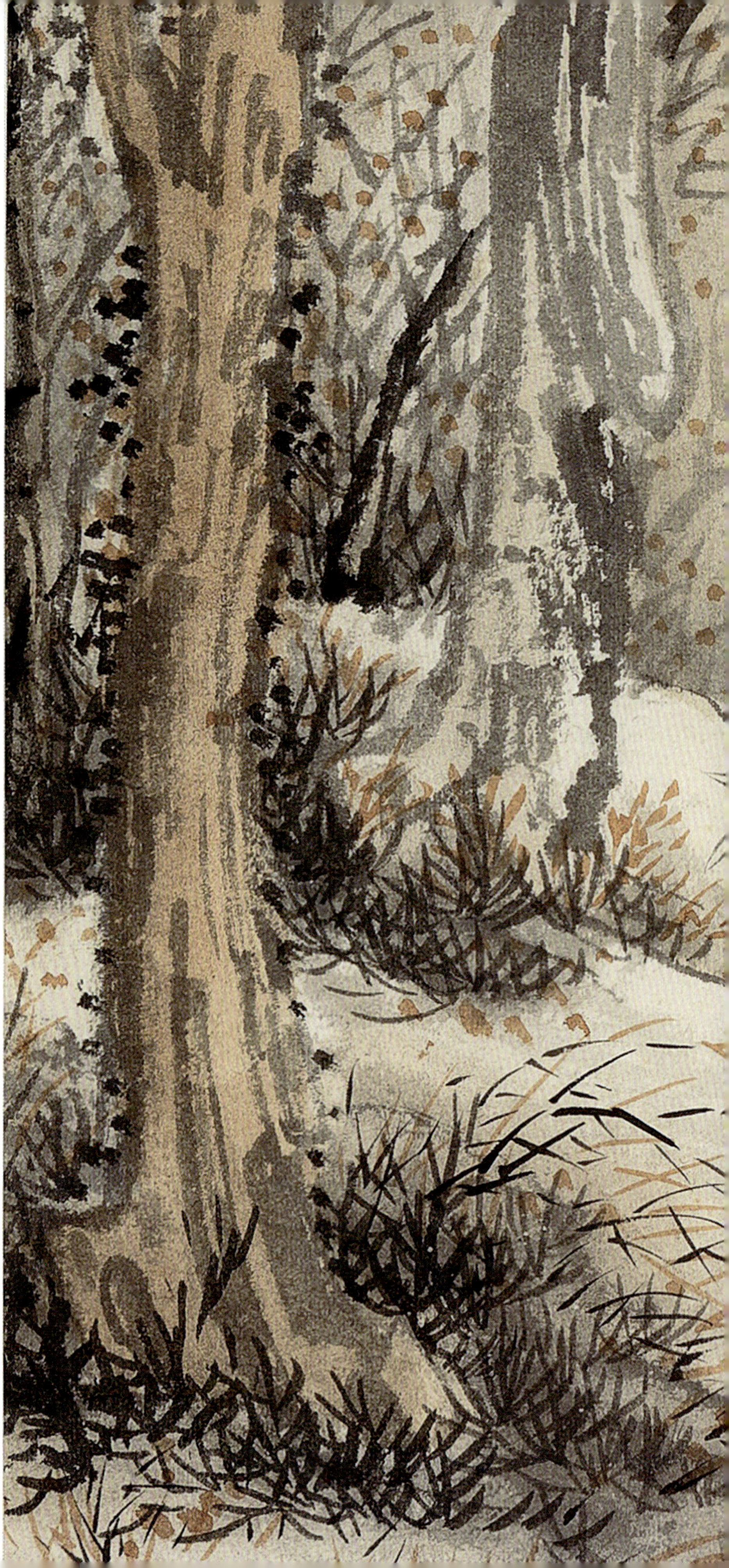

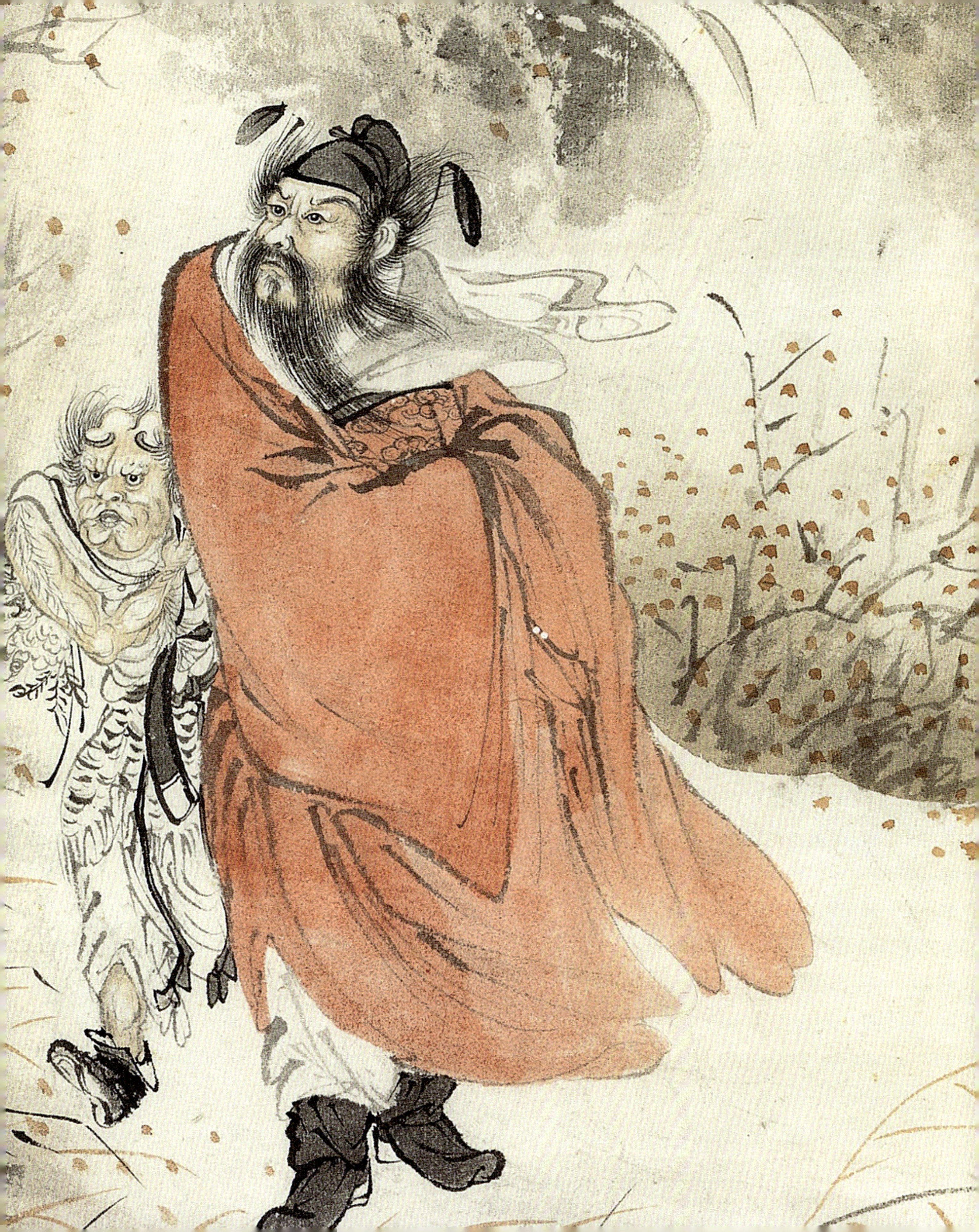

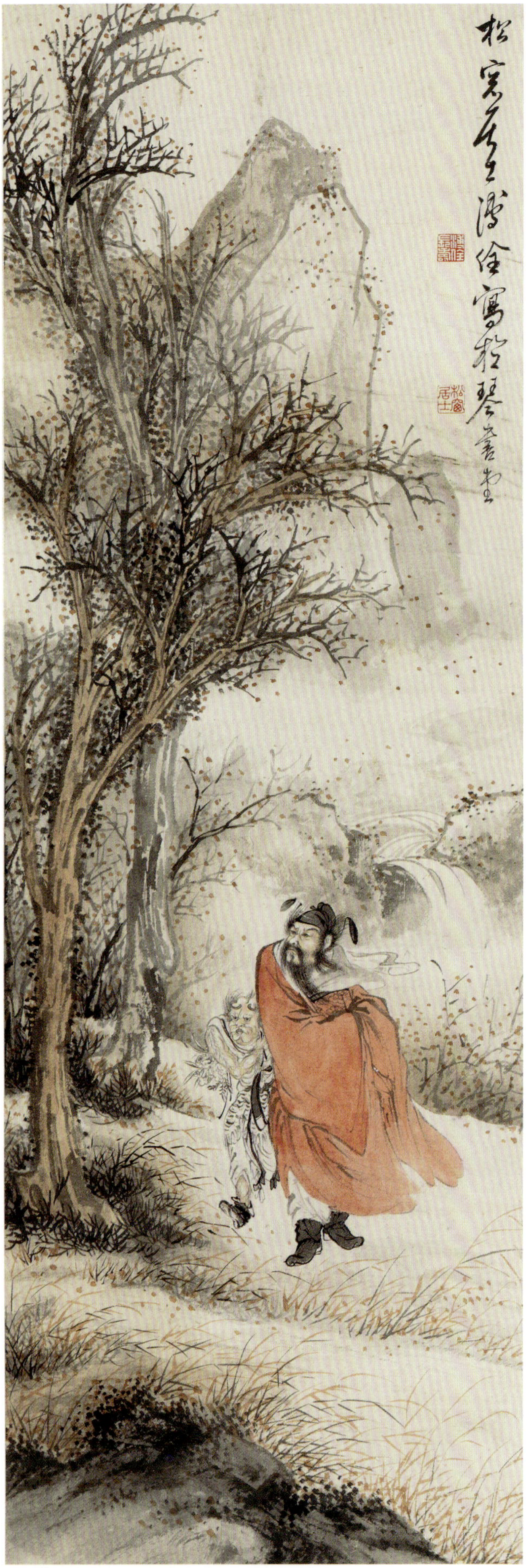

Artist:
Pu Quan

Medium:
Color on silk, Hanging scroll

Dimensions:
99 cm × 32 cm

Red-Robed Zhong Kui

Inscription:
Written by Lay Scholar Songchuang Pu Quan in the Qingshu Hall.

Seal:
Pu Quan Longevity, Lay Scholar Songchuang

Aisin Gioro Pu Quan (1913–1991)
Styled as Songchuang, he was a member of the Qing imperial clan and the great-great-grandson of Emperor Daoguang, renowned as a modern painter and calligrapher.

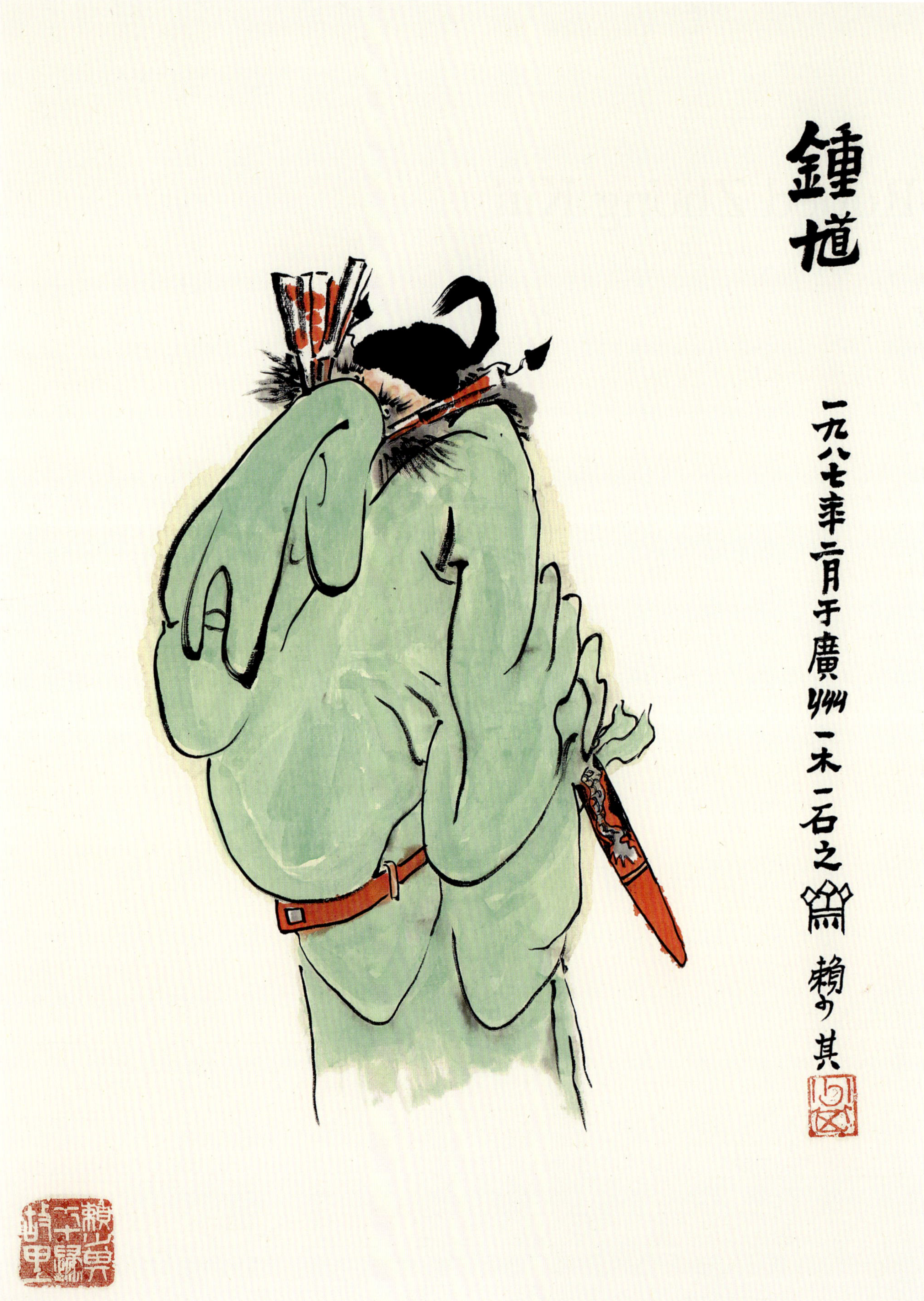
鍾馗
一九八七年二月于廣州一木一石之齋
賴少其

Artist:
Lai Shaoqi

Medium:
Color on silk, Hanging scroll

Dimensions:
55 cm × 38 cm

Green-Robed Zhong Kui

Inscription:
Zhong Kui. February 1987, at Guangzhou Wood and Stone Studio, by Lai Shaoqi.

Seals:
Shaoqi, Lai Shaoqi returns to hometown at seventy

Lai Shaoqi (1915–2000)
Lai Shaoqi, a native of Puning, Guangdong, and known by his studio name "Mushi Studio," was a renowned printmaker, traditional Chinese painter, calligrapher, seal carver, and a writer and poet. As one of the leading figures in contemporary Chinese art, he was often referred to as the "Sage of the Art World" and known in Japan as the "Chinese Painting Master." Lai Shaoqi pioneered the unique "white-over-black" technique, positioning him as a principal founder of the Neo-Huizhou style printmaking.

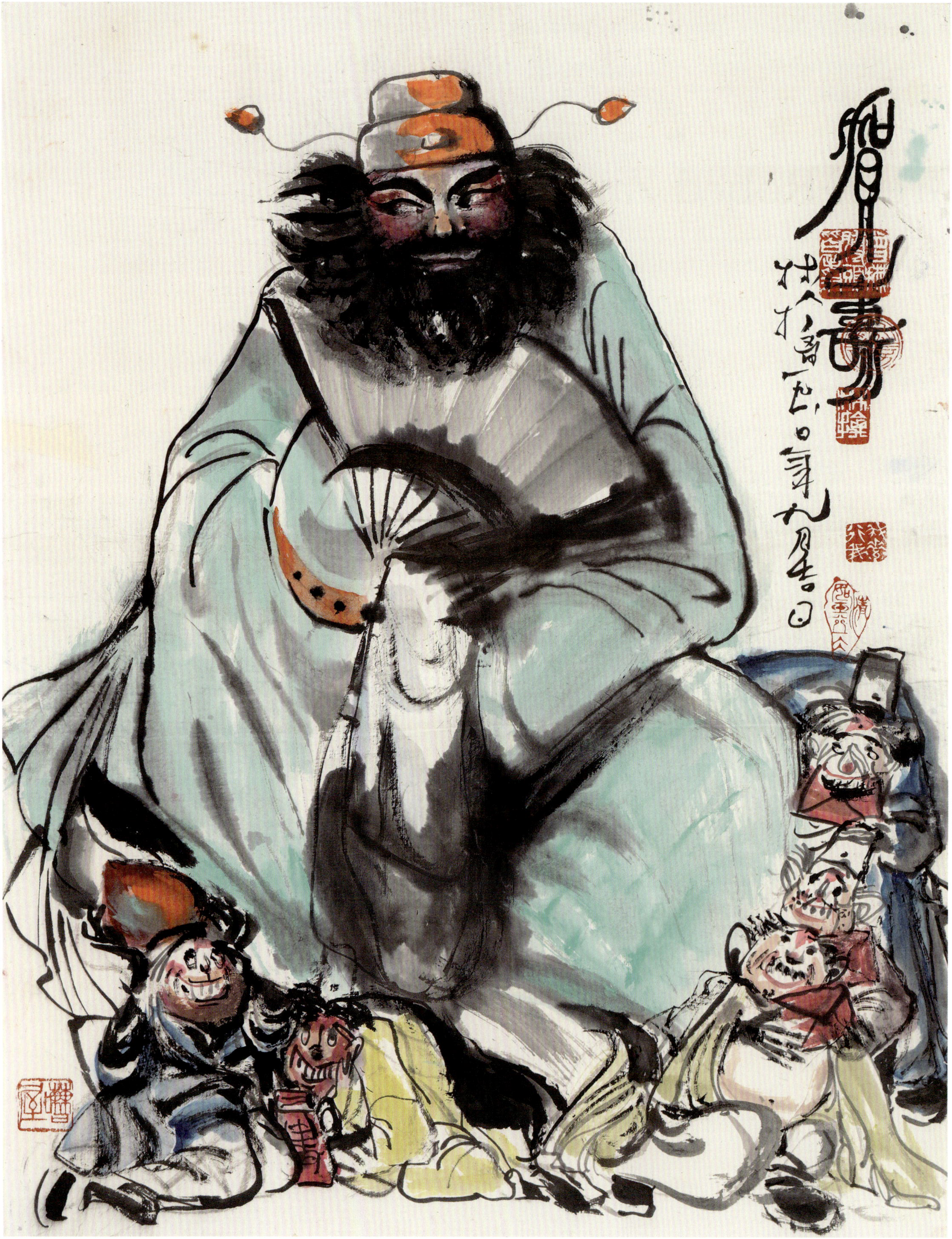

Artist:
Lin Qin

Medium:
Color on paper, Framed piece

Dimensions:
67.5 cm × 51.5 cm

Celebrating Longevity

Inscription:
Celebrating Longevity. Written by Lin Qin on an auspicious day in September 1980.

Seal:
Lin Qin, My nature my way, All who nudged my arm are dear friends, Pure as jade cup ice, Clamorous house

Lin Qin
A Hong Kong director and producer, a pioneer in the Hong Kong comic industry.

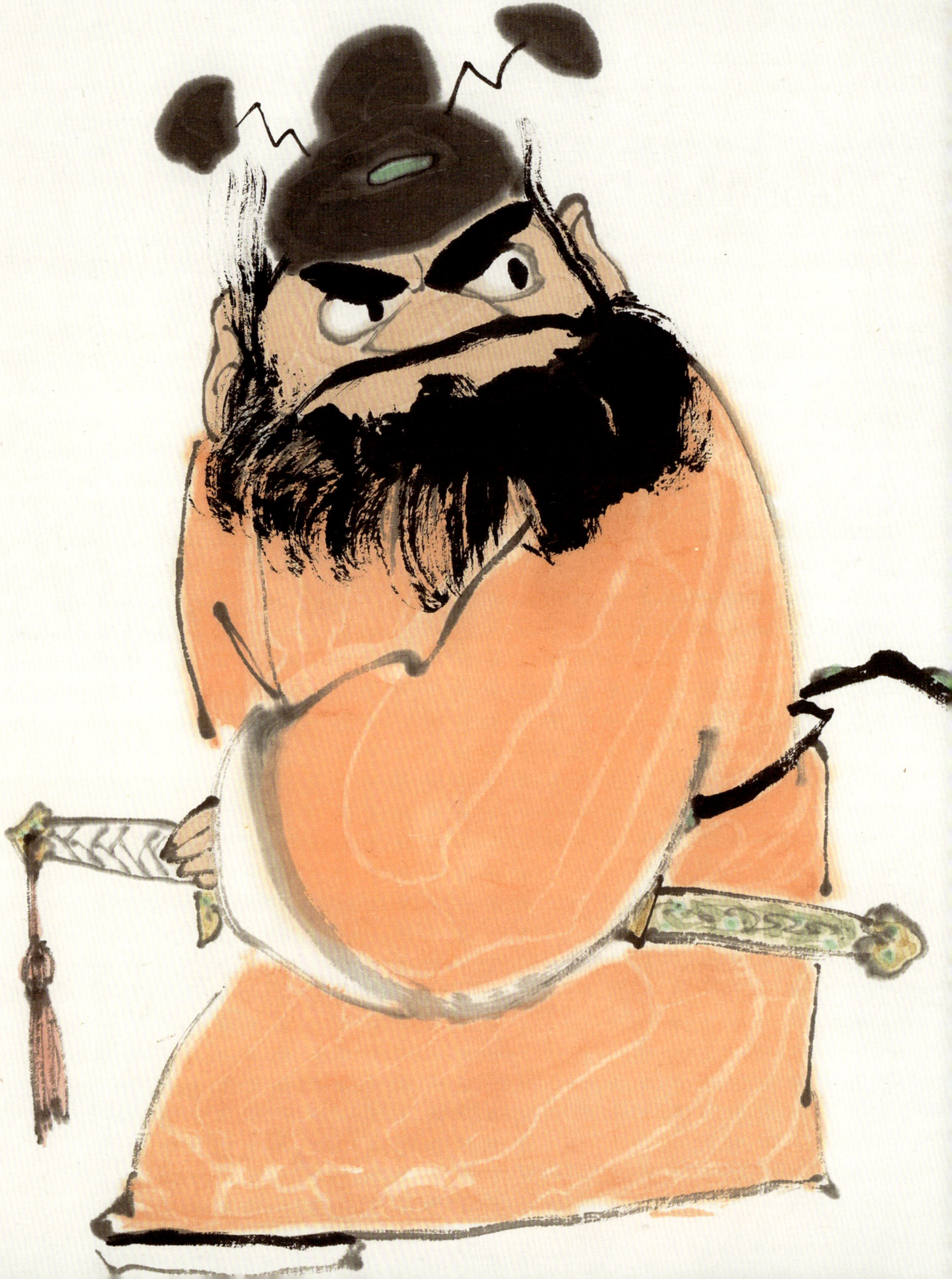

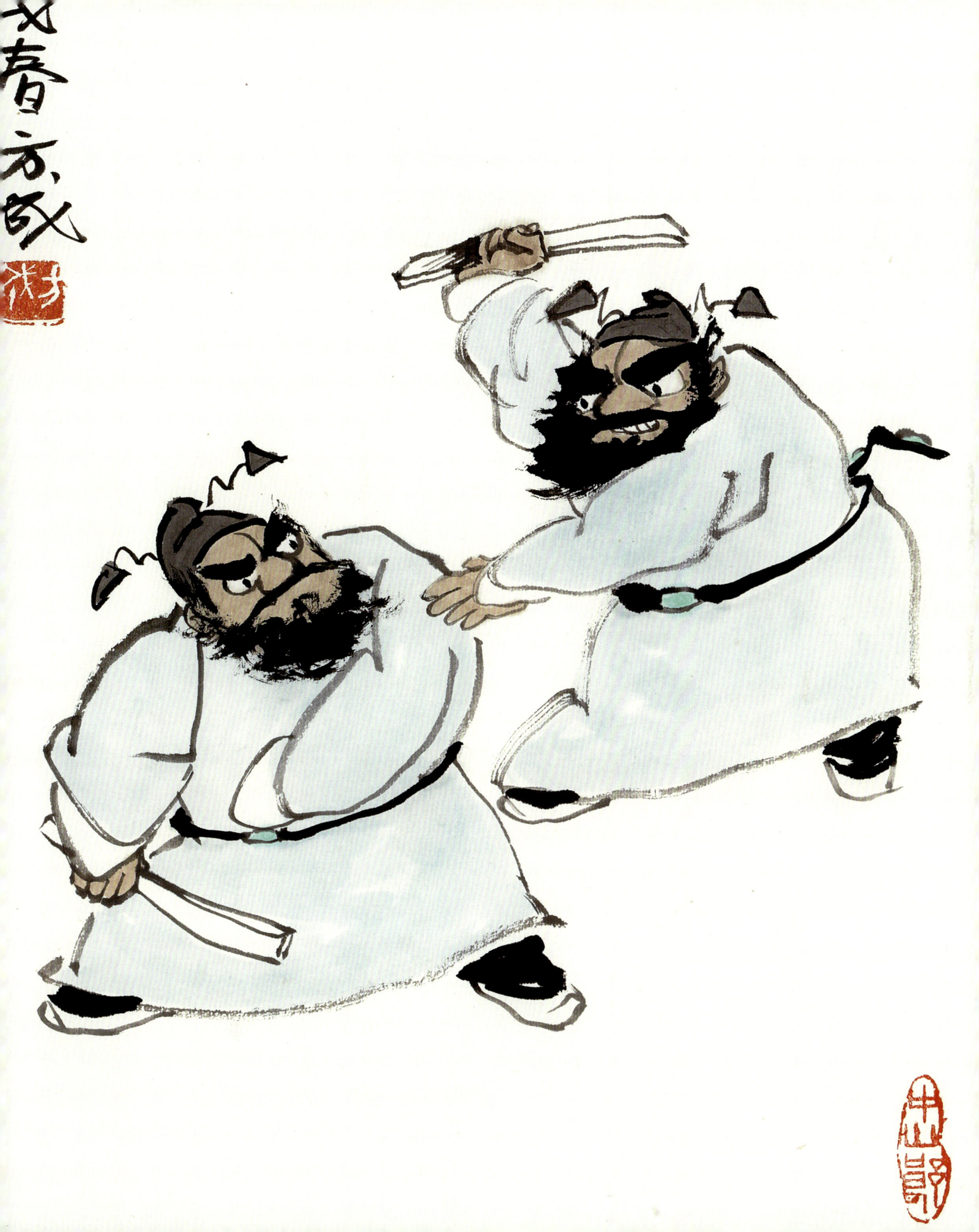
春方成

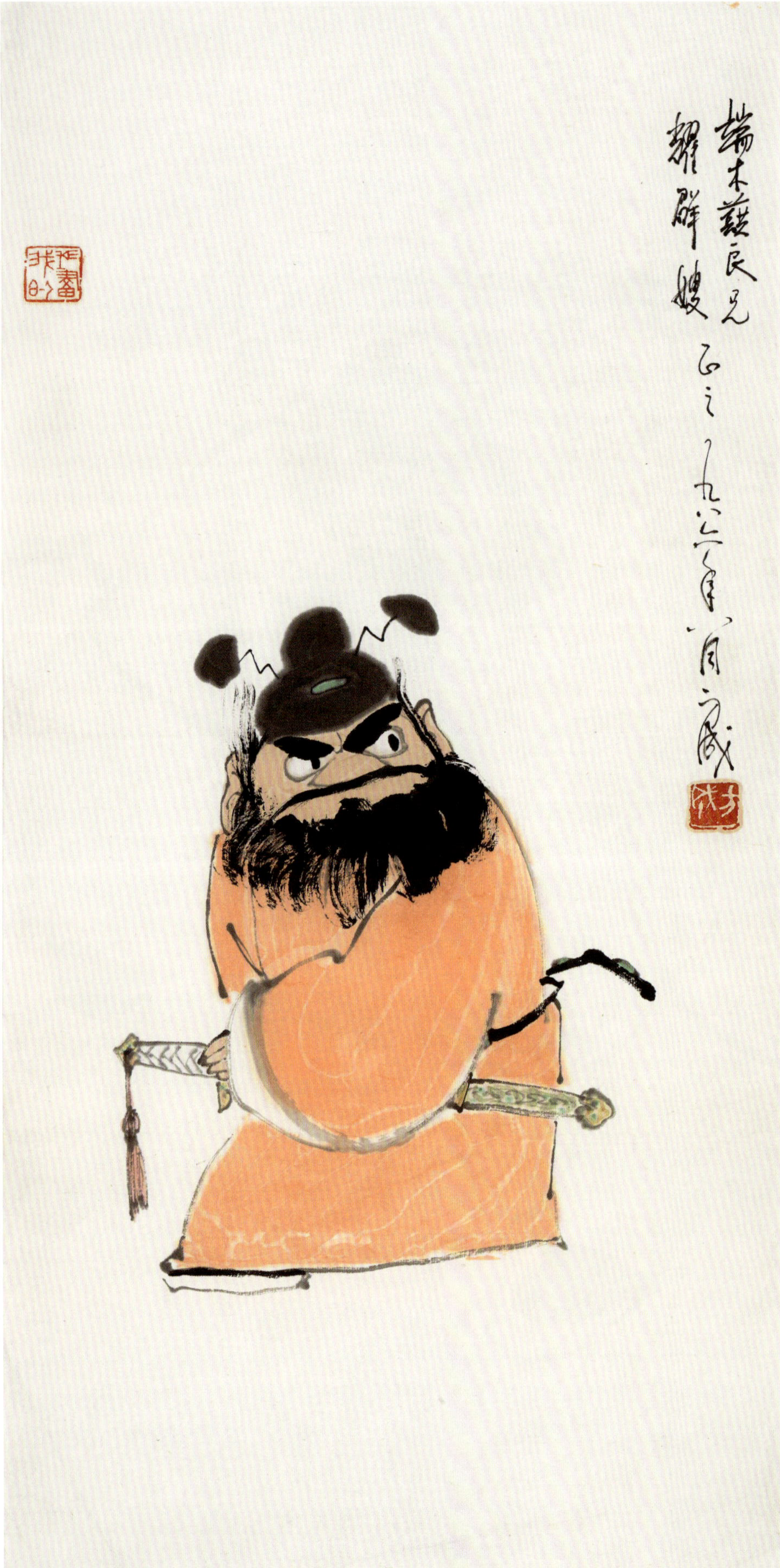
端木蕻良兄
耀群嫂 正之
一九八六年八月 方成

Artist:
Fang Cheng

Medium:
Color on paper, Framed piece

Dimensions:
70 cm × 34 cm

Red-Robed Zhong Kui

Inscription:
Commissioned by Elder Brother Duanmu Hongliang and Sister-in-law Yaoqun, this was completed by Fang Cheng in August 1986.

Seal:
Fang Cheng, I paint my own

Fang Cheng (1918–2018)
Originally named Sun Shunchao with the pen name Zhang Hua for essays, he was of ancestral origin from Zhongshan, Guangdong, born in Beijing. A cartoonist, essayist, and expert in the study of humor theory.

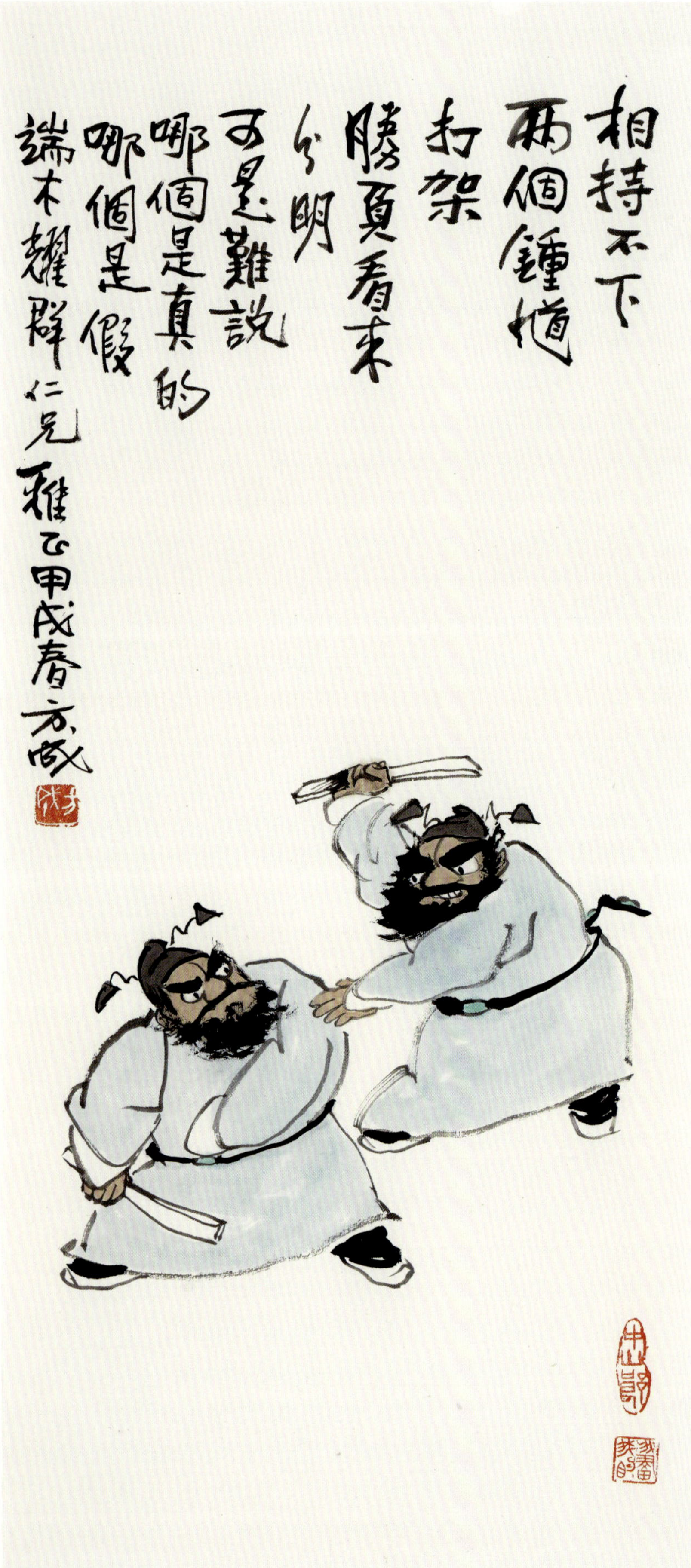
相持不下
兩個鍾馗
打架
勝負看來
分明
可是難說
哪個是真的
哪個是假
端木耀群仁兄
雅正甲戌春方成

Artist:
Fang Cheng

Medium:
Color on paper, Framed piece

Dimensions:
70 cm × 34 cm

True and False Zhong Kui

Inscription:
An impasse, two Zhong Kui figures in combat. The victory seems clear, yet it's hard to discern which is real and which is false. Commissioned by friends Duanmu and Yaoqun for their refined rectification, in the spring of Jiaxu, by Fang Cheng.

Seal:
Fang Cheng, The gentleman from Zhongshan, I paint my own

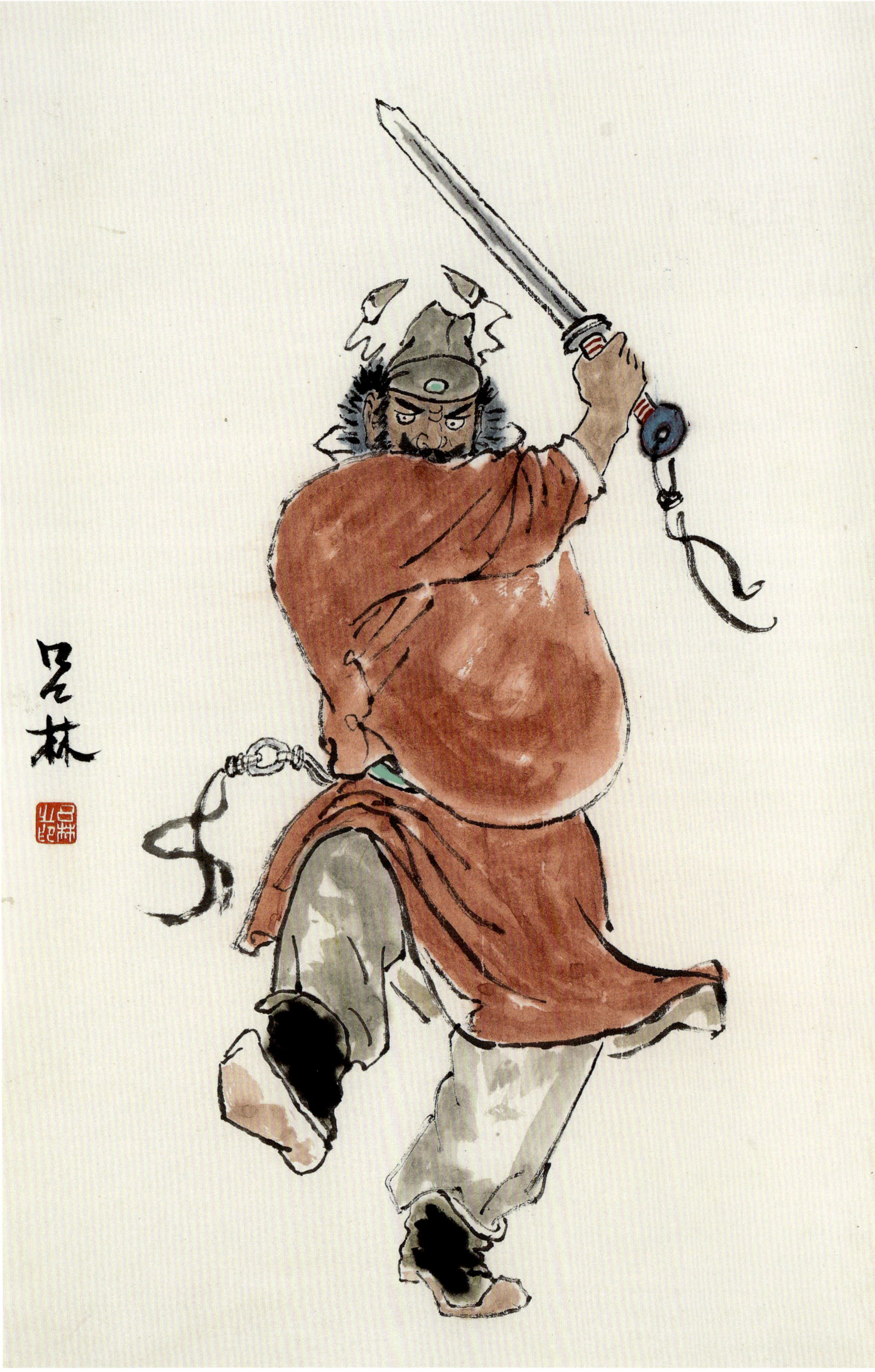
吕林

Artist:
Lü Lin

Medium:
Color on paper, Hanging scroll

Dimensions:
65 cm × 42.5 cm

Zhong Kui Wielding Sword

Inscription:
Lü Lin

Seal:
The seal of Lü Lin

Lü Lin (1920–1994)
A native of Jixian, Shanxi, he was skilled in printmaking and Chinese painting. He served as the head of the Fine Arts Department at the Northwest Art Academy, the Southwest People's Art Academy, as the vice-president of the Sichuan Academy of Poetry, Calligraphy, and Painting, and as vice-chairman of the Sichuan branch of the China Artists Association.

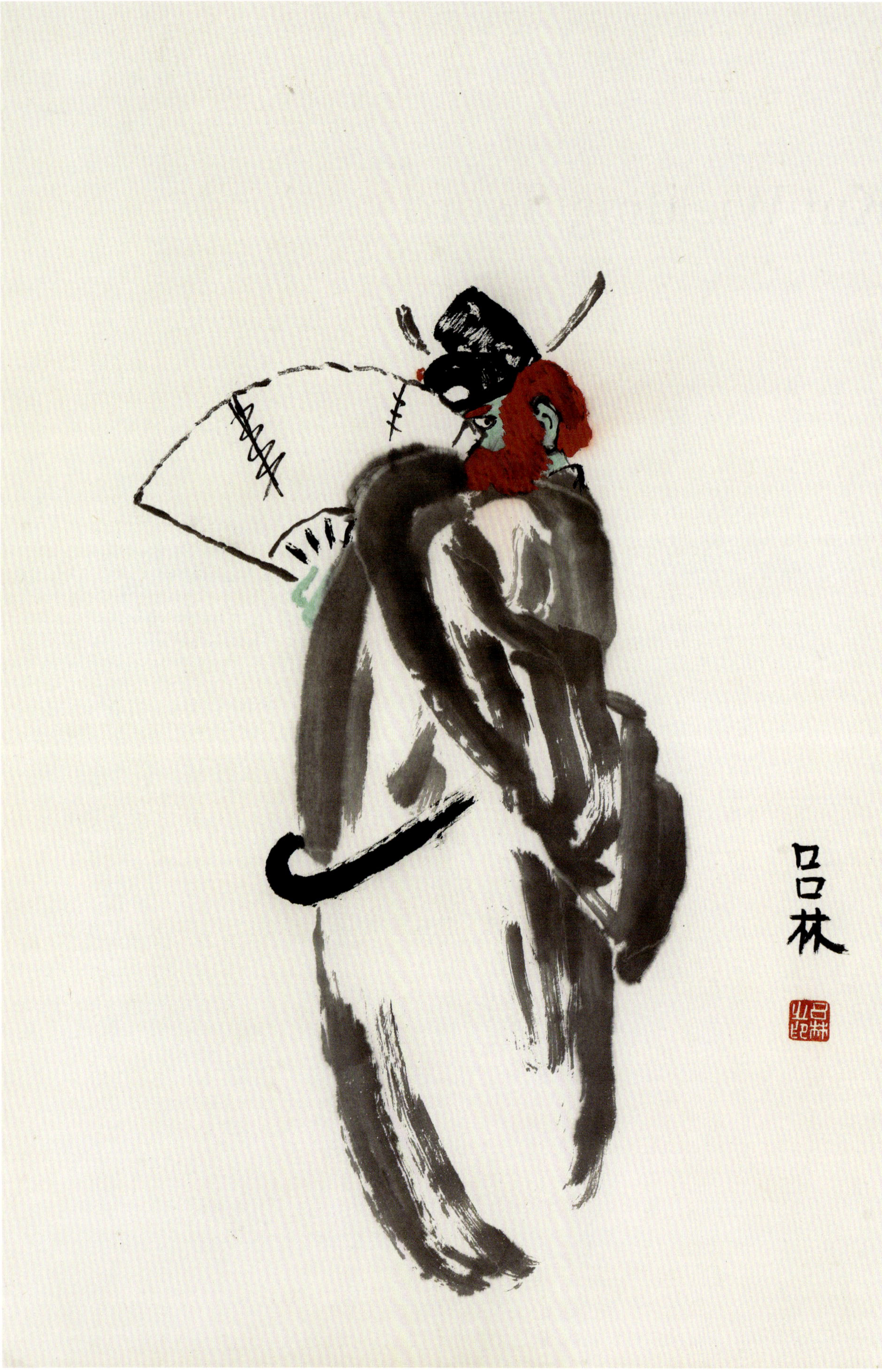
吕林

Artist:
Lü Lin

Medium:
Color on paper, Hanging scroll

Dimensions:
67 cm × 43.5 cm

Zhong Kui Holding Fan

Inscription:
Lü Lin

Seal:
The seal of Lü Lin

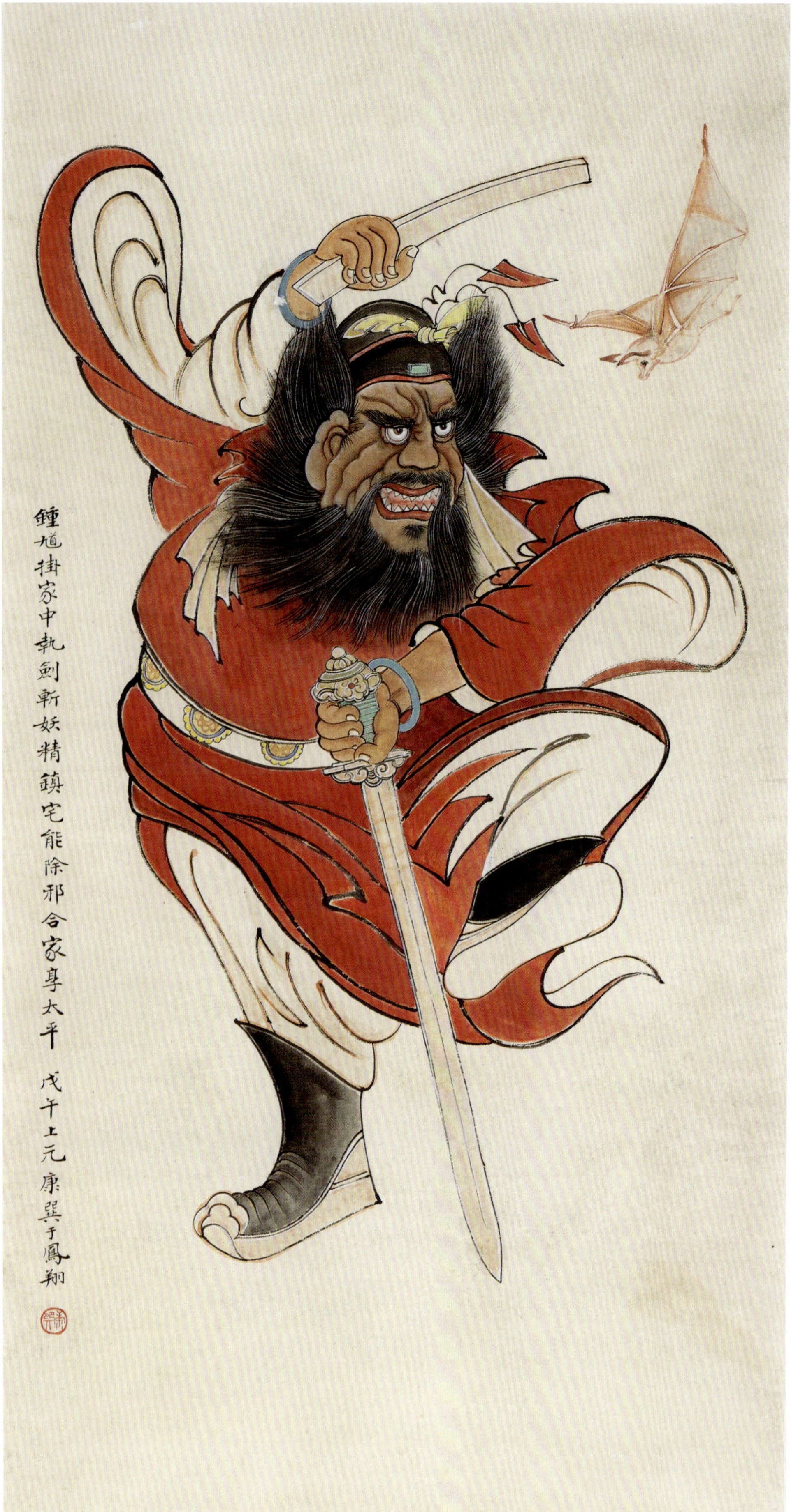
鍾馗掛家中執劍斬妖精鎮宅能除邪合家享太平
戊午上元康巽于鳳翔

Artist:
Kang Shiyao

Medium:
Color on paper, Framed piece

Dimensions:
131 cm × 67 cm

Zhong Kui with Sword

Inscription:
Zhong Kui hangs in the home, his sword slashing through demons. His presence wards off evil, bestowing peace upon the household. On the Lantern Festival of the Wuwu year, by Kang Xun in Fengxiang.

Seal:
Kang Xun

Kang Shiyao (1921–1985)
Pen name Kang Xun, a native of Bo'ai, Henan. He was proficient in Chinese painting and one of the leading artists of the "Chang'an School of Painting." He held posts as a standing director of the Shaanxi Artists Association, vice director of the Folk Arts Committee of the China Arts and Crafts Society, and vice president of the Shaanxi Traditional Chinese Painting Academy.

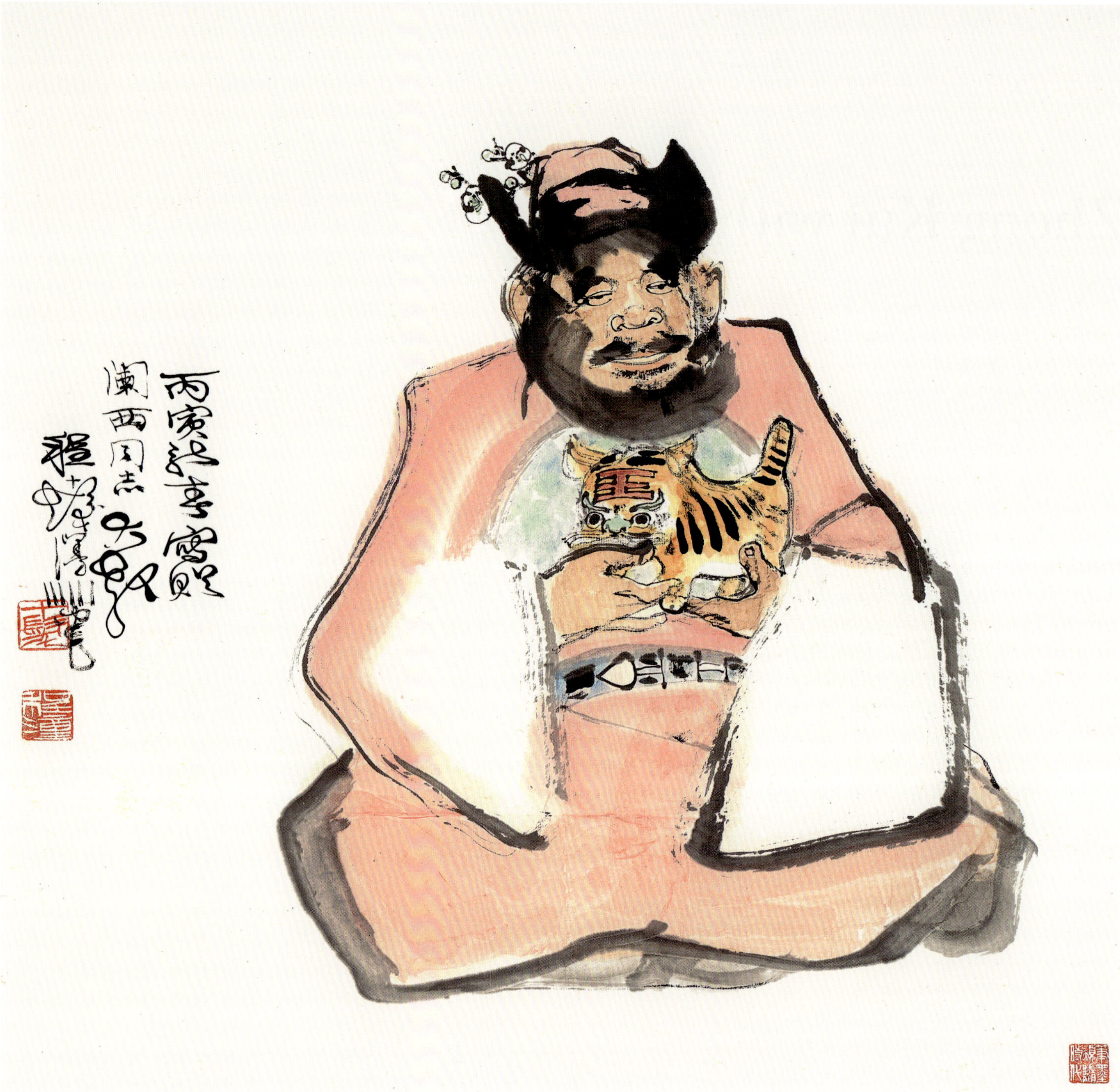

Artist:
Cheng Shifa

Medium:
Color on paper, Hanging scroll

Dimensions:
66 cm × 67 cm

Bingyin Zhong Kui

Inscription:
In the early spring of the Bingyin year, this piece is penned as a gift to comrade Lanxi, the great teacher, with a casual brush by Cheng Shifa.

Seal:
Shifa, Cheng Tong, The brush and ink must follow the times

Cheng Shifa (1921–2007)
Originally named Cheng Tong and styled as Shifa, he was a native of Songjiang, Shanghai. He used various studio names, initially "Bujing Studio" and "Never idle retreat," later adopting "San Fu Study" and "Bamboo Grove and Distant Mountains Studio." Renowned as a Shanghai School painter and calligrapher, he excelled in depicting figures and birds-and-flowers. Cheng's versatility extended to comic strips, New Year pictures, and illustrations, where he displayed considerable skill. In calligraphy, he drew strength from Qin and Han dynasty wooden slips and Huai Su's cursive scripts, adeptly integrating cursive, seal, and clerical scripts. In 1957, he contributed to the founding of the Shanghai Chinese Painting Academy, eventually becoming its director in 1984, focusing on Chinese painting.

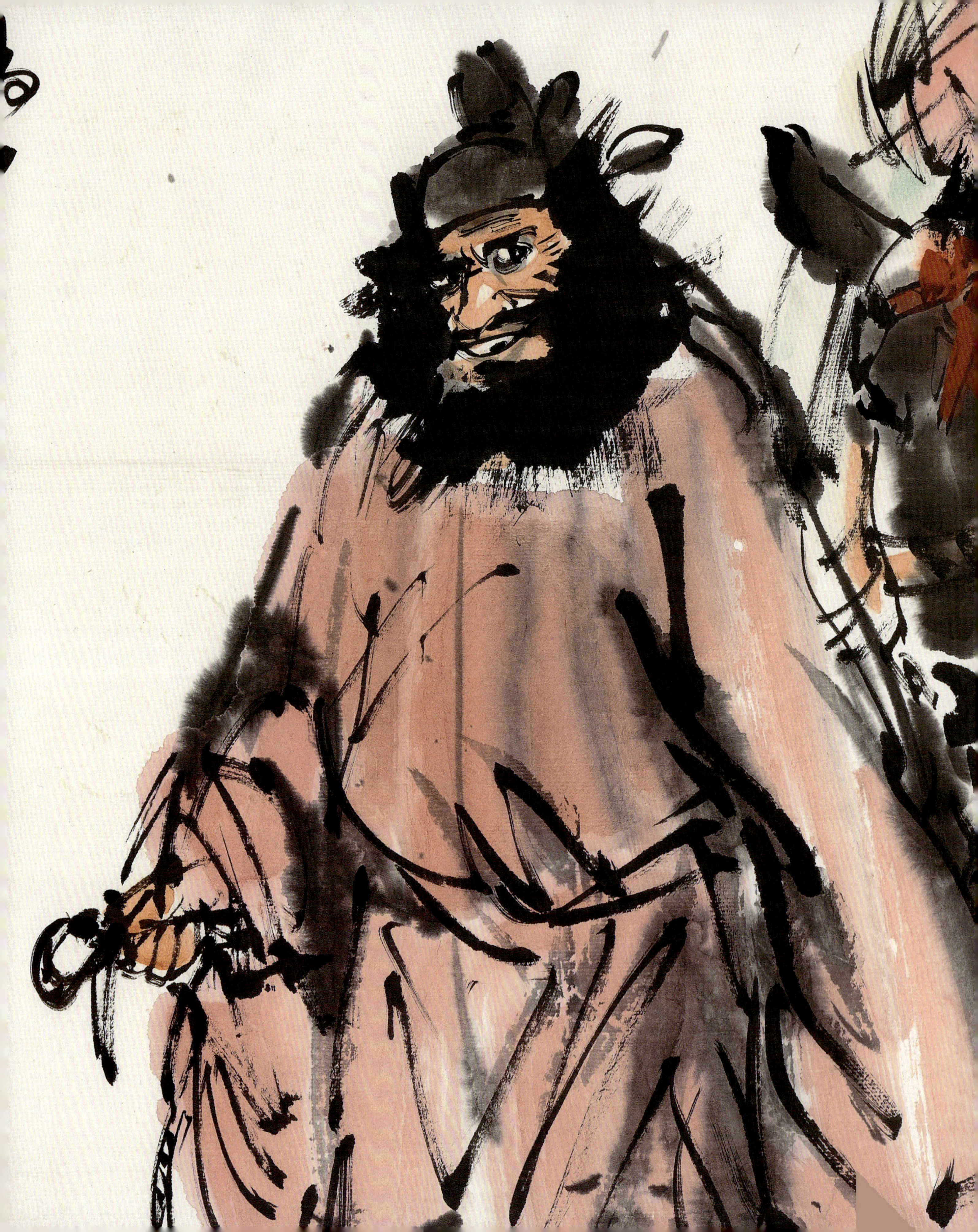

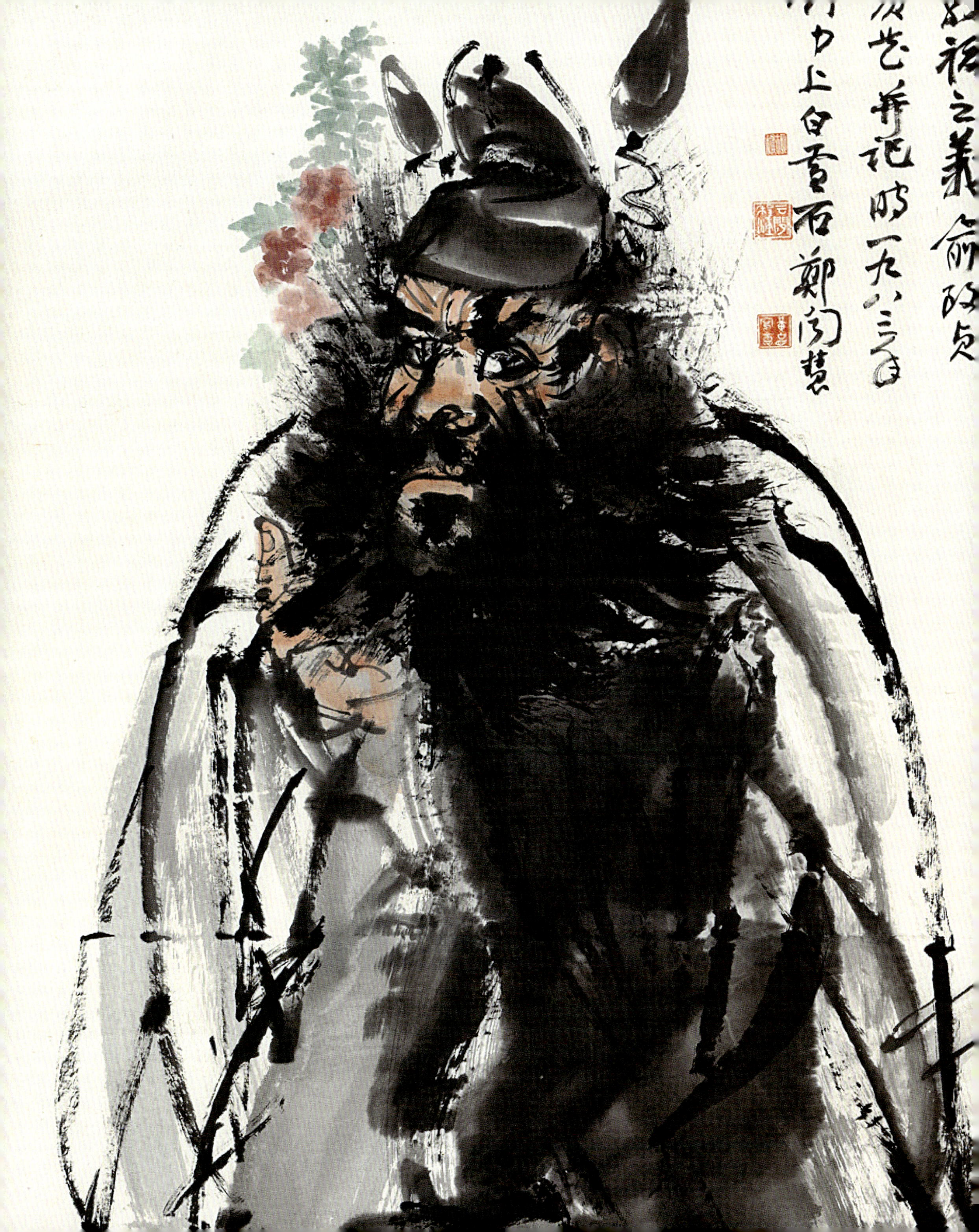

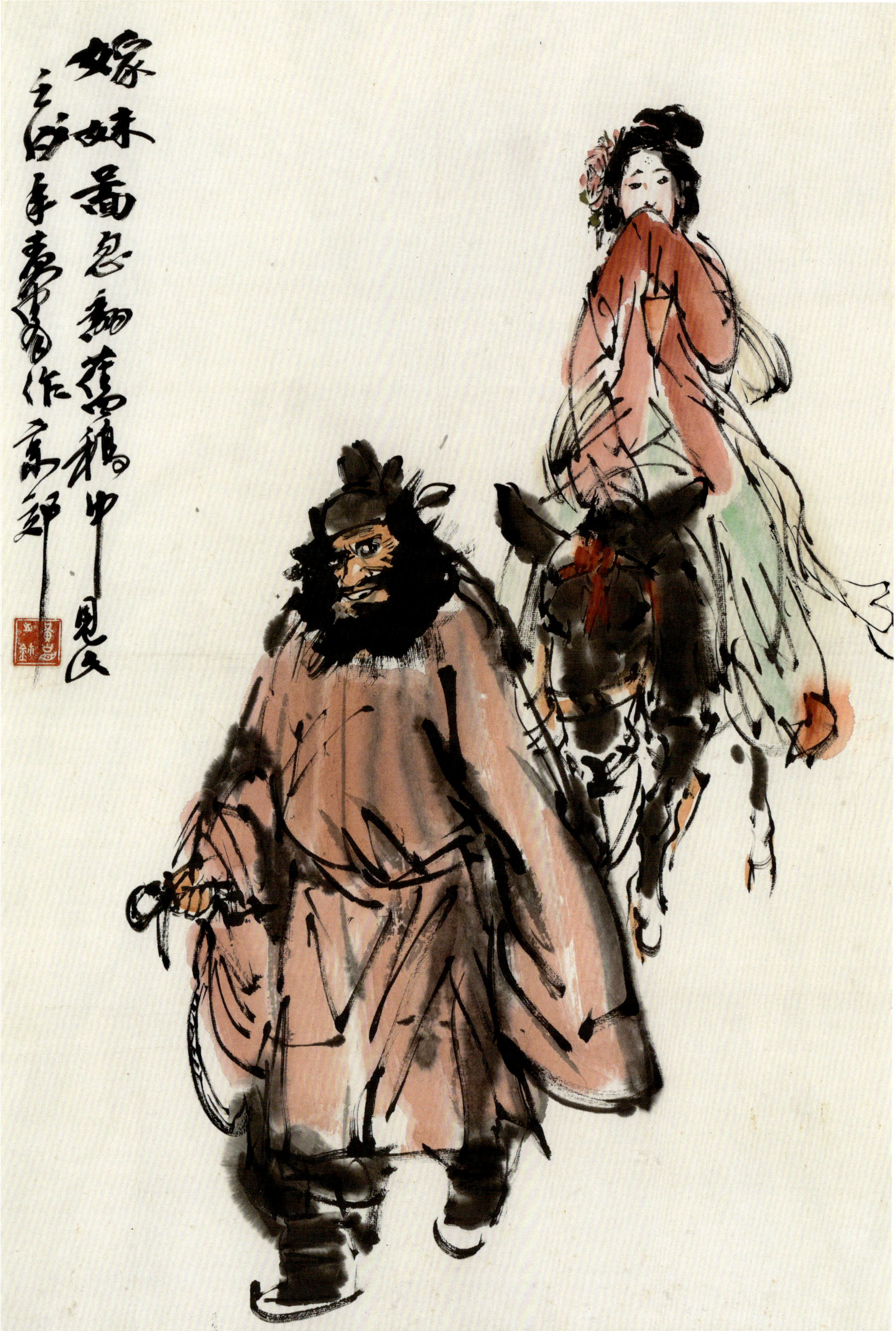

Artist:
Huang Zhou

Medium:
Color on paper, Framed piece

Dimensions:
68.5 cm × 46 cm

Zhong Kui Marrying Off His Sister

Inscription:
Zhong Kui Marrying Off His Sister. Suddenly found this among old drafts. Created by Huang Zhou in the year Renxu, in the suburbs of Beijing.

Seal:
The carving of Huang Zhou

Huang Zhou (1925–1997)
Styled Yingzhai, from Li County, Hebei. A representative figure of the Chang'an School, a master of Chinese painting, social activist, and collector. He served as vice president of the Chinese Painting Research Institute, a member of the National Committee of the Chinese People's Political Consultative Conference (CPPCC), a standing member of the CPPCC, and a standing director of the China Artists Association.

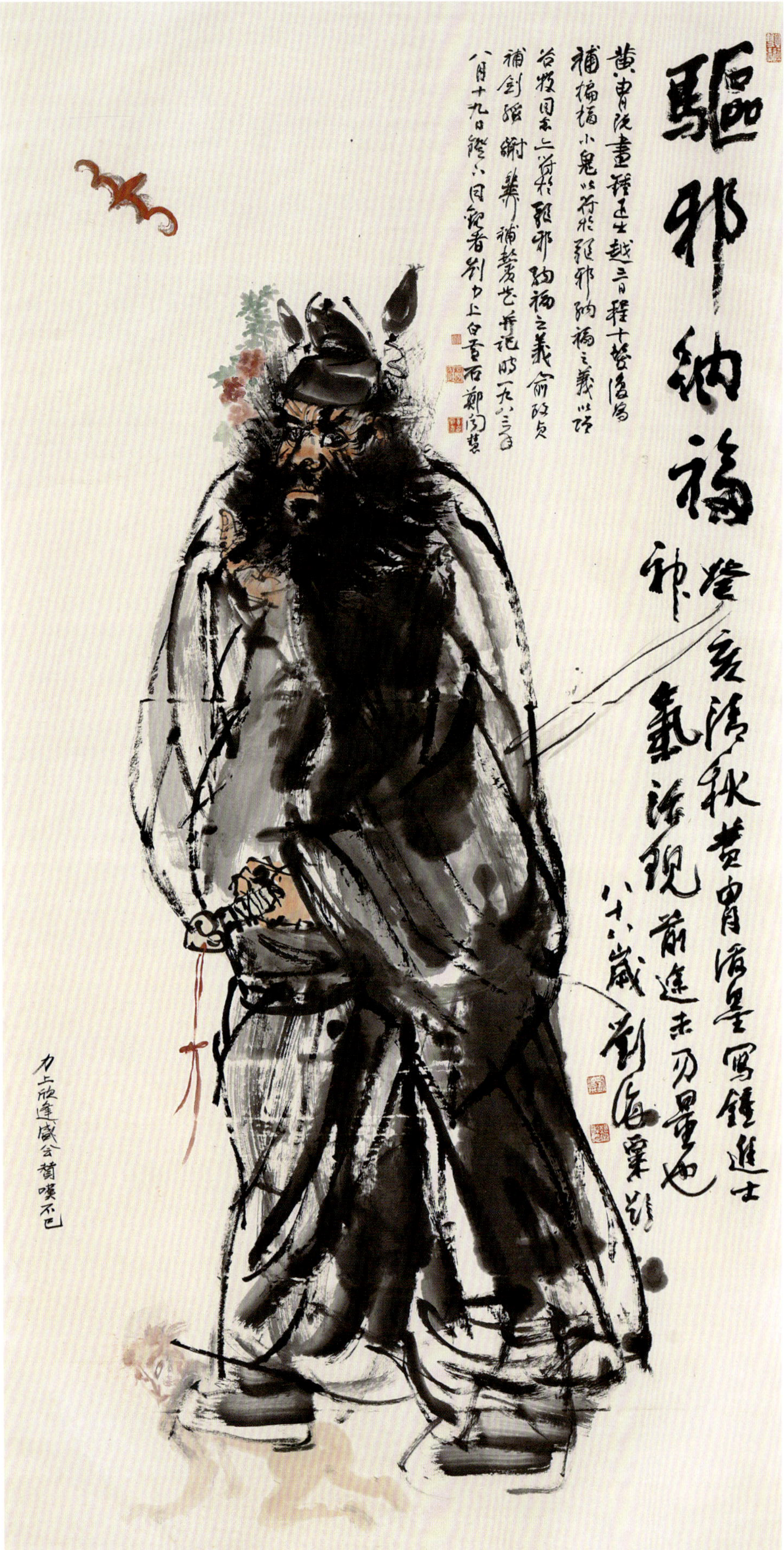
驅邪納福

Artist:
Huang Zhou | Inscribed by Liu Haisu, Cheng Shifa, Yu Zhizhen, Xie Zhiliu

Medium:
Color on paper, Hanging scroll

Dimensions:
248 cm × 124 cm

Expelling Evil and Attracting Blessings

Inscription:
Expelling Evil and Attracting Blessings. In the clear autumn of the Guihai year, Huang Zhou splashed ink to depict Zhong Kui, vivid with spirit, his future not easily predicted. At the age of eighty-eight, Liu Haisu inscribed this.

Seal:
Liu Haisu, Artistic rebel

Inscription:
After Huang Zhou painted Zhong Kui, three days later, Cheng Shifa additionally drew bats and little demons to complement the theme of exorcising evil and attracting good fortune, as a gift to Comrade Gu Mu, also in line with the theme. Yu Zhizhen added the sword, and Xie Zhiliu added the temple flowers, recorded on August 19, 1983, as observed by Liu Lishang, Bai Xueshi, and Zheng Wenhui under the light.

Seal:
Zhiliu, Yunjian Chengtong, Huang Zhou's freehand brushwork, Double purity of heart and deed

Inscription:
Lishang rejoiced at the grand gathering, full of admiration.

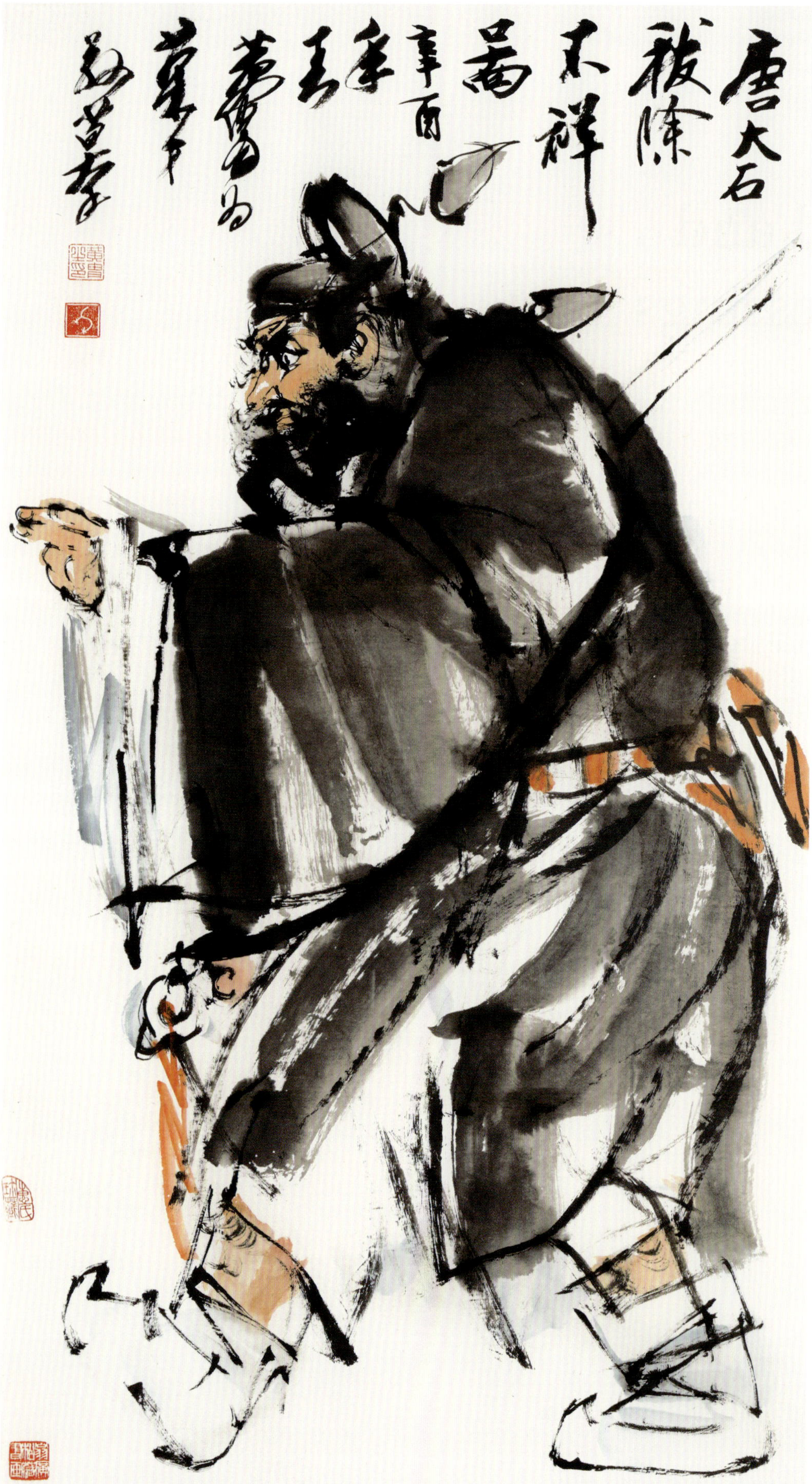

Artist:
Huang Zhou

Medium:
Color on paper, Hanging scroll

Dimensions:
95 cm × 51 cm

Imitating Tang Yun's "Exorcising Misfortune"

Inscription:
Tang Dashi's "Exorcising Misfortune". In the spring of the Xinyou year, Huang Zhou respectfully emulated this for Rongcai.

Seal:
The seal of Huang Zhou

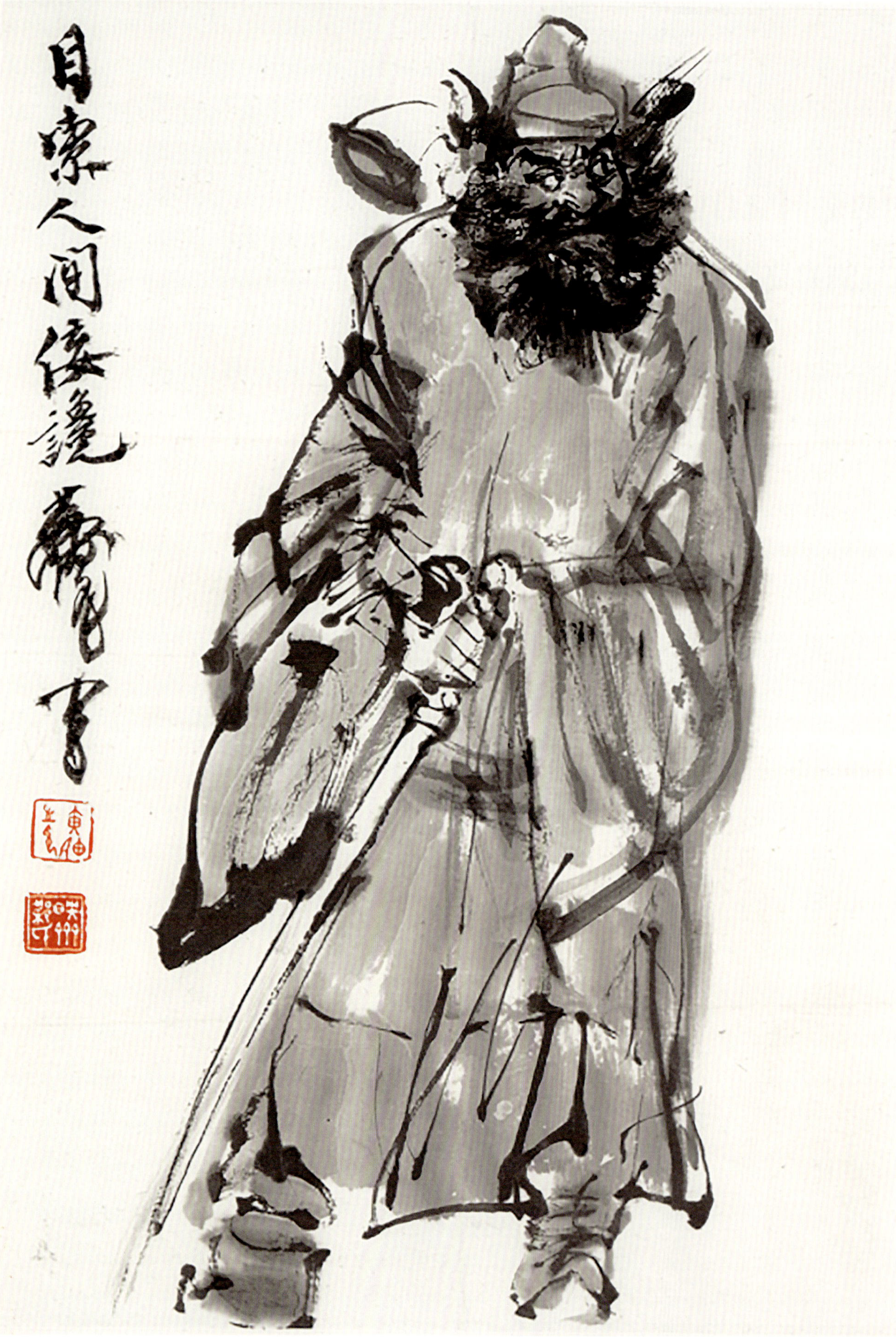

Artist:
Huang Zhou

Medium:
Ink on paper, Hanging scroll

Seeking Out Flattery and Deceit in the Human Realm

Inscription:
Seeking Out Flattery and Deceit in the Human Realm.
Painted by Huang Zhou.

Seal:
The seal of Huang Zhou, Liang clan of Yingzhou

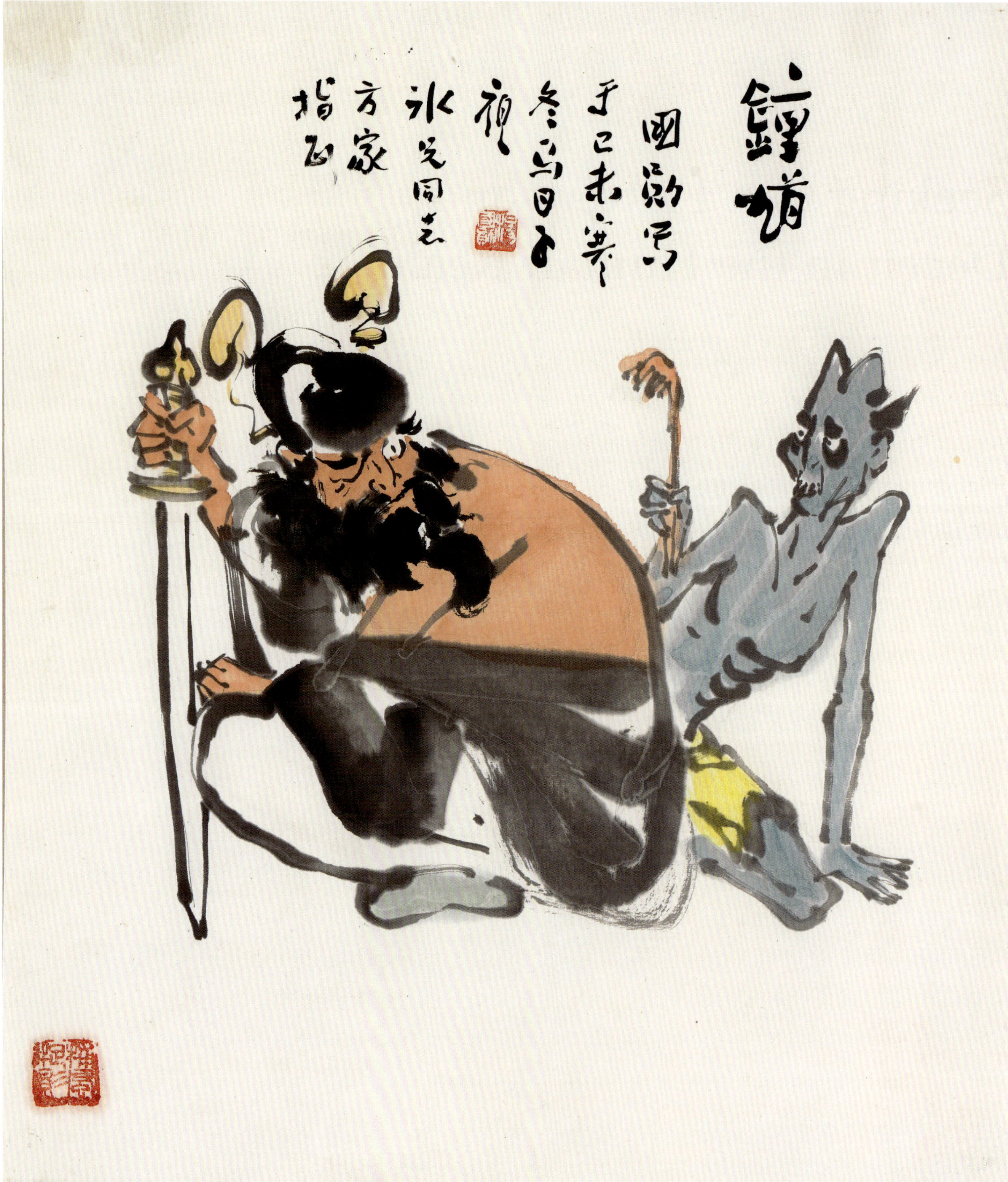
鍾馗
冰兄同志
方家
指正

Artist:
Yang Guoxun

Medium:
Color on paper, Hanging scroll

Dimensions:
53 cm × 44 cm

Zhong Kui

Inscription:
Zhong Kui, penned by Yang Guoxun on a frigid night of the 21st day in the Jiwei winter, with brother Bing, a comrade of the Fang family, provided corrections.

Seal:
Yang Guoxun, Grasping at shadows

Yang Guoxun (1930–1996)
A painter from Fenghuang, Hunan, he excelled in painting opera characters.

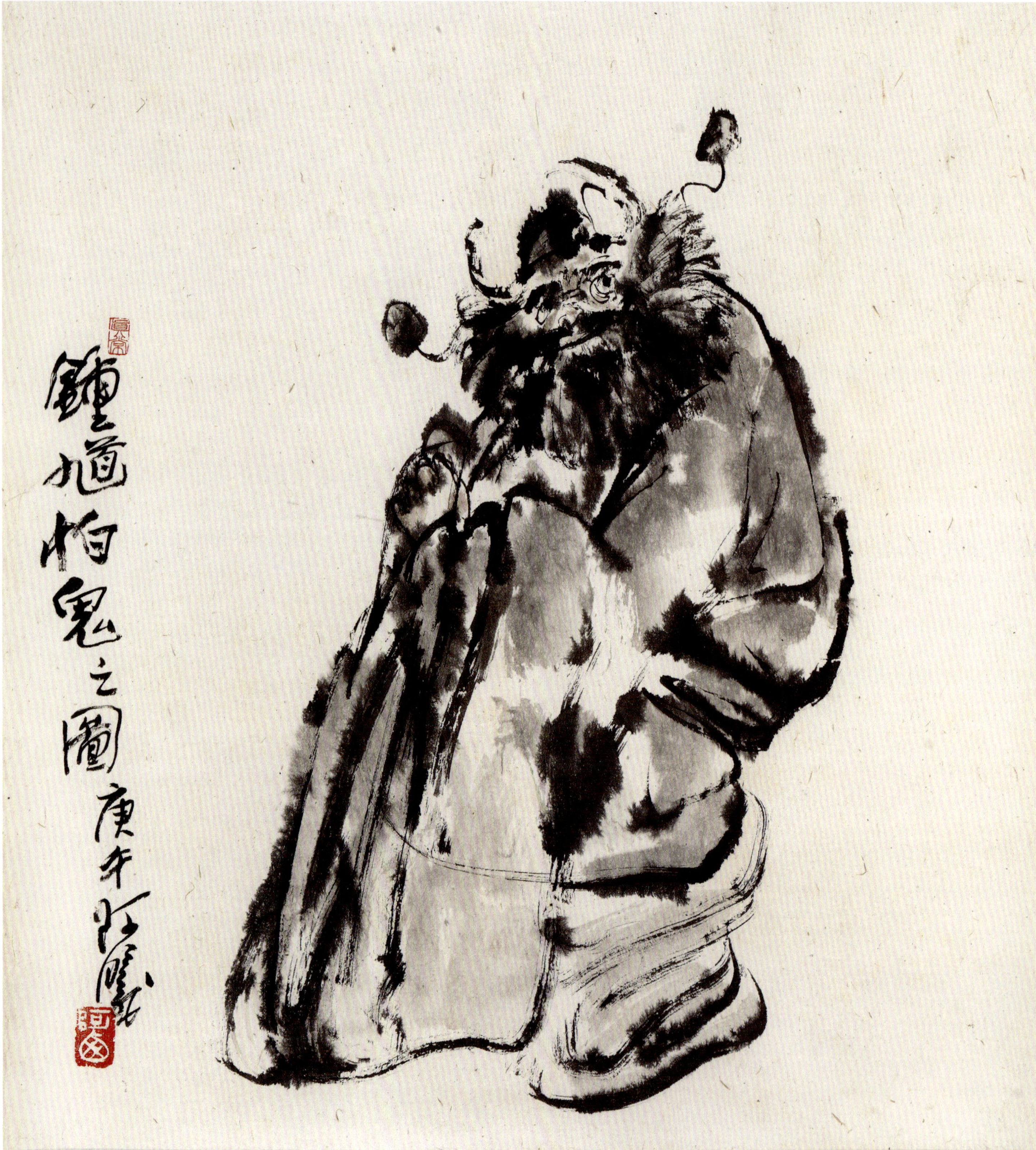

Artist:
Chen Dexi

Medium:
Color on paper, Hanging scroll

Dimensions:
57 cm × 51 cm

Zhong Kui Fearing Ghosts

Inscription:
The painting of Zhong Kui Fearing Ghosts, by Xi in the year of Gengwu.

Seal:
Xi, Zhenchang

Chen Dexi (1936–2012)
A native of Shantou, Guangdong. Graduated from the East China Art College (now Nanjing University of the Arts) in 1957 and taught there until 1981. He later resided in Hong Kong, where he held teaching positions at institutions including the Chinese University of Hong Kong.

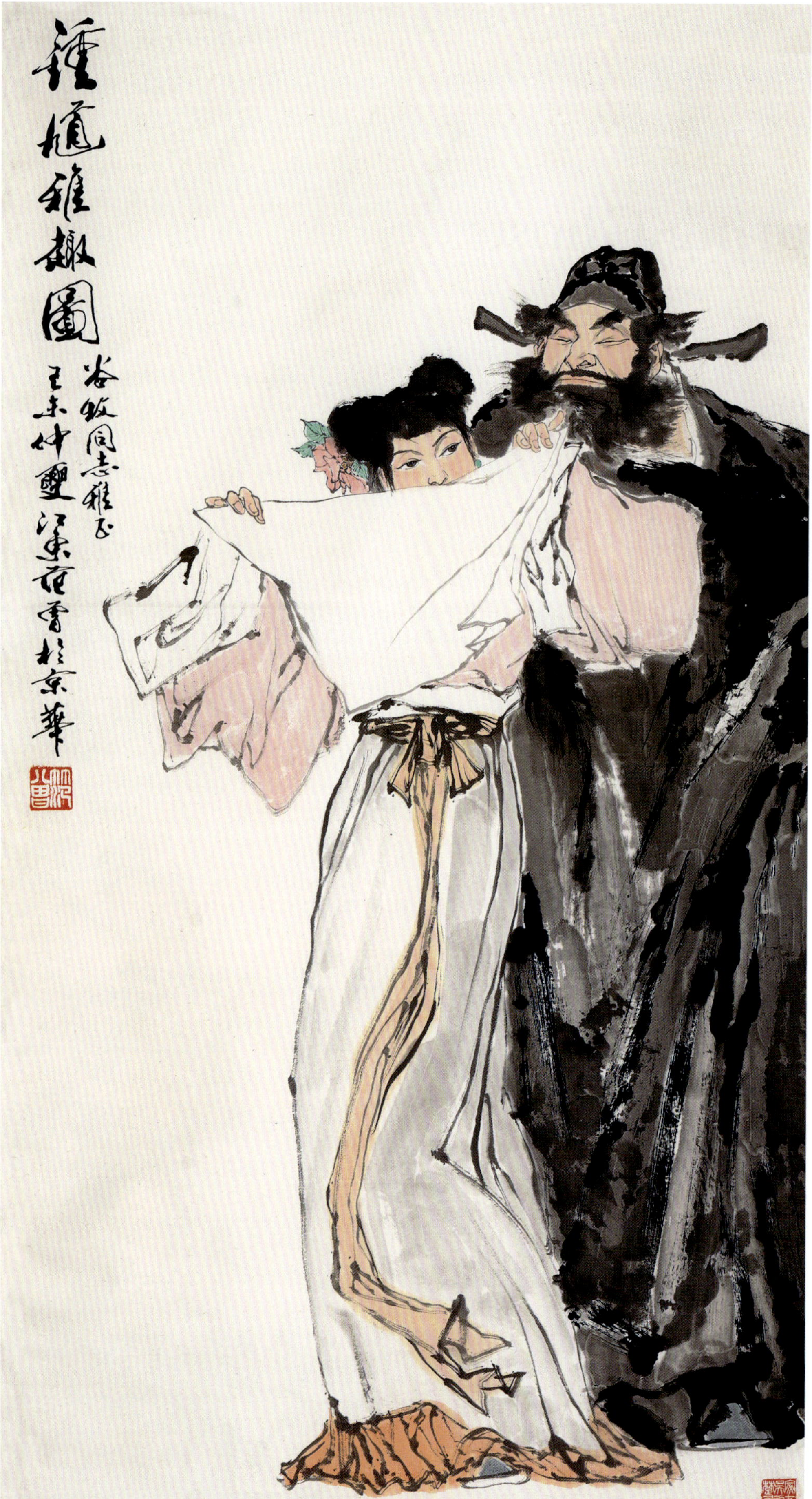
鍾馗雅趣圖
谷牧同志雅正

Artist:
Fan Zeng

Medium:
Color on paper, Hanging scroll

Dimensions:
180 cm × 97 cm

Zhong Kui with Elegant Interests

Inscription:
Zhong Kui with Elegant Interests. Commissioned by Comrade Gumu for his distinguished rectification, Fan Zeng painted this in mid-summer of the Jiwei year in the eastern part of the Yangtze, in Jinghua.

Seal:
Fan Zeng, Home Between Wu and Chu

Fan Zeng (b. 1938)
Styled Shi Yi, a native of Nantong, Jiangsu. A Chinese painter specializing in figure painting and a calligrapher. Currently a member of the China Artists Association, a doctoral supervisor and researcher at the Chinese National Academy of Arts, as well as a lifetime professor and doctoral supervisor at Nankai University.

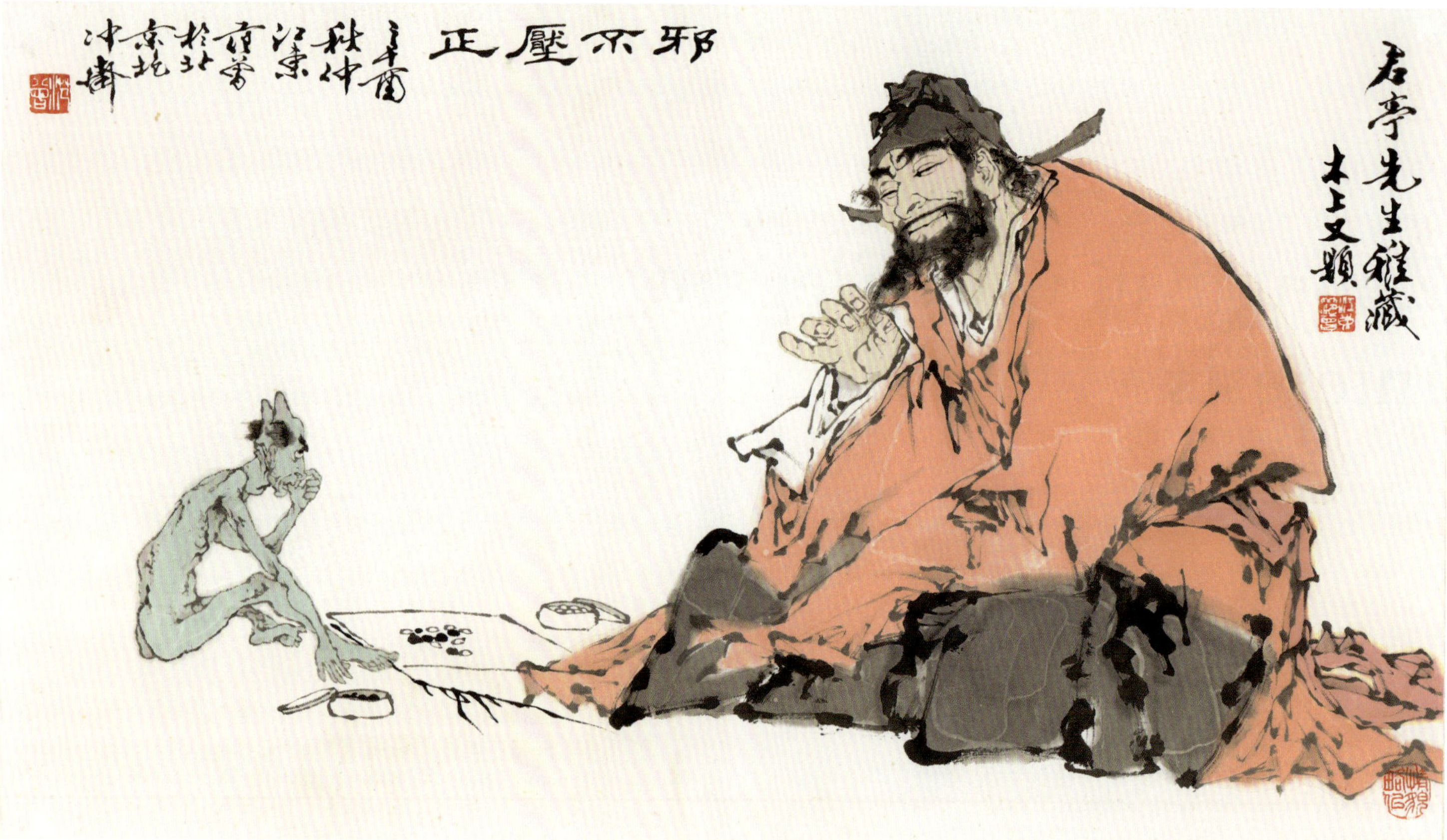
邪不壓正

Artist:
Fan Zeng

Medium:
Color on paper, Framed piece

Dimensions:
109 cm × 42.5 cm

Evil Cannot Suppress the Righteous

Inscription:
First, "Evil Cannot Suppress the Righteous." Created by Fan Zeng from Jiangdong, in mid-autumn of the Xinyou year, at Baochong Studio in Beijing.
Second, Mr. Junting's distinguished collection. Further inscribed by Mushang.

Seal:
Fan Zeng, Jiangdong Fan Zeng

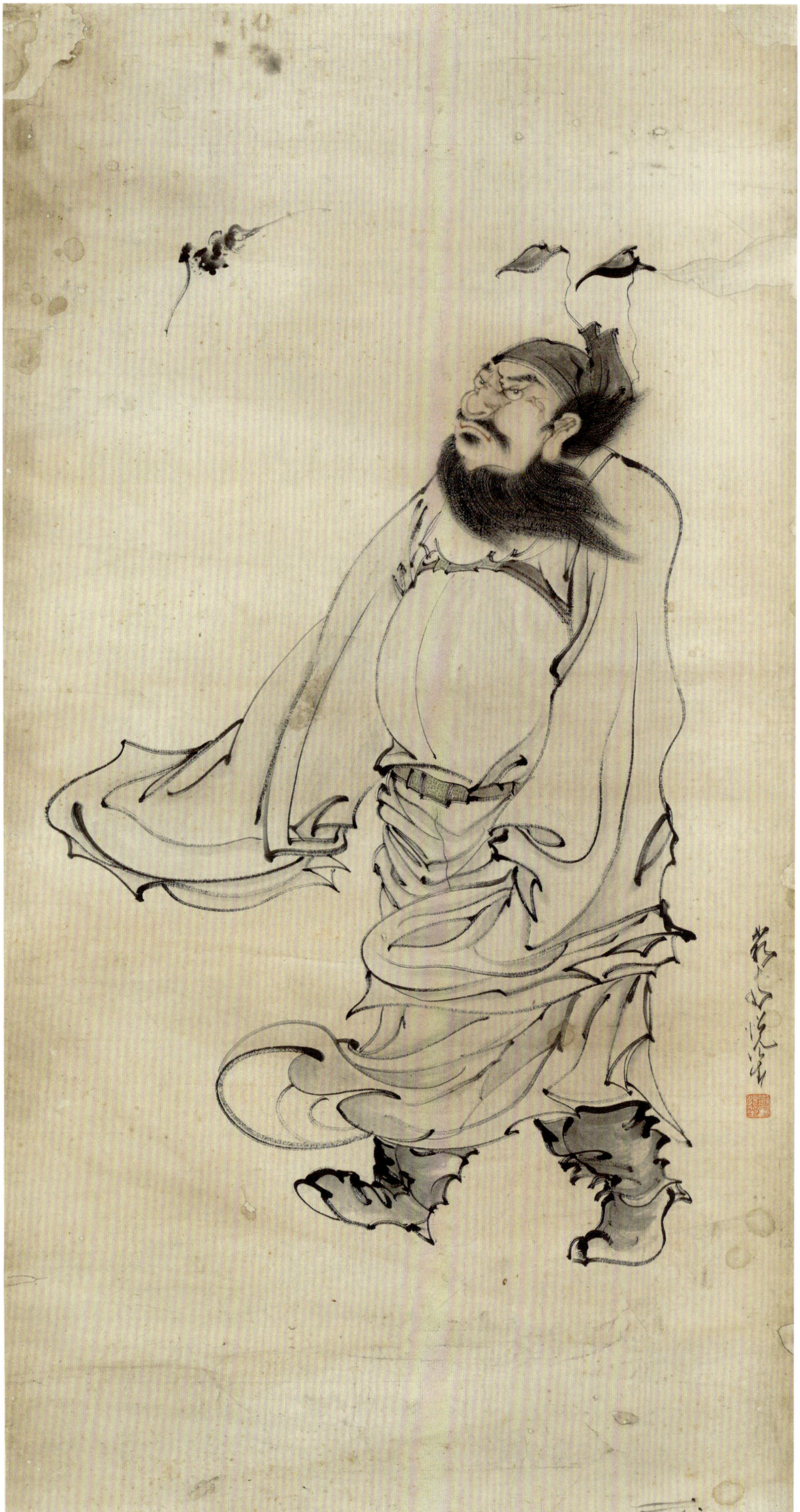

Artist:
Liu Yuesheng

Medium:
Color on paper, Framed piece

Dimensions:
99 cm × 50 cm

Zhong Kui Welcoming Fortune

Inscription:
Lingnan Yuesheng.

Seal:
The seal of Liu Yuesheng

Liu Yuesheng (b. 1941)
A native of Guangzhou. He began his Chinese painting studies under Jiang Chengzan and founded the Gengzi Yishe society, later becoming a disciple of Li Lingjia from Minhou.

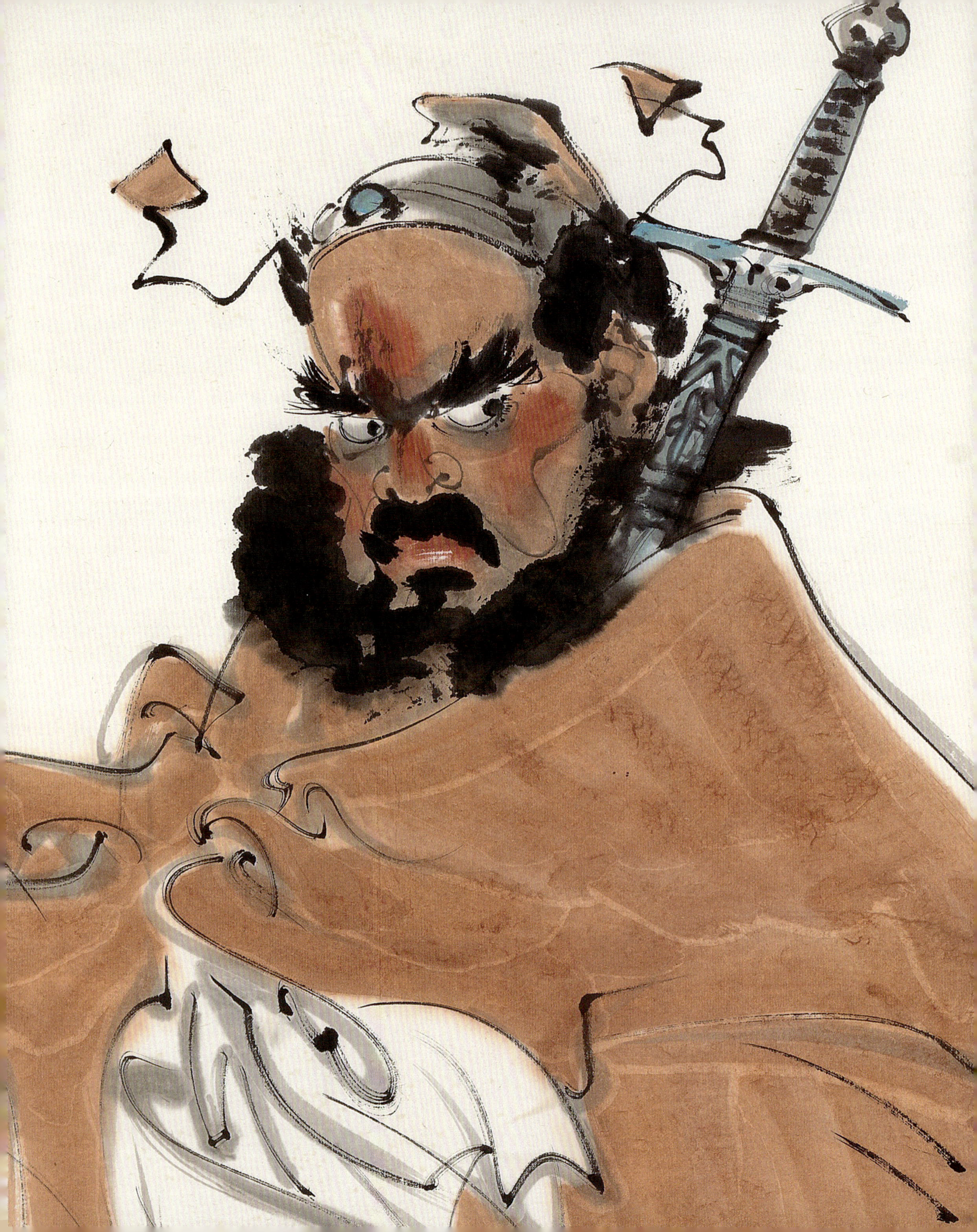

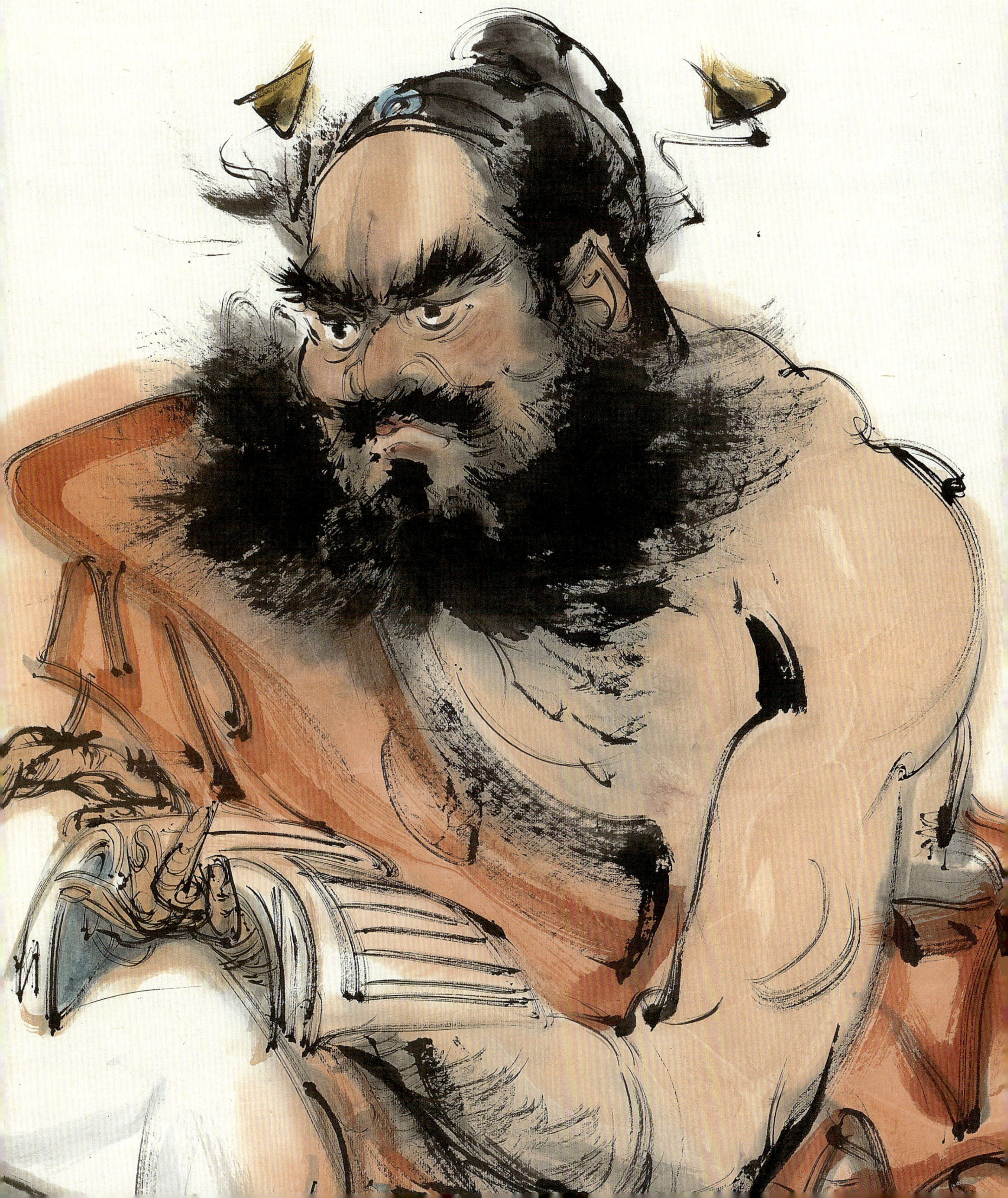

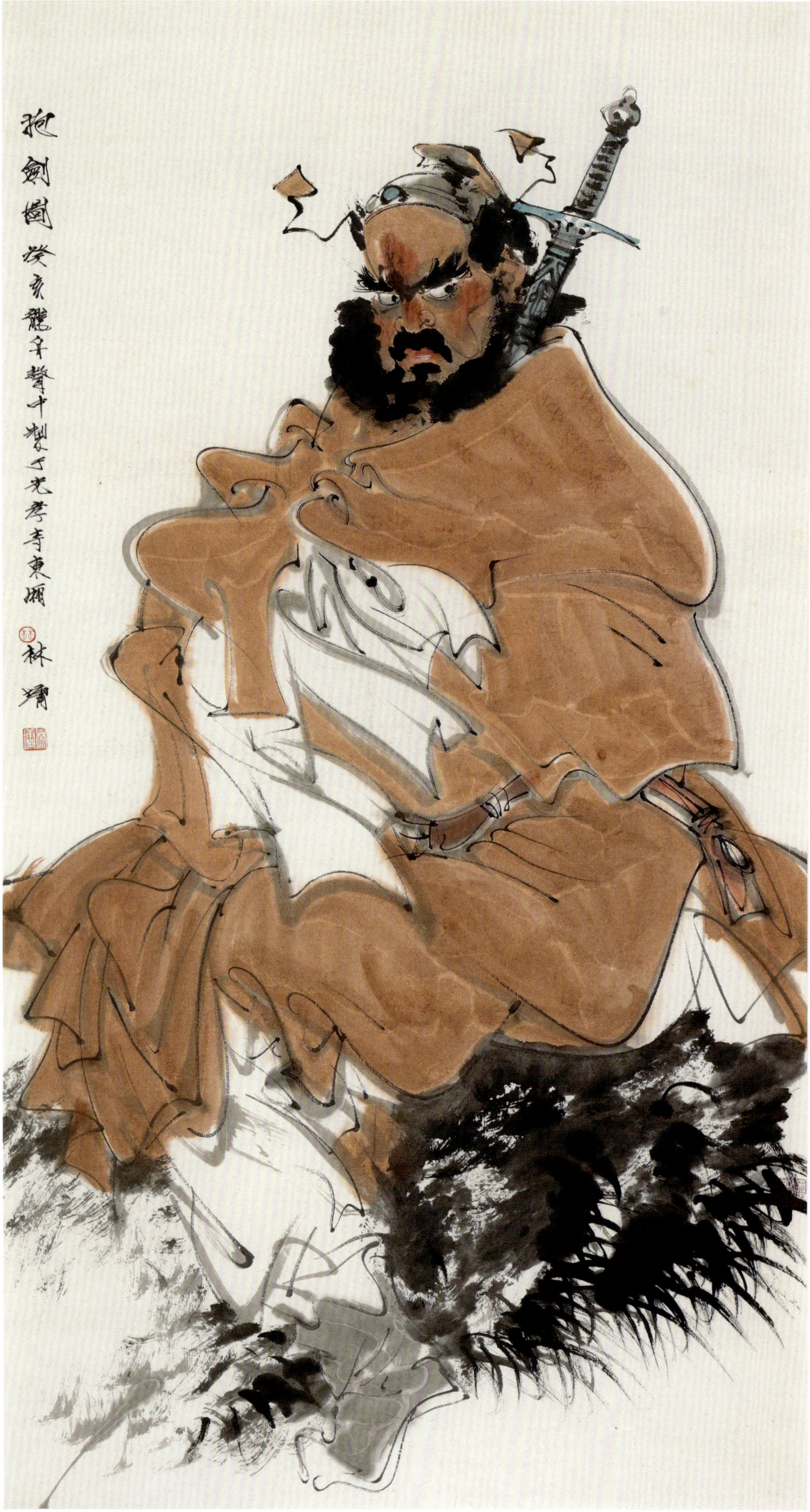
抱劍圖
癸亥龍年驚蟄中製于光孝寺東廂
林墉

Artist:
Lin Yong

Medium:
Color on paper, Hanging scroll

Dimensions:
135 cm × 68 cm

Holding the Sword

Inscription:
Holding the Sword. Created by Lin Yong amidst the sounds of dragon boats in the eastern wing of Guangxiao Temple during the Guihai year.

Seal:
Lin, Lin Yong

Lin Yong (b. 1942)
From Chaozhou, Guangdong, he is a national first-class fine arts master, adept in figure and flower-and-bird painting, known for a style that is free, fresh, and bright. He also excels in literary criticism and illustration. He has served as the vice-chairman of the China Artists Association, president of the Guangdong Painting Academy, chairman of the Guangdong Artists Association, a member of the executive committee of the Chinese Painting Research Institute, and vice-president of the Guangdong Federation of Literary and Art Circles.

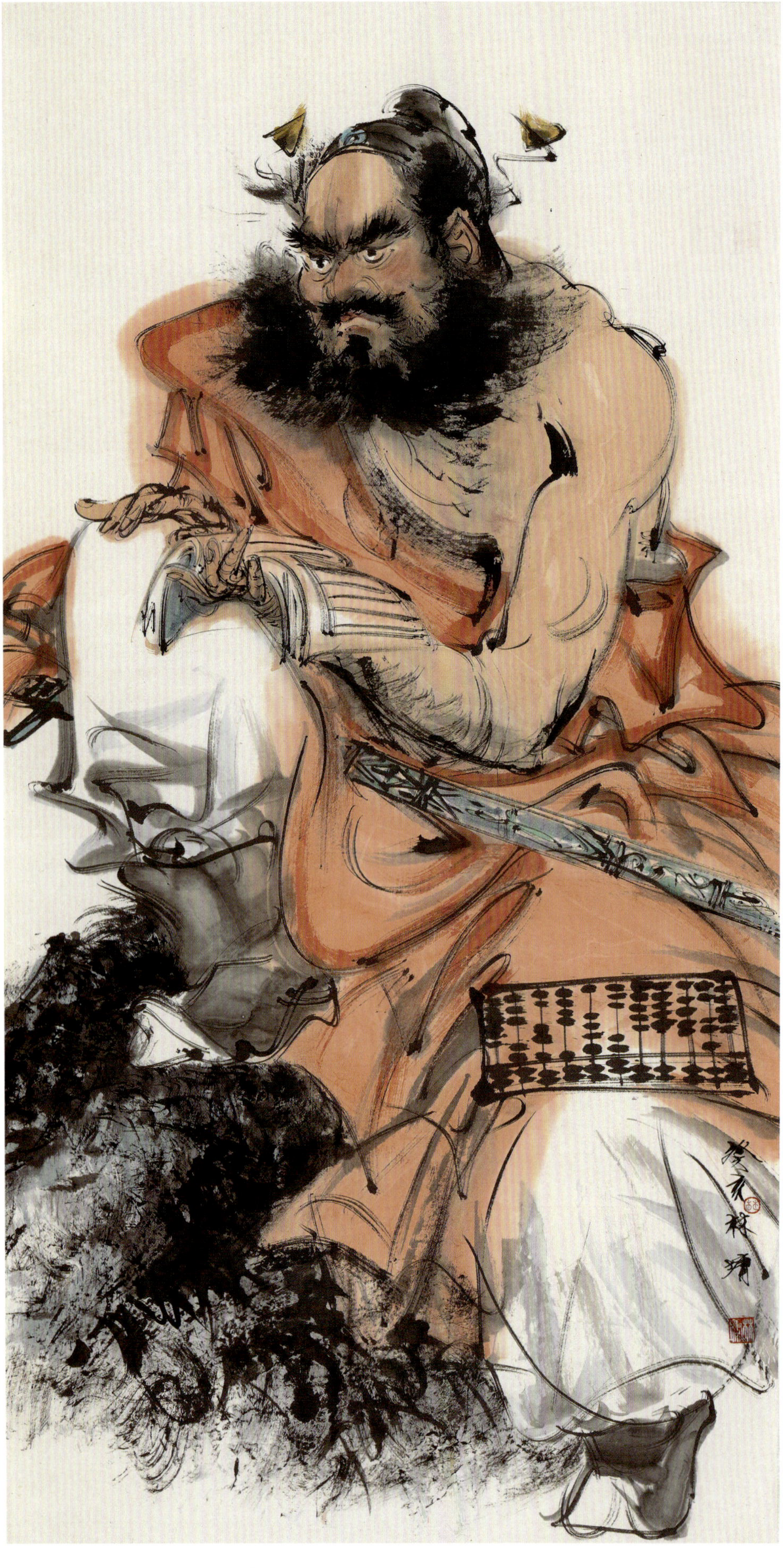

Artist:
Lin Yong

Medium:
Color on paper, Hanging scroll

Dimensions:
134.5 cm × 67 cm

Zhong Kui Settling Accounts

Inscription:
Guihai, Lin Yong

Seal:
Lin Yong, Lin

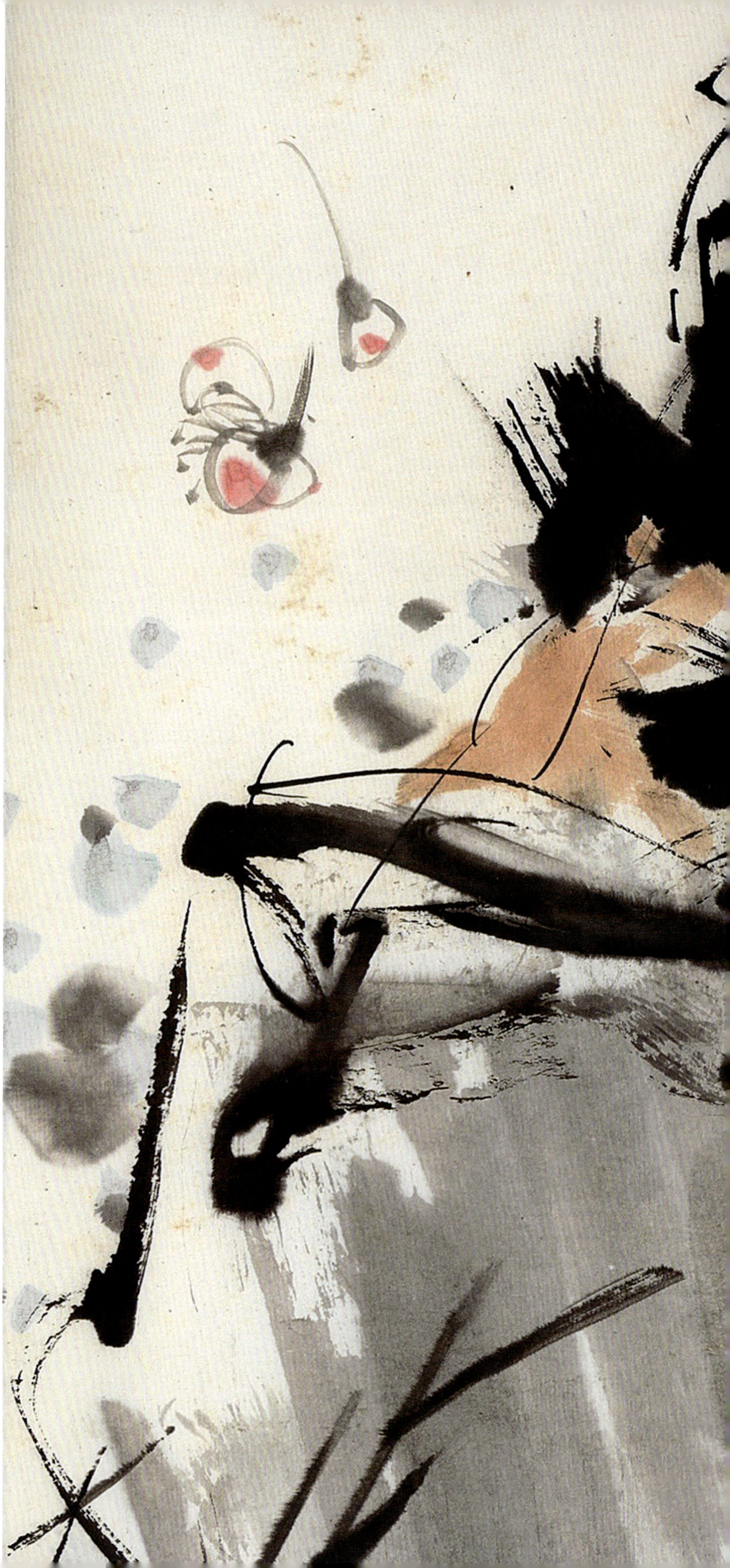

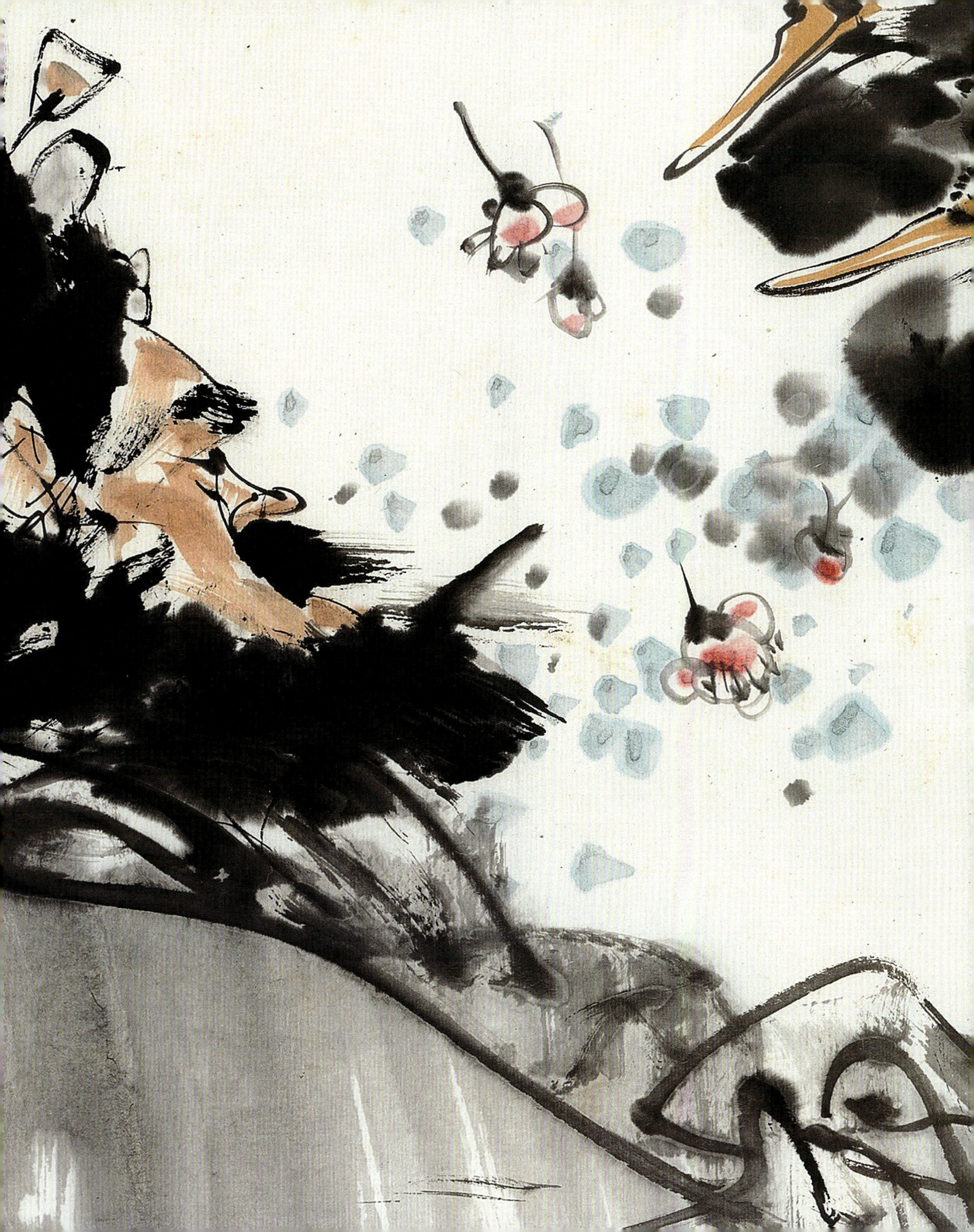

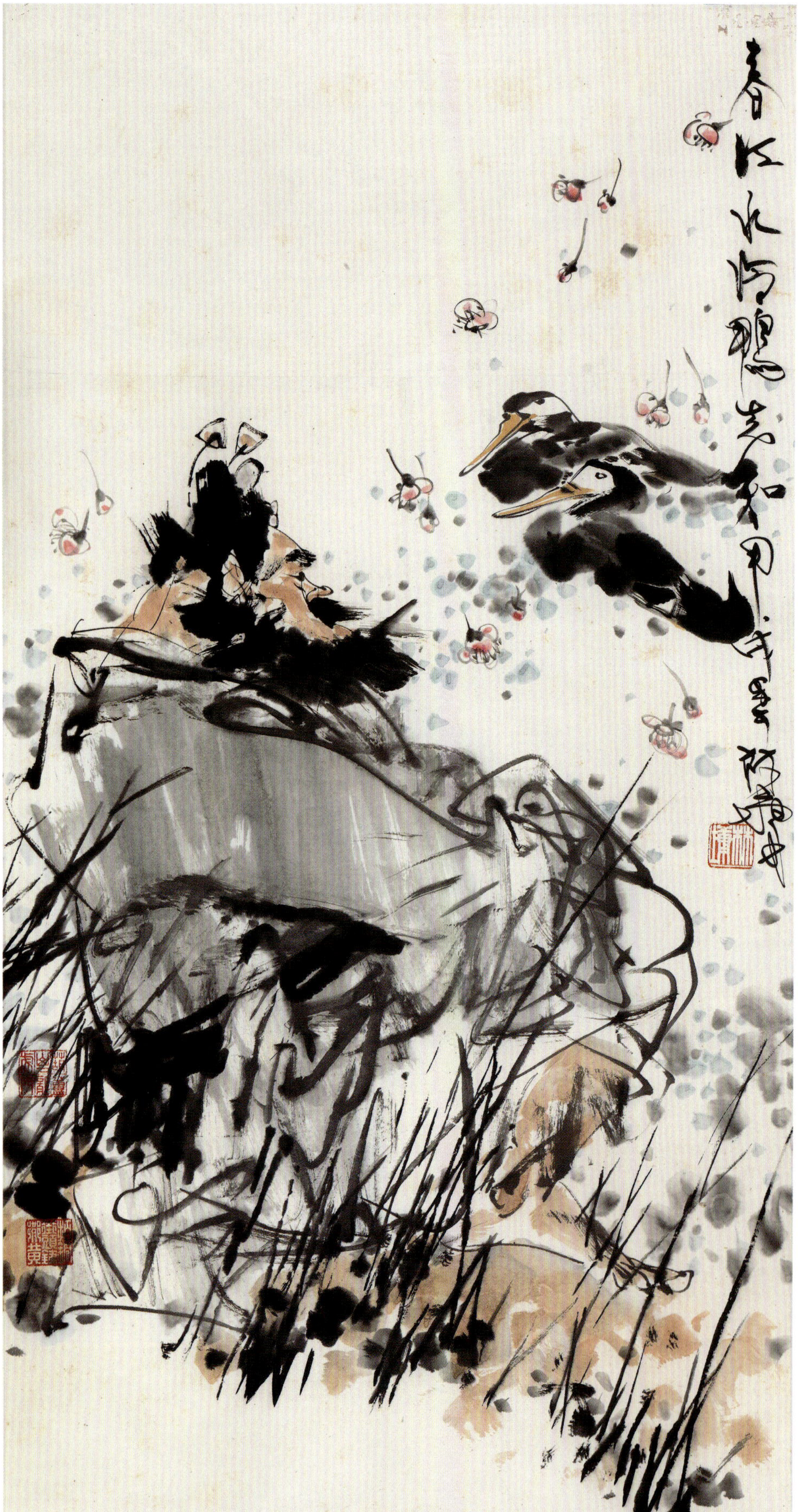

Artist:
Lin Yong

Medium:
Color on paper, Hanging scroll

Dimensions:
133.5 cm × 67.5 cm

Zhong Kui Watching Ducks

Inscription:
The duck knows first when the waters of the spring river grow cold. Created by Lin Yong in the spring of the Jiaxu year.

Seal:
Lin Yong, Under the Gourd Mountain by Dragon Tiger Gate, From the copper-beating street in the ironworking village, Huang

爆竹無聲便過年耳根
清靜亦欣然乾坤廣大容
我醉新喜黃花上鬢邊

戊寅新正試筆觀齋於榴堂

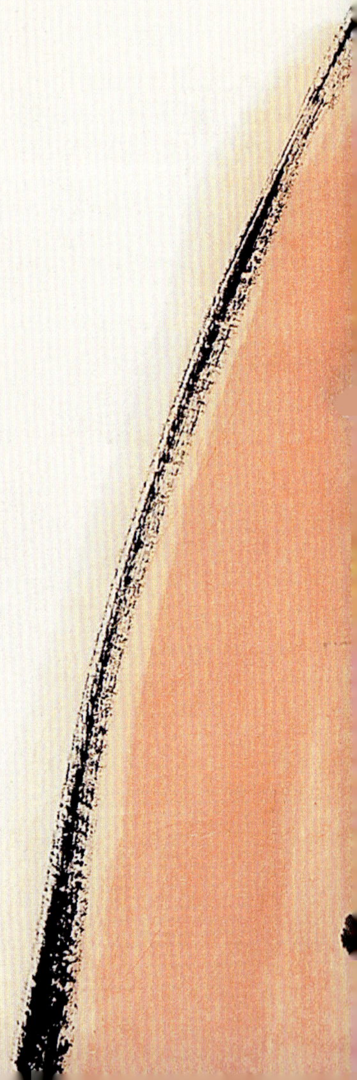

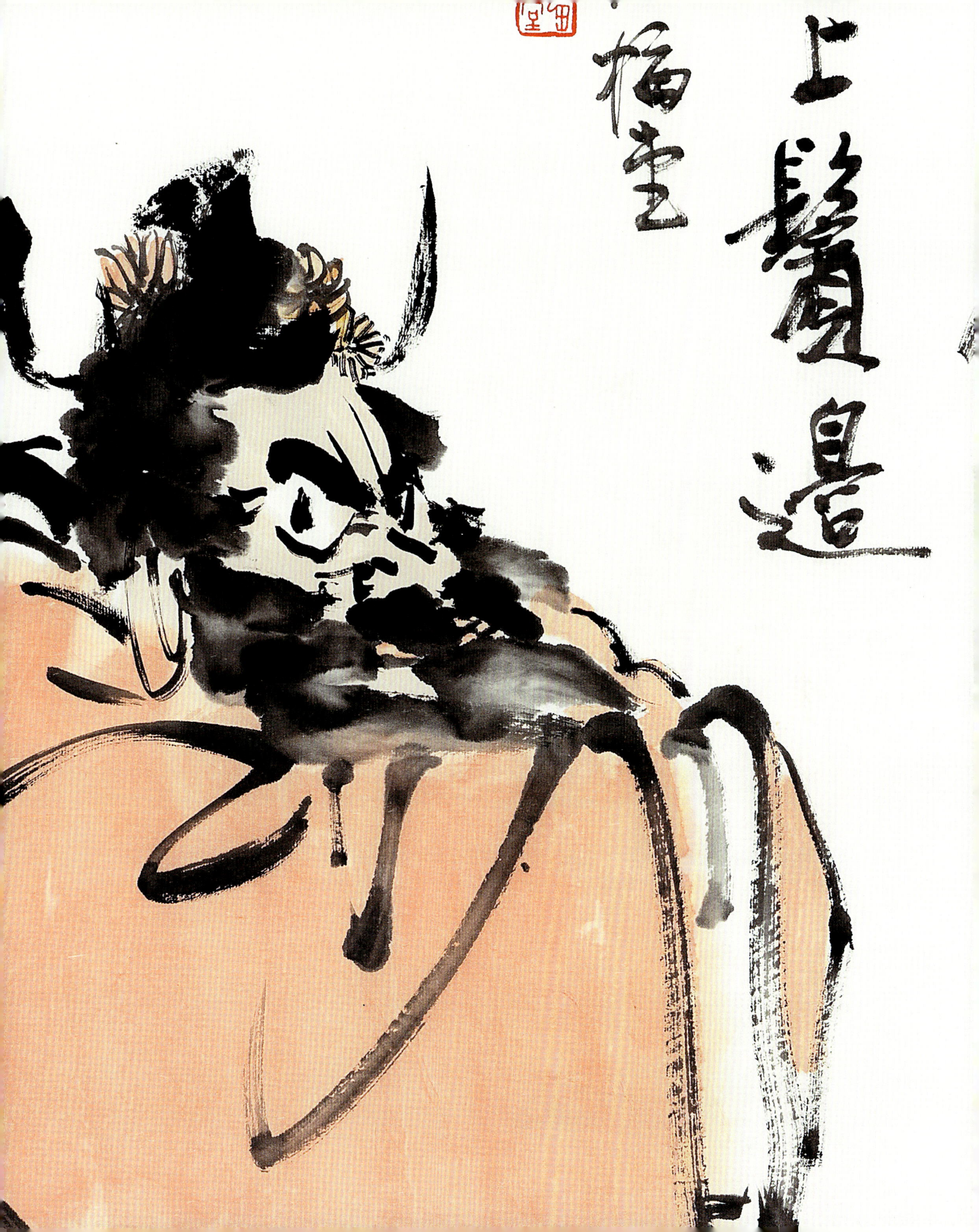

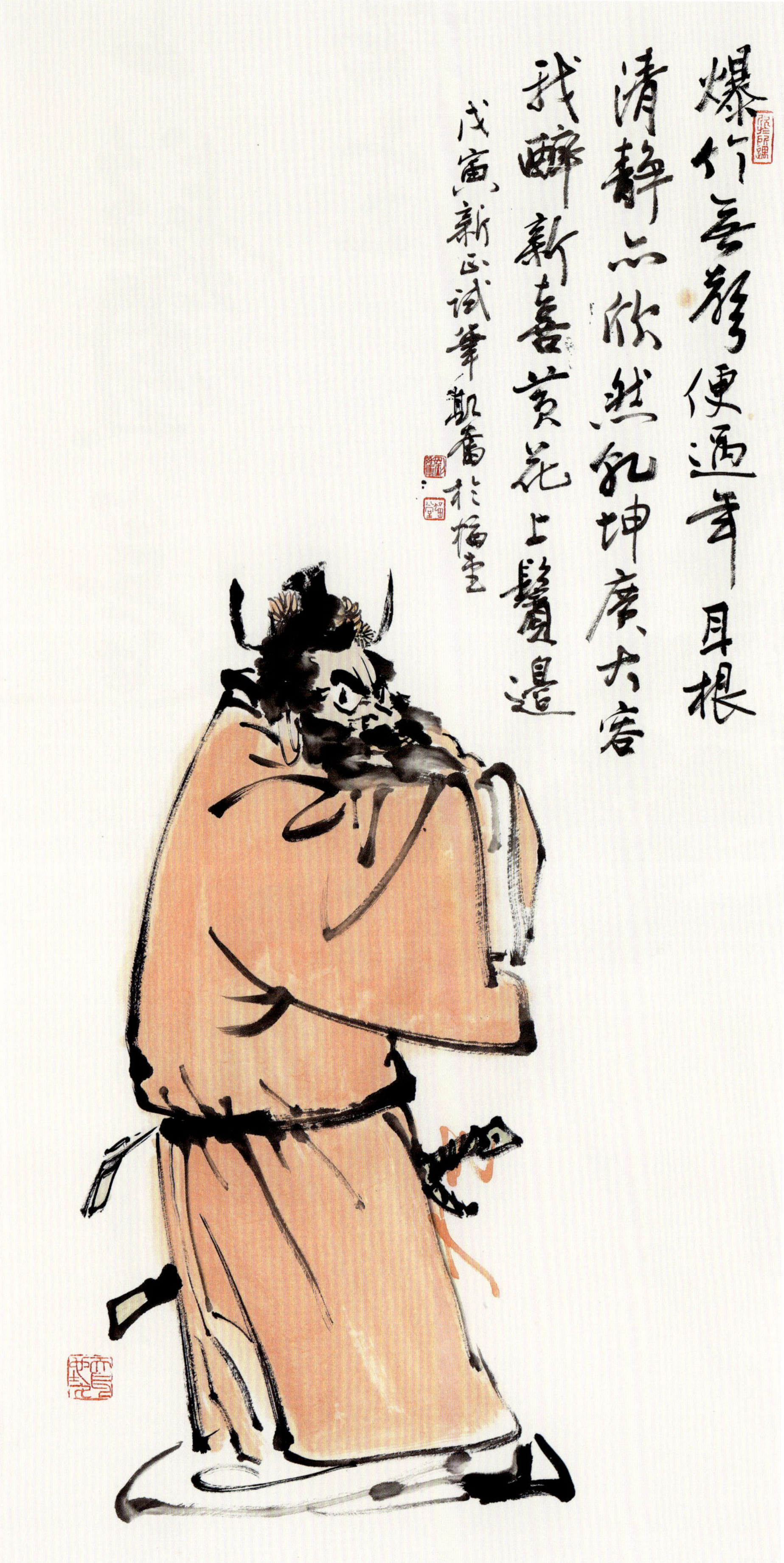

爆竹無聲便過年耳根
清靜亦欣然乾坤廣大容
我醉新喜黃花上鬢邊
戊寅新正試筆凱齋於福堂

Artist:
Liu Sifen

Medium:
Color on paper, Framed piece

Dimensions:
135 cm × 66 cm

Zhong Kui with Flowers in His Hair

Inscription:
Firecrackers silent, the New Year passes by,
Ears at peace, a joyous tranquility I find.
In this vast universe, there's room for my drunken sway,
Fresh joy adorns with golden blossoms gracing my temples' gray.
Testing the brush on the New Year of Wuyin, by Sifen at the Bat Hall.

Seal:
Liu Sifen, Bat Hall, Delighted with what one encounters

Liu Sifen (b. 1944)
Styled Bat Hall, a native of Zhongshan, Guangdong. He has served as the Chairman of the Guangdong Federation of Literary and Art Circles, President of the Guangdong Academy of Painting, a member of the China Writers Association, and a director of the China Artists Association.

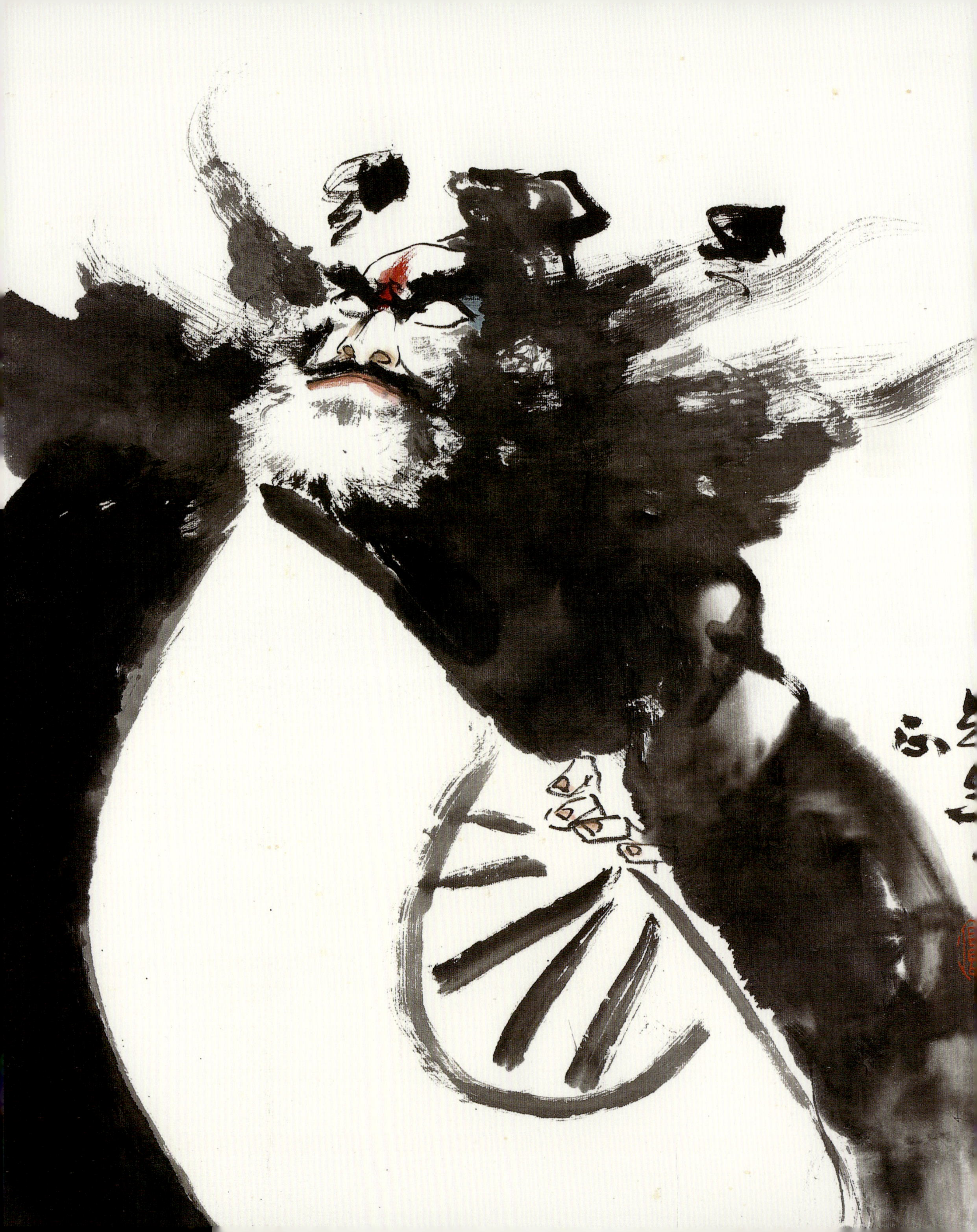

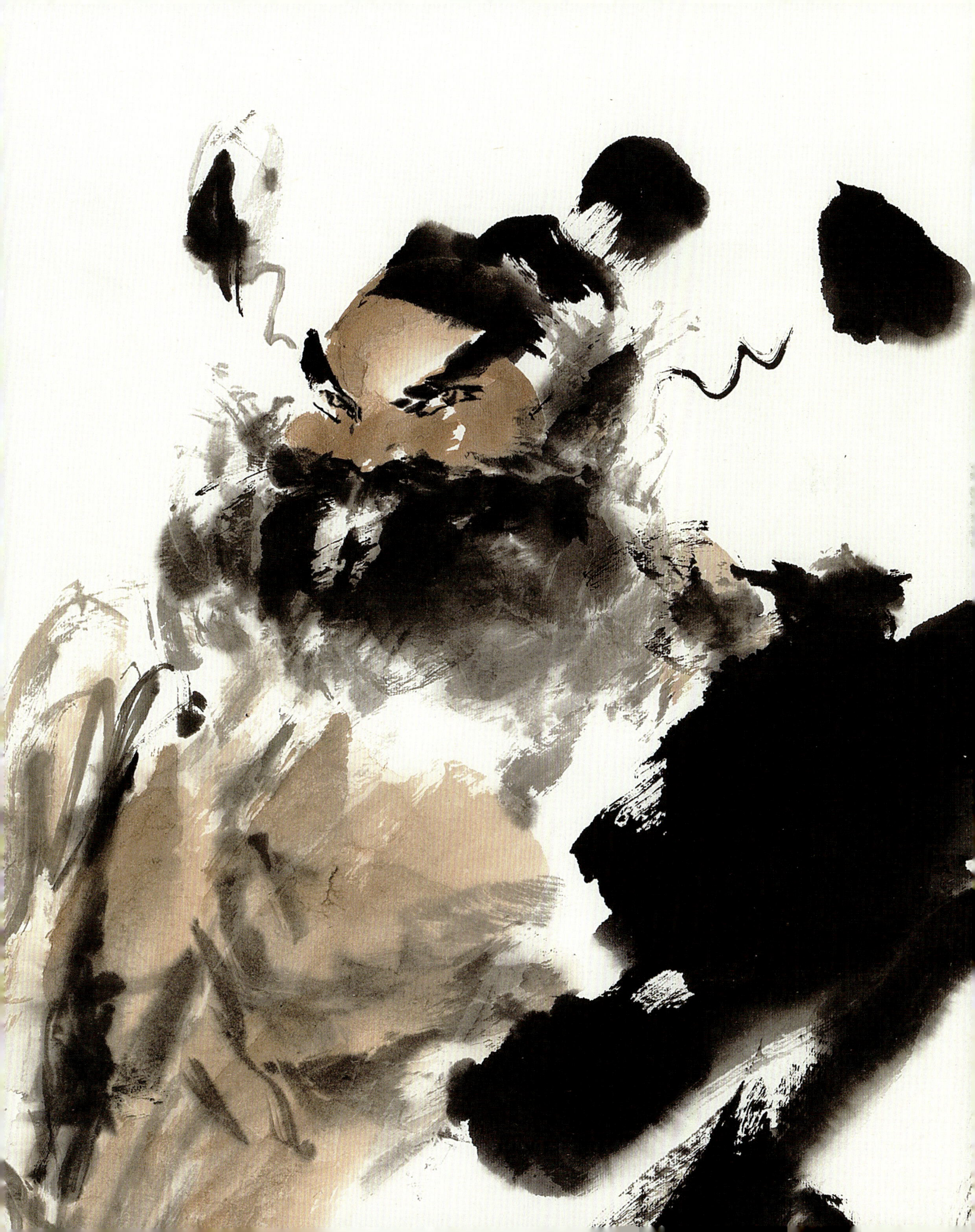

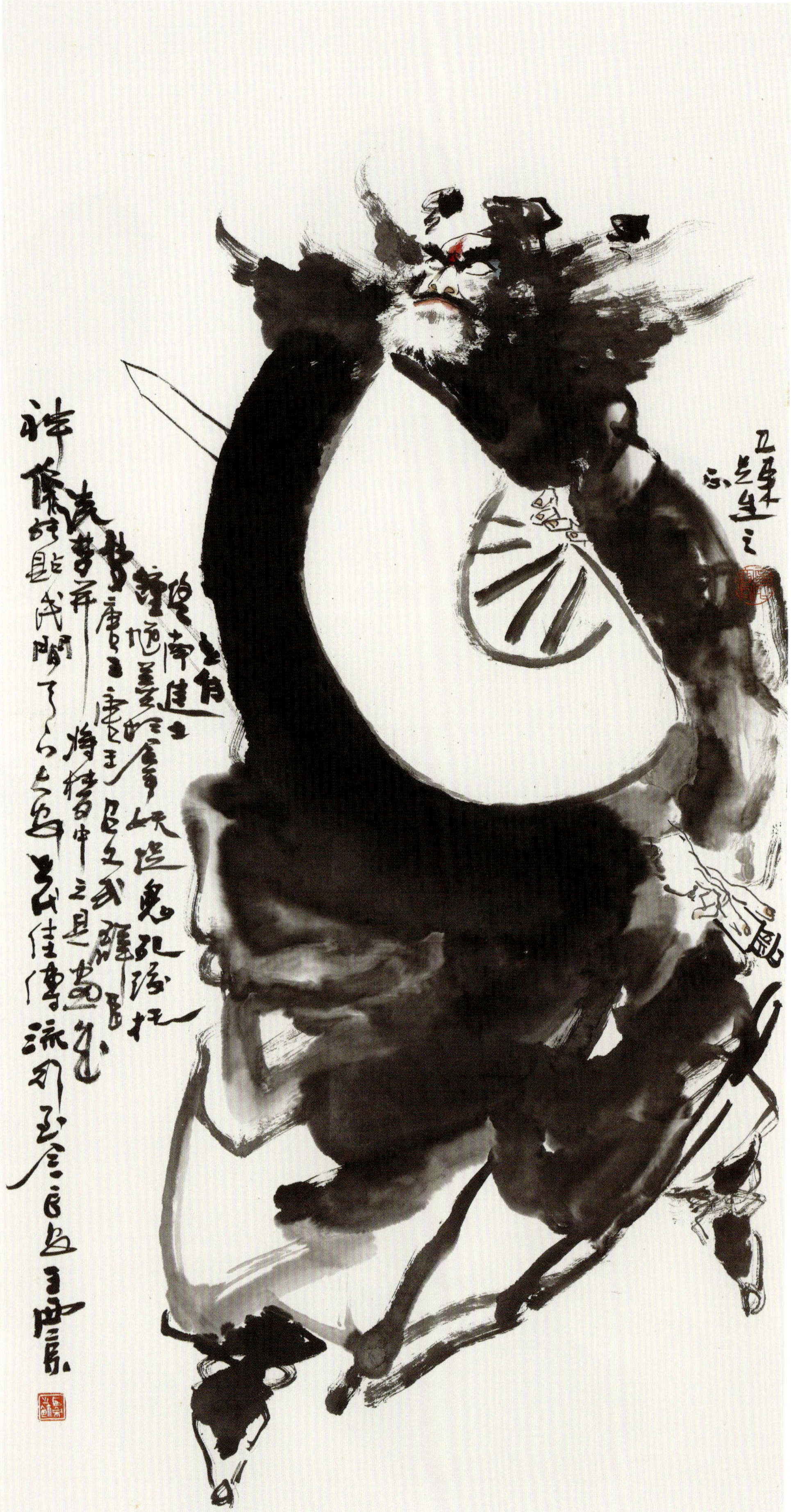

Artist:
Wang Xijing

Medium:
Ink on paper, Framed piece

Dimensions:
137 cm × 68 cm

Zhong Kui Welcoming Fortune

Inscription:
In the world, there exists Zhong Kui, the Jinshi from Zhongnan, known for capturing demons and ghosts. After his death, he appeared in a dream to the Tang Emperor. The Emperor summoned his ministers to discuss the dream and had the image seen in the dream painted as an icon. Spread among the people, it brought peace to the world. A fine tale passed down through generations, popular to this day. Created by Wang Xijing of Chang'an. Righted by Mr. Li Dong.

Seal:
The seal of Xijing, Impromptu

Wang Xijing (b. 1946)
A native of Xi'an. A painter and national first-class artist, he has held positions including Director of the China Artists Association, Member of the Chinese Painting Art Committee of the China Artists Association, Vice Chairman of the Shaanxi Federation of Literary and Art Circles, President of the Shaanxi Artists Association, President of the Xi'an Academy of Chinese Painting, and Chairman of the Xi'an Artists Association.

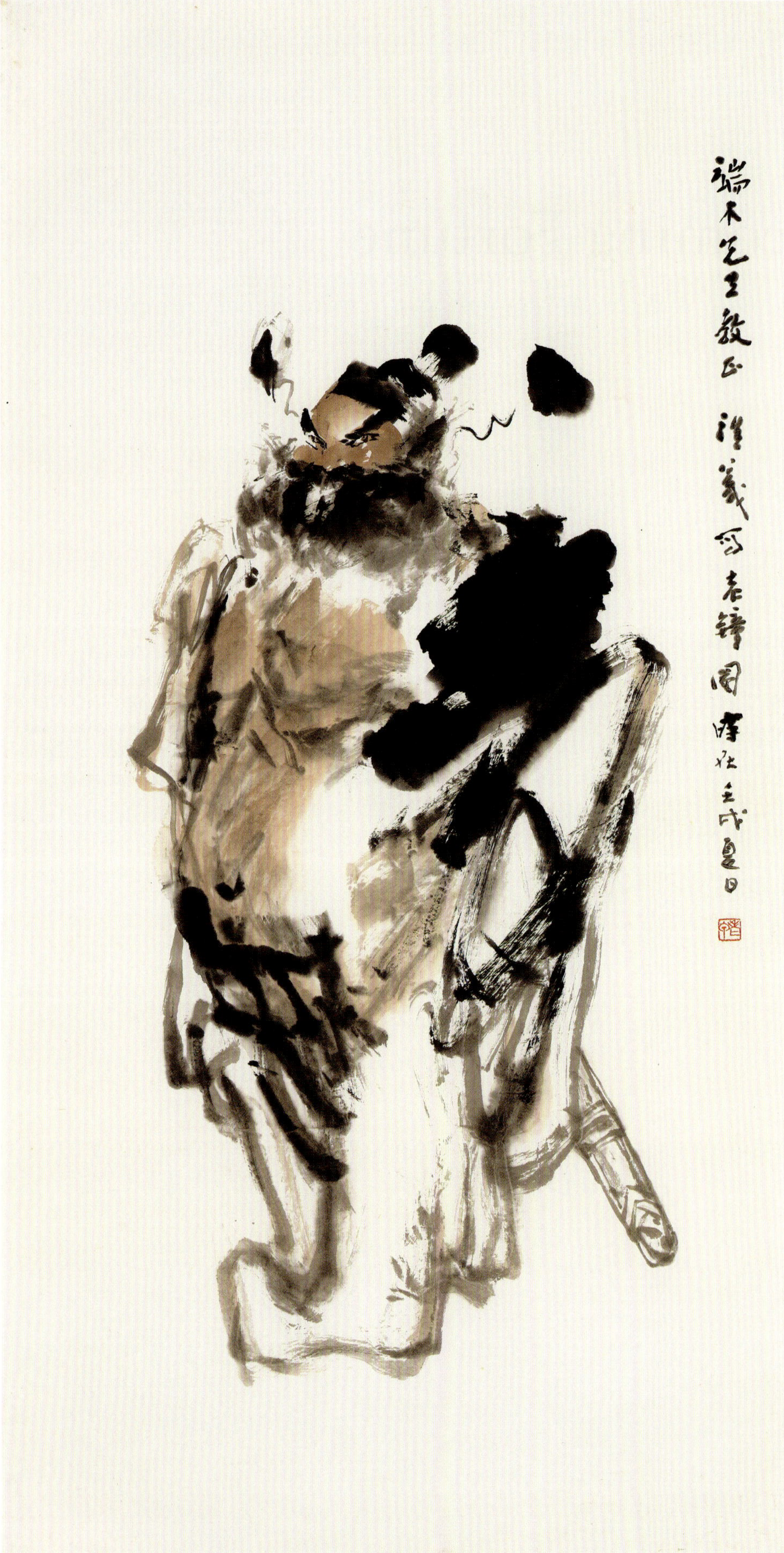

Artist:
Jia Haoyi

Medium:
Color on paper, Framed piece

Dimensions:
135 cm × 67 cm

Zhong Kui

Inscription:
Corrected by Mr. Duanmu, the depiction of old Zhong Kui was written by Haoyi on a summer day in the year of Renxu.

Seal:
Lao Jia

Jia Haoyi (1938–2022)
Also known as Lao Jia, a native of Zunhua, Hebei. A graduate of the Beijing Academy of Arts, he is a national first-class artist, a member of the China Artists Association, a researcher at the National Academy of Chinese Painting, a special researcher at the Art Creation Research Center of the Chinese National Academy of Arts, a member of the Arts Committee of the Central Academy of Culture and History, and the director of the Lao Jia Art Museum.

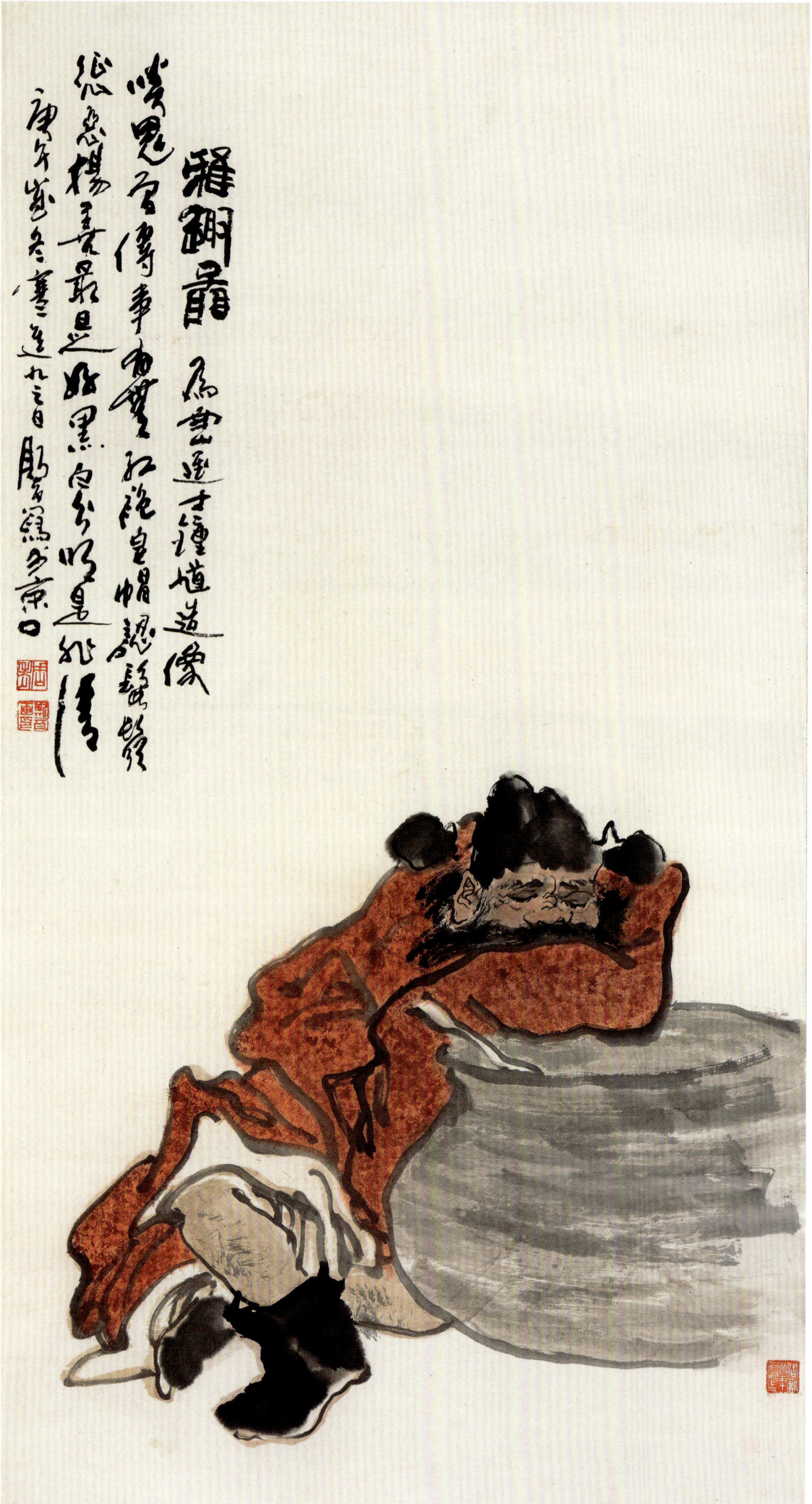

Artist:
Zhou Siyin

Medium:
Color on paper, Hanging scroll

Dimensions:
104.5 cm × 55.5 cm

Elegant Interests

Inscription:
A humorous depiction created for Tang Jinshi Zhong Kui. Debates of his ghost-eating tales, recognized by his red robe and black hat, beard and mustache. Best known for punishing evil and promoting good, his actions make the distinction between right and wrong clear. Written in Jingkou on a cold winter's day in the year of Gengwu, by Siyin.

Seal:
Zhou Lao, Siyin's painting seal, Works by Zhou Siyin after fifty

Zhou Siyin
Formerly the Deputy Director of the Zhenjiang Museum.

Compilation of Zhong Kui Resources

Zhong Kui is the name of a deity.

Qieyun

by Wang Renxu of the Tang Dynasty

The Taoist scripture speaks: At the grand gateway, the ghostly official is known as Dazhen Duke, while at the lesser portal, the ghostly official is called Xiaozhen Duke. The guardian of the chambers is named Yiwen, the guardian at the rear is Wanlun, the keeper at the kitchen gate is Yanjing, and the watcher over the paths is called Shigong. Along with these are various spirits, great and small, presiding over the fortune and calamity within the abode, and the spirits of men and women who have perished by water, fire, metal, and wood, each with their designated roles. Now, what spectre comes to afflict the living? In times of peril and distress, the Most High dispatches mighty warriors and red-armoured soldiers to slay myriads of ghosts. Armed with swords to bind the spectres, Zhong Kui triumphs in their slaying and delivers them to the abode of evil's banishment.

The Divine Incantations Scripture

by Du Guangting of the Five Dynasties

At the start of each new year, it has become customary for families to paste the image of Zhong Kui on their doors... Shen Cunzhong wrote in *Dream Pool Essays* that it is uncertain when this tradition began. During the Huangyou era, a grave was unearthed in Jinling containing a stele, which belonged to Lady Zheng, the mother of Zong Que from the Song of Southern dynasties. The inscription mentioned Lady Zheng's sister named Zhong Kui, leading some to speculate that the image of Zhong Kui may have ancient origins. Moreover, the Zhong Kui that Emperor Xuanzong of Tang dreamed of during his illness cannot be considered conclusive proof; it was simply a coincidence that Lady Zheng's sister shared the name, and it does not necessarily mean she was associated with that ghost-catching Zhong Kui. The trend of mutual imitation among contemporary households extends beyond this practice alone. But now, in the depictions of Zhong Kui, a female figure is also often included, referred to as Zhong Kui's little sister, a testament to the extent of the misinterpretation.

The Record of Affirmed Truths

by Zhao Shuxiang of the Song Dynasty

In recent festivals, the markets have been bustling with the sale of Door Gods, Zhong Kui, peach wood boards, taofu, as well as wealth-inviting dull donkeys, prosperity stone deer and horse, and Tianxing Script.
On New Year's Eve, a grand Nuo folk religion is held in the palace, with trusted officials from the Imperial City and guards from various departments donning masks, wearing colourful embroidered garments, and wielding golden spears and dragon banners. Meng Jingchu, the Commissioner of the Music Office, of imposing stature, is fully clad in gold-plated copper armour, assuming the role of a general. Two others, garbed in armour as well, portray the Door Gods. A grotesquely ugly and corpulent man from the Music Bureau is dressed as the judge. Additionally, characters such as Zhong Kui, his little sister, the Lord of the Land, the Kitchen God, and others, amounting to over a thousand people, proceed from the inner palace to exorcise malevolent spirits, marching out of the Nanxun Gate and around the Dragon Bend. This rite, known as the "Burying of Malevolence," marked the end of the ceremony.

The Eastern Capital: A Dream of Splendor

by Meng Yuanlao of the Southern Song Dynasty

Suddenly, a sound as loud as thunderclap, known as "exploding firecrackers," marked the retreat of those barbarian shield-bearers. Following this, fireworks were set off in grand fashion. Some individuals entered the stage with masks and dishevelled hair, spewing fireworks that resembled wolf teeth, appearing as ghastly deities. They wore short jackets embroidered with gold on green and gold-adorned black trousers, barefoot, each carrying a large brass gong[1], moving forwards and backwards in a dance, an act called "embracing the gong." They circled the arena several times, occasionally setting off fireworks on the ground. Another thunderous bang, and the musicians started playing a slow tune to pay homage to the crescent moon. Characters with faces painted in blue-green and gold-eyed masks, adorned with leopard skins and brocade sashes, were termed "stiff ghosts." Some brandished knives and axes, others hammers and clubs, assuming postures that mimicked the chasing and capturing of spirits. Yet another bang, and a figure with a masked, bearded face, draped in a green robe and carrying a whip and scrolls like the image of Zhong Kui, entered with an accompaniment of a small gong and dance steps, known as the "dance partner." This was followed by two or three gaunt individuals, coated in powder with golden eyes and white faces, resembling skeletons, dressed in brocade waistbands and carrying soft clubs. They made humorous gestures, running about, their actions like a rehearsal for a play, referred to as the "Mime Zaju."

The Eastern Capital: A Dream of Splendor

by Meng Yuanlao of the Southern Song Dynasty

With the New Year drawing near, merchants have displayed a variety of goods, creating and selling images of Door Gods and Taofu[2], along with banners to welcome spring. Shops specializing in paper horses feature prints of Zhong Kui, horses symbolizing wealth, and horses looking backwards, offered as gifts to customers. From this month onward, groups of impoverished individuals, typically in threes or fives, take to the streets. They impersonate deities, ghosts, judges, Zhong Kui, and his sister, beating drums and gongs, begging from door to door. This custom, commonly referred to as "Da Ye Hu," carries with it the intention of expelling evil spirits.
Families of all social standings sweep the streets clean before their doors, removing dust and dirt to cleanse their courtyards, replacing the images of Door Gods, hanging depictions of Zhong Kui, nailing up peach talismans, and affixing placards to welcome spring, all while paying homage to their ancestors. On New Year's Eve, the imperial palace hosts an elabourate exorcism ceremony, with officials from the imperial city donning masks and multi-coloured embroidered attire, brandishing golden spears, silver halberds, patterned wooden swords, and banners of multicoloured dragons and phoenixes. Entertainers, soldiers, talisman officers, judges, Zhong Kui, the Six Ding, divine soldiers, emissaries of the five directions, the Kitchen God, the Lord of the Land, Door Gods, and other deities are invoked, with drums and wind instruments playing within the palace, expelling malevolent spirits all the way out of the Donghua Gate, circling the Dragon Pond, concluding with the "Burying of Malevolence" ritual.

Dreams of a Millet Dream

by Wu Zimu of the Southern Song Dynasty

---

[1] A traditional percussion instrument in China

[2] Peach wood charms..

Since October, within the capital's Chaotian Gate, there has been a bustling trade of various brocades, new calendars, a range of door god paintings both large and small, peach talismans, Zhong Kui, mythical creatures such as suangi[3], tiger heads, along with gold-threaded flowers, spring festival stickers, and colourful banners, making for a thriving market. On the thirtieth day, the night of the grand festival, there are performances of young girls exorcising evil spirits through ritual dances, depicting Taoist protective deities such as the Six Ding, the Six Jia[4], and various other gods, largely as described in *The Eastern Capital: A Dream of Splendor*.

Tales of Lin'an
by Zhou Mi of the Southern Song Dynasty

The ancient people placed great importance on the Nuo ritual for expelling epidemics, a practice upheld from the Han through to the Tang Dynasty, even within the imperial palace and forbidden precincts, with over a thousand children participating. As expressed in Wang Jian's poem: "On New Year's Eve, the Jinwu Guards present the names for the Nuo ritual, as figures in painted trousers and red robes march in four columns." However, such practices are no longer found even among the common folk today, and only the traditions of painting Zhong Kui and setting off firecrackers remain.

Miscellany of Five Assorted Offerings
by Xie Zhaozhe of the Ming Dynasty

The common belief that Zhong Kui (钟馗) originated from a dream of Emperor Xuanzong of Tang is incorrect. In fact, Tang people invented stories about Zhong Kui, fabricating them just as they did with fictional characters like Mao Ying and Tao Hong. According to the *History of the Northern Dynasties,* there was a man named Yao Xuan, whose real name was Zhong Kui (钟葵), courtesy name Bi Xie. Later generations depicted Zhong Kui (钟葵) on doors as a charm against evil, hence the association. In the Song Dynasty, Zong Que's sister was named Zhong Kui (钟葵), and subsequent painters created works of Zhong Kui's (钟馗) sister getting married, leading to another association. However, the characters Kui (葵) and Kui (馗) in their names are different. Additionally, Zhong Kui (终葵) refers to a type of vegetable. In *Rites of Zhou, Office of Winter*, it is said that the top of Da Kui (大圭) resembles Zhong Kui (终葵). The commentary explains that Zhong Kui (终葵) means a mallet, and in the region of Qi, a mallet was referred to as Zhong Kui (终葵). In the *Book of Rites, Yu Zao,* it is noted that the son of heaven holds a sceptre. The commentary indicates that this sceptre, also called Da Kui (大圭), is three feet long with a widened top resembling a mallet head, signifying that it is unbending and straight.

The Compendium of Cinnabar and Lead Annotations
by Yang Shen of the Ming Dynasty

The Rites of Zhou, Office of Winter states that the top of Da Kui (大圭) resembles Zhong Kui (终葵). The annotation clarifies that Zhong Kui means mallet is named by the people of Qi as Zhong Kui (终葵), suggesting the head of Da Kui (大圭) is similar to a mallet. The Record of Metal and Stone indicates that during the Jin and Song dynasties, the name Zhong Kui (终葵) was used and later became erroneously known as Zhong Kui (钟馗). Folk artists commonly affix images of a deity to the top of doors, where he is depicted wielding a mallet to strike ghosts. Those who are fond of the supernatural then add their own interpretations, claiming that Zhong Kui (钟馗) has the power to devour ghosts. Artists also created paintings of the New Year's Eve excursion of Zhong Kui (钟馗) and Zhong Kui's (钟馗) marrying off his sister, further distorting the truth. Literary figures whimsically created The Legend of Zhong Kui (钟馗), claiming he was a Jinshi from the Kaiyuan era, whom Emperor Xuanzong of Tang dreamed of and commissioned a portrait, an entirely baseless story. The collections by Sun Di and Zhang Shuo contain the *Acknowledgment for the Imperial Bestowal of Zhong Kui Painting and the Calendar*, which predates the Kaiyuan era by a significant period. It is similar to the name "Shi Gandang" found in *Jijiupian*—both are names without actual historical figures behind them. Common people set up stones at their doors inscribed with "Shi Gandang of Mount Tai," and literati even composed tales of Shi Gandang, which were mere fabrications and playful fiction. Over time, these fabrications were transmitted among the folk, and eventually, people came to believe in their real existence.

Notes from the Shaoshi Mountain Studio
by Hu Yinglin of the Ming Dynasty

The name Zhong Kui is believed to have originated during the Six Dynasties. In tradition, names of deities and spirits are often enigmatic and beyond inquiry. People have always sought the origins of such names to affirm their authenticity; if not fabricated, they were later rationalized. Tales of Zhong Kui (钟馗) predate the Six Dynasties, with longstanding legends of his ghost-catching. Yao Xuan was originally named Zhong Kui (钟葵), and Zong Que's sister was also named Zhong Kui (钟馗), both named after spiritual entities. Hence, Yao Xuan's appellation, Zhong Kui (钟葵) with the courtesy name Bi Xie, was derived from the belief in Zhong Kui's (钟馗) power to expel evil. Later generations, unable to trace Zhong Kui's (钟馗) origins and seeing Yao Xuan's name Zhong Kui (钟葵) with the courtesy name Bi Xie, mistakenly attributed his origin to this, a clearly far-fetched connection. Continuing to read Long Shu's *Pure Land Texts*, there was a Tang individual named Zhang Zhongkui (钟馗), possibly also a namesake of the deity, akin to Yao Xuan and Zong Que's sister, whose corroborative presence bolsters my confidence that what I have observed is not fabricated.

Notes from the Shaoshi Mountain Studio
by Hu Yinglin of the Ming Dynasty

The *Rites of Zhou, Office of Winter* mentions that the top of Da Kui (大圭) resembles Zhong Kui (终葵). The annotation explains that Zhong Kui (终葵) is also known as a mallet. In *The Correct Rhymes of the Hongwu Era* as Kui (葵), which may also be written as Kui (揆). *Yangzi's Chalice Words* suggest that even if the error regarding Zhong Kui (馗) originated here, there seems to be no concrete evidence. If one were to argue based on phonetic similarity, then the *Zuo Zhuan* mentions the Zhong Kui (终葵) clan, and *Erya, Shicao* lists both Zhong Kui (终葵) and Zhong Kui (中馗) as names of grasses — surely these cannot be twisted as proof? Some say Zhong Kui (馗) should be written as Zhong Kui (终夔), implying an ultimate, exhaustive meaning as in the lexicon of the Chinese character classification. In ancient texts, Kui (夔) is sometimes written as Kui (馗), and the *Jiyun* dictionary clarifies that the characters Kui (馗), Kui (夔), Kui (逵), and Kui (匮) are interchangeable. Kui (夔) refers to a mountain spirit, the strange beings of earth and stone mentioned in the *Annals of Confucius and His Descendants*. Kui (夔) also denotes mythical creatures

[3] Originally referring to a lion and later known as one of the nine sons of the dragon, is a mythical creature often depicted in ancient Chinese literature.

[4] Gods who safeguard immortals and followers, overseeing the good and evil of the human world.

like Mōryō. Named Zhong Kui (终夔) for his role in subduing evil spirits, this too is speculative. If so, using Zhong Kui (钟馗) would also be acceptable since Zhong (钟) conveys a sense of gathering, so why change Zhong (钟) to Zhong (终)? Folk paintings depict Zhong Kui (钟馗) wielding a ghost to protect the home, and *Peiwen Yunfu* states that Zhong Kui (钟馗) is not a ghost's name.

Notes from the Shaoshi Mountain Studio
by Hu Yinglin of the Ming Dynasty, as quoted by Chen Xinshu

In *Rites of Zhou, Office of Winter,* a Da Kui (大圭) is recorded to be three chi[5] long, with a Zhong Kui (终葵) at its shuttle's end (original note: Zhong Kui (终葵), which is also a mallet, symbolizing the straight and unbending top of the shuttle). Similarly, in the Book of *Rites, Yu Zao* mentions Zhong Kui (终葵) as a mallet. *Fangyan* records that people from Qi referred to a mallet as Zhong Kui (终葵). In Ma Rong's *Ode to Guangcheng*, he writes of "wielding the Zhong Kui (终葵), akin to hoisting the guardian's axe high" (original note: "Zhong Kui" (终葵) is being used in a cultured manner). The ancients used mallets to drive away ghosts, similar to grand exorcism rituals. Nowadays, people paint images of Zhong Kui on doors, who was said to be a ghost catcher seen in Emperor Xuanzong's dream, although this account in *Supplementary Discourses to the Dream Pool Essays* is debated (original note: *The History of the Five Dynasties: The House of Wu-Yue* depicts artists offering paintings of Zhong Kui fighting ghosts on New Year's Eve). The *Book of Wei* records that Yao Xuan's original name was Zhong Kui (钟葵), courtesy name Bi Xie, signifying the ancient practice of using Zhong Kui (钟馗) as a talisman against evil. There were also figures like the son of Wang Tuo in Huainan named Zhong Kui (钟葵), Yang Zhongkui (钟葵), Qiu Zhongkui (钟馗), Li Zhongkui (钟馗), Murong Zhongkui (钟馗), and Qiao Zhongkui (钟馗) (original note: in the *History of the Northern Dynasties*, the *Biography of the Sui Commoner Liang* refers to him as Qiao Zhongkui (终葵); however, at the end of the *Biography of En'xing* mentions Gong Zhongkui (钟馗), with the character "Kui" (馗) presented in two forms. Yet, in the Biography of Yang Yichen, the name remains Qiao Zhongkui (终葵). Others include Duan Zhongkui (钟葵), Yu Jin's courtesy name Zhongkui (钟葵), and Zhang Zize originally named Zhongkui (钟葵). In *The Book of Tang*, General Zhang Zhongkui (钟葵) under Wang Wujun is recorded (original note: in *Zizhi Tongjian* as Zhong Kui (钟馗). The prevalence of this name suggests either an association with its form or its meaning of exorcising evil. In the *Zuo Zhuan*, during the fourth year of Duke Ding's reign, it is recorded that the Yin people were divided into seven clans, including the Zhong Kui (终葵) clan. However, the rationale behind this particular naming remains unclear.

Daily Knowledge Record
by Gu Yanwu of the Qing Dynasty

Yongxiu (Yang Shen)'s account, compared to that of Renbao (Lang Ying), provides a more detailed explanation that the name Zhong Kui is indeed an error arising from Yao's character Zhong Kui (终葵) for "Bi Xie," which has its reasons. As for how the Zhong Kui (终葵) of Da Kui (大圭) transformed into the personal name Zhong Kui (终葵), its significance is not seen. Gu Ning cites Ma Rong's *Ode to Guangcheng*: "Wielding the Zhong Kui (终葵), as if lifting a jade axe," which refers to the ancient practice of using a mallet to chase away spirits, akin to brandishing spears and shields in grand exorcism rituals. This explanation is closer to the truth. Originally, Zhong Kui (终葵) was used to chase away spirits, and due to its function of warding off evil, it was later adopted as a personal name. Over time, its original meaning as an object to ward off evil was forgotten, and it was mistaken for a person who chased ghosts, leading to the belief that there was actually a person with the surname Zhong and given name Kui who consumed ghosts.

Various Investigations from My Remaining Collection
by Zhao Yi of the Qing Dynasty

Beggars are clad in tattered armor, impersonating Zhong Kui, and dance along doorways to drive away spirits. This tradition commences at the start of each month and culminates on New Year's Eve, known as "Zhong Kui Dance"… Inside the hall, a painting of Zhong Kui is displayed for a month to banish malevolent spirits and spectres.

Record of Qingjia
by Gu Lu of the Qing Dynasty

In *Records of Local Customs* by Xueting from our family, the attire for those embodying Zhong Kui and judges, styled after the Fang Xiang clan, involves donning bear skins, wearing four golden eyes, and wielding halberds and shields. This practice is rooted in ancient rites aimed at expelling the residual miasma of epidemics from homes.

Record of Qingjia
annotated by Gu Lu of the Qing Dynasty

Each Dragon Boat Festival, shops in the market cover sheets of yellow paper with vermillion seals, some adorned with images of the Taoist Master Zhong Kui, others with talismans depicting the five poisonous creatures. These images are hung for sale, and the citizens of the capital vie to purchase them, affixing them to their central doors as a ward against calamities and malevolence.

Annals of Beijing's Seasonal Customs
by Fucha Dunchong of the Qing Dynasty

Your humble servant has received the imperial envoy with the sacred edict, bestowing upon me a painting of Zhong Kui and a scroll of the new calendar. Such an honour has descended upon an insignificant individual like myself, bringing glory to my private abode. I hereby express my deepest gratitude. In this new era of celestial cycles and harmonious seasons, all nations celebrate the joyous occasion, and even the heavens are steeped in the grace of dew. This grace has also been extended to a lowly servant like me, receiving such a distinct gift. I will hang this painting to expel evil spirits and maintain peace at home. At the appropriate time, I will unfurl the calendar scroll and respectfully study it. By nature, I am but a simple scholar, ill-suited for my post, yet the Holy Majesty, in his mercy, has placed his trust in me, burdening me with honour and a sense of unworthiness. I am filled with shame for my deficiencies and awe for the imperial grace. Never would I have imagined such light to shine upon me, to be counted among the meritorious and the noble. The bestowed honour is cherished, and with deep gratitude, I hold it as dear as life itself.

Acknowledgement for the Imperial Bestowal of Zhong Kui Painting and the Calendar
by Zhang Shuo of the Tang Dynasty

---

[5] The Chinese "chi" (尺) is an ancient unit of length. Traditionally, it was considered equivalent to the width of an average person's thumb at the knuckle, while modern measurements equate it to approximately one-third of a meter or roughly one foot.

Your humble servant hereby reports: A distinguished official of high rank delivered the holy imperial command, gracing me with a painting of Zhong Kui and a scroll of the new calendar. As the celestial cycle renews, even at the twilight of the year, such a radiant favour has abruptly been bestowed, making it feel as if spring has arrived. I am deeply thankful for this esteemed honour. With the painting, I shall ward off malevolent forces, and with the calendar, I shall dutifully mark the passage of time. This not only enhances the distinction of my household but also serves as a cherished treasure, constantly held in esteem. In beholding and seeking, all can see the sanctity of the grace, a sentiment I wear with utmost joy and reverence.

Acknowledgement to Duke Du of Huainan for the Imperial Bestowal of the Zhong Kui Calendar
by Liu Yuxi of the Tang Dynasty

The imperial palace has long possessed a painting of Zhong Kui by Wu Daozi, prefaced with an inscription by a Tang dynasty individual that reads: "Emperor Xuanzong of Tang, during his martial exercises at Li Mountain in the open year, returned to the palace by the end of the year feeling discontent and subsequently fell ill. As the illness persisted for nearly a month, no physician or sorcerer could bring about a recovery. One night, he dreamt of two ghosts, one large and one small. The smaller one, with a red calf's nose, wore one shoe and was barefoot with the other, carrying the spare shoe, and stealing Yang Guifei's purple sachet and the Emperor's jade flute while running around the palace. The larger ghost, in a hat and blue robe with one arm bare and both feet shod, caught the smaller one, gouged out its eyes, then tore it apart to devour. The Emperor inquired who the larger ghost was, to which it replied: 'I am Zhong Kui, a man who failed the military examinations but swore to rid the world of demons for Your Majesty.' Upon awakening, the Emperor found his illness had miraculously improved, and his vigour renewed. He then commanded the painter Wu Daozi to depict the scene from his dream, saying: 'Try to paint for me as seen in the dream.' Wu Daozi followed the decree, and as if having witnessed it himself, quickly completed the painting and presented it. The Emperor, gazing at it intently, said: 'It's as if you shared the dream with me. How strikingly similar it is!' Wu Daozi approached and said: 'Your Majesty, your constant labours day and night, often at the expense of meals, brought on the illness. If evil spirits were indeed dispelled, it was to protect Your Sacred Virtue.' Then, dancing, he wished the Emperor tens of thousands of years of life. The Emperor, overjoyed, rewarded him with a hundred gold pieces and decreed: 'The divine spirit responded in a dream, and the affliction was completely cured. A valiant man who expels demons truly deserves commendation. Since the painting is extraordinary, let it be shown to the officials. Used at the year's end to drive away evil, it should be easily recognized. To remove demonic influences and calm the malevolent atmosphere. Let it be known throughout the land, and let all be informed.' In the fifth year of Xining, the Emperor ordered the painting to be replicated and engraved on printing plates, and printed copies were bestowed upon each of the ministers of the two bureaus. That year on New Year's Eve, the imperial officer Liang Kai was sent to the eastern and western bureaus to distribute the images of Zhong Kui." Reading this inscription, it seems that the tradition of depicting Zhong Kui began during the Kaiyuan period. During the Huangyou years, a tomb was unearthed in Jinling's Shangyuan County, containing a stele for the tomb of Lady Zheng, mother of the general Zong Que of Song of the Southern dynasties. Lady Zheng was the daughter of Zheng Zhong, a Minister of Finance of the Han dynasty. Zong Que had a sister named Zhong Kui. There were individuals named Li Zhongkui during the Later Wei dynasty, and generals named Qiao Zhongkui and Yang Zhongkui during the Sui dynasty. Therefore, the name Zhong Kui has long existed, not originating from the Kaiyuan period; it was only during Kaiyuan that paintings of Zhong Kui began. The character for 'Zhong Kui (钟馗)' is sometimes also written as 'Zhong Kui (钟葵)'."

Supplementary Discourses to the Dream Pool Essays, Volume 3
by Shen Kuo of the Song Dynasty

In the depiction of Zhong Kui, the ancient painter Wu Daozi portrayed him in a blue robe, standing on one foot, with one squinting eye, a command tablet at his waist, and dishevelled hair, seizing a demon with his left hand and gouging out its eyes with his right. The brushwork was vigorous and powerful, truly a masterpiece of painting. When someone presented this painting to the ruler of Shu, he greatly treasured it, often hanging it in his bedroom. One day, the ruler summoned the artist Huang Quan to appreciate the painting. Upon seeing it, Huang Quan immediately praised its brilliance. The ruler then suggested, "If Zhong Kui were to pinch the demon's eye with his thumb, it would appear even more forceful. Try modifying it for me." Huang Quan took the painting back to his quarters, and after several days, feeling hesitant to alter the original, he instead painted a new Zhong Kui on a fresh silk canvas, indeed pinching the demon's eye with the thumb. The next day, he presented both the original and the new painting to the ruler. The ruler asked, "I asked for a modification, why did you paint a new one?" Huang Quan replied, "The strength of the entire body, the aura, and the expression in Wu Daozi's Zhong Kui were all concentrated in the second finger, not the thumb, thus I dared not change it rashly. Although my painting cannot compare to that of the ancient masters, the strength of the whole body is focused on the thumb, hence I dared to paint anew." The ruler of Shu, impressed and appreciative, rewarded him with rich brocades and precious vessels, recognizing his originality.

Records of Picture Seeing and Hearing
by Guo Ruoxu of the Song Dynasty

Huang Quan, known as Yaoshu from Chengdu, was famed for his painting from an early age. At seventeen, he became an attendant to the Houzhu of Former Shu (the last lord of Former Shu), Wang Yan. Advancing through the ranks, he was appointed as the Inspector of the Imperial Treasury under Meng Chang and later became a vice official in the capital. Wang Yan once summoned Huang Quan to observe Wu Daozi's depiction of Zhong Kui, and remarked, "In Wu Daozi's painting, Zhong Kui gouges the ghost's eye with the second finger of the right hand. It would appear more forceful if the thumb were used instead." He instructed Huang Quan to make this alteration. However, Huang Quan did not alter Daozi's original but instead submitted a new painting where Zhong Kui used his thumb to gouge the ghost's eye. Surprised by the unexpected submission, Wang Yan questioned him. Huang Quan responded, "In Master Daozi's painting, the essence and intent are captured in the second finger. In my painting, they are captured in the thumb." Wang Yan was pleased, acknowledging that Huang Quan's brushstrokes were not made in vain.

Xuanhe Painting Catalog
by the Song Dynasty

Yang Fei, a native of the capital, travelled through Jiangsu and Zhejiang, eventually settling in the regions of the Huai and Yangtze rivers. He excelled in painting Buddhist scriptures, studying under the style of Wu Daozi, and was capable of creating large Buddhist images. Once, at the Puzhao Temple on the banks of the Si River, he painted *The Two Deities*, towering over three zhang[6] in height, with a robust and imposing quality that commanded awe. His depiction of Zhong Kui was also skillful. Though many recent artists have depicted Zhong Kui, the original source is debated. Some say, "Emperor Xuanzong, suffering from malaria, dreamt of Zhong Kui dancing before him, banishing the disease. Subsequently, his likeness was transcribed and came to be known in the world, marking the origin of Zhong Kui's image. Over time, though the portrayals underwent minor transformations, the general depiction remained consistent, with variations only in how the Danqing artists chose to adorn it." Another account mentions, "An ancient stele from the Six Dynasties was once found among ruins and tombs, bearing the name Zhong Kui, suggesting that the character did not originate from the Kaiyuan period." But no definitive evidence confirms this. Presently, the imperial collection includes two: a standing Guanyin and a portrait of Zhong Kui.

Xuanhe Painting Catalog
by the Song Dynasty

During the Kaiyuan era, Emperor Xuanzong of Tang, suffering from illness and residing in his chamber, dreamt of a mischievous ghost clad in one shoe, the other hanging at its waist, stealing Yang Guifei's purple sachet and tooting on a jade flute, causing a raucous disturbance. The Emperor admonished it, and the ghost responded, "I am a spirit of depletion." The Emperor, irate and on the verge of summoning his warriors, beheld a larger ghost, clad in a blue robe with a tattered hat and girdled belt, who promptly seized and blinded the smaller ghost before devouring it. Inquiring about the identity of this formidable spectre, the response came: "I am Zhong Kui, a Jinshi from Zhongnan Mountain. I died after failing the imperial exams, tripping over the palace steps. By imperial decree, I was buried in a green robe and vowed to rid the world of prodigal and malevolent spirits." Upon awakening, the Emperor found his malady miraculously cured. He thus commanded the master painter Wu Daozi to depict the vision. Marvelling at the painting's divine quality, he awarded Daozi a hundred gold pieces, setting a precedent for people to hang Zhong Kui's image on their doors for protection.

Records of the Origins of Matters and Things
by Gao Cheng of the Northern Song Dynasty

During the Kaiyuan era, Emperor Xuanzong of Tang, disheartened after martial exercises at Li Mountain, became ill and dreamt by day of a little ghost, with a red nose and one foot bare, the other shod, and an extra shoe dangling from its waist. The impish spirit, wielding a large fan, had stolen Yang Guifei's purple sachet and the Emperor's jade flute, playfully darting before the palace. Upon being rebuked by the Emperor, the small ghost replied, "I am but a spirit of depletion." The Emperor said, "I have not heard of such a spirit." The ghost explained, "As 'depletion,' I steal frivolously as if it's a game, turning joy into sorrow in people's homes." The Emperor was enraged and called for guards. suddenly, a larger ghost appeared, in a ragged hat and blue robe, wearing court shoes. It seized the smaller one, gouging out its eyes before consuming it. When asked its name, it declared, "I am Zhong Kui, a Jinshi of Zhongnan Mountain. Ashamed after failing the exams during the Wude era, I tripped on the palace steps and died. Buried in a green robe by imperial decree, I swore to help Our Majesty eradicate such spectres." Upon awakening, the Emperor's sickness miraculously abated. He commanded the artist Wu Daozi to paint this dream vision. Following the order as if he had witnessed it himself, Daozi completed the painting swiftly and presented it. The Emperor, observing it for a long time, exclaimed, "This is as if you shared my dream!" He then rewarded Daozi with a hundred pieces of gold.

Tianzhong Records
by Chen Yaowen of the Ming Dynasty

During the Tang Dynasty, Wu Daozi created the "Zhong Kui Entering the Palace" painting, while Zhang Wo depicted "Zhong Kui Holding Hu." From the Five Dynasties, Mou Yuande is known for the "Zhong Kui Striking Ghosts" painting. In the Song Dynasty, Shi Ke produced "Zhong Kui and His Little Sister," Sun Zhiwei offered "Zhong Kui in the Snow," Li Gonglin composed "Zhong Kui Marrying Off His Sister," Liang Kai created "Zhong Kui Seeking Plums on a Lame Horse," and Ma Hezhi gave us "Zhong Kui Reading Under the Pine." From the Yuan Dynasty, Wang Meng painted "Zhong Kui in the Chilly Woods," Qian Gu portrayed "Old Zhong Kui Relocating," Guo Xu presented "Zhong Kui Kicking a Ball," and Chen Hongshou illustrated "The New Year's Eve Excursion of Zhong Kui." No one had ever painted a drunken Zhong Kui before, so I, using the Zen practice of mixing rice juice with ink, sucked the brush and depicted Zhong Kui inebriated. This painting not only serves to exorcise evil and ward off malevolence, but its portrayal of drunkenness is charmingly endearing, evoking the image of a jubilant scholar from Mount Zhongnan revelling in the festive celebrations of a golden age, basking in the peace of prosperous times. In the past, people would paint small images of Zhong Kui to offer to officials at year's end to dispel inauspiciousness, but now it is customarily done on the fifth day of the fifth month. On a summer day of the Xinwei year, this painting was presented as an offering to Gao Zhai, known as the Hermit of Crane Pavilion, a distinguished official of the Imperial Court.
The inscription was made by the esteemed Jin Nong from Hangzhou, renowned for his extensive learning and eloquent words, at the venerable age of seventy-five.

Inscription on "Zhong Kui"
by Jin Nong of the Qing Dynasty

Chen Shizeng, beyond Buddhist figures, also painted "Zhong Kui." With bold and expressive strokes, he depicted Zhong Kui standing sideways, holding a Hu in both hands, eyes gazing upwards as if beseeching. The brushwork and spirit of this painting bear a resemblance to Jin Dongxin. The inscription reads: "With towering hat and wide belt, his face is fierce and strange. With angry beard bristling, all evils retreat and hide away." The painting was created at the Tian Zhong Festival (Dragon Boat Festival) in the year of Xinyou (1921).

Chen Shizeng
by Yu Jianhua

---

[6] A "zhang" (丈) is an ancient Chinese unit of measurement that is approximately equivalent to 3.3 meters or 10.8 feet in the current metric system.

Upon completing the painting, Huang[7] burned incense and bowed deeply, expressing his wish for such a person as Zhong Kui to be ever-present.

Qi Baishi's inscribed painting of Zhong Kui

The old master was skilled in depicting both deities and ghosts, as seen in the work "Zhong Kui's Sister Wishing Longevity to Her Brother", where he illustrated several ghosts. It is told that Zhong Kui had a younger sister who, wishing to celebrate her brother's birthday, presented a load of ghosts as a gift, playfully suggesting that the large ghost carrying the load could also be part of the offering if it seemed too modest. The painter's works, whether of gods or ghosts, were underpinned by a reflection of reality, further accentuated by exaggeration to create these supernatural beings. These creations often had allegorical depths, portraying the hardships of life. The thin and skeletal ghosts within the basket, and the grimy, woebegone appearance of the larger ghost, with one foot in a straw shoe and the other barefoot, represent the destitute farmers, a visual metaphor for their almost ghostly existence under the harsh dominion of landlords. Thus, peasants from the old society, upon encountering such vivid self-portraits in temples, would naturally be deeply stirred.

Qi Baishi's Painting Techniques and Appreciation
by Hu Peiheng and Hu Tuo

I recall hearing from the old master Qi Baishi that in his youth, he painted many murals of gods and spirits for local temples, which greatly appealed to the peasant masses. Thus, monks and Taoists were eager to form connections with Baishi. Regrettably, these works were destroyed in the wars. The only surviving piece from his middle age is "Zhong Kui Slaying Ghosts" for Mr. Li Jinxi. In it, Zhong Kui's fierce expression, with wide eyes and open mouth, is intimidating. Zhong Kui, deeply rooted in folk culture as a symbol of justice, is known for capturing ghosts and banishing evil. The old master's intent in painting Zhong Kui was a wish for such righteous beings to always exist. Such divine images naturally drew the attention of peasants in temples and inspired a sense of justice. Out of curiosity, I requested the old master to recreate a few divine images based on drafts from thirty or forty years ago.

Qi Baishi's Painting Techniques and Appreciation
by Hu Peiheng and Hu Tuo

Strength can rid the grain of mice and waste,
Ultimately, he's a man of scholarly taste.
On the fifth day of the fifth lunar month of the Gengxu year, in imitation of Master Dongxin.

Inscribed by Chen Banding on *"Zhong Kui Drunk on Rocks."*

[7] Huang, a name given by his teacher, is one of the aliases of the renowned Chinese painter Qi Baishi.

A Collection of Poetic Inscriptions on Portraits of Zhong Kui by Renowned Masters

The scribe of Jinan[8], now his beard frosted white,
Finds Zhong Kui in green, a seasonal sight.
His hand lifts to heavens, pleased at snow's gentle grace,
Yet treads o'er the frost in worn shoes - such a case.

Time's torrent sweeps on, to yellow dust it's cast,
Sixty plus six years, the old man holds fast.
His children forbid him to fade with the night,
While the silver jug soaks the creamy delight.

Inscription on an Ancient Portrait of Zhong Kui
By Su Zhe of the Song Dynasty

In biting winds, the moon casts forth a grievous, sour dismay,
Owls take wing, foxes call through ruins where the spectres play.
Brambles tangle amidst the stones, shrouding mists at twilight's cusp,
Ancient alters lie in ruins, while dead trees to the earth succumb.

Below, three phantoms gather, their cries through silent fields spread,
Inflicting on some hapless home the fevered, swollen dread.
Pain, heat, and bloated sickness, soon erupt in heaving sighs,
Witches called, shamans plead, under dark and brooding skies.

With ritual tools and anxious haste, the elders do prepare,
Straw figures, herb-filled boats, and meals laid out with solemn care.
In disarray the offerings stand, as ghosts now grasp their due,
While living hearts hold vigil, dine, and watch the spectral view.

Suddenly, 'midst the terror's grip, a figure grand they see,
A deity astride a bull, his visage stern and free,
With children front and back to aid, his ghostly prey to catch.
Zhong Kui feasts from dawn to dusk, yet hunger's match not met.

Disturbed by his mighty glare, the ghosts in panic flee,
No time to warn, no time to hide, their fate is sealed, they see.
Wine spills, meat scatters, in the filth their forms collapse,
Their souls dispersed, their bodies fall into death's final lapse.

One beneath the timber's shade, still clutching cup in fright,
One in hiding met his end, his gaze locked in the night,
And with a breath, the god ensnares, his power bound them tight.
Not ten steps from his mighty snare, they meet their final plight.

Why did you, Pu Sheng, chance upon this scene to thus convey?
With strokes that filled your scroll with none amiss, so artists say.
Your ink with monstrous fears aligns, a gift to me, but why?
I wave it off, no bribe I'll take, though many might apply.

In times to come, those seeking verse may frequent my door,
I write these lines to tell the tale of what the painting bore.

On Pu Sheng's Painting of Zhong Kui
By Wen Tong of the Song Dynasty

In heartland's embrace, Lord Zhong had his place,
"Whither to wander," he mused, "in open space?"
"Not for petty hunt, sans hound nor hawk's grace,
But for leisure's pursuit, with kin to embrace."

His sister's beauty, sheep's charm on her face,
Suits well the darkest rouge, in pastoral taste.
At inns along paths, they sought brief respite's trace,
Whose ancient abode offers food, drink, a base?

Red cap, bird-adorned cloak, simple pleasures encased,
Yet purest blood of beauty remains chaste and chased.
Better to savor homebrewed Zhongshan's embrace,
Drunken for years three, worldly ties to erase.

Yet, one dread looms, of high brow's mocking face,
Aunt's lavish spending on others' displaced space.
Awaiting his sobering, to tidy up the place,
At Ma Wei's[9] riches, now vanished without a trace.

Some say that ink demons[10] are but casual strokes of the brush, a grave misconception indeed. For these are the revered cursive sages of calligraphy. As Bian Shifeng once observed, "Those not skilled in proper script may yet excel in cursive; in times past, adept painters of ink demons like Gu Zhen, Zhao Qianli, and Ding Xianggui were indeed remarkable. Alas, their departure from traditional figure painting was too great, leading observers to dismiss their work as mere dalliance." While Gu Zhen's ink demon is exquisitely crafted, his intentions veer towards the vulgar, going so far as to depict the noble Zhong Kui as a wild boar chased by a staff-wielding girl. What is the meaning of this? And now, I present my own painting, "Zhongshan Going on Excursion"...

Self-Inscription on Painting "Zhongshan Going on Excursion"
By Gong Kai of the Song Dynasty

A soul of loyalty beyond the mortal call,
In dreams, imperial robes from heaven fall.
Alive, he shunned a thousand measures of grain,
In death, his valour for nations does remain.

With hands that tore asunder mountains steep,
His spirit quelled the ghastly cries that crept in sleep.
Imagine him, with sister by his side astride twin fawns,
Drunk beneath the autumn moon, until the break of dawn.

Portrait of Zhong Kui
By Tang Su of the Yuan Dynasty

---

[8] Jinan, a city in the central and western part of Shandong Province, China.

[9] Ma Wei (马嵬): Refers to Mawei Slope, a historical site near Xi'an, famous as the place where the Tang Dynasty concubine Yang Yuhuan, known as one of the Four Beauties of ancient China, was forced to hang herself during a military rebellion.

[10] In traditional Chinese art, "墨鬼" (Mogui), or "ink demons," refers to a distinctive and free-form style of ink painting that emphasizes emotional expression and artistic spontaneity over meticulous detail and conventional technique. The subjects, often abstract and exaggerated, embody dynamism and expressive power.

In twilight years, the sun dims as thunder slays the light,
Within jade halls, the spectres wail, recoiling from the sight.
Barefoot 'cross celestial bounds, on dragon's tail he treads,
Secretly, 'neath autumn's waves, red lotuses he shreds.

Scholar of Zhongnan, cap askew, his green robe snugly tied,
With boots of black that span so wide, through haunts of ghosts he strides.
With mouth agape and dripping red, he swallows spirits' gall,
Amidst the crisp, bronze clashing sounds, autumn's sorrows fall.

Great demons leap, while lesser fiends let out their mournful cries,
The pig-shaped dragon chews on gold, as hunger in him lies.
His rage, not cooled by passage of time, his gaze stern and direct,
With bristled beard like spears arrayed, his fierce eyes demons check.

Ode of the Zhongnan Scholar
—— Inscription on Ma Lin's Portrait of Zhong Kui, for Li Wufeng
By Sa Duci of the Yuan Dynasty

Sturdy Zhong Kui stands, a pair of ghosts upon his broad back borne,
One, bloated with a bag that casts a slanted shadow, looking worn.
Another bears a sword, his tasseled cap askew, his presence scorned,
While yet a double-horned spectre with a skull, all norms has torn.

His lady glides in her sedan, with ghostly maids her grace ensuring,
Holding feline treasures close, their beauty in the shadows luring.
With their coffers dark and deep, in sable sleeves the mystery enduring,
Attendants in resplendent dress, with vermin and scorpions their clothes adorning.

Bearing packs, they march; the heaviest luggage for the ghosts a boon,
Even spectral infants are adorned, in finery they're richly hewn.
With bags that house a lute, as if to serenade the distant moon,
And gourds that dangle sadly there, as if their fate's a woeful tune.

Spirits climb with poles in hand, their weary ascent can't be foreseen,
The last in jars confined, around the columns tightly they are lean.
The starving dead still shuffle on, though flesh has fallen, stark and keen.
A multitude of monsters throng, unceasing in the scene.

Since the divine Yu[11] cast his cauldrons, how many years have slid?
Yet still the mythical Mōryō flutters here, as though bid.
Alas, and woe, I ask myself, amidst these phantoms hid,
Where do such oddities come from, in this portrait's cryptic grid?

Portrait of Zhong Kui
By Feng Zizhen of the Yuan Dynasty

One must chuckle at Lord Gong's jest with spirits and ghosts,
His bold strokes craft visions that rival celestial hosts.
In poverty, I dare not unveil such art to gaze,
Lest in jest, they find in me, a subject to amuse and amaze.

Zhongshan Going on Excursion
By Li Mingfeng of the Yuan Dynasty

An ancient figure with fearsome gait, through brambles of the living strays,
His chair of vines on ghostly shoulders lays, as both his trembling knees obey.
Before him, darkened sprites of portly shape, short, stout, not from the elder's drapes;
His motley retinue in servile capes, bear ghostly offerings for his escape.

Starved spectres grow not fat, though plenty spread, with elder's hands the feast is shred;
The gaunt amongst them, cloaked in ragged dread, too weak to serve, by heavy tasks are led.
The rest, a myriad of grotesque mien, designed to make the living lean,
Gong of Chu[12], fierce aged, not of their scene, how might one know his form unseen?

One fancies Gong's eyes sparkling in the dark realm, walking dead of a separate helm;
The rich, in death no less, their fats overwhelm, to feed the elder's banquet realm.
No summons calls Gong forth to declare his state, nor can demonic cries negotiate;
With the empire's luminous fate, untouched by blight, the people celebrate longevity's gate.

Zhong Kui Commanding Ghosts
By Zheng Yuanyou of the Yuan Dynasty

In times when the Tang's glory dimmed, the siblings rose in day,
The palace courtyards echoed with the fiends they'd flay.
Where was she when Zhong Kui fought, not seen in fray?
Adorned in splendor, beauty veiled in spectral sway.

Whither went her visage known, to what unknown stay?
Even demons bow to her, their gazes shy away.
Sword in hand, on steed she leaps, with brother at the play,
Guarding homes, her presence promised safety's ray.

Poor old Han once bound by want, his plight would always weigh,
His vessel bound, for years untold, by night it lay.
Had she chose to join her kin in ghostly hunt's array,
I, too, would pledge my wealth in gold without dismay.

Portrait of Zhong Kui's Sister
By Zheng Yuanyou of the Yuan Dynasty

Zhong Kui's glare pierces, with bristled beard and halberd raised,
His sister, adorned anew, her face with black lacquer glazed.
Their carriages follow in tandem, but to what end do they strive?
Empty but for skeletons, in chariots standing alive.

The Emperor of Kaiyuan's realm in human cares has ceased,
The haunted palace seeks the strength of this ghost-subduing beast.
Gong of Chu, with peculiar love for the dark and the strange,
Left a legacy in his art, where eerie forms never change.

Zhongshan Going on Excursion
By Wang Xiaoweng of the Yuan Dynasty

---

[11] Yu, also known as the Great Yu (大禹), is a legendary ruler in ancient China famed for his control of the floods. He is often credited with founding the Xia dynasty and is celebrated for his creation of a system of flood controls.

[12] The phrase "Gong of Chu" likely refers to the connection of Gong Kai (also known as Gong Cuiyan) with the region of Chu, or it may emphasize his cultural characteristics or identity. The land of Chu is often depicted in history and literature as a place filled with mystery and exotic charm, which resonates with the themes of the supernatural and the peculiar in Gong Kai's works.

Fengdu's[13] mountains veiled in shadows, autumn rains softly wail,
A throng of spectres mourn en masse, their cries cold and frail.
Elder Kui, his beard abounding, in ancient turban dressed,
At the sound of ghostly whispers, his craving hardly repressed.

Astride his phantom carriage, Kui roams through the night,
Flanked by demons bearing swords and hats against the dim twilight.
Gnarled figures, hair unkempt, their skeletal bodies lean,
His sister too, her sullen face, her garments finely seamed.

Turning back, old Kui observes, their eyes in silent battle,
Seeming not to scorn Kui's looks, nor by his visage rattled.
A female ghost trudges behind, laden with quilt and cushion,
Perhaps Kui's weary from his journey, for slumber he seems to wish in.

Bearing jugs amidst the biting cold, his presence stark and bold,
Might he press these fiends into a brew, their essence to be sold?
Rendered speechless, I stand, my words restrained by fear,
As blood is shed where spirits are bound, their fate draws ever near.

Are we to mince these devils to feed our ghostly fare,
While my hands, though able, clasp only empty air?
A calm spirit and a steady heart might just be a ruse,
For now I trust the poet's stroke, which freely he does use.

The Cuiyan hermit, his mind serene and plain,
Why knows he so the hearts of ghosts, their sentiments and pain?
Behold, his brush strokes frighten those from the nether ring,
Once the poem is complete, we'll hear the spectres sing.

To this day, upon this scroll, a chill wind still does blow,
Where's the clan of old Kui from, which land did they bestow?
Legends tell in Tang's court, his form was once espied,
But was it ever real, what in dreams Cao Cao[14] confide?

Spirits of the palace shattered, on Ma Wei's dust laid thin,
Suddenly, through azure skies, thunder strikes begin.
With myriad monsters felled by Heaven's furious might,
Mount Fengdu crumbles, seeing day from night.

Old Kui, starving, finds no ghost to sate his need,
Forsaken in the mortal realm, by the door he stands to heed.

Inscription on Gong Cuiyan's "Zhongshan Going on Excursion"
By Song Wu of the Yuan Dynasty

In the portrait where spirits dwell and wild tempers flare,
Eyes pierce souls, and bristling beards slice through the air.
Desolate hills embrace the dusk, the sun in silent gloom,
Winds whirl with ghostly flames amidst bamboo's secret room.

Since Wei and Tang, the visage meant to banish foul spirits near,
Before the palace, reeling steps follow the flute's faint cheer.
A warrior in azure appears, as if from dream's own thread,
His presence in this silken work perplexes the beholder's head.

Though legends of Zhongshan bear a tint of the surreal,
Its guardian's figure still wields power to protect and heal.
The artist's heart, vast as the sea, who could its depths explore?
Each stroke he lays is poised with might, sharp as a warrior's lore.

The radiant glow from Heaven's court shines forth to clear the dim,
Thirty-six emperors aloft partake in celestial hymn,
Amidst spring's warmth, the chill of shades casts down a dismal sheen.
For you, I wield my brush and strive to leave the world unseen;
A single thought, it wanders far, as on a grand boulevard serene.

Inscription on Gong Cuiyan's "Zhongshan Going on Excursion"
By Han Xing of the Yuan Dynasty

The northern wind hurls sand that bids our gaze to shield,
As palace willows, tinged with gold, sweep o'er the brook's field.
A scholar from Zhongnan stands with sudden, stubborn mien,
Deep in thought, his grin like a hedgehog, teeth unseen.

Clad in blue with horned belt, his figure looms immense,
His black hat shadows his face, boots baring digits hence.
The Bai Ze[15] by his side, its mouth quivers in suspense,
Its tread as weighty as the Qilin's[16] steps so dense.

In his grasp, divine scripts fill the paper to the brim,
As if to decree, "This New Year shall blessings bring to him."
With a burst, the bamboo cracks, all else becomes dim,
Come morrow, spring's radiance will stretch beyond the rim.

Portrait of Zhong Kui
By Ling Yunhan of the Ming Dynasty

Before him strides the bearded man, the dusky dame in tow,
The winter ghosts are grains to haul, the others bear the load.
Rainbows serve as reins and thunder rumbles as the coach,
Why task the ghosts to shoulder sedan, in such reproach?

Behold, old Kui may not be just, in fairness does he lack,
With power clutched, self-interest taints, the laws to crack.
Dark clouds hang low with eerie shades, the spectres stack,
Oh Kui, mighty Kui, what's your plan of attack?

Inscription on "Zhong Kui Marshalling Ghosts for Relocation"
By Liu Ji of the Ming Dynasty

---

[13] Fengdu (酆都): A famous cultural and historical site located on the northern bank of the Yangtze River in China, known as the "City of Ghosts" with temples and shrines dedicated to the afterlife in Chinese folklore.

[14] Cao Cao (曹操): A key warlord and statesman in the late Eastern Han Dynasty, later the founder and the first ruler of the state of Wei in the Three Kingdoms period. He is often portrayed as a cunning yet wise leader and is a central figure in the historical novel *Romance of the Three Kingdoms.*

[15] The Bai Ze (白泽) is a legendary creature in Chinese mythology known for its ability to discern all supernatural beings.

[16] The Qilin (麒麟) is a mythical creature in Chinese culture that symbolizes good luck and is said to appear with the arrival or passing of a sage or ruler.

In mountains bare, where no souls tread, the night is cold and stark,
A horde of ghosts their wails let loose, the west wind bites and barks.
The scholar in his robe of green leans on his sword so long,
His slanted hat casts shadows dim, his black boots broad and strong.

Lanterns unlit reflect on streams that cross the land askew,
His rage cleaves through the demon's head, their essence burns anew.
The greater demons leap and bound, the lesser wail and howl,
Like cormorants too heavy, grounded, unable to take flight or prowl.

Now in the city's heart, the ghosts begin their eerie stroll,
Even 'neath the blue sky and bright sun, their chirps from shadows toll.
Oh, how we yearn for him to rise and take up his righteous role,
To slay the myriad demons would also make my soul whole.

Portrait of Zhong Kui Slaying Demons
By Liu Pu of the Ming Dynasty

The scholar in green, his angry whiskers heaved,
Finds ghosts as sweet as honey when hunger is relieved.
Sour winds and bitter rains disturb the light of day,
He seeks to relocate to where the mountain shadows lay.

His sister, face like polished jet, follows close behind,
Her gaze, piercing as beads, can dazzle any mind.
Myriad forms of ghostly slaves and consorts align,
With crab-fiends and cat-spirits, in solitude, they shine.

His might commands the ghosts, ensuring they comply,
While mocking skulls trail after, sneering at Zhong Kui's high.
A hero stands, a mountain of bones piled to the sky,
Do not rely solely on the sceptre in thy hand, so nigh.

Inscription on "Zhong Kui Relocating"
By Li Ye of the Ming Dynasty

From Zhongnan's peaks, a scholar true, in martial prowess delights,
Wild goblins, mountain sprites, all ranked within his sights.
Through fields he'd chase with seasons' wheel, a hunting quest so grand,
His vigour echoed like the drums that stirred the land.

The cymbals' clash portended splits across the earth's own face,
As darkened banners rose aloft, wind's proud embrace.
A limping donkey, whip-defied, would keep a steady pace,
Why leash a loyal dog whose tail sways with such grace?

Not yet the hawk's leash loosed to soar, nor tiger freed from binds,
Ghosts leapt like pawns, while an old sage their strategy divines.
Some turned as wolves, spears at the back; some, as monkeys, axes tried.
The owls' hoot matched bows pulled taut, snakes with crossbows at their side.

With shield in spin, he artfully parried threats from all around,
His hammer flew, a dance of war, without a single bound.
Seated, he struck where none could meet, his prowess did astound,
In advance or retreat, his moves a steed's pride confound.

His waking yawn reveals a snarl, teeth bared in daylight's yawn,
So nimble, one might think his arms had sprouted feathers, dawn.
No chariot needed in his chase, nor nets for beasts withdrawn,
He knows the worldly courts endure, where mortal law is drawn.

His power rivals that of gods, within the earthly courts,
Artists mimic those before, their brushes their resorts.
Gone is Master Wu[17], and Yan[18] delights in ancient sorts,
The I Ching shows one's path, while Han[19] poverty reports.

Such scenes are hard to fathom, and harder to portray,
Yet they're kept for year's end rites, as old gives way to day.
With firecrackers' single blast, spring claims its bright array.

Ghost Hunting
by Ling Yunhan from the Ming Dynasty

A venerable man with whiskers wide, meets spectres with delight, not spite,
Through Zhongshan's drunken springtime nights, his wandering spirit takes its flight.
His beard betrays a dragon's soul, a spectre's guise his ancient role,
Surrounded not by mortal kin, but spirits that from legends stroll.

Lone was Gong of Chu in death, his life unknown, bereft of breath,
Why bother with the ghostly throng, when life to men did not belong?
Beware the sacred cauldrons' gaze, those secrets that the heavens praise,
This painting should be cherished deep, through ages let its magic stay.

Zhongshan Going on Excursion
By Master Zongyan of the Yuan Dynasty

A chill wind whistles, its mournful cry brings the cold to rise,
As old Kui treads the mountain paths where night rain lies.
He laments not enforcing laws at the empire's heart,
Vowing in death he'd never spurn the Tang's sartorial art.

His dream of Li Mountain[20] shattered with a single glance behind,
He prays the Deity spares the trouble of the Six Ding's[21] assigned.
All demons and spectres submit beneath his whip's command,
Triumphantly he rides the donkey, hands sleeved, across the land.

An Ode to "Zhong Kui Riding a Donkey", Composed for the Grand Judicial Commissioner Zhou Ke
By Cheng Mingzheng of the Ming Dynasty

With a tiger's maw and bristled whiskers fierce,
How can he not untie the fiends that humans pierce?
To pilfer blooms and flutes, mere trifles they beseech,
Can he endure a ghoul's mischief on the bridge that spans so reach?

Inscription on Liang Kai's Painting of Zhong Kui
By Jiang Zhuxiao of the Ming Dynasty

---

[17] Wu Daozi, a famed painter from the Tang Dynasty, known for his mastery of brushwork.

[18] Yan Zhenqing, a Tang Dynasty calligrapher known for his distinctive and forceful style.

[19] Han Yu, a prominent poet and essayist of the Tang Dynasty, known for his contributions to classical prose.

[20] Li Mountain (骊山), historically known as the burial site of China's First Emperor, Qin Shi Huang, is associated with imperial power and the afterlife.

[21] The Six Ding (六丁) are divine beings in Chinese mythology that are often invoked for their strength and assistance.

The ancient Zhong Kui from Mount Zhongnan, appears fierce and bold, in tiger skin boots, a black hat, and a duck-green robe. He refuses to emerge in the bright light of day, choosing instead Lantern Festival night to commence his wanderings. With the moon high above the Ghost Gate, he rides a black ox as steady as an elephant. Ghostly women adorn their cheeks with rouge, and ghostly children hang a single braid; their entourage's noise is loud and chaotic. Guided by a spirit maiden's banner, flanked by a Dashi sword[22]. One holds a whip to the left, another a bow to the right. Leading the way is one with a black lacquer lantern, and following is another with a yak hair banner. Carrying, shouldering, and handling various items, their grotesque and fierce appearances inspire fear, resembling a mix of tigers, gibbons, and other wild beasts. The ghosts, wounded in battle, their blood turned into phosphorescent flames, twinkling on the ground like burning oil. The chilly wind whistles over the desolate moor, and all manner of strange creatures hold their breath, daring not to make a sound. Zhong Kui warns them to keep their distance, declaring his desire to drink their blood, as sweet as the finest ale, to feast on their flesh, as tender as lamb. He will not tolerate these spirits' greed in the world any longer. Alas! Old Zhong Kui is indeed a hero among spectres. Hence, the Tang Emperor, envisioning his likeness, decreed Wu Daozi to paint it with a brush of five colours. Recalling the days of the Tang Dynasty's Tianbao era, when ghosts were in abundance; Yang Guifei seduced with her fox-like charm in the Palace of Eternal Purity[23], and An Lushan roared in the imperial halls. Had Zhong Kui been present, these two spectres would not have escaped, surely bound and delivered to the Envoy of the Cang Water[24], wrapped in red silk. Their carcasses offered to the heavens, locked in the beast's prison; their skins flayed, furs plucked, to experience the toil of a day. This would have fouled the hot springs and left Li Mountain overgrown with weeds. It would have removed the Tang family's century of misfortune, while Zhong Kui received a millennium of praise in the Tang annals. Yet, on Lantern Festival night, he returns, allowing all to light lamps and beat gongs freely.

The New Year's Eve Excursion of Zhong Kui
By Wu Kuan of the Ming Dynasty

Within the palace of Kaiyuan, ghosts hailed a mother's name,
The chancellors and viceroys indulged in hexes, to their shame.
The Emperor bestowed upon Lord Zhong, the Yellow Thearch's fame,
Yet unrewarded ghostly chases, doomed him to the brine.

Who's the crone in mountain's nook, by cobwebs densely spun?
Carrying infants and bags, across the Zhou paths[25] they run.
Skulls chatter in mournful whispers, their lamentations spun,
By midnight, 'tis old Sang who's vexed to boil under the none.

Lord Zhong looks back, to where he liked, with just one glance behind,
Wooden guests[26] cavort on beams, as mountain sprites entwined.
If thou would not stay, my solace in thine exit I'd find,
Together we'd uphold the spirit of Shubao, enshrined.
When next we meet, let not our hearts with mutual grief be lined.

A Playful Inscription on Qian Shubao's Rendering of Zhong Kui's Relocation
By Wang Shizhen of the Ming Dynasty

Rising to the heavens, poised as if a dragon in flight,
Who would say this noble sir lacks a visage bright?
Even armed for war, he's not outshone by Jiao Manqian's[27] light,
In striking foes, he'd rather Duan Sinong's[28] fierce might cite.

Self-Inscription on "Zhong Kui Watching a Sword"
By Gao Qipei of the Qing Dynasty

With a serene gaze, his mind as vast as the skies above,
The feast concludes in the Pearl Palace[29], the wine at its ebb.
No need this day to frequently check the sword by my side,
Endless spring beauty pervades Chang'an[30], far and wide.

Self-Inscription on the "Metamorphic Forms of Zhong Kui" Series: The Banquet's Conclusion
By Gao Qipei of the Qing Dynasty

With furrowed brow, he faces a mountain of human sin,
White hairs might well descend his cheeks, for all within.
He hopes his righteous image in a Qin mirror[31] stays,
To deter the brazen wraiths from venturing out their ways.

Self-Inscription on the "Metamorphic Forms of Zhong Kui" Series: Reflection in the Mirror
By Gao Qipei of the Qing Dynasty

---

[22] A type of sword that was introduced to China from Arabia during the Tang Dynasty.

[23] A palace in the Tang Dynasty's imperial complex, associated with Yang Guifei.

[24] The Envoy of the Cang Water refers to a mysterious figure who claims to be the deity in charge of the waters.

[25] The "Zhou path" in the context of the poem could be interpreted as an allusion to the paths of the Zhou Dynasty, symbolizing ancient or traditional ways.

[26] Wooden guests (木客) in Chinese folklore are mystical beings that inhabit secluded mountainous regions. They are described as small, humanoid figures with sharp claws for climbing, and possess intelligence and skills in crafting, sometimes interacting with humans through trade.

[27] Jiao Manqian (焦曼倩) is a figure known for his handsome appearance in Chinese folklore.

[28] Duan Sinong (段司农) is a legendary Chinese warrior celebrated for his strength.

[29] Pearl Palace (珠宫) refers to the Dragon Palace, a legendary undersea abode of the Dragon King in Chinese mythology. It is also a term used to denote Taoist temples or Buddhist monasteries, symbolizing places of spiritual or religious significance.

[30] Chang'an (长安) was the ancient capital of many Chinese dynasties, notably the Tang dynasty. It is known today as Xi'an and is celebrated for its rich cultural heritage.

[31] The Qin mirror refers to an ancient type of bronze mirror associated with the Qin Dynasty, often inscribed with mystical symbols believed to have protective powers.

When hunger strikes, a ghost devoured fills the belly round,
The rest are mounted, riding high across the heavens' bound.
The poor scholar on the streets, in pleasant banter found,
Why fret for lack of coin to hire a donkey's homeward bound?

Self-Inscription on the "Metamorphic Forms of Zhong Kui" Series: Riding the Ghost
By Gao Qipei of the Qing Dynasty

In rage, his crown thrusts skyward though his head is bare,
His sword's chill could make even June's warmth rare.
Against the mightiest spring gales, his gaze fixed and stark,
Where he'll ascend the altar remains yet in the dark.

Self-Inscription on the "Metamorphic Forms of Zhong Kui" Series: Ascending the Altar
By Gao Qipei of the Qing Dynasty

Flags and staffs in the clouds gleam atop the celestial dais,
Seen as blessings bestowed by heavenly officers, a fortunate praise.
Yet fearing these gifts may be squandered, dispersed in many ways,
He stirs his visage to summon the wind and thunder's formidable gaze.

Self-Inscription on the "Metamorphic Forms of Zhong Kui" Series: The Wind and Thunder
By Gao Qipei of the Qing Dynasty

Enveloping mists and fogs press near, a shrouding embrace,
Delight in slaying fox spirits that leap across mountain's face.
With hand on cheek and steady gaze, he whistles soft and low,
Where lightning strikes, it leaves but ash, in its brilliant glow.

Self-Inscription on the "Metamorphic Forms of Zhong Kui" Series: Subduing the Demon
By Gao Qipei of the Qing Dynasty

Embracing knees, he softly chants, relaxed in repose,
Seated wide, his bright eyes open, in calmness he glows.
He knows now, the true talisman that evil defies,
Is not found in the flames of burning yellow paper ties.

Self-Inscription on the "Metamorphic Forms of Zhong Kui" Series: Embracing Knees
By Gao Qipei of the Qing Dynasty

He who banishes ghosts, if not a god, must surely be divine,
Wretched are the wraiths that steal names, their fate to pine.
The seal he sets, displayed for all in the Jade Tower's keep,
No need for bones of spite to fill the brushwood's heap.

Self-Inscription on the "Metamorphic Forms of Zhong Kui" Series: The Sealing Scroll
By Gao Qipei of the Qing Dynasty

A gentle spring breeze flutters the new green of his robe,
Bountiful blessings he bestows, aiding the good across the globe.
Occasionally, he can't help but laugh behind his hand,
Amused by those seeking fortune, burning gold as their demand.

Self-Inscription on the "Metamorphic Forms of Zhong Kui" Series: The Muffled Laugh
By Gao Qipei of the Qing Dynasty

Since ancient times, mountain spirits have mocked the dwarfed,
Yet dare they near the scholar's seat, in corners deftly left.
It's not to sneak a view of texts denying their own breath,
But suspect they're perusing tomes of old, despite death's theft.

Self-Inscription on the "Metamorphic Forms of Zhong Kui" Series: Reading
By Gao Qipei of the Qing Dynasty

Amidst wild graves, blooms boast their charm, beneath the faint moon's spell,
The grasses whisper, as the dusk's moon oversees the dell.
If one but wakes and merely looks, without discerning gaze,
He's not the one who's skilled in casting malevolent spirits away.

Self-Inscription on the "Metamorphic Forms of Zhong Kui" Series: The Doze
By Gao Qipei of the Qing Dynasty

Whose guardian deity hangs upon the door,
With blade in hand, suddenly takes flight to soar?
If only he could slay the demons of dismay,
With him, I'd share the gift of immortality's stay.

Self-Inscription on the Zhong Kui Album
By Gao Qipei of the Qing Dynasty

His whiskers bristle, fury unsettled, discontent,
In broad daylight, he longs to clash with spirits malevolent.
He sighs at hordes of goblins and sprites that together band,
Resolved to purge all blue-faced demons from the land.

Portrait of Zhong Kui
By Hua Yan of the Qing Dynasty

Light chariots race with the gusting wind, sharp and swift,
Bright lanterns flicker, cradling clouds in a celestial drift.
Leaping and capturing, with commanding shouts so bold,
It is he with the beard, Zhong Kui, as the stories told.

Scroll of Zhong Kui Marrying Off His Sister
By Hua Yan of the Qing Dynasty

From the world he retreats to the depths of Zhongnan's grace,
Among mountain sprites and wooden guests, he finds his place.
Though many scorn my visage as less than human form,
Their hearts, judging by face, can't know my spirit's norm.

Portrait of Zhong Kui
By Li Fangying of the Qing Dynasty

As Dragon Boat Festival nears, stormy rains do throng,
Mature wheat in fields lies fallen, swamped in mud along.
Yet Zhong Kui still has spare coins, his purse is never light,
It seems that while men may be poor, spirits take no plight.

Wind and Rain Zhong Kui Painting, Two Days Before the Dragon Boat Festival in the Tenth Year of Qianlong's Reign
By Li Fangying of the Qing Dynasty

I do not depict Zhong Kui as he strides toward the hall,
Rather, him tapping his sword hilt, reciting poems tall.
Now the capital's at peace, its environs serene and sure,
No need for you, dear sir, to lure demons obscure.

Self-Inscription on "Zhong Kui"
By Ren Bonian of the Qing Dynasty

His brows and beard like spears, he scolds the sly fox sprite,
Looking back at the scene before the hall, a perfect sight.
Ghosts on the road are mocked, they cannot make their flight,
Wishing your sacred blade blurs with the blood of this plight.

The fox, skilled in mimicking a fair lady's guise,
Finds her magic foiled by old Kui, much to her surprise.
Ha! How laughable, her tricks meet their demise.

Inscription on Ren Yi's "Scholar Zhong Slays the Fox Spirit"
By Wu Changshuo of the Qing Dynasty

A jug of liquor spent, youth cast away in zest,
Staggering steps provoke chagrin, a dramatic jest.
A scholar's life drowned in ceaseless drunken spree,
Yearns for Liu Fen[32], the sole man awake to see.

Commissioned by Master Zhuanxuan, I usually have little skill in portraiture, yet this painting came to be with a brush inspired by the ancestral temple portraits from the era of Emperor Wu of Han. Su Dongpo once said, "My calligraphy is crafted without method," and so it is with my painting.

Self-Inscription on "Zhong Kui"
By Wu Changshuo of the Qing Dynasty

Robed in blue with sleeves vast, Zhong, a scholar from Zhongnan cast.
Aou-head not won, his anger vast, Rage surges like the Winnowing Basket's[33] blast.

Sword unsheathed, shining sway, Demons cut, to their dismay.
Appeared in dreams to Emperor's delight, His illness cured, ended the fright.

"I am your servant, Zhong is here," Protection given, no need to fear.
Emperor's health, now hearty and clear, All weakness and wasting disappear.

Recorded by the Emperor for his feat, Ordered his likeness, none can cheat.
What look bears he against the breeze? Whiskers like dragons, they do please.

Wu Daozi, his brush divine, As Qin[34] decreed this portrait line.
All under heaven followed the sign, Evil banished by his might's shine.

Majestic light in all directions cast, In the court, shadows vast,
Like dragons humming, tigers roar, Zhong Kui's image, we adore.

During the Tang Dynasty, Emperor Xuanzong once dreamt of Zhong Kui slaying the ghost of wastefulness, which led to the healing of his illness. Consequently, he commissioned Wu Daozi to paint the likeness of Zhong Kui and disseminate it throughout the realm. Upon seeing the painting, Emperor Xuanzong remarked, "It is as if you have shared my dream; the resemblance is striking indeed." This testifies to Wu Daozi's divinely inspired artistic ability, although over time, the copies made across the land gradually lost the authenticity of the original. The paintings from Lingbi County, however, often retained Wu Daozi's original style, and hence were widely esteemed until they too eventually altered. In essence, the most appreciated works are those that capture the vigourous and valiant spirit, not necessarily conforming to Lingbi's particular style. In Hangzhou lived Dong Xu, adept at painting Zhong Kui. A patron presented me with a painting for my inscription, and thus I composed these words. Similarly, Wu Yuehu's portrayal of Zhong Kui did not fall short of Dong Xu's, and I also applied this inscription to his work, which subsequently became a common practice.

In Praise of the Portrait of Zhong Kui from the Duplicate Collection of Mingshan
By Qi Zhouhua of the Qing Dynasty

---

[32] Liu Fen, an official and political essayist of the Tang Dynasty.

[33] The Winnowing Basket (箕宿) is a sector in the Chinese constellation system, part of the Twenty-Eight Mansions. It lies within the eastern quadrant associated with the Azure Dragon.[33] Liu Fen, an official and political essayist of the Tang Dynasty.

[34] "Qin" refers to Emperor Qin Shi Huang. Here, it likely employs hyperbole, suggesting that the beauty and reverence of Wu Daozi's paintings are as if decreed by Emperor Qin himself, compelling everyone to emulate them.

Not below, yet scratching there; not above, still itches to bear.
Thou art but outside the skin, how couldst thou feel where my itch lies within?

In the Bingyin year, I discussed and inscribed for the fifth time upon the painting "Zhong Kui Scratching His Back."

Inscription on "Zhong Kui Scratching His Back"
By Qi Baishi

Reeds and rushes, thin as hair, birds in slanted flight almost disappear.
Why not depict Zhong Kui, who rests from ghost-slaying by this pine so sheer,
Sword sharpened, sitting calmly here, immersed in reading, without fear.

The Old Pine in Autumn
By Qi Baishi

Beneath his feet, the water glistens wide,
At the bridge's end, his sword like frostbite bides.
Should he pass like this, ponder with care,
With caution in every step, and a measured stare.

Note: Beneath the bridge hides a little demon.

Inscription on "Zhong Kui Crossing a Bridge"
By Qi Baishi

With his official cap on, he should heed not a petty itch,
Yet in the midst of scratching, Fengdu is turned into a chaotic pitch.
There dwell souls in Fengdu, who loathe to leave their pear blossoms which,
Though sparse they bloom, their love for them remains without a switch.

Inscription on the Portrait of Zhong Kui
By Qi Baishi

Worn official hat, a robe of crimson hue,
Steps leisurely taken, fan swaying too.
Mocked as the scholar from Zhongnan, it's true,
Whose charms against demons hold greater value?

This is a newly composed poem. My disciple Ruiguang made a larger version of the painting on an old porcelain piece, which I have slightly revised and kept. I have also affixed the seal "Three Hundred Stones Wealthy Man[35]."

Self-Inscription on "Zhong Kui"
By Qi Baishi

Gaunt as dry wood, claws sharp as hooks,
Brows lifted high, stepping on rocks, he overlooks all woes.
Yet in this world, some still seek blessings to invoke,
His bearded visage befitting the head of ghosts he dutifully smote.

Inscription on "Zhong Kui Scratching His Back"
By Qi Baishi

Tattered cap and blue robe, he deems worldly matters slight,
Yearly painting him requires meticulous might.
How much of the world's hidden rage can be brought to light?
'Tis he, Master Zhong, who drives off ghosts with brusque right.

Scholar Zhong
By Zhang Daqian

Reed wine drained dry in every home, not a drop left to spare,
Feasting on oddities, bellies full beyond compare.
Drunk, plucking pomegranate blossoms, in hair they're placed askew,
Old Zhong Kui, in such a mirth, appears youth anew.

In the Renxu year of seventy-one, the octogenarian[36] took delight in jesting with colloquial bite.

Inscription for the Portrait of Scholar Zhong
By Zhang Daqian

[35] Qi Baishi was very thrifty. He used found stones for his seals and, to economize, carved on every side of each stone, amassing a collection of multi-faceted seals. Thus, he humorously referred to himself as the "Three Hundred Stone Wealthy Man".

[36] The poet, Zhang Daqian, refers to himself as an "octogenarian" (an eighty-four-year-old elder) in this line.

ISBN 978-1-913536-57-2

ACS LIGHTH USE

PORTRAITS OF ZHONG KUI BY TIMELESS MASTERS

Publisher: Lu Jican
Chief Editor: Zhou Ziqing
Executive Editor: Li Kun
Compiled by Xu Xiwen and Dai Xinwei
Translator: Zhu Liya
Art Designer: Chen Ting
Cover design: Xiong Libo

6 Prospect Way, Royal Oak Industrial Estate,
Daventry Northamptonshire, NN11 8PL, UK
Tel: + 44(0) 1213 146196 -1
Fax: + 44(0) 1213 146196 -2

Web: www.lighthousebooks.net
Sales & Distribution: sales@lighthousebooks.net
Press & Editorial Submissions: press@lighthousebooks.net

Printed and bound in China.

First published in 2024 by © Lighthouse Publishing (UK) Limited – ACS
Original Edition © Guangdong Lingnan Fine Arts Publishing House Co., Ltd.

This English edition is authorized by Guangdong Lingnan Fine Arts Publishing House Co., Ltd.